CULINA MUNDI

With recipes from 40 countries

CULINA MUNDI

With recipes from **40** countries

h.f.ullmann

We wish to thank all the restaurants, people and organizations whose gracious collaboration has made it possible for us to bring this project to fruition.

Abbreviations and quantities

1 oz = 1 ounce = 28 grams
1 lb = 1 pound = 16 ounces = approximately 450 g
1 cup = 8 fluid ounces = approximately 250 ml (liquids)
4 cups = 1 quart = approximately 1 liter
16 cups = 4 quarts = 1 gallon = 3.8 liters
1 g = 1 gram = 1/1000 kilogram
1 kg = 1 kilogram = 1000 grams = 2¼ lb
1 liter = 1000 milliliters (ml) = approximately 1 quart
125 ml = approximately 8 tablespoons = ½ cup
1 tbsp = 1 level tablespoon = 10–20 g * (see below) = 15 ml (liquids)
1 tsp = 1 level teaspoon = 3–7 g * (see below) = 5 ml (liquids)

The weight of 1 cup or 1 tbsp of a dry ingredient varies significantly depending on its density, e.g. 1 cup flour weighs less than 1 cup butter.

Measurements of dry ingredients always refer to the ingredient as described in the wording immediately following, e.g. 1 tbsp chopped onion or ½ cup grated cheese.

Quantities of ingredients have been rounded up or down for convenience, where appropriate. Metric conversions may therefore not correspond exactly. It is important to use either American or metric measurements within a recipe.

Degree of difficulty of the recipes:

★   easy
★★   medium
★★★ difficult

Photography: Didier Bizos

© for the original French editions: Fabien BELLAHSEN and Daniel ROUCHE

Title of the German edition: *Culina Mundi*
ISBN 978-3-8331-2169-2

Copyright © 2011 for this English edition:
Tandem Verlag GmbH
h.f.ullmann is an imprint of Tandem Verlag GmbH

Special edition
Adaptation and editing of the English edition: Brett Jocelyn Epstein, Eric Martinson, Dr. Pippin Michelli, Tammi Reichel for APE Intl., Richmond VA

Translation and typesetting: APE Intl., Richmond VA

Cover design: rincon² medien GmbH, Cologne
Cover photo: © StockFood.com / Nilsson, P.

Project coordination: Isabel Weiler

Overall responsibility for production: h.f.ullmann publishing, Potsdam, Germany

Printed in China

ISBN 978-3-8331-6119-3

10 9 8 7 6 5 4 3 2 1
X IX VIII VII VI V IV III II I

www.ullmann-publishing.com
newsletter@ullmann-publishing.com

Contents

Foreword

"Tell me what you eat and I will tell you what you are", quipped the renowned French gastronome Jean Anthelme Brillat-Savarin two centuries ago. Some people appreciate a piece of meat cooked to medium-rare perfection, while others categorically refuse to eat meat and swear by medleys of grains and vegetables. Some are delighted by foods bathed in sauces, while others prefer to steam their food. In the end, everyone has their own ideas about the right way to eat, which is related to our physiology and our approach to life.

What is true for individuals also applies to societies. We can make a slight change in the saying coined by the author of the famous book *Physiology of Taste* and say "Tell me what you eat and I will tell you where you come from". We can observe that certain nations consume great quantities of fresh fish and hardly any dairy products, while others are inclined to bake foods au gratin or don't consider a meal complete unless it includes meat that has been cooked slowly, with a wealth of spices.

Culina Mundi invites you to discover other cultures through the prism of gastronomy, a universal and undeniable marker of identity and culture. This book of cuisine, one of a kind, gathers more than 350 recipes from 60 famous chefs. These ambassadors of national or regional culinary traditions invite you on a fabulous voyage from the Americas to the Far East, with stopovers in Europe and Africa. A place of honor is naturally given to countries such as France, Italy, India, Thailand, Vietnam, Lebanon or Mexico, whose foods have become widely known in the whole world, but it also explores the less familiar cuisine of countries such as Croatia and Slovenia, situated between the Mediterranean and Slavic cultures, or the culinary richness of South America.

The cuisine of each country is represented by signature recipes that have already crossed national boundaries, such as guacamole, sushi, couscous, brownies or baklava. There is no need to translate or explain these names. But because cooking is an art, each chef has also presented some of his or her own creations, the products of national or regional culinary tradition, as well as their personal talent and know-how.

To further persuade you, *Culina Mundi* highlights the close links between a country's cuisine and the foods that grow and are produced there: the recipes are paired with interesting information about the vegetables, fruits and spices used in that land, the breeding of animals or the diverse ways ingredients can be prepared apart from the recipe at hand. The descriptions of products typical in other places but difficult to find at home help you successfully adapt and recreate the recipes.

You will also be fascinated to see the long voyage undertaken by certain foods, now commonplace in places far away from each other geographically. From the Mediterranean basin to Scandinavia, for example, pastry chefs could hardly do without nuts and dried fruits. Spices such as cinnamon and cumin have also spread well beyond their original home in Asia.

This tour of the culinary world also allows you to discover the context in which foods are usually eaten: as everyday fare at the family table, on festive or religious occasions, or between meals as snacks. You will notice that the order or time of day when certain foods are served varies quite a lot. Pastries and sweets that might be the crowning touch to a meal in France might be teatime treats in other countries, or even breakfast!

In a time when fast foods and industrially prepared foods are commonplace, *Culina Mundi* seeks to promote the culinary heritage of the world. Indeed, in some ways the very globalization that has allowed certain foods to travel around the world and enrich the gastronomy of many countries is a double-edged sword. By making certain foods "stars" of the planetary food scene, in the long term don't we run the risk of considerably impoverishing regional and national cuisines?

Finally, whether you are making dinner for your family or inviting guests for a celebration, putting together just the right meal is an art that combines research into the best dishes with the affection we feel for those who will eat them. *Culina Mundi* aspires to be a source of inspiration for you in this noble enterprise.

Christèle Jany

Hot & Cold Appetizers

Antilles

Preparation time: 15 minutes
Cooking time: 25 minutes
Soaking time, salt cod: 24 hours
Difficulty: ★

Serves 4

For the pumpkin accras:
ca. 200 g/7 oz giraumon or pumpkin
3 cloves garlic
3 chives
1 chili pepper tip
2 or 3 sprigs parsley
1 sprig thyme

1 tbsp flour
150 g/5¹/₂ oz malanga
salt
pepper

For the cod accras:
250 g/9 oz salt cod
250 g/1³/₄ cups flour
3 cloves garlic
3 chives
2 or 3 sprigs parsley
1 sprig thyme
1 chili pepper tip
2 egg whites
oil for frying

Accras made with fish are famous little crusty croquettes served warm that go perfectly with *ti-punch*, a rum-based drink. Though not as famous, pumpkin *accras* made with giraumon can be found at family gatherings in the West Indies. Creole chefs also call them *marinades* or fried candy.

These fritters were first introduced to the West Indies by African slaves. In the Ewe language spoken in Ghana and Togo, the word *accras* means vegetable fritters. Everything needed for making them is available in the West Indies: *chou coco* (heart of coconut palm), christophines, breadfruit, zucchini, eggplant, little fish called *pisquettes* and shrimp.

Giraumon is a West Indian pumpkin shaped like a large pear. Either green or white, it can weigh anywhere from 2 to 15 kg (4½–33 lb) and its flesh can be anywhere from dark yellow to bright orange. It is delicious in purées, soups, au gratin or in a stew called *carry* or *colombo*, depending on the spices used. Recently, giraumon has been used in flans and cakes as well. Malanga, a starchy cousin of manioc, gives off an ideal odor for seasoning pumpkin *accras*. In Guadeloupe, malanga can be found with either pink or white flesh. Like potatoes, it goes well with meat topped with cheese or mousseline sauce. When peeled and cut into pieces, it cooks easily in 10 to 15 minutes. In this recipe, the malanga makes the batter smoother.

If desired, the egg whites can be omitted from the cod batter. Using yeast will make them puffier and crisper. Do not hesitate to use chopped onion for flavor. To perfect the flavor of the batter, make a test batch, then taste it and make any needed changes before frying the *accras*.

1. The day before serving, put the cod in cold water for desalting. Let it soak for 24 hours. The day of serving, cut off the top of the pumpkin and remove the seeds. Cut it into large slices and then cubes. Cut the peel off each piece.

2. Prepare the various ingredients for the pumpkin accras: peel and crush the garlic, finely chop the entire chives (green and white), chili pepper and parsley.

3. Purée the pumpkin in a blender, then tip into a bowl. Add the garlic, chives, chili pepper, parsley, crushed thyme and flour. Mix well, then add salt and pepper. Grate the malanga over the top and mix until it is a smooth paste. Form small balls with the mixture.

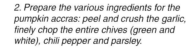

Accras

4. Poach the cod in boiling water for 5 minutes. Take it out and place it in a strainer. Put the cod on a chopping board and gently remove the skin, spine and any other bones, and then tear the meat into small pieces.

5. To make the cod accras, put the flour in a mixing bowl. Add 125 ml/1 cup cold water and whisk with a fork. Add the garlic, chives, chopped parsley and thyme, chili pepper, and the bits of cod. Blend well.

6. Beat the two egg whites and add them to the cod paste just before frying. With a spoon, drop the accras into a fryer at 160°C/340°F. Fry the pumpkin accras after the cod accras are finished.

Marinated Anchovies

Preparation time: 10 minutes
Marinating time: 13 hours
Chilling time: 3 hours
Difficulty: ★★

Serves 4

500 g/generous 1 lb fresh anchovies
250 ml/1 cup wine vinegar
salt
pepper
200 ml/generous ¾ cup virgin olive oil

For the raspberry oil:
100 g/generous ¾ cup raspberries
300 ml/1¼ cups olive oil

For the garnish:
cherry tomatoes
blades of chive
lettuce

Olive oil is the star in this anchovy dish, which is extremely popular throughout Spain. Spain was already exporting olive oil in the time of the Roman Empire, and today it is refined throughout the entire country. It becomes so pure that it can be poured over salads and fish without altering their taste. It is especially useful for preserving foods such as sardines and anchovies.

The purest and most familiar olive oil is produced in the Seuta region. It is produced from small, round olives with a very delicate skin. Only half a spoonful of olive oil is needed to make a marinade fruity and acidic. Cherries or strawberries will blend nicely with its flavor as well.

Anchovies get their popularity on the Iberian Peninsula from the Basque region, in the north of Spain. This small, silvery fish is either salted or preserved in a jar with oil. When freshly caught, it has bright eyes and glossy skin. Their fillets must be removed with agility, but also with delicacy because their fine meat must stay completely intact in the marinade. A single swift movement is needed to remove both the head and the spine. The anchovies are quickly rinsed off and cleaned, then placed on a plate skin-side down. They should be placed in a marinade made of water and vinegar to ensure that the meat stays intact. The vinegar cleans the fish and gives it its firmness and sheen. After marinating for 10 hours, they are strained and olive oil is poured over the anchovies before being put back into the marinade for three more hours.

These little fish go through all this without being harmed. Fresh and shiny as the day they were caught, they are then arranged on a serving platter and covered with a little raspberry oil just before they are served. Sardines could be prepared the same way.

The raspberry oil will stay fresh for two weeks if stored in an airtight glass jar. Perfect on salads, it can add some sophistication to cold meats as well.

1. Make the raspberry oil: purée the fresh raspberries. Strain in a chinois or other strainer. Add 3 spoonfuls of the raspberry purée to the olive oil and put into a bottle. Set aside.

2. Cut the anchovies just behind the head. Remove the head and spine all at once. Gently open the fish into two halves. Rinse them quickly under running water.

3. Place the anchovies skin-side down in a dish with fairly high sides. Cover them with water and pour the wine vinegar over them. Let them marinate for 10 hours.

in Raspberry Oil

4. Take the anchovies out of the marinade after the time indicated has passed. Wipe off the excess marinade. Place them on a plate and season with salt and pepper. Pour over olive oil and refrigerate for 3 hours.

5. Place them skin-side down on absorbent paper and let the marinade drain onto the paper for about 10 minutes.

6. Arrange the anchovies meat-side down on a serving platter. Decorate with the cherry tomatoes and blades of chive. Add a few lettuce leaves to the presentation. Generously pour raspberry oil over the platter.

Vegetable

Preparation time: 15 minutes
Cooking time: 40 minutes
Difficulty: ★

Serves 4

2 red peppers
2 cloves garlic
10 basil leaves, choppped
olive oil
¹/₂ chili pepper
salt
pepper

300 g/11 oz eggplant
3 tbsp tomato sauce
100 ml/7 tbsp white wine
300 g/2³/₄ cups sliced zucchini
100 ml/7 tbsp peanut oil
4 globe artichokes
juice of 1 lemon
200 g/2¹/₂ cups sliced mushrooms
12 cherry tomatoes
200 g/7 oz mozzarella cheese
1 ball scamorza cheese (optional)
1 or 2 sprigs parsley

The best way to begin an Italian meal is with colorful antipasti. The name literally means "before the meal", because it stimulates the taste buds before the main course.

Italian cooks in the Renaissance used to begin and end their meals with cold platters, ancestors of antipasti. As a result of the work in the kitchen done by Bartolomeo Scappi, chef of the popes, the habit of eating an antipasto spread throughout Europe around 1570.

There are three different groups of antipasti. *Affetati*, the most popular, is composed of deli and dried meats. It is frequently made with San Daniele or Parma ham, dried beef called *bresaola*, *felino* sausage and *pancetta*, the unsmoked bacon rolled in pepper. The vegetables used by our chef belong to the *antipasto misto* group, which includes many dishes without meat. These vegetables are served fried or grilled. In fact,

restaurants serve *antipasto misto mare* with seafood, including fish and shellfish.

Gustavo Andreoli served eggplant with tomato sauce as one of his starters. Eggplant, or aubergine, is consumed mostly in southern Italy. It is grown in Puglia, in Campania, in Sicily, in Calabria and in Sardinia. Italians make all sorts of delicious dishes with eggplant: fritters, eggplant stuffed with anchovies and capers, roulades and meatballs.

Our chef uses one cheese that has two distinct flavors to accompany the vegetables: mozzarella. One type is made from water buffalo milk and has a fruity flavor, and the other type is made from cow's milk and is called *scamorza*. This caramel colored cheese is shaped like a pear and has a smooth and delicate rind.

1. Sear the peppers for 10 minutes on the stovetop. Put them in a bowl and cover so the steam loosens their skins. Peel them and cut into strips. Add to the bowl 1 clove garlic, chopped basil, a drop of olive oil, crushed chili, salt and pepper.

2. Rinse the eggplant and cut it into small pieces. Fry it for 5 minutes in 50 ml/3¹/₂ tbsp hot olive oil. When the eggplant starts to brown, add the tomato sauce and the white wine. Let this cook for 10 minutes.

3. Wash the zucchini, dry it off, then cut it into thin slices. Heat the peanut oil in a frying pan and add the zucchini slices. Allow to brown for 10 minutes in the oil.

Antipasti

4. Remove the leaves from the artichokes. Let the hearts soak in lemon-flavored water, then cut into thin strips. Put them in a bowl and add the lemon juice, a drop of olive oil, salt and pepper.

5. Heat 50 ml/3^1/$_2$ tbsp olive oil in a frying pan. Add the thinly sliced mushrooms, 1 clove garlic and some chopped basil. Season with salt and pepper. Let this cook for 4 or 5 minutes and then let cool.

6. Cut the cherry tomatoes in two and the cheese into thin slices. Arrange the different antipasti on a serving platter: peppers, mushrooms, eggplant with tomato sauce, artichokes, cherry tomatoes and mozzarella.

Spider Crab

Preparation time: 1 hour
Cooking time: 25 minutes
Difficulty: ★

Serves 6

6 spider crabs
300 g/11 oz prawns
10 g/1 tbsp mustard
150 g/1⅓ cups grated cheese
100 g/¾ cup chopped fresh parsley
3 tbsp fine breadcrumbs

1 tbsp butter
sea salt
pepper

For the béchamel:
1 liter/1 quart milk
30 g/2 tbsp butter
30 g/3 tbsp flour
1 pinch nutmeg
salt
pepper

In 1520, when Portugese explorer Ferdinand Magellan discovered the strait that is named for him today, the "Land of Fire", Tierra del Fuego, was populated with nomad Indians who were still living much as they had in the Stone Age. Among them, the Alakalufs and the Yagans were spending their lives on the water in canoes, eating crabs, mussels and fish. These Indians were decimated before the start of the twentieth century. Today, the people of Ushuaia and Punta Arenas make their living by fishing or working in crab, shrimp, scampi or fish factories.

The spider crab is one of the favorite local catches. Argentinans call this shellfish belonging to the crab family *Centollo*. It has a pink, pinkish yellow or reddish shell that is prickly and long and delicate legs with no pincers. It can live in sandy bottoms up to 50 meters (165 feet) deep. Its meat has a subtle flavor that is not as strong as that of crab.

It is important to choose a lively spider crab that reacts energetically to having its legs or antennae touched. Make sure that it has plenty of meat, determined by its weight and volume. It should have a hard shell resistant to barnacles (this signifies that it hasn't become thin from recent sloughing). If turned over, the underside of the shellfish should be swollen and near transparent.

For this recipe, our chef partially shells the spider crab. To fully cook a small spider crab in a salted court-bouillon takes 15 minutes, and about 25 minutes for a large one. To give the spider crab more flavor, add herbs and white wine to the bouillon. Fried mushrooms or marinated mussels can add flavor to this recipe as well. If your local fish market does not sell spider crab, this same dish au gratin will taste just as good made with large crabs.

1. Separate the crab shells from the meat and legs. Scrape off and rinse the skeletons and set aside. Cook the meat and legs together for 5 to 6 minutes in salted boiling water. Crumble the meat into small pieces. Shell the prawns and chop them.

2. For the béchamel, bring the milk to the boil. Melt the butter in a saucepan. Whisk in the flour and then add the hot milk. Whisk for 10 minutes over low heat to obtain a béchamel sauce. Add salt, pepper and a little nutmeg.

3. Put the béchamel in a bowl. Add the crumbled crab meat and the chopped prawns. Mix well with a spoon.

"Tierra del Fuego"

4. Add the mustard, chopped parsley and grated cheese to the filling. Add salt and pepper to taste. Mix until the filling is smooth.

5. With a brush, coat the inside of the shells with melted butter. Tap the breadcrumbs into the shells so that they are distributed evenly throughout.

6. Fill the shells with the béchamel filling. Even out the top with a spatula. Sprinkle breadcrumbs on top and cook in the oven for 10 minutes at 190°C/370°F. Garnish with fresh parsley and serve hot.

Mechelen Asparagus

Preparation time: 45 minutes
Cooking time: 25 minutes
Difficulty: ★★

Serves 4

2 bunches green asparagus
$1/2$ carrot, sliced in disks
1 rib celery, chopped
juice of 1 lemon
12 large scampi, uncooked
sea salt

For the zabaglione:
150 g/$^2/_3$ cup butter
4 egg yolks
330 ml/scant $1^1/_2$ cups Hoegaarden beer
salt
pepper

For the garnish:
1 bunch watercress
1 bunch chervil

Imagine: tender asparagus covered with scampi from the North Sea and enveloped in a beer zabaglione—this is a starter that should be savored slowly.

Well known in Egyptian times and loved by the Romans, asparagus grows exceedingly well on the Belgian terrain. Asparagus from Mechelen is the primary crop in the city. This hardy plant has the tendency to have a strong and slightly bitter flavor in its tips. Other varieties of asparagus will work just as well as Mechelen asparagus. Fresh asparagus must be firm, have a bold color, and the tips must break off easily, because they are the most edible part.

Chef Pierre Fonteyne uses his creativity in this recipe, as he substitutes a common vinaigrette with a zabaglione to accompany this entrée. Cooked in a double boiler, the zabaglione is ready when the eggs combine with the beer and form a smooth blend. The most expert chefs use a whisk to achieve the best effect: the eggs must never cook, but need to thicken when mixed with the Hoegaarden beer.

This delicious beer, as its name indicates, comes from the Flemmish town of Hoegaarden, Belgian capital of wheat beers. Made in a bottom fermentation process at a temperature of less than 10°C/50°F, it is pale yellow in color and its flavor is that of hops, spices and citrus. A pinch of brown sugar in the sauce will eliminate some of its bitterness.

Scampi are known by several names, including Dublin Bay prawns and, the French term, langoustines.

Pierre Fonteyne also suggests another presentation of this dish. He reconstructs the scampi with its head and legs, and arranges the asparagus, coated in zabaglione, around them. He dresses this dish up with watercress and chervil.

1. Peel the asparagus. Remove any dirty, stringy parts. Rinse and drain. Cook for 15 minutes in 1 liter/1 quart salted water. Allow to cool and then set aside. Rinse the watercress and chervil for the garnish, then drain them.

2. In 2 liters/2 quarts salted water, boil the sliced carrot and celery. Add the lemon juice. As soon as the water boils, add the scampi to the pot. Allow to cook for 3 minutes over high heat. Remove and let cool.

3. Take the scampi out of the pot and place them on a plate. Remove their shells, clean out the heads, but leave the legs intact. Set aside the legs and heads for garnishing later.

with Scampi

4. For the sabayon, cut the softened butter into pieces. Break the eggs into a saucepan. Add the beer to the eggs while whisking.

5. Place the saucepan in a container filled with water over medium heat. Let it thicken in the double boiler, whisking constantly.

6. When the sauce is somewhat thickened, add the butter, salt and pepper, still whisking. Remove from heat when the sabayon is smooth. Place 2 or 3 asparagus spears on a plate and top with the scampi and sabayon. Garnish with the watercress and chervil.

Eggplant with

Preparation time: 20 minutes
Cooking time: 1 hour
Difficulty: ★

Serves 5

1 kg/2¼ lb eggplant
6 cloves garlic

4 tbsp tahini
2 tbsp olive oil
juice of 2 lemons
2 tsp ground cumin
salt
pepper

Hardy under its purple cover, the eggplant is most prevalent in recipes from the Mediterranean basin, although it is native to Pakistan. This vegetable can be grilled, baked, found in fritters, moussaka and ratatouille—the number of possibilities is countless. If Lebanon uses it lavishly in an assortment of *mezze*, or appetizers, Egypt uses it frequently in *baba ghanoush*, so this dish of grilled eggplant, puréed and then mixed with sesame cream, has a different name in Egypt and Lebanon. The seasoning is the only difference between the countries—and of course the palaces!

For Mohamed Fawzi Kotb, selecting the eggplant is very important. The largest and oldest vegetables have more seeds, so a smaller variety is the way to go. Try a mini-eggplant with shiny, smooth skin that is almost black with firm flesh. After poking several holes in the eggplant with a fork or a knife, it takes about an hour to bake in the oven. The flesh must be cooked, but not to the point where it starts to break apart.

If larger eggplants are desired, these can take about 20 minutes longer to cook. After the eggplant cools and is separated from its skin, it is first cut into large pieces and then chopped. Garlic is added to intensify its flavor. Baba ghanoush must have a smooth texture, but is not puréed.

Famous in the Middle East, *tahina* or tahini, a paste of ground sesame seeds, enriches the eggplant with the velvet smoothness of its volatile oil. As for the cumin, let its acrid aroma penetrate the eggplant's lemon-flavored skin.

In Egypt, it is customary to serve Eggplant with Sesame Cream with a bowl of tahini. Each guest can add as much cumin and lemon juice as they like.

1. Prick the skin of each eggplant with a knife or fork. Put them in a baking dish and bake at 200°C/390°F for 1 hour. Place the cooled eggplants on a chopping board. Split down the middle with a knife. Open and completely remove the flesh.

2. Put the eggplant flesh in a pile on the chopping board. Chop it into large chunks with a knife.

3. Peel and chop the garlic, then toss it onto the pile of eggplant. Finely chop the mixed garlic and eggplant. Save this mixture in a salad bowl.

Sesame Cream

4. Put the tahini in a small pitcher. Pour it onto the garlic and eggplant mixture and stir together with a whisk.

5. When the sesame cream is mixed well with the eggplant, pour the olive oil over the top and whisk together.

6. Juice the lemons into a small bowl. Pour the juice into the mixture. Sprinkle the cumin, salt and pepper on top and whisk vigorously. Serve in small dishes.

Eggplant au

Preparation time: 15 minutes
Cooking time: 25 minutes
Difficulty: ★

Serves 6

3 large eggplants
3 cloves garlic
1 bunch parsley

6 tbsp breadcrumbs
300 g/11 oz feta
salt
pepper
7 tbsp olive oil
3 tsp vinegar

This Eggplant au Gratin recipe comes from Macedonia, a region in the north of Greece. An inventive chef allowed himself a day of experimentation with that jewel, eggplant, and decided to cut it in half and broil it, fill it with garlic and cheese and serve it browned on top.

Zucchini, eggplant and tomatoes are the preferred vegetables of the Greeks. Greek eggplant, with an elongated shape, is cultivated almost everywhere in the country. Eggplant is the principal ingredient in moussaka, for example. Greeks stuff them with small vegetables, grill them and fry them, transforming them with caviar or *tourlou*, which is something like ratatouille. Indeed, they even candy eggplant by soaking them in a brine or sugared syrup.

In the *Odyssey*, Homer tells the story of the hero Ulysses, a shepherd, who makes cheese with the milk of his ewes. The word *feta* dates back to the seventeenth century, a time when Venice occupied Greece. Derived from the Latin word *fette*, it meant that one would cut this cheese into slices to preserve in barrels of brine. Today, it is one of the most popular cheeses in the world. A slice of feta, black olives and bread make a popular *mezze*, or starter. It is also used in salad and au gratin recipes. Of all the Greek cheeses, only feta will work well with this recipe owing to its flavor and its ability to melt.

Greek olive oil brings out the flavor of the Eggplant au Gratin. Our chef recommends using oil from Crete, because it is the most reputable. It is clear green with a light, fruity flavor. Olive oil from Kalamata in the Philippines is darker green with a thicker texture and is slightly bitter. Also very reputable, *halkidikiès* oil produced in Halkidiki in northern Greece is just as clear green and is very light, but also bitter.

1. Prick the eggplant skins with a fork. Put them on a broiling pan and broil or grill for 15 minutes. Peel the garlic and chop it along with the parsley.

2. Put the bread crumbs, crumbled feta and chopped garlic into a bowl. Using your hands, toss until everything is finely crumbled.

3. When the eggplants are cooked, cut each in half. Break the flesh into pieces using the tip of a knife.

Gratin with Feta

4. If desired, add salt and pepper to the eggplant. Sprinkle each eggplant half liberally with several dashes of olive oil, moving the bottle so as to distribute the oil evenly.

5. Place the eggplant halves on a flat baking dish. Sprinkle with chopped parsley and fill them with feta.

6. Bake the eggplant halves in the oven at 200°C/390°F for 10 minutes. When they are browned, remove from the oven and pour 3 tsp of vinegar and 3 tsp olive oil over the top. Serve hot.

Cod

Preparation time: 40 minutes
Cooking time: 50 minutes
Soaking time, cod: 12 hours
Difficulty: ★

Serves 6

250 g/9 oz salt cod
500 g/2 or 3 potatoes

150 ml/²/₃ cup milk
2 onions
1 bunch parsley
4 eggs
salt
pepper
oil for frying

There is still a demand for salt cod, an excellent representative of Portuguese food. Dried and salted cod cannot be found in the Mediterranean, however, so fishermen must transport it during long voyages from the Northern Seas to Lusitanian lands. It was in the fifteenth century when the cod saga began, as the Portuguese landed on the coasts of Canada. In the water, they discovered a godsend: a wealth of lively cod! Over the course of four centuries, ships from Aveiro, Setúbal, the Azores and the Algarve set out together for six months in search of this delicious creature. They traveled all the way to Newfoundland and Greenland. Lightly salted, this fish can easily be transported and travels all the way to Portugal without fear. There, it is washed, desalinated and then dried. After a period of decline, cod fishing has found new ways to expand in the twentieth century.

As for the potato, introduced from the New World, it has replaced bread and been a star of the table for centuries. A simple and robust accompaniment for meat and fish dishes, it can also be found in simmering stews as well as in delicious soups such as the *caldo verde* of Minho. Potatoes are the perfect partner for cod, usually cooked with their skin and served *coup de poing*, which means lightly mashed. In today's world, a victim of style like everything else, potatoes increasingly take the form of French fries.

Unlike a few similar dishes, these cod fritters are particularly light and low in fat. In fact, since they are made of pre-cooked ingredients, they fry very quickly, giving the oil just enough time to brown them without penetrating the interior.

1. Place the cod in cold water for 12 hours to desalinate, changing the water frequently. Drain it. Cook the potatoes for 30 minutes in lightly salted water. Peel and mash them.

2. Pour the milk into a saucepan and add an equivalent amount of water. Bring this mixture to the boil and add the cod. Allow to cook for 8 to 10 minutes. Drain, then remove the skin and spine.

3. Using a fork, separate the fibers from the meat while tearing it into pieces: they should come apart easily.

Fritters

4. Peel the onions and cut them into small dice. In a mixing bowl, mix the mashed potatoes, crumbled cod and diced onions.

5. Chop the parsley and sprinkle it on top of the mixture. Break the eggs over the top and add the pepper. Mix well with a whisk.

6. Make the quenelles with the help of two wet spoons: take a little of the mixture on one spoon and use the other to mold the dumpling. Brown the quenelles in the olive oil. Drain them on paper towels.

Brik with

Preparation time: 30 minutes
Cooking time: 10 minutes
Difficulty: ★

Serves 4

1 medium onion
¹/₂ bunch flat-leaf parsley
2 tbsp olive oil
4 sheets brik pastry
or phyllo dough or spring roll wrappers

50 g/¹/₃ cup capers
¹/₂ can chunk tuna in water
4 eggs
2 tsp salt
2 tsp pepper
olive oil for frying
1 lemon, to garnish

Crusty, savory *brik* turnovers contribute greatly to the well-deserved influence of Tunisian cuisine: of Levantine origin, *brik* pastries pander to the pickiness of gourmands and gourmets. Everyone has their own means of folding it: round, triangular, square or rolled up like a cigar. *Brik* may have salty or sweet fillings, as desired.

Called *warka* or *malsouka* in Tunisia, the thin pastry is made from fine semolina dough. Well kneaded, the dough is cooked on the heat of a special device that makes extremely fine sheets. Today, the complex hand-made process has become mechanized. Sheets of *brik* pastry, sometimes even pre-folded, can be found easily in Tunisian stores.

To make *brik* with egg, Kafik Tlatli suggests choosing sheets that are relatively thick. When folded, a sheet of *malsouka* can hold a heavy filling: in this case, tuna, egg, onions and capers.

A thick sheet folded in four makes the center stronger and the raw egg can be broken without worrying about piercing the dough. Particularly appreciated by the people of Tunisia, capers are added to many dishes. Their vinegar flavor goes deliciously with tuna. There are very small capers with a subtle flavor called *nonpareilles*. Their flavor is quite understated inside the *brik*.

In a deep fryer or a frying pan, the filled *brik* is placed in very hot, yet not boiling olive oil. When brown, it is removed from the fryer and put on a plate covered in paper towel to eliminate any excess oil.

It is tradition to enjoy *brik* with creamy egg in the middle, sometimes without capers and without tuna, but with shrimp, beef, or potatoes. Others prefer to bite into browned *brik* with slices of hard-boiled egg inside.

1. Peel and finely slice the onion. Remove the parsley stems and dice the leaves. Heat 2 tbsp olive oil in a frying pan and brown the onion on high heat for 2 minutes. Add the parsley. Brown for 5 minutes or until all the oil has evaporated.

2. Spread a sheet of pastry over a plate. Fold the 4 sides into the center to make a square.

3. Add the capers to the onion-parsley filling. Put some of the filling, in the shape of a crown, in the middle of the brik. Evenly spread crumbled tuna on the crown.

Egg and Tuna

4. Break an egg over the center of the crown. Add salt and pepper.

5. Fold one side of the sheet of pastry over the egg to form a triangle. Prepare more brik in the same way. Heat olive oil for frying the brik.

6. When the oil is very hot, gently add the brik. Let each side cook for 2 minutes, turning frequently. Allow to drain on paper towels. Serve very hot with lemon quarters.

Ceviche

Preparation time: 20 minutes
Marinating time: 60 to 90 minutes
Difficulty: ★

Serves 6

1 kg/2¼ lb fresh coalfish fillets
6 limes
100 g/3–4 oz pitted green olives
750 g/3¼ lb tomatoes
500 g/generous 1 lb onions

1 bunch flat-leaf parsley
50 g/⅓ cup capers
200 ml/generous ¾ cup olive oil
salt
pepper

Ceviche consists of raw fish pieces that have been marinated in lime juice and are then accompanied with tomatoes, onions, olives, capers and parsley. It is a regional recipe from the state of Guerrero, Mexico, famous for its languid Acapulco beaches on the Pacific Ocean.

In this recipe, the fish does not actually cook. The acidity from the lime juice naturally cures the flesh. Usually, Mexican chefs prepare *ceviche* with *sierra*, a local blue fish, cousin to the barracuda and yellowtail snapper. Bass or burbot can also be used in this recipe. Our chef prefers using coalfish (or coley), because the meat remains firm.

Mexicans have access to around 10,000 km (6,200 miles) of coastline along the Pacific and the Gulf of Mexico. On the Pacific, they catch crayfish, swordfish, bass or sharks. The Gulf of Mexico offers fish that can be found throughout the Caribbean: barracuda, yellowtail snapper, royal sea bream and a wide variety of shrimp. In Mexico, fish is prepared and eaten in the simplest of ways: typically, it is grilled, fried or marinated in lime juice.

Seasoning based on tomatoes, onions, olives and capers is characteristic of Mexican cuisine. Tomatoes were cultivated by the Aztecs and Incas, who called them *tomatl*. Because of the richness of the soil and the hot climate that lasts the entire year, this vegetable is grown in abundance and in many varieties.

Great citrus fruit producers, notably in the Vera Cruz region, Mexicans often opt to use limes in the preparation of marinades. Their very flavorful juice serves well to marinate both fish and meat. Lime juice is an element in many cocktails that include tequila, and is also found in the delicious avocado purée known as guacamole.

1. On a chopping board, cut the coalfish into small cubes with a knife. Put the cubes in a high-sided dish.

2. Juice the lime and pour it over the diced fish. Allow to marinate for 1 to 1½ hours in the refrigerator.

3. During this time, cut the olives into little disks. Finely dice the tomato. Peel and chop the onions. Cut the parsley into fine strips.

4. In a mixing bowl, combine the tomatoes, olives, onions, parsley and capers. Store them in the refrigerator.

5. After the fish has marinated, remove it from the marinade and drain. Put it in the mixing bowl with the vegetables and parsley. Mix well with a spoon.

6. Add the olive oil to this ceviche mix. Season with salt and pepper. Mix well and serve well chilled.

Rhine Salmon

Preparation time: 1 hour
Cooking time: 25 minutes
Marinating time: overnight + 2 hours
Chilling time: 2 or 3 hours
Difficulty: ★★

Serves 4

1 bunch dill
1 bunch parsley
1 bunch chervil
40 g/3 tbsp sugar
80 g/¹/₄ cup sea salt

400 g/14 oz salmon fillet, with skin
1 lemon
100 g/²/₃ cup flour
125 ml/1 cup milk
2 eggs
fine salt
freshly ground pepper
oil and butter for frying
200 ml/generous ³/₄ cup thick
crème fraîche, *or* sour cream
2 cucumbers

Crêpes rolled in jam are what inspired chef Otto Fehrenbacher to create this original and colorful Salmon Charlotte recipe. Coated in jam, confectioner's crêpes from Chantilly are filled and sliced into roundels. On the same principle, our chef presents an entrée in which he coats crêpes with crème fraîche (or sour cream) and salmon marinated with dill and lemon and then rolls them. After cutting them into slices, he places them in molds and fills the gaps with cubes of salmon and cucumber. He then removes them from the molds just as for a charlotte. This is a very light dish, ideal for a spring or summer meal.

Sometimes, he serves these rolled and stuffed crêpes as appetizers, without really making a true charlotte. Chantilly crêpes can also be coated with horseradish, and then the charlotte need only be filled with cubes of salmon.

In our chef's region, north of the Black Forest, salmon was reintroduced to the Rhine around five years ago, and then it started coming back up the rivers. When there is no salmon in the Rhine (it continues to be rare), Otto Fehrenbacher prefers to prepare an excellent wild Scottish salmon from the Shetland Islands or a trout that comes from regional fishing, rather than using farm-bred salmon.

Germans always serve cucumber raw, as a salad. After soaking it in water, they mix it with mustard, vinaigrette, dill and a little fresh cream.

It is important to fill the crêpes generously with thick cream before adding the salmon. The final preparation will be very tasty. If time permits, it is a good idea to leave the filled crêpes in the refrigerator overnight. This will firm up the crêpes and their filling, making them easier to slice.

Generally, our chef pours gelatin into the gaps in the charlotte mold, and serves the whole topped with a dab of cream.

1. Chop the dill, parsley and chervil, and mix them with the sugar and sea salt. Remove the bones from the salmon with tweezers. Place them in a tub and add the juice of ¹/₂ lemon. Sprinkle the herb mixture on top and allow to marinate overnight.

2. Blend the flour with a little milk and then whisk in the eggs. Add the rest of the milk along with salt and pepper. Make 6 crêpes in a frying pan with hot oil and butter. Skin and thinly slice the salmon. Spread some cream over the crêpes and cover it with slices of salmon.

3. Quickly roll the crêpes around their filling. Cover them in several layers of plastic wrap, being careful to seal them completely. Chill in the refrigerator for 2 to 3 hours.

Charlotte

4. Dice the remaining salmon that has been marinating. Peel the cucumbers, deseed, and dice to match the salmon. Mix the salmon and cucumbers with the juice of the second lemon half, dill, salt and pepper. Add the remaining cream. Allow to marinate for 2 hours.

5. Unpack the refrigerated crêpes and slice them into roundels. Line small teacups with plastic wrap. Line them with the crêpe roundels.

6. Put the salmon-cucumber mixture in the center of the teacups lined with crêpe. Fill all the way to the top and pack them down tightly with the back of a spoon. Turn the teacup over and unmold its contents on a bed of cucumber slices. Garnish with sprigs of the fresh herbs.

Tucumán and

Preparation time: 1 hour
Cooking time: 2 hours
Chilling time: 1 hour or more
Difficulty: ★★★

Serves 6

For the chicken turnover pastry:
1 kg/7 cups bread flour
100 g/7 tbsp butter, softened
20 g/1 tbsp salt
oil for frying

For the chicken filling:
1 chicken, uncooked
5 liters/5 quarts white wine vegetable bouillon
¹/₂ onion

250 g/1¹/₄ cups lard
1 small potato
200 g/7 oz pitted olives
100 g/³/₄ cup raisins, soaked in wine

4 eggs
1 pinch paprika
salt, pepper

For the spicy turnover pastry:
600 g/4¹/₄ cups plain or cake flour
200 ml/generous ³/₄ cup oil
200 ml/generous ³/₄ cup milk

For the spicy filling:
1 kg/2¹/₄ lb fillet of beef
1 pinch cumin
1 pinch *aji molido* (yellow chili paste)
200 g/1 cup lard
1 onion
1 pinch paprika
3 eggs

In the Tucumán province, the fertile plain that stretches east of the Cordillera in the Andes is situated next to tall plateaus that are bordered with high and majestic mountains. San Miguel of Tucumán, the regional capital, is among the most beautiful cities in the country owing to its many historic buildings. This is where delicious chicken turnovers can be enjoyed. Salta, where the spicy turnovers come from, is also a colonial gem. The town hall of 1582, the convent of San Bernardo and the church of San Francisco are all places visitors should see.

The people of South America are very fond of stuffed turnovers called *empenadas*, and they serve them as starters or between meals. Argentians prepare them with egg, chicken, spinach, cheese and ham. The original recipe was imported from Galicia by Spanish immigrants, who filled them with chicken, onions and peppers.

Farms throughout Argentina provide plenty of space for their chickens to run about freely. Corn yields are very abundant so it costs little to keep people nourished. In the preparation of *puchero*, for example, it is added to a chicken, potato and carrot stew. And it is featured in the sweet corn gratin that is part of the meat dish called *pastel choclo*.

Aji molido (yellow chili paste) adds flavor to the beef turnovers and is a typical flavor from Buenos Aires. Spicy peppers are put out to dry in the sun for many days, and then they are crushed coarsely.

Our chef recommends letting the pastry rest for at least four to six hours. It must be very firm so that it can be worked well. If not made correctly, the turnovers will open in the deep fryer or crumble in the oven.

1. Mix the flour and butter to prepare the pastry for the chicken turnovers. Use the fingertips to mix. Knead the dough with 300 ml/1¹/₄ cups salted water and form a ball. Cover it with plastic wrap and set aside for 1 hour. Boil the potato for 30 minutes. Boil all 7 eggs for 10 minutes.

2. For the spicy turnover pastry, mix the flour with 200 ml/generous ³/₄ cup water. Add the milk, begin mixing together, and finally add the oil. Knead it like pie dough. Leave it to sit for 1 hour in the refrigerator.

3. Poach the chicken for 1 hour in the vegetable bouillon. Remove the bones and skin, and chop the meat into pieces. Chop separately the olives, onion, raisins and hard-boiled eggs, and cut the potato into small cubes.

Salta Turnovers

4. For the spicy turnover filling, chop the beef and add the aji molido and cumin. Brown the onion for 5 minutes in some lard. Add the beef and let brown for 8 minutes. Away from the heat, add the paprika, salt, pepper and 3 chopped eggs. Let this cool.

5. For the chicken turnover filling, heat some lard in another frying pan and brown the chopped onion. When browned, remove from the heat and add the chicken, paprika, potato cubes, chopped green olives, 4 hard-boiled eggs, salt and pepper. Let this cool.

6. Make flat disks from the two pastries. Fill the butter pastry with the chicken filling. Seal the pastry disks and fry for 10 minutes. Fill the water pastry with the beef filling. Form turnovers. Glaze the surface with beaten egg yolk and bake in the oven for 20 minutes at 180°C/355°F.

Spinach

Preparation time: 30 minutes
Cooking time: 1 hour 20 minutes
Difficulty: ★★

Serves 4

2 large onions
200 ml/generous ³⁄₄ cup peanut oil
1 kg/2¹⁄₄ lb ripe tomatoes
4 Tourteaux or common crabs

200 g/7 oz bewolés (Cameroonian herb)
or fresh spinach leaves
1 pinch cayenne pepper
salt
pepper

Our chef has developed a recipe of stuffed crab with *bewolés* that is actually not very typical of the way crabs are enjoyed in Cameroon. In reality, the people of Cameroon usually prepare crabs very simply, rather than stuffed.

Cameroonians who live along the coast are able to find two types of crabs that are caught throughout most of the country on the Atlantic: small green crabs and large red crabs that resemble common crabs, called *tourteaux*. They appreciate these big crabs simply seasoned in a court-bouillon, simmered in a sauce with gumbo, or in a soup, mixed with various fish. For the preparation of this recipe, common crabs work best, but spider crabs or preserved crab meat works fine as well.

Marie Koffi-Nketsia combines crab meat with *bewolés*, a local herb that is related to spinach in its taste. The people of Came-

roon often combine *bewolé* leaves with tomatoes and shrimp or simmer them in a peanut sauce. Another typical variety of spinach, *ndolé* with a bitter taste, constitutes the national dish.

In Cameroon, peppers are used in a majority of dishes. Two main types share the favor of the country's chefs: the large yellow pepper called *teclar*, very flavorful with a fiery taste, and a large, round red pepper that is very spicy. Generally, our chef uses fresh peppers. In this recipe, we preferred to use dry cayenne pepper to adapt to different palates.

We have served the filling in the shells of crabs for a classic presentation. Of course, it can also be served in small casserole dishes or in little pastry pies. To make them even more appetizing, sprinkle them with breadcrumbs or butter and cook them au gratin in the oven.

1. Peel and chop the onions. Brown half of them in 50 ml/3¹⁄₂ tbsp of the peanut oil for 10 minutes in a covered saucepan.

2. Remove the skin from the tomatoes. On a chopping board, chop the tomatoes with a knife. Add them to the onion saucepan. Let brown for 20 minutes on high heat. Plunge the crabs into boiling water, cook for 15 minutes, then remove the meat.

3. Blend the meat in a mixer. Brown the rest of the onions in 50 ml/3¹⁄₂ tbsp oil for 5 minutes. Add the crab meat, chili, salt, pepper and another 50 ml/3¹⁄₂ tbsp oil. Let brown for 10 minutes, stirring constantly.

Stuffed Crab

4. Blanch the spinach for 5 minutes in salted boiling water. Refresh in cold water, then drain them well. Finely chop the spinach on a chopping board. Add salt and pepper, then sauté for 5 minutes in a covered frying pan with the remaining oil.

5. When the spinach is wilted and dry, add it to the saucepan containing the crab and tomatoes. Adjust the seasoning, depending on the desired flavor. Let cook for 10 to 15 minutes, stirring often.

6. With a spoon, fill each crab shell with the filling. Pack the filling well and serve hot.

Janina Crêpes

Preparation time: 1 hour 15 minutes
Cooking time: 40 minutes
Resting time, dough: 1 to 2 hours
Difficulty: ★★★

Serves 4

120 g/4 oz dried wild mushrooms
300 ml/1¼ cups oil for frying

For the crêpe dough:
250 g/1¾ cups flour
350 ml/1½ cups milk
40 g/2½ tbsp butter
2 whole eggs
2 egg yolks
2 g/½ tsp salt

For the ravioli dough:
250 g/1¾ cups flour
2 eggs
1 tsp salt

For the filling:
1 small onion, minced
50 g/¼ cup lard
500 g/generous 1 lb cooked sauerkraut
200 ml/generous ¾ cup beef stock
1 egg
50 g/½ cup breadcrumbs
1 tsp each: salt, pepper

For the breadcrumb topping:
4 eggs
1 tbsp oil
300 g/3 cups fine breadcrumbs
salt
pepper

From North to South and East to West, it is not unusual to find chefs preparing a recipe in honor of their native country. Arkadiusz Zuchmanski's Janina Crêpes and Ravioli are a famous appetizer that is presented in two different forms, made from a light dough, a rich filling and an irresistible breadcrumb topping.

A long time ago, many Italians were attracted to a flourishing Poland and immigrated there. Certain Italians left monuments, while others taught local people the art of working with dough. Crêpes and ravioli adapted to Polish fillings of cabbage with beef or white cheese.

When making the crêpe dough, add the flour to the mixture last, sprinkling it on like rain. Whip vigorously until a light and airy dough is formed. The cooked crêpe can also be folded over the filling. They can undergo a second frying and remain just as light. The breadcrumb topping will brown them.

The ravioli dough will have a thicker texture than that of the crêpes. The salted flour is mounded on a working space and the eggs broken in the center. Then 30 ml (2 tbsp) of water or oil are gradually added. The dough needs to be worked with gently by hand, constantly pushing the ingredients toward the center. After it is well kneaded and in the shape of a ball, the dough is covered with a wet cloth and chilled. It becomes supple and homogeneous this way.

To prepare the ravioli, place a small amount of dough on a flour-covered table. Roll it out as thin as possible and put 2 tbsp filling in the center, then seal by pinching the edges together. Round, squared or in croissant form, the ravioli are poached rapidly. Our chef suggests covering the ravioli in breadcrumbs and then quickly browning them in a fryer with a drop of hot butter. A mushroom sauce boasting the colors of fall will accompany this recipe well.

1. Rehydrate the dried mushrooms in lukewarm water. Mix all the crêpe dough ingredients together vigorously. Separately, knead all the ingredients for the ravioli dough together with 30 ml/2 tbsp water. Refrigerate both for 1 to 2 hours.

2. Over low heat, cook the onions in the lard for 3 minutes in a covered pot. Add the sauerkraut and mix well. Add half of the drained and minced mushrooms and the beef stock. Cook 10 minutes on low heat. Combine the breadcrumbs, eggs, salt and pepper in a bowl.

3. Make the crêpes in a hot, oiled frying pan. Lay out each crêpe on a work surface. Top each one with a large spoonful of filling and spread it the width of the crêpe.

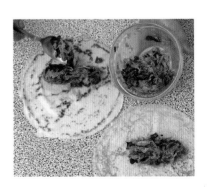

and Ravioli

4. Fold the left and ride sides of the crêpe over the filling. Fold the top and bottom toward the center, forming a square, and then roll it up. In a bowl, whisk 4 eggs with 1 tbsp oil and 1 tbsp water. Put the breadcrumbs in a dish.

5. Roll the filled crêpes thoroughly in the eggs and then in the breadcrumbs. Prepare the ravioli and fill them with the rest of the stuffing. Cook them for 3 minutes in boiling water and keep hot.

6. Cook the remaining dried mushrooms 5 minutes in boiling water. Blend them in a mixer. Deep-fry the crêpe rolls for 1 minute. When they are golden brown, use a skimmer to remove them from the oil. Serve the crêpes and ravioli covered in mushroom sauce.

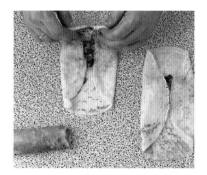

Ham and Chicken

Preparation time: 40 minutes
Cooking time: 35 minutes
Difficulty: ★

Serves 4

100 ml/7 tbsp whole milk
1/3 stick cinnamon
1 pinch nutmeg
black peppercorns
250 g/9 oz chicken breast

5 onions
1 liter/1 quart olive oil
250 g/9 oz Iberian ham
500 g/3 1/2 cups flour
100 g/1 cup breadcrumbs
2 eggs
salt
1 head of lettuce

Spanish cuisine honors the famed béchamel by using it in one of its specialties, possibly the most popular and appreciated throughout the country. Because, for the Spanish, the preparation of croquettes is tradition. In a form more or less oval, the thin, crusty exterior of breadcrumbs mixed with beaten eggs is stuffed with various fillings, some more refined than others, from all different regions. Common elements throughout all these fillings are chicken, ham, tuna or vegetables.

This dish is an appetizer that is generally served with a salad. In Spain, *croquetas* also refer to cod fritters, which are also served as a starter. Inspired by a traditional croquette recipe, chef Alberto Herráiz's croquettes distinguish themselves from the others because of their most generous size.

Like Serrano ham, Iberian ham or *jamón ibérico*—sometimes called *pata negra* because of the black legs of the variety of semi-wild pig that it comes from—is without doubt one of the most famous in Spain. It is so popular that its reputation has extended beyond the borders of Spain. The secret of its flavor, discovered in the sixteenth century, resides in the feeding of the pigs with roots, herbs and olives, completed by a fattening up with acorns.

Breeding grounds of Iberian pigs remain cork oak forests and the green forests of Extremadura and Andalusia. Rare and expensive, these swine possess distinctive signs that can be easily picked out, as its meat is blue-veined and streaked in fat. To fully appreciate the delicate flavor of hazelnut in this pork, it is served simply in *tapas* and with white bread. If the pig is presented on a *jamonera*, a plank of wood or metal, it is carved according to precise rules.

With wine, the presence of the cinnamon in this recipe will be taken into account. Opt for a fine sherry or other types of wine that are aromatic and fruity.

1. Bring the milk to the boil with the cinnamon, a pinch of nutmeg and a few black peppercorns. Add the chicken breast and allow to cook for 10 minutes on low heat.

2. Peel and mince the onions. Fry them gently in 400 ml/1 2/3 cups of the olive oil. Drain the chicken breast and set aside the milk. Dice both the chicken and the ham. Add the flour to the onions and mix well.

3. Strain the milk into the pan with the onions (remove the cinnamon). Blend well.

Croquettes

4. When the mixture is thickened, add the cubes of chicken and ham and stir so that nothing sticks. Add salt and pepper, to taste. Remove from the stovetop and let cool.

5. Prepare the large croquettes: take a handful of the mixture for each croquette, pressing them firmly into shape so they do not fall apart during cooking. Make them in the shape of large sausages.

6. Heat the remaining oil to 160°C/320°F. Beat the eggs. Roll the croquettes in the egg and then in breadcrumbs. Fry them until golden brown, then drain. Serve right away, accompanied with a salad.

Fawn Medallions

Preparation time: 20 minutes
Cooking time: 25 minutes
Chilling time: 1 hour
Difficulty: ★★

Serves 4

600 g/1¹/₄ lb fawn tenderloin

For the vinaigrette:
1 tbsp balsamic vinegar
salt
1 tbsp olive oil
1 tbsp peanut oil
1 tbsp walnut oil
pepper

For the mushroom marinade:
250 g/9 oz assorted wild mushrooms
¹/₂ tbsp olive oil
30 g/3 tbsp coriander seeds
1 shallot, finely diced
¹/₂ tbsp dry white wine
juice of 1 lemon
salt
peppercorns

For the garnish:
chervil sprigs
toasted sandwich bread (optional)

Thin shavings of meat in the form of *carpaccio* is a great idea for an hors-d'oeuvre that should delight fans of game. If fawn is very infrequently eaten and hard to locate, doe meat, venison and young boar meat are just as delicate as that of fawn.

The important aspect of this recipe is the particular flavor of the game that blends perfectly with the aromas of the wild mushrooms. Whether made with beef or fawn, *carpaccio* is eaten raw, in extremely thin slices, generally carved from a piece of meat without fat. Tenderloin, sirloin or the leg of the fawn will all make a delicately flavored treat.

In order to help cut the game thinly enough, Michel Haquin suggests deep freezing the piece of meat an hour before slicing it. This makes it firmer and thus easier to slice into nice, thin rounds that are quite even in size. In regards to choosing which

mushrooms to use, they must be a good match for the taste of the meat that has been chosen: chanterelles, morels or *pieds-de-mouton* (meaty, cream-colored wild mushrooms) will all be perfect with a *carpaccio* of game. On the other hand, porcini and button mushrooms work better with beef.

Nevertheless, the cooking time will vary slightly depending on which mushrooms are chosen. The chanterelle mushroom, because of its fragility, cannot be cooked for very long. It is suggested to remove it from heat in the middle of the cooking time. As for the *pieds-de-mouton*, they take longer to cook and must be cut into two. This recipe suggests an amazing marinade of cooked mushrooms in a Mediterranean-flavored juice. A smart trick is to use lemon juice, because it will prevent the mushrooms from darkening prematurely.

1. Put the fawn tenderloin in the freezer for 1 hour. Pour the vinegar and a little salt into a small bowl. Add the three oils. Whisk together well, add pepper, and set aside for later.

2. Wash the mushrooms. In 100 ml/7 tbsp water, bring to a boil the olive oil, coriander, chopped shallots, salt, pepper, white wine and lemon juice.

3. As soon as it boils, add the mushrooms. Allow to cook, uncovered, for 20 minutes. Turn the mushrooms into a mixing bowl and let cool.

with Marinated Mushrooms

4. Place an 8-cm/3-in metal ring in the center of each plate. Fill the circle with the cooled mushrooms (without their cooking juices). Set aside.

5. Take the fawn tenderloin out of the freezer and cut it in extremely thin slices, approximately 5 mm/¹/₈ in thick. Arrange them nicely around the rings.

6. Using a brush, cover each slice of meat with the vinaigrette. Season with the peppercorn, sea salt and coriander. Remove the rings from the mushrooms and garnish with chervil.

Lobster in

Preparation time: 35 minutes
Cooking time: 25 minutes
Difficulty: ★★

Serves 4

For the lobster:
1 lobster, ca. 1.5 kg/3¼ lb
or 4 small lobsters of 400 g/14 oz
500 ml/2 cups white wine
1 onion
1 carrot

For the garnish:
1 head frisée
½ head raddichio
150 g/5½ oz lamb's lettuce
12 new carrots
100 g/⅔ cup peas
1 bunch young onions
dill (optional)

For the raspberry vinaigrette:
50 ml/3½ tbsp sherry vinegar
100 ml/7 tbsp olive oil
100 g/¾ cup raspberries
salt
pepper

It is without a doubt the largest, finest and most appreciated of crustaceans: if the male lobster is known for having a refined taste, the female, who is heavier, is only more flavorful. Equipped with a pair of powerful pincers and a solid shell, the lobster can be cut either when raw or after it has been cooked. In this recipe, our chef plunges it into boiling water while it is still alive. It is preferable to tie the claws together to prevent struggle in the hot water.

Highly sought after by chefs, the meat in the claws is the smoothest. When cutting the lobster, the innards must be removed. You can prepare the lobster mince for this recipe only with claw meat, if you prefer: the preparation of the court-bouillon will be the same, but you will need to cook the claw meat for 6 minutes after it comes to the boil.

This dish is best served at the beginning of spring. Choose fresh onions, still quite small in size, as these have a more subtle taste than fully grown onions later in the season. They should be minced once cooked to make the dish more refined. The young carrots' outline can be enhanced by giving them a nice shape. Peel the carrot with one hand, while turning it around in the hollow of the other. The ends are rounded with the blade of a small paring knife. Cooked separately, these tender vegetables should be plunged immediately in cold water to preserve their color.

The choice of lettuces will vary depending on the season; the most important aspect is that it is fresh and crisp. Avoid leaving the lamb's lettuce in water for too long or it will become water-logged.

The lovely red color of the sauce comes from blending the raspberries to serve with the lobster. If they seem a bit acidic, add 1 tbsp sugar to the vinaigrette to make them sweeter.

1. Put 1 liter/1 quart cold water in a large pot. Add the white wine, chopped onion and carrot. Bring to a boil. Add the lobster and allow to cook 10 minutes.

2. Remove the lobster from the pot and run it under cold water. Separate the claws from the body by cutting at the joint. Detach the head from the tail. Break the legs and pull out the meat. Save the tail meat and the empty claws for the final presentation.

3. Trim and wash the lettuce. Peel the young onions. Peel the carrots and cut in half lengthwise. Shell the peas, if needed. Cook the vegetables in 1 liter/1 quart salted water, one vegetable at a time. Drain and set aside.

Raspberry Vinaigrette

4. Blend the raspberries in a mixer. Add the vinegar and blend again. Pour in the olive oil and blend one more time. Season with salt and pepper and set aside.

5. Cut the lobster tail meat in half lengthwise. With the point of a knife, devein. Cut each half into three escallops.

6. Arrange the lettuce hearts to form a rose shape. Place the lobster escallops and claws on either side with an assortment of vegetables. Pour the raspberry vinaigrette over the top and garnish with dill.

Escargot

Preparation time: 30 minutes
Cooking time: 1 hour 40 minutes
Rising time: 2 hours
Difficulty: ★★

Serves 4

For the escargots:
72 fresh escargot (small land snails)
1¹/₂ onions
1 or 2 cloves
1 small sprig thyme
1 bay leaf
1 bulb fennel
1 shallot
2 cloves garlic
6 anchovies

75 g/2¹/₂ oz uncooked ham
30 g/¹/₃ cup crushed walnuts
100 ml/7 tbsp olive oil
3 tomatoes

1 pinch cayenne pepper
1 splash pastis [anise-flavored alcohol]
salt, pepper

For the bread galettes:
350 g/1²/₃ cups mashed potatoes
120 g/³/₄ cup spelt or sweet chestnut flour
120 g/³/₄ cup wheat flour
4 eggs
40 g/3 tbsp brewer's yeast
120 ml/¹/₂ cup milk
butter for frying

For the garnish:
4 sprigs chervil
4 blades of chive
purslane leaves or fresh spinach

These small escargots come straight from Languedoc, and more specifically from the Sommières region where there are, according to Georges Rousset, just as many escargot recipes as there are towns. Everything is simple and authentic in the preparation of this dish. Only the rinsing and cooking of the land snails takes a bit of time.

Put the escargot, already well cleaned, in a saucepan with cold water that has been flavored with onion, clove, thyme, bay leaf, fennel and olive oil. The cooking begins on a very low heat, as the escargots begin to leave their shells. Next, increase the heat, but be sure not to touch the saucepan so that the escargots do not retreat back into their shells. Skim and allow to cook on low heat for 1¼ hour. Drain the escargots, keeping 500 ml/2 cups of the cooking juice to add to the sauce. Once out of their shells, save the escargots in their juice.

If cooking these gastropods does not sound like a process you want to be part of, escargots can often be bought in a box already cooked and often out of their shells. They will have to be drained and can then be put directly in the sauce to simmer for three minutes. Sometimes, however, the labeling on the escargot boxes is wrong or misleading: make sure that they are true small escargots and not the larger, chewy escargots imported from Asia.

It can be useful to prepare the potato purée the night before, especially if taking on the task of cooking fresh escargots the next day.

The dough for the galettes must rest for two hours at room temperature so that the yeast has time to do its work in making the dough rise. The dough is made from wheat flour or sweet chestnut or spelt flour. A long time ago, the peasants in poor lands used both of these types of meal to make their bread in regions where flour was expensive or hard to obtain.

1. Rinse the escargots. Allow to cook for 1–1¹/₄ hour in a large pot with 1 onion, clove, thyme, bay leaf, fennel, salt, pepper and 1 dash of oil. Once cooked, drain and remove them from the shell. Chop the ¹/₂ onion, the shallot and the ham.

2. Heat 1 tbsp olive oil in a frying pan. Add the ¹/₂ onion, shallot, crushed garlic, ham, walnuts, and the (desalinated) anchovies to the pan. Let brown for 2 to 3 minutes.

3. Blanch and dice the tomatoes. Add them to the previous mixture. Wet with a few spoonfuls of the juice from cooking the escargots.

Sommièroise

4. Add the escargots to the frying pan. Season with salt, pepper and cayenne pepper. Let simmer for 2 minutes on low heat (the cubes of tomato must remain whole). Add a dash of pastis. Set aside.

5. For the galettes, mix together the flours, mashed potatoes and eggs. Add the brewer's yeast, dissolved in the milk. Mix well to form smooth dough. Wrap in plastic wrap and let rise for 2 hours at room temperature.

6. Heat up a blini pan or small frying pan; grease it lightly. Cook 2 tbsp of the galette batter at a time, letting each brown for 5 minutes. On each plate, arrange purslane leaves, escargots in the sauce, chervil and chives. Accompany with the galettes.

Asparagus Pastry

Preparation time: 1 hour
Cooking time: 20 minutes
Difficulty: ★

Serves 4

40 green asparagus
100 g/7 tbsp butter
100 ml/7 tbsp crème fraîche
4 or 5 sprigs chervil
250 g/9 oz puff pastry
flour for dusting
sea salt, table salt
pepper

Pastry forms a culinary base that allows for the preparation of many hot appetizers. It seems that puff pastry was devised in the Middle East and brought to Europe by the crusaders. Many have laid claim to the marvelous pastry with thousands of "leaves": among them, the most famous perhaps, is Claude Gelée. An apprentice pastry chef in the beginning of the seventeenth century, he later became the famous landscape painter, Claude Lorrain. His preparation demanded know-how and patience: the base dough is filled with butter and then folded over itself multiple times in order to form the multi-layered pastry that allows it to rise so enticeingly while baking. Our chef nicely joins the puff pastry with fine asparagus of distinct flavor. Three major types of asparagus are sold in markets from April until the end of July. Green asparagus, which features this color from the stem to the tip, is cultivated in fresh air in open fields. It is gathered once it has reached a height of 10 cm/4 in above the soil. One advantage of this type of asparagus is that it does not need to be peeled. White asparagus is not exposed to light, as it is well hidden under a knoll and not discovered until it pushes through. Purple asparagus is simply a form of white asparagus that has pushed through the knoll. Its tip takes on a purple tint when it makes contact with the sun.

Whatever the color, these vegetables must be fresh, clean and shiny. When the stem is broken, the cut must be neat and some sap released. Once bought, it is important to cook them as soon as possible, because they dry out quickly. In the worse case, preserve them in the vegetable drawer in the refrigerator for two or three days, well wrapped in a damp cloth.

1. With the help of a small knife, gently scrape beneath the asparagus tips to remove its little leaves. (Avoid cutting into the green of the asparagus).

2. With caution scrape the heel of the asparagus (down to the white part) using a peeler. Carefully rinse them, then drain.

3. On a chopping board dusted with flour, cut the puff pastry into 4 pieces, each 11 x 7 cm/4^1/$_2$ x 2^2/$_3$ in. Bake the pastry in the oven at 200°C/390°F for 15 to 20 minutes. Meanwhile, cook the asparagus for 15 minutes in salted water.

with Chervil Butter

4. Chop the chervil into large pieces. Remove the asparagus from its cooking water and keep warm. Reduce the liquid, then add the cream and pepper to taste. Add the butter, a piece at a time. Stir in the chopped chervil.

5. Open the pastries, still warm, in half. Reheat the asparagus and cut to a length of about 15 cm/6 in, so they are longer than the pastry pieces. Cut the asparagus ends into small cubes.

6. Place half of a pastry on a plate. Fill with the chopped asparagus and place several long asparagus pieces on top of them. Cover with the other pastry half. Coat the plates with the chervil sauce.

Rabbit Liver

Preparation time: 15 minutes
Cooking time: 25 minutes
Difficulty: ★

Serves 4

1 leek
100 g/7 tbsp butter
salt
pepper

500 ml/2 cups thick crème fraîche
100 ml/7 tbsp wine vinegar
100 g/²/₃ cup chopped shallots
3 rabbit livers
300 g/11 oz puff pastry
100 ml/7 tbsp Cognac

Rabbit Liver in Puff Pastry with leeks is the creation of Fredy Girardet, a famous restaurateur in Crissier, which is near Lausanne. He has been elected the best cook in Switzerland and granted three stars by the elite Michelin Guide.

Creamed leak is almost mythical in the Vaud region, where Fredy Girardet was inspired to offer rabbit liver as a topping. In one of his books that addresses this recipe, Girardet compares it to another leek preparation favored in Vaud: "Here, the leeks are cooked the same way, but not as long, cut very thinly and no potatoes are used." The Swiss are just as crazy about leeks as Alsatians are about sauerkraut. Notably, they prepare them in soups and quiches with a lot of Gruyère cheese, and they enjoy mashed potatoes topped with sausage and a cloud of creamed leeks. The versatile vegetable can also be used as a topping for fish from Lake Leman.

Fredy Girardet's pastries are very famous and their popularity has spread far and wide. They are intended for those who embrace the unorthodox, because rabbit is not eaten often in the Vaud region. Rabbit legs, however, are served with beer or mustard sauces. In the region of Tessin, which is strongly influenced by Italians, *coniglio alla ticinese* simmers in a sauce of white wine, tomato, bay leaves, sage and rosemary. It is served with polenta.

When filling the pastries, the creamed leeks may be too cool and thick. Our chef suggests mixing it with a little cold water. Warm it up a bit and then add it to the pastries. This dish can also be served with duck liver or preserved poultry and the puff pastry can be made from scratch. Puff pastry that is sold in stores is certainly very practical, but be aware that the pastry rises differently depending on the manufacturer.

1.Clean the leek and separate the white from the green part. Cut each color into rings. Let soak in a pot of cold water and then drain it in a strainer.

2. Melt half of the butter in a large saucepan. Once it begins to sizzle, add the leek rounds. Add salt and pepper. Cook on low heat for 10 minutes, stirring frequently.

3. When the leeks are nicely browned and have started to soften, add the crème fraîche. Blend well over low heat and add the vinegar for seasoning.

in Puff Pastry

4. Peel and finely chop the shallots. Cut the rabbit liver into small dice. Slice the puff pastry into 4 large rectangles of the same size. Bake for 10 minutes according to package instructions.

5. Melt the remaining butter in a frying pan. Add the rabbit liver and chopped shallots. Allow to cook for 5 minutes until everything is browned. At the last minute, deglaze with the Cognac. Mix quickly with a spatula.

6. Divide each pastry in half and lightly hollow out the interior. Fill 4 pastries with the creamed leak, then the rabbit liver with shallots. Top with the remaining pastry.

Fine Moroccan

Preparation time: 1 hour
Cooking time: ca. 2 hours 30 minutes
Marinating time: 6 hours
Difficulty: ★

Serves 4

For the winter squash:
3 kg/7 lb red winter squash
350 g/1²/₃ cups granulated sugar
1 pinch saffron
15 g/1¹/₂ tbsp gum arabic crystals
3 cinnamon sticks
100 ml/7 tbsp peanut oil
For the candied tomatoes:
2.5 kg/5¹/₂ lb tomatoes
1 pinch saffron

20 g/2 tbsp gum arabic
2 cinnamon sticks
400 g/1³/₄ cups granulated sugar
100 ml/7 tbsp peanut oil

For the grilled vegetables (taktouka):
1 kg/2¹/₄ lb fresh tomatoes, sliced
4 cloves garlic
10 leaves each: cilantro, parsley
1 tsp each: cayenne pepper, cumin
salt, pepper
2 tbsp olive oil
500 g each red, green bell peppers
For the eggplant:
8 leaves each: parsley, coriander
1 tsp cayenne pepper
1 tbsp tomato purée
4 cloves garlic
vinegar
1 tsp cumin
100 ml/7 tbsp peanut oil
4 small eggplants

Moroccans love to make salads with cooked vegetables, such as *taktouka*. On the table, salads are served at the same time as tajines and *méchoui*, and they are not topped with European style dressings. Hundreds of different varieties of salads can be found on Moroccan menus, most of them with vegetables.

The winter squash *mâassel* ("sweet") is used in salads and couscous. It can be found throughout the year in Moroccan markets. The variety from Doukala, close to El-Jadida, is the most familiar. In the markets, Moroccans can find round, red winter squash as well as long, red winter squash that is shaped like a large pear. *Slaoui*, an enormous squash, grows in many home gardens and plays a large part of the culture in the Salé region. Its flesh is green and its peel is smooth with a whitish-grey tint.

Tomatoes and eggplant are included in practically all Moroccan salads. Tomatoes that are grown in open fields are culti-

vated on a large scale and eaten in great abundance. Moroccans reserve plum tomatoes, however, for the sole purpose of exportation. According to our chef, the most flavorful local tomatoes are those that grow around the sides of peduncles. During Ramadan, all families prepare a popular soup called *harira* that requires a lot of tomatoes. The demand for tomatoes in the markets rises during this time, causing prices to be rather unstable. Some women take precaution in the summer by buying tomatoes and then canning or deep-freezing them in a tomato coulis.

Moroccan olive trees grow predominantly around Meknès and Marrakech. The olives are cultivated in October. They produce oil that is strong in flavor and a little bitter, and has a dark color. Moroccans like to eat olive oil on bread for breakfast with a cup of tea.

1. Cut the winter squash in sections. Peel it and cut into small pieces. Put them in a large pot with the sugar, saffron, gum arabic, cinnamon and oil. Cover the pot and simmer for 60 to 80 minutes until it becomes a jelled purée.

2. For the candied tomatoes, first blanch the tomatoes. Cut them into round slices. Add the saffron, gum arabic, cinnamon, sugar and peanut oil. Bake in the oven at 150°C/300°F for 1 hour to 1¹/₄ hours until the tomatoes are candied.

3. For the taktouka, mix the slices of raw tomato with the chopped garlic, cilantro and parsley, cayenne pepper, cumin, salt and pepper. Pour the olive oil over top. Let reduce for 20 to 25 minutes over low heat.

Salads

4. Blister the skin of the peppers on a grill or a stovetop. Dip them in cold water and then peel. Cut into thin strips. Add them to the tomato mixture (for the taktouka). Cook for 5 minutes.

5. In a mixing bowl, prepare the chermoula by mixing chopped parsley and cilantro, cayenne pepper, 2 crushed cloves garlic, vinegar, cumin and oil. Mix with a spoon to obtain smooth paste.

6. Halve the eggplants and cook for 20 minutes in salted water flavored with garlic. Drain, then cover with chermoula. Let marinate for 6 hours. On each plate, arrange quenelles of candied tomato, winter squash, taktouka and the eggplants with chermoula.

Fried Duck Foie Gras

Preparation time: 20 minutes
Cooking time: 45 minutes
Difficulty: ★

Serves 4

For the quince compote:
2 quinces
30 g/2 tbsp softened butter
2 tbsp acacia honey
1 pinch quatre épices (white pepper, nutmeg, cinnamon and clove blend)
1 tbsp sherry vinegar

For the foie gras:
320 g/11 oz duck foie gras
1 tsp fine sea salt from Guérande
crushed pepper
1 pinch four-spice blend

For the sauce:
100 ml/7 tbsp port wine
1 tbsp sherry vinegar
1 pat butter

For the garnish:
chives
fine sea salt from Guérande

Whether from goose or duck, foie gras is one of the most exquisite dishes of all. Depending on the animal and how it was fed, the color of the liver varies from ivory to pinkish-white, but it is always darker in color if from a duck.

Choose a foie gras of medium size, because if it is too large, it will melt while cooking. Foie gras is used in a variety of ways: terrines, pâtés, fillings… When served raw, it is considered a delicate and refined dish that always gains particular attention. Always cooled before serving, it is able to preserve its unique flavor and will be much easier to cut.

Michel Roth has chosen to serve flavorful escallops of fried foie gras with small cubes of quince, a fruit that has a beautiful bright yellow color. Its bitterness will compliment the delicate foie gras. Also, our chef has prepared a sweetened compote with acacia honey. Not very flavorful, the honey adds a bit of

sweetness to the fruit without altering its flavor. Everything is seasoned with *quatre épices*, a four-spice blend. *Quatre épices* of excellent quality will include seeds of crushed black cumin, but it is more frequently substituted with a blend of pepper, cinnamon, nutmeg and clove. It is often a seasoning found in stew with meats and dishes with game or pork.

Reduced by half over high heat, the port wine and sherry vinegar form a sugary-acidic mixture in the preparation of the syrup. This syrup transforms into a sauce when a bit of butter is added to the mixture after it is removed from the heat. Blend it with a spoon for a minute, return to high heat, and the sauce will become a delicious topping with a nice brown color.

Our chef says that poultry and veal foie gras can also be accompanied with quince compote. Port wine replaces red or Maury wine.

1. Peel and cut the quinces into small cubes. Heat the butter in a pan and add the quince. Stir in the honey and a pinch of the quatre épices blend. Mix well. Add the sherry vinegar and blend again. Over low heat, stew this mixture for 30 minutes. Set aside on a plate.

2. Cut the raw foie gras gently on the diagonal, in slices that are 1 cm/¹⁄₃ in thick and weigh ca. 40 g/1¹⁄₂ oz. Add salt, pepper and season with the quatre épices blend.

3. Heat a frying pan with no fat and add the foie gras. Sear the pieces on high heat for 30 seconds each side, using a spatula to keep them from sticking to the pan. Drain them on paper towels.

and Quince Compote

4. Remove the grease from the frying pan and deglaze the pan first with the port wine and then the sherry vinegar. Reduce by half for 5 minutes over high heat to form a syrup.

5. Away from the heat, add 1 pat of butter to the syrup. Return the pan to the heat and stir constantly until a thick and smooth sauce is obtained. Set aside.

6. Serve each person two foie gras scallops, each plate accompanied with a quenelle of quince compote. Cover with the sauce. Garnish with chives and fine sea salt.

Guacamole

Preparation time: 20 minutes
Difficulty: ★

Serves 6

6 avocados
1 lime
4 tomatoes
1 medium onion

olive oil
salt
pepper
1 bunch cilantro
1 small red chili pepper (optional)
1 small green chili pepper (optional)

Guacamole is extremely widespread throughout Mexico, and very popular in the United States, as well. This fine avocado purée with a bright green color is nicely blended with lime juice, onions, cilantro, tomatoes and olive oil. Enthusiasts of hot foods add chili pepper.

Very easy to make, guacamole is served in Mexico as a cold appetizer or as *encas*: generally, a piece of meat is placed on a corn tortilla, guacamole is spread on top and the tortilla is rolled up to form a taco.

Originally from Mexico, avocados were eaten by Indians more than 10,000 years ago. This fruit is cultivated from Veracruz to Yucatan and grows on large trees. There are only two harvests each year. Their flesh has a wonderful flavor and their leaves, which taste like aniseed, are used as a condiment. Common-sized avocados have two types of peel: green and smooth or black and crumpled. Mexicans also eat a large type called "butter avocado" that has an especially creamy taste. They are often stuffed with crab or shrimp, added to soups at the last moment or used to garnish meat dishes.

To avoid discoloration of the avocado purée once it comes into contact with air, add lime juice to the mixture. If it is not eaten immediately, our chef suggest adding Vitamin C to it. This will not alter the flavor of the guacamole and it will retain its beautiful color for many hours.

The avocado flesh can be mashed with a fork, but our chef prefers to beat it vigorously with the end of a small whisk, a technique that is much quicker and provides for easy cleanup.

Our chef serves this wonderful paste with fried tortillas that have been cut into triangles. A small glass of tequila is the perfect drink to accompany it.

1. Cut the avocados in half lengthwise and remove the pit. With a spoon, remove the flesh inside the shell and put it in a mixing bowl.

2. With a small whisk, vigorously beat the avocado flesh just until it is a smooth purée.

3. Press the lime and add its juice to the avocado. Mix with a spoon until it is well blended with the purée.

4. Rinse and drain the tomatoes. Cut them into small cubes and add to the avocado purée. Blend everything together.

5. Peel the onion, dice it finely and chop the cilantro. Add them to the avocado and mix well.

6. Add a drop of olive oil to the guacamole along with salt and pepper. Gently mix one more time. Serve very cold.

Herring

Preparation time:	20 minutes
Cooking time:	20 minutes
Difficulty:	★

Serves 4 or 5

1 large carrot
2 medium potatoes
2 eggs
1 large salted herring

1 red beet, cooked
1 large onion
2 tbsp oil
1 cucumber
fresh chives (to garnish)
fresh dill (to garnish)

Herring with Vegetables is among the most mouth-watering cold appetizers in Russia. It is served in the middle of *zakouskis*, an assortment of dishes served in small portions, taking on the role of building up the appetite before the arrival of the main entrée. On the table, the frozen fish dishes combine their colors and flavors with vegetables in brines or salads.

Herring comes from the family of fish called *clupeids* and is frequently caught in cold seas. In Russia, they can be found in the Baltic Sea and north of the Pacific coast. It is a product that requires long preparation, as it needs to marinate in brine for several months in barrels. A long time ago, Russians always took herring with them during long horse and carriage voyages. Two types of herring are served today: one is less salty, and the other one is extremely salty and must be soaked in milk to eliminate some of its sodium. Russian gourmands enjoy cooking many herring recipes, including "herring in a fur coat": the fish meat is inserted between a layer of eggs, beets, potatoes, onions and mayonnaise. When mixing the meat with bread and onions, a filling for the eggs is obtained. Russians also enjoy herring hors d'oeuvre where the herring is spread onto rye bread that has been buttered and seasoned with scallions. It is also served hot, with steamed small potatoes rolled in butter with dill.

When removing the skin, use caution so that the fat underneath the skin is not scratched, because it protects the fillets. The skin brings its own flavor to the dish, but be sure not to add too much oil to the meat.

Do not hesitate to vary the assortment of vegetables used in this dish, adding vegetables that inspire you, including peas or cucumber cubes.

1. Boil the carrot, potatoes and eggs until the eggs are hard-boiled. Cut off the head of the herring. Open the belly and remove the innards. Gently split the back and remove the skin. Use the tip of a finger to remove the fillets.

2. Peel the potatoes and beets. Cut them in small dice and do the same with the carrots. Peel the onion and finely mince it.

3. Peel the hard-boiled eggs and cut each egg into four equal quarters.

with Vegetables

4. Arrange a line of potato slices in the center of the serving platter. On top, add a double layer of herring slices and brush them with oil. Garnish the ends of the dish with the head and the tail of the herring.

5. Cover the middle of the herring with a line of sliced onion.

6. Fill the sides with the carrot cubes, then potatos and lastly the beets. Season the carrots with finely chopped scallions and dill. Garnish with thin slices of cucumber and hard-boiled egg quarters.

Fried Herring with

Preparation time: 40 minutes
Cooking time: 10 minutes
Difficulty: ★

Serves 4

8 small herring
100 g/²/₃ cup flour
oil for frying

For the frying batter:
2 egg whites and 1 egg yolk
250 g/1³/₄ cups flour
150 ml/²/₃ cup beer
50 ml/3¹/₂ tbsp olive oil

For the whipped butter:
200 g/14 tbsp butter
juice of 1 lemon
salt
pepper
4 sorrel leaves

For the lemon vinaigrette:
100 ml/7 tbsp olive oil
100 ml/7 tbsp white vinegar
2 shallots
lemon zest

A long time ago, herring was the most popular staple food in Sweden. In the south of the country it is called *sil*. The small fish, low in fat, is caught on fine lines between the islands of Gotland and Öland. Herring has the lovely name of *strömming* in the local tongue.

At midday, just about all Swedish restaurants serve herring fillets with mustard and dill or coated with flour and fried in brown butter. Herring is also nicely accompanied by mashed potato and blueberries.

This dish is a main feature of a *smörgåsbord*, a buffet with a number of small dishes that has become symbolic of Swedish cuisine. The number of ways to serve herring is limited only by your imagination: fresh herring marinated in salt and sugar, young herring *matjes* with sour cream, *strömming* marinated with vinegar, smoked herring, fresh poached herring served with tomato sauce, curry mayonnaise or mustard sauce, in salad with onions, potatoes and red beets… Enthusiasts of strong flavors add *surströmming*, herring fermented until it has an unmistakable taste. That is prepared in the Höga Kusten region, on the banks of the Gulf of Bothnia.

A traditional Christmas feast would include an extravagant presentation of a dozen herring dishes, several types of salmon, as well as a choice of a meat dish, a cabbage dish… Beer and schnapps are served to fill in any gaps in the meal. The sale of alcohol is strictly regulated and is limited to state-owned stores called *systembolaget*. Supermarkets only sell beer with a low alcohol content.

When dipping the herring into the frying batter, wait a few seconds before frying it so that the excess batter drips off. Then lower the fish into the hot oil, and immediately after frying put it on a paper towel to absorb the excess oil.

1. For the frying batter, whisk the egg whites until stiff. In a second bowl, whisk the flour with the egg yolk, beer, 250 ml/1 cup water and the olive oil. With a spatula, carefully fold the egg whites into the beer and flour mixture.

2. Gut the herrings and remove the heads. On a plate, roll each fish in flour. Balance the herring on a soup spoon and quickly dip into the frying batter.

3. Heat the oil for deep-frying. Drop a batter-covered herring in the hot oil and cook 2 to 3 minutes. Prepare each herring the same way.

Butter and Lemon

4. For the whipped butter, brown the butter in a small saucepan. Add the lemon juice little by little while whisking continuously. Season with salt and pepper. Let cool.

5. Set the bowl with the butter in a larger bowl filled with ice cubes. Whisk vigorously just until it becomes a thick, beige paste.

6. For the lemon vinaigrette, mix the chopped shallots, lemon zest, olive oil and white vinegar. Arrange the fried herring on plates with the lemon sauce and a sorrel leaf filled with whipped butter.

Hummus

Preparation time:	15 minutes
Cooking time:	1 hour 30 minutes
Soaking time:	24 hours
Difficulty:	★

Serves 4

500 g/2¹/₂ cups dried chickpeas
1 tsp baking soda
150 g/scant ²/₃ cup tahini
2 lemons
2 tsp salt
2 cloves garlic
olive oil to garnish

A great favorite on tables as an hors d'œuvre or *mezze*, hummus holds a privileged place in Lebanese cuisine. With or without garlic, flavored with lemon or *tahina* (sesame seed paste), olive oil or peanut oil, this chickpea purée is served in all Mediterranean countries. Lebanese, Egyptians, Israelites, Syrians, Turks and Greeks all claim that they were the original source of this fabulous dip or spread.

The chickpea is a product typical of the Mediterranean basin. This legume holds within its pods round seeds, small "chicks", which are beige in color. This pea is found in foods everywhere from the East to the West, served hot or cold, in salads or in puréed form as well as in couscous dishes.

Always eaten cooked, chickpeas need to be soaked in cold water for 24 hours before cooking, making it more digestible. Adding a spoonful of baking soda to the water will speed up the cooking process.

High in energy, yet with a bitter taste, the chickpea's flavor always comes through, no matter what it is blended with. This is why this recipe combines the chickpea with a smooth cream that has a slightly sweet flavor, *tahina*. Made from crushed sesame seeds, tahini is used in many eastern dishes to enrich salads, fish and grilled meat. This cream is sold in jars at every Middle Eastern market. Shake the jar before opening it, so as not to lose the sesame oil that has separated.

Hummus and tahini blend perfectly to form a thick paste that becomes a little more fluid once the lemon juice is added. A pinch of salt should be added along with a dash of garlic, depending on taste.

By tradition, hummus is never served by itself on Lebanese tables: it is nicely garnished with cubes of turnips that have been marinated in vinegar, crunchy red radishes and mint leaves to cleanse the palate.

1. Put the chickpeas in a bowl of cold water to soak the night before preparing the hummus. After 24 hours of soaking, drain them. Put them in a saucepot with 2 liters/ 2 quarts water and add the baking soda.

2. Start the cooking over high heat, just until foam forms on the surface. Remove this foam and reduce the heat. Allow to cook for 1¹/₂ hours, skimming frequently. With a skimmer, remove the chick peas from the cooking liquid, drain them and transfer to a bowl.

3. Pass the chickpeas through a vegetable mill until they become a thick purée.

4. To this purée, add a pinch of salt and then the tahini. Blend well.

5. Peel and finely mince the garlic. Stir it into to the mixture. Press the lemons and pour the juice over the mixture. Blend again.

6. With a spoon, smooth small amounts of hummus to form a layer lining the inside of a bowl. Add a dash of olive oil in the center and eat chilled.

Hot Oysters

Preparation time: 30 minutes
Cooking time: 6 minutes
Difficulty: ★★

Serves 4

24 oysters

For the garlic butter:
100 g/7 tbsp butter
2 cloves garlic
1 bunch flat-leaf parsley
1 small shallot
salt
pepper

For the sauce:
500 ml/2 cups thick crème fraîche
or heavy cream
1 pinch saffron
1 pinch cayenne pepper
1 tsp tomato purée
2 tsp potato flour or cornstarch
2 tsp milk
100 g/scant 1 cup grated Emmental cheese
salt
pepper

Oysters have been appreciated by gourmands for many years, even centuries. Whether firm or fatty, they are most often eaten raw and still alive, served with buttered mixed-grain bread. It is also possible, of course, to cook them. In the eighteenth century, the master chefs were already serving delicious oyster dishes au gratin.

Sold by the dozen or in crates, French oysters come from Atlantic ports and the English Channel. To make sure they are fresh, test their liveliness by poking the muscle with the tip of a knife. If they retract, they are still very much alive. The oyster must be full of water and giving off an iodine odor. When in doubt, it is better to play it safe and discard it.

When using an oyster knife, be careful not to hurt yourself: first, hold it in your hand using a towel. Open the oyster by the side or where the two shells are hinged together and separate the muscle that attaches the two shells. This process must always occur just before the meal.

To make the hot oysters, place them on a dish on pleated aluminum foil so that they are protected during cooking and the sauce will not overflow into the dish. Our chef has chosen to accompany them with a garlic butter, which has the advantage of being able to stay fresh for several days or frozen for months. The extra garlic butter can be used to stuff mussels, land snails or scallops.

When pouring the sauce over the top, be generous and be sure to fill the oysters completely with it. For a smooth, thick, creamy sauce, add a spoonful of potato flour that has been diluted in a little milk and cream. The oysters should not be cooked on the grill for any longer than 3 minutes, or else they will become indigestible and lose their flavor.

1. Hold each oyster shell firmly in your hand and twist the blade of a knife between the two shells. Separate the muscle. Open the oysters and remove any remaining shell remnants from them. Empty any water from them.

2. Fold a large sheet of aluminum foil and place it in the bottom of a baking dish. Arrange the oysters in the dish one by one. Set aside.

3. In a food processor, blend all the ingredients for the garlic butter just until they form a smooth paste. Place 1 nut-sized portion of garlic butter on each oyster.

Au Gratin

4. Bring the cream to the boil (or just below) for 3 minutes. Add the cayenne pepper, saffron, salt, pepper and the tomato purée. Whisk over low heat.

5. When the cream begins to boil, add the starch diluted in milk. Let thicken over high heat while whisking.

6. Completely cover each oyster with the sauce. Sprinkle them with grated Emmental cheese and brown for 3 minutes under a very hot grill. Serve them immediately.

Oysters

Preparation time: 45 minutes
Cooking time: 25 minutes
Difficulty: ★★

Serves 4

16 oysters
3 tbsp butter
1/2 onion
1 rib celery
1 bunch spinach
1/4 tsp tarragon

2 or 3 sprigs parsley
1 tsp salt
1/4 tsp pepper
rock salt for the platter

For the breadcrumb topping:
3 tbsp butter
30 g/1/4 cup breadcrumbs
2 or 3 sprigs parsley
2 dashes Tabasco sauce
1/2 tsp salt

The original version of this Oysters Rockefeller recipe was created in 1899 in New Orleans by Jules Alciatore, chef at the restaurant *Chez Antoine*. According to the story, a customer commented after tasting the dish that it was just as rich in taste as the Rockefellers were in wealth. The term "rich" is a play on words, referring to foods with many ingredients and full flavor, and often a lot of calories, as well as commenting on the personal wealth of great families like the Rockefellers.

Although the origin of the sauce that covers the oysters in this recipe is unknown, it is similar to the garlic butter sauce that is served with escargot. Our chef has chosen to serve a modern version of this recipe that first appeared in 1920, in which the oysters blend well with the flavors of buttered cream spinach and pastis.

The majority of American oysters come from the Atlantic Ocean, along the East Coast. They are caught by boat with the help of large rakes. In the Chesapeake region, oyster farming was developed around 1850. Since all the oysters are of the same species (*crassostrea virginica*), they are distinguished from each other by where they live and are caught. In the United States, a chef who wishes to prepare Oysters Rockefeller may well choose very famous Blue Point oysters. They generally come from the Great South Bay in New York, in the center of the East Coast. Because Blue Point oysters are so large, they can be stuffed generously.

The oysters are stuffed with spinach, a vegetable that Americans are very fond of. They eat it fresh in salads, fried and in a number of different fillings. The spinach here is seasoned with pastis and Tabasco sauce, a hot sauce made from pepper, salt and vinegar that is made in Louisiana. If any filling remains, it can be used to liven up pasta.

1. Open the oysters by inserting a knife between the shells and twisting. Hold half of the oyster in one hand and remove the meat with the tip of a small knife. Follow the same process for the rest of the oysters.

2. Chop the onion and celery. Melt the butter in a frying pan and add the onion and celery. Brown for 5 minutes on medium high heat.

3. Rinse and drain the spinach. Add the whole leaves to the frying pan and cover the pan. Cook for about 5 minutes, then raise the lid and allow any excess liquid to evaporate.

Rockefeller

4. Add the chopped parsley and tarragon, salt, pepper and finally the pastis. Continue to cook until the ingredients are blended and then chop everything together.

5. Prepare the breadcrumb topping by combining in a mixing bowl the melted butter, chopped parsley, breadcrumbs, salt and a few drops of Tabasco sauce. Mix with a spoon.

6. Arrange the oysters on a platter that has been covered in rock salt. Stuff them with the spinach mixture and then the bread-crumb topping. Heat them for 10 minutes in a warm oven.

Imam

Preparation time: 20 minutes
Cooking time: 45 minutes
Difficulty: ★

Serves 6

6 eggplants
1 long green pepper
1 onion
4 cloves garlic
1 medium tomato
¹/₂ sprig parsley

¹/₂ lemon
100 ml/7 tbsp olive oil
1 tsp salt
1 tsp sugar
oil for frying

Legend tells of a story that took place during the time of the Sultans: An imam, a Muslim leader, married a young woman and received a dowry of twelve jars of excellent olive oil. Two weeks later, there wasn't a drop of olive oil left in the house. The very religious husband fainted when he learned that his wife had used all the olive oil to prepare her stuffed eggplant. The recipe is therefore called "the unconscious imam". A familial dish, *Imam Bayildi* is served either as a cold appetizer or as the main dish when the chef fills the vegetable with ground lamb.

A long time ago, the almost excessive passion of the people of Istanbul for eggplants often provoked *patlican yangini*, or "eggplant fires", a true horror in a city where most of the houses were made of wood. In the summertime, wind from the south would blow the embers from eggplant grills and spread the fire throughout the old neighborhoods.

Our chef favors using *kemmar* eggplants, which are long and thin, for this recipe. They are cultivated near Istanbul. Small round eggplants called *top* are used as garnish for hot dishes. The best season falls between spring and summer. Today, they are produced in greenhouses all year round near Ankara and on the shores of the Black Sea. Specialists of Turkish cuisine are able to publish entire cookbooks that contain nothing but eggplant recipes. Whether in moussaka, fried, stuffed with meat and rice, in purée form, in *turşu* (vegetables with vinegar) or in jam, this vegetable is utterly central to Turkish cuisine.

Certain Turkish chefs prepare a lighter preparation and poach the eggplants in water with lemon, brown them in the end with very a little oil and then cook them in a large fryer. You may want to try out both of these two methods and choose which you prefer.

1. Peel the eggplants. Slice off the skin with a large knife, cutting from the top to the bottom and turning the eggplant. Cut the pepper in very fine strips and set aside.

2. Heat a deep-fryer and lower the whole eggplants into the hot oil. Allow to cook just until the flesh is nicely browned. Remove the eggplants from the oil with a slotted spoon.

3. Cut open the eggplants and remove the seeds. Place them on a baking tray and set aside.

Bayildi

4. Peel and slice the onion and garlic. Heat the olive oil in a saucepan and fry the onion and garlic, covered and over low heat, for 5 minutes.

5. Dice the tomato and finely chop the parsley. Add both to the onions. Add the salt, sugar and incorporate the juice from half a lemon. Cook for another 5 minutes.

6. Fill the eggplants with the tomato and onion mixture. Garnish with the finely sliced green pepper. Bake in the oven at 180°C/355°F for 30 minutes.

Involtini

Preparation time: 25 minutes
Cooking time: 25 minutes
Standing time: 1 hour or more
Difficulty: ★★

Serves 6

300–400 g/11–14 oz long eggplant
200 g/7 oz Parma ham
1 whole mozzarella
200 g/7 oz ewe ricotta
4 or 5 leaves basil

500 g/generous 1 lb cherry tomatoes
virgin olive oil
salt
pepper

For the garnish:
dried oregano
fresh parsley
mixed lettuce
black olives

Our chef shares with us that his mother makes these succulent eggplant and meat "packages" in the springtime with ricotta cheese made from the first milk of ewes, after the lambs have been sold. That is the right moment for the very best ricotta, because the ewes graze on tender herbs that taste of pastures.

Ricotta, mozzarella, … Donato Massaro combines these two cheese temptations in these eggplant rolls to create a wonderful flavor in the mouth. The mozzarella that can be found in stores is made entirely from cow's milk. The milk is acidified with whey, which is the liquid that remains after milk coagulates the night before, and curdled with rennet. This curdled milk must be worked to obtain the consistency of large seeds, like nuts, cut into strips and melted in hot water. The resulting paste is smoothed out and then formed into small balls. The cheese is then washed with salted, cold water.

Campania and Latium are home to mozzarella made with water buffalo milk. This milk contains 53% fat, however, and fresh mozzarella must be consumed within three days or it will become overly acidic.

Do not forget the small dash of oregano as a final touch for this dish. This lively plant, whose name in Greek means "the joy of the mountains", livens up innumerable sauces, tomato soups, pasta and of course pizza. Oregano will work the best in this dish when dried, but its aroma is very strong and just a small pinch will suffice.

Our chef also suggests a trick to making the eggplants release their bitter liquid. Make sure to salt the eggplant with fine salt, and let the eggplants stand for one or two hours, if possible. In case you are going to use sea salt, you must rinse the eggplant slices for a long time after they have been coated with it. After tasting *Involtini alla Lucania* wrapped in ham, there will be no stopping you from preparing different variations of this dish, perhaps using slices of fried zucchini or fine pork escallops.

1. Slice the eggplants lengthwise. Place the slices on a grill and sprinkle them liberally with salt. Let stand for 1 hour. When the eggplants have released much of their liquid, put them on a paper towel.

2. Pour some oil for frying in a frying pan. Brown the eggplant slices for 5 minutes on each side in the hot oil. Place them on paper towels to absorb any excess oil.

3. Cut ¼ of the ham in very small dice and set aside the rest to be used for the rolls. Thinly slice the mozzarella. Chop the basil. Mix the ricotta, diced ham, basil, salt, pepper and some oil into a smooth filling.

alla Lucania

4. Take a small bit of filling on the end of a metal spatula. Place it on the end of the eggplant slices nearest you. Top each mound of filling with a slice of mozzarella.

5. Form an eggplant roll by starting at the end nearest to you. Lay out a thin slice of ham next to the roll. Place the eggplant on the ham and roll them up together to form the involtini.

6. Blanch the tomatoes, dice them, add salt and pepper and sauté for 5 minutes. Tip into an oiled dish with the involtini. Brown for 10 minutes in the oven at 250°C/480°F. Sprinkle with chopped parsley and oregano and accompany with olives and mixed greens.

Spinach

Preparation time: 35 minutes
Cooking time: 25 minutes
Difficulty: ★

Serves 4

200 g/generous 1¹/₃ cups flour
500 ml/2 cups oil
200 g/7 oz spinach
1 tsp garam masala
¹/₂ tsp cumin
salt
pepper
oil for frying

Even though our main concern is food, we cannot forget the fast, a period of purification of the body and soul and means of prayer for the people of India. The ancestral art of combining spices with vegetables, bread or meat is anchored in the fact that vegetarians and inveterate fasters get to choose everything that they eat in accordance with their lifestyles, while appreciating the pleasure of eating well.

Fresh spinach combined with an airy and spicy dough is perfect for satisfying small pangs of hunger that occur throughout the course of the day. These round, browned fritters are exquisite either as an appetizer or as an entrée followed by lamb curry or chicken tandoori. The main spice used is *garam masala*, in fact a blend of several spices: curry, nutmeg, cumin, pepper, clove… It has become a staple in Indian cuisine.

Mentioning only one type of preparation of *garam masala* is impossible, because its mixture varies from one region to another. Certain regions make it sweet, others strong, measuring out as much of this magic mixture as they want; only the people of India know its secret.

Small *kachori* are an example of salted fritters, but they can be made other ways, notably stuffed with soft, fresh cheese or kneaded with onions and seasoned with cumin seeds.

Kachori are a specialty more strongly associated with northern India, but they are known throughout the country and it's rare that someone from the south is unfamiliar with them. The variations made in the south they tend to be more rustic and especially richer in spices. There is no dispute among Indians about the place of fritters in Indian cuisine, because they are more than delicious.

From north to south and east to west, gourmands of the world will know to appreciate these fritters simply as a delight of Indian cuisine.

1. Tip the flour into a mixing bowl, then the oil and 120 ml/¹/₂ cup water. Add a pinch of salt. Begin to knead the dough just until it is flexible, light and elastic. Form the dough into a large ball and cover with a damp cloth. Set aside while preparing the spinach.

2. Blanch the spinach in salted boiling water. When the water returns to boiling, remove the spinach and rinse it under cold water. Drain and cut into large pieces.

3. Slowly brown the spinach in a frying pan with oil and season it with the garam masala, pepper and cumin. Stir well for 2 minutes.

Kachori

4. Take out the dough and press it into a circle that is fairly thick. Put the spinach in the center of the dough and fold it down over the spinach. Flour your hands and knead the dough to incorporate the spinach well.

5. Form 16 balls of spinach dough. Roll each ball between your hands and set aside on a clean cloth.

6. Heat oil in a saucepan. Drop the dough balls into the oil for 15 minutes. Turn over each fritter with a skimmer. Remove them and place on paper towels. Serve hot, warm or cold.

Kipper

Preparation time:	45 minutes
Cooking time:	1 hour 25 minutes
Chilling time:	24 hours
Difficulty:	☆

Serves 4

2 smoked herring
2 onions
200 g/7 oz bacon
250 g/9 oz Bintje potatoes
1 egg

2 g/1 tsp quatre épice (four spice blend)
30 ml/2 tbsp Drambuie
20 ml/4 tsp whiskey
salt
pepper

For the garnish:
mixed lettuces
cherry tomatoes
red radishes
lard to cover the top (optional)

Kipper Pâté comes straight from Scotland, a rugged country of fishermen and miners where people know how to prepare simple dishes that keep well. Kippered herring, onions (rare vegetables from a country where the sun does not often shine), local whiskey and bacon can be found in this recipe and are greatly appreciated in all the Nordic countries, as well.

Kippers, which begin as herring from the Baltic Sea, are smoked along the coast of Scotland. The herrings are cut in half, gutted, salted and hung from long lines. Basements of homes are equipped for the purpose of smoking herring, and grilled kippers are found on the breakfast menu in many a respected hotel in London.

The Scots claim that their whiskey is world-famous because of the purity of their water sources. A mash resulting from the fermentation of barley is the first step in the creation of whiskey, which is distilled a second time to make Drambuie. The brew master adds some honey, heather and aromatic herbs to achieve this slightly syrupy liquor that retains the flavor of whisky. The Scots drink Drambuie as an aperitif with ice. In this Kipper Pâté recipe, the sweet flavor of Drambuie counterbalances the Scottish whiskey, which has a much dryer feel in the mouth.

For this preparation, we have served the pâté in slices, but it is also excellent served as quenelles on toast. Our chef suggests removing the crust from several slices of white bread, then cutting two triangles from each slice. Toast them before serving.

To prepare a truly perfect dish, the Kipper Pâté must rest in the refrigerator for 24 to 48 hours. This preparation does not contain a lot of water, because the smoked fish and bacon are very dry and the onions lose their water while cooking. If you cover the surface of the pâté in lard, it may be stored up to ten days.

1. Lay out the herrings in a roasting pan. Put them in the oven for 10 to 12 minutes at 200°C/390°F. Set them aside. Cook the potatoes in salted water, in their skins, for 30 minutes. Let them cool.

2. Peel and mince the onions. Cut the bacon into large cubes. In a saucepan, fry the bacon for 4 minutes over high heat. Add the onions and brown for 8 minutes. At the end of the cooking time, season with the four-spice blend.

3. Remove the spine from the cooked herrings. Uncover the fillets by removing any small or large bones that remain. Hold the fish by the tail and remove the skin. Discard the skin.

Pâté

4. In an electric food mill, alternate the potatoes, bacon with onions and crumbled herring. When everything has been chopped, put the ingredients through the mill a second time.

5. Add the egg, Drambuie and whiskey to the pâté. Salt and pepper to taste. Beat vigorously with a wooden spoon just until the filling is nice and smooth.

6. Fill a loaf pan with the pâté. Put the loaf pan in a covered pot and place that in a large pan half filled with water. Bake in this water bath for 30 minutes on low heat, then refrigerate for 24 hours. Serve the pâté in slices garnished with the mixed lettuce, radish and cherry tomatoes.

Vegetable

Preparation time: 30 minutes
Cooking time: 25 minutes
Difficulty: ★

Serves 4

For the lasagne noodles:
400 g/scant 3 cups flour
4 eggs
1 tbsp olive oil
salt

For the stuffing:
200 g/7 oz artichoke
400 g/14 oz eggplant

300 g/11 oz tomatoes
400 g/14 oz zucchini
2 fennel bulbs
200 g/7 oz mushrooms
200 g/7 oz mozzarella
1 bunch basil
60 g/generous ¹/₂ cup grated Parmasan
1 shallot
1 lemon
butter
olive oil
salt
pepper

There are many lasagna recipes that are favored by Italians. The classic recipes include lasagna with meat, tomatoes and béchamel sauce, but they also prepare lasagna with fish, only one vegetable or even stuffed with roasted game. Our chef has chosen a traditional dish and has made it lighter, as he does not use béchamel and does not make it into an au gratin dish, as many lasagnas are. This way, it is easy to taste the distinct flavors of the vegetables, Parmesan and basil.

The artichoke is a typical Mediterranean food. It comes from a wild thistle that has become edible due to successive cross breeding. What we refer to as the "core" or "heart" of the vegetable is really the unopened flower bud. The leaves that are edible are in fact the "shells", or the actual leaves, which grow in the form of large rosettes and can be found at the base of the stem. Italian chefs of the Renaissance offered recipes with artichokes among their culinary repertoire.

In Italy, small globe artichokes are very popular and only their very tender heart is eaten. They are cultivated in the area near Rome. Make sure to drop the hearts in water with lemon added so that they do not lose their color.

If you are preparing lasagna noodles for the first time, an ordinary rolling pin will suffice for making the pasta. If you are pleased with the results and want to experiment further with homemade pasta, you may want to consider buying a pasta maker for your home. Chefs are finding it easier and easier to use a pasta maker. When using a pasta maker, pass the dough through the machine several times in order to obtain extremely thin and smooth strips of lasagna.

To refine the final presentation, garnish each lasagna with a basil leaf. Immediately cover the lasagna with a sauce made from olive oil and finely chopped basil.

1. Tip the flour onto your work space in a circle. Break the eggs into the center. Pour over the olive oil and add a pinch of salt. Vigorously knead this pasta dough, roll it out, and make thin bands for the lasagna noodles.

2. Cut off the artichoke leaves and set the hearts in water with lemon added. Mince them. Peel and finely dice the eggplants. Cut the tomatoes, zucchini and fennel into similar dice and slice the mushrooms.

3. Peel the shallot and mince it. In a frying pan, heat a mixture of butter and olive oil. Sweat the shallots for 2 to 3 minutes.

Lasagna

4. When the shallots begin to brown, add the diced artichoke hearts along with the eggplant, fennel and zucchini. Add 100 g/ generous ½ cup of the tomatoes and the mushrooms. Salt and pepper and allow to cook for 10 minutes on low heat.

5. Lay out the lasagna noodles on a work surface. Cut the pasta into circles using a metal ring that is 10 cm/4 in around. Cut the mozzarella into cubes. Partially fry the remaining diced tomatoes for 5 minutes; cook the lasagna noodles for 5 minutes in a pot of boiling water.

6. On each plate, place a circle of pasta and cover with the vegetables, mozzarella, Parmesan and chopped basil. Cover with a second circle and make a second layer of the same ingredients. Finish with a third pasta circle. Garnish with the fried tomatoes and basil.

Scampi and

Preparation time: 40 minutes
Cooking time: 25 minutes
Resting time, dough: 5 minutes
Difficulty: ★★

Serves 4

For the pasta:
500 g/3¹/₂ cups flour
8 egg yolks
50 ml/3¹/₂ tbsp olive oil
15 g/1 tbsp salt

For the accompaniment:
12 scampi
500 g/2¹/₂ cups cooked lentils
3 cloves garlic
300 g/11 oz cherry tomatoes
200 ml/generous ³/₄ cup olive oil
50 g/3¹/₂ tbsp butter
salt
pepper

A Neapolitan insists on taking the time to make the pasta for this dish yourself at home. Massimo Palermo reveals the secret to pasta that is infallible, simple and full of goodness. Infallible? A drop of olive oil gives the pasta its elasticity. A cloud of flour on marble causes the pasta to spread very thinly without any problem, with the help of a rolling pin. To make this pasta, wrap most of it around the rolling pin, leaving only the part of the *malfatti* to be indented outside of the roller. Goodness? *Malfatti* signifies "poorly made." You can imagine the many lengths and forms this pasta can take when being creative with it: long, wide, short, *malfatti* pasta is a very cheerful dish, re-sembling the streets of Naples where it comes from. Its name varies depending on that shape the pasta is given: tagliatelle, fettucine and *pappardelle*, ribbons of pasta that are usually combined with crème fraîche, basil and Parmasan cheese.

In our recipe, small brown lentils accompany the pasta. You may cook them in advance: 10 to 15 minutes in two liters/two quarts of salted water. In Italy, vegetables and pasta are often eaten al dente, literally "to the teeth", meaning they still offer a little resistance when you bite into them. For those that like their lentils a little softer, add ½ cup water to the sauce. *Poco ma non troppo* (enough but not too much), because the lentils will start to become mash if cooked too much.

Malfatti pasta with lentils goes very nicely with scampi from Naples: large prawn or any other crustacean will add a nice flavor to the pasta. To preserve the rich flavors that are very important to Neapolitans, the legs of the scampi are cracked so that the flavor of the sauce is intensified. The wonderful aro-mas of this dish will make guests hungry, and you can give them a true taste of Italian flavors.

1. Mound the flour on a marble counter. Tip the egg yolks in the center. Pour on the olive oil and 50 ml/3¹/₂ tbsp water little by little, as needed. Add the salt. Knead with the palms of your hands into a smooth and moist ball of pasta. Cover with a cloth. Let rest for 5 minutes at room temperature.

2. Roll out the pasta dough as thinly as possible. Wrap the pasta around the rolling pin and unroll part of it on a chopping board. Cut the pasta with the tip of a knife. Cut large bands of all different sizes. Do the same thing with the rest of the pasta.

3. Lay the scampi on their backs. Split open the entire body, cutting them in half. Open them wide. Gently cut the legs and set them aside.

Lentil Malfatti

4. Brown the crushed garlic in the olive oil and remove it; replace with the lentils, cherry tomatoes, basil, salt and pepper. Cook for 10 minutes over low heat. Place the scampi on top of this mixture and cover the pan. Cook another 10 minutes, then set aside the cooked scampi.

5. Boil 2 liters/2 quarts salted water in a saucepan. As soon as it starts boiling, gently drop the pasta into the water. Allow to cook 5 minutes over medium heat. Remove the pasta from the water and drain it in a strainer.

6. Add 50 g/3 1/2 tbsp butter to the lentils. Bring to a boil and add the cooked pasta, stirring immediately. Arrange the lentils in a crown on the plates. Add the pasta, scampi, cherry tomatoes and basil, and serve.

Eggplant

Preparation time: 35 minutes
Cooking time: 45 minutes
Soaking time: 1 hour
Difficulty: ★

Serves 4

1 large eggplant
oil for frying
salt

For the salad:
2 tomatoes
1 green pepper

1 red pepper
1 yellow pepper
2 cloves garlic
1 small can tomato purée
1 pinch paprika
1 pinch caraway
1 dash hot chili sauce
salt
pepper

For the garnish:
1 bunch cilantro
50 g/scant ¹/₂ cup pine nuts
10 black olives

Full of Mediterranean flavors, this vegetarian entrée can be eaten warm or cold, depending on your preference. Very easy to prepare, Eggplant Medallions accompanied by Jewish salad is a nice homage to these sun-loving vegetables.

Mainly cultivated in the Arava and Jordan valleys, eggplants are found in plenty in Israelite markets. Available the entire year, they have certainly found their place among various Mediterranean and Middle Eastern dishes. Originally from India, these vegetables rich in potassium are particularly loved by Israelites.

To prepare the medallions, make sure to purchase large eggplants that have a rich purple color. Choose those with no blemishes, with smooth and firm skin, that are not wrinkled around the peduncle, and as fresh as possible.

It is imperative to salt them and let them stand for at least an hour before frying them; this prevents the flesh from absorbing too much oil. The temperature of the oil must be extremely hot

so it sears the eggplants. When you remove them from the pan, immediately place them on paper towels.

In dressing the eggplants with Jewish salad, Ledicia Renassia demonstrates her artistry in creating plates with warm, sparkling colors from the Mediterranean. This combination of flavors is marvelous and very successful.

Very popular in Sephardic Jewish families, this salad is often eaten for the evening meal on the sabbath, or *Shabbat*. This delicious salad composed of tomatoes and peppers is familiar to many people.

Known for their inventive methods and techniques in the fields of agriculture and irrigation, Israelites cultivate tomatoes and peppers in greenhouses. Both of these are found in the salad and bring touches of color and warmth to the dish. After topping the eggplant medallions with the salad, don't forget to pour the juices remaining from cooking the salad around the medallions.

1. Wash and cut the eggplant into round slices about 1 cm/¹/₃ inch thick. Salt both sides of each slice and set them on a wire rack to steep for 1 hour.

2. For the Jewish salad, wash all the peppers and cut them into strips. In a frying pan, heat the olive oil and sauté the pepper strips. When they begin to soften, add salt and pepper. Continue to cook for about 10 minutes.

3. Wash and cut the tomatoes into quarters. Add to the pepper mixture. Cook over low heat for about 15 minutes.

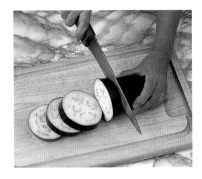

Medallions

4. Chop the garlic and add it to the mixture along with a dash of hot chili sauce.

5. Stir in the caraway, paprika and tomato purée. Let simmer and reduce for about 15 minutes. After cooking, add the olives.

6. Rinse and drain the eggplant slices. Brown them in olive oil in a frying pan. Put them on paper towels. Toast the pine nuts. Place some Jewish salad in the center of each eggplant medallion and garnish with the remaining olives, pine nuts, cilantro and the sauce.

Spinach and Ricotta

Preparation time: 30 minutes
Cooking time: 25 minutes
Difficulty: ★★

Serves 4

For the stuffed mussels:
100 g/3¹/₂ oz spinach
24 large mussels
3 sprigs fresh basil
100 g/6 tbsp ricotta
2 eggs

fresh nutmeg
1 lemon
salt
pepper

For the sauce:
800 g/1³/₄ lb cherry tomatoes
5 cloves garlic
5 basil leaves
200 ml/generous ³/₄ cup olive oil

Green, red and white are the bold colors of this traditional recipe. This spectacular appetizer is a flavorful gift from generous Italy.

The green comes from spinach, whose flavor counts as many detractors as it does fans. You should use the summer variety, nice and green, as it will be sweeter than the winter kind. Wash the spinach well, then blanch it briefly and be sure to strain it completely, pressing against the strainer to squeeze out all the water. This will give the stuffing an even consistency. You can substitute Swiss chard or, as a last resort, use frozen chopped spinach in place of fresh.

Cherry tomatoes supply the red, and bring their character and subtle flavor to the sauce. Aromatic grape tomatoes or firm little olive tomatoes will both work nicely in this recipe. The olive oil and tomatoes cook together over a high flame. The garlic and basil are kept in the sauce so they won't lose any of their flavor.

The white comes from ricotta, which binds the stuffing and makes it creamy and sweet. This typical Neapolitan cheese works wonders in any sauce, whether savory or sweet.

You will need mussels with large shells to accommodate a generous portion of the filling. Aluminum foil will hold them closed during cooking—you don't want to lose a bit of the precious mixture.

The aromas of basil and oregano proclaim the dish as coming from Naples. In the words of passionate Neapolitan chauvinist Massimo Palermo, "Only one city can rival Naples when it comes to culinary flavor, but no one knows what city that is…"

1. Blanch the spinach 5 minutes in salted water. Drain and set aside. Scrape the mussels clean and rinse them several times with clean water. Slip a knife blade between the shells to open them, but leave them attached at the hinge.

2. Mince the spinach. In a bowl, mix the basil leaves, spinach, ricotta and eggs. Add a little grated nutmeg and lemon zest. Season with salt and pepper.

3. Stir with a whisk until you obtain a stiff mixture. Use a spoon to portion out the mixture into the mussels.

Filled Mussels

4. Fill the mussels with stuffing. Cut up strips of aluminum foil the width of the shells. Band each mussel closed with a strip of foil and set them aside.

5. Slice the cherry tomatoes in half. Heat the olive oil in a saucepan. After crushing them in the palm of your hand, brown the garlic cloves. Add the tomatoes (remove the garlic halfway through the cooking). Cook over high heat for 5 minutes, stirring gently. Add fresh basil toward the end.

6. Carefully place the stuffed mussels one by one in the sauce. Cover and let cook 15 minutes over low heat. To serve, put some tomato sauce in each bowl first, then arrange stuffed mussels in it, with their foil band removed.

Matsunaga

Preparation time: 25 minutes
Cooking time: 55 minutes
Difficulty: ★★

Serves 4

1 daikon (Japanese radish)
10 cm (4 in) leek (whites and greens)
1 small can fois gras

For the miso soup:
2 strips konbu seaweed
800 ml/3¹/₃ cups cold water
30 g/1 oz dried bonito
100 g/3¹/₂ oz miso
1 egg yolk
60 g/4¹/₂ tbsp sugar
1 tbsp sake
1 tbsp rice wine

Long Japanese daikon radishes and miso, a fermented soybean paste, have both been part of Japanese cuisine for centuries. Kiyotaka Matsunaga added his own touch to this traditional preparation by stuffing the radishes with European foie gras. The Japanese can import this foie gras, but it is quite expensive. To meet this new demand, duck farms have been established around the Japanese countryside.

The daikon, a type of long, white root somewhere between a turnip and a radish, is regularly used in everyday meals. Because it can be grown in any garden, it is one of the few vegetables available in winter. After being harvested, it is preserved in salted rice water and is one of the many vegetables, called *tsukemono*, served in brine. Close to one million tons of daikon are consumed in Japan each year!

The simplest Japanese meal is comprised of steamed rice seasoned with marinated daikon. This Japanese condiment is also added into melted sauces, used to decorate *sashimi* dishes (thinly sliced raw fish), is shredded for seasoning, is pickled, or is added as small, raw strips in salads.

The miso paste that seasons the daikon was brought to Japan by the Chinese during the eighth century. To prepare it, the Japanese ferment the soy by using a special mold with a mixture of boiled soybeans, rice, water and salt. The resulting paste should be soft with a distinct flavor and can be any color ranging from white (*shiromiso*, which is soft and slightly salted) to yellow (*shinshumiso*), to red (*akamiso*, which is very strongly salted) and finally to chocolate.

Miso can also be prepared with a combination of soy and barley (*mugimiso*) or simply with soy (*mamemiso*). It complements Japanese breakfast soups, salads, vegetables and fish. It is also excellent when used to preserve food.

1. In a saucepan, cover the konbu with the cold water. Heat for 15 minutes over low heat. Just before it starts to boil, remove the seaweed and add the tuna. Lower the heat and cook until it sinks to the bottom of the pot. Then remove the tuna from the water by straining it through a sieve.

2. Cut the daikon into 4 pieces about 3–4 cm/1¹/₄–1¹/₂ in long. Peel each piece into a very fine spiral using a small, well-sharpened knife to create 4 similar pieces.

3. Bring water to the boil in a saucepan. Place the radish spirals in the water, boil for 30 minutes, and then drain.

Radishes

4. Combine the miso, egg yolk and sugar in a small saucepan. Pour in the sake and rice wine. Stir for 2 to 3 minutes over low heat. Pour this mixture into the tuna stock to complete the miso soup.

5. Take one leek, with both the white and green parts, and chop it into the thinnest slices possible, about 5 cm/2 in long.

6. Hollow out the tops of the daikon spirals with a melon baller. Fill with miso. With the same tool, make balls of fois gras and pan-fry them. Garnish each radish with fois gras, place them in a bowl with miso soup and decorate with leek slices.

Pork

Preparation time: 30 minutes
Cooking time: 3 to 4 minutes
Soaking time,
mushrooms & vermicelli: 20 minutes
Difficulty: ★

Serves 4

50 g/1³/₄ oz dried black mushrooms
200 g/7 oz carrots
2 onions
200 g/7 oz bean sprouts
200 g/7 oz Vietnamese vermicelli

500 g/generous 1 lb boneless
pork spareribs
1 drop nuoc mam fish sauce
1 pinch sugar
salt
pepper
50 ml/3¹/₂ tbsp beer
1 package square Vietnamese rice paper
oil for frying

For the garnish:
1 head Batavia lettuce
1 bunch mint

Pork Spring Rolls are among the most popular Vietnamese dishes. People who enjoy this traditional dish are treated to "a little bit of luxury" that can also be stuffed with crab, shrimp or beef.

Pork is the least expensive meat in Vietnam. The black pigs grow quickly and are easy to raise because they only need be fed the household's leftovers. Even in the suburbs, people may raise a few pigs to be sold eventually.

Spring rolls are always wrapped with rice paper made of rice flour, salt and water, and then cooked like crêpes and dried. The best spring rolls remain crisp when cooked. The Vietnamese know exactly where to get the best rice paper in their neighborhood. Outside of Vietnam, you can ensure a certain crispiness by moistening the rice paper with a mixture of beer and water before filling the rolls and frying them. The Vietnamese use small sheets of rice paper for the spring rolls and cut the larger sheets, which they fry and add to salads and rice vermicelli.

These quite nutritious rice noodles are sold in two forms: when they are not used for preparing spring rolls, the thinnest noodles are boiled and then spread out into thin sheets and topped with scallion oil. You can also easily mix them with pork, sautéed beef or grilled shrimp and wrap it all with a lettuce leaf to dip into a sauce. As for the largest noodles, they are cooked like spaghetti and enjoyed with lettuce and *nuoc mam*, the Vietnamese fermented fish sauce.

When you prepare your spring rolls, it is important to reinforce them by using two triangular-shaped rice sheets to form the outer layer. After moistening them, you need to dry them very carefully. Cook the spring rolls the same way you cook French fries: the first frying seals them, and the second gives them a golden-brown color and makes them nice and crisp.

1. Soak the mushrooms in water for 20 minutes. Peel and quarter the carrots and onions, and then put them in a food processor with the raw bean sprouts, noodles and mushrooms. Blend together until the mixture becomes a batter.

2. Grind the spareribs in a meat grinder. Pour the ground meat into the vegetable and noodle batter. Season with nuoc mam, sugar, salt and pepper.

3. Add water to a small saucepan and bring to the boil, then add the beer. Place two triangular rice sheets on top of each other. Quickly submerge them in the boiling liquid and dry them carefully with a cloth.

Spring Rolls

4. Spread out the two triangles on a completely dry cloth. Add a heaped teaspoon of filling.

5. Pinch together the left and right sides of the rice paper over the filling. Starting with the base of the triangle facing you, roll it up to create a cylinder. Prepare all the spring rolls in this same way.

6. Using a skimmer, fry the spring rolls in boiling oil. Take them out of the fryer; this is the "pre-cooking" stage. Just before serving, refry the rolls to brown them. Arrange them in small dishes garnished with lettuce and mint and serve hot.

Nine

Preparation time: *45 minutes*
Cooking time: *35 minutes*
Difficulty: ★★

Serves 4 or 5

For the pancakes:
300 ml/1¼ cups water
130 g/scant 1 cup flour
1 pinch salt
vegetable oil

For the filling:
10 dried black wood ear mushrooms
1 carrot

½ cucumber
10 fresh shiitake mushrooms
100 g/3½ oz bean sprouts
vegetable oil
3 eggs
200 g/7 oz beef fillet
3 tsp soy sauce
1 clove garlic, chopped
2 or 3 green onions, chopped
1 tsp sesame oil
½ tsp sugar
1 pinch pepper

Nine Delights adorns Korean tables like a brightly colored flower. Guests can taste no fewer than nine different dishes displayed like petals on a large, compartmented tray. Instead of choosing what to cook and hoping your guests will like it, guests can choose their favorite dishes and place them on top of small pancakes on their plates. They then roll up the pancakes with their chopsticks. All that is left is to enjoy! In Korea, the average life expectancy is 60 years. Because of this, a person's sixty-first birthday is an occasion for great festivities on which Nine Delights is traditionally served.

Beef is a good choice when preparing the nine delights, particularly because Koreans truly enjoy this meat. Chef Kim suggests that you use a tender beef fillet, the cut consumed most frequently in Korea, along with sirloin.

A serving of Nine Delights includes a range of vegetables typical of those grown in Korea. These include carrots, zucchini, cucumbers and spinach, and are grown particularly in the suburbs of Seoul to provide the capital city with fresh produce. There are also huge fields of large, white turnips and cabbage that are used in the production of *kim-chi*, a fermented dish similar to sauerkraut.

Complementing the vegetables are shiitakes, Asian mushrooms that have been eaten for over 200 years. Korea, China and Japan have made them an important agricultural crop. Shiitake mushrooms are the second most cultivated mushroom in the world after button mushrooms. Of course, Koreans today do not always have the time to prepare nine individual dishes. Like them, you can vary the number of choices. Do not hesitate to prepare a stack of large, thin crêpes that you fill with any sort of ingredient and roll up. Cut the rolls into small bite-sized pieces that you can arrange by color on a plate.

1. Mix 300 ml/1¼ cups water with the flour and salt to form a very thin crêpe batter. Set it aside. Soak the dried mushrooms in cold water.

2. Heat the oil in a large frying pan. Pour in 1 tbsp of the batter and cook, forming a small crêpe about 5 cm/2 in around. Cook multiple crêpes at the same time—this should take about 20 minutes.

3. Peel the carrot and julienne it. Cut the cucumber into large pieces. Take one section in your hand and slice in a spiral. Place several pieces of cucumber on top of one another and julienne them as well.

Delights

4. Drain the dried mushrooms and slice into long, fine pieces. Cut off the shiitake stems and mince the caps. Remove the tips of the bean sprouts. In a frying pan, cook separate crêpes with the egg whites and egg yolks.

5. Heat some oil in two frying pans. Brown the shiitakes, black mushrooms, carrots and cucumbers individually for 5 minutes each. Mince the meat and fry it with the soy sauce, garlic, onions, sesame oil, sugar and pepper.

6. Thinly slice the egg crêpes and cut them into thin strips. On a decorative serving plate, arrange the ingredients in small groups according to color. Place vegetables and/or meat in the small crêpes and enjoy.

Oi-Sonn

Preparation time: 30 minutes
Cooking time: 12 minutes
Soaking time: 15 minutes
Difficulty: ★★

Serves 4

3 small thin cucumbers
100 g/3¹/₂ oz beef fillet
3 fresh shiitake mushrooms
1 egg
oil
1 tsp soy sauce

¹/₂ clove garlic
1 green onion, chopped
10 g/1¹/₂ tbsp pine nuts
¹/₂ tsp sesame oil
1 pinch pepper
1 pinch sugar
salt

For the sauce:
¹/₂ tsp salt
2 tbsp white vinegar
2 tbsp sugar

Fried cucumber served with eggs, mushrooms and beef is a very elegant dish from South Korea with quite aristocratic origins. In the past, in fact, it was among the famed "royal dishes": only royalty and nobles, who had a large kitchen staff, had the privilege of serving this demanding dish.

However, more often than not, Koreans enjoy cucumber fresh rather than fried. They soak pieces of it in a pepper dip, or serve it in salad with minced garlic, pepper, chopped leeks, salt and sometimes vinegar. When fermented, they prepare it as *kimchi*, a spicy hot Korean condiment that is more commonly made with cabbage.

Cucumber, a vegetable from the *Cucurbitacea* family, is one of the oldest cultivated vegetables. It most likely originated in the northern Himalayas; there, archeologists have discovered cucumber seeds over 9,500 years old. This refreshing vegetable quickly spread from the Himalayas throughout Asia, and then moved from Egypt to Greece and Rome. The Romans grew

cucumbers in large basins and ate them coated with honey. You should choose small ones that are smooth and firm with bright green skin. When preparing this recipe, our chef suggests adding the sauce just before serving so that the vegetable's bright green color doesn't fade.

Always aware of the appearance of a dish, our chef explains that pancakes made of egg white and egg yolk respectively are a lovely addition to a platter that is otherwise difficult to garnish with color. Eggs are used frequently in Korean cooking because of their lovely yellow-white contrast. Pay close attention when preparing these very thin egg pancakes, because the egg yolks should never spill onto the egg whites.

Prepare the cucumbers by cutting three grooves and filling them with garnish. You can vary the presentation of this dish by serving a range of appetizers with 2 cm (¾ inch) pieces of cucumber. Stuff each piece with a different-colored ingredient, and you will create a rainbow assortment of starters.

1. Cut the cucumbers in half lengthwise. Then cut them at a 45° angle into pieces 4 cm/1¹/₂ in long, and cut three slits into each piece. Soak them for 15 minutes in cold, lightly salted water.

2. Slice the beef into thin strips, then stack them and cut them again into julienne. Chop the mushroom caps into julienne, 2.5 cm/1 in long.

3. Separate the egg. Lightly beat the yolk. Heat the oil in a non-stick frying pan and pour in the egg yolk. Cook it into a thin pancake, 3 minutes on each side. Prepare the egg white in the same way.

4. Mix the soy sauce, garlic, chopped green onion, pine nuts, mushrooms and meat. Add the sesame oil, pepper and sugar. Mix well and fry the mixture for 5 minutes, stirring constantly. Quickly fry the cucumbers for 2 to 3 minutes per side over high heat.

5. Cut the egg pancakes into thin strips. Take a piece of cucumber. In the first slit, place a bit of the egg yolk pancake, in the second some meat filling, and in the last some of the egg white pancake.

6. In a bowl, prepare the sauce by mixing the salt, vinegar and sugar. If it seems too bitter, gradually add small amounts of water. Place the stuffed cucumbers on a large serving plate and top with vinegar sauce.

Omelette

Preparation time: 30 minutes
Cooking time: 25 minutes
Difficulty: ★

Serves 4

300 g/11 oz smoked haddock
400 ml/1³/₄ cups heavy cream
salt
pepper
24 quail eggs

For the Mornay sauce:
10 g/1 tbsp finely diced celery
10 g/1 tbsp finely diced leeks

10 g/1 tbsp chopped fennel
20 g/2 tbsp finely diced onion
800 ml/3¹/₃ cups milk
1 bouquet garni
1 pinch grated nutmeg
50 g/3¹/₂ tbsp butter
50 g/¹/₃ cup flour
salt
pepper
30 g/¹/₄ cup grated Gruyère cheese
100 ml/7 tbsp heavy cream
1 egg yolk
dill

Arnold Bennett was a regular at the *Savoy Hotel*, one of the largest luxury hotels in London, established by Cesar Ritz and Auguste Escoffier at the end of the nineteenth century. Bennett always ordered an omelette prepared with cream, which now bears his name. Many English restaurants have honored special clients by naming a dish for him or her.

Great Britain remains a true hunting country, abounding in game from Scotland to the south of England. Due to its low altitude, wind and sea currents cross the country, and migratory paths for birds follow them. One famous bird is the pileated woodpecker that is sought after in Yorkshire and the north-west. Other favorites of English hunters include quails, ducks, pheasants, partridges, woodcocks, rabbits and hares. The famous grouse is pursued from the third Thursday of August through mid-November. Scotland and the Midlands, the Nottingham coast and the region around Sheffield are all known for their abundance of game. The quail eggs that you will find in markets are all farm-raised.

In Victorian times, the English were accustomed to eating haddock for breakfast in the form of kedgeree, a sort of casserole with rice and eggs. Customers at the *Connaught* enjoy Monte Carlo haddock poached in milk and served with a side of tomatoes and a poached egg.

In this recipe, the leeks add a slight bitterness, the celery a note of freshness, and the onion brings sweetness. Our chef suggests baking the haddock in the cream so that it adds its flavor to the cream, while slowly softening.

Make sure the Mornay sauce has cooled before adding the whipped cream and egg. If the sauce is too hot, the cream will start to melt and the egg will begin to cook. The egg helps the sauce thicken and stay on the plate, while the whipped cream gives the sauce the appearance of a glaze.

1. Remove the skin from the haddock. Remove all of the small pieces that have bones. Cut the flesh into slices, then into small cubes.

2. Combine the finely diced or chopped celery, leek, fennel and onion to form a mirepoix. Pour the milk into a saucepan and add the vegetables, bouquet garni and nutmeg. Bring to the boil.

3. Melt the butter in a small pan. Stir in the flour with a wooden spoon to make a roux. Strain the hot milk through a sieve to remove large pieces of herbs or vegetables, then pour the milk into the roux and whisk. Cook for 10 minutes, stirring constantly, until you get an even béchamel sauce.

Arnold Bennett

4. When the sauce is thick and even, add salt, pepper and the grated Gruyère. Whisk briskly just until the cheese is completely incorporated. Let the resulting Mornay sauce cool down.

5. Pour the 400 ml/1³/₄ cups cream into a small saucepan. Add the haddock. Bring to the boil and season with salt and pepper. Cook for 3 minutes. Cook the quail eggs for 3 minutes in boiling water, just until they become soft. Peel them carefully.

6. Whip the heavy cream. Fold into the Mornay sauce, then add one egg yolk. Whisk briskly. Spoon hot haddock cream into individual serving dishes. Top with quail eggs, then with Mornay sauce. Quickly set into a glaze by heating with a small hand-held torch. Sprinkle with fresh dill.

Hungarian

Preparation time: 45 minutes
Cooking time: 40 minutes
Difficulty: ★

Serves 4

2 potatoes
4 eggs
50 g/3¹/₂ tbsp butter, softened
1 small bunch parsley, ground
1 tsp mustard
1 tbsp anchovy cream
salt
pepper
green lettuce
parsley

For the tartar sauce:
1 egg yolk
100 ml/7 tbsp oil
20 ml/4 tsp vinegar
1 tsp sugar
¹/₂ lemon
30 ml/2 tbsp light cream
1 tsp mustard
salt
pepper

For the garnish:
1 small potato
2 carrots
1 large Golden Delicious apple
3 or 4 cornichons
100 g/²/₃ cup small peas, cooked

This recipe for stuffed eggs has been around since the 1930s, but it did not become popular until the 1970s when it started showing up on restaurant menus, both in cities and the countryside. Hungarians particularly enjoy these stuffed eggs in the summer because they are so refreshing. Although they are typically homemade, they are so popular that they are often found pre-made in supermarkets.

Hungarians eat lots of eggs, starting with their first meal of the day. They like to settle their stomachs by eating hearty omelettes filled with bacon, sausage and onions. One of the most famous egg-based Hungarian dishes is called *rakott krumpli*. It is a type of casserole with hard-boiled eggs, sausage and potatoes separated by layers of an egg and sour cream sauce. The entire dish is then baked in the oven. Hard-boiled eggs are also used for stuffing lamb chops, which are sliced and beautifully garnished with a side of vegetable salad.

Potatoes are also a fundamental part of Hungarian cuisine. They are often prepared as fries, mashed potatoes, or used in soups. However, there is also a traditional Hungarian side dish of "sour potatoes", or *burgonyafozelek*. Potatoes are boiled in salted water, mashed with flour that has been browned in fat, and then thinned with a little water and sour cream. The resulting dish has a consistency somewhere between that of soup and purée.

Hungary also produces a large quantity of pickles. Hungarians especially eat large pickles that are long, like cucumbers. In the summer, cucumbers of a more moderate size are preserved in water, bread, dill and salt. They are marinated for six days in the sun. Hungarians then use them in salads, or chop them into small pieces to serve with vegetable blends as accompaniment for various roasts.

1. Boil the potatoes and carrots together for 30 minutes. Hard boil 4 eggs for 10 minutes and set everything aside. For the tartar sauce, prepare a mayonnaise with the egg yolk, oil and vinegar. Mix in the remaining tartar sauce ingredients and put in the refrigerator to chill.

2. Peel the potatoes and put 1 aside with the carrots for the garnish. Peel the eggs. Cut in half, remove the yolks and set aside the whites. Mash the yolks and 2 of the cooked potatoes on a strainer resting on top of a plate.

3. Melt the butter and blend it into the egg-potato mixture by using a fork.

Stuffed Eggs

4. Add the parsley, mustard, anchovy cream, salt and pepper to the filling. Mix again with a fork.

5. Using a pastry bag with a notched tip, fill each egg white half with the filling. Peel the apple. Chop it into very fine dice along with the carrots, remaining potato and the pickles.

6. Add the peas, carrots, apple, potatoes and pickles to ¾ of the tartar sauce. Place a rounded scoop of vegetable tartar sauce and the stuffed egg halves onto each plate and top with the rest of the tartar sauce. Garnish with lettuce and chopped parsley.

Pappardelle with

Preparation time: 1 hour
Cooking time: 10 minutes
Difficulty: ★★

Serves 4

For the pappardelle:
1 kg/7 cups flour
3 whole eggs
6 egg whites
5 tbsp olive oil
3 g/¹/₂ tsp salt

For the sauce:
1 zucchini
6 dried tomatoes
15 cherry tomatoes
¹/₂ clove garlic
¹/₄ onion
salt
¹/₂ tsp black pepper
10 basil leaves
100 ml/7 tbsp white wine
grated Parmesan, to taste

Pasta reigns supreme in Italy: whether thin, cylindrical, flat, rectangular, tubular, spiral or elbow-shaped, it is served at every meal and for all occasions. Green, yellow or red, their lovely names pay homage to their mother tongue: *orecchiette*, *farfalle*, *fettuccine*, *agnolotti*… Each variety is equally seductive when paired with the likes of Parmesan with foie gras, or seafood with cherry tomatoes.

Large and flat, pappardelle noodles are well-suited to all kinds of sauces. In general, however, you should choose pasta according to the ingredients used with it. The thinner the sauce, the more hollow and absorbent the shape of the noodle will be. To prepare a light pasta, our chef Francesca Ciardi suggests that you use natural wheat flour and egg whites.

Because it uses many eggs, fresh pasta does not keep for more than two days. Pappardelle prepared with dried eggs is sold in many Italian grocery stores. It takes much longer to cook dried

pasta than freshly prepared, and this is the very key to the quality of Italian pastas: the cooking time and preparation.

When cooking fresh pasta, you should follow this exact process. Place the noodles in a strainer, then place them directly in salted boiling water, strainer and all. After three minutes, quickly drain the excess water and immediately pour the pasta into the sauce. This Italian "golden rule" guarantees the success of your fresh pasta.

Dried tomatoes and cherry tomatoes give these pappardelle a Mediterranean flavor. Because dried tomatoes are already salted, you may not need any additonal salt in the sauce. To achieve the best flavor, pluck the basil leaves directly from the sprigs into your frying pan. Great pasta is never served without Parmesan cheese; crumble fresh Parmesan generously over the steaming hot pappardelle.

1. Mound the flour on a work surface and make a well in the center. Break the eggs into it. Mix the eggs with the flour, then add the other ingredients. Knead into a dough. Pass the dough through a pasta machine three times, folding it in thirds after each round, until it is 2 mm thick.

2. For the sauce, cut the zucchini and dried tomatoes in thin strips and slice the cherry tomatoes in half. Finely chop the garlic and onion. In a frying pan coated with oil, fry the garlic without browning it. Add the onion, cherry tomatoes, zucchini, dried tomatoes, salt and pepper.

3. Sauté everything for 1 minute. Tear the basil leaves by hand into the frying pan. Immediately pour on the white wine. Simmer for 2 minutes. Add salt and pepper and remove from heat.

Tomatoes and Zucchini

4. With a knife or pastry wheel, cut strips 2 cm/³/₄ in wide from the dough to form pappardelle noodles. Unfold the pasta and set the noodles aside in a sieve.

5. Bring 2 liters/2 quarts water to the boil in a pot. Place the sieve with the pappardelle into the boiling water for 3 minutes. Immediately take the sieve out of the water and drain the pasta.

6. Once the noodles have drained, tip them into the frying pan with the sauce. Serve right away, steaming hot and garnished with basil leaves and sprinkled with grated Parmesan cheese.

Quail Breast

Preparation time: 40 minutes
Cooking time: ca. 25 minutes
Difficulty: ★★★

Serves 4

For the quail salad:
6 quails
salt, ground pepper
50 g/3¹/₂ tbsp butter
2 or 3 sprigs rosemary
60 g/2 oz alfalfa sprouts
60 g/2 oz wheat sprouts
60 g/2 oz red cabbage shoots
60 g/2 oz onion shoots
180 g/6 oz Brussels sprouts, blanched
50 ml/3¹/₂ tbsp peanut oil

For the pumpkin sauce:
200 g/7 oz pumpkin
50 ml/3¹/₂ tbsp port
100 ml/7 tbsp apple juice

For the balsamic glaze
20 ml/4 tsp balsamic vinegar
100 ml/7 tbsp apple juice
100 g/7 tbsp sugar

For the salsify "tagliatelle"
300 g/11 oz salsify
salt, oil for frying

For the sauce:
60 ml/¹/₄ cup soy sauce
1 tbsp puréed mango
3 tbsp balsamic vinegar
3 tbsp sushi vinegar
60 ml/¹/₄ cup olive oil
1 pinch each: sugar, dried ginger
dab of wasabi paste

With his creative Euro-Asian accents, Marcel Vanic serves a dish that combines excellent quails, pumpkin, plant sprouts and balsamic vinegar that is produced in Austria. Foods from more exotic origins are brought out in a Japanese-inspired sauce with soy, sushi vinegar and wasabi.

Austrians love to cook with grain-raised quail from the countryside. Generally, cooks buy the quail breasts ready to fry at a market or in specialized butcher's shops, and serve them on a bed of green salad. They can also be found already boned and stuffed with stale bread mixed with eggs, milk and herbs. For our recipe, you will need to remove all the boneless meat from the carcass and scrape along the vertebrae with a knife. You can use the remaining pieces to prepare a succulent stew.

Austrian gourmets are lovers of plant sprouts that they can easily buy very fresh, well packaged in small containers. Although we have selected wheat grain, alfalfa, onion and red cabbage sprouts, there is no reason you can't prepare an equally delicious one with lentil, soy, radish, Lucerne or mung bean sprouts. They can embellish many salads, sandwiches and all types of hors d'oeuvres.

In his sauce, our chef uses exceptional Golles balsamic vinegar. Made by a small family enterprise in Riegersburg in Styria, this product is based on fermented white grapes and ages tranquilly for many years in wooden barrels before acquiring its superb flavor.

1. Split open the quails on both sides. With a small, sharp knife, remove all the meat, leaving a small piece of bones. Salt and pepper the meat. In a hot, oiled pan, brown the meat for a few minutes until golden. Add the butter and rosemary, then remove from heat and set the meat aside.

2. Cut the pumpkin into large pieces, peel and cut the flesh into small cubes. Tip them in a saucepan. Add the port and apple juice, bring to the boil, then reduce. Purée, then season with salt and pepper and cool.

3. For the balsamic glaze, mix the ingredients in a saucepan. Bring to the boil. Lower the heat to moderate and reduce until it has a thick, syrupy consistency.

with Crisp Sprouts

4. With a vegetable peeler, carefully peel the salsify. Cut the salsify along the length of the root in order to form very thin strips of "tagliatelle". Blanch them quickly in salted water, then fry in a little oil.

5. For the sauce, combine the soy sauce, an equal amount of water, the mango purée, balsamic vinegar, sushi vinegar, olive oil, sugar, wasabi, ginger, salt and pepper. Whisk well.

6. Mix the sprouts, Brussels sprout leaves and the sauce. Place a small circle of salad in the center of each plate. Top with quail meat and salsify "tagliatelle". Surround with pumpkin sauce and balsamic glaze.

Potted Mackerel

Preparation time:	40 minutes
Cooking time:	50 minutes
Chilling time:	24 hours
Difficulty:	★★★

Serves 4

For the potted mackerel:
1 large crab (or 8 claws)
100 ml/7 tbsp white wine
1 sprig thyme
1 bay leaf
1 bunch flat-leaf parsley
salt, pepper
2 small mackerel
50 g/3^1/$_2$ tbsp butter

20–30 ml/1^1/$_2$–2 tbsp balsamic vinegar
20 leaves gelatin
3 shallots, chopped

For the gribiche sauce:
1 egg yolk
150 ml/^{2}/$_3$ cup olive oil
1 tsp vinegar
1 tsp mustard
1 pinch salt
1 pinch pepper
1 tsp capers, chopped
2 gherkins, chopped
1 shallot, chopped
3 chives
3 tarragon leaves
3 sprigs parsley

Mackerels and lisettes, a fish of the same family but much smaller and less fatty, are rarely served as a terrine. They are more commonly served in a white wine marinade or a mustard sauce. In certain countries, mackerel is soaked in brine before being eaten.

Here, our chef mixes browned mackerel fillets and flaked crab with shallots and parsley. The mackerel can be replaced with fillet of sole, lisette or turbot. The butter is heated just until it is very hot and begins to foam, and at that instant the mackerel is added to the pan to seal the skin.

The plentiful meat from the large crab called "toureau" comes apart easily, thus adding to the wonder of the terrine. After cooking the crab, save the broth to add to the gelatin later. To simplify, you can use crab claws instead. Cooked in boiling water for 15 minutes, they break easily at the joints and the meat comes free without a problem. For enthusiasts of quick work in the kitchen, canned crabmeat is a welcome time-saver. It is enough to just drain the contents of the can and add it to the other ingredients.

Our chef has a few surprises in store when cooking the savory gribiche sauce for your terrine. Used like mayonnaise, this well-regarded sauce accents a range of meats and fish. The addition of condiments such as gherkins, capers, chives, tarragon and parsley has earned this sauce's status among the ranks of classic gastronomy. Because the sauce is based on raw eggs, this dish cannot be saved for more than a day, so eat it all!

1. Cook the crab for 40 minutes in 1 liter/ 1 quart water with the wine, thyme, bay leaf, 2 or 3 parsley leaves, salt and pepper. Wash and gut the mackerels. Lift out the fillets. Brown them in 30 g/2 tbsp clarified butter for 3 minutes on the skin side. Salt, pepper and deglaze with balsamic vinegar.

2. Prepare the gribiche sauce: whisk the egg yolk with the oil. Blend in the vinegar, mustard, salt and pepper. Add the capers, gherkins, shallot, chive, tarragon and some of the minced parsley. Cover in plastic wrap and put in the refrigerator.

3. Cover the inside of a terrine mold with a large piece of aluminum foil. Evenly distribute the rest of the parsley leaves in the form.

and Crab

4. Place two of the mackerel fillets in the mold over the parsley, with the skin side down. Shell the cooked crab and strain the resulting stock.

5. Soften the gelatin in warm water. Dissolve it in the stock and reheat. Brown the shallots in 20 g/1^1/$_2$ tbsp butter. Grind the remaining parsley. Blend the shallots and parsley with the crabmeat. Stir in 750 ml/3^1/$_4$ cups of the gelatin crab stock.

6. Pour this mixture in the terrine. Cover with the other two mackerel fillets, skin side up. Pour the remaining stock on top. Refrigerate for 24 hours. Remove from the terrine and serve in slices with gribiche sauce.

Smoked Fish

Preparation time: 45 minutes
Cooking time: 20 minutes
Marinating time: 3 hours
Chilling time: 24 hours
Difficulty: ★★★

Serves 10

6 leaves gelatin
750 ml/3¼ cups fish stock
1 tbsp tomatoes, puréed
3 egg whites
100 ml/7 tbsp Riesling
100 ml/7 tbsp Noilly Prat
salt
pepper

For the sauce:
300 ml/1¼ cups heavy cream
1 lemon
60 g/¼ cup grated horseradish (jar)

For the fish:
250 g/9 oz each: pickerel, eel, sturgeon
and salmon fillet
300 g/11 oz sliced smoked salmon
300 g/1 cup coarse sea salt
150 g/⅔ cup sugar
a few stems of dill, chives, chervil
and tarragon

For the garnish (optional):
mixed lettuces
quail eggs
lumpfish roe
cherry tomatoes
dill, chervil, chives
vinaigrette

Presskopf, which translates as "headcheese," was originally an elaborate terrine made from the head of a salted, boiled and pressed pig. The animal, naturally fattened on the fertile land in Alsace, supplied country families with food. Various pork dishes and *Presskopf* remain specialties of Alsace.

But cuisine evolves: the pork was replaced by fish, pressed into a terrine and spiced with horseradish. To make this recipe, it is best is to buy fish that has already been smoked, although you can also smoke fresh fish yourself. Smoking is a very ancient means of food preservation. The fish must always be salted first. The sugar and salt in the marinade permit the fish to retain water. Carefully rinse and wipe the fish, and they can then be smoked on a grill. Do not be surprised if their color

darkens. Not only fish, but poultry, pork and game as well, can be smoked and made into any terrine you might care to devise. To facilitate turning out of the headcheese, line the mold with some plastic wrap before adding the ingredients. Once cooled, the terrine becomes easy to cut. Lift the plastic wrap and slice the headcheese into equal pieces.

Very popular in Alsace, the French word for horseradish, *raifort*, literally means "strong root". Fragrant, fresh and sharp, this powerful condiment should be added sparingly to the whipped cream.

Add quail eggs, some red and black lumpfish roe on the horseradish, cherry tomatoes and herbs for color, and you have *Presskopf* in gala attire.

1. Soften the gelatin in cold water. Warm the fish stock and stir in the tomato purée and egg whites. Strain. Add the gelatin to the hot stock and dissolve it by whisking over high heat. Cool. Add the Riesling, Noilly Prat, salt and pepper.

2. Whip the cream until thick. Gently add several drops of lemon juice and horseradish according to taste. Salt and pepper. Leave at room temperature until serving.

3. Cover all the fish with sea salt and sugar. Marinate for 3 hours, then remove the salt and sugar. Carefully dry the fish with paper towels.

Headcheese

4. If the fish is already smoked, skip this step. If the fish is fresh, place it on a smoking grill. Light the wood (or sawdust) and smoke the fish. Cut into thin slices and steam for 3 minutes.

5. Cover the sides and bottom of a mold with plastic wrap. Soak the slices of smoked salmon in the gelatin liquid. Place them on the bottom and sides of the mold.

6. Place 3 long strips of one kind of fish in the mold, then alternate chopped herbs and slices of various fish. Cover with the gelatin, fold the smoked salmon over everything and cover the terrine with plastic wrap. Refrigerate for 24 hours. Remove from the mold, slice and serve with sauce.

Pot-au-Feu Ravioli

Preparation time: 45 minutes
Cooking time: 35 minutes
Resting time, dough: 4 to 24 hours
Difficulty: ★★

Serves 4

For the ravioli dough:
160 g/scant 1 1/4 cups flour
20 ml/4 tsp olive oil
1 whole egg
5 g/1 tsp fine salt
20 ml/4 tsp water
1 egg yolk

For the filling:
120 g/4 1/2 oz beef, boiled *pot-au-feu* style
1 pat butter
1 clove garlic, chopped

20 g/2 tbsp chopped shallots
3 sprigs parsley, chopped
100 ml/7 tbsp white wine
2 tbsp crème fraîche

For the sauce:
50 ml/3 1/2 tbsp poultry stock
20 ml/4 tsp crème fraîche
60 g/1/4 cup butter
salt
pepper

20 g/1/4 cup horn of plenty mushrooms
1 pat butter
2 sprigs chervil

Pot-au-feu is a traditional French family meal consisting of beef and vegetables slowly cooked into a flavorful stock, and there are almost invariably some leftovers. The bouillon can also be used in soup, and vegetables make soups thick and tasty. But what can you do with the beef? Jacky Morlon brings out the best of this strongly flavored boiled beef in his small ravioli of incomparable taste, yet recognizable in great, long-simmered dishes.

The olive oil in the pasta gives the ravioli their Mediterranean flavor. The pasta dough is chilled for four hours, or even overnight. A fine pasta dough makes the ravioli light.

Pot-au-feu is generally prepared with shoulder of beef, top round, flank steak or chuck roast flavored with carrots, leeks, onions, cloves and herbs. It must cook for at least two hours.

Experts use oxtail, which requires much patience to be boned, but the result is an absolutely exceptional ravioli filling.

However, you may not have prepared pot-au-feu before. Merely boiled, a piece of shoulder or leg is satisfactory. Cut into strips, the meat is browned before being made into the ravioli filling. This filling must be cool and very compact while you form the raviolis so that the very thin pasta does not burst while cooking. An egg yolk serves to seal the ravioli shut, but a little bit of cold water can do the same task.

Adding some horn of plenty mushrooms, also known by their French name, *trompette de la mort* ("trumpet of death"), gives this dish a beautiful autumn color. Porcini or chanterelle mushrooms may also be used. Quickly cooked in butter, they complete this delicious hot appetizer.

1. Combine all the ingredients for the ravioli dough, except the egg yolk. Form a ball. Chill the dough between 4 and 24 hours. Roll out the dough to a thickness of 2 mm. With a corrugated cookie cutter, cut circles with a diameter of 8 cm/3 in. Set aside.

2. Shred the meat. Melt the butter in a saucepan and brown the meat. Add the garlic, shallot and parsley. Mix. Stir in the white wine and crème fraîche. Reduce for 10 minutes over low heat. Take off the heat.

3. With a spoon, fill the center of each ravioli with filling. Whisk the yolk and brush the outer edge of each circle.

with Mushrooms

4. Close the ravioli by pressing the edges together with damp fingers. Set aside.

5. Boil 1 liter/1 quart lightly salted water. Immerse the raviolis in the boiling water and poach for 5 minutes over high heat. Remove them with a skimmer and set aside on a plate.

6. Reduce the poultry stock by one third over high heat. Pour in the crème fraîche, stir, and reduce for 5 minutes. Add the butter and keep stirring. Salt and pepper. Sauté the mushrooms in some butter. Serve the raviolis covered in sauce with mushrooms and chervil.

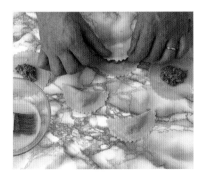

Fried

Preparation time: 40 minutes
Cooking time: 5 minutes
Difficulty: ★

Serves 4

200 g/7 oz shrimp
4 scallions
8 slices white bread
100 g/3½ oz thickly sliced boiled ham

salt
pepper
1 pinch sugar
sesame oil
oil for frying

Fried shrimp rolls are a savory mix of Chinese and European culinary traditions. These crisp, delicious mouthfuls of white bread are filled with luscious shrimp paste, scallions and ham. When the rolls are cut, the beautiful green and pale pink interior is exposed.

The Chinese have shrimp of all sizes at their table every day: small shrimp are used to make fillings and large shrimp are barbecued. Depending on the type of shrimp, the shell may be white, pink or striped. They are most often sautéed with vegetables, pork or chicken, or used to garnish Cantonese soups and rice. Indeed, the Chinese use the largest shrimp with vegetables such as mushrooms, onions and green peppers on brochettes or use them in fritters.

When the shrimp are puréed, you can adjust for any excess moisture by adding a little starch to the filling. Our chef has enveloped this filling in slices of white bread, a food that originated in the West, but is found more and more often in China. Actually, bread seldom plays a role in a typical Chinese diet, where rice or rice noodles accompany every meal. To prepare the rolls, our chef softens the slices of bread with steam to allow them to easily mold around the filling.

The boiled ham is also Occidental. The Chinese raise pork in large quantities, but prefer to eat it in the form of cutlets, fillet, ribs, and so on. However, the city of Chin-Hua, in the Shanghai region, has developed a unique ham specialty. There ham is cooked with numerous spices and has a pronounced flavor.

1. Remove the shrimp heads. With your fingers, remove the shells. Put the meat in a small dish.

2. Cut the scallions to the length of the slices of bread. Cut the ham into fairly thin, long strips.

3. Put the shrimp in a food processor. Add salt, pepper, sugar and sesame oil. Blend it all into a thick paste. Bring water to a boil in the bottom of a steamer.

Shrimp Rolls

4. Cut the crusts off the bread and cut the pieces into squares. Place the bread in the upper basket of the steamer and steam for 30 seconds.

5. Spread shrimp paste on each slice of softened bread. Place a piece of scallion and a slice of ham on top. Roll each piece of bread around its filling and seal with a little more shrimp paste.

6. Heat the oil in a fryer. With a skimmer, immerse the rolls in oil for 5 minutes. Once they turn golden brown, drain. Cut each roll into 3 pieces and serve hot.

Molded

Preparation time: 1 hour 30 minutes
Cooking time: 3 hours 20 minutes
Chilling time: 4 hours or more
Difficulty: ★★

Serves 4

1 kg/2¼ lb ripe tomatoes
2 cloves garlic, chopped
1 sprig rosemary
2 bay leaves
2 or 3 sprigs parsley
1 red bell pepper
500 ml/2 cups olive oil + 1 tbsp
1 tbsp brown sugar

300 g/9 oz fresh tuna
20 g/2 tbsp flour
salt
pepper
1 onion
½ carrot
1 rib celery
150 ml/⅔ cup sherry vinegar
125 ml/½ cup fish stock
50 g/1¾ oz pitted black olives
8 quail eggs
4 gherkins
4 green onions
4 sprigs basil
coarse salt (optional)

A signature of Mediterranean cuisines, and notably Spain, *escabeche* is a mix of cooked fish and a flavorful marinade, often served chilled. Here our chef has combined tuna with tomatoes, the leading ingredient in the Spanish diet. Traditionally preserved and canned in the countryside in the summer months, the tomato provides a full year of lovingly prepared, delicious dishes.

To improve this salad, which is ideal for summer meals, chef Alberto Herráiz replaced the customary preserves with tomato confit. This change accounts for the particularly long cooking time. The tomatoes must be ripe and firm; if they are soft, they might become compote when cooked. Served cold and accompanied by nothing more than some white bread, this salad from the Mancha region has become a specialty appreciated by the gourmands around Murcia. The chef proposes that you

complement this delicious salad with a Macabeo white wine from La Mancha.

Tuna, which most Spanish people use in its canned form, often comes from Basque country and Galicia. For this recipe, however, it needs to be fresh and either white or red. When choosing the fish, make sure the flesh is bright and firm. Cooked here in a frying pan, it can also be browned in olive oil, then baked in the oven at 250°C/480°F for five minutes. It is equally possible to replace the fresh tuna with canned, natural or *escabeche* tuna. Those who enjoy fresh sardines may prefer to use them instead of the tuna. As for the fish stock, it can be replaced with tuna juice or simply water.

If quail eggs are not available, chicken eggs will be fine. Quail eggs require a relatively long cooking time. To shell them more easily, add some salt to the water.

1. Skin and de-seed the tomatoes. Place them on a plate and sprinkle with the garlic, rosemary, bay leaves and parsley. Skin, de-seed and slice the red pepper. Add to the tomatoes. Pour in 250 ml/1 cup oil and the sugar. Cook in the oven for 3 hours at 80°C/175°F

2. Take out the central bone from the tuna and remove the skin. Cut the fish into thick slices, then large chunks. Sprinkle all the surfaces with flour, salt and pepper. Set aside.

3. Peel the onion and carrot. Chop the onion and julienne the carrot and celery. Brown together in 1 tbsp olive oil. Deglaze with the vinegar and reduce. Mix with the fish stock and let simmer over low heat.

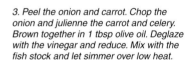

Tuna Salad

4. Heat 200 ml/generous ¾ cup olive oil. Brown the tuna for 3 minutes on each side; the flesh should be pink on the inside. Add the tuna to the stock and cook for 5 minutes over high heat.

5. Purée the black olives until very fine, add 50 ml/3½ tbsp olive oil and emulsify. Pass through a sieve if you wish. Hard boil the quail eggs. Mince the gherkins and spring onions.

6. Line four round molds with tomatoes. Fill with tuna, peppers, onions, gherkins and quail egg halves. Top with more tomatoes. Chill at least 4 hours, then remove from the molds and decorate with olives, basil and some coarse salt.

Ciego de Avila

Preparation time: 30 minutes
Cooking time: 30 minutes
Difficulty: ★

Serves 4

1 chicken, ca. 700 g/1¹/₂ lb
200 g/7 oz potatoes
100 g/3¹/₂ oz pineapple
1 onion
30 g/1¹/₂ tbsp salt

For the mayonnaise:
2 egg yolks
1 tbsp mustard
2 tbsp vinegar
150 ml/²/₃ cup oil
salt
pepper

Every morning in Moron, a large, sculpted rooster wakes the town's inhabitants with its electric cock-a-doodle-doo. This is just one sign of its popularity in Cuba, though pork and fish are eaten just as often.

From their Spanish ancestors, Cubans inherited the recipe for *arroz con pollo*, a rice dish with tomatoes and sweet peppers mixed with juicy roasted chicken. They also prepare chicken fricassée; *chicharrones de pollo*, which involves chicken fritters marinated in a lime and soy sauce; and *pollo barbacoa*, or chicken smoked over mangrove wood. Every Cuban family raises a few chickens for meat and eggs, even in cities, in a small cage in a corner.

The potatoes cultivated in Cuba come from Canadian seeds, and can be a substitute for rice. Cubans prepare stuffed potatoes with ground beef or make croquettes. However, they prefer rice and black beans.

The pineapples in the third part of the recipe are cultivated in the center of the island, in the Ciego de Avila region. Pineapples come from an herbaceous plant of the *Bromeliaceae* family. It produces a crown of rigid leaves where the fruit grows. The pineapples found in markets are divided into three categories: Cayenne pineapples, fat with pale yellow flesh and soft leaves; bottle pineapples that have an elongated shape; and finally Victoria pineapples, small and very sweet with thorny leaves. In Cuba, they are cultivated from seedlings.

Your chicken stock will be nice and clear if you take care to skim it several times while the chicken boils. By doing this, you eliminate much of the fat and any impurities.

Enrique Hernandez Hernandez advises you to serve your salad in a bed of lettuce leaves and to decorate it with tomatoes and pineapples.

1. Cut the chicken in half. Remove all the skin. Separate the wings and remove as many bones as possible. Boil the chicken in salted water for about 30 minutes.

2. Peel the potatoes. Cut them into thick slices and then into smaller pieces. When the chicken has cooked for 10 minutes, add the potatoes to it. Cook until the potatoes are just tender.

3. With a skimmer, remove the chicken. De-bone each piece, then cut the meat into very small pieces.

Chicken Salad

4. Slice the pineapples in half. Remove the skin with a sharp knife. Carefully remove the small black pips, then cut the fruit into pieces, avoiding the hard core at the center.

5. Peel and mince the onion, slicing it finely.

6. Use the listed ingredients to prepare a mayonnaise. Combine the chicken, pineapples, onion and potatoes. Stir in the mayonnaise and serve cool.

Brazilian

Preparation time: 35 minutes
Cooking time: 2 to 3 minutes
Chilling time: 1 to 2 hours
Difficulty: ★

Serves 4

150 g/5¹/₂ oz fresh goat cheese
200 ml/generous ³/₄ cup olive oil
salt
pepper

10 large shrimp
2 hearts of palm
2 large tomatoes
1 melon
2 tsp wine vinegar
12 fresh basil leaves

Brazilian Salad, or *salada brasileira*, is a traditional dish from the tropical coasts in the north of Brazil. Brazilians combine many ingredients in their salads, such as hearts of palm, tomatoes, onions, gherkins, beets or hard-boiled eggs. Popular restaurants offer grand salad and meat buffets. Brazilians generally eat a mixed salad with their meat, and accompanied by pasta or potatoes.

Hearts of palm are the uncontested stars of Brazilian salads. They come from a palm tree that grows abundantly in Brazil's hottest region. In the past, those who hunted in the forest collected them for their personal consumption. The industrialization of this product is relatively recent; now hearts of palm are available already cooked and canned.

Cheese is one of the typical products of the state of Minas Gerais, in central eastern Brazil. The ancestors of the current inhabitants of this region made cheese from cow's and goat's milk in their homes; its industrial production dates back less than a generation. The most renowned cheese of Minas Gerais is a very thick ricotta type called *pañ de queijo*, which is cut into small cubes to garnish salads.

Usually for this dish, our chef uses a very large tomato variety that comes from the south of Brazil. They contain a lot of flesh and very few seeds. Beefsteak tomatoes can also be used for this recipe, just be sure they are fully ripened. The use of melon is optional, and you can also add apples, mangoes or avocados. Instead of an ordinary wine vinegar, a few drops of balsamic vinegar can lend additional color and a particular flavor to this refreshing salad.

1. In a bowl, mash the goat cheese with a fork. Add a drizzle of olive oil and mix with the fork. Salt and pepper. Mix one last time. Put in the refrigerator.

2. Poach the shrimp for 2 to 3 minutes. Cut the hearts of palm into chunks. Rinse the tomatoes and slice them.

3. Arrange the tomato slices on a plate in an attractive pattern. Place some heart of palm on each tomato slice.

Salad

4. Cut the melon into sections. Peel it and slice each section lengthwise, then cut again into small triangles.

5. Cut off the shrimp heads. Carefully remove their shells. Blend the vinegar with salt and pepper.

6. With an ice cream scoop, mold balls of the goat cheese mixture and place them in the center of the plates. Surround the cheese with the shrimp and place melon triangles between the tomatoes. Top with the vinaigrette and decorate with fresh basil leaves.

Caesar

Preparation time: 30 minutes
Cooking time: ca. 5 minutes
Difficulty: ★

Serves 4

3 cloves garlic
120 ml/$^1/_2$ cup olive oil
2 tbsp butter, softened
$^1/_2$ loaf stale bread, cubed
1 head romaine lettuce
$^1/_2$ tsp salt

4 anchovies
1 lemon
2 eggs
$^1/_2$ tsp Worcestershire sauce
50 g/$^1/_2$ cup Parmesan, grated
1 pinch black pepper

On Independence Day in 1924, Caesar Cardini, a restaurateur in Tijuana, a city on the Mexican border, received so many clients that he was left with almost nothing to serve for dinner. He improvised a salad with lettuce, garlic, anchovies, croutons, olive oil and eggs. The clientele included numerous Californians and Hollywood stars who had crossed the border to have a drink legally (the sale of alcohol was illegal in the United States at the time). They enjoyed the meal so much, they helped make it a success across the United States. These days, the Caesar has become the preferred salad for a large number of Americans.

In elegant restaurants, the head waiter may mix the lettuce and season it in front of the guest, since it should not sit before being served. Caesar Salad is served as an appetizer or as the main dish for a light lunch. Grilled chicken, shrimp or poached salmon can be added.

Caesar salad would not be truly authentic without the barely cooked, almost raw, coddled eggs—they are steeped in simmering water for precisely one minute, then rinsed under cold water to stop the cooking process. When the American Board of Health decreed that raw eggs are a potential source of salmonella infection, restaurateurs started to use pasteurized eggs. Furious, elected officials in San Francisco broke the law and served their citizens the largest Caesar salad ever made.

To prepare the salad, cooks use romaine lettuce with its long, bright, lightly grooved green leaves. They serve the leaves whole or torn into narrow pieces. For a refined presentation, shape the lettuce into a bowl and pour the dressing inside. Our chef suggests that you make all the dressing in a salad mixer, so it will be easier to crush the anchovies and garlic. Croutons added at the last minute retain their crispiness.

1. Peel the garlic and chop it finely. Heat 60 ml/$^1/_2$ cup of the oil and the butter in a large frying pan. When hot, sauté 1 clove of the garlic.

2. When the garlic begins to brown, add the bread cubes. Brown them over relatively high heat, tossing regularly.

3. Rinse the lettuce and spin it. Tear the leaves coarsely and put them in a large bowl.

Salad

4. Put the remaining garlic in the serving bowl with the salt and anchovies. Crush with a wooden spatula to make a paste. Squeeze the lemon.

5. Poach the eggs for 1 minute, then rinse in cold water. Peel and add to the paste. Add the lemon juice and Worcestershire sauce and mix. Pour in the rest of the oil gradually, energetically mixing until the liquid is mayonnaise-like.

6. Add the torn lettuce to the sauce, then the croutons and Parmesan. Toss rapidly with salad spoons, sprinkle with freshly ground pepper and eat immediately.

Crisp Salad

Preparation time: 30 minutes
Cooking time: 55 minutes
Soaking time: 15 minutes
Difficulty: ★

Serves 4

1 chicken
20 dried black mushrooms
oil
2 large handfuls cashews
2 tsp Szechuan pepper

2 cm/³/₄ in piece fresh ginger
5 sprigs chives
1 sprig cilantro
salt
pepper
1 cucumber
3 tbsp hoi sin sauce
4 tsp sugar
2 tbsp cold water
1 tbsp soy sauce
1 tsp cayenne pepper

During Chinese meals, appetizers consist of an assortment of hot or cold foods, presented to the guests, who serve themselves small portions. For a celebratory meal, the table of appetizers is decorated with vegetable sculptures, such as swans or phoenixes, which are not eaten.

The number of dishes offered depends on the wealth of the host. Chicken salads might be served with crab rolls, marinated cabbage or cucumbers, fried eggs wrapped in pork, or even "crisp seaweed" (Swiss chard). Every effort is made to stimulate the guests' appetites.

A day never passes without a Chinese swallowing a few pieces of chicken in a bowl of broth and noodles. They appreciate this bird on New Year's as a symbol of happiness.

Presented "with all the sauces" in Chinese cuisine, chicken is titled "imperial" when it is cooked in the company of bamboo shoots, black mushrooms and red and green peppers. It be-

comes satiny in a ginger sauce with chives. It also appears steamed in tea vapor, sautéed in thin strips with noodles, or in fried rolls that are a favorite at family celebrations. Finally, in the Szechuan, chicken breast with peanuts is served alongside other sweet recipes which combine poultry with a melon cream or mandarin zest.

The fresh, woody and slightly spicy flavor of Szechuan pepper seasons this crisp yet tender salad. This rosy-colored spice is also called anise pepper or fagara, as well as by its Latin name, *Xanthoxylum piperitum*. It comes from a species of thorny ash tree and does not have a botanical tie to the ordinary pepper. The Chinese grill Szechuan peppers to release their flavor, then grind them.

A tiny pinch of Szechuan pepper suffices to marvelously flavor a marinade for pork spareribs.

1. Bring a large pot of water to the boil. Meanwhile, empty and rinse the chicken under running water. Plunge the chicken into the pot. Cover and cook 50 minutes. Skim the surface of the water while it is cooking.

2. Place the black mushrooms in a bowl of warm water to soak for around 15 minutes.

3. Heat the oil in a frying pan. When it is boiling hot, arrange the cashew nuts on a slotted spoon and immerse them in the oil for 5 minutes, until the nuts are well browned.

with Spicy Chicken

4. Grind the szechuan pepper. Peel the ginger and mince it with the chives and cilantro. In a bowl, combine all the spices with salt and pepper. Drain and chop the mushrooms. Dice the cucumber.

5. Carve the cooked chicken, discard the skin and remove the meat from the bones. Slice the meat into thin strips, then cut it into small pieces. Add them to the spice mix along with the cucumber, mushrooms and cashews.

6. Whisk the hoi sin sauce with the sugar and cold water. Pour it over the chicken and add the other ingredients. Blend and serve.

Thai

Preparation time: 30 minutes
Cooking time: 5 minutes
Difficulty: ★

Serves 4

For the salad:
5 small tomatoes
1 cucumber
1 red onion
10 g/1 tbsp minced coriander root
2 sprigs cilantro

3 sprigs fresh mint
10 g/1½ tbsp lemongrass
120 g/4 oz beef

For the sauce:
1 red pepper
2 cloves garlic
2 lemons
10 g/1½ tbsp powdered sugar
25 ml/1½ tbsp fish sauce
40 ml/2½ tbsp white vinegar

Fairly nicknamed "the little princess of Asia", Thailand delights in its gastronomy. Constantly concerned about their well-being, Thais try to be frugal, but they also know how to earn a profit from fish and meats. With one of the most important bovine herds in southeastern Asia, Thais also create unique and varied dishes with tender beef. Whether it is a salad or a sauce, spiced sweet or sour, each accompaniment is a perfect mix of flavors with beef. And for a simple salad, nothing is left to chance.

Honoring his native cuisine, Oth Sombath and his wife chop, mince and weigh each ingredient, so that no flavor risks overshadowing another. The queen of the flavors, Chinese citronella, or lemongrass, is cut into thin round slices. The top of its green stem releases an intense citrusy flavor. Only use the top 10 cm (4 in) of the plant.

Different from European coriander, Thai coriander, called *hom nam*, grows as large green leaves that are often used whole in soups or curry sauces. Chop the *hom nam* the whole length of the leaf. The root can be used in the salad if it has a very fresh, white color.

Omnipresent in Thai cuisine, garlic is one of the three principal flavors of soups and curries, along with *hom nam* and peppercorns. Thais always use it finely minced. For truly authentic flavor, it is preferable to weigh the ingredients once they have been cut and minced. Take the time to prepare them separately in small dishes, as the Asians do. Add them one at a time to the diced meat, then let the flavors slowly blend, in the rhythm of the Thai people.

1. Cut the tomatoes and cucumber into round slices. Peel and chop the onion. Mince the root and leaves of the coriander. Pluck the mint leaves off the stems and chop the stems, but reserve the leaves for decoration. Cut the lemongrass into rings. Set aside on a plate.

2. Heat a thick-bottomed pan over high heat, with no oil. When it is very hot, sear the meat for 2 minutes on each side. Take the pan off the heat.

3. To prepare the sauce for the salad, chop the red pepper in half. Remove the seeds. Mince it, then peel and mince the garlic. Combine pepper and garlic in a bowl.

Beef Salad

4. Squeeze the lemons and pour the juice into a small bowl. Add the sugar, fish sauce and then the lemon juice to the pepper and garlic.

5. Remove the meat from the pan. On a cutting board, slice the meat in half lengthwise. Cut each half into strips 1 cm/¹/₃ in thick, then dice the strips.

6. Arrange the meat and vegetables on a plate. Top with the sauce, then the vinegar. Serve the salad warm, decorated with mint leaves.

Fjord Shrimp

Preparation time:	30 minutes
Cooking time:	30 minutes
Difficulty:	★

Serves 4

2 tbsp butter
4 sheets brik pastry or phyllo dough
10 g/4 tsp cumin seeds
200 g/7 oz shelled shrimp
juice of 1 lime
salt
1 pinch sugar
12 green asparagus

½ bunch chervil
½ bunch dill
2 tbsp olive oil

For the lemon coulis:
2 lemons
1 pinch sugar
300 ml/1¼ cups Sauternes dessert wine
1 tsp arrowroot
salt
pepper
Tabasco sauce (optional)

Denmark is largely made up of 300 islands, and there are fjords where fresh water mixes with salt water. The Roskilde fjord, close to Copenhagen, provides a large quantity of small shrimp that are greatly prized by gourmands. Our chef advises you to spice these delicate crustaceans with both sugar and salt, and then serve them between crispy sheets of pastry with cumin and lemon coulis.

In Denmark, shrimp are caught from May until August, sometimes even September if the weather is still mild. They measure at the very most 1 cm (⅓ inch) once shelled. The best are marketed in the spring and at the end of the season. The Danes enjoy their shrimp on cumin bread, with lemon. Among the *smørrebrød*, the open-faced sandwiches typically eaten for lunch, *rejesalat* merits special mention: cooked shrimp on a bed of mayonnaise, with hard-boiled egg, dill and lemon, all on white bread.

In the country, dishes are essentially seasoned with cumin, dill and chervil. Cumin is the aromatic seed of a plant that grows approximately 30 cm (12 inches) high, with mauve or pink flowers. It often flavors cheeses, bread or even pigeon stews.

Dill, a member of the *Umbelliferae* family, is known for its leaves, which have a very strong anise-like flavor, and for its seeds, with their digestive value. It goes well with all kinds of fish, and blends nicely with clarified butter to top small boiled potatoes. Dill is an indispensable ingredient in Scandinavian cuisine.

The Danes still pretend that chervil originated in their country, even though historians place its origins in southern Russia, instead. Wild chervil does grow in Denmark and sprigs of it make their way into many fish recipes and soups.

1. Melt the butter in a small dish. Lay out 2 sheets of pastry on a cutting board. Using a brush, rub them with the butter.

2. Sprinkle the surface with cumin. Cover each sheet with a second one and brush them with melted butter. With a chef's knife, cut them in 2 equal pieces, then into triangles, just as you would a cake.

3. Place the triangles on parchment paper on a baking sheet. Cover them with a second sheet of paper and then a second baking sheet. Bake for 10 minutes at 180°C/355°F. Put the shrimp in a bowl, and add a little lime juice, salt and sugar.

and Asparagus Salad

4. Cook the asparagus for 10 minutes in salted, boiling water. Chop the chervil and dill. For the coulis, squeeze the juice from 1 lemon. Zest the other lemon in strips, slicing from top to bottom, leaving all of the white skin. Mince the zest.

5. Remove the flesh from the lemons. Pour the water, sugar, lemon juice and lemon pieces into a pot. Cook and reduce for 10 minutes. Add the Sauternes and arrow-root, and continue cooking until the sauce is completely blended. Strain, then add the zest, salt and pepper.

6. Slice the asparagus into 3 or 4 pieces. Brown them quickly in olive oil. On a plate, arrange the asparagus, shrimp and cumin pastry. Sprinkle with chervil and dill, and accompany with lemon coulis and Tabasco sauce.

Palm Salad

Preparation time: 30 minutes
Difficulty: ★★

Serves 4

400 g/14 oz hearts of palm
1 lemon
40 ml/2¹/₂ tbsp olive oil
salt
pepper

200 g/7 oz pineapple
100 g/3¹/₂ oz sliced smoked marlin
1 large tomato
3 or 4 sprigs chive
greens
butter (optional)
toast (optional)

The nickname "millionaire salad" suits this dish well. To make it, it is in effect necessary for a royal palm tree to grow for five to seven years until it reaches a height of 8 to 10 m (22–36 ft). Once the tree is cut down, the bared heart at its core produces at the most three or four portions, and the price for this is rather high. A heart of palm is a little crisp and tastes of hazelnuts and green almonds. Our chef likes to prepare hearts of palm au gratin, or poached like asparagus and covered with hollandaise sauce. He also suggests *achards* of palm, flavored with turmeric, mustard, lemon juice, garlic and ginger in olive oil.

Victoria pineapples magnify the flavor of this tropical salad. This small fruit weighs only 600 to 800 grams (21–28 oz), with hard, yellow skin and thorny leaves, and is cultivated on the island of Mauritius in the domains of Montagne-Longue and Crèvecoeur. The people of Mauritius Island mix it into salads with green mango, chopped green pepper and salt, and enjoy its fresh juice mixed with crushed ice and water.

A migratory fish, marlin is caught around Mauritius from November to August. The months of December and January see the arrival of international fishing champions, some of whom catch marlins that weigh up to 500 kg (over 1,000 lb)! This cousin of swordfish comes in many varieties, such as blue marlin, black marlin, striped marlin and winged marlin. It is as delicious fresh as it is marinated in *carpaccio*, or as a steak, in a curry, in *vindaye* with mustard or in a stew. On the island, a few canning factories specialize in the preparation of smoked marlin. It is wonderful in salads or on toast!

To preserve all the flavor of the heart of palm, pineapple and marlin, our chef advises you not to dress the salad with a vinaigrette, which would dominate all the other subtle flavors. A simple sauce of good olive oil and lemon juice would be just the thing.

1. Peel the heart of palm, then cut it into very thin, round slices. Put the slices in a bowl.

2. Squeeze the juice from the lemon. Quickly pour this juice over the palm slices to prevent them from discoloring. Add the olive oil, salt and pepper, and mix with a spoon.

3. Cut off the top and bottom of the pineapple. Cut it into large pieces and peel with a small knife. Slice the large pieces, then cut them into very small sticks.

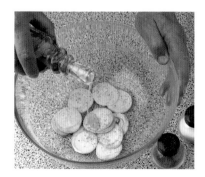

with Smoked Marlin

4. Julienne the slices of smoked marlin. Cut the tomato in half, remove the seeds, then cube it. Chop the chives.

5. Mix the heart of palm with the pineapple, chives and tomatoes.

6. Decorate the plates with greens and arrange the salad and the marlin on top. Serve accompanied with buttered toasts.

Kerkannah Islands

Preparation time:	*45 minutes*
Cooking time:	*30 minutes*
Maceration time:	*10 minutes*
Difficulty:	★

Serves 4

1.5 kg/3¼ lb octopus
1 clove garlic
salt
½ bunch flat-leaf parsley
3 tomatoes

1 onion
3 lemons
100 ml/7 tbsp olive oil
ground black pepper
1 pinch cumin
1 head lettuce
black olives
2 hard-boiled eggs

Every civilization has its tree of knowledge. For the Chinese, it is the sacred blackberry bush, for the Scandinavians, the ash tree, and for the Tunisians, the olive tree, a plant adapted to the Mediterranean climate. Olive trees spread as far as the eye can see from Sousse to Sfax.

Across from Tunisia, the archipelago of Kerkannah draws its outline in the blue of the sea. Families in Kerkannah, who reside almost entirely on the islands of Gharbi and Chergui, live in a realm of palm trees and fishing. For the island inhabitants, who are quite isolated from the rest of the world, octopus represents a true "gift from God". Fishing takes place at night, but it is in the morning that the cephalopod mollusk meets its sad end. Out of the water, laid on the sand and beaten with the branch of a palm tree, the octopus from Kerkannah spreads its tentacles, offering its delicate flesh.

Nothing is wasted from this animal: blanched for five minutes, it is rapidly found in a dish of well-spiced couscous, and its extremities enrich chickpea soup, while its tentacles are cooked in a most delicious salad. Mohamed Boussabah insists on using beaten octopus, because it never loses its tenderness, even after it has been cooked a long time. If you cannot find it, choose small octopi with delicate flesh and cook them for a short time. Much appreciated by gourmets, the suckers of the mollusk can be removed.

Tomatoes and onions are discreet in this salad. Finely chopped, the mild, white onion leaves only its aroma. The firm-fleshed tomatoes do not expel their juice. Add pepper and cumin to taste, and finally, lettuce and hard-boiled eggs complete this delicious appetizer. Poured in moderation over the salad, olive oil from Sfax lends the octopus its pleasing qualities.

1. Carefully wash the octopus and dry it with a paper towel. Cook it for 30 minutes in a pot of boiling water, then drain it. Cut the tentacles into large cubes and set aside.

2. In a mortar, crush the garlic and salt into a compact paste. Rinse the parsley and set aside the leaves. Peel and dice the tomatoes.

3. Peel the onion and cut it in half. Chop it very finely with a small knife. Mince the parsley.

Octopus Salad

4. Juice 2 lemons and slice the third. In a bowl, combine the octopus, onion, parsley and tomatoes. Add the lemon juice and a drizzle of olive oil.

5. Season with salt and pepper, then let macerate for 10 minutes in a cool place, stirring occasionally. Add the cumin. Wash the lettuce leaves and keep them cool.

6. Cover a plate with lettuce and arrange the octopus salad in the center. Garnish with black olives, hard-boiled eggs, tomatoes and lemon slices. Serve cold.

Kibbutz

Preparation time: 30 minutes
Difficulty: ★

Serves 4

2 pink Jaffa grapefruit
250 g/9 oz firm cherry tomatoes
1 fennel bulb
2 small Israeli cucumbers
100 g/3¹/₂ oz salted Israeli cheese
or feta cheese
1 Carmel avocado

For the sauce:
1 bunch cilantro
1 clove garlic, peeled
¹/₂ lime
50 ml/3¹/₂ tbsp olive oil
salt
pepper

1 bunch mint
10 black olives

With origins in a utopian dream, the communal experience of the *kibbutzim* has demonstrated over and over again the efficiency of this way of life. Stemming from a typically Israeli tradition, it is a lifestyle choice. Based on the principles of shared production and consumption, along with the economic equality of all the members, this agrarian business model has transformed the Israeli countryside. Thanks to the work of these pioneers, this country's land is now fertile and produces an abundant variety of fruits and vegetables.

The Kibbutz Salad is a lovely homage to the men and women who work tirelessly outdoors and whose daily meals consist mainly of fresh produce they have grown. This very refreshing dish contains avocados, grapefruit, cucumbers and salted cheese. It is a savory meal perfect for the summer months.

This salad is served in grapefruit rinds, more evidence of its originality. Ledicia Renassia, who came up with this idea,

recommends cutting the citrus fruit with the tip of a knife and scooping out the insides with a spoon. Choose any type of Jaffa grapefruit, all of which are well known for their exceptional flavor.

As for the Carmel avocados, which are a delicacy around the world, they are mainly grown on plantations in northern and central Israel. These fruits, which have a slightly nutty taste, are an excellent source of potassium. They also give the salad a soft and delicate consistency. However, they are quite fragile and must be handled carefully.

This delicious salad is a remarkable combination of tastes, the aniseed flavor of the fennel mingling with fresh mint. Enhanced with an Oriental sauce, thanks to the coriander, Kibbutz Salad is a true delight for the taste buds.

1. Cut the grapefruit in half. Scoop out the flesh without damaging the rinds. Remove the white pith from the rinds. Set aside.

2. Wash the vegetables. Cut the cherry tomatoes in half and the fennel bulb into long thin slices. Set aside.

3. Cut the cucumbers into thin slices; do not peel them.

Salad

4. Cut the cheese into cubes. Quarter and peel the avocado. Chop the mint into small leaves.

5. Make the sauce by placing the coriander and the garlic clove in a blender. Juice the lime and add its juice to the sauce. Blend together, adding the olive oil, salt and pepper.

6. Mix the grapefruit, tomatoes, fennel, cucumbers, cheese and avocado together in a large salad bowl. Fill the grapefruit rinds with the salad, olives and mint. Serve with the sauce.

Savoyard

Preparation time: 15 minutes
Cooking time: 45 minutes
Difficulty: ★

Serves 4

For the salad:
mixed fresh greens
250 g/9 oz slab bacon, not smoked
4 average potatoes
4 slices of bread, crusts removed
1 pat butter
50 ml/3¹/₂ tbsp oil
500 ml/2 cups water
1 dash vinegar

1 egg
200 g/7 oz Gruyère cheese

For the dressing:
1 egg
1 shallot
1 clove garlic
salt
pepper
1 tbsp mustard
150 ml/²/₃ cup peanut oil
60 ml/¹/₄ cup wine vinegar
150 ml/²/₃ cup walnut oil
5 sprigs parsley

Curly endive, escarole, oak leaf, lettuce, radicchio, or fresh and crispy Batavia, green, brown, red or white, greens never cease to inspire and stimulate new ideas.

Savoyard Salad includes three authentic types of farm produce: eggs, cheese and bacon. The egg is soft-boiled, halfway between soft-cooked and hard-boiled. The fresher the eggs are, the more magnificent the poached eggs will be, and the more the whites congeal in the boiling water without falling apart. Cooking them requires extreme precision. There are two ways to soft-boil them: poach them for 3 minutes in unsalted water, or place the eggs in their shells in salted water for 4 minutes. This method is immediately followed by immersing the eggs in cold water.

Whether smoked or salted, the bacon should be blanched in boiling water for 3 minutes. When diced and browned, the meat is crispy. Emmental, Gruyère, Comté … whichever cheese you use, cut it just before serving so that it does not become too soft. As for the potatoes, they are cooked slowly in their skins for half an hour. They are then peeled while still hot and cut while warm.

But there is no such thing as a good salad without a good dressing, and as for choosing the dressing, to each his own. Bernard Collon sticks with tradition: shallot, pressed garlic, a pinch of salt, wine or sherry vinegar or some peanut oil. He whisks everything together into a rich mixture with a delicate flavor. The poached egg enriches the vinaigrette. When it has been whipped, it is blended with 1 tbsp of walnut oil as a finishing touch. The second poached egg can be put in the vinaigrette or on top of the salad. You can also simply serve a soft-boiled egg to each guest.

1. Wash the greens 2 or 3 times in water, then set them aside. Dice the bacon and blanch the meat for 3 minutes. Cook the potatoes for 30 minutes. Let them cool somewhat before peeling and cutting them.

2. To make croutons, chop the bread into cubes. Brown the butter and oil in a pan. Add the bread and cook until it is golden. Then, in the same pan, brown the meat cubes for 5 minutes, then set them aside.

3. Boil the water with the vinegar. Crack the eggs into a small bowl. Place them one at a time into the boiling water and poach them for 4 to 5 minutes, then plunge them in cold water to stop the cooking.

Salad

4. Peel and mince the shallot and garlic. In a bowl, combine them with the salt, pepper and mustard. Add the peanut oil, wine vinegar and walnut oil and whisk.

5. Using a paper towel, carefully dry off the poached eggs. Mash an egg into the vinaigrette. Chop the parsley and sprinkle some of it over the dressing.

6. Cube the cheese. Place the greens in the center of the plates and top with the potatoes, meat, cheese, croutons and the rest of the parsley. Add the soft-boiled egg and dressing.

Vietnamese

Preparation time: 40 minutes
Cooking time: ca. 10 minutes
Marinating time: 15 to 20 minutes
Difficulty: ★

Serves 4

1 green papaya
200 g/7 oz soy sprouts
1 tomato
2 small fresh chili peppers
1 clove garlic
1 banana flower
1 cucumber
1 pinch salt

1 chicken, ca 500 g/1 generous lb
1/4 white cabbage
200 g/7 oz carrots
1 mint stalk
3 or 4 sprigs basil

For the sauce:
1 small fresh chili pepper, chopped
1 clove garlic, chopped
3 tbsp sugar
100 ml/7 tbsp nuoc mam (fish sauce)
50 ml/3 1/2 tbsp lime juice
200 ml/generous 3/4 cup water
50 ml/3 1/2 tbsp vinegar

peanuts

There is nothing like a fresh chicken salad with vegetables to whet your appetite, especially if you live in south Vietnam with its hot and humid tropical climate. This salad and another, made with vermicelli rice, sautéed beef and cucumbers, all bathed in soy sauce, are equally popular.

Crispy and crunchy are the key words in Vietnamese cuisine, and carrots, white cabbage, cucumbers, soybean sprouts and green papaya give an indispensable crispiness to this dish. Papayas grow in bunches right on the trunk of especially fast-growing trees. The papaya is a large, long, bright green fruit that is picked before it is fully ripe. Its flesh, which is hard and filled with large seeds, is usually cut into thin slices or grated like carrots to add to salads. The Vietnamese also cook papayas in large slices. The skin of a ripe papaya is yellow and its flesh bright orange. The sweetness of papaya makes it an ideal ingredient for fruit salads.

Our chef has given a nice touch to his salad by adding some banana flowers. This large, dark red flower has a base that is covered with little purple receptacles. These receptacles are used to garnish this salad. Vietnamese people also enjoy sprinkling them over soups. Vietnam produces many bananas because they can be grown in just three or four months. They are eaten when green or when ripe, with both the leaves and the flowers, which are added to rice while it cooks. Banana leaves can also be used in place of aluminum foil to cover rice and small cakes.

The preparation of the sauce is vital for preparing a good chicken salad. Add sugar and vinegar according to your taste, so that all of the ingredients remain balanced. Do not hesitate to season the dish with some lemongrass.

1. Cut the papaya in half, remove the seeds from the center, and peel the fruit. Blanch the soy sprouts. Chop up the tomato, chili peppers, garlic and banana flower. Set aside.

2. Slice the papaya and unpeeled cucumber, then julienne the flesh. Place the pieces in a pot.

3. Sprinkle the cucumber and papaya with salt and let stand for 15 to 20 minutes.

Chicken Salad

4. In a large pot, bring some water to the boil. Place the chicken in the boiling water and cook for 10 minutes. Meanwhile, cut the white cabbage into long, thin slices.

5. Remove the chicken from the water and finely slice the meat. Peel and cut the carrots. Combine both with the tomato, chili peppers, garlic, banana flower, mint and basil.

6. For the sauce, mix the chili pepper, garlic, sugar, nuoc mam, vinegar, lime juice and water. Mix the salad with some of this sauce in individual serving bowls. Garnish with peanuts and serve with a small bowl of additional sauce.

Salad with

Preparation time: 40 minutes
Marinating time: 24 hours
Difficulty: ★

Serves 4

1 red bell pepper
1 green bell pepper
2 cloves garlic
salt
pepper
250 ml/1 cup olive oil
8 sardines, preferably Portuguese
2 sprigs coriander, chopped

Being a country with an abundance of sunshine, Portugal is an ideal place to enjoy salads, especially during the summertime. During this season, hearty soups are replaced with lighter meals that include plenty of vegetables seasoned with onions, garlic and spices. Salads are sprinkled with olive oil, and sometimes lemon juice or vinegar.

Bell peppers, sometimes a vibrant green and other times a deep warm red, whether quartered, thinly sliced or finely diced, add color, texture and flavor to many different dishes. The pepper is one of the more popular vegetables in Portugal, and it is a perfect partner with tomatoes, potatoes, onions, garlic and many other vegetables and spices. And though it is particularly used in salads, it is also paired with fish, for example in the traditional Portugese *caldeirada* fish stew. Peppers marinated in olive oil and seasoned with garlic are one of the most flavorful appetizers and can even be served as a snack.

In Portugal, sardines are caught in fishermen's nets in great quantities and eaten by the mouthful. Large sardines are grilled, marinated with salt and lemon juice, or made into a pâté or a mousse. They are then served as an appetizer, along with slices of bread and accompanied with bits of cheese, olives, fritters and meats such as sausage and ham.

Our chef has used small, tinned sardines that are readily found at nearly any grocery store. If you have the chance, though, try to find some that come from Portugal. You can also replace them, however, with anchovies or jack.

1. Grill the bell peppers with a torch, scorching all the skin. If you do not have a torch, broil them, turning regularly until all the skin is blackened.

2. Place the grilled peppers in cold water so they will be easier to peel; the skin should come off by itself. Peel them.

3. Cut the peppers in quarters, then carefully remove the seeds and white membranes.

Peppers and Sardines

4. Place the peppers in a large baking pan. Peel and chop the garlic and sprinkle it over the peppers.

5. Season the peppers with salt and pepper and drizzle with the olive oil. Cover the pan with a sheet of parchment paper and refrigerate for 24 hours.

6. Take the peppers out of the refrigerator 30 minutes before serving time. Open the sardines and remove the center bone. Place the peppers on plates, sprinkle them with the marinade and serve with the sardines. Garnish with chopped coriander.

Warm

Preparation time: 30 minutes
Cooking time: 35 minutes
Difficulty: ★

Serves 4

For the carrot salad:
1 kg/2¼ lb carrots
8 cloves garlic
1 sprig parsley
1 sprig cilantro
4 tbsp olive oil
½ tsp cumin
salt
pepper

For the sweet potato salad:
1 onion
1 clove garlic
5 tbsp olive oil
½ tsp ginger powder
1 pinch saffron threads
½ tsp ginger powder
1 kg/2¼ lb sweet potatoes
2 or 3 sprigs parsley
1 tbsp coriander
1 pinch cinnamon
salt
pepper

It is a Moroccan tradition to have several small appetizers at a meal. Moroccans especially enjoy appetizers before a meal of meat, chicken or fish. One that our chef suggests is made of slightly crunchy carrots with garlic and parsley. It is a dish bursting with flavor and color, typical in this magical country whose cuisine never ceases to charm. For a special touch, you can cut the carrots with a curved tool, which makes them even more appealing.

Sweet potatoes, the stars of the second salad, are particularly nice in appetizers; they can also be served at the end of the meal or as an afternoon snack. Appetizer? Dessert? Moroccans eat this tuber anytime. Lahoucine Belmoufid offers many different ways to prepare them, such as slightly sugared sweet potato with beef or lamb, or sweet potatoes caramelized and served as a side dish with meat dishes. Here, the chef lets us

choose and offers it with salt, sugar and spice. This recipe is of Jewish origin, demonstrating that the history of cohabitation between these people has blended great culinary traditions.

When the recipe is intended to be a dessert, it can be served with mint tea. Saffron, the red gold of gastronomy, colors and seasons the dish, while the parsley decorates it and gives it a pleasant scent. If you'd like to grow your own sweet potato, place one in a vase of water and let its leaves spread throughout your kitchen, or even your garden.

The pair of appetizers our chef has prepared are brought to the table in small quantities in two dishes so that every guest can be sure to have a taste of each. Instead of clearing them from the table, let them remain until the end of the meal so that guests can continue to help themselves to a fork-full every now and then.

1. For the carrot salad, peel and cut the carrots into thin, round slices. Peel the garlic and remove any sprouts.

2. Boil the garlic and carrots for 10 minutes. They should remain somewhat crisp. Turn off the heat, remove the garlic cloves and crush them. Drain the carrots.

3. Chop the parsley and coriander. In a bowl, mix the olive oil, parsley, cilantro, garlic, cumin, salt and pepper. Pour this sauce over the carrots.

Fez Salads

4. For the sweet potato salad, peel and chop the onion and garlic. Brown them in olive oil for 15 minutes, then sprinkle them with ginger and saffron.

5. Peel the sweet potatoes and rinse them in cold water. Pat them dry and cut into thick, round slices. Add them to the onions.

6. Pour a glass of water over the potatoes and onions and simmer for 5 minutes. Cook for another 3 minutes over medium heat. Remove from the heat and add the parsley, coriander, cinnamon, salt and pepper. Serve lukewarm or cool with the carrot salad.

Valero-Style

Preparation time: 45 minutes
Cooking time: 50 minutes
Difficulty: ★★

Serves 4

12 large sardines
salt
pepper
1 pinch nutmeg
1 tsp paprika
1 pinch dried thyme
2 bay leaves
olive oil

2 red bell peppers
2 green bell peppers
8 onions
1 sprig thyme
500 ml/2 cups red wine

For the tomato compote:
5 large tomatoes
1 onion
4 cloves garlic
olive oil
several basil leaves, chopped
1 tsp sugar
salt
pepper

Spanish cuisine has a masterful way of making succulent dishes out of simple ingredients. The proof is seen in recipes such as these Valero-Style Sardines. The success of this dish lies in the choice of fish. Small, grilling sardines that harden quickly are not the best for this recipe; here, large sardines are king. They have the most desirable qualities: fatty flesh that does not dry out quickly and remains soft in the pan, and they can also be filleted without much trouble.

In northeast Spain, people like to eat sardines baked in the oven with breadcrumbs, herbs and spices. The small, silver fish are held in high esteem among the Spanish. When cooked as fillets, they are perfect for tapas. When grilled or braised, they make a wonderful, light summer meal.

To fillet the sardines, our chef suggests making an incision near the head and detaching the fillets from there all the way down to the tail.

Tomatoes and peppers from Mexico arrived in Spain in the sixteenth century via the conquistadors. The best variety of pepper comes from Navarre and Rioja. Long and pointed, it is known as *pimiento piquillo* and is outstanding when stuffed with fish or vegetables. The large green or red pepper is known as *morron*. As for the paprika, it is made of a mixture of many varieties of dried and ground chili peppers.

1. Scale and fillet the sardines.

2. Place the fillets, skin-side down, on parchment paper on a baking tray. Season them with salt, pepper, nutmeg, paprika, dried thyme and 1 bay leaf. Moisten with a little olive oil. Set aside.

3. Finely dice the peppers and onions into a mirepoix. Sweat them with the fresh thyme and the other bay leaf, crumbled, over low heat in 2 tbsp oil for 10 minutes. Add the wine, salt and pepper. Cook over low heat until soft, then set aside.

Sardines

4. To prepare the tomato compote, peel the tomatoes, cut them into quarters, de-seed and dice them. Peel and chop the onion and garlic. Brown them in oil with the tomatoes. Add the basil, sugar, salt and pepper. Let the liquid evaporate.

5. Heat the oven to 200°C/390°F. Strain the onions and peppers, then the tomato compote. Pour the juice into a pan and reduce until a syrupy sauce is obtained. Shape the tomato compote into small quenelles.

6. Spread some of the onion and pepper mix on half of the fillets, and top with a second fish fillet. Heat in the oven for about 5 minutes. Arrange the stuffed sardines on plates with quenelles of the tomato compote and decorate with the sauce.

Lebanese

Preparation time: 20 minutes
Difficulty: ★

Serves 4

4 bunches flat-leaf parsley
2 to 3 sprigs fresh mint
1 medium onion
1 kg/2¹/₄ lb tomatoes
60 g/7 tbsp bulghur wheat

1 tsp salt
1 tsp pepper
3 lemons
150 ml/²/₃ cup olive oil

For the garnish:
lemon slices
quartered tomatoes

In the 1920s, the Lebanese often served an assortment of twenty different *mezze* as appetizers, each served in its own little dish. Today, the number of hot and cold appetizers can reach fifty. An authentic *mezze* table will always include a tabbouleh dish.

In the West, tabbouleh has been transformed into a cold appetizer made from couscous, to which each cook adds whatever is at hand. Tired of such confusion, Hussein Fakih returns the dish to its original four ingredients: parsley, bulghur wheat, tomatoes and onion.

Perfected over the course of 6,000 years, the technique used for cracking wheat is a precise act: softened in water, the grains then slowly dry in the Lebanese sun before being cracked and transformed into cracked wheat and bulghur (they are similar, but not identical). Bulghur can be prepared in several ways: raw in tabbouleh or in ground meat stuffing, or cooked in a number of stews and fish dishes. Only a small quantity of it is added to tabbouleh. Without being cooked, it brings a little crunch to the tomatoes and the parsley.

Flat-leaf parsley and fresh mint are abundant in Lebanon. With a subtler flavor than its curly cousin, flat-leaf parsley gives fragrance to many Lebanese dishes. The chef chops it, a whole bunch at a time, with a precise and efficient gesture. The tomatoes are chosen for their round firmness, so as to make chopping them easy work. The onion, tomatoes and parsley are all tossed into a deep salad bowl. The grains of bulghur are then scattered on top of the green mixture. Then, at this final moment, the oil and lemon are called upon to season the dish.

1. Cut the stalks from the parsley and then chop the leaves finely with a knife, along with the mint leaves.

2. Peel the onion and chop in half. Cut into slices and then chop.

3. Cut the tomato into slices, then into strips and finally small dice.

Tabbouleh

4. Tip the tomatoes, onion and the chopped mint and parsley into a large salad bowl. Sprinkle with the bulghur, salt and pepper.

5. Squeeze the lemons and pour the juice into a small bowl. Pour it over the tabbouleh mixture along with the olive oil.

6. Mix all the ingredients together and adjust the seasonings. Pour into a pretty, deep serving dish. Garnish with tomatoes and slices of lemon. Enjoy immediately.

Malsouka

Preparation time: 30 minutes
Cooking time: 1 hour
Difficulty: ★

Serves 4 to 6

450 g/1 lb lamb
salt
pepper
1 pinch saffron
8 eggs
2 onions

100 ml/7 tbsp olive oil
400 ml/1²/₃ cups water
3 bunches parsley
100 g/1 cup grated Gruyère cheese
50 g/3¹/₂ tbsp butter
8 sheets malsouka (phyllo dough
or spring roll wrappers can substitute)
1 lemon (optional)

The Malsouka Tajine is the most refined of the Tunisian tajines. Moroccan tajines are stew-like in nature, whereas the Tunisian tajine is a gratinéed dish. They are prepared with lamb or chicken and peas, ricotta, spinach, with a salad of potato with tomatoes and grilled peppers, or even various cheeses. A tajine may be served as a warm appetizer, as an alternative to vegetable salad. Tunisian mothers prepare this dish for family celebrations, or to honor a guest.

The leaves of *malsouka*, the dough used to wrap *brik*, have given the dish its name. Expert cooks gently touch a ball of dough to a white-hot baking griddle, leaving just enough on the griddle to make unimaginably thin sheets. These sheets of dough are so delicate and difficult to prepare that often one prefers to buy ready-made ones. They are hard to find outside Tunisia, but phyllo or spring roll wrappers will do the job. These sheets of *malsouka* can be used in savory or sweet dishes. Dough with eggs, thin, cigarette-shaped *zriga*, *hourta*

stuffed with hazelnuts, *samsa* with vegetables or meat, stuffed fingers with hazelnut cream…

Our chef has stuffed her tajine with a mixture of lamb shoulder, eggs and onions with saffron. Beldi Tunisian lamb has the advantage of being very lean, and most of its fat is concentrated near the tail of the animal. The lamb shoulder is used in the preparation of couscous, and roasted lamb with potatoes, saffron and *smen* (a type of fermented butter with a characteristic aroma.)

So that your tajine does not burn in the oven, Manoubia Hassairi suggests that you cover it with an extra sheet of dough that will protect the rest of the dish. You can easily peel this layer off if it is really too burnt.

Our chef is in the habit of finishing the recipe by piercing a small hole in the crust of the tajine, through which she dribbles lemon juice. She decorates the dish with slices of lemon sprinkled with herbs and serves it on a bed of lettuce.

1. Cut the piece of lamb into thick slices and then into cubes. Tip the meat into a large saucepan. Salt and pepper and add a generous pinch of saffron. Boil 5 of the eggs for 10 minutes, then peel.

2. Peel and chop the onions. Heat the oil in a pan and sauté the onions for 10 minutes without letting them brown. Add the onions to the pan with the meat.

3. Pour 400 ml/1²/₃ cups water into the mixture. Cook for 25 minutes on high heat until the meat is tender and the sauce is reduced. Strain the meat to separate it from its juices and then add it to the chopped hard-boiled eggs, 3 raw eggs, chopped parsley, and the grated cheese.

Tajine

4. Melt butter in a small saucepan. Brush the pastry sheets with the melted butter. Place 4 sheets on the bottom of a deep pie pan.

5. Pour the meat stuffing onto the sheets. Spread it out with the back of a spoon. Fold the sheets over the stuffing and brush them with melted butter.

6. Cover the tajine with 4 new sheets coated in butter. Lift the tajine on each side and fold the sheets under the edge. Bake for 15 minutes at 140°C/285°F. Remove from the pan and serve in wedges drizzled with lemon juice.

Mussels Tart

Preparation time: 30 minutes
Cooking time: 1 hour 10 minutes
Difficulty: ★

Serves 4

1.5 liters/1½ quarts mussels
2 shallots
½ carrot
½ stalk celery
2 tbsp butter
½ tsp corn oil

250 ml/1 cup dry white wine
2 or 3 sprigs parsley
fresh pepper
1 ready-made pie crust, not baked

For the white sauce:
1 onion
2 tbsp butter
2 tbsp flour
salt
pepper
50 g/scant ½ cup grated Swiss cheese

The Mussels Tart recipe provided by Richard Bizier comes from the French territory of Saint-Pierre and Miquelon, which is geographically and culturally close to the Canadian island of Newfoundland. Beginning in the sixteenth century, Saint-Pierre and Miquelon was populated by fishermen from Basque country, Brittany, Normandy, Acadia and Newfoundland, who had come to fish cod on the banks. They developed a rich but little-known culinary repertoire that includes such varied foods as seafood and sea urchin, stuffed squid, Basque sausage, stuffed pumpkin…

In former years in the region, the fishermen were only interested in catching cod, which was all the rage, and would simply throw the mussels back into the ocean. Mussels have become quite a fad in the last twenty years. They are enjoyed prepared in various ways, *marinière*, in *poulette* sauce or green pepper sauce, stuffed and tied with string, or as a savory cream with fennel.

To prepare the tart, our chef generally uses blue mussels from Prince Edward Island or Madeleine Islands. Their abundant, plump flesh has an excellent salty flavor. Using rather small mussels with bright orange and very flavorful flesh will make a delicious tart.

According to taste, you may replace the mussels with shrimp, small shellfish or lobster, because the basic recipe is simple and adaptable.

Thin the roux that forms the base of the sauce with the cooking juices from the mussels, adding a little milk or bouillon as necessary. Cook the white sauce, stirring constantly over low heat until it thickens. Cooked and drained mussels should not add too much liquid to the sauce, but it is best to be careful.

The filling is poured onto the pie crust in the traditional way. However, you are welcome to try preparing this Mussels Tart from Miquelon in a puff pastry shell.

1. Pull the beards off and rinse the mussels. Brown the mirepoix of shallots, carrot and celery in a mixture of butter and oil in a large pot. When they begin to soften, pour in the white wine. Add the chopped parsley and pepper. Let simmer briefly.

2. Pour the mussels into the pot with the vegetables. Cover and let cook until they are well open.

3. Let the mussels cool to lukewarm temperature. Shell them carefully and put aside in a small bowl. Filter the cooking juices. Keep the juice separately from the vegetable, herbs and spice mixture.

from Miquelon

4. Brown the chopped onion in butter and sprinkle in the flour to make a roux. Thin with 250 ml/1 cup of cooking juices from the mussels. Whisk over low heat until the sauce whitens. Add salt, pepper and the grated cheese.

5. Tip the mussels into the sauce and then add the vegetable mixture. Mix well.

6. Line the bottom of a buttered pie pan with a prepared crust. Gently pour the mussels in sauce into the crust. Bake the mussels tart at 180°C/350°F for 45 minutes.

Tempura

Preparation time:	40 minutes
Cooking time:	30 minutes
Rehydration time:	10 minutes
Difficulty:	★★

Serves 4

18 large tiger shrimp
several drops mirin (sweet sake)
6 sheets yuba
12 green asparagus stalks
6 shiso leaves
frying oil

For the tempura batter:
2 egg yolks
200 ml/generous ³/₄ cup water
120 g/³/₄ cup + 2 tbsp flour

For the sauce:
1 or 2 laces of konbu seaweed
30 g/1 oz dried bonito flakes
200 ml/generous ³/₄ cup mirin
2 tbsp soy sauce
3 cm/1 in piece fresh ginger
3 cm/1 in piece daikon

Tempura, very popular in Japan, came from recipes brought by Portuguese missionaries in the sixteenth century. The cook dips pieces of various types of food—eggplant, carrots, shiitake mushrooms, shrimp, white fish, cuttlefish, beef or pork—in a dough made from equal parts of water and flour and with egg yolks, then puts them in a deep fryer.

The Japanese serve tempura on a board, accompanied with a bit of fresh ginger and grated daikon radish to cleanse the palate. They accompany the tempura with rice and a sauce made from seaweed, dried bonito and soy sauce.

Our chef has enveloped shrimp paste in yuba leaves. These large, very thin leaves that resemble a pasta dough are derived from a soy paste. The soy beans are soaked, ground, steamed, then mashed and mixed with rice water. The skin that forms on the surface when they cool is peeled off and dried so as to form

yuba. The yuba leaves must always be rehydrated for ten to fifteen minutes before use.

The Japanese consider shiso to be indispensable to the tempura dish. These are the jagged edged, soft green leaves of a black variety of nettle. Its fresh taste reminds one of mint and lemon balm, a plant which could be used to replace the shiso. Shiso is as common in Japanese gardens as parsley is in European ones. It is used as a spice, but also for medicinal, coloring and decorative purposes. In order to preserve its form and color, only coat one side of the leaves with tempura batter.

The paper the tempura is presented on is indispensable to soak up the last traces of oil. Also present a small dice of grated daikon radish, topped with a bit of ginger. Daikon aids in the digestion of fats and the ginger brings a spicy accent. Add more or less to the sauce according to taste.

---

1. Peel the shrimp; set 8 aside. Slit the backs of 12 shrimp. Turn them onto their backs and make several cuts at an angle on the sides. Turn them back over onto their bellies. Crush the shrimp on a cutting board with the tips of your fingers while stretching them out.

2. Toss 6 more shrimp with several drops of mirin and set aside. Transfer the crushed shrimp into a mortar. Crush energetically with a pestle until you obtain a gray, somewhat sticky paste.

3. Rehydrate the yuba for 10 minutes in hot water. Use a sponge to remove excess water, then cut into even rectangles. Peel the asparagus. Spread the shrimp paste at the bottom of the yuba rectangles, top with an asparagus spear and then roll up together. Close the ends with tooth picks.

4. Whisk the egg yolks with the water. Add 100 g/7 tbsp of the flour and whisk again to obtain a tempura batter. Add the konbu seaweed to 800 ml/3⅓ cups cold water and warm it for 15 minutes. Discard the konbu, bring the bouillon to the boil and add the bonito.

5. Return the bouillon to the boil, then remove from the heat and strain. Pour 4 ladles of bouillon into a small saucepan. Bring to the boil. Add the mirin and soy sauce and simmer for 10 minutes on low heat.

6. Dip the whole shrimp, the remaining asparagus and the floured shiso into the tempura batter. Immerse them in a deep-fat fryer, along with the shrimp and yuba rolls. Let cook until all pieces rise to the surface. Serve the rolls in small sections with the sauce, grated daikon and fresh ginger.

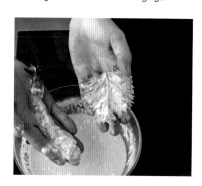

Cod and

Preparation time: 30 minutes
Cooking time: 45 minutes
Soaking time, salt cod: 12 hours
Chilling time: 6 hours
Difficulty: ★★★

Serves 4

For the terrine:
1 kg/2¹/₄ lb salt cod
400 g/14 oz potatoes
salt

For the jelled cream:
2 sheets gelatin
or ¹/₂ of a ¹/₄-oz packet granulated gelatin
100 ml/7 tbsp heavy cream
100 g/7 tbsp butter
2 egg yolks
3 tbsp walnut oil
3 tbsp sherry vinegar
5 sprigs parsley
5 stalks chives

For the sauce:
2 tsp yellow mustard
2 tsp sherry vinegar
1 tbsp walnut oil
200 ml/generous ³/₄ cup heavy cream

Here is a nice terrine recipe, simple and easy to prepare. The only difficulty, which cannot be avoided, is the soaking of the cod. It is preferable to let the fish soak overnight under a thin stream of water. However, you can also soak the fish in a bath of cold water that you change often. Fresh cod may also be used, but the terrine will lose its salty flavor.

The quality of potatoes is important, and Charlotte or Ratte potatoes are well-suited to this terrine. They should be cooked no longer than 30 minutes so as to keep them tender yet firm. They should then be cooled, drained, peeled, cut into thick slices and then placed carefully into the bottom of a loaf pan. The careful arrangement of the potatoes has its importance for it prevents the cream from seeping into the terrine.

The gelatin should be softened in cold water, dissolved on low heat, then mixed with the melted butter. This mixture makes the terrine hold its shape while the beaten egg yolks bind it together. The vinegar gives the dish acidity, while the walnut oil brings an autumn flavor. Finally, chopped parsley and cut chives add a bit of green to the very white cod.

Although removing the terrine from the mold can cause anxiety to some, it becomes child's play when the terrine has been refrigerated for six hours beforehand. Nicole Fagegaltier places the pan in a bath of hot water for about ten minutes and then empties it onto a serving dish without any trouble.

To add a fresh touch to this appetizer, the slices of cod and potatoes can be accompanied by a small bouquet of tender young lettuce leaves. The capucine flower provides a beautiful touch and can be eaten.

1. Let the cod soak overnight in a bath of cold water. The next day, place the fish in a large pot, cover with water and let cook for 10 minutes.

2. Wash the potatoes. Cook them, in their skins, in 2 liters/2 quarts salted water for 30 minutes. Drain and then peel. Cut into rounds 2 cm/³/₄ in thick. Set aside.

3. For the jelled cream, dissolve the gelatin in a little water over low heat. Add it to the cream. Stir in the melted butter, whisk, then let cool. Mix everything together in a blender or food processor, adding the egg yolks, vinegar and walnut oil.

Potato Terrine

4. Flake the cooked and drained cod, making sure to eliminate all the bones. Place in a large bowl. Season with the mixture from the blender. Sprinkle in chopped parsley and chives.

5. Prepare the sauce by whisking together the mustard, vinegar and walnut oil. Pour in the cream and blend to obtain a homogenous consistency. Incorporate this sauce into the cod mixture.

6. Cover the bottom of a loaf pan with plastic wrap. Arrange a layer of potatoes, then the cod cream. Layer again with potatoes and cod cream. Press down, refrigerate 6 hours, remove from pan and cut into slices.

Danish

Preparation time: 50 minutes
Cooking time: 35 minutes
Difficulty: ★★

Serves 8

1 kg/2¼ lb fresh salmon
1 kg/2¼ lb smoked salmon
12 eggs
150 ml/⅔ cup heavy cream (18% fat)
5 young leeks
1 smoked eel
2 smoked herrings
½ red onion

4 sprigs dill
1 cucumber
10 radishes
salt
pepper
1 small glass salmon roe
Tabasco sauce (optional)
lemon (optional)

For the sauce:
200 ml/generous ¾ cup plain yogurt
without gelatin
3 saffron threads
1 cm/½ in piece horseradish
300 ml/1¼ cups heavy cream

When dining in a restaurant, the Danish often enjoy a plate which combines herring, eel, salmon, mackerel and smoked fish roe. Charles-René Madsen has brought together all of these products to make a savory and very colorful terrine and to show the glory of Danish fishing. A triangle of browned salmon skin as decoration is the chef's touch.

Danish fishermen have developed a veritable industry of salting and drying fish. Today the island of Bornholm, situated between the south of Sweden and Poland, is a true paradise of smoked herring. From May to October, hundreds of thousands of fish are cleaned and then marinated overnight in brine. Slipped one by one onto a rod, they are then smoked over an alder wood fire.

According to our chef, Danish salmon has lost much of its aura since it is now farm-raised. In his restaurant, Charles-René

Madsen uses salmon from the Arctic Ocean, which has gray, firm flesh. A fish whose flesh is too bright orange has been fed with food that is artificially colored.

The preparation of the eel demands a few precautions. Slit the fish along the belly and the back. Pass your knife along the skin to melt the fat a bit. Then delicately lift the skin, holding it as you go with the handle of a spoon so that it does not come off all at once.

Decorate your serving dish in a unique way by drying the salmon skin. Remove it gently and then cut it into triangles. Spread it out on parchment paper placed on a baking sheet. Cover with another sheet of paper and another baking sheet to hold it in place. Bake for 30 minutes at 160°C/320°F. You may add the fresh radish leaves to the salad.

1. With a sharp knife, remove the skin from the salmon and smoked salmon. Set aside the smoked salmon. Using tweezers, remove the bones from the fresh salmon and cut it into large cubes. Mix the fish with some salt in a food processor.

2. When the mixture reaches a fine consistency, add the eggs and 50 ml/3½ tbsp of cream. Mix again until blended. Rinse the leeks, cut the green part into strips, and blanch for 5 minutes in salted water.

3. Slide your knife along the skin of the eel to warm the fat. Lift off the skin and then cut the flesh. In a terrine lined with leek strips, layer the fish cream and pieces of smoked salmon and eel. Cook for 30 minutes in a water bath. Cool in the refrigerator.

Smoked Fish Terrine

4. Scrape the skin and top layer of fat from the herrings. Take a herring fillet in your hand. Gently pull up the spine, taking care not to leave small bones on the fish. Prepare the other herring in the same way.

5. Peel the red onion and chop it along with the dill. Cut the cucumber in two, scoop out the seeds, and cut into small dices. Wash and cut the radishes lengthwise. Mix everything together with the herring and 100 ml/7 tbsp cream. Salt and pepper.

6. Mix the yogurt, saffron, grated horse-radish and cream. Remove the terrine from the mold and slice. On each plate, arrange a slice of terrine, a spoonful of vegetables in cream, small mounds of salmon roe and the horseradish sauce. Decorate with a slice of salmon skin dried in the oven.

Ricotta and

Preparation time: 30 minutes
Cooking time: 20 minutes
Chilling time: 4 hours or more
Difficulty: ★★

Serves 6 to 8

2 green peppers
2 zucchini
6 tomatoes
5 sheets gelatin
or 1¼ ¼-oz packages granulated gelatin

600 g/2½ cups ricotta
3 or 4 cloves garlic
1 bunch basil
1 drizzle olive oil
salt
pepper
1 yellow bell pepper

For the decoration (optional):
mixed salad
cherry tomatoes
fresh basil

Our chef was inspired by products from his region in Italy, Basilicata, to put together this recipe. In this mountainous region of southern Italy, goat raising is very common and goat milk is made into pecorino or ricotta cheese. Vegetables are also abundant in this area.

The making of ricotta ensues from that of pecorino. When the goats have finished raising their kids around Easter time, they are milked for the production of pecorino. The curds that will form the cheese are pressed and the whey is collected. This whey is cooked along with milk until ricotta rises to the surface. Ricotta is produced fresh, plain or lightly salted. It can be eaten in its natural form as a cheese, or it can be used as a stuffing for pasta, in spinach or vegetable pies, in roulades, or in cakes or pies. Sometimes it is even dried for two or three days, then breaded and pan fried, or further refined in the same way as goat cheese. Industrial ricotta made from cow's milk is

gradually replacing the traditional preparation of sheep's milk ricotta. It no longer has the same taste or texture but it does stay fresh longer. One must take the precaution of mixing it in the blender or passing it through a sieve, because it often has a granular texture.

This terrine could not exist without the extraordinary presence of basil. The word basil comes from the Greek *basileus*, signifying "king". Basil meets all the challenges of multiple preparations: tomatoes, spaghetti, soup, fish, salad, sauces and oils. We recommend buying it fresh and carefully examining its quality. The leaves should be bright green and should fairly burst with health.

You will also make a delicious terrine by substituting eggplant slices for the zucchini. The eggplant will go well with the basil and the peppers.

1. Preheat the oven broiler. Arrange the green peppers on the grill and broil for 10 minutes until their skin blisters. Wash the zucchini, remove the ends, and cut lengthwise in slices 3–4 mm/⅛ in thick.

2. Put water on to boil in a steamer. Steam the zucchini slices for 8 minutes, then dry them on paper towels. Place the tomatoes in the steamer and cook for 2 minutes.

3. Soak the gelatin in a little water. In a blender or food processor, blend the ricotta, peeled garlic cloves, basil (reserve several leaves for the tomato sauce), a trickle of olive oil and the gelatin. Salt and pepper.

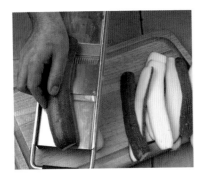

Vegetable Terrine

4. Peel and seed peppers and tomatoes. Cut 2 tomatoes in half and split each piece gently by flattening with your hand. Arrange the zucchini slices so as to line a terrine dish. Spread the basil cream along the bottom, then top with tomato pieces.

5. Next, alternate green peppers and basil cream. Finish with slices of zucchini and then refrigerate the terrine for 4 hours or more. Then remove the terrine from the mold and cut into slices.

6. Cut the yellow pepper and blend with olive oil, salt and pepper, and set aside. Then blend the remaining 4 tomatoes with basil, salt and pepper. Serve the terrine accompanied by the purée of yellow pepper and tomatoes.

Vaud Tomme

Preparation time: 25 minutes
Cooking time: 20 minutes
Difficulty: ★

Serves 4

180 ml/³/₄ cup walnut oil
6 slices bread
1 clove garlic
2 egg yolks
4 Vaud Tomme cheeses
50 g/3¹/₂ tbsp butter

500 g/generous 1 lb dandelion stems
150 g/5–6 oz smoked bacon
100 g/generous ³/₄ cup walnut halves
320 ml/1¹/₃ cups wine vinegar

Our chef offers this recipe, prepared in the Lausanne and Montreux areas of Switzerland, as a delicious warm appetizer, served on a bed of salad. Tomme cheese is served whole or cut, and the center is soft or runny when pierced with the point of a knife.

The Vaud tomme used by our chef is a kind of small, round, flat Camembert-style cheese, made from cow's milk in the canton of Vaud. Its maturation lasts seven to nine days. Among the different varieties, the milk used to make the Fribourg tomme benefits from the highest altitude and the best pastures. The Payerne tomme is seasoned with cumin and molded into rectangular loaves. Of course, an industrially produced tomme differs from its country cousin, which is made from raw milk and cream. Cooks also have the choice between full fat, three quarters fat, and half fat cheeses.

The high season for dandelion is in April and May. This bright yellow flower is considered a weed by many a home owner, yet the Swiss appreciate the pale yellow, buried stems that are cut 10 cm (4 inches) from the roots. The dark green leaves are edible, but according to our chef, they can be thick and rather bitter. His compatriots also eat the *rampon*, a type of lamb's lettuce that grows in vineyards.

The Vaud tomme has a rather thick crust and does not get runny even when it is baked. You could replace it with a not-too-ripe Saint-Marcellin, or any other small, soft cheese. As it is sometimes difficult to overcome certain people's reticence to try the dandelion stem salad, our chef suggests placing the breaded tommes on a bed of lamb's lettuce or arugula as alternatives. In the Vaud canton, some like to splurge by cooking potatoes and bacon that they add to the salad. Garnish it with parsley and halved cherry tomatoes.

1. Pour about 100 ml/7 tbsp walnut oil on the slices of bread. Rub with a peeled garlic clove, then toast for 10 minutes under a broiler or grill. Crush the bread crumbs to obtain a breading.

2. Beat the egg yolks well with a fork. Brush the egg yolk on the tomme cheeses.

3. Pour the bread mixture in a small shallow dish. Place the tommes in the dish and turn them several times until they are well coated.

with Dandelion Stems

4. Heat some butter in a pan. When it sizzles, brown the tommes on both sides, for 5 minutes. Cut the dandelions 10 cm/ 4 in from the roots; keep the leaves and rinse them in a salad spinner. Discard the bitter roots.

5. In another pan, brown the bacon with the walnut halves for about 5 minutes, until everything is nicely golden. Deglaze the pan with 100 ml/7 tbsp vinegar, scraping the bottom of the pan with a spatula.

6. Prepare a vinaigrette with 220 ml/scant 1 cup vinegar and 80 ml/¹/₃ cup walnut oil. On small plates, arrange the salad, the bacon and walnuts. Pour on some of the deglazing liquid and some of the vinaigrette. Place the tommes on top and enjoy warm.

Fernández Family

Preparation time: *30 minutes*
Cooking time: *40 minutes*
Difficulty: ★

Serves 6

1 kg/2¼ lb potatoes
2 onions
2 small zucchini
4 tbsp olive oil
10 eggs

200 g/7 oz pink shrimp, cooked
1 tsp salt
¹/₂ tbsp pepper

For those who understand the word "picnic" as a synonym for "rejoice," for those who are tired of chips and sandwiches eaten on the beach, here is the warm and appetizing tortilla of a family from Seville. More than a simple omelette, this tortilla blends eggs, potatoes and onions as its main ingredients. The rest is left up to the imagination of each family.

It is on Saturday night that Spanish mothers beat eggs at length to prepare Sunday's tortilla. It will be cooked at the last minute before the family's departure for the beach. Apparently easy and quick to prepare, the tortilla needs several simple but necessary steps: the potatoes are peeled and cut, wiped without being washed. For a Spanish look, choose large potatoes. Then, onions and potatoes are cooked together in a covered pan, without browning. Small zucchinis should be cooked quickly so as to preserve their fragile skins. Small or large, zucchinis

contain a lot of water: let them cook uncovered for total evaporation. Eggplant, mushrooms or tomatoes can be substituted for the zucchini and cooked in the same way for an equally delicious result. Aficionados of the most purely flavorful tortilla can keep the oil left from sautéeing the vegetables and pour it onto the cooked and turned tortilla before serving. Others should follow the taste of the chef, and all should use a fork or whisk to beat the eggs at length.

The olive oil should be very hot but not boiling, and in sufficient quantity to prevent it from burning. Shake the pan gently so as to mix all the ingredients well. Carefully flip the cooked tortilla in a final gesture: choose a flat plate larger than the diameter of the pan. This helpful hint can be used for any omelette: when cooked on both sides, the tortilla should double in volume.

1. Peel the potatoes and onions. Cut the potatoes in three parts lengthwise. Keeping the three pieces together, cut along the width to dice. Do the same with the onions and the unpeeled zucchini.

2. Fry the potatoes in 1 tbsp hot oil. Add the onions, stir well, cover and let cook for 15 minutes on low heat. Add the zucchini. Continue cooking for 5 minutes, uncovered. Strain the mixture in a sieve.

3. Tip the cooked vegetables into a dish and set aside. Break the eggs into a large mixing bowl. Beat them with a fork, gently at first, then energetically for 10 minutes.

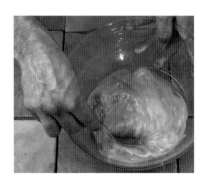

Tortilla

4. Peel the shrimp and cut them in half. Mix them in with the vegetables. Pour onto the beaten eggs. Add salt and pepper and mix.

5. In a large frying pan with high sides, heat 3 tbsp olive oil. When it is very hot, pour the egg mixture in all at once. Spread it out on the bottom of the pan and cook for 5 minutes on high heat, uncovered.

6. When the tortilla starts to puff up, place a large plate on top of the pan. Take off the heat and flip the pan and the plate so that the tortilla is resting on the plate. Slide the tortilla from the plate back into the pan. Continue cooking for 5 minutes on low heat. Serve lukewarm.

Anchovy, Porcini

Preparation time: 30 minutes
Cooking time: 25 minutes
Difficulty: ★★

Serves 4

30 to 40 fresh anchovies
350 g/³/₄ lb potatoes
250 g/9 oz fresh porcini mushrooms
4 slices crusty bread
3 cloves garlic
1 small bunch flat-leaf parsley
1 small sprig thyme
1 pinch oregano

¹/₂ lemon
1 pinch pecorino cheese
salt
pepper
extra virgin olive oil

For the tomato sauce:
500 g/generous 1 lb cherry tomatoes
2 cloves garlic
1 basil leaf
1 pinch oregano
salt
pepper

In the Basilicata region of Italy, mamas prepare many *tortinos* at a time on a large baking sheet. We have baked them in circular forms to give them a more contemporary presentation.

Basilicata is a region in which pecorino is produced. This hard cheese is made from sheep's milk and has a pronounced and somewhat spicy aroma. In Italy, all the mountainous areas have their own type of pecorino. The most well known are the Roman and the Sardinian pecorinos. This cheese is made from Easter through the summer. Lamb's rennet is added to sheep's milk and warmed, then allowed to curdle. The curds are then divided, put into molds, pressed, drained and finally salted. After five days of salting, the cheeses are rinsed and put to dry in a cellar for five to eight months. Before being sold, the crust of the cheeses are coated in oil for the final presentation.

Porcini mushrooms are also a favorite element of many foods, valued throughout Italy. Dried or packed in oil, they make an excellent sauce for pasta. Anchovies are more of a regional specialty of the coasts, because in times past, the difficulty of transporting fish from the coast to inland towns prevented people in the Basilicata mountains from eating much fish apart from dried eel.

For a fully successful preparation of this recipe, you must use an excellent, crusty loaf of savory country bread. Our chef's mother makes her own bread: each loaf weighs between 2 and 3 kg (4½–6½ lb) and it keeps for a week. If no such bread is available, replace it with breadcrumbs.

If you would like to prepare the *tortino* in larger quantities by using a baking sheet, allow about ten minutes additional baking time. You should also feel free to use your imagination and vary the layered ingredients, for example using tomatoes in place of the porcini.

1. Rinse the anchovies. Detach the head and insert a finger in the body to open and remove the backbone. Peel the potatoes and cut them into very fine slices along with the porcini.

2. Remove the bread crusts and crush the remaining bread with a sieve. Pour the crumbs into a dish with the chopped garlic and parsley. Add thyme, oregano, pecorino, lemon juice, salt and pepper. Pour a thin stream of olive oil until the mixture is combined.

3. Fry the potatoes in a pan with olive oil for 5 to 7 minutes. Place the cooked slices on paper towels to remove the excess oil.

and Potato Tortino

4. Oil a baking dish, then place circular forms in it. Put a layer of potatoes at the bottom of each form. Sprinkle with the herbed breading. Top with some of the sliced porcinis.

5. Cover again with herbed breading. Arrange several rounds of potatoes on top. Sauté the peeled, diced tomatoes, the chopped garlic and basil, the oregano, salt and pepper.

6. Place the anchovies on the top of the tortino. Sprinkle with breading. Bake in the oven at 200°C/390°F for 15 minutes. Remove the tortino from the mold, place on individual plates, and present with tomato sauce.

Tyropita

Preparation time: 30 minutes
Cooking time: 10 minutes
Difficulty: ★

Serves 6

350 g/³/₄ lb feta
20 mint leaves
2 sprigs basil
150 g/5¹/₂ oz kasseri cheese

pepper
3 eggs and 1 egg yolk
12 sheets phyllo dough
150 g/²/₃ cup butter
sesame seeds

From appetizers to main courses to desserts, phyllo dough is integral to many Greek dishes. These very thin sheets of pastry are made simply from wheat flour and water. Our chef's mother still prepares them in her village, but most Greeks buy them ready-made. Phyllo means "leaf" in Greek. These sheets of dough beautifully wrap a wide variety of fillings and are used in the making of baklava, small cakes dripping with honey syrup. If fresh, phyllo dough should be wrapped in a moist towel because it dries out very quickly. It keeps for two months in the freezer.

The feta and Kasseri cheeses melt deliciously in these savory pastries. Along with *kefalotyri*, they are the three most popular cheeses in Greece. Made from sheep's milk, never cow's milk, Kasseri resembles a pale yellow Gruyère, very compact but creamy, without holes or crust. It is most often eaten grated

over pasta. It can also be sliced, breaded and fried in olive oil, and it is used in the stuffing of small peppers and pies.

The inhabitants of ancient Greece associated basil with rites of love and death. This royal plant called *vasilikos* was considered sacred and women were not allowed to pick it. It is used infrequently in Greek cuisine today. However, many Greeks decorate their window with a little potted basil plant to chase away snakes and mosquitoes. They also like to run their hand over the plant to bring out the fresh aroma.

Before making these delicate flaky pastries, our chef advises that you rinse the feta under running water to soften its salty taste. Do not add any salt to the stuffing. It is up to your imagination to vary the stuffing by trying different combinations of feta, Kasseri and *kefalotyri*; or alternately making a white sauce with feta and dill.

1. Cut the feta into little cubes. Finely chop the mint and basil. Combine them all in a dish. Grate the kasseri on top. Add pepper and 3 eggs and mix well with your hands until thoroughly combined.

2. Spread a sheet of phyllo dough on your work surface. Brush the dough with melted butter. Cover with a second sheet, aligned exactly on top of the first.

3. Cut the dough into 4 equal rectangles. Place 1 tbsp of the cheese filling at the bottom of each rectangle.

4. Fold over the bottom of the rectangle. Fold in the left and right sides slightly. Brush with melted butter, then roll up, beginning with the side nearest you. Complete the others in the same fashion.

5. Beat the egg yolk with a fork. Brush the tops of the rolls with egg yolk. Butter a baking tray.

6. Arrange the rolls on the buttered tray. Sprinkle with sesame seeds. Bake at 180°C/355°F until golden. Eat while hot.

Soups

Creole-Style

Preparation time: 1 hour
Cooking time: 1 hour 50 minutes
Difficulty: ★★

Serves 4

1 kg/2¹/₄ lb spare ribs
100 g/3–4 oz cassava
100 g/3–4 oz yams
100 g/3–4 oz sweet potatoes
100 g/3–4 oz pumpkin

2 cobs of fresh corn
1 plantain
30 g/1 tbsp chopped garlic
30 g/3 tbsp chopped onions
30 g/2 tbsp tomato paste
30 g/1¹/₂ tbsp salt
50 ml/3¹/₂ tbsp oil

Taino Indians already enjoyed the *ajiaco* when Christopher Columbus disembarked in Cuba on October 12, 1492. They would take advantage of the hunting seasons and periods of abundance to organize celebrations when they would regale themselves with *ajiaco*. This is still a very popular dish that lends itself wonderfully well to social gatherings.

People in Cuba organize great neighborhood meals where everyone brings a dish to complement a giant *ajiaco*. Indeed, the term *ajiaco* is also used in Cuba to designate all kinds of cultural mix, such as combinations of music and literature.

The *ajiaco* prepared by our chef is enriched with spare rib off-cuts. These are rib pieces surrounded by meat and fat that have been cut in long strips from the upper side of the pork.

With its rich garnish, this dish is a veritable anthology of Caribbean vegetables. The yam is a tuber very similar to the potato, with dark brown skin and white flesh, which constitutes the base of a climbing plant.

Yams, cooked like potatoes, taste markedly different depending on the variety. The sweet potato is another tuber, with a pinkish brown color, that yields a vigorous herbaceous plant. Its subtly sweet taste recalls chestnuts. It is eaten with salt when boiled, mashed or fried but it is sweetened for cakes and jam.

The third tuber in this dish is the cassava, also called manioc, which comes from a tropical shrub. Its flesh is white, yellow or reddish and its thick peel is brown. Here, our chef has used sweet cassava which has a thick brown skin that peels off easily from the white flesh. The bitter kind of cassava is used to prepare cassava flour and tapioca.

Last of all is the plantain, which is longer than the common dessert banana, with thicker skin and firmer flesh. It is eaten green or yellow, fried, grilled, boiled or steamed, and often accompanies meat and fish. It is a staple food of the West Indies and Africa: 30 million tons of plantain are consumed every year worldwide.

1. Set a large pot of water to boil. Separate the spare ribs and then tip them into the boiling water. Allow to cook for 1 hour on low heat.

2. Peel the cassava, yams, sweet potatoes and pumpkin. Dice the tubers and pumpkin coarsely. Shuck the corn cobs, rinse and cut into disks. Keep the plantain separate.

3. Strain the boiled spare ribs. Cut into large dice (remembering to remove the bones) and set aside.

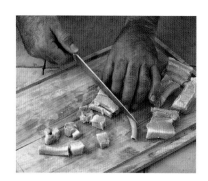

Ajiaco

4. Tip the meat, yams, sweet potatoes, cassava, pumpkin and corn into the stock. Bring to the boil.

5. Sauté the chopped garlic and onions in hot oil for 5 minutes until golden. Add them to the pot. Then stir in the tomato paste and salt, and allow to cook 30 to 40 minutes.

6. Cut the plantain into disks and fry for 5 minutes in the hot oil. Add to the soup immediately prior to serving, piping hot, in a nice soup tureen.

Spiced

Preparation time: 30 minutes
Cooking time: 50 minutes
Difficulty: ★★

Serves 4

3 onions
1 clove garlic
1 carrot
1/2 leek
1/2 rib celery
2 tomatoes, peeled
50 ml/3 1/2 tbsp oil
3 tbsp vinegar
50 ml/3 1/2 tbsp dry white wine

salt, pepper
1 pinch quatre épices (ground ginger, nutmeg, clove and white pepper blend)
2 cloves
1 bay leaf
1 lobster
20 ml/1 1/2 tbsp tomato paste
500 ml/2 cups liquid crème fraîche
1 chili pepper
1 tbsp aged rum

For the bouquet garni:
2 or 3 sprigs parsley
1 chive
1 bay leaf
1 sprig thyme

Lobster bisque is just about always available in the excellent restaurants of Martinique. Here, our chef presents the basic recipe which is a medley of lobster, tomatoes, onions, garlic and a bouquet garni. It is part of a rich tradition of soups based on seafoods, and can be prepared in a similar way using shrimp, crabs, conchs, fish etc.

In Martinique, lobsters are held in tanks full of water until purchased andsold fresh. Generally, to make economical use of the whole lobster, only the head is used in the soup. The tail, which contains most of the flesh, is reserved for nobler use. For a more sophisticated presentation, however, we cut the lobster flesh into medallions and poached them as a garnish for the soup. It is worth mentioning that lobster tails are a very popular barbecue item on the island. They are served with a Creole sauce or a *sauce-chien*, a sort of marinade flavored

with lime, onions, garlic, green peppers and aromatic herbs. It is often accompanied by a delicious gratin of *christophines* (chayote).

The bisque is delightfully perfumed with a little aged rum. As it ages, the rum, which is won through distillation of sugar cane juice, gradually develops its perfume and acquires an amber color. It is called "aged rum" because it spends at least three years in its cask. Alternatively, Cognac may be used to flavor the soup.

While frying the vegetables with the lobster head, do not hesitate to add a little water to the pan from time to time to prevent the mixture from sticking to the bottom of the pan.

If a whole lobster was used for this recipe, our chef's suggestion can be followed for the final flourish, or the flesh can simply be dropped into the bisque just before it is finished.

1. Peel the onions, garlic and carrot. Prepare the bouquet garni. Chop 2 of the onions, the carrot, leek, celery, tomatoes and garlic. Heat the oil and fry a few onion rings for 5 minutes. Then add all the other chopped vegetables and the bouquet garni. Allow to simmer for 10 minutes.

2. When the vegetables start to soften, deglaze with the vinegar, then white wine. Stir, remembering to scrape the bottom of the pot. Add salt and pepper, the pinch of quatre épices and the cloves. Cook for 15 minutes.

3. Detach the head from the lobster. Cut the head in several pieces. If desired, cut the flesh into round pieces and poach them 5 to 6 minutes with 1 onion and 1 bay leaf. Set aside to use as garnish.

Lobster Bisque

4. Add the pieces of lobster head to the pot with the vegetables. Allow to cook until the lobster pieces redden and the vegetables blend into a sauce. While cooking, add the tomato paste.

5. Transfer the pieces of lobster head to a food processor. Holding the processor firmly, blend until the contents look like a pink paste.

6. Pass the mixture through a very fine sieve, scraping as much through as possible. Add to the pot with the bisque, crème fraîche, ground chili pepper and aged rum. Whisk briefly over low heat and serve hot. Garnish with the lobster medallions, if desired.

Muscovite

Preparation time: *30 minutes*
Cooking time: *55 minutes*
Difficulty: ★

Serves 5 or 6

1.5–2 liters/1½–2 quarts meat stock
200–250 g/7–9 oz white cabbage
150 g/5–6 oz smoked bacon
2 large raw red beets
butter
1 tbsp sugar
1 tbsp red wine vinegar

1 or 2 onions
2 tomatoes
1 or 2 carrots
salt
2 cloves garlic
2 tbsp lard
rye bread
1 pinch cayenne pepper
100 ml/7 tbsp crème fraîche
1 bunch curly-leaf parsley
1 bunch dill

The family dish par excellence in Russia, borscht is popular throughout the world today. This traditional soup is easy to prepare, for it is made mainly with ingredients grown in Russian kitchen gardens. Historically, it is a Ukrainian dish consisting of a mixture of red beets, cabbage and lard; the Russians added the smoked meat. The recipe is very old, and Russian cuisine is very conservative: cooks frequently prepare dishes with origins that go back to the eighteenth and nineteenth centuries.

There are many local variants of borscht. Sometimes dry prunes, beef, potatoes cut in cubes or turnips are added. Today, no one hesitates to present this quite humble dish at the start a special meal.

Beets, of course, are the definitive ingredient of borsch: they provide its signature color and flavor. They are cultivated in the summer and harvested in the fall, just before the first snow arrives. During the winter, Russians store them somewhere cool, buried in sand. They also preserve them as pickles. Cordon-bleu chefs use them as cold appetizers ("beet caviar" is very popular) as well as in a number of different soups. Beets are also enjoyed smothered in a white sauce as an accompaniment to cold meats.

In former times, when vinegar was still unknown in Russia, they would add a dash of *kvas* (or *kvass*) to the borscht. *Kvas* is the national beverage of Russia, a fermented drink made from rye bread or wheat bread, yeast, diverse fruits, sugar and water (it is also made using beets). The vinegar can also be replaced with lemon juice.

For a more substantial soup, add some chopped carrots and browned onions.

1. Heat the stock in a large pot. Meanwhile, cut away the hard part of the cabbage. Shred the rest with a sharp knife. Add the pieces of bacon to the warm stock. Bring to the boil.

2. Add the shredded cabbage to the stock. Allow to cook about 10 to 15 minutes.

3. Peel the beets, then cut into halves and slice into small sticks. Melt some butter in a saucepan. When it is hot, add the beets. Cover and cook lightly for a little while, then add the sugar and vinegar and allow to gel.

Borscht

4. Peel the onions, tomatoes and carrots. Dice finely. Fry in hot butter in a separate pan for 10 minutes, then stir them into the beets. Pour in the stock and then add salt. Cook for another 15 minutes.

5. Peel the garlic. Crush 1 clove together with the lard in a mortar to form a paste. Add it to the borscht after 10 minutes and leave to finish cooking.

6. Cut the bread into square slices and brown them in a skillet. Sprinkle with the remaining crushed garlic clove and cayenne pepper. Spoon the soup into bowls and top with crème fraîche and chopped herbs. Accompany with the garlic rye bread.

Brazilian

Preparation time: 20 minutes
Cooking time: 1 hour 35 minutes
Difficulty: ★

Serves 4

½ chicken
3 chicken bouillon cubes
1 onion
3 potatoes
1 green bell pepper
1 red bell pepper
2 tomatoes
2 cloves garlic

2 tbsp peanut oil
100 ml/7 tbsp dry white wine
½ tsp salt
¼ tsp fresh ground pepper
½ cup rice
100 g/generous ½ cup green peas
(from a jar or can)

For the accompaniment:
grated Parmesan cheese
parsley
8 slices white bread

Brazilian soups are frequently prepared with a chicken stock base. In this recipe, our chef blends the flavors of chicken stock, bell peppers, potatoes, tomatoes and onions.

Today, Brazil is the world's third most important producer of chicken, and the local cooks also transform it into a multitude of delicious small dishes. In one traditional recipe, the fowl is stuffed with cassava flour mixed with olives, raisins, cheese, prunes, bacon and vegetables. Even more surprising, the Brazilians have developed a dish called *cuscuz de galinha* which, despite its name, has only a distant connection with North African couscous. It is a mixture of chicken and cornmeal cooked in a mold and garnished with herbs, chorizo sausage, olives, hard boiled eggs, tomatoes and palm hearts.

In Brazil, beans and rice appear on the table every day. It was Portuguese colonists who brought the rice, sugar cane, olive oil, coriander and pork to the country. Rice is generally cooked in a tightly covered pan with very little liquid.

To accompany the national dish, *feijōada* with black beans and pork, cooks prepare *arroz brasileira*: rice cooked with broth and then fried with onions, garlic, tomatoes, parsley and coriander. But Brazilians are also happy to boil rice with coconut milk, thus producing *arroz de coco*, to accompany meat, fish or beans. There is also *arroz de marisco*, a northern recipe based on fried rice with seafood.

Brazil also produces white wines and is the third most important viticultural region of South America. The 58,000 hectares (23,500 acres) of vines, from Italian stock, are found almost entirely in the south, in the state of Rio Grande do Sul. Of course, any good dry white wine will suit this soup well.

1. Plunge the half chicken into a large pot of cold water. Add the bouillon cubes and onion (whole). Cover and allow to cook for 1 hour.

2. Peel the potatoes and dice them finely along with the red and green bell peppers. Blanche the tomatoes, peel and dice them. Peel and crush the garlic.

3. Pour the oil into a large pot. Add the potatoes, bell peppers, tomatoes and garlic. Pour in the white wine, salt and pepper. Stir and cook for about 15 minutes until the potatoes are almost cooked and the wine has evaporated somewhat.

Chicken Broth

4. At this stage, add the rice and green peas to the pot. Cook, stirring, for about 2 minutes.

5. Remove the chicken from the stock with a slotted spoon. Detach and shred the white meat. Stir into 500 ml/2 cups of the bouillon from step 1.

6. Pour this mixture into the pot with the vegetables. Allow to cook for 20 minutes until the rice is tender. Sprinkle with the parmesan cheese and chopped parsley, and serve the soup with toasted bread.

Chicken Broth with

Preparation time: 40 minutes
Cooking time: 1 hour 30 minutes
Difficulty: ★★

Serves 6

For the broth:
750 g/1³/₄ lb chicken pieces
200 g/7 oz beef shoulder with bone
1 onion
1 carrot
1 rib celery
1 leek
2 or 3 cloves
1 bay leaf

salt
4 black peppercorns
1 handful chives

For the corn rosettes:
60 g/¹/₄ cup butter
125 g/³/₄ cup + 2 tbsp cornmeal
salt
4 eggs
3 g/1 tsp dried yeast

For the cheese filling:
200 g/generous ³/₄ cup cottage cheese
1 egg
1 tsp breadcrumbs
salt
white pepper

This Chicken Broth with Filled Corn Rosettes comes from the northern part of Slovenia, from the coast of Gorenska and Prekmuerje in the Alpine mountains. It is considered a festive dish, as it takes a long time to prepare.

As far as the Slovenians are concerned, pork is the meat they generally prefer to eat. Also enjoyed are chicken, then beef, and mutton is a distant last (although it was a more common part of the diet around a hundred years ago). Chicken features in a wide range of Slovenian dishes. It is stuffed with bread, chicken livers, smoked pork belly and, most recently, wild mushrooms, as well. But contemporary taste tends to favor lighter fare that is not as rich.

In the summer, huge fields of corn cover the Slovenian plains. These crops are mostly used to feed the Slovenian people and their livestock. Corn and potatoes were both introduced to the country in the eighteenth century. Slovenians like polenta served with milk or various sauces. Among their favorite dishes is *žganci*: cornmeal is boiled until almost dry, then allowed to stand and broken into flakes with a fork. These are eaten with bits of pork or lard. Also a specialty is a kind of savory pie with alternating layers of polenta and gorgonzola.

Before adding an onion into the broth, the Slovenians roast it on a griddle to bring out the flavor. Originally they would set this on top of their wood-burning stoves but an electric griddle will work just as well.

After cooking, our chef recommends soaking the chicken pieces in cold water to refresh the meat for easier slicing. It will also be necessary to press the cottage cheese through a sieve to obtain a smooth filling for the cornmeal rosettes.

1. Place the chicken and beef in a large pot, cover with water and bring to the boil. Skim, then add the peeled onion, peeled carrot, celery stick, leek, cloves, bay leaf, salt and peppercorns. Allow to cook gently for 1 hour.

2. Drain off the chicken pieces and strain the broth. Put the pieces on a chopping board and dice the meat evenly. Reserve the beef for some other recipe.

3. Prepare the corn rosettes. Set a pan with 250 ml/1 cup water to boil. Add the butter, cornmeal and a little salt. Stir with a spatula.

Filled Corn Rosettes

4. Mix in the eggs, one by one, and then the yeast powder. Stir again over a low heat to produce a lovely yellow batter.

5. Put the batter into a pastry bag with a star nozzle. Dot a non-stick baking sheet with small star-shaped dabs of corn batter. Bake for 12 to 15 minutes in the oven at 160°C/320°F.

6. For the filling, mix the cottage cheese, eggs, breadcrumbs, salt and white pepper. Scoop out the centers of the rosettes with the point of a knife. Use a pastry bag to fill the rosettes. Serve the soup garnished with diced chicken, finely chopped chives and the stuffed rosettes.

Tortmech

Preparation time: 30 minutes
Cooking time: 1 hour 10 minutes
Difficulty: ★★

Serves 4

For the chorba:
1 chicken
salt
pepper
saffron
1 handful green peas
4 sprigs parsley
2 carrots, peeled and sliced
1 rib celery, chopped
2 potatoes, diced

1 egg
1 lemon

For the tortmech:
250 g/1³/₄ cups fine semolina
salt
cornstarch
150 g/5–6 oz ground lamb
1 pinch saffron
¹/₂ onion, minced
pepper
3 or 4 sprigs parsley, chopped
1 tbsp butter
150 g/1¹/₃ cups grated Gruyère
olive oil for frying

Tortmech Chorba is a sophisticated soup of Turkish origin, now proper to the region of Tunis. It is generally made only for special occasions because it demands a great many ingredients and a degree of skill and experience. Spicy and nourishing, *chorba* in all its variations is of the foods traditionally served at the end of fasting during the holy month of Ramadan in Maghreb countries.

The classic Tunisian *chorba*, red in color, is prepared with lamb, celery, parsley, carrots, tomatoes, potatoes and harissa (a hot chili sauce). The meat and vegetables, which vary depending on what's available, are always finely diced.

The soup presented here includes *tortmech*, which are a kind of fried stuffed pastry akin to Italian tortellini. They are either served in a separate bowl, or tipped into the soup at the very last minute before serving. They should not be left in the soup, as they will absorb too much liquid and fall apart.

Tortmech Chorba is made with chicken. In Tunisia this fowl is transformed into fricassée with green olives and glazed lemons; and into *melmes* which are cooked with chickpeas, onions, tomatoes and leeks; or simply roasted whole with a side dish of rice.

Saffron and turmeric were introduced from the Middle East during the Turkish occupation of Tunisia. They flavor and color all traditional dishes, from couscous to soups, chicken, fish and more. Saffron is actually the stigma of a variety of crocus, and must be harvested by hand. It is the oldest known cooking spice and had already been cited 3,500 years ago in an Egyptian papyrus. 100,000 flowers produce just one pound of saffron, which explains why it is the most expensive spice in the world.

The *chorba* is completed by adding egg yolk beaten with lemon into the hot soup, giving it a wonderful color.

1. Cut the chicken in half. Then cut it into pieces and add to a cooking pot with salt, pepper and saffron. Add 2 liters/2 quarts water, the green peas and parsley, then the carrots, celery and diced potatoes. Cover and allow to simmer for 30 minutes.

2. To make the tortmech, mix the semolina, salt and 100 ml/7 tbsp water. Knead the mixture, then gather into a ball and roll out with a rolling pin. Cut out circles with a cookie cutter or glass (4 cm/1¹/₂ in around) and sprinkle the pieces with cornstarch.

3. Mix the ground lamb, saffron and minced onion, then add salt and pepper. Cook for 30 minutes until all liquid is evaporated. Add the parsley and butter and return to low heat for 2 minutes. Blend well. Stir the grated cheese into the filling.

Chorba

4. Put small balls of the filling onto the pastry circles. Set them to one side of each circle so the dough can be folded in half.

5. Using a brush, spread the free half of each circle with beaten egg white (keep the yolk). Fold the tortmech very carefully to cover the filling, sealing the edges well with your finger tips so they remain closed during cooking.

6. Remove the chicken from the pot, shred the meat and return it to the soup. Fry the tortmech for 5 minutes in olive oil. Beat the egg yolk with the juice of 1 lemon and pour into the soup. Whip vigorously. Serve the soup with a plate of tortmech or put a few in each bowl immediately before serving.

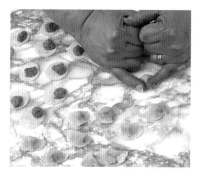

Clam

Preparation time:	1 hour
Cooking time:	50 minutes
Difficulty:	★

Serves 4

1 liter/1 quart small clams
1 liter/1 quart medium-size clams
500 ml/1 pint mussels
1 small onion
1 rib celery
1 leek

200 ml/generous ¾ cup white wine
2 bouquet garni
100 g/7 tbsp butter
salt
ground pepper
50 g/⅓ cup flour
2 liters/2 quarts poultry stock (skimmed)
1 liter/1 quart fish stock
450 ml/scant 2 cups light cream
1 small, firm potato
dill for garnishing

Clam chowder, a delicate and creamy clam soup with diced potatoes, is very popular from old England to New England, on the east coast of the United States. Creamy soups are popular in Britain, where pubs serve a range of vegetable, fish, shellfish and meat-based soups. Likewise, every London hotel offers a *soupe du jour* on its menu.

The United Kingdom's gourmands have at their disposal a wide variety of mollusks to enrich soups and seafood platters. Since time immemorial, the coasts of Ireland have been famous for an abundance of wild cockles and mussels. Irish mussels are now also raised in the sea specifically for our consumption. They are frequently prepared stuffed with garlic and parsley butter. The English also enjoy shellfish platters filled with lobster, Dublin Bay prawns, Devon crab, Irish oysters and small shellfish.

The potato ranks high among Ireland's foremost culinary specialties. It was introduced to the country in 1545 by the former pirate turned admiral, Sir Walter Raleigh. Among the most popular varieties we find the King Edward, ideal for mashing; the Maris Pipper, with its firm flesh; or the delicate Royal Jersey, similar to the little Noirmoutier potato. The English could not do without their fries for the favorite fish and chips, or without the baked potato. Another very popular dish, called "bangers and mash", consists of sausages, beans and mashed potatoes.

The shellfish used in this soup can vary according to the season and your wishes: scallops, shrimp, mussels or a combination; all will be welcome. Do not hesitate to season your clam chowder with a pinch of saffron or curry.

1. Peel and rinse the shellfish. Put them into a soup pot. Chop the onion, celery and leek. Add the white wine, a bouquet garni, half the chopped vegetables and half of the butter (cut in small pieces) to the pot. Salt and pepper. Cover and allow to cook for 5 to 6 minutes.

2. Have two small bowls ready by the side of the soup pot. After cooking, shuck the mussels and clams, depositing the shells in one bowl and the meats in the other. Reserve the cooking water. Discard the shells.

3. Put the shellfish, the other half of the vegetables and second bouquet garni in a saucepan. Sweat them 5 minutes in the remaining butter. Sprinkle and stir in the flour while continuing to cook another 2 minutes, without browning the flour.

Chowder

4. Add the stock that came from cooking the shellfish initially, the fish stock and the chicken stock. Bring to the boil, then reduce heat and cook 30 minutes, reducing the volume by about a third.

5. Pour in 350 ml/1½ cups of the cream, using a whisk to incorporate it well into the soup. Bring the soup to the boil once again, then strain to remove the garnish.

6. Dice the potatoes, then cook 5 minutes in the soup. Bring the remaining cream to the boil, season with pepper and add the shellfish. Serve the clam chowder garnished with shellfish and dill. Accompany with hot peppered cream on the side.

Northern Seas

Preparation time: 45 minutes
Cooking time: 1 hour 25 minutes
Marinating time: 12 hours
Difficulty: ★★★

Serves 4

400 g/14 oz ocean trout
1 tbsp brown sugar
1 tbsp white sugar
4 large Dublin Bay prawns
1 kg/2¹/₄ lb fresh shrimp
2 shallots
1 carrot
150 g/5–6 oz celeriac

¹/₂ leek
1 bouquet garni
2 liters/2 quarts fish stock
200 ml/generous ³/₄ cup Cognac
1 bunch dill
salt
pepper
olive oil for browning

For clarification of the consommé:
5 egg whites
1 onion
1 carrot
2–3 ribs celery
1 leek

Danish people tend to enjoy a wide variety of soups, frequently as their main course. They are typically prepared from chicken stock, with potatoes or dumplings added. Many soups include yellow peas, fried bacon or sausage. An equally popular soup is a close Danish cousin of bouillabaisse Provençale, made with trout.

In Denmark, trout is raised in conditions identical to those in which salmon is bred. Fortunately, streams rich in wild trout flow in that country, to the great benefit of professional fishermen and to the delight of amateur ones. The calm waters of Jutland (the continental part of Denmark), as well as those of Gudenåen, in the heart of the kingdom, are famous for their abundance of trout. The Danish like this fish smoked, wrapped in foil and cooked with small vegetables and dill, or marinated in a mustard sauce.

Dublin Bay prawns, also known as scampi, are a significant part of the diet in Denmark. Often simply steamed, they are eaten on white bread with lemon and a mayonnaise with a hint of mustard blended in. The Danish seacoast is surrounded by sand banks, beyond which lie shoals. Danish scampi, which inhabit frigid waters, are caught with lobster pots in the depths of the Kattegat and Skagerrak Seas.

While clarifying this consommé, be sure to stir it continuously over a low heat until the impurities rise in the form of a foam, almost like a mousse. The process of clarification yields a perfectly clear consommé. The proteins of the egg whites coagulate when they cook, trapping all the dregs and bringing them to the surface. Furthermore, the addition of aromatic vegetables enhances the flavor.

1. Prepare the trout: remove the skin and bones. Cut the meat in two equal pieces, then slice each half on the diagonal. Place the fish in a dish with a little cold water.

2. Mix the brown sugar, white sugar and salt in a bowl. Dust the top of the fish with this mixture with your hands dipped in the water. Sprinkle with chopped dill. Allow to marinate at least 12 hours.

3. Chop the carrots, shallots, celery and leek. Brown them in oil for 10 minutes in a soup pot. Add the unpeeled shrimp and the bouquet garni. Brown these slowly for 5 minutes, flambé with Cognac, then pour in the fish stock. Add salt and pepper and cook 30 minutes.

Consommé

4. To clarify the consommé, in a food processor, chop the leek, carrot, onion and celery. Add 5 egg whites and blend. Poach the prawns quickly, just until the water boils.

5. Blend the soup in a food processor. Re-heat 10 minutes to reduce it, then pass it through a sieve. Pour the clarifying mixture into the soup. Heat 30 minutes more, jiggling it regularly until the impurities form a thick granular coating on the surface.

6. Cover a tureen with a cloth. Ladle the soup in, passing it through the cloth. Add the trout and prawn tails, and pour the clear bouillon over them. Decorate with chopped herbs.

Cream of Broccoli Soup

Preparation time: 1 hour
Cooking time: 40 minutes
Chilling time: 1 hour
Difficulty: ★★

Serves 4

For the soup:
8 snow pea pods
1 leek
1 small onion
20 g/1¹/₂ tbsp butter
800 g/1³/₄ lb cauliflower florets
1 liter/1 quart chicken stock
400 g/14 oz broccoli

300 ml/1¹/₄ cups light cream
salt
pepper

For the crab chartreuse:
2 slices smoked salmon
200 g/7 oz crabmeat
2 chives
10 g/1 tbsp salmon roe

For the cocktail sauce:
1 egg yolk
1 tsp sherry vinegar
200 ml/generous ³/₄ cup grape seed oil
1 tbsp fine mustard
2 tbsp ketchup
¹/₂ tsp Worcestershire sauce
3 drops Tabasco sauce

Michel Roth never stops creating, revising and combining aromas, textures and colors throughout the course of the seasons. Soups previously clear become creamy, salmon gets prepared *à la chartreuse*, and mayonnaise puts on the airs of cocktail sauce. It all starts with a compote of leeks and onions mingling in butter without browning. Then comes the cauliflower—small white florets that will retain their crispness even after cooking. They will take only fifteen minutes to cook in the chicken stock.

Tender, healthful and quick-cooking, broccoli has made a strong comeback in today's cuisine. It is served raw, perhaps with mayonnaise, steamed, in salads and accompanied by fish or meat. Once cooked, it will be puréed and have crème fraîche added. Next throw on some crumbled florets and—why not?—a bit of grated Gruyère cheese. At this point, we can pause and sample the cream of broccoli either cold or hot.

But Michel Roth has drawn attention to the center of the dish by placing a superb salmon and crab chartreuse there. The chartreuse is a classic preparation inspired, so they say, by the dietary regime followed by Carthusian monks. It typically consists of partridge or pheasant stuffed into a domed mold lined with multicolored vegetables, then cooked in bain-marie. For his part, our chef has given the name of chartreuse to his little forms filled with crabmeat and cocktail sauce, then encircled in strips of thinly sliced smoked salmon. These salmon bands are fit into a pastry ring and then filled with the crab stuffing.

If you do not have pastry rings, you can use ramekins lined with plastic wrap or fasten the bands of salmon end to end and fill them with the stuffing. The chartreuses will be easier to remove from the molds if they are chilled in the refrigerator for an hour or more.

1. Blanch the snow peas, then set aside to cool. Wash the leek and peel the onion. Finely chop the white part of the leek and the onions, then sweat 4 to 5 minutes in the butter.

2. Add the cauliflower. Pour in the chicken stock to cover. Bring to the boil and cook 15 minutes. Remove and discard the stems from the broccoli florets. Add the heads to the soup and cook 10 minutes.

3. Slice the smoked salmon into regular 2-cm/³/₄-inch strips. Fit the salmon strips into the pastry rings and set aside.

with Crab Chartreuse

4. To prepare the cocktail sauce, make a mayonnaise by beating together the egg yolk, sherry vinegar, grape seed oil and mustard. When it has thickened, mix in the ketchup, Worcestershire sauce and Tabasco.

5. Crumble the crabmeat and mix it into the cocktail sauce. Add the minced chives. Set aside and keep cool. Purée the soup. Add the cream and season. Chill 1 hour.

6. After the soup has cooled, stuff the salmon molds with the crabmeat mixture. Fill your bowls with soup and unmold a chartreuse into the center of each. Decorate each chartreuse with pea pods wrapped around salmon roe.

Cream of Pumpkin Soup

Preparation time: 30 minutes
Cooking time: 1 hour 10 minutes
Difficulty: ★

Serves 4

1.5 kg/3¼ lb pumpkin or winter squash
250 g/9 oz firm potatoes
50 g/3½ tbsp butter
salt
pepper

For the quenelles:
50 g/3½ tbsp butter
125 g/4–5 oz porcini mushrooms
50 g/4 tbsp diced dry-cured ham
125 ml/½ cup whipping cream
25 g/3½ tbsp shelled walnuts
walnut oil

Here is a simple and delicious soup that nicely brings out the chestnut flavor of pumpkin. Concealed beneath the skin of a pumpkin is a juicy, ochre flesh that lends itself well to many soup preparations. As in preparing squash, you first quarter the pumpkin. Next, peel the thick skin, and keep in mind that members of the family *Cucurbitaceae* don't like to be kept waiting. Once it is peeled and the seeds are removed, it should be cooked promptly to assure the best flavor.

Quickly browned in butter, the diced pumpkin should retain its crispness. Then it should be cooked slowly and gently—for an hour—so the cubes don't break up. Try to use starchy potatoes, as the starch in the pumpkin and potato gives the soup its velvety character.

During the cooking, there should always be enough water to cover the vegetables, so add more if necessary. The soup will be puréed right in the cooking pot in order to preserve all the juices and flavors of the vegetables.

The whipped cream should be refrigerated for ten minutes before being delicately blended with the walnuts, cubed ham and mushrooms to prepare the quenelles. The quenelles are what make this Cream of Pumpkin Soup so very special. They are prepared at the last moment as a simple and unexpected gesture. You will need two small spoons to put the polish on this delightful appetizer: with one spoon, take a dollop of the quenelle mixture, then cover the dollop with the second spoon. The two spoons shape the quenelle before you to release it into the soup.

Nicole Fegegaltier serves her creation in cups. A couple of tender, young burnet leaves will give the soup an uncommon flavor reminiscent of cucumber.

1. Cut the pumpkin in 8 pieces. Remove the seeds, then peel and dice. Melt the butter in a soup pot and sweat the pumpkin for 3 minutes in it. Pour in 2 liters/2 quarts of water to cover. Meanwhile, peel and dice the potatoes.

2. When the water starts boiling, add the potato and some salt. Cook uncovered for 1 hour over low heat.

3. Using a mixer, blend the pumpkin and the potatoes directly in the cooking pot until you obtain a smooth mixture. Stir and keep hot.

with Walnuts and Porcini

4. Melt the butter for the quenelles in a skillet. Add the diced mushrooms and some salt. Brown them over high heat, then add the minced ham. Stir for a minute on low heat and set aside.

5. Whip the cream well, until firm. Chill for 10 minutes to stiffen it. Gently blend in the ham, mushrooms and walnuts. Adjust the seasoning.

6. Pour the soup into cups. Top each cup with a little porcini, ham and walnut quenelle; then garnish with a splash of walnut oil.

Cream of Tomato

Preparation time: 20 minutes
Cooking time: 40 minutes
Difficulty: ★

Serves 4

3 large onions
1 clove garlic
3 tbsp olive oil
1 kg/2¹/₄ lb tomatoes
3 potatoes
2 tsp paprika
salt
pepper

1 sugar cube
1 sprig cilantro
2 sprigs fresh mint
3 tbsp arak (anisette)
1 tbsp sour cream
or crème fraîche (optional)
whiting (optional)

For the garnish:
mint leaves
cilantro

Extremely refreshing, this is a dish full of original flavors and can be enjoyed hot or cold. The recipe is an adaptation by Ledicia Renassia, who, being fond of Mediterranean flavors, wanted to enhance this family favorite with the anise flavor of *arak*.

Prized in the Sephardic Jewish community, *arak* is a strong liquor similarly popular throughout the Middle East. Its name comes from the Arabic word *araq*, which means "juice" or "sap". You can substitute Greek *ouzo*, Turkish *raki* or simply anisette; each will give slightly different results.

A comfort food, this anise-flavored cream of tomato soup is ideal for a family with children. The alcohol evaporates during cooking, leaving just the distinctive flavor of the anise.

As with the famous Spanish gazpacho, the star of this soup is the tomatoes. Benefiting from Israeli irrigation techniques in arid land, tomatoes grown with brackish desert well water are prized for their extremely sweet flavor.

Native to Peru, this "fruit-vegetable" was imported to Spain in the sixteenth century. Considered by Europeans to be poisonous, the tomato had to wait until the twentieth century to become indispensable.

For this recipe, try to use round, firm, fleshy and glossy tomatoes, preferably of uniform color. Do not forget to add the sugar cube—it is essential to counteract their acidity.

Marrying mint to anise brings out all its freshness. This aromatic plant is rich in calcium, iron and vitamins. Choose mint that is very green without any blackened leaves and with firm stems.

If the mood strikes you, augment this dish with bits of whiting or make it creamier with a dab of sour cream or crème fraîche.

1. Peel the onions and garlic. Chop the onions and crush the garlic with the flat of a knife blade. Brown them in a soup pot with 3 tbsp of olive oil.

2. Blanch the tomatoes briefly and remove the skins. Cut them in chunks and add to the onions and garlic.

3. Wash and peel the potatoes. Cut in large cubes and add to the pot. Sprinkle the paprika, salt and pepper over the vegetables. Continue cooking 5 minutes, stirring occasionally.

Soup with Anise

4. Add 2 liters/2 quarts water and the sugar. Cook covered for about 25 minutes.

5. Add the leaves of the cilantro and mint, coarsely chopped. Stir in the arak and cook 5 minutes.

6. Transfer the mixture to a blender or food processor and purée. Adjust the seasoning. Pour the soup into a tureen. Garnish with mint leaves and minced cilantro.

Creamy

Preparation time: 20 minutes
Cooking time: 1 hour 10 minutes
Difficulty: ★

Serves 4

2 or 3 leeks
1 kg/2¼ lb potatoes
1 large onion
1 head celeriac
50 g/3½ tbsp butter
2 liters/2 quarts chicken stock (cube)

500 ml/2 cups light cream
chopped chives
salt
pepper

In the nineteenth century, Grimod de la Reynière, a pioneer in French gastronomy, declared to food lovers that "soup is to a meal like a beautiful entryway is to a house!" Puréed made creamy, thickened with egg or ennobled in the form of bisque, soups have diversified in both homes and restaurants.

Originating in the very center of France, vichyssoise is among the most classic soups. Leeks, potatoes and celery constitute the base of the recipe. Some chefs add carrots and garlic to vary the flavors. Use only the white part of the leek, as it is more tender and has a subtler flavor than the green part. As it often has soil lodged in its root, be sure to wash the leek thoroughly before slicing it. Either winter leeks or the smaller spring ones can be used for making vichyssoise.

A legendary tuber, the potato comes in so many varieties that they can no longer be counted. Native to South America, it has a thousand and one uses and stands up to all manner of cooking. The varieties with firmer flesh, such as the Bintje and Belle de Fontenay, are well-suited for salads. Other types are excellent au gratin, puréed in soups or as mashed potatoes. Whatever the variety, all potatoes must be stored away from light and have any buds or green parts removed.

Generally, the soup vegetables are cooked in water. Here, the chicken stock adds an additional bit of flavor.

Vichyssoise is served in two versions: if it is not puréed it is served very hot, or it is puréed and made very creamy. However you plan to serve it, vichyssoise has the advantage of keeping well—it can be kept 48 hours in the refrigerator with no problem.

1. Rinse the leeks, and remove and discard the green part. Peel the onion and celeriac. Chop everything finely.

2. Melt the butter in a pot. Add the sliced vegetables and sweat for 10 minutes over high heat, stirring and not letting them brown.

3. Meanwhile, prepare the chicken stock from a bouillon cube. Pour the stock over the vegetables until the pot is ¾ full. Bring to the boil.

Vichyssoise

4. Peel the potatoes. Cut them into chunks and add to the other vegetables. Season with salt and pepper. Cover and simmer for 50 minutes on medium heat.

5. Take the pot off the burner. Using an electric mixer, purée the soup right in the cooking pot.

6. Add the cream, stirring it in with a whisk. Heat the soup to just before the boil. Serve hot or cold, garnished with chopped chives.

Parsley Root

Preparation time: 1 hour
Cooking time: ca. 1 hour 15 minutes
Difficulty: ★★★

Serves 4

For the consommé:
1 carrot
¼ head celeriac
200 g/7 oz parsley root (or parsnips)
½ leek (white part)
100 g/3½ oz beef shank
2 egg whites
1 liter/1 quart cold beef stock
salt
pepper

For the marrow crêpes:
100 g/⅔ cup flour
125 ml/½ cup milk
4 whole eggs
100 g/3½ oz beef bone marrow
100 g/1 cup breadcrumbs
10 sprigs flat-leaf parsley
salt
pepper
oil for the pan

Our chef loves to consult old cookbooks. It was in of one of these venerable works that he came upon the recipe for the crêpes stuffed with beef marrow that compliment this consommé. A recipe typical of the Swabian region of Germany adds strips of crêpe to the soup. In the "wedding soup" served in the Frankish region of Germany, the cook adds little round dumplings of bone marrow and of liver as well.

Stefan Rottner's consommé is noteworthy for its parsley root flavor. The root comes from bulbous parsley, widely used in German, Austrian, Russian and Hungarian cuisine. This ancient vegetable is delicious in soup, as an accompaniment to game and in purée.

To make clarifying the consommé easier, ask your butcher to grind the meat for you. It is very important to salt the mixture from the start because the salt and egg whites will join forces to entrap the undesirable particles. The egg white tends to diminish the taste of the soup. It is for this reason, as well, that the salt and plenty of aromatic vegetables are added.

In this recipe, the chef mixes the aromatic vegetables with the cold consommé. Then he heats the mixture very gently, stirring regularly until a mousse full of particles rises to the surface. Alternatively, you could hot-clarify the soup by pouring the boiling hot bouillon over the vegetable mixture. The finer you chop the ingredients, the quicker the clarification process.

Afterwards, you will strain the consommé through a damp cloth. If it were dry, spaces between the fibers might be obstructed by detergent residues, and the liquid would have a hard time passing through. The resulting bouillon should be a lovely golden color. According to a German expression, "we should be able to drop a coin in and still be able to read its value."

1. Peel the carrot, celery and parsley root, then chop them finely. Clean and mince the leek. Put everything in a soup pot. Add the ground beef, egg whites, salt and pepper. Pour in the beef stock. Heat 10 minutes over high heat.

2. Once it boils, reduce the heat and simmer another 20 minutes. When the ingredients rise to the surface in a thick mousse, the soup has been clarified.

3. Prepare the crêpe batter: in a bowl, combine the flour and milk, then gradually beat in two eggs.

Consommé Rottner-Style

4. Heat oil in a big skillet. When it is hot, cook the crêpes until golden. Break up the marrow bones and extract the marrow. Using a fork, mash it in a small bowl with 2 eggs and the breadcrumbs. Add the chopped parsley.

5. Blend the bone marrow mixture with a whisk until it is a smooth filling. Add salt and pepper. Spread the filling on the crêpes with a spatula. Roll them carefully.

6. Wrap each roll in aluminum foil and poach for 15 minutes in hot, not boiling, water. Take them out of the water and let cool in the foil. Take the rolls out of the foil and slice into rounds. Disperse these in the soup.

Fassolada

Preparation time: 30 minutes
Cooking time: 1 hour 25 minutes
Difficulty: ★

Serves 6

400 g/2 cups dried white beans
4 carrots
2 onions
4 or 5 ripe tomatoes
2 ribs celery

salt
pepper
1 or 2 bay leaves
1 pinch dry oregano
scant 1 cup olive oil
1 leek

Konstantinos Stamkopoulos prepares this *fassolada* in memory of his aunt, who made a marvelous version of it. It is the most often eaten soup in winter, a veritable national institution that sparks polemics among cooks. Should we put in carrots? What about tomatoes? Garlic? This *fassolada* is so hearty that it can be served as a main course. It is surrounded with all sorts of *mezze*: small white onions, smoked herring, olives and cubes of salty feta cheese.

Soup in Greece is almost always a main dish. Greeks typically serve *fakies*, a lentil soup; *psarosoupa*, based on fish; or *kratosoupa*, with meat, carrots, potatoes, celery and leek. In the ports, the fishermen prepare a rockfish soup called *kakavia*.

Religious orthodoxy and poor soil gave rise to a diet prevalent in starchy foods and vegetables. In the past, on Wednesdays,

Fridays and during Lent, the faithful could not consume anything else because meat, fish, milk, cheese and eggs were forbidden. Nowadays, the Greeks are the largest consumers of vegetables in Europe, and red meat, fish and chicken are eaten in moderate amounts, rather than at every meal. In addition to beans, they enjoy other starchy foods such as lentils, chickpeas and potatoes.

Our chef advises you to use nice, ripe, juicy tomatoes if possible, otherwise canned tomatoes with some tomato paste. The beans will cook best if you use bottled water; they do not like hard water or salt at the start of cooking. You can enhance the soup with a splash of olive oil, large black olives or pieces of fried leek. It will be even more delicious if prepared a day ahead of time and then reheated.

1. Put the beans in a large pot and cover with cold water. Bring to the boil and simmer 10 minutes. Drain the beans, then pour in hot water to cover them.

2. Peel the carrots, onions and tomatoes. Chop the onions, celery and tomatoes; slice the carrots crosswise.

3. Add all but the tomatoes to the beans. Season with salt and pepper. Cook covered for an hour on low heat.

4. Now incorporate the tomatoes into the bean soup. Then add the bay leaves, dried oregano and some olive oil. Cover and cook another 10 minutes on low heat.

5. Peel the leek, then wash and pat dry. Mince the green part very finely with a chef's knife.

6. Fry the leek strips in a pan with olive oil. Serve the bean soup in individual bowls. Garnish them with fried leek and a splash of olive oil.

Lamb

Preparation time: 20 minutes
Cooking time: 2 hours 25 minutes
Difficulty: ★

Serves 4

200 g/7 oz lamb
1 tbsp sweet paprika
1 tsp ground coriander
salt
pepper

3 cloves garlic
50 ml/3¹/₂ tbsp olive oil
2 tbsp tomato paste
1 rib celery
100 g/²/₃ cup frick (green wheat flour)
50 g/¹/₄ cup chickpeas, soaked

For the garnish:
¹/₂ lemon
¹/₂ bunch cilantro (optional)

Since ancient times, Tunisia has known how to put fertile land to good use. The Romans turned the Tell region into the greatest granary in the country. The Tunisians have refined the art of cooking grains: they roast, sift, grind and grade their grains with great attention to detail. From wheat to barley, from *borghul* to semolina, the small grains are cooked with loving care in the heat of the *kanoun*.

Frick is a preparation of green wheat: harvested before maturity, the grains are crushed in a mortar or a mill. Sifting yields the green wheat flour. The remaining screened-out fragments, or *frick*, are conserved and commercialized for the preparation of soups. Nowadays they are produced industrially.

Quick and delicious, this energetic soup is prepared in no time at all. Rafik Tlatli suggests you start off with all the necessary spices and seasonings at hand because "flavor doesn't wait".

Originally from America, paprika does wonders for stews and soups. Its flavor comes out best with meats and in foods that are not cooked.

Tunisian chefs would not know what to do without cilantro and coriander. The Hebrews used this spice to season their pastries, the Romans to preserve meat. The lamb in this recipe will absorb a lot of the coriander's distinct flavor if you let it stay in contact with the spices for a few minutes.

A major player in Tunisian cuisine is tomato paste, which lends itself to any sauce. As it is concentrated, it needs to be diluted with a glass of water. Then it should be cooked a bit to reduce its acidity.

During cooking, the *frick* grains tend to soak up the bouillon. It's best to keep an eye on the liquid level in the pot, which should remain three-fourths full.

1. Dice the lamb, removing any excess fat, into 1-cm/¹/₃-inch cubes. Put the meat in a bowl.

2. Sprinkle with the paprika, coriander, salt and pepper. Use a wooden spatula to stir and make sure the meat is well covered with the spice mixture.

3. Peel and crush the garlic. Heat the olive oil in a soup pot and brown the garlic. Add the spiced meat, then brown for 3 minutes over a high heat, stirring continuously.

Frick

4. Dilute the tomato paste in a glass of water, then pour over the lamb meat. Add the celery, diced. Simmer 10 minutes over low heat without covering.

5. Add 2 liters of water, season with salt and pepper, then bring to the boil.

6. Sprinkle the frick into the soup while stirring, then add the chickpeas. Cover and cook 2 hours over low heat. After the cooking is complete, squeeze half a lemon into the soup. Serve hot in bowls garnished with fresh cilantro.

Andalusian

Preparation time: 1 hour
Cooking time: 5 minutes
Difficulty: ★

Serves 4

2 kg/4¹/₂ lb tomatoes
1 cucumber
1 large or 2 small red bell peppers
1 large or 2 small green bell peppers
¹/₂ onion
2 cloves garlic
4–5 ribs celery

salt
pepper
1 small green chile pepper (optional)
1 liter/1 quart olive oil
4 tbsp sherry vinegar

For the garnish:
1 red bell pepper
1 green bell pepper
1 cucumber
2 ribs celery
150 g/5¹/₂ oz Serrano ham
¹/₂ stale baguette
2 tbsp olive oil

Since time immemorial, both cold and hot soups have been the prelude to meals in Spain. In summer as in winter, custom soup is customarily the first to go on the table. One of the most renowned concoctions remains garlic soup, made up of almonds, garlic and water blended into a delicious emulsion.

Renowned among soups is the Andalusian Gazpacho, always a temptation to any gourmet on a quest for freshness. Be sure to refrigerate this soup before serving, as it should be served ice-cold. Traditionally made from fresh tomatoes, onions, garlic and olive oil, over time it came to include additional ingredients such as cucumber, bell pepper and celery. Ever since, its reputation has crossed Spanish borders to seduce food lovers everywhere.

Spain gets the credit for one of the most celebrated hams in the world's culinary patrimony. Made from the meat of black-footed pigs that feed on acorns, mountain Serrano ham is a particularly fine meat, firm and tasty. It is used to flavor certain soups and is eaten as an appetizer. It is also ideal simply sliced thinly and served on a piece of grilled bread rubbed with garlic and olive oil.

For this recipe, our chef insists on tomatoes that are ripe and meaty, with firm, not watery flesh. Adding ice cubes before serving is considered a sacrilege; they should be banned because they tend to make the soup watery.

If you would like to preserve the rustic character of the recipe, there is no need to remove the seeds from the vegetables. On the other hand, if you do, you will obtain a smoother and creamier preparation. For those who enjoy wine with soup, a glass of fine sherry makes a good companion to this refined version of gazpacho.

1. Peel the tomatoes, cucumber and bell peppers. Remove the seeds and chop the vegetables. Peel and dice the garlic and onion. Chop the celery.

2. Purée the vegetables. Add salt and pepper and, if desired, the chile pepper, halved and cleaned.

3. Resume blending, while slowly pouring in the olive oil, then the vinegar. Keep mixing until you obtain a homogeneous mixture.

Gazpacho

4. Pass the purée through a strainer. Check the seasoning, then chill in the refrigerator.

5. Prepare the garnish for the gazpacho: clean out the peppers and peel the cucumber. Finely dice them and the celery. Cut the ham into small pieces.

6. Cut the bread into cubes. Brown them in a skillet with olive oil for 5 minutes. Serve the gazpacho well chilled and garnished with the diced vegetables, bread and ham.

Harira

Preparation time:	35 minutes
Cooking time:	1 hour 40 minutes
Soaking time,	
chickpeas and lentils:	overnight
Difficulty:	★

Serves 4

100 g/ ¹/₂ cup yellow lentils
200 g/1 cup chickpeas
2 onions
1 bunch cilantro
1 bunch parsley
1 rib celery
250 g/9 oz beef (blade or eye of round)

5 tomatoes
1 tsp smen (rancid butter)
1 tsp saffron
1 tsp ground ginger
1 chicken bouillon cube
150 g/³/₄ cup orzo
150 g/generous ¹/₂ cup tomato paste
100 g/²/₃ cup flour
salt
pepper

For the garnish:
8 dates
8 figs (optional)
lemon (optional)

For Moroccans, *harira* is inseparable from their gastronomic patrimony. This traditional soup, always made from meat, chickpeas, lentils, tomatoes and celery, is eaten by every family during Ramadan. It is also made in honor of a young bride the morning after her wedding.

Very nourishing, this dish, a cousin of Hungarian goulash, varies by region and family. But for many Moroccans, the genuine article is *Harira Fassia*, the version from Fez (*fassia* means "of Fez"). This imperial city, guardian of traditions, boasts fourteen centuries of culinary heritage. Fez has contributed many recipes worthy of its famous name to the country's repertoire. Fassia gastronomy, known for being elegant and elitist, is distinguished for its savoir-faire and refinement.

Easy to prepare, *Harira Fassia* is a subtle blend of flavors, and thus requires a long cooking time. Celery, or *krafece* in Moroccan, is a marvelous flavor enhancer in soups, stews and sauces. Valued for its crunchy texture, this garden vegetable is available year round in market stands. Choose stalks that are nicely green and firm, without any withering or yellowing near the base. It keeps very well in the refrigerator. *Harira* is unthinkable without lentils and chickpeas. The latter, native to western Asia, have a slight hazelnut flavor. Very nourishing and hearty, they retain their shape when cooked. Do not forget to soak them for twelve hours and to remove their little husk.

A succulent dish, *Harira Fassia* is always eaten with sweets such as dates and figs.

1. The night before cooking, soak the lentils and chickpeas. Remove the husks of the chickpeas. Peel and thinly slice the onions. Chop the cilantro, parsley and celery.

2. Cut the beef in small cubes. Blanch and peel the tomatoes. Cut them into fine dice, then set aside.

3. Begin cooking by sweating the onions in the rancid butter. Add the diced meat, saffron and ginger. Salt and pepper. Dissolve the bouillon cube in a glass of water and pour it into the pot. Add the chickpeas and simmer the mixture.

Fassia

4. Add water, then the parsley, cilantro and celery. Cook for about 30 minutes. Next add the lentils, cook another 20 minutes, then add the tomatoes, cover and cook 20 minutes more.

5. Add the orzo. Allow to cook for 5 minutes. Dilute the tomato paste with water, add the flour and blend together.

6. Add this mixture to the pot and cook uncovered about 15 minutes, stirring occasionally. Pour the harira fassia into a tureen and accompany with dates, figs and lemon.

Royal

Preparation time: 30 minutes
Cooking time: 1 hour 20 minutes
Soaking time, chickpeas: overnight
Difficulty: ★

Serves 6

200 g/7 oz beef
1 small onion
¹/₂ rib celery
¹/₂ bunch cilantro
¹/₂ bunch parsley
100 g/¹/₂ cup chickpeas
100 g/¹/₂ cup lentils
500 g/generous 1 lb fresh tomatoes
2 tbsp tomato paste

2 tbsp oil
200 g/generous 1¹/₃ cups flour
50 g/3¹/₂ tbsp butter
1 egg
¹/₂ tsp ground ginger
¹/₂ tsp cinnamon
1 packet saffron
red food coloring
2¹/₂ tsp gum arabic
1 tbsp salt
¹/₂ tsp pepper

For the accompaniment (optional):
fresh lemon
dates

The queen of Moroccan cuisine, *harira* is truly used "for all occasions." It is found on every table in the Moroccan community during Ramadan, when each evening the faithful "break" their fast after the sun sets. At weddings, it fortifies the tired guests at dawn, before they go to bed. In more modest families that do not have the benefit of three solid meals a day, *harira* frequently constitutes the evening meal.

The word *harira* evokes in Arabic a thickened liquid, as opposed to the other well-known Moroccan soup, *chorba*, which is more fluid. Certain cooks prepare *harira* with corn, or with barley semolina. For an enhancement, our chef advises you to make your beef choice between bottom round, tip roast or brisket.

The combination of dried legumes, or *koutnia*, gives this soup a lot of nutritional value. Moroccans consume lentils, chick-peas, red or white beans, fava beans and split peas during the cold season. Winter can be harsh in Morocco, especially in the mid-Atlas region, where the thermometer can descend to between –5 and –8 °C (15–23 °F). To the lentils, cooks add meat that was dried or preserved during summer. The chickpeas are cooked for a long time with beef or mutton feet. This produces a fairly gelatinous mixture that is eaten hot.

Moroccan cuisine is extremely rich in spices of all sorts whose subtle flavors and aromas mingle beautifully: cinnamon, saffron, ground ginger, cumin, paprika, nutmeg and pepper are characteristic. Some of them arrived in the Middle Ages from the East; others during the period of the great discoveries, when boats loaded with spices would run aground on Moroccan coasts. Nowadays only cumin, saffron and paprika are produced in the kingdom.

1. The night before cooking, put the chickpeas to soak in cold water and leave overnight. When you are ready to begin, cut the beef into long pieces. Using a chef's knife, slice these into small cubes.

2. Shred the tomatoes with a grater over a bowl. Chop the cilantro and parsley; keep separate. Peel the onion, then finely chop it and the celery.

3. Pour 3 liters/3 quarts water into a pot. Add the tomatoes, parsley, onion, celery, lentils, drained chickpeas, tomato paste, cinnamon, ginger, saffron, gum arabic, red coloring, salt, pepper, butter and oil. Cover and cook 45 minutes to 1 hour on low heat.

Harira

4. Mix the flour with 100 ml/7 tbsp of water in a small bowl. Whisk until well blended, then add to the soup and mix it in well. Cook another 5 minutes, stirring until the soup has thickened.

5. Next sprinkle the soup with the chopped cilantro. Cook another 2 to 3 minutes.

6. Beat an egg. Pour it into the soup, whisking vigorously. Continue cooking 5–10 minutes, stirring constantly. Serve the harira in a decorative soup tureen, accompanied by a bowl of dates and lemon slices.

Iota from

Preparation time: 45 minutes
Cooking time: 1 hour 40 minutes
Soaking time, beans: overnight
Difficulty: ★

Serves 6

200 g/1 cup dried borlotti beans
400 g/14 oz dried pork filet
80 g/ca. 4 slices bacon
500 g/generous 1 lb sauerkraut
300 g/11 oz potatoes

3 cloves garlic
peppercorns
2 bay leaves
salt
1 "Turk's Turban" squash (optional, to use as soup bowl)

Viljam Cvek presents a typical soup from the Istrian coast in the northern part of Croatia. This invigorating and hearty dish based on dried beans and pickled cabbage, or sauerkraut, is frequently served as a main course.

Traditionally, every Croatian meal starts with a soup that is usually a type of beef or chicken bouillon with vermicelli. The lady of the house also makes cream of vegetable soups into which they might add mashed potatoes or croutons. They also occasionally add dried meat, which simmers for hours with the vegetables.

The coast of Croatia is certainly paradise for fish soups, while the mountains of the interior are home to thicker stews containing a fair amount of meat and crème fraîche, inspired by Central European recipes.

In Croatian cuisine, dried beans are frequent ingredients in winter soups, salads and stews. The bortlotti beans used by our chef are beige-colored and stippled with brown. They have to be soaked overnight in cold water. Frequently, a part of the cooked beans will be made into a salad and the other used in a soup that will be served at the same meal.

Croatian cooks use white and red beans interchangeably, either baked au gratin with pork ribs and onions, or simmered with cured pork belly.

The sauerkraut used by our chef is made from smooth-leafed green cabbage that Croatian families marinate in brine. Ordinary sauerkraut made from white cabbage is also suitable. There are as many recipes for Istrian Iota with cabbage as there are villages along that coast. Some cooks will cut the potatoes differently, while others serve the soup with the meat in large chunks.

1. Soak the beans overnight. The next day, drain them and put them into a heavy pot. Add water to cover and bring to the boil to blanch the beans. Drain them, add cold water again to cover. Boil for 30 minutes.

2. Cut the pork and bacon across the grain into large chunks. Put the meat and sauerkraut into another heavy pot. Pour in water to cover, then cook for 30 minutes with the pot covered at a good boil.

3. Peel the potatoes and dice them small. Peel and chop the garlic. Switch the cabbage and pork to a larger pot, then pour in the beans with their water.

Istria

4. To this mixture, add the peppercorns, potato, bay leaves, garlic and salt. Cover and cook another hour.

5. Remove the meat from the pot and transfer it to a cutting board. Steadying the meat with a carving fork, break it up with the tip of a knife.

6. Slice the "lid" off the squash and hollow out the inside to make a bowl. Pour the soup into the squash and add the meat shreds. Serve immediately.

Krupnik

Preparation time: 50 minutes
Cooking time: 3 hours 40 minutes
Marinating time: 1 hour
Difficulty: ★

Serves 4

For the stock:
300 g/11 oz boneless beef
300 g/11 oz veal or beef bones
150 g/5¹/₂ oz chicken gizzards

For the soup:
2 carrots
100 g/3¹/₂ oz celeriac
1 leek
120 g/10 tbsp pearl barley
200 g/7 oz potatoes
4 small dried wild mushrooms
salt

For the garnish:
¹/₂ bunch parsley
¹/₂ bunch dill

Krupnik is a traditional rural recipe that brings together left-over meat and several garden vegetables. This soup requires above all an excellent meat stock. Tender veal bones release a flavorful gelatin into the stock. Bone marrow lovers will tend to use beef bones. Whichever you choose, soak them in water an hour before cooking the *krupnik* so the mineral matter detaches from the bones.

Like many familial recipes, *krupnik* is adaptable to the mood of the moment; make it with a tender and gelatinous shank of beef, a melt-in-your-mouth veal plate or a chicken—whole or chopped in pieces—cooked right in the soup. You can make a very Polish variant of *krupnik* by using oxtail and pieces of pork. In order to obtain a nice, clear broth, it is best to keep skimming it all during cooking, which should be gentle. Cooking on too high a heat can toughen the meat and spoil the

flavors. After a long cooking time, meat has to rest for a while to firm back up again. Let it cool down on a chopping board before slicing it.

A big favorite in Poland, dried wild mushrooms find their way into many dishes. Very tasty, they can be added to the broth without having to re-hydrate them; fresh chanterelles or porcini mushrooms can be used as well, after a quick rinse.

Abundantly cultivated in Poland, barley remains as always the country's most popular grain. Pearl barley is used instead of the unprocessed groats for a shorter cooking time. After cooking the barley in salted water, our chef adds it to the broth to thicken it. Alternatively, it can be served in a separate bowl. A lump of butter will make it extra creamy. Minced dill and parsley add color to the *krupnik* and make it more attractive.

1. Soak the beef, bones and gizzards in cold water for 1 hour. Drain and transfer to a pot. Cover with 3 liters/3 quarts water. Simmer 3 hours over low heat. Take the beef and gizzards out from the stock and allow to cool down on a chopping board. Keep the stock warm.

2. Slice the beef into pieces 1 cm/¹/₃ in thick, then into strips 1 cm/¹/₃ in wide. Do the same with the gizzards. Remove the bones from the stock.

3. Wash and peel the vegetables. Separate the green and white parts of the leeks and slice both finely. Chop the carrots in 4, then slice into small sticks. Do the same with the celeriac. Boil the barley for 5 minutes in salted water. Drain and set aside.

with Barley

4. Put all the vegetables and the sliced mushrooms into the meat stock, then add the cooked barley. Bring the soup to the boil.

5. Add the sliced meat to the soup. Cover and cook 15 minutes over low heat. Meanwhile, peel and dice the potatoes in small pieces.

6. Turn up the heat. When the soup reaches the boil, add the diced potatoes. Cook 15 minutes, then transfer to a nice soup tureen. Garnish with minced parsley and dill and serve quite hot.

Locro

Preparation time:	1 hour
Cooking time:	3 hours 25 minutes
Soaking time:	24 hours
Difficulty:	★★

Serves 6

250 g/1¹/₂ cups white hominy
250 g1¹/₄ cups dried white beans
500 g/generous 1 lb osso buco
500 g/generous 1 lb tripe
250 g/9 oz white cabbage
300 g/11 oz sweet potatoes

300 g/11 oz butternut or winter squash
500 g/generous 1 lb flank steak
1 red chorizo sausage

For the chile sauce:
¹/₄ scallion
1 red bell pepper
100 g/7 tbsp lard
1 pinch paprika
1 pinch ground aji chile
70 ml/5 tbsp stock

Locro comes to us from northern Argentina. In the language of the Andean natives, the expression *chanuna* is used interchangeably to mean either "to cook" or "to make *locro*". It is a sort of stew where you throw whatever you have on hand into the pot, whether it's vegetables, pork, rabbit or beef. Formerly, the gauchos would dig a hole in the ground and build a fire in it. Over this they would place a brazier called a *fogon*, on which they heated the pot of *locro* for their meal.

Hominy, one of the ingredients of *Locro*, is prepared in a very particular way. The white or yellow grains of corn are removed from the ears, dried and then the skin is eliminated. The final product resembles shards of rice. It must be soaked before it is used and requires a long cooking time.

The most famous dish made from hominy is called *masamorra*, a type of corn pudding with sweet milk. During the 1810 revolution, clever merchants circulated around the city hall of Buenos Aires with trays of *masamorra*, which was greatly appreciated by the protestors. Since then, every May 25th small stands are set up along the parade routes for the independence celebrations, offering *masamorra*, *locro*, fritters and more.

The Spaniards and Italians who populated Argentina brought along their culinary traditions. The very popular chorizo used in our *Locro* is made from pork and sold fresh or dried. It gets its red color from its high pepper content. Argentineans also make a fine, sweet sausage called *salchicha* and a sort of blood sausage they call *morcilla*.

If you'd like, you can shorten the preparation time for *Locro* by using canned white beans. Decorate the finished soup with quick-fried shreds of leek greens.

1. A day ahead, put the corn and beans in cold water to soak (separately). The next day, cook the beans for 2 hours at a simmer. Set aside. Blanch the osso buco and tripe together for about 5 minutes.

2. Remove the meat from the stock and let it dry off and cool until lukewarm. Dice it and the raw steak.

3. Bring 4 liters/4 quarts water to the boil in a stockpot. Pour the corn into the boiling water. When it reaches the boil again, take it off the heat and add 250 ml/1 cup of cold water.

4. Put the steak, osso buco and tripe into the pot of corn. Cover and bring to the boil, then lower the heat and cook 30 minutes.

5. Peel the squash and sweet potatoes. Cut them into large cubes and slice the cabbage thin. Slice the chorizo into disks. Put it, the vegetables and the beans into the pot with the corn. Cook another 30 minutes.

6. For the chile sauce, slowly brown the chopped scallion and diced red pepper in the lard. Dissolve the ground aji and paprika in some bouillon, then add the mixture to the skillet and stir. Serve the locro in individual soup bowls with a small side of the spicy sauce.

Minestrone

Preparation time: 30 minutes
Cooking time: 1 hour 15 minutes
Difficulty: ★

Serves 4

¹/₂ red cabbage
¹/₂ Savoy cabbage
200 g/7 oz Swiss chard
200 g/7 oz winter squash
¹/₂ rib celery
1 medium zucchini
4 carrots

1 small red bell pepper
1 small green bell pepper
200 g/7 oz tomatoes
200 g/1¹/₂ cups fresh green peas
1 large potato
2 onions
2 tbsp olive oil
pepper
sea salt
200 g/generous 1 cup cooked red beans
1 bunch basil
bread for the croutons (optional)

Each region in Italy gives a personal touch to its soups according to that region's taste or the specialty of the province. Here Francesca Ciardi presents us with a basic minestrone. In general, this soup consists of a fairly dense broth with a lot of colorful diced vegetables. In this case, our chef has abandoned the soup bowl for a hollowed-out round loaf of rustic bread, in which she serves the soup.

The choice of vegetables can vary according to the season. You should avoid using leeks, however, because their strong taste could take away from that of the other vegetables. Red or white beans, green peas, Swiss chard, spinach; all sorts of fresh and dried vegetables can enrich your minestrone. Dice the fresh vegetables into small cubes and cook the greens whole.

Preparing a minestrone of the highest quality requires time and patience. This allows the vegetables to take on the flavor of the olive oil and the onion. Vegetables contain a high proportion of water. Take the time to let much of this evaporate before adding the cooking water.

Following their own tastes, cooks frequently add some pasta, a potato or some rice to thicken the minestrone; in our recipe, Francesca Ciardi has opted for potato. Broken up at the end of cooking, its starch will discretely permeate the soup without altering the taste of the vegetables. This soup can also be enriched by adding beef or bacon along with the vegetables at the beginning. Finally, take the time to add water little by little to the minestrone as it slowly cooks, keeping the vegetables barely covered with water. Let your diners pour a splash of olive oil and sprinkle grated parmesan cheese over their soup once it's served.

1. Core the cabbages and shred the leaves. Separate the leaves from the ribs of the Swiss chard. Dice the winter squash, chard ribs, celery, zucchini, carrots, bell peppers and tomatoes. Shell the peas. Peel the potato and set it aside whole.

2. Peel the onions and dice them small. Pour the olive oil into a large pot. Heat it over high heat. Add the onions and sweat them while stirring.

3. Before the onions change color, add all the cut vegetables. Stir carefully so the vegetables all get coated with oil. Season with salt and pepper. Allow to cook over low heat.

4. Cover the vegetables with cold water. Add the beans and place the whole potato in the middle of the vegetables. Cover the pot partially. Cook the minestrone for 1 hour over low heat.

5. Uncover the pot. With a fork, crush the potato inside the pot. Mix it in with the rest of the vegetables. Adjust the seasoning.

6. Shred the basil leaves over the soup. Stir them in and let the soup rest for 5 minutes off the heat. Serve quite hot, with croutons if you wish.

Mascarene Island

Preparation time: 20 minutes
Cooking time: 15 minutes
Difficulty: ★

Serves 4

1 potato
300 g/11 oz watercress
60 g/¹/₄ cup butter

600 ml/2¹/₂ cups chicken stock
100 ml/7 tbsp light cream
or liquid crème fraîche
salt
pepper

A blending of multiple cultures in Mauritius has produced a great variety of soups there. Vegetable soups like this one with watercress and potato rub elbows with Chinese such as crab bouillon and chayote or squash leaf soups, as well as with *moulouktani*, a very spicy Indian soup with taro leaves, curcuma, chili pepper, ginger and fenugreek.

On the island of Mauritius, watercress grows naturally in the wild. It is also cultured in basins where water circulates on its way to irrigate sugar cane plantations. The Mauritian people consume the somewhat bitter red-stem watercress as well as the more neutral-tasting white-stem watercress. They typically cook the leaves in the same manner as spinach: sautéed to accompany potatoes and fish. They also make soups and sauces with it and use it to color mayonnaise.

It is worth mentioning that Mauritians have demonstrated a penchant for cooking herbs. On the island, any edible-looking leaf is called *brède*: the leaves of watercress, spinach, sorrel, *mouroungue* (chard), Chinese cabbage, *giraumon* (winter squash), *chouchou* (tiny cabbage similar to Brussels sprouts), or of an aquatic root called *songe*. They boil the leaves, prepare them in *étouffés* (spicy Cajun stews) and make excellent, economical stocks from them to flavor rice or use in curry.

Potato cultivation on Mauritius does not have a long history; the island has a monoculture of sugar cane on practically all its fertile lands. As a part of a program of agricultural diversification, sugar producers began to plant potatoes between the rows of sugar cane in the 1980s.

If you like, you may want to embellish your watercress soup with sautéed veal sweetbreads, small pieces of porcini mushrooms or even sautéed shrimp.

1. Wash the potato and the watercress. Peel the potato and slice it into small, thin pieces. Chop the watercress with a cook's knife. Melt half the butter in a pot. Add the watercress and stir.

2. Add the potato to the pot and season with salt and pepper.

3. Pour in the cold chicken stock. Bring to the boil and cook 5 minutes.

Watercress Soup

4. Run the soup through a vegetable mill into a bowl.

5. Put the soup back into the pot. Bring it to the boil. Stir in the cream and return the soup to the boil.

6. Cut the remaining butter into small pieces, then gradually add to the soup, whisking it in well. Finish blending the soup with a mixer. Serve it nice and hot in an attractive soup tureen.

Split Pea Soup

Preparation time: 15 minutes
Cooking time: 55 minutes
Soaking time: overnight
Difficulty: ★

Serves 4

For the soup:
250 g/1¼ cups split peas
1 thick slice Ardennes ham

1 leek
1 rib celery
1 large white onion
1 liter/1 quart skimmed poultry stock (optional)
50 g/3½ tbsp butter
salt
pepper

For the accompaniment:
2 slices of white bread
30 g/2 tbsp butter

Forgotten for a long time, the split pea has retaken its place of honor in this soup descended directly from family kitchens. Nutritious, simple and quick to prepare, it cooks in less than one hour and can be served with or without croutons and ham; briefly puréed or strained to make it smoother.

Marked by the vicissitudes of history, Belgian gastronomy has profited from foreign influences, as seen in certain preparations influenced by Spanish cuisine and in products such as the famous Ardennes ham.

This cooked ham, with its strong smoked flavor, is a top-shelf meat product known even back in Roman times. It has inspired many tasty little dishes among Belgian chefs.

A stickler for authentic cuisine, Michel Haquin uses this ham for just one thing that is essential to the soup: its flavor. It is important to take the ham out before puréeing the soup. For charcuterie lovers, Bayonne ham or smoked bacon can also nicely compliment the flavor of the split peas.

Choose smaller peas for a shorter cooking time, and soak them in cold water for twelve hours beforehand along with the slice or chunk of ham. Note that the ham will contribute its saltiness to the soup, so add salt sparingly.

The fact that split peas are considered simple, everyday fare does not mean they are undistinguished. Three options present themselves for finishing this soup: puréed and cooked down to half its original volume, it will warm you up and fill an empty belly; blended and then strained, it's good with lightly browned croutons; and finally, you can mix some flour in a little water and blend it in to make the soup creamy and slightly thicker. Serve it with bits of pancetta and croutons either scattered in the soup or in a bowl on the side.

1. Fill a large bowl with water. Soak the split peas and the piece of ham in it overnight.

2. Wash and thinly slice the leek, celery and onion. Sweat them 10 minutes in butter, over high heat, stirring constantly.

3. Drain the peas. Add them and the ham to the onion and leek.

with Ardennes Ham

4. Pour in stock or water to cover, season with salt and pepper. Cook for 40 minutes uncovered over a moderate heat.

5. Take the soup off the stove and mix it right in the pot with a hand-held blender. Pass it through a strainer to obtain a smooth liquid. Keep it hot.

6. Remove the crust from the bread slices. Slice them into small cubes. Brown these in a skillet with some butter, turning as necessary. Serve the croutons in the soup or on the side.

Black Bean

Preparation time: 15 minutes
Cooking time: 1 hour
Difficulty: ★

Serves 4

250 g/1¼ cups black beans
½ green bell pepper
1 bay leaf
2 cloves garlic
3 onions
5 g/2 tsp oregano

5 g/2 tsp ground cumin
200 ml/generous ¾ cup olive oil
200 ml/generous ¾ cup red wine
30 g/1½ tbsp salt

Black beans are the great specialty of Cuba, and Black Bean Soup is a particularly popular dish. These black, smooth-skinned legumes have a creamy texture and are used to prepare numerous sauces and stews in the Caribbean, Central America and South America. They are frequently cooked in the oven with ham or salt pork, garlic, cumin and chile peppers.

Cubans make a dish called *moros y cristianos*, which consists of black beans and rice cooked together. This starchy preparation originated in Africa and at one time was used to feed the slaves in Cuba, who simply cooked it in water. Cuban children are given a black bean purée called "African purée".

On the island, beans are cultivated as abundantly as rice and cassava for basic everyday nourishment. They are grown between rows of sugar cane, where their roots help oxygenate the soil. After the harvest of the beans, the dried stalks and leaves are recycled with the cane leavings to feed livestock.

This recipe has relatively mild flavors, as Cuban cuisine is not particularly spicy. The spices routinely used include cumin, bay leaf, garlic, onion and bell peppers.

In comparison to their neighbors on the other Caribbean islands, Cubans do not make as much use of chili pepper, *massalé*, curry or *colombo*. According to our chef, this is due to centuries of Spanish colonial heritage. The cumin really gives this Black Bean Soup a marvelous flavor. It comes from the seed of an annual plant with mauve flowers that grows to about 30 centimeters (1 ft) tall.

Cumin flavors the cuisines of the Middle East and the Mediterranean basin as well. It undoubtedly migrated to the Americas with the conquistadors, for it is found not only in a large number of Cuban dishes, but is also omnipresent in Mexican cuisine.

1. Put the black beans in a soup pot and cover with hot water. Add the bell pepper and the bay leaf. Pour in hot water to cover and cook 30 minutes.

2. When the beans are tender, mash them a bit in their cooking water using the back of a ladle.

3. Peel two of the onions and the garlic. Mince both with a chef's knife. Sweat 5 minutes in a frying pan with hot oil.

Soup

4. When they are well browned, add the garlic and onion to the beans.

5. Add the wine. Cook another 15 minutes to reduce the soup and give it consistency. Now sprinkle the soup with cumin, oregano and salt.

6. Peel the remaining onion for the final garnish. Dice it finely and sweat for 5 minutes in hot oil. Serve the black bean soup with these small cubes of fried onion.

Dried Beef

Preparation time: 30 minutes
Cooking time: 1 hour 10 minutes
Soaking time: 30 minutes
Difficulty: ★

Serves 4

80 g/6 tbsp pearl barley
60 g/2 oz dried beef
1 carrot
60 g/2 oz celeriac
1 small onion
1 potato

1 small leek
30 g/2 tbsp butter
1 bay leaf
1 or 2 cloves
2 liters/2 quarts chicken stock
100 ml/7 tbsp heavy cream or crème fraîche
1 egg yolk
salt
pepper

In French-speaking Switzerland, they say *souper* rather than *diner* (sup rather than dine), because soup is an almost obligatory meal that can come in the form of consommé, vegetable soup or a cream of pea potage. Here Marc Imbs offers up a dish from the region of Grisons, near the corner where Switzerland meets Austria and Italy.

The dried beef from Switzerland is quite renowned. In the past, mountain peasants brought along this conserved meat for extended treks in the Alps. It is prepared from beef rump, a choice meat free of nerves, rich in muscle and nicely marbled. The pieces are first marinated in brine with herbs, then pressed in special forms. Next, the meat is hung to dry for three to four months in *spychers*—elevated lofts where the dry mountain air can circulate freely. During this process, the beef loses half of its moisture.

Sliced just before serving, the dried beef shows a beautiful dark red color. It has to be sliced very finely so it will reconstitute in the soup. In Switzerland, this beef is eaten with delight on buttered rye bread called *Roggenbrot*.

This old-fashioned soup is very creamy thanks to the pearl barley. The grains of barley are hulled, then polished into little round pearls as they pass several times between millstones. They are used in preparing baby cereal, stews and soups. Even after the initial milling, this grain takes a relatively long time to cook.

You can thicken your soup with crème fraîche or heavy cream. Cooking a ham heel in with the vegetables will give a rustic touch to the soup, but take it out once the soup is cooked. The dried beef, on the other hand, goes in at the last minute as it will harden when cooked.

1. Warm up 500 ml/2 cups water and pour it into a bowl. Stir in the barley and soak for 30 minutes.

2. Cut the beef in very thin slices. Slice these into fine strips, then cut the strips into tiny squares. Set aside the beef until you are ready to serve the soup.

3. Peel the carrot, celeriac, onion and potato. Clean and trim the leek. Slice the vegetables very finely, then cut them into tiny cubes for a mirepoix.

Soup

4. Melt the butter in a large pot. Add the vegetables, bay leaf and clove. Sweat this mirepoix for around 5 minutes. In a different pot, heat the chicken stock for 10 minutes.

5. When the vegetables become tender, add the hot chicken stock and barley. Season with salt and pepper. Cook for 45 minutes. Remove the bay leaf and clove.

6. Right before serving, beat the crème fraîche and egg yolk in a bowl. Pour this into the soup all at once, whisking well. Add the dried beef and serve while hot.

Potage

Preparation time: 20 minutes
Cooking time: 45 minutes
Difficulty: ★

Serves 4

whites of 4 leeks
80 g/¹⁄₃ cup butter
500 g/generous 1 lb potatoes

sea salt
pepper
¹⁄₂ baguette
50 g/7 tbsp grated Gruyère cheese
chervil sprigs

Very simple to prepare, *Potage à la Parisienne*, an elegant way of saying Parisian Soup, is the base for all potato soups. First, leeks and potatoes cut in *paysanne* style are cooked in water. In the *paysanne* preparation, the potatoes are sliced first into sticks, then these are sliced crosswise into fine dice. The leeks are sliced lengthwise into two or four long pieces, depending on their diameter, then minced with a chef's knife. To preserve their starch, the potatoes should not be washed after being sliced.

Closely related to onion and garlic, the leek was already in use in Assyrian, Egyptian and Hebrew kitchens. The Roman emperor Nero was known as "the porrophage" because he would consume large amounts of leek bouillon to clear his throat. Grown year-round in many varieties, the best leeks comes around between October and March. It should look freshly cut, the color a strong bluish-green. The ideal ratio is one-third white, two-thirds green. Try to stick with medium-sized leeks because the larger ones have tough and stringy outer leaves. Washed and dried off, it will keep for several days in a sealed container.

Brought over from the Andes around 1535, potatoes did not succeed in establishing themselves in European kitchens until the end of the eighteenth century. Potatoes such as the Bintje, Estima or Manon will work well in our *Potage à la Parisienne*. Developed in 1935, the Bintje is the most commonly used variety of potato in the world. Registered in 1981, the Estima is almost as universal as the Bintje; it is good for mashing, baking, in soup, as fries and in stews. As for the Manon, it was introduced more recently, in 1987. It is perfect for soups and French fries.

If you like, garnish your *Potage à la Parisienne* with fresh croutons browned in butter.

1. Prepare the leeks. Wash and dry them, then mince finely to release their full flavor.

2. In a good-sized pot, melt the butter and sweat the leeks. You may add a little water to keep them from burning.

3. Meanwhile, peel and clean the potatoes, then slice lengthwise and cut into sticks about 1 cm/¹⁄₃ inch square. Chop these evenly into small pieces. Do not rinse the potatoes after slicing.

à la Parisienne

4. Pour 1 liter/1 quart cold water into the leek pan. Add some pepper and a pinch of sea salt. Bring to the boil and cook 15 to 20 minutes.

5. Add the potato to the leeks. Bring to the boil again and cook about 10 minutes.

6. Pour the soup into a tureen. Bake or broil some thin slices of baguette covered with grated Gruyère cheese. Serve the soup topped with these and decorated with sprigs of chervil.

Pekinese

Preparation time: 20 minutes
Cooking time: 15 minutes
Soaking time: 15 minutes
Difficulty: ★

Serves 4

3 or 4 large dried black mushrooms
2 chicken breasts
1 can bamboo shoots
50 g/1¾ oz tofu

2½ tbsp soy sauce
1 tsp potato flour
3 eggs
3 tsp vinegar
1 tsp minced chives for garnish
1 tsp salt
pepper

Chinese soups generally consist of very clear broths in which the cook has briefly simmered vegetables, meat or fish (or sometimes all three) that have been sliced or shredded. The seasoning and garnish are added just before serving.

As opposed to Western custom, soup in China often arrives at the close of a copious meal. Chicken, tomato and black mushroom soups with egg; soups with carp or tofu; and pork soup with mushrooms, cabbage and bamboo shoots all share favor among Chinese gourmets.

Our chef's suggestion comes from the region of Beijing, the capital of China. People there love to comfort themselves with a nice spicy soup after having confronted the region's rigorous climate. Beijing cuisine uses soy, wheat, millet and a few vegetables. It is a paradise of pastas, lacquered duck, lamb stew with ginger and meats grilled on a sizzling platter. In winter, vegetables are largely limited to potatoes, cabbages, onions and turnips. Soy sauce, vinegar and chili pepper provide the flavor. Fortunately the summer brings tomatoes, green cabbages, eggplants, cucumbers and colorful squash back to the markets.

The Chinese have cultivated mushrooms for at least 2,000 years. Down south in Yunnan, more than 200 varieties of "domesticated" mushrooms can be found. The black mushrooms used here are also called wood ears, tree ears or cloud ears. Look for them in Asian markets in dried form. They will triple or quadruple in volume after they have been soaked for a while. Their gelatinous texture is very good for soups and quick-frying.

Products from the soy plant are commonly used all across China. As beans, sprouts, tofu (commercially produced bean curd); and in a variety of colored sauces, soy appears in many Chinese dishes.

1. Soak the mushrooms for 15 minutes in a bowl of warm water. Bring some water to the boil in a pot. Simmer the chicken breasts in it for 10 minutes.

2. Drain the mushrooms. Slice the bamboo shoots, mushrooms and tofu into fine strips. Cut the chicken diagonally across the grain into regular strips.

3. Put all these ingredients in a pot and mix them together.

Soup

4. Pour in the stock from cooking the chicken. Bring it to the boil, then add the soy sauce and salt.

5. Dilute the starch in cold water in a small bowl. Using a spoon, add the mixture to the simmering soup and stir will. Beat the eggs in a separate small bowl.

6. Add the vinegar to the soup, then the eggs, stirring briskly. Serve very hot in an attractive soup tureen. Sprinkle with pepper and chopped chives.

Salmorejo

Preparation time: 15 minutes
Cooking time, eggs: 10 minutes
Chilling time: 20 minutes
Difficulty: ★

Serves 4

For the salmorejo:
1/3 red bell pepper
500 g/generous 1 lb tomatoes
2 slices white bread
5 g/2 tsp minced garlic

20 ml/4 tsp white wine vinegar
250 ml/1 cup virgin olive oil
4 g/3/4 tsp salt

For the garnish:
2 eggs
100 g/3 1/2 oz ham, diced

Salmorejo was created in the ancient city of Cordova. At first, the preparation of this delicious soup strangely resembles that for gazpacho, another famous Andalusian soup: sweet red bell peppers with their earth-tone color and sun-drenched Seville tomatoes seasoned with a bit of zesty garlic, to which we sometimes add cucumber and green bell pepper.

However, the texture of *Salmorejo* is thicker than that of gazpacho because the vegetables are puréed with bread. Using white bread will yield a thinner consistency, while whole grain bread will make it thicker. Do not forget to remove the crust.

The virgin olive oil will bring a fullness to the flavor of the *Salmorejo*. Pure, healthful and fragrant, the Spanish olive oil should be added gradually to the vegetables. José Luis Tarín Fernández suggests putting half in at first before beginning to purée the vegetables. The mixture thickens at once with the influence of the oil. Then pour the rest in a thin stream into the mixer before covering it and continuing to blend. Like a mayonnaise sauce, the soup starts out thick and homogeneous, then becomes a fluid, light and creamy *Salmorejo*.

The same effect can be achieved by pouring the oil through the chute of a food processor, permitting a gradual blending without having to open the machine. Sherry vinegar in place of white will strengthen the flavor of the soup.

Nothing remains now but to pass the soup through a strainer, taking the time to crush the remaining vegetable chunks at the bottom of it so the soup will retain as much color, flavor and vitamin content as possible.

Let inspiration be your guide for the final garnish: serve the soup cool, with cubes of boiled or Serrano ham, flakes of tuna, or hard-boiled eggs either halved, sliced or diced. This soup has the advantage of being able to keep up to three days in the refrigerator.

1. Cut the bell pepper in 2-cm/3/4-in pieces. Quarter the tomatoes. Peel the garlic and cut it in half. Boil the eggs for the garnish 10 minutes and set them aside.

2. Stack the slices of bread on a cutting board, cut off the crusts, then cut the bread into cubes.

3. Put the bread in a food processor. Add the tomatoes and bell pepper, then the garlic.

4. Pour in the vinegar and half of the olive oil. Add salt. Close the processor and blend until you obtain a thick, homogeneous purée.

5. Open the processor. Add the remaining olive oil gradually. Cover the processor again and blend the soup until you obtain an emulsion.

6. Place a strainer over a bowl. Pour the soup through it, using the back of a ladle to press through as much pulp as possible. Refrigerate the resulting Salmorejo for 20 minutes. Serve cool, decorated with halved hard-boiled eggs and ham.

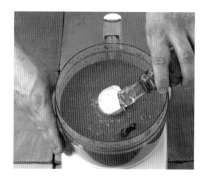

Beer

Preparation time: 10 minutes
Cooking time: 15 minutes
Difficulty: ★

Serves 4

2 liters/2 quarts chicken stock
250 g/9 oz (ca. 6 slices) white bread
330 ml/scant 1½ cups beer
salt
pepper

1 pinch cinnamon
freshly ground nutmeg
100 ml/7 tbsp light cream or crème fraîche
75 g/⅓ cup butter
salt
pepper

For the garnish (optional):
pine nuts
chopped chives

Alsatian gastronomy is far from limiting itself to its famed sauerkraut. Here Franck Mischler and Mickaël Wolf represent a simple soup, strong in flavor and a worthy representative of this region's authentic cuisine.

Beer soup has its origins in peasant tradition. A natural chicken stock will give some nice flavor to the soup, so be sure to start with that. Simply boil a chicken carcass in 2 liters (2 quarts) of water with an onion, salt and pepper. Then strain the skimmed stock and throw in the pieces of bread.

Sliced white bread, country bread or stale; all are good for this soup as long as the crust is removed. If stale, the bread will take a little more time to saturate. The bread can tend to rise to the surface of the soup; don't hesitate to use a spoon or other utensil to hold it down after you have poured in the beer.

While Alsace boasts a solid reputation when it comes to wine, it has also offered a great variety of beers for centuries. Hearty and generous as the Alsatians themselves, their beer finds its way into numerous dishes. Pure water, quality barley and fine hops are the essence of good beer. Beer lovers have their preferences: dark, blonde or red; the color matters little in this soup. The beer will serve to bind the bread and the broth.

Very aromatic and sweet, nutmeg adapts to any taste. Professionals grate their own with the help of a small, sharp rasp. More practical is the ground form, but its flavor is more fleeting. In order to preserve all its flavor, add the nutmeg at the end of cooking—and the cinnamon, as well. If the soup seems too thick, a little more beer added after cooking will help thin it a bit.

1. In a soup pot, boil the chicken stock for 5 minutes over high heat. Cut the bread into 3-cm/1¼-inch cubes.

2. Put in the pieces of bread and pour the beer over them. Allow to cook for 20 minutes over medium heat.

3. Take the pot off the heat. Liquefy the soup right in the pot with a hand-held mixer until it is velvety smooth.

Soup

4. Season the soup with salt and pepper. Add a pinch of cinnamon and grate in the nutmeg, then whisk them into the soup.

5. Put the pot over low heat. Thicken the soup with the cream or crème fraîche, beating it in well. Season to taste.

6. Stir in the softened butter. Serve the soup quite hot, sprinkled with toasted pine nuts and chopped chives.

Sauerkraut and

Preparation time: 30 minutes
Cooking time: 30 minutes
Difficulty: ★

Serves 4

50 ml/3¹/₂ tbsp oil
500–600 g/1–1¹/₄ lb raw sauerkraut
1 carrot
200 g/7 oz celeriac
1 onion

2 tbsp butter
1 tbsp wheat flour
2 liters/2 quarts beef stock
5 or 6 porcini mushrooms (jar)
1 bay leaf
peppercorns
2 or 3 cloves garlic
salt
100 ml/7 tbsp sour cream
1 bunch dill
1 bunch curly-leaf parsley

Cabbage soup might be the oldest of all Russian soups. In the summer it's made with fresh cabbage, in the winter with sauerkraut. Historically, this dish has been enjoyed at all social strata. In days gone by, it would be eaten as much in the tsar's family palace as it was in the *isbas* of the poorest peasants. In more privileged households it was prepared with a nice beef stock, to which small pieces of meat were added. The peasants had to be content with water, but they supplemented the dish with mushrooms gathered in the forest. When the tsar went hunting, he would bring along frozen sauerkraut soup and cook it in big cast-iron pots throughout his travels.

Prepared in the autumn with shredded fresh white cabbage and sea salt, Russian sauerkraut is then marinated in oak barrels for several months.

The heads of cabbage are also salted and put in the bottom of the barrel. During the fermentation process, small holes are pierced to release the fermentation gases. A cover is placed atop the barrel to pack it down. Other ingredients might be added, such as carrot sticks or slices of green apple.

Rural Russians like to gather mushrooms in the forest to liven up the everyday fare. Our chef uses fresh porcini mushrooms, but you can use conserved or dried mushrooms in this recipe with little loss of flavor.

Do not hesitate to add flavor to your soup with an old central European trick: brown half an onion and half a carrot on a grill, then simmer them in the beef stock.

1. Heat the oil in a soup pot. Add the sauerkraut to it and grate in the carrot. Brown until the cabbage is golden, stirring enough to prevent sticking. Add a glass of water, cover andlet simmer 1¹/₂ to 2 hours.

2. Meanwhile, peel the celeriac and onion and dice them into small cubes. Brown them in the hot butter. When they begin to turn golden, sprinkle in the flour. Stir for a few minutes over low heat.

3. 15 minutes before the sauerkraut is done cooking, add the onion and celeriac mixture. Finish cooking.

Porcini Soup

4. Heat the beef stock. Slice the mushroom heads into strips and add them to the stock.

5. Add the sauerkraut mixture, the bay leaf and the peppercorns to the stock. Simmer 30 to 40 minutes.

6. Near the end of this time, peel and shred the garlic, then mix it with some salt. Sprinkle this into the soup 4 to 5 minutes before it is ready. Serve the soup in a tureen, topped with sour cream and sprinkled with chopped parsley and dill.

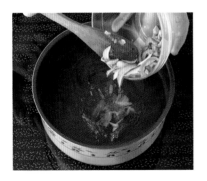

Újházi

Preparation time: 40 minutes
Cooking time: 2 hours 15 minutes
Difficulty: ★

Serves 4

1 chicken, ca. 1 kg/2¼ lb
1 onion
1 clove garlic
1 Hungarian green pepper
1 small tomato

pepper
salt
6 to 8 peppercorns
3 carrots
1 white turnip
1 celeriac
80 g/generous ½ cup green peas
100 g/3½ oz cauliflower
80 g green cabbage
50 g/1¾ oz small button mushrooms
1 chicken bouillon cube
80 g/3 oz vermicelli

This chicken and vegetable soup gets its name from the Hungarian author Ede Újházi, who lived from 1844 to 1915. Easy to prepare, it is served both in restaurants and at home, either as an appetizer or, because it has a generous amount of meat, as the main course. It is a traditional dish at weddings. Hungarians typically enjoy the bouillon first, then eat the meat topped with one of several sauces: tomato, sorrel, Morello cherry or apple.

Soup is common in Hungarian meals, often as the main course, especially in the evening. Another soup that is very popular in that country is *lebbencsleves*, from the town of Hortobágy. This recipe consists of pan-frying pancetta with onions, then adding paprika, water, diced potatoes, tomatoes and green bell peppers and cooking it all together. At the same time, fine

pastas are prepared with eggs, flour and water, then dried, browned in oil and added to the soup at the last moment.

What Hungarians call a green pepper is a narrow, elongated pepper of a pale green color approaching yellow. Its Hungarian name is *zöldpaprika* (literally, "green pepper"). The apple pepper, small and round, is called *almapaprika*. There is also an even smaller pepper called *cseresznyepaprika*. The bigger varieties are stuffed with green cabbage or ground pork with tomato sauce. They are all used in numerous soups, meat stews and salads. Hungarian peppers used for eating as such are products of the same regions as those which produce paprika, near Szeged and Kalocsa.

When you serve your soup, you can either leave the pepper in or remove it, savouring just its flavor.

1. Cut the chicken into eight pieces of about the same size. Then cut the wings, legs and breasts into 2 or 3 pieces each. Peel the onion and garlic. Slice the pepper into rings and dice the tomato.

2. Put the chicken in a pot with cold water. Bring to the boil. Add the whole onion, tomatoes, pepper and salt; then the garlic and peppercorns wrapped in cheesecloth. Allow to simmer 1½ to 2 hours. Filter the stock back into a pot, removing the garlic and peppercorns.

3. Peel the carrots, turnip and celeriac. Slice them in strips. Add them and the peas to the soup.

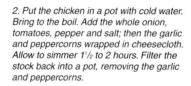

Soup

4. Break the cauliflower into small florets. Mince the cabbage and quarter the mushrooms. Put all into the soup and bring to the boil. Simmer 10 minutes, until the vegetables are tender.

5. Crumble the bouillon cube into a small pan of boiling water. Add the vermicelli, cook 3 to 4 minutes, then drain.

6. Put pieces of chicken into soup bowls. Pour on some vegetable bouillon. Just before serving, add the cooked vermicelli.

French

Preparation time: 30 minutes
Cooking time: 1 hour 45 minutes
Difficulty: ★

Serves 4

4 onions
150 g/²/₃ cup butter
1 pinch flour (optional)
1.5 liters/1¹/₂ quarts veal stock

salt
pepper
250 g/9 oz Gruyère cheese
¹/₂ baguette, slightly dry

Onion soup has been on the menu since medieval times and has survived all the trends. In those days, the term *soupe* referred to the slice of bread that one dunked in the soup. Around the turn of the last century, Parisian partyers would converge on Les Halles at the end of the night, where they would try to cut through the alcoholic haze with a nice hot bowl of French Onion Soup. This tradition is carried on today in late-night restaurants and to conclude nighttime festivities.

The onion, native to the plateaus of Iran, was used by the Chaldeans for their magic rites. During antiquity it was considered sacred, representing true wealth for the Egyptians. Universally enjoyed, onions are eaten in many varieties and at all stages of development. Before the bulb develops it's known as a scallion, then as a green onion once it forms a small, elongated bulb. The mild, young *oignon blanc*, or "white onion", is ubiquitous in France. When fully mature, onion bulbs have a yellow, white or reddish color depending on the species. When you are caramelizing the onions, take care to stir them regularly to keep them from sticking to the pan. Ideally you want to sweat them for two hours. For the cheese, feel free to choose between real Swiss Gruyère cheese, Emmental, Comté or Beaufort; or use a combination and add a little Parmesan.

There are many regional variations that have evolved from this basic recipe. In Normandy, the cooks replace the meat stock with milk. In the department of Landes, the region's version of onion soup is topped with slices of baguette spread with a cheese béchamel sauce. In Bordeaux, they use milk to make their *tourin* and thicken it with egg yolks and crème fraîche. In Lyon, when the onion soup comes out of the broiler or grill, cordon-bleu chefs take a mixture of 4 egg yolks and 100 ml/7 tbsp each of cream and old Madeira and slide it under the cheese into the soup.

1. Peel and halve the onions. On a cutting board, slice them thinly.

2. Melt the butter in a large soup pot. Add the onions. Sweat for 1 hour, uncovered, over very low heat until they are completely soft. Stir in a pinch of flour if you like.

3. Pour on the veal stock and season with salt and pepper. Bring it to the boil, then lower the heat and cook 20 minutes more, still uncovered.

Onion Soup

4. On a cutting board, cut the baguette into thin slices. Dry these in the oven.

5. Skim the surface of the soup so it is clear. Pour the soup into individual bowls, then place two slices of bread into each.

6. Sprinkle the grated Gruyère cheese generously over the soup. Broil or grill for about 10 minutes and serve hot.

Christmas

Preparation time: 30 minutes
Cooking time: 15 minutes
Difficulty: ★★

Serves 6

36 oysters
4 shallots
1 carrot
1 clove garlic
2 sprigs parsley
3 or 4 celery leaves

4 tbsp butter
1 tbsp corn oil
60 ml/¹/₄ cup dry white wine
125 ml/¹/₂ cup fish stock
2 liters/2 quarts milk
salt
pepper
1 pinch paprika
12 saltine crackers

The cuisine of Quebec, Canada and the United States offers many variations of oyster soup. In nineteenth-century cookbooks from Quebec, many recipes call for oysters, which were plentiful in the salt-water part of the Saint Lawrence River. They were cooked on steak, used in turkey stuffing and in sauces. In her 1878 cookbook, Reverend Mother Caron suggested poaching these mollusks in rabbit consommé!

Unfortunately, pollution coming from the Great Lakes has decimated the wild oyster population in the St. Lawrence. Our chef recommends using cultivated oysters: the *malpèque*, with its craggy, elongated shell, from Prince Edward Island; and the *caraquète*, with a deeper, rounder shell, from New Brunswick. Available from September through December, these oysters are consumed fresh on the half shell.

This recipe offered by Richard Bizier is one of the dishes typically enjoyed at Christmas. The traditional meal starts with an oyster or mussel soup, followed by a turkey stuffed with meat and bread (or possibly potatoes, savory and giblets), and finishes with a Yule log (cake) or an English-style fruitcake.

When you poach the oysters in the fish stock, do not leave them in for more than 30 seconds. They should just have turned white and be barely cooked because they will be put into the hot soup at the end. If overcooked, they will shrink and be less aesthetically pleasing.

Just before serving, our chef sprinkles the soup with crushed crackers. In Canada these salty and light crackers are also called soda biscuits and are generally found at hors d'oeuvre time. They add a nice crunchy touch to soups.

1. Open the oysters and keep them cool on the half shell. Peel the shallots, carrot and garlic. Mince them, the parsley and the celery leaves very finely.

2. In a skillet, lightly brown the vegetables and herbs in the butter and oil until tender.

3. Deglaze with the white wine and bring to the boil.

Oyster Soup

4. Detach the oysters from their shell with the tip of a small pointed knife. Using a slotted spoon, dunk the oysters in the cooking soup. Poach them only briefly, then set them aside.

5. Add the fish stock and milk, both luke-warm. Bring the soup to the boil. Add salt and pepper.

6. Pour the hot soup into shallow soup bowls. Add the poached oysters and a knob of butter. Sprinkle with paprika and cracker crumbs.

Aztec

Preparation time: 25 minutes
Cooking time: 15 minutes
Difficulty: ★

Serves 6

6 tomatoes
3 garlic cloves
1 onion
1 pinch cumin
2 tsp dried oregano
¹/₂ tsp black pepper

¹/₂ tsp cayenne pepper
3 tbsp tomato paste
50 ml/3¹/₂ tbsp oil
1 liter/1quart chicken stock
4 or 5 fresh lamb's-quarters
(or goosefoot) leaves

For the garnish:
250 g/2¹/₄ cups grated Emmental cheese
5 corn tortillas
100 ml/7 tbsp oil
150 g/5¹/₂ oz feta cheese
200 ml/generous ³/₄ cup light cream

Aztec Soup is a typical recipe from Mexico City. The Aztecs founded their empire in Mexico in the fourteenth century and thereafter expanded their power throughout all of Central America. The tomatoes, cayenne pepper, lamb's-quarters and corn found in this recipe were already part of the daily diet of this people.

The Mexicans have access to naturally ripened tomatoes all year long, whether they are round or elongated, red, green or yellow. They are used the same way here as in Europe: in salads, soups, sauces to accompany meat, and more.

Tony Spinosa, our chef, could put the tomato paste directly into the blender when he starts making his soup; instead he prefers to simmer it in olive oil first to bring out all its flavor.

Among the herbs that season the soup, the one called *espazote* in Mexico contributes the mint and lemongrass tones that make it unique. Called lamb's quarters or white goosefoot in the US,

it is considered a weed, but the leaves are edible and were used in many ways in earlier centuries. Now it is only used in Mexican and Indian cuisine.

Aztec Soup is garnished with strips of fried tortilla. Made simply of cornmeal, salt and water, tortillas are cooked like pancakes, but without any fat. Mexicans prepare them at home or buy them in specialized shops called *tortillerias*.

Our chef recommends cutting them in strips as soon as you take them out of the package, because they quickly dry out and become hard. To make the work go faster, stack them and slice a few at a time. While you prepare your soup, the strips can dry as they please—they will be easier to fry and absorb less oil.

Our chef uses feta cheese to garnish his soup because it is similar to the fresh goat and cow cheeses that are produced in Mexico. One can also find cheeses that are akin to Cantal and Emmental.

1. Peel and quarter the onion and garlic. Chop up the tomatoes. Pour everything in a blender or food processor. Add the cumin, oregano, cayenne and black peppers and a splash of cold water. Blend to obtain a pink sauce.

2. Heat 50 ml/3¹/₂ tbsp oil in a saucepan and simmer the tomato paste in it for a few minutes, stirring regularly. Add the tomato and onion mixture.

3. Add the minced lamb's quarter and then the chicken stock. Adjust the seasoning. Simmer for about 10 minutes.

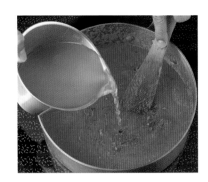

Soup

4. With kitchen scissors, cut the corn tortillas into strips.

5. Heat 100 ml/7 tbsp oil in a frying pan. When it is very hot, add the tortilla strips and brown them for around 3 minutes, turning them often so they cook evenly.

6. Put the grated Emmental in the bottom of your soup tureen and then pour the soup in. Garnish with the strips of fried tortillas and small cubes of feta. Drizzle over several drops of cream and serve warm.

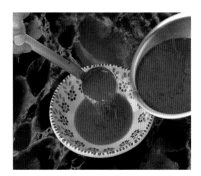

Chinese Chicken

Preparation time: 20 minutes
Cooking time: 15 to 20 minutes
Difficulty: ★

Serves 4

100 g/3¹/₂ oz chicken fillets
150 g/scant 1 cup corn kernels
salt
pepper

1 pinch sugar
peanut oil
sesame oil
1 tsp starch
2 eggs

Chicken and Corn Soup is among the simplest and most economical dishes in Chinese cuisine. It is served as an appetizer, following the fried starters. Other popular soups include combinations of all sorts of sliced vegetables such as bamboo shoots, tomatoes, black mushrooms, button mushrooms, cabbage or water chestnuts. To these, fine noodles are often added.

Chicken consumption in China lags just behind that of pork. Cooked in brochettes, sautéed, marinated in brine, fried, steamed, put in soups … there are hundreds of recipes. The preference, however, leans toward marinated chicken because its meat is savory and very tender. Food lovers in China value every bit of the chicken. The feet are rolled in soy sauce and steamed. The tongues, believe it or not, are marinated with many spices and then sautéed. The gizzards are sautéed or poached with a mix of imperial spices—aniseed, cumin, pepper and cinnamon—and are enjoyed chopped up in soups. An especially delectable morsel called the parson's nose, the pope's nose or the oyster, has a pronounced flavor and is reserved for the grandparents as a sign of respect. The heads are offered to guests to wish them good luck in life.

Our chef suggests you try another recipe he particularly enjoys. Take a chicken and rub the interior with salt, sugar and star anise powder. Then roast it in the oven for an easy, practical and delicious dish.

Corn is not used much in Chinese cuisine except in soup or mixed with other vegetables. It is primarily used to decorate and add color to the plate. That said, the Chinese do consider corn on the cob to be a delicacy.

1. Put the chicken fillets into a pot of boiling water. Poach them for about 10 minutes. Take the chicken out and leave the broth in the pot.

2. Finely chop the chicken meat.

3. Tip the chicken pieces back into its broth and add the corn.

and Corn Soup

4. Season with salt and pepper. Sprinkle in the sugar, then pour in a dash of peanut oil and a few drops of sesame oil. Bring the soup to the boil.

5. Dissolve the starch in a little cold water. Pour into the soup, stirring briskly. Allow to thicken for 2 to 3 minutes over high heat, stirring continuously.

6. Beat the eggs in a small bowl. Pour the eggs into the soup and whisk for 2 to 3 minutes over low heat. Serve very warm.

Georgia

Preparation time: 20 minutes
Cooking time: 50 minutes
Difficulty: ★

Serves 8

150 g/scant 1¼ cups roasted peanuts
1 onion
1 rib celery
2 tbsp butter
2 tbsp flour
2 liters/2 quarts chicken stock

175 g/²/₃ cup peanut butter
1 bay leaf
1 tbsp honey
200 ml/generous ¾ cup thick sour cream
salt
pepper
1 red bell pepper

Originally from Georgia, the Peanut Soup recipe suggested by our chef is also known in Virginia. Today, half of the peanuts in America come from Georgia. This crop caught the attention of the world when Jimmy Carter was elected president of the United States in 1976; he owned a large peanut plantation in his home state. They are also grown throughout the southern United States, in rotation with cotton. In this recipe, we use the nuts in a soup that takes advantage of their delicious taste as well as their high protein and fat content.

Peanuts have grown for millennia in southern North America and in Central America. According to archeologists, Amerindians were already cultivating them 5,000 years ago! In the seventeenth century, the Spanish explorers of the New World exported them to Africa to feed their slaves. The Africans liked them so much that they brought them back to North America. Americans tend to think of their favorite snack as a nut. In truth, it is a leguminous plant related to peas and beans; its seeds are harvested from pods that grow underground. Around 1900, the chemist Georges Washington Carver, an African American, discovered more than 3,000 uses for the peanut!

After shelling the peanuts, carefully peel off their brownish-pink skins, then run them briefly through a food processor to crush coarsely. To make a garnish for the soup, put the crushed peanuts into a hot skillet and dry-roast them in their own fat.

In preparing this soup, our chef has added the flavor of natural peanuts with that of peanut butter. Americans love peanut butter and use it in many ways. This very nutritious food has been produced in the United States since 1890.

1. Peel the skin off the peanuts, then crush them and set aside. Peel and chop the onion. Mince the celery. Melt the butter in a soup pot and slowly brown the celery and onion in it until they begin to soften.

2. When the onions are transparent, sprinkle the flour into the pot and pour in a little of the chicken stock. Cook for 5 minutes, stirring constantly.

3. Pour in the rest of the chicken stock and stir it in. Cook for several minutes over low heat.

Peanut Soup

4. Add most of the crushed peanuts, keeping a few for the garnish. Stir in the peanut butter and the bay leaf. Bring to the boil, then lower the heat and cook for 30 minutes. Strain the soup.

5. Stir in the honey. Bring the sour cream to room temperature by scooping it into a bowl.

6. Incorporate it into the soup with a whisk. Season with salt and pepper. Reheat briefly, beating the soup with the whisk. Sprinkle with pan-roasted crushed peanuts and small cubes of bell pepper.

Bangkok

Preparation time: 30 minutes
Cooking time: 20 minutes
Difficulty: ★

Serves 4

600 g/1¼ lb farm-raised duck breast fillet
50 g/1¾ oz galangal (galanga root)
several stalks Chinese lemongrass
100 g/3½ oz button mushrooms
1.2 liters/5 cups (3 cans) coconut milk
350 ml/1½ cups chicken stock

4 fresh bergamot leaves
1 tsp ground red chili pepper
2 limes
100 ml/7 tbsp nam pla sauce
2 sprigs fresh cilantro
2 coriander roots (hom nam)

Baptized ages ago with the sweet name of *muang thai*, "the country of free men", Thailand was never colonized by European nations and took in peoples of neighboring countries while preserving its own identity. Influenced in turn by the Chinese, Cambodian and Indian cultures, Thai cuisine has evolved into one that is delightful at any time.

Thais undoubtedly learned the art of preparing duck from the Chinese. Forgoing the splendor of glazed duck, Oth Sombath bestows upon the bird a medley of the colors found in the markets of Bangkok. Chicken or beef can be substituted for this premium meat. Once the meat is cut in small cubes, cooking any of them will be identical.

In Thai cuisine, precision in measuring ingredients is essential to balancing the flavors. Under the attentive eye of Buddha, each Thai person is duty bound to respect this culinary art. Our chef thus recommends patiently weighing each ingredient and keeping them in separate little bowls.

Equivalent to Vietnamese *nuoc mam*, *nam pla* is a sauce made from small shrimp and small fish, salted and left in the sun to ferment. The sauce takes on a brown color and a strong flavor—a few drops can transform ordinary rice into something exotic. *Nam pla* replaces salt in Asian food, so you will not need salt for this recipe.

Nam pla, lime juice and fresh chili pepper make an audacious trio of seasonings for your soup. Lemongrass and galangal, a potent form of ginger, are cut in round, transparent slices. When very fresh, the galangal does not need to be peeled.

As for the coconut milk, it is used generously in Asia as well as the West Indies. Made from the pulp of coconut, it is poured in a bowl before being used to give it a homogenous consistency. Added all at once to the bouillon, it lends sweetness and flavor to the soup.

1. Place the duck fillet skin-side down on a chopping board. With a chef's knife, make fine slices in one direction, about as wide as the meat is thick. Repeat in the other direction to obtain cubes of around 2 cm/¾ in.

2. Slice the galangal in very thin rounds (ca. 5 mm/¹⁄₅ in), then cut each round in half. Repeat with the lemongrass, from the tips of the leaves to 10 cm/4 in before the bulb. Keep the bulbs.

3. Carefully rinse and pat dry the mushrooms. Separate the caps from the stems. Peel the caps delicately and quarter them. Set aside.

Duck Soup

4. Put the coconut milk in a bowl and the chicken stock in a large pot. Heat the stock over high heat. When it begins to simmer, add the coconut milk all at once. Whip the mixture and bring it to the boil.

5. As soon as it boils, lower the heat. Shred the bergamot leaves into the soup; add the diced duck, galangal, chili pepper, lemongrass, quartered mushrooms, lime juice and the nam pla sauce. Return to the boil.

6. Cook until the duck is done about halfway, then reduce the heat and cook an additional 2 to 5 minutes. Remove from the heat. Cover the bottom of each soup bowl with the diced meat and ladle soup over it. Sprinkle with leaves and slices of coriander root.

Green Cabbage

Preparation time: 1 hour
Cooking time: 45 minutes
Marinating time: 1 hour
Rising time: 30 minutes
Difficulty: ★★

Serves 4

For the green cabbage soup:
400 g/14 oz green cabbage
2 shallots
1 clove garlic
50 g/3½ tbsp butter
thyme, cumin, salt and pepper
400 ml/1⅔ cups vegetable stock
200 ml/generous ¾ cup cream

For the lobster:
2 lobsters
100 ml/7 tbsp olive oil
1 onion, 1 carrot, 1 rib celery

thyme, bay leaf, parsley
2 tbsp tomato paste

For the pickled ginger:
2 ginger roots
100 ml/7 tbsp white vinegar
100 g/7 tbsp natural cane sugar

For the skillet bread:
500 ml/2 cups milk
50 g/3½ tbsp butter
12 g/1 tbsp baking yeast
2 tsp baking powder
2 tsp caramel
120 g/¾ cup + 2 tbsp all-purpose flour
500 g/3½ cups pastry flour
1 tsp sugar

The Swedish love to eat cabbage soup in winter, when it is offered as a main course. Green cabbage appears in three or four different forms among the foods that are featured in the great *smörgåsbord* buffet eaten at Christmas. Cabbage is great served with ham hocks and sausages, or seasoned with mustard sauce. Swedes love this vegetable, and just as often will eat white or red cabbage, kale, or Brussels sprouts, which they serve with game.

Our chef has come up with a popular combination by introducing the luxurious lobster into this soup. This crustacean, with its blue or black shell and impressive claws, is caught from small boats working the Kattegat Sea off of Gothenburg. The restaurateurs of Malmö, such as our chef, do not hesitate to buy their lobsters from nearby Danish fishermen.

To accompany this dish, Stefan Linde has brought back the tradition of *spistunnbröd* or "skillet bread." Depending on the

ingredients and how long you cook the bread, it can be soft or hard. Chefs also like to bake homemade bread with yogurt. Leavened solely by the yogurt, they take two or three days to rise.

Nowadays of course, Swedish bakers also offer French-style baguettes and Italian *ciabattas*, but the real star of Swedish breadmaking is *knäckebrod*, which can be translated as "bread that breaks". This flat, very hard bread keeps a long time and is enjoyed at breakfast with jam, cheese, or herring. Its dough is rye- or wheat-based and has many holes so the heat of the oven can disperse efficiently throughout the dough during its very brief baking time.

This Green Cabbage Soup with Lobster is served with small, pan-fried shreds of cabbage.

1. Wash the cabbage. Slice it thinly and mince the shallots and garlic. In a saucepan, heat the butter and brown the chopped vegetables gently for 5 minutes with thyme, cumin, pepper and salt. Add the vegetable stock and the cream.

2. Dispatch the lobsters with a single knife blow between the head and the body. Chop them into big pieces. Boil them 5 minutes in a large pot of water with the olive oil, onion, carrot, celery, parsley, bay and thyme.

3. Add the tomato paste and enough water to cover. Let simmer 15 to 20 minutes over low heat. Pass this stock through a strainer. Set aside the lobster and keep the stock in a saucepan. Reduce it for 10 minutes to obtain a thick sauce.

Soup with Lobster

4. Peel the ginger and slice it into fine strips. Place them in a bowl and pour over the white vinegar. Sprinkle the cane sugar over them with a small spoon. Mix well and let marinate for 1 hour.

5. Heat the milk with the butter in shavings until it reaches body temperature. Remove from the heat and whisk in the yeast and baking powder, caramel, both flours and the sugar. Blend with an electric mixer. Knead the dough and let it rise for 30 minutes.

6. Roll out the bread dough thinly and slice it in triangles. Brown them on both sides in a skillet. Remove the lobster meat from its shell. Accompany the cabbage soup with a plate of lobster decorated with the ginger, the skillet bread and a bit of sauce.

Shrimp and

Preparation time: *45 minutes*
Cooking time: *15 minutes*
Difficulty: ★

Serves 4

8 jumbo shrimp
40 g/1½ oz Chinese lemongrass
40 g/1½ oz galangal (galanga root)
750 ml/3¼ cups chicken stock
150 g/5–6 oz button mushrooms
40 ml/2½ tbsp fish sauce

1 lemon
3 sprigs fresh cilantro
4 dried bergamot leaves
4 cayenne peppers

In Southeast Asia between the Sea of China and the Gulf of Thailand, no fewer than 15 different varieties of jumbo shrimp can be found. Sought for its savory and firm flesh, this crustacean never ceases to feed the imagination of Thai cooks.

Popular all through Thailand, Shrimp and Lemongrass Soup, or *tom yam kung*, illustrates the refinement of flavors in Thai culture. Substituting ingredients is not an option for this recipe. In any case, Asian food has become so popular these days that it would be surprising not to find the necessary ingredients in either a supermarket or a specialty Asian market.

Chinese lemongrass comes in stalks. Called *serai* or *va kral*, its bulb looks like a small onion. Do not use the stalk past about 10–15 cm/2½–3¾ inches from the bulb. Its powerful lemony flavor calls for very fine slices, as with galangal, also called galanga root.

Resembling ginger but lighter in color, galangal must be used in moderation as its strongly peppery taste can disagree with certain palates. Our chef strongly recommends peeling it before use.

Whether you use Thai straw or button mushrooms is your choice. Cook them from two minutes for "al dente" up to five minutes for well done.

Because Asian culture is inspired more by wisdom than by rigor, its gastronomy is imbued with subtlety. Beyond merely cooking, each ingredient takes the time to get acquainted with the flavor of the others right up until serving time. As a final refinement, you will shred cilantro over the hot *tom yam kung*. Now, aromatic to the last drop, the soup enchants the palate. Fresh cayenne peppers and lemon juice are served on the side for an exotic taste sensation.

1. Peel the shrimp and set them aside.

2. Slice the lemongrass and galangal very finely, across the grain. Bring the chicken stock to the boil in a pot. Once boiling, add the lemongrass and galangal. Simmer over a low heat.

3. Meanwhile, carefully rinse and pat dry the mushrooms. Peel and quarter them, then add to the broth. Let the flavors mingle for 2 to 5 minutes over high heat.

Lemongrass Soup

4. Add the fish sauce and allow it to blend into the soup without stirring. Squeeze the lemon and pour the juice into the pot.

5. Drop the peeled shrimp into the soup. Add 2 sprigs of fresh coriander. Cook 2 minutes on low heat.

6. Add the whole leaves of bergamot, then the chili peppers. Bring just to the boil, then remove from heat. Serve the soup right away, garnishing the bowls with cilantro.

Prawn Soup

Preparation time: 30 minutes
Cooking time: 2 hours 10 minutes
Difficulty: ★★

Serves 4

2 chicken legs
500 g/generous 1 lb large prawns
50 g/1³/₄ oz tamarind paste
1 dash nuoc mam

¹/₂ fresh pineapple
2 tomatoes
100 g/3¹/₂ oz bean sprouts
1 sprig basil
1 small fresh chili pepper (optional)
1 stalk Chinese lemongrass
2 lemons

Prawn Soup with Lemongrass is very common in Vietnam. Local varieties frequently have a two-pronged hot and sour flavor, provided in this case by the chili pepper and tamarind. For their daily meal, the more well-off Vietnamese will start off with a soup, then have a rice dish with fish or meat; while those of more modest means do with just soup and rice.

Vietnamese waters abound with both fresh- and salt-water shellfish. Our chef, who in this recipe uses prawns from the sea, loves to cook with the bluish-clawed river ones from the Mekong. He finds them very flavorful and believes the "coral", or egg sac, located inside their large heads, gives a nice taste to the soup. The Vietnamese equally enjoy crab and scampi, and these can substitute for the prawns in your soup.

Tamarind paste has a sour flavor and comes in the form of a violet-brown pulp. The pod-like fruit from which it is extracted looks like a fat brown bean with fibrous flesh. In Vietnam, tamarind paste is used widely to flavor soups. Tamarind is also sold fresh, dehydrated, in juice, in syrup, pickled or candied.

Chinese lemongrass is present in most Vietnamese dishes. The Vietnamese call it *xa*. Its thick, pale green stems rise from a white bulb and release a delicious flavor of lemon rind. They are used to enrich soup, stews and salads. Lemongrass is sold fresh or dried. Don't hesitate to freeze some fresh so you'll always have it on hand.

In preparing the soup stock, you can substitute a chicken carcass for the legs, or use giblets or pork bones.

1. In a stockpot full of boiling water, simmer the chicken legs for 2 hours.

2. Meanwhile, pull the heads off the prawns and set them aside. Peel the shell from the bodies, starting from the "neck" down.

3. Slice open the prawns down the length of the back and de-vein them.

with Lemongrass

4. Cook the heads in the boiling chicken stock for 3 minutes.

5. Add the tamarind paste bit by bit into the bouillon, then the nouc mam. Continue simmering for another 5 minutes. During this time, peel and cube the pineapple, and quarter the tomatoes.

6. Mix the pineapple, tomatoes, bean sprouts, basil, minced chili and minced lemongrass. Add this mixture to the soup just before serving, then add the prawns and cook 2 to 3 minutes. Accompany the soup with lemon quarters.

Hungarian

Preparation time: 30 minutes
Cooking time: 1 hour 40 minutes
Difficulty: ★

Serves 4

400 g/14 oz beef fillet
2 medium onions
3 tbsp lard
2–3 tbsp paprika
2 green peppers
1 large tomato

salt
ground pepper
1 clove garlic
ground cumin
400 g/9 oz potatoes

For the pasta dough:
1 egg
80 g/9 tbsp flour
salt

Hungarian Goulash remains a delight of Hungarian gastronomy. In the local language, *gúlyás* are the cowherds who watch over the cattle on the great plain of Röna, a region of Puszta, in the eastern part of the country. Outside of Hungary, there is still confusion over the term "goulash". The *gúlyás lavasc* served in the country is a beef and paprika soup, and not the stew most Europeans associate with the term goulash. In Hungary, a stew of beef and paprika is called *pörkött*, and resembles a Burgundy-style preparation with green peppers, onions and tomatoes. It is served with gnocchi, potatoes or small soup pastas.

The small pasta that is added to this soup is prepared at home. Its Hungarian name is *csipetke*; which means "tear into little pieces". In the old days, Hungarians prepared goulash in enor-mous crocks capable of feeding a large extended family. This tradition is continued today at village festivals.

Meat consumption has changed over time in Hungary. Centuries ago, peasants raised pigs, which require relatively little feeding and space. Only large landowners possessed herds of cattle. Nowadays, land ownership has equalized and poultry farming is in expansion. In the year 896, the Huns settled in the Carpathian basin and are said to have brought with them the gray *szürkemarha* cow. Well-adapted to the climate and flora of the Puszta, where they roamed free, they all but disappeared with the advent of industrial cattle breeding. Today this species is being re-established.

In your goulash, you can substitute lamb, chicken, or even rabbit for the beef.

1. Place the beef fillet on a cutting board and slice it into small cubes with a chef's knife.

2. Peel and chop the onions. Heat the lard in a saucepan and sweat the onions for 5 minutes. Remove from the heat and stir in the paprika.

3. Chop the peppers and tomato into a brunoise. Add them and the meat to the pan. Season with salt and pepper. Lightly brown for 5 minutes over moderate heat. Peel and crush the garlic.

Goulash

4. Stir the garlic and cumin into the pot. Add water to cover everything, then cover the pot and simmer for 1½ hours. Add the diced potatoes for the final 15 minutes.

5. Prepare the pasta: in a bowl, mix the egg with the flour and salt. Knead the dough with your fingers until it loses its stickiness.

6. With thumb and index finger, tear off tiny pieces of dough over a plate. Cook the pasta in the soup for about 1 minute. When it rises to the surface, it is done. Serve the soup very hot.

Lentil Soup with

Preparation time: 30 minutes
Cooking time: 40 minutes
Difficulty: ★

Serves 4

700 g/3¹/₂ cups lentils
500 g/generous 1 lb Swiss chard
2 bunches cilantro
25 g/3¹/₂ tbsp minced garlic
350 g/³/₄ lb onions

250 ml/1 cup olive oil
35 g/2 tbsp salt
1 pinch pepper
75 g/¹/₃ cup flour
juice of 2 lemons

Whether brown or yellow, round or flat, warm or cold, lentils have been tempting palates since the dawn of time. Since Biblical times, when Esau sold Jacob his birthright for a plate of lentils, this energy-rich legume has nourished millions of hungry people. The Romans imported the small grains from Egypt by the boatload. In Lebanon, Lentil Soup with Swiss Chard and Lemon sometimes takes on religious significance. During Lent, the patriarch of the house makes it a point of honor to share this food with his guests.

In this recipe, the lentils borrow a little style from the delicately flavored Swiss chard. This plant is enjoyed as much for its green leaves, with a less pronounced taste than spinach, as for its white ribs, typically cooked in their own juice or au gratin with béchamel sauce. In this soup, the chef uses both parts of the Swiss chard. He separates the ribs from the leaf and removes the filament in the rib. He freshens up the leaves under a cold water before chopping them.

For preparing the soup, the lentils start off in cold water and will have a longer or shorter cooking time depending on their size. The chopped onions will brown in oil together with the garlic and fresh cilantro. It would be difficult to substitute the latter with coriander seed, which has a more fruity flavor akin to orange zest. If necessary you might use Vietnamese cilantro, which has a more lemony flavor.

Midway through the cooking of the lentils, you add the Swiss chard so their flavors can mingle. When they are almost done, the browned cilantro-onion-garlic mixture is added as well, and permeates the soup with its intense flavors.

1. Put the lentils to cook in a pot with 2 liters/2 quarts salted water. Wash the Swiss chard and separate the ribs from the leaves. Slice the ribs lengthwise and chop them into small sticks. Slice the leaves crosswise.

2. 15 minutes into the lentils' cooking time, add the chard leaves and ribs. Stir and cover. Cook 10 minutes over moderate heat.

3. Meanwhile, remove the stems from the cilantro. Peel and slice the garlic and onions. Mince them and the cilantro with a chef's knife.

Swiss Chard and Lemon

4. Heat the oil in a large skillet. Once it is hot, add the mixture of garlic, onions and cilantro. Season with salt and pepper. Brown for 5 minutes over high heat. Dilute the flour in some water, and stir this into the skillet.

5. While still hot, add the contents of the skillet to the lentil soup. Let it cook another 5 to 10 minutes to blend the flavors. Add the lemon juice and adjust the seasoning.

6. Serve the lentil soup nice and hot in an attractive soup tureen or in individual bowls.

North Sea

Preparation time:	45 minutes
Cooking time:	15 minutes
Difficulty:	★

Serves 4

50 g/3¹/₂ tbsp butter
2 onions, chopped
1 small celeriac, peeled and chopped
1 rib celery

1 bunch parsley
1 sprig thyme
1 bay leaf
2 cloves garlic, peeled
2 kg/4¹/₂ lb Golden Zeeland mussels
1 bunch water cress
250 ml/1 cup liquid crème fraîche
salt
pepper

Sold by the quart in a basket or punnet, mussels are being farmed in increasing numbers in France, Holland and Spain. This small shellfish, several species of which are on the decline, are popular with chefs and diners worldwide. But the greatest consumers of mussels remain the Belgians, who know how to use them well in a multitude of recipes.

Our chef Pierre Fonteyne can be found in Knokke-Heist, in the northernmost reaches of the Belgian coast. He is not far from the Netherlands or the coasts of Zeeland, famous for their production of large mussels. More than 100,000 tons are raised each year in the deep Dutch waters!

Among the mussels of the North Sea, our chef favors the Golden Zeeland, which offers a well-rounded shell, streaked with black, containing a thick, yellow flesh. If you cannot find them, replace them with common mussels, smaller but very fragrant. Choose them well, because there is the secret to our soup: good-quality mussels emit aroma and fluids when they are cooked, thus deliciously flavoring the soup, which requires very little water. Natural aroma guaranteed!

Reserve a few mussels in their shells to decorate the plates. Pierre Fonteyne leaves nothing to chance: the chopped celery, diced into tiny pieces, blends perfectly with the flavor of the mollusks in a subtle equilibrium.

By design, the parsley serves two functions in this kind of soup: the stems of parsley flavor the broth, while the leaves tint the pale mussels with green, served on a plate or in a bowl.

Whenever Brussels celebrates, people treat themselves to the pleasure of a soup made with mussels, accompanied by a Belgian beer and French fries, crisp and flavorful. Simple is usually best!

1. In a large pot, melt the butter and sweat the onions, celeriac, half the celery (chopped), the parsley stems (reserve the leaves to garnish), thyme, bay leaf and garlic.

2. Scrape and rinse the mussels. Pour them over the aromatic garnish, and add pepper to taste. Cover. Allow to cook over high heat until the mussels open completely, while stirring from time to time to mix the ingredients well.

3. As soon as all the mussels are open, remove them from the pot. Tip them into a colander and strain (reserve the juice). Shell them. Reserve several whole mussels for garnish.

Mussel Soup

4. Pour the mussel cooking juices into a pot. Add the washed water cress, parsley leaves and crème fraîche. Mix well. Bring to the boil over high heat, and remove from the heat as soon as it boils. Season to taste. Keep hot.

5. Wash the remaining piece of celery. Remove any strings and cut the pieces into small sticks 3 cm/1¼ in long, then divide in half, and then into small cubes. Blanch them briefly.

6. Cover the bottom of each soup dish with the shelled mussels and some of the celery. Top the soup with the reserved mussels, still warm.

Pennsylvania Dutch

Preparation time: 30 minutes
Cooking time: 1 hour 30 minutes
Difficulty: ★

Serves 8

1 roasting chicken
2 carrots
2 medium onions
1 rib celery
10 peppercorns
6 ears fresh corn

1 pinch saffron threads
125 g/4–5 oz tagliatelle
6 sprigs parsley
salt
$1/_4$ teaspoon black pepper

Eric Beamesderfer spent his childhood in the Pennsylvania Dutch area not far from the northeast coast. He remembers with delight the chicken pot pie his mother used to prepare for him, a chicken and corn soup to which she added large squares of noodle dough and potatoes. In the seventeenth century, German and Swiss colonists expelled from the Rhine Valley for religious reasons came to populate the Lancaster area. A dish of chicken and vegetables in a pie plate cooked under pasta counts among their culinary specialties: it is the origin of chicken pot pie. These pioneers adapted the recipe to include foods they discovered in their new home, such as corn, and put the pasta in the broth. Our chef has slightly modified his mother's recipe and added long tagliatelle rather than large pieces of pasta.

The Pennsylvania Dutch conserve to this day a traditional, agriculture-based way of life and their recipes celebrate good, natural food. Their family soups and stews have become so famous that they are now served in many restaurants. In the supermarkets, products stamped with the words *Pennsylvania Dutch*, including noodles, are synonyms of quality for American consumers.

Pennsylvania farms produce large quantities of corn. Our chef nostalgically remembers accompanying his grandfather in the hills looking for sweet corn. At the time of harvest, they used to produce enormous quantities of chicken soup with corn. Harvested for at least 5,000 years in North America, it now represents the most cultivated indigenous American plant in the United States.

In our recipe, the corn is paired with small, tender pieces of chicken. Bordering Pennsylvania, the tri-state *Delmarva* region (an abbreviation for Delaware, Maryland and Virginia) produces close to 11 million chickens per week. Sussex county has become the leading American supplier of chicken.

1. Rinse the chicken under running water. Place it in a large pot with 3 liters/3 quarts cold water.

2. Peel the carrots and onions. Cut them into small cubes, as well as the celery. Add the vegetables and peppercorns to the pot. Cover. Bring to the boil, lower the heat and let cook for at least 1 hour.

3. Take the chicken out of the broth. Bone it and cut the meat into very small cubes. Strain the broth and reserve it.

Chicken Noodle Soup

4. Take an ear of fresh corn and with a chef's knife, slice along the ear from top to bottom, to detach the kernels. Continue in the same way for the other ears.

5. Pour the chicken broth into a saucepan, add the saffron and bring to the boil. Add the tagliatelle to the hot chicken broth and allow to cook slowly over low heat.

6. Finally, add to the broth the corn with its juice, the minced parsley and the cubes of chicken. Salt and pepper. Allow to cook for 5 more minutes, then serve hot.

Roman

Preparation time: 30 minutes
Cooking time, broth: 40 minutes
Cooking time, filling: 35 minutes
Difficulty: ★

Serves 6

For the vegetable broth:
2 or 3 carrots
1 rib celery
1 large onion
2 cloves garlic
1 leek

For the soup garnish:
2 cloves garlic
$1/2$ sprig rosemary
olive oil
40 g/$1^{1}/_2$ oz fatback
salt
pepper
300 g/$1^{1}/_4$ cups canned chickpeas
200 g/7 oz peeled tomatoes
200 g/7 oz fresh tagliatelle

This exquisite chickpea soup flavored with tomatoes and rosemary originated in Latium, around Rome. It is also found in Tuscan cuisine. The Italians are not especially fond of soup, preferring to start their meals with rice or pasta. The most famous Italian soup, of course, is minestrone.

The Latin name for chickpeas, *cicer arietinum*, suggests the irregular form of the peas, which they used to compare to a ram's head. *Arietinum* in effect means "little ram". This is a highly appreciated legume all around the Mediterranean basin. The Italians only grow chickpeas in the very south of the country. They do not consume many of them, but they do know how to prepare them in a wide variety of ways: in salads with olive oil, in stews and in soups. In Lombardy and Piedmont, *pasta e cecci* is a dish that mixes pasta and chickpeas. They are also served puréed with fried bacon, and chickpea flour is the base of *farinata*, a flat bread prepared in Ligurie.

Additionally, the inhabitants of Palermo make fritters with this legume. If dried, they must be soaked anywhere from eight hours to overnight to rehydrate, then they need a full three hours to cook. It is for this reason, to save time, that our chef recommends choosing canned chickpeas that have already been cooked.

Gustavo Andreoli pairs the peas with pasta in order to embellish the soup. Of course, you can make fresh pasta yourself and then cut it into 5 cm (2 inch) squares. But there is no reason not to use dry packaged pasta, either in squares or maybe in the form of letters.

Rich and savory thanks to the tomatoes, this soup would be disappointing without the flavor of rosemary to support it. In Italy, this plant also flavors chicken, lamb and veal. The stems of rosemary hold up well when dried.

1. Combine the vegetables for the broth in a pot, cover with water and cook for 40 minutes. Meanwhile, cut the fatback into long, thin strips, and then into tiny cubes.

2. Peel the garlic, and slice it finely. Break the rosemary into three small pieces. Heat 50 ml/$3^{1}/_2$ tbsp olive oil in a pan, and fry the fatback, garlic, rosemary, salt and pepper for 4 to 5 minutes.

3. Crush the peeled tomatoes. Stir them into the pot with the garlic, rosemary and browned fat. Cook another 3 to 4 minutes to flavor the preparation.

Chickpea Soup

4. *Drain the chickpeas. Add them to the pot of tomato sauce. Mix well.*

5. *Strain the vegetable broth and remove the vegetables. Pour 500 ml/2 cups of it into the tomatoes and chickpeas. Allow the soup to simmer for around 20 minutes.*

6. *Cut the pasta into small squares and pour them into the soup. Allow to cook another 5 or 6 minutes. Serve hot.*

Kornati Island

Preparation time: 40 minutes
Cooking time: 20 minutes
Difficulty: ★

Serves 6

1 carrot
1 onion
1 potato
2 cloves garlic
1 sea bream
1 hog fish

1 celery leaf
white peppercorns
olive oil
1 bay leaf
sea salt
1 tbsp tomato paste
100 ml/7 tbsp white wine
1 sprig parsley
1 lemon

A national park located off the coast of Croatia facing Zadar, the Kornati archipelago consists of a hundred islands. Most of the small Adriatic islands remain completely wild. Boaters also appreciate the Kornati Islands because there is an abundance of charming coves.

The few inhabited islands are so rocky that the activity revolves entirely around fishing. It is a family matter, carried out during the day on small boats with rather flat bottoms, 8 or 9 meters (25 to 30 feet) in length. Therefore, the fishermen of the Kornati Islands nuanced this succulent soup which blends the fine flesh of local fish, tomatoes, onions and potatoes with a sauce flavored with eminent Mediterranean accents.

The waters surrounding the Kornati Islands are packed with all sorts of fish, such as sea bream, hog fish, John Dory, monkfish, redfish, catfish, red mullet, and we shouldn't forget the blue fish, such as mackerel and sardines. On the other hand, in the depths of the ocean, the rocky bottoms do not provide very favorable habitats for the survival of flat fish such as sole or Greenland halibut.

The islanders of Kornati consume fish most often in the form of soups so substantial that they often constitute the main dish, or simply grilled over a fire of vine shoots or olive wood. On the Croatian coasts, the people just as often serve other fish soups such as *brodetto* which is a thin broth, and also *gregada*, which more resembles a stew.

Our chef's soup, a distant cousin of the *bouillabaisse* from Marseilles, reminds us just how highly the fishermen of the various Mediterranean countries valued the range of fresh fish they have brought in on their boats through the centuries.

1. Peel the carrot, onion and potato then slice them finely. Peel and mince the garlic. With a large, sharp knife, cut the sea bream and hog fish into 3 large pieces.

2. Put the fish pieces in a large pot. Cover with water. Add the celery, carrot, onion, potato, peppercorns, a splash of olive oil, bay leaf and sea salt. Cook 15 minutes over moderate heat.

3. When they are well cooked, take the fish out of the pot using a skimmer. Set aside on a plate. Collect all the vegetables, keeping them separate from the fish, and set aside the pot of stock.

Fish Soup

4. Take each piece of fish and carefully remove the fat and bones.

5. Pour the vegetables into a food processor. Blend to form a pale orange purée. Put the fish back in the stock. Lastly, stir in the vegetable purée.

6. Add the tomato paste, white wine, garlic and a dash of olive oil. Bring to the boil. Sprinkle with chopped parsley and squeeze in some lemon juice. Serve immediately.

Rock Fish Soup

Preparation time: 45 minutes
Cooking time: 40 minutes
Difficulty: ★

Serves 4

Soup:
2 leeks
2 onions
2 tomatoes
1 sprig fennel
1 clove garlic
1 red pepper
1 bay leaf
3 sprigs flat-leaf parsley
1 piece orange zest

1 kg/2¼ lb rock fish (conger eel, gurnard, weever, rainbow wrasse, etc.)
salt, pepper
1 pinch saffron
1 tbsp olive oil
300 g/11 oz ditalini pasta (optional)

For the rouille:
2 cloves garlic
2 Spanish chili peppers
1 slice bread without crust
2 tbsp olive oil
200 ml/generous ¾ cup fish bouillon

For the croutons:
1 stale baguette
1 clove garlic

Soups have been keeping people warm on a daily basis for centuries. But ordinary soup is transformed into a truly celebratory dish when you let the most succulent rock fish simmer in it: red gurnard (called *galinettes* in the south of France), conger eel, rainbow wrasse and gurnard delicately mix together in a very flavorful broth.

Caught in large, fine-meshed nets, rock fish delight seasonal fishermen of the French Riviera, from Carry-le-Rouet to the Italian border. None of these fish need to be gutted. A quick rinse under cold water suffices.

Next, stew the aromatic garnish. For best success, this soup must be made in the following order: first are leeks and onions well stewed in olive oil to tone down the iodized taste of the fish. Then follow the crushed bay leaf, crushed tomatoes, pepper, a whole sprig of flat-leaf parsley, minced garlic, bulb

or leaf fennel and orange zest. When this aromatic mix is fully cooked down, add cold water, then the fish.

To give this recipe its characteristic beautiful yellow color, it needs a spice as brilliant as gold: saffron. From the earliest times, this was a commercial high flier. Today it is still the most expensive spice in the world. Highly prized by the Asians, saffron "makes chicken sing, gilds seafood, fish and shellfish, and enlivens red meat".

Perfect as a starter, this fish soup becomes satisfying enough for a complete meal when the tiny *ditalini* pasta, shaped like miniature cylinders, is cooked for three minutes in the broth. Give the dish an added touch with little croutons rubbed with garlic and the peppered rouille, a sauce with the consistency of mayonnaise that is prepared much the same way.

1. Slice the leek, onions, tomatoes, fennel, garlic and pepper. In a pot, brown the leeks and onions in 1 tbsp oil, add the tomatoes, pepper and crushed bay leaf. Stew lightly for 5 minutes until the vegetables soften.

2. Pour on 1 tbsp water to steam the tomatoes and add 3 sprigs of flat-leaf parsley. After 1 minute of cooking, add the minced garlic, fennel and orange zest. Stew for 10 minutes.

3. Tip the fish into the stewed vegetables. Sprinkle with salt, pepper and saffron. Pour in 2 liters/2 quarts water for each 1 kg/2 lb of fish. Boil for 20 minutes over medium heat. Adjust the seasoning.

with a Light Rouille

4. Strain the broth. Crush the fish in the bottom of the sieve to extract all the juices. If the soup is too thin, add a little flour mixed with 1 tbsp olive oil. Keep warm.

5. For the rouille sauce, crush the garlic and red chili peppers in a bowl. Add the crust-less bread, soaked in water with the excess pressed out. Stiffen the sauce like a mayonnaise with 2 tbsp olive oil. Thin down with some of the fish broth.

6. Slice the stale baguette on the diagonal. Quickly fry, grill or broil the slices. Rub the croutons with garlic. Serve the soup accompanied by the rouille and the croutons.

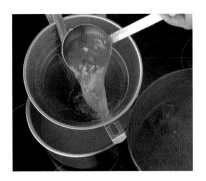

Maruzzara-Style

Preparation time: 20 minutes
Cooking time: 30 minutes
Difficulty: ★

Serves 4

2 carrots
2 onions
1 stem celery
200 ml/generous ³/₄ cup olive oil
2 garlic cloves

100 g/3¹/₂ oz fat from Parma ham
or from Italian prosciutto
2 pepper birds (also called Thai chile)
600 g/1¹/₄ lb small octopus
500 g/2 cups tomato purée
500 g/2³/₄ cups cooked red beans
salt
pepper
flat-leaf parsley to decorate

Each more excellent than the last, Italian specialties are not limited only to pasta, risotto, gelato and pizza. Among the old recipes that are still consumed today throughout Italy are polenta, copied from the porridge eaten by the famous legionnaires of Julius Caesar, and Maruzzara-Style Soup.

In the past, cooks have used snails in this sauce with red beans and prosciutto. Today, octopi replace the snails in a more modern presentation.

It should be remembered that the smaller the octopus, the tenderer the flesh will be. The whole small octopus will be put in the soup. Only the tentacle ends of a large octopus, on the other hand, should be left in the soup.

Red beans or white beans go well with this delicious mollusk. Soaked for twelve hours in cold water, these dried beans can be cooked a day ahead of time in three liters or quarts of salted water. After two hours of cooking, strain them and leave in the refrigerator until the next day.

Bacon or fatback can be used instead of the Parma ham or Italian prosciutto. Only the fat of that illustrious Italian cooked pork with the local name *Prosciutto di Parma* is used here, which will not actually be eaten. But it will bring its exceptional flavor to the soup and its tenderness to the red beans and octopus pieces. There are other varieties of cured Italian ham of excellent quality, such as San Daniele, which can also be used to flavor the soup.

For a complete and harmonious meal, prepare some spaghetti with garlic and pesto as an entrée.

1. Peel the carrots and onions. Chop the carrots, onions and celery into very fine, even dice.

2. Pour the olive oil into a large pot, covering the bottom. Add the garlic, peeled and crushed, the prosciutto fat and pepper birds. Allow to brown, then remove from the heat.

3. Cut the octopuses into pieces of about 2 cm/³/₄ in. Add them to the pot.

Octopus Soup

4. Return the pot to the heat. Brown for 5 or 6 minutes over high heat. Remove the cooking fat.

5. Add to the pot the diced vegetables and the tomato purée. Tip in the red beans, then season with salt and pepper. Add water to cover. Simmer for 10 minutes, uncovered, over low heat.

6. Mince the parsley and sprinkle over the soup. Serve hot in a soup tureen or individual bowls.

Marmitako

Preparation time: 1 hour
Cooking time: 1 hour 30 minutes
Difficulty: ★★

Serves 4

¹/₂ green bell pepper
¹/₂ white onion
2 tbsp olive oil
3 small pepper birds (Thai chile)
1.5 kg/3¹/₄ lb potatoes
7 dried red chorizero peppers

200 g/7 oz cherry tomatoes
salt
pepper
1 liter/1 quart fish stock
600 g/1¹/₄ lb fresh tuna steaks

In Spain as elsewhere, the summer brings celebrations and festivities. But in Laredo, a very special celebration takes place on August 16. Early in the morning, the small swimming station situated on the Gulf of Gascoigne sees chefs, villagers and myriad cauldrons disembark at its port. The competition for the best Marmitako begins, and the pots receive into their depths everything that seems good to eat.

Rufino Manjarrés here presents a Marmitako with a tuna base. However, poultry, beef, pork or all three are sometimes combined in its making. Potatoes and tomatoes always appear in the original base. Large winter potatoes are chosen, peeled and then cut into large pieces which withstand long simmering without falling apart. Sometimes, small new potatoes can be used: they are cooked for five minutes, stirred often, then taken out of the pot.

In Spain, the term *pimiento* describes the sweet pepper as well as the spicy peppers. The *chorizero* (or choricero) peppers, with a red-brown color, are much appreciated in Spain. After a meticulous harvest, they are dried in the sun, draped in long garlands on balconies. Rehydrated and then split, the *chorizero* is then carefully scraped to extract the pulp, an indispensable element of the Marmitako. To make the task easier, well-stocked grocery stores offer bottles of *carne de pimiento chorizero* (chorizero pepper flesh), containing the pulp of the pepper ready to use.

Marmitako is never stirred. When Rufino Manjarrés adds the fish stock, he suggests lightly moving the pot over the stovetop to detach any particles that have settled on the bottom. Although categorized as a soup, the Marmitako does not have to be liquid in the final presentation.

1. Finely mince the green pepper and onion. Brown 2 minutes over low heat in the olive oil, with the pepper birds. Set aside.

2. Peel the potatoes. Cut them into large pieces. Add to the onion and pepper mix. Cook for 5 minutes, stirring often. Soak the dried red peppers for 5 minutes in a bowl of hot water.

3. Drain the rehydrated pepper pulp. Purée the cherry tomatoes. Stir together the pepper pulp and puréed tomatoes. Tip this mix into the potatoes. Add salt and pepper. Cook for 3 minutes over low heat while stirring.

Tuna Soup

4. Heat the fish stock. Pour it over the potatoes. Simmer for 15 minutes over low heat.

5. Slice each tuna steak horizontally to produce two slices, then dice into 2 cm/ ³/₄ in cubes.

6. Add the cubes of tuna to the soup pot. Adjust the seasoning. Cook uncovered for 1 hour over very low heat. Remove from the heat as soon as the potatoes are cooked. Serve hot.

Bride and

Preparation time: 20 minutes
Cooking time: 2 hours 20 minutes
Difficulty: ★★

Serves 6

500 g/generous 1 lb neck of lamb, in slices
1 small onion
1 small carrot
100 g/6 tbsp strained yogurt
1/2 medium lemon
50 g/1/3 cup flour

1 egg
salt
ground pepper
25 g/11/2 tbsp butter
1/2 tsp paprika

Wedding ceremonies in Turkey are exceptionally splendid, and can last up to five days. On the third day, called henna night, a large meal brings together many guests after the bride has her hands decorated with henna. Traditionally, this banquet includes Bride and Groom Soup, called *düğün çorbası* in Turkish, roast lamb, rice *pilav* and *zerde*, a dessert made with sugared rice and milk covered with a saffron sauce. The banquet also makes use of the less noble pieces of lamb such as neck, though the leg and shoulder are offered barbecued.

Lamb is the principal meat consumed in Turkey. A number of regions are favorable for raising sheep. Lamb from Thrace, in European Turkey, is particularly appreciated, as well as those raised between Balikesir and Bandirma, south of the Marmara Sea, in the *kivircik* or "Black Sea Cowlick", or even lamb of Karaman, coming from central Anatolia. Lamb is prepared

everywhere in the form of roast leg, *döner kebab* (slices of meat piled up and grilled on a vertical spit, by now familiar to people outside of Turkey) and *cice-kebab* (skewers).

It is no surprise that the soup should be made with yogurt, since the Turks invented this dairy product in the Middle Ages. A mix of boiled cow's and sheep's milk is heated to 25°C/77°F and a leaven of leftover yogurt is added. Then it is left to rest for a few hours in a hot place. The yogurt obtained in this way accompanies fried eggplant and zucchini, *pilav* rice, stuffed vegetables or even ravioli. Thinned with water and sprinkled with mint, it becomes a refreshing drink called *ayran*. Turkish yogurt can be prepared lightly creamy or strained. However, our chef feels that a good Turkish yogurt should be thick enough to be cut with a knife.

1. Place the neck of lamb slices in a pot of cold water. Bring to the boil and cook until the first bubbles rise. Peel the onion and carrot.

2. Drain the lamb. Place it in a pot of hot water. Add the onion and carrot. Cook covered for at least 2 hours.

3. Drain the contents of the pot (reserve the juice and let the meat cool). Take a slice of lamb in your hand. Break the meat apart, then shred it. Repeat with the other slices.

Groom Soup

4. Pour the strained yogurt into a bowl. Squeeze the juice of half a lemon into the bowl. Sprinkle with flour, then break the egg in the center. Whisk it all together.

5. Thin the preparation with a little of the stock from cooking the meat. Whisk into a homogenous cream. Pour this mix into the pot of stock placed over low heat. Whisk vigorously for 5 minutes until the cream thickens. Salt and pepper.

6. Melt the butter, add the paprika and brown 2 to 3 minutes while stirring. Add the meat to the soup and stir it in. Add 1 tbsp of the paprika butter and whisk off of the heat. Pour the soup into bowls and decorate with drizzles of paprika butter.

Soup of

Preparation time: 30 minutes
Cooking time: 40 minutes
Difficulty: ★

Serves 6

2 green bell peppers
2 red bell peppers
16 green asparagus
salt
4 tomatoes
12 slices bread

1 head garlic
olive oil
2 liters/2 quarts chicken broth
pepper
4 or 5 sprigs flat-leaf parsley

In spring, the inhabitants of Malaga make a delicious meal of assorted vegetables in stock cheerfully called "Soup of Seven Palms", *sopa de siete ramales*. Its name evokes Holy Week and the celebration of Palm Sunday, a week before Easter.

Red and green bell peppers, tomatoes, garlic and asparagus constitute the small vegetables of this soup. If available, Xavier Valero recommends using wild asparagus. With a color that fluctuates between green and mauve, wild asparagus has a thin stalk and a strong, characteristic flavor that is much appreciated by the Spaniards.

More commonly sold in markets, cultivated green asparagus replaces the wild asparagus in our recipe. In Spain, green asparagus is the pride of the farmers of Navarre, who harvest it from April to June. Before peeling, be sure to cut off the end of each stalk, which is hard and fibrous. After poaching the

asparagus, plunge it into a bowl of ice water to conserve its bright green color. As for the tomatoes, blanch them, then cut them into quarters. Pass the blade of a small knife between the flesh and the seeds to eliminate them. You will obtain "petals", as our chef likes to say.

All the ingredients will be immersed in chicken stock and poached. A bouillon cube can be used instead for speed, but a completely homemade stock will taste far better: brown the crushed carcass of a chicken with an aromatic garnish (onion, cloves, carrots, bay leaves, celery or leeks) and add water. Simmer for about 1 hour 30 minutes and then strain.

To serve, the vegetables will be arranged on small plates, and the garlic croutons and the broth presented separately. Alternatively, pour it all into a large bowl or deep dishes.

1. Place the peppers on a baking sheet covered with a sheet of aluminum foil and grill for 10 minutes under the broiler. Then peel them with a small knife and cut into fine strips.

2. Rinse and dry the asparagus. Peel, starting below the tip and continuing to the end of the stem. Then poach for 5 minutes in salted, boiling water.

3. Dip the tomatoes into a bowl of boiling water. When the skin lifts, take them out and put them in a bowl of ice water. Take the tomatoes in your hand and remove the skin with the tip of a knife. Then cut them into petals.

Seven Palms

4. Slice the bread into small pieces. Cover with a few drizzles of olive oil. Put them on a baking sheet and toast under the preheated grill or broiler. Then rub each slice with a clove of peeled garlic.

5. Bring the chicken broth to the boil. Put in the asparagus, tomatoes, red and green peppers. Salt and pepper. Poach the vegetables for 5 minutes. Remove from the broth with a skimmer.

6. Brown slivers of garlic in a pan of very hot oil. When it bubbles, sprinkle with minced parsley. Serve the broth in small soup dishes and the vegetables on a plate with the croutons. Drizzle with the garlic and parsley oil.

Baleares

Preparation time: 30 minutes
Cooking time: 1 hour 35 minutes
Difficulty: ★

Serves 4

4 carrots
2 turnips
2 salsify roots (oyster plants)
1 head lettuce
2 sprigs thyme
2 sprigs rosemary

2 sprigs marjoram
250 g/1¾ cups fresh peas
olive oil
4 pinches salt
1 pinch pepper
2 pinches sugar
1 liter/1 quart fish stock
8 thin slices baguette

For chef Xavier Valero, there is no Spanish cuisine without soup. This particular one features on the menu of his restaurant in Neuilly, *San Valero*, which figures among the best establishments specializing in Spanish gastronomy. From his frequent trips to the Iberian Peninsula, Mr. Valero brings back new ideas, discoveries of traditional and unpublished recipes and unexpected, original combinations to please the palates of all who taste them.

Soups of herbs are part of the daily fare in Spain, sometimes embellished with fish and shellfish such as lobster, or various meats; sometimes enriched with vegetables such as cabbage and tomatoes. In the Balearics, soup is mixed with the aromatic tips of fresh marjoram leaves. They give the broth unequalled flavor, making it worth savoring both hot and cold.

The inhabitants of the Balearics always attribute culinary, therapeutic and even magical importance to the many plants of their environment. Among these, marjoram has fine stems covered with small, bright green leaves. Its odor is reminiscent of mint, basil and lemongrass. Commonly used in Mediterranean cuisine, it also flavors lamb, game filled with vegetables, fish and eggs.

To refine this very simple and delicious soup, go ahead and play up the sobriety using a simple lettuce. In place of classic-sized turnips, you can choose to use small turnips, with fine flesh and a more refined taste.

The chef recommends accompanying this herb soup with a white wine from Galice *Ribeiro* or *Rias Beixas*.

1. Peel and chop the carrots, turnips and salsify.

2. Wash the lettuce and cut it into strips.

3. Place the carrots, turnips, salsify and lettuce in a soup pot.

Herb Soup

4. Add the thyme, rosemary, marjoram leaves and then the peas. Cover with water. Add 2 tbsp olive oil, salt, pepper and sugar. Bring to the boil. Lower the heat and let the liquid evaporate for 1 hour; hardly any water should be left.

5. Add the fish stock to the soup. Simmer for 25 to 30 minutes.

6. In a pan, brown the baguette slices in oil. Arrange them in the bottom of deep dishes, then pour in the soup. Add a drizzle of olive oil and serve at once.

Moroccan

Preparation time: 30 minutes
Cooking time: 2 hours 5 minutes
Soaking time: overnight
Difficulty: ★

Serves 4

90 g/7 tbsp chickpeas
60 g/5 tbsp lentils
250 g/9 oz shoulder of lamb, cubed
1 large onion
80 g/⅓ cup unsalted butter
40 g/2½ tbsp salted butter
1 tbsp peanut oil

½ tsp ground cinnamon
½ tsp ground ginger
1 pinch saffron threads
red food coloring powder
salt
ground black pepper
4 sprigs celery leaves
500 g/generous 1 lb tomatoes
1 tbsp flour
20 sprigs parsley
20 sprigs cilantro
250 g/9 oz dried dates
200 g/7 oz dried figs
2 lemons

Harira, or "village soup", is one of the Moroccan national foods and Moslems' favorite dish during Ramadan. This comforting and satisfying meal is very welcome every night, following the fast from sunrise to sunset.

Everyone squeezes a little lemon juice into their soup, which is accompanied by dates, dried figs and sometimes the braided pasta called *chbakkia*. After the *harira*, the hosts serve coffee, tea and little *mlaoui* crêpes. After marriage celebrations, which go on for days, the guests enjoy it for breakfast. In some regions, the soup is thickened with eggs.

In order to make this soup, thrifty chefs take care to collect all the scraps of lamb that cannot be used in other dishes. The best Moroccan lamb comes from the Atlas Mountains. The most widespread breed is the Shawiya sheep, or *serdi*. Their white heads are partially covered in black wool. During the Festival of the Sacrifice, every bit of the animal is of value. The leg and

shoulder are used in barbeques and couscous, the neck is cooked in tajines, the head is steamed, and the tripe and giblets are used in stews.

In this soup, our chef uses a typical and unique Moroccan salted butter called *smen*. This sheep's milk butter is melted, clarified, then salted. After two or three weeks, it ferments and is poured into jars. It can keep for up to ten years! Since it is seldom found in our stores, it can be replaced with ordinary salted butter.

The variations on this soup are truly countless. According to your taste, you can add broad beans in place of the chickpeas, beef in place of the lamb, *kefta* (ground meat) meatballs, vermicelli, rice or even large-grain couscous for *m'hamsa*. You can use pre-soaked canned chickpeas. In spite of all the possibilities, our chef vows that his mother's recipe will be the best of all.

1. Soak the chickpeas overnight. The day of the meal, put them into a pot with the lentils, meat, chopped onion, butters, oil, cinnamon, ginger, saffron, red coloring and chopped celery. Season with salt and pepper.

2. Add 3 liters/3 quarts cold water. Mix everything well. Cook, covered, for 1 hour to 1 hour 15 minutes.

3. Blanch the tomatoes. Remove the seeds and crush the flesh. When the chickpeas and lentils are tender, add the crushed tomatoes to the pot. Continue to cook, covered, for 20 minutes.

Harira

4. Place the flour in a bowl. Pour in some water and whisk to produce a smooth mixture. Thin with a little of the hot broth.

5. Pour this mixture little by little into the soup, whisking vigorously all the time. Continue to cook for another 15 minutes.

6. Sprinkle the soup with minced parsley and cilantro. Cook another 15 minutes, covered. Serve the harira in a pretty soup bowl, accompanied by dates, dried figs and lemon quarters.

Chilled

Preparation time: 20 minutes
Chilling time: 20 minutes
Difficulty: ★

Serves 4

750 g/1³/₄ lb strawberries
1 green bell pepper
1 red bell pepper
1 onion
2 cloves garlic
1 tsp salt

1 tsp pepper
30 g/¹/₄ cup powdered sugar
200 ml/generous ³/₄ cup olive oil
100 ml/7 tbsp sherry vinegar

For the decoration (optional):
diced red pepper
diced green pepper
croutons

Colorful, fresh and full of vitamins, this Chilled Strawberry Soup by José Luis Tarín Fernández showcases the creativity of Hispanic cuisine. Inspired by the famous *gazpacho* from Andalusia, the subtlety of tomatoes will be replaced by the sweetness of strawberries. This soup is so original that you cannot substitute other fruits for the strawberries. Only true fans of tartness would risk adding a hint of raspberries.

To make sure the soup is sweet, look for nice summer strawberries rich in flavor and with a firm texture. In the market, choose large, ripe fruits without spots. With such delicate flesh, strawberries do not appreciate being handled: a brief pass under running water, followed by a gentle draining will suit them perfectly.

A safe bet for Spanish cuisine, peppers are used in all sauces. The acidic green peppers and the sweeter red peppers should have a rich color and a brilliant, smooth skin when they are fresh. The fine white membranes found inside and the tiny seeds must be removed as they are not very digestible.

The strong sweetness of the flesh of the red pepper can overwhelm that of the strawberries. Thus it is no accident that the chef suggests lightly acidifying the soup with sherry vinegar. A famous wine from Andalusia, *Jerez* or sherry has been made since the twelfth or thirteenth century in the region of Jerez de la Frontera, close to Cadiz. Sherry gives vinegar a full-bodied aroma. However, its thick texture is difficult to dissolve: pour it into the soup a little at a time to obtain a perfect blend. If you cannot find such vinegar, add a few dashes of balsamic vinegar instead.

Puréed, emulsified and then strained, the strawberry soup is placed in the refrigerator to cool for twenty minutes, before being served with small croutons.

1. Hull the strawberries; lightly pull on the stem of the fruit without touching the flesh. Rinse the strawberries quickly under cold water. Let them drain in a strainer, then cut into quarters.

2. Wipe the peppers. Cut them in two lengthwise. Remove the white membrane inside and deseed. Cut them in four, then into 3 cm/1¹/₄ in pieces. Do the same with the onion. Cut the peeled garlic cloves in two.

3. Tip the peppers, onion, garlic and strawberries into a food processor. Add salt, pepper, sugar. Start by blending gently for 2 to 3 minutes to produce a thick, even mixture.

Strawberry Soup

4. Open the bowl of the mixer. Pour half the olive oil into the preparation. Mix vigorously then add the rest of the olive oil. Mix again for 2 to 3 minutes until it looks emulsified.

5. Place a sieve over a large bowl. Pour the soup through a little at a time to filter it, pressing with the back of a ladle to get the most out of the pulp.

6. Pour in the sherry vinegar. Stir to incorporate it into the soup. Adjust the seasoning. Refrigerate for 20 minutes. Serve cool but not frozen, decorated with diced peppers and accompanied by croutons.

Cold

Preparation time: 30 minutes
Cooking time: 10 minutes
Difficulty: ★

Serves 4

100 g white grapes
350 ml/1¹/₂ cups extra virgin olive oil
350 g/generous 2¹/₃ cups blanched almonds

¹/₂ stale baguette
1 clove garlic
5 tbsp sherry vinegar
salt
pepper
4 chive blades

It is a habit of the Spanish to "dress up" their everyday bowls of soup with diverse and varied garnishes. Inescapable, they serve as a first course or a main dish for the nightly meal. Always simple and flavorful, they are most often made with fresh vegetables. The succulent almond soup presented here, a specialty of the city of Malaga, is an exception. Deceptively simple, it calls for quality ingredients, which are the object of close attention.

The almonds, first of all, should be chosen dried and not fresh. It is in January that the white flowers of almond trees bloom. Most of the almonds in Spain come from the plantations in the country. These extend, in fact, from Tarragon to Valencia and as far as Malaga, and they are also found near Granada and Almeria, and as far as the Canaries. The huge number of

almond varieties show an incredible range of forms, from elongated to heart-shaped. A fruit for everything, almonds are cracked as an aperitif or eaten to dull the appetite or help ease nausea. They are integrated into a wealth of cakes, confections and various desserts. They used to be a source of essential protein in the diet, and keep in mind that although almonds contain 54% fat, they are rich in iron, calcium, phosphorus and vitamin B. The olive oil should be slightly acidic.

To obtain a smoother preparation, we recommend straining this soup. Traditionally, it is served with bread, individual grapes and thin wedges of melon. The grapes in the decoration can be replaced with green melon from Spain. To give this rustic soup a more sophisticated presentation, the chef prefers to serve it in attractive glasses with stems.

1. Remove the grapes from the bunch. Using a knife, carefully peel them. Cut them in half, then deseed with the tip of the blade.

2. Heat 50 ml/3¹/₂ tbsp olive oil. Fry the blanched almonds in the oil until nicely browned.

3. Remove the crust from the stale baguette, cut it into sticks, then cut each stick into 3 cm/1¹/₄ in cubes.

Malaga Soup

4. Peel and trim the garlic. Run the almonds and the garlic through a food processor.

5. Add the diced bread to the mixer. Mix while gradually incorporating the vinegar, and then 300 ml/1¼ cups olive oil. When the blend is smooth and even, add 1 liter/1 quart water. Salt and pepper.

6. Pour the almond soup into cups or wide glasses with stems. Decorate with grapes and chopped chives.

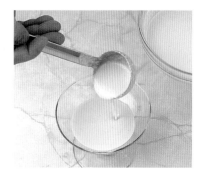

Japanese

Preparation time: 25 minutes
Cooking time: 35 minutes
Difficulty: ★★

Serves 4

1 lobster
1 duck breast

For the dashi bouillon:
2 strips konbu algae
30 g/1 oz dried bonito tuna flakes
4 large oyster mushrooms
12 gingko biloba nuts

For the acompaniment:
soy sauce
sake
1 lime

Using a familiar stock called *dashi*, made from dried bonito tuna flakes, our chef has composed a more elaborate recipe that showcases the superb lobster. Curiously, this autumn dish was originally created to feature the *matsutaké* mushroom, similar to porcini. We have replaced it in this instance with oyster mushrooms.

The Japanese lobster soup is served in a small, very special container that resembles a tea kettle, designed under the name *do bin*. In the tea houses of Kyoto, an entire ceremony is linked to the use of the *do bin*. The small bowl serving as the lid is turned over and filled with a little of the stock from the "tea kettle". With their chopsticks, the guests search out the ingredients in the *do bin* and quickly soak them in the stock before tasting.

The best Japanese lobsters come from the Gulf of Isé, south of Nagoya. They are caught in the wild and also raised commer-

cially. Rather small, they offer a beautifully bright red shell. However, in Japan as in Europe, lobster remains a luxury product. It is prepared roasted, boiled, steamed or cut into fine strips and served raw in the form of *sashimi*.

Like the mushrooms, the gingko biloba nuts are a typical product of the autumn in Japan. Surrounded by a shell, they are dried for three days under the sun, shelled, rinsed and placed to dry another three days before being fit to eat. Typically, chefs grill them like chestnuts.

Duck meat is consumed in Japan primarily due to the influence of Chinese cuisine. But far fewer ducks are raised to be eaten than chickens. In fact, the Japanese primarily raise them as an ornamental animal. However, they particularly like the wild duck dish that they call *kamo*.

1. Insert the end of a knife into the junction between the head and shell of the lobster. Cut to remove the head. Split the ventral side of the lobster. Cut the tail into small sections.

2. Slice the duck breast. Bring a pot of water to the boil. When it begins to boil, blanch 4 strips of the breast. Cool immediately over ice.

3. To make the dashi bouillon, put the konbu in a pot of cold water and heat 15 minutes. Just before it reaches the boil, remove the konbu and replace it with the bonito flakes. Lower the heat and cook until they fall to the bottom. Then strain the stock.

Lobster Soup

4. In a small saucepan, bring the bonito stock to the boil. Put in the pieces of lobster to poach for around 15 minutes.

5. Shell the lobster pieces and cut the meat. Tear the oyster mushrooms into 4 or 5 strips each.

6. Using chopsticks, arrange in each container 4 strips of mushroom, 2 to 3 pieces of lobster, 3 gingko biloba nuts and 1 strip of duck. Pour over a little stock. Accompany with soy sauce, sake and lime quarters.

Frothy

Preparation time: 30 minutes
Cooking time: 1 hour 15 minutes
Soaking time: overnight
Difficulty: ★

Serves 4

300 g/1¹/₂ cups yellow split peas
1 onion
300 g/11 oz smoked bacon
20 g/1¹/₂ tbsp butter
500 ml/2 cups poultry stock
1 bouquet garni
100 g/3¹/₂ oz celeriac

1 carrot
1 large turnip
2 parsnips
1 bay leaf
300 g/11 oz Danish pork sausage
¹/₂ bunch chervil
¹/₂ bunch marjoram
300 ml/1¹/₄ cups heavy cream
100 ml/7 tbsp cumin schnapps
salt
pepper
300 g/2 cups fresh peas
100 ml/7 tbsp milk

Pea soup is one of the most traditional Danish dishes. Its consistency can be rather light, as in the recipe presented here, or much thicker. In the winter version, the peas are cooked for a long time with small pieces of meat until the whole reaches the consistency of porridge.

Danish split peas are yellow. Today, they are considered inexpensive provincial food, and many young people scorn them in favor of other foods deemed more modern and attractive. These peas must soak overnight in cold water before they are cooked.

The Danish are such fans of pork products that they could not do without the sausages in their purée of peas. One well-known sausage is called *medisterpølse*. Either white or grey and rather peppery, it can be very long or tied at regular intervals. There is

also a smoked version. This sausage must be boiled before being pan-fried.

In Denmark, the cumin brandy which flavors herb mousse is one of many strong spirits given the slang name *snaps*. It is also called *aquavit*, derived directly from the Latin expression *aqua vitae* ("water of life"). The Danes like to drink it in a quick, single gulp at the bar. It consists of a rather strong alcohol made from potatoes and distilled grains, flavored with cumin or with other spices such as fennel, aniseed and coriander. Cumin *snaps* accompanies the majority of old Danish dishes that were devised at a time when the use of wine was unconventional, or even unknown. In our recipe, the alcohol must be placed in the freezer before use, allowing it to integrate especially well into the very cold whipped cream.

1. The day before, set the split peas to soak. Peel and chop the onion. Cut the smoked bacon into pieces. Brown half of them in the butter in a large pot for 10 minutes (set aside the other half). Add the chopped onions. Continue to cook 5 minutes.

2. Pour in the poultry stock, split peas, green peas and bouquet garni. Simmer for at least 1 hour, covered.

3. During this time, peel the celeriac, carrot, turnip and parsnip. Dice them. In a pot of water, cook the sausage with the bay leaf for 20 minutes. Brown the rest of the bacon 5 minutes in a pan, and add the sausage, cut into pieces.

Danish Pea Soup

4. Next pour the carrot, celeriac, turnip and parsnip dice into the pan with the sausage and bacon. Cook 10 minutes while stirring, so that the vegetables cook and brown a little in the butter.

5. To make the herb mousse, chop the chervil and marjoram very finely. Whip the cream. Fold the herbs into the whipped cream, then the brandy. Season with salt and pepper and blend very delicately, using a spatula.

6. Drain the cooked peas and pour into a blender or food processor. Add the milk and purée, then briefly reheat. Pour into a pretty dish. Arrange the browned vegetables and pieces of sausage in the center. Garnish with a dollop of the herb mousse.

Savoyard

Preparation time: 20 minutes
Cooking time: 1 hour
Difficulty: ★

Serves 4

2 leeks
1 turnip
1 rib celery
3 potatoes
salt
pepper

500 ml/2 cups milk
50 g/3¹/₂ tbsp butter
¹/₂ baguette for the croutons
100 g/scant 1 cup grated Gruyère cheese

Savoyard Soup is a more sophisticated version of a rustic country soup. Here, the vegetables cook for a very long time in boiling salt water, until they absorb all the cooking water. This method serves to rehydrate the vegetables and to rebuild their moisture level. The Savoyards love soup very peppery and commonly thin it with a generous amount of milk. Then they pass the cooked vegetables and milk through a vegetable mill on medium setting.

Those who enjoy a smooth soup will appreciate the full value of Savoyard Soup. Those who prefer it with a coarser texture, as in Savoy, can use their judgment to augment the soup with some remaining cooked vegetables. It can also be thickened with an egg yolk, blended first into a large spoonful of liquid crème fraîche.

With a simple, robust charm, this soup offers a number of possibilities to satisfy everyone's taste. Each guest has the pleasure of breaking an egg into his or her plate of hot soup. To perfect its authentic taste, you can add some leeks and celeriac in place of the turnips. Traditionally used in the past in place of turnips, celeriac is an ideal ingredient for soups. While the turnip is mild to the palate, celeriac sharpens the taste of the soup with a powerful and strong flavor.

Served in individual bowls or in a large soup dish, Savoyard Soup is always enjoyed very hot. Add grated Gruyère cheese and croutons and place it under the broiler or grill for a few minutes to make it even more appetizing.

Followed by a country omelet filled with potatoes and bacon, and accompanied by a Gamay de Savoy white wine, Savoyard Soup makes an ideal hot meal on a winter's night.

1. Wash the leeks, turnip, celery and potatoes. Cut the peeled potatoes in four, and the turnip in half.

2. Place all the washed and cut vegetables in 2 liters/2 quarts boiling salt water. Season with pepper. Boil 40 minutes, covered. The vegetables must be very tender and have soaked up practically all the water.

3. Pass the well-cooked vegetables through a vegetable mill on a medium setting. Add a little of the cooking water, if any remains, to obtain a thick soup.

Soup

4. Let the soup reheat over a low heat. Pour in the cold milk, half at a time. Adjust the consistency of the soup. Stir in the butter. Heat 15 minutes over low heat.

5. Prepare the croutons: cut the baguette into thin slices, 3 per serving. Toast them under the grill or broiler for 2 minutes.

6. Present the soup in bowls or deep dishes. Arrange the croutons and grated Gruyère on the soup, or serve them on the side.

Slovenian Porcini

Preparation time: 50 minutes
Cooking time, soup: 40 minutes
Baking time, bread: 35 minutes
Rising time: 2 hours 30 minutes
Difficulty: ★★

Serves 6

50 ml/3¹/₂ tbsp peanut oil
40 g/¹/₄ cup chopped onion
vinegar
200 g/7 oz porcini
1 pinch wild savory
2 pinches parsley
1 pinch marjoram
20 g/2 tbsp flour
2 cloves garlic

1 bay leaf
3 tbsp buckwheat
1 liter/1 quart beef stock
salt, pepper
2 tbsp liquid crème fraîche

For the bread bowls:
300 g/2¹/₂ cups rye flour
150 g/1 cup wheat flour
50 g/3¹/₂ tbsp margarine
1 pinch cumin
15 g/1 tbsp salt
25 g/2 tbsp baker's yeast
100 ml/7 tbsp milk
butter for the circles
1 egg

Porcini and Buckwheat Soup is a specialty of the mountainous region of Gorenska, in the northwest of Slovenia. When chefs make this soup in the month of June during the first harvests, they use what are called "wheat porcini"; in the autumn, they enrich it with "buckwheat porcini", which appear in October when buckwheat is harvested. Our chef saw an easy parallel between the "buckwheat porcini" and the buckwheat that he added to this soup.

Mushroom picking is a truly popular pastime in Slovenia, a country where half the land is covered in forests. An old local expression asserts "mushrooms are the meat of the poor", and truly, the markets boast an amazing abundance of porcini, chanterelles, parasols, morels, lactaires, russulas and clavaria that find their way to the family tables. The pick of the basket are the rare and thus rather expensive, delicate Caesar's mush-

rooms and black and white truffles. The recipes for mushroom soup are therefore particularly varied. Small porcini are dried, marinated in salted and vinegary water, flavored with bay leaves and coriander, then conserved in jars. A good cordon-bleu chef in Slovenia must know how to prepare excellent preserved mushrooms.

Buckwheat, or black wheat, is an essential component in the daily lives of Slovenians. Popular songs commonly evoke the buckwheat harvest. Many families carry the name *Ajdovec*, derived from *ajda*, meaning precisely buckwheat. The plant has been grown since the eighteenth century throughout the countries in this region.

The browned onions can be deglazed with vinegar or white wine. Just before serving, some people like to add a little lemon juice to their soup.

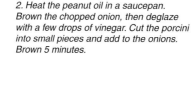

1. Prepare the bread bowls. Combine the 2 flours, margarine, cumin and salt. Dissolve the yeast in the milk and add to the dry mixture. Thin with 1 cup cold water. Knead into a smooth dough. Roll it into a ball, cover with a towel and let rise for 2 hours at room temperature.

2. Heat the peanut oil in a saucepan. Brown the chopped onion, then deglaze with a few drops of vinegar. Cut the porcini into small pieces and add to the onions. Brown 5 minutes.

3. Chop the wild savory, parsley and marjoram. Sprinkle the flour, minced garlic, wild savory, marjoram, 1 pinch of parsley, bay leaves and buckwheat into the pan. Stir well to combine.

and Buckwheat Soup

4. Finally, pour on the beef stock. Season with salt and pepper. Bring to the boil and simmer 30 minutes.

5. Butter 6 metal rings. Place them on parchment paper set on a baking sheet. Divide the raised dough in 6 balls and put 1 in each ring. Decorate with additional dough. Cover with a towel, and let rise for 30 minutes. Glaze with a beaten egg and bake 35 minutes at 180°C/355°F.

6. Cut the "hat" off each of the breads. Spoon out the inside to hollow them out. Fill with the porcini soup. Garnish with crème fraîche and chopped parsley.

Old Viennese

Preparation time: 20 minutes
Cooking time: 45 minutes
Difficulty: ★

Serves 4

600 g/1¼ lb potatoes
2 orange carrots
2 yellow carrots
60 g/2 oz celeriac
1 onion
3 cloves garlic

30 g/2 tbsp butter
60 g/2 oz sliced smoked bacon
1 liter/1 quart poultry stock
salt
pepper
1 bunch marjoram
120 g/4 oz porcini
1 bunch flat-leaf parsley

In Austrian gastronomy, this soup takes the name *Alt-Wiener Kartoffelsuppe*, or Old Viennese Potato Soup. It appears in the repertoire of highly traditional Viennese cuisine, made up of dishes that are at once simple and fortifying: roast beef with onions, goulash with paprika, meatballs, and so on. Today, creative chefs simplify these, for example, by replacing lard with butter or olive oil.

Devotees of the daily soup, Austrians like their soup thick with puréed vegetables, which they enrich with crème fraîche. In the soup presented by Marcel Vanic on the other hand, the little cubes of yellow and orange carrots, celery, potatoes and porcini appear in a cascade of colors in a base of clear stock.

It is important to choose a type of potato that will not fall apart during cooking and that contains a lot of starch. In Austria,

they prefer to use the *Dita* variety. These will be combined with the yellow carrots, which are less common outside Austria. Their taste does not differ from that of regular carrots.

The favorite mushrooms in Austria are porcini and chanterelles. Our chef prefers to make this recipe with fresh porcini, which he places in the soup uncooked. The small strips of flavorful porcini float on the surface of the stock when it is served. Out of season, porcini preserved in brine will suffice, although the taste is a little different and the texture sometimes a little slimy. Our chef strongly advises against using dried mushrooms, which give their bitterness to the soup.

The porcini may also be replaced with other fresh mushrooms of high quality such as chanterelles or meadow mushrooms.

1. Peel the potatoes, orange and yellow carrots and celeriac, then cut them into fine dice for a mirepoix. Peel and mince the onion and garlic. Brown the onion in a pot with butter.

2. Add the diced bacon and chopped garlic. Let it all brown, stirring to prevent sticking.

3. Pour the diced vegetables into the pot. Mix with a wooden spatula for a moment over low heat.

Potato Soup

4. Pour in the poultry stock. Bring to the boil.

5. Now add the potato chunks to the soup. Salt, pepper. Sprinkle with marjoram. Allow to cook 20 minutes, until the vegetables are very tender.

6. Slice the porcini into strips and add to the soup. Finish cooking for a few minutes. Pour into bowls, and decorate with fresh marjoram and parsley leaves.

Cuttlefish and

Preparation time: 30 minutes
Cooking time: 50 minutes
Soaking time: overnight
Difficulty: ★

Serves 4

50 g/¼ cup chickpeas
1 kg/2¼ lb cuttlefish
salt
2 small bay leaves
2 lemons
1 onion
100 ml/7 tbsp olive oil

2 tomatoes
1 tbsp tomato paste
1 clove garlic
3 cloves
1 pinch ground caraway
1 pinch turmeric
1 pinch ground coriander
1 pinch sweet paprika
4 green bell peppers
pepper
100 g/1 cup grilled and crushed barley
20 g/2½ tbsp dried mint
1 pinch ground cumin

In Tunisia, babies' food is still homemade, and everybody finds their place in the home kitchen: the women, experts in precise gestures, take up residence there, gourmands and connoisseurs pace the markets, and children joyously help with the peeling and other chores. Contrary to what some believe, Tunisian cuisine is not fattening. Healthy and nutritionally balanced, it meets everyone's needs. Nutritious and flavorful grains such as wheat, sorghum and barley play an important role in the everyday diet.

Harvested before complete maturity and threshed with a stick to separate the grains, the grains of barley are seived to sort by size. The largest grains end up in the steam of a couscous cooker, while the smallest find themselves poured into delicious soups.

Famous for the quality of their fish, the fishermen of Sfax net cuttlefish with a delicate flesh. To mix the mollusk with the

barley was easy: *tchiche bil chouabi*, or Cuttlefish and Chick–pea Soup, was born of this happy marriage, producing a soup with subtle flavors, full of vitamins and color.

Many spices typical of Tunisian cuisine are found in this soup. Flavor it according to taste with varying amounts of coriander, caraway, turmeric, cumin and sweet paprika.

Only when the cooking is complete should you add the tiny leaves of dried mint. When they have lent their fresh flavor to the soup, they may be removed just before pouring the soup into serving dishes.

The cumin with its acrid taste does not take well to being cooked, which would make the soup overly bitter. Hence it is sprinkled onto the soup as a final flourish. The soup could almost do without this last gesture because of the presence of the cuttlefish, which enriches this scarlet soup with its particular flavor.

1. A day ahead of time, soak the chickpeas overnight. Rinse the cuttlefish carefully and remove the interior bone. Blanch the cuttlefish in 2 liters/2 quarts water seasoned with salt, bay leaf, and 2 or 3 lemon slices. Drain and chop the cuttlefish into small dice. Set aside.

2. Chop the onion. Sweat for 3 minutes in the hot olive oil. Add the diced cuttlefish, rehydrated chickpeas and diced tomatoes. Cook for 5 minutes over high heat.

3. Stir in the tomato paste. Add the peeled garlic, cloves, caraway, turmeric, coriander, paprika and green peppers cut into large pieces. Season with salt and pepper. Simmer 5 minutes over low heat.

Chickpea Soup

4. Add enough water to cover and bring to the boil. Simmer over low heat for 20 minutes. The water must be completely absorbed.

5. Add water to the soup, filling the pot ³/₄ full. Stir in the barley, stirring constantly. Cook 8 to 10 minutes, uncovered, over low heat. Adjust the seasoning.

6. When it is ready, sprinkle the mint into the soup. Cook an additional 5 minutes while stirring. Add a little pepper and a pinch of cumin. Remove from the heat. Serve very hot with quarters of lemon.

Warsaw-Style

Preparation time: 1 hour
Cooking time: 2 hours
Difficulty: ★★

Serves 4

For the tripe soup:
2 large onions
80 g/¹⁄₃ cup butter
200 g/7 lb boneless beef
200 g/7 lb calf or beef bones
1 bay leaf
1 celeriac
1 rib celery
2 carrots
1 leek

1 kg/2¹⁄₄ lb cooked beef tripe (double-fat)
30 g/3 tbsp flour
1 tbsp tomato paste

For the spices:
2 tsp sweet paprika
2 tsp allspice
2 tsp white pepper
1 tsp ground nutmeg
2 tsp salt
2 tsp black pepper
2 tsp ground ginger

1 tsp dried marjoram
slices of baguette (optional)

Warsaw, nicknamed Siren City because of the mermaid it takes as its emblem, was once a flourishing city. Palaces, sciences and the arts made it a very prosperous intellectual center. Often coveted, conquered and destroyed, Warsaw courageously withstood the vicissitudes of its history. Strongly influenced by Jewish culture, the gastronomy of the city secretly preserves these tragically underrated culinary traditions.

Substantial but light, at once salty and sweet, mild and strong, tripe soup or *flaki* has been popular in Poland for over 600 years. As early as the beginning of the fifteenth century, Queen Hedwig and her spouse the grand-prince of Lithuania, Ladislas Jagellon, King of Poland, enjoyed this beverage. Traditionally, Polish families made this dish to seal marriages.

We recommend pre-cooked tripe for a quicker cooking that is well-adapted to contemporary cuisine. Very easy to find, they often need to be blanched before use. Raw tripe, on the other hand, needs meticulous cleaning, followed by four hours' cooking to be thoroughly blanched and enjoyable. Highly appreciated in Poland, tripe is often served in a simple poultry stock for a quick *flaki*, or tripe soup.

Flaki has many variations. The onions, caramelized in a pan for our recipe, can also be cut in two and roasted directly on the stovetop, in the fashion of the Eastern countries. They may be removed from the stock before serving. For a lighter consommé, omit the roux. There is no necessity to add the meat from the beef, but the bones, tender and gelatinous, should be kept for the stock.

Gourmets in Warsaw often to accompany their *flaki* with pork or veal meatballs, and always offer a few slices of baguette for more enjoyment.

1. Caramelize the chopped onions in 50 g/3¹⁄₂ tbsp butter. Put the beef and bones in a soup pot and fill it to ³⁄₄ with cold water. Add the bay leaf. Bring to the boil and simmer for 1 hour, skimming often, adding the cooked onions after 30 minutes.

2. Meanwhile, julienne the celeriac and celery, carrots and leek, and also the cooked tripe. When the beef is cooked, remove it from the stock and dice it. Combine both meats and the vegetables in a deep pot.

3. Measure 1 liter/1 quart of the skimmed stock and add it to the deep pot, filling it to ³⁄₄ full. Bring to the boil. Simmer 30 minutes over low heat, uncovered.

Tripe Soup

4. Prepare a roux: gently melt 30 g/1 tbsp butter in a small pan. Gradually add the flour to the hot butter and stir vigorously. When the mix becomes golden, remove the roux from the heat. Allow to cool.

5. Pour the cooled roux into the hot stock with the meat. Whisk vigorously to obtain a smooth mix without lumps. Allow to thicken for 10 minutes over very low heat, stirring constantly.

6. Prepare the spices separately on a plate. Add a pinch of each to the soup. Thin the tomato paste with 1 tbsp warm water and add it to the soup. Stir gently. Simmer for 5 minutes. Sprinkle with chopped marjoram and serve.

Carrot Cream

Preparation time: 10 minutes
Cooking time: 35 minutes
Difficulty: ★

Serves 4

800 g/1³/₄ lb carrots
60 g/¹/₄ cup butter
¹/₂ tsp ground cumin
¹/₂ tsp turmeric
salt
pepper
¹/₂ tsp chili powder

A mosaic of cultures, religions and traditions, India presents an interesting anthology of cooked dishes, desserts and varied meals. Vegetables and fruits blend together and harmonize in a whirling country dance of spices and flavors. Hence, vegetables become fruits, fruits become vegetables, and soups transform into dessert. So goes all of Indian cuisine and all its nuances.

Is this Carrot Cream Soup with Cumin a main dish or a dessert? An awkward dilemma for gourmets, but quickly resolved: serve it chilled as an appetizer, or hot for a light dinner accompanied by small *nan* breads filled with cheese, or browned *chapatti* cakes, and without forgetting a glass of *lassi*, the refreshing Indian yogurt-based drink.

Traditionally, this soup is made with pumpkin. Pumpkin or carrot, the color remains the same although the flavor and texture change: the hint of sweetness in carrots replaces the more neutral flavor of the pumpkin, while the alliance with cumin introduces a further subtlety.

Those who dine at an Indian restaurant without knowing much about the gastronomical culture and its associated philosophy may not realize that, enveloped in the gentle magic of an Indian dinner, they will not leave untouched on the spiritual plane. The relaxation generated by the flavored round of bowls of preserves and sweet and salty seasonings, as well as the graceful motions of those who serve the food, provide food for thought about a distant world that is worthy of our attention.

Indian cuisine is not only the art of eating well, but also involves the art of thought. Indians do not separate cooking from spirituality; to do so would be a distortion of their ethics, their food culture, and above all their approach to living.

1. Peel the carrots, then cut them in quarters or eighths depending on their size. Regroup the sticks and cut them into small dice.

2. In a buttered pot, sweat the carrots while stirring constantly with a spatula for 5 to 6 minutes over medium heat. They must not stick.

3. Over the same medium heat and stirring continually, add the cumin, turmeric, salt, pepper and finally the chili powder, sprinkling over all the carrots. Stir and toss the carrots to coat them with all the spices.

Soup with Cumin

4. Pour 800 ml/3¹/₃ cups water over the simmering carrots and stir. Cook for 30 minutes or more over medium heat, watching that the little bit of stock does not reduce completely.

5. Purée the soup with a hand-held mixer to obtain a creamy and smooth velouté. If you do not have a blender, you can use a vegetable mill or food processor.

6. Serve the thick soup hot in cups or bowls, or even in a large dish presented at the table.

Werner Matt's

Preparation time: 40 minutes
Cooking time: 30 minutes
Difficulty: ★★

Serves 6

6 celeriac, 800 g/1³/₄ lb each
60 g/¹/₄ cup butter
50 g/generous ¹/₄ cup shallots
salt
pepper
oil for frying

500 ml/2 cups white wine
80 ml/¹/₃ cup white port
1 liter/1 quart poultry stock
1 lemon
400 ml/1²/₃ cups heavy cream
1 rib celery
white truffle oil (optional)

Presenting us with this exceptional recipe for Celeriac Velouté, Marcel Vanic pays homage to his spiritual cuisine-master, Werner Matt. Our chef was his student for four years, in the kitchens of *Vienna Plaza*. The velouté created by Werner Matt has become so famous that clients leave clutching the recipe decorated with a humorous illustration.

Served in its hull complete with a proud plume of greens, this soup recalls the better known cream of pumpkin soup served in little pumpkins, or chilled tomato soup poured into enormous Moroccan tomatoes.

Austrian chefs work much more often with celeriac than with celery. In this recipe, celery is only used as greenery on the top of the celeriac. Commonly grown in the country, this strongly flavored root transforms into wonderful purées, salads, soups or even chips.

Hollowing the celeriac takes a little care. After cutting off a lid from the top of the vegetable, mark out the inner edge of the future container with a pastry cutter or small knife. Then hollow out the flesh with a melon-baller, exactly as for a melon. This should produce a container the size of a coffee cup. Some of the removed flesh will be used to make the soup. The rest is cut into julienne and fried. To complete the lid, cut a small hole in the center, and decorate it with a plume of celery greens.

Our chef adds to this velouté a very dry white wine that boasts a good acidity, such as *Veltliner*, produced in the south of Styria.

The soup, which can be embellished with white truffle oil, or even grated truffles, is generally topped with the plumed celeriac lid.

1. Remove the hard base of each celeriac in a slice, to create a flat base. With a chef's knife, cut off a "hat" about 3 cm/1¹/₄ in from the top of each one.

2. Drive a pastry wheel or knife into the interior of the celeriac to mark the edge well. Then, using a melon-baller, scoop out the flesh to produce a container for the soup.

3. Chop 550 g/1¹/₄ lb of the celeriac. Brown it in butter with the chopped shallots. Salt and pepper. Separately, cut a little raw celiac into very fine sticks. Deep-fry them to a sort of "hay", and set aside on paper towels.

Celeriac Velouté

4. Pour the white wine, port, poultry stock, and juice of the lemon into the pot of shallots and celeriac. Season with salt and pepper. Bring to the boil, and simmer for 20 minutes.

5. Blend the cooked soup in a food processor. Whip the cream. Incorporate it gently, using a whisk, into the hot but not boiling soup. Mix vigorously and pour immediately into the hollowed celeriacs.

6. Insert a few stems of a celery sprig into the celeriac lids. Place over the soup or on the side. Decorate with the fried celeriac hay and little drizzles of white truffle oil, and serve hot.

Mushroom Velouté

Preparation time:	20 minutes
Cooking time:	40 minutes
Difficulty:	★★

Serves 4

For the soup:
400 g/14 oz button mushrooms
200 g/7 oz chanterelle mushrooms
200 g/7 oz horn of plenty mushrooms
50 g/3¹/₂ oz porcini
50 g/3¹/₂ tbsp butter
salt
pepper
1 liter/1 quart poultry stock
2 cloves garlic
1 sprig thyme

1 bay leaf
300 ml/1¹/₄ cups liquid crème fraîche
or heavy cream

For the garnish:
80 g/3 oz raw duck liver, sliced
50 g/3¹/₂ tbsp butter
100 g/3¹/₂ oz button mushrooms
100 g/3¹/₂ oz chanterelle mushrooms
100 g/3¹/₂ horn of plenty mushrooms
50 g/1³/₄ oz porcini
1 tbsp olive oil
¹/₂ bunch chives
¹/₂ bunch chervil

For decoration:
chives, chervil

While they live, mushrooms pull their meager sustenance from the ground to survive. Often hidden in the shadows of the forests, they are born in the greatest secrecy and perish, ravished by a few avid devotees who hasten to put them into their cooking pots.

While hundreds of varieties exist (of which many are inedible), Michel Roth's Mushroom Velouté with Foie Gras includes only the most popular. The chanterelle, an excellent edible mushroom with a bright yellow color and thick flesh, is recognizable by its pleasant odor. The horn of plenty mushroom gets its French name, *trompette-de-de-la-mort* (trumpet of death), from its abundance around Halloween. Not very fleshy but very flavorful, they are easily dried and thus keep well. The porcini, also called cep or boletus, remains the most sought-after mushroom. Infused with a slight aroma of the oaks under which it grows, it has a slightly sweet flavor.

Generally, mushrooms are fragile. Once rinsed, drain them and dry them quickly. An over-long soaking in water will impair their texture, which needs to stay firm during cooking. While the mushrooms are sautéed vigorously in the pan, when the poultry stock is added to the pot and the flavor is intensified by garlic, thyme and bay leaf, you will need to stir them to blend everything well. The soup is transformed into a purée that is then enriched with crème fraîche or cream. Pass it through a sieve, and the texture becomes smooth. The traditional frying of mushrooms sets up the garnish. They are cooked twice, first in olive oil, and secondly in browned butter.

Michel Roth describes this hot velouté as so tantalizing that it makes his mouth water. You can enjoy it sprinkled with Parmesan, or follow it with fish and game for truly special occasions, especially when strips of duck liver grace the soup with their presence.

1. Rinse the mushrooms well. Dry them. Slice the porcini and button mushrooms lengthwise. Cut the chanterelles and horn of plenty mushrooms into strips. Set aside a few porcini and 100 g/3¹/₂ oz of each of the other types for the final frying.

2. For the soup, melt the butter and add the sliced chanterelles, porcini, horn of plenty and button mushrooms. Salt and pepper. Sauté 2 to 3 minutes over high heat, without letting them brown.

3. Pour 1 liter/1 quart poultry stock over the mushrooms. Add 2 whole cloves of garlic, the thyme and bay leaf. Simmer 30 minutes, uncovered, over low heat.

with Duck Liver

4. Thoroughly blend the cooked mushrooms to obtain a smooth, thick mixture. Stir in the crème fraîche and keep hot.

5. Sear thin slices of liver in the hot butter for a few seconds over high heat. Set them aside. Separately, brown the reserved chopped mushrooms for 3 minutes in olive oil. Then fry them a second time for 2 minutes in lightly browned butter. Add the chopped herbs.

6. Spread 2 spoonfuls of sautéed mushrooms in the bottom of each soup dish. Cover with the very hot velouté. Decorate with a few strips of mushrooms and fried liver. Garnish with chervil and chives.

Chestnut

Preparation time: *30 minutes*
Cooking time: *50 minutes*
Difficulty: ★

Serves 4

1 leek
1 sprig celery
1 carrot
1 onion
1 clove garlic
50 g/3¹/₂ tbsp butter

500 g/generous 1 lb chestnuts
salt
pepper
200 ml/generous ³/₄ cup heavy cream

Soups, potages, veloutés, consommés and stocks have long constituted the most common first course of a French meal. The word "supper" was born back when the nightly meal consisted of a vegetable soup poured over a thick piece of bread.

Many talented chefs give quite specific names to their soups depending on their texture and the ingredients used. Over time, many of the hearty soups characteristic of certain regions have fallen out of favor in lieu of more sophisticated cream soups and veloutés.

Dominated by the flavor, texture and color of the chestnuts, the soup presented by our chef is puréed and then blended with cream to transform it into a velouté. It can also be delicately thickened with a beaten egg yolk, which will give it a smoother and glossy finish. But it is also possible to leave the soup un-blended to preserve a more authentic regional character. If

chestnuts are not in season, go ahead and use frozen or vacuum-packed chestnuts.

The quantity of water added to the soup varies according to whether you prefer a very thick or more fluid end result. It is preferable to add enough water to cover the vegetables to start them cooking at first, and to add more liquid according to the desired consistency toward the end.

Jacky Morlon refines this traditional recipe with a cloud of whipped cream. Chestnuts and cream are a favorite combination of many gourmets. It is so easy to make the seasoned whipped cream that it would be a pity to leave it out. A very cold cream of good quality, seasoned with a spoonful of salt, a little pepper and even some chopped fresh parsley is vigorously whipped to obtain a light and firm mousse. Refrigerate for 5 to 10 minutes before placing it on the velouté.

1. Separate the white and green of the leek and pare the celery. Peel the carrot, onion and garlic. Cut all the vegetables into pieces 2 x 2 cm/³/₄ x ³/₄ in long.

2. Melt the butter in a large pot. Pour all the vegetables into the hot butter. Cook for 5 minutes over high heat, without browning.

3. Shell the chestnuts. Pour 2 liters/2 quarts water over the vegetables.

Velouté

4. Add the chestnuts to the vegetables and bring to the boil. Season with salt and pepper. Simmer 45 minutes, covered, over medium heat. Meanwhile, whip 100 ml/ 7 tbsp of the cream. Salt and pepper. Set aside in the refrigerator.

5. Off the heat, purée the soup directly in the pot, using a hand-held mixer, to obtain a smooth cream.

6. Pour the remaining cream into the soup and whisk to blend. Adjust the seasoning. Serve hot in a soup dish, decorated with a spoonful of seasoned whipped cream.

Pumpkin Velouté

Preparation time: 25 minutes
Cooking time: 40 minutes
Difficulty: ★★

Serves 6

1 kg/2¼ lb pumpkin
1 taro or cocoyam root
3 cloves garlic
2 green onions
1 red pepper tip
4 tbsp olive oil

5 g/2 tsp cumin seeds
salt
pepper
12 freshwater prawns
50 ml/3½ tbsp old rum
100 ml/7 tbsp crème fraîche

Traditional Pumpkin Velouté with Freshwater Prawns is particularly appreciated on Good Friday, after a week of fasting. Many soups in Guadeloupe are so filling that they constitute a main dish in themselves. The most fortifying is *soup à Congo*, which includes a variety of tubers (yam, sweet potato, taro, Madeira), fresh vegetables and legumes enriched with meat (pork tails, snout or fat, salted beef). Fishermen also prepare soups of fish, shellfish and small bivalves called *chobettes*.

The local *giraumon* pumpkin is used in a number of Antillean soups. It is a green pumpkin marked with flecks, with a delicate orange flesh and a very sweet flavor. Like melons, it grows in humid regions on creeping stems that can reach 5 meters (15 feet) long. In the past, Creole women used its oil and seeds to make beauty products. Outside the Antilles, it may be replaced with a common pumpkin. The starch in the taro (also known as cocoyam) helps thicken the soup. It may be replaced with yam, sweet potato or even parsnip.

Favorite companions of this soup, the freshwater prawns are very close cousins in Guadeloupe to the *z'habitants* of Martinique. These smooth-shelled blue crustaceans are larger than Mediterranean prawns and equipped with two large pincers, like miniature lobsters. They once frequented the rivers and seas of Guadeloupe, but pollution has made them disappear. In order to satisfy demand, they are raised in Pointe-Noir and Petit-Bourg.

To flavor everything, our chef uses green onion, a virtually indispensable plant in all savory Antillean foods. It has a long green stem with a white section leading to the root. Shallots can be used instead of green onion, if you prefer.

For added sophistication, we recommend scooping the flesh from the pumpkins to make decorative soup bowls, rather than simply chopping and peeling them as described below.

1. Cut the pumpkin into large chunks. Then cut these into smaller pieces and peel them. Do the same for the cocoyam. Now dice both vegetables. Peel the garlic, and chop it along with the spring onion and red pepper.

2. Heat 2 tbsp oil in a pot. Tip the pumpkin and cocoyam into the hot oil, stir with a spoon and cook for 10 minutes, long enough for the pumpkin to soften.

3. Add half the green onion, half the garlic and the cumin. Pour in a cup of water. Stir well and simmer for 10 minutes.

with Freshwater Prawns

4. Using a hand-held mixer, blend the soup in the pot. Adjust the consistency by adding a little water if necessary. Salt and pepper.

5. Fry the freshwater prawns 5 minutes in a pan with 2 tbsp hot oil. Add the remaining green onions and chopped garlic. Allow to simmer for 10 minutes, adding water regularly so the shellfish don't stick. Then flambé with the rum.

6. Pour the soup into a food processor or blender, add the crème fraîche, and blend. Reheat for a few moments. Serve the soup in bowls or a hollowed-out pumpkin, and garnish with the prawn tails.

Mussel

Preparation time: 30 minutes
Cooking time: 7 minutes
Difficulty: ★

Serves 4

2 kg/4¹/₂ lb mussels
1 onion
50 g/3¹/₂ tbsp butter
2 or 3 sprigs thyme
1 or 2 bay leaves
1 bunch flat-leaf parsley

500 ml/2 cups white wine
salt
pepper
600 ml/2¹/₂ cups crème fraîche
2 egg yolks

For the garnish:
sprigs of fresh chervil

Well known for their low calorie content and their richness in calcium, iron and iodine, mussels are very popular in French cuisine. They can be prepared in various ways: marinated, creamed, fried, sautéed, stuffed in an omelet or au gratin. Some of the more complex preparations, such as mussel stew or roasted mussels, made a reputation for certain port towns. But France does not have a monopoly on the exploitation of mussels. They can be found in Spanish paella and English soups, not to mention the famous *moules-frites* (fried mussels) of Belgium.

Philippe Fouchard chose to present the mussels in the form of an appetizing velouté that is gastronomically excellent. The tiny farm-raised mussels lend themselves favorably to this smooth, sophisticated soup. The mussel beds are lines of chain posts, half buried in the sea bed. *Boucholeurs* (mussel farmers) collect seed mussels from the sea on ropes that are then wound round the posts. The mussels continue to grow on these mussel beds, sometimes covered and sometimes uncovered with water, depending on the tide. This method of mussel cultivation, practiced from Charente-Maritime to Cotentin, produces small mussels that are fleshy, tender and very flavorful. The method was invented around 1290 by an Irishman, Patrick Walton, who developed it in the Bay of Aiguillon.

Weary of hearing that in Normandy people only think of crème fraîche, butter and eggs, our chef based his velouté on this trilogy of products from Normandy, and then added the flavorful mussels from Barfleur.

But the refined flavor of the velouté also derives from the mix of egg yolks and crème fraîche added to the filtered stock. If this mix of crème fraîche and eggs seems too thin, boil it over high heat while whisking vigorously for three minutes. Thus fortified, it will regain its aromatic smoothness.

1. With the tip of a small knife, scrape the shells of the mussels to remove the embedded barnacles, and cut off the protruding filaments. Rinse the mussels under running water, then drain them in a colander.

2. Brown the chopped onion in a large pot, in the hot butter. Add all the mussels, the thyme, bay leaf, parsley, white wine, salt and pepper. Cook for about 3 minutes over high heat, until the mussels open. Remove the mussels from the heat as soon as they open.

3. Using an empty shell to form a pincer, open all the mussels. Remove the flesh and place it on a plate.

Velouté

4. Pour the juice from cooking the mussels in a large bowl. Filter it over a pot to eliminate the herbs and small debris. Keep this stock hot for making the velouté.

5. Whisk together the crème fraîche and the egg yolks. Pour this mix into the hot stock, whisking vigorously. Cook the resultant velouté over low heat 4 minutes, stirring continually.

6. To serve, put a few shelled mussels into the bottom of soup bowls and cover with very hot velouté. Decorate with remaining mussels and a few sprigs of chervil. Enjoy while hot.

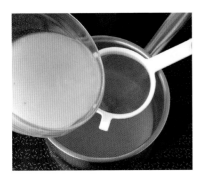

Sorrel

Preparation time:	*45 minutes*
Cooking time:	*55 minutes*
Difficulty:	★

Serves 4

For the velouté:
2 large potatoes
2 onions
2 leeks
50 g/3¹/₂ tbsp butter
2 small bunches sorrel
1 sprig thyme

1 bay leaf
4 tbsp flour
1 liter/1 quart chicken stock

For thickening:
3 egg yolks
250 ml/1 cup milk
salt
pepper

For the garnish:
1 smoked eel
1 bunch watercress (optional)

Rich in potassium and consumed for its therapeutic virtues, sorrel has long been a staple of the Flemish diet. Its curative power against gout used to relieve the rural population. Since then, the green leaves of this edible plant have been a delightful part of many preparations. The most traditional remains the Sorrel Velouté.

Similar to spinach, sorrel has a somewhat more acidic flavor. There are many varieties of it. The leaves used for the velouté may be large or small, but must be glossy and firm, with a pure bright green color. Some of them will be reserved: all softened in butter, the small leaves will garnish the bottom of the plate, where they will be joined by chunks of smoked eel.

This fish with the appearance of a snake was already much appreciated by the Romans. Since then, the eel has been highly valued in a many countries. They are caught by fishermen when they leave the rivers to make a long migration to the Sargasso Sea, their spawning ground.

The smoked eel should be covered with a brilliant, almost black skin. Very easy to skin, they contain a fatty but flavorful flesh. The Belgians make wonderful meals with them: pan-fried, grilled and especially *au vert* ("in green"), in a sauce comprising an assortment of flavorful herbs. Well-preserved cold smoked eel can be spread on toasts to make a sophisticated accompaniment to the Sorrel Velouté. But a number of other smoked fish can easily replace it, such as julienned mackerel or salmon.

Egg yolks and milk bind the soup, transforming it into a sumptuous velouté. Our chef strongly recommends pouring the thickening into the soup away from the heat, otherwise the eggs will cook out as ugly lumps.

1. Peel the potatoes and onions and cut them into large pieces. Chop the whites of the leeks. Sweat these vegetables for 10 minutes in butter with 20 leaves and stems of sorrel, the thyme and the bay leaf. Remove from the heat, sprinkle on the flour, and stir.

2. Replace the pot on the heat for 1 minute and stir. Add the chicken stock. Bring to the boil and simmer for 40 minutes over high heat, stirring occasionally.

3. Meanwhile, melt a pat of butter in a saucepan. Chop the remaining sorrel, tip it into the hot butter and brown over low heat.

Velouté

4. Remove the skin from the smoked eel. Remove 2 fillets. Cut the meat into large pieces, then into strips, and then into sticks 4 cm/1¼ in long. Set aside.

5. Cover the bottom of the soup dishes with pieces of eel and some of the sautéd sorrel. Mix the sorrel soup in a blender separately. Reheat it for 5 minutes.

6. Make a thickening agent by beating the egg yolks in a small bowl with milk, salt and pepper. Add to the sorrel velouté. Whisk vigorously, and pour into the prepared plates. Decorate with watercress leaves.

Couscous Soup

Preparation time: 20 minutes
Cooking time: 30 minutes
Difficulty: ★

Serves 4

4 cloves garlic
50 ml/3¹/₂ tbsp olive oil
4 tbsp tomato paste
1 rib celery
1 tbsp ground caraway
ground pepper

1 tsp dried mint
1 tsp hot chili sauce (optional)
100 g/²/₃ cup fine couscous
1 preserved lemon, quartered
50 g/¹/₃ cup capers

As the Tunisian sun attracts tourists in search of the warmth of its rays, there are many who believe that the land of olive groves never sees a day of winter. Although unquestionably milder than most, winter still exists, however, and surprises even the Tunisians, like an eclipse in a cloudless sky. Deprived of light, even their food suddenly loses its color. The heat of this invigorating soup takes the place of refreshing fresh salads and honeyed pastries.

In Tunisia, couscous is the star: its texture may be fine like a meal or rolled into medium- or large-grained couscous. In any size and whether made from hard wheat or barley, it is used on every occasion. Traditionally, the couscous is sprinkled with oil and worked by hand until the grains are well-coated, then cooked in the steam of a *couscousière* (steamer). It is also a delicious element in many soups.

To make this Couscous Soup, look for a fine semolina. Often destined for a porridge for young babies just learning to eat,

this form of semolina makes the soup light and smooth. Avoid pouring the semolina into over-hot stock, because it will thicken too quickly. Our chef recommends pouring it in little by little after adding the cold water. Then bring to the boil slowly, stirring constantly. The couscous must be perfectly diffused throughout the water.

Ever-present in Tunisian cuisine, tomato paste is generally used in sauces and soups. As it is thick, dilute it with a little warm water before pouring it into the hot oil. In Tunisian homes, it is used in preparations that are conserved during the summer. It is kept in the larders of all good Tunisian homes, with the jars of capers and preserved lemons. Those who dislike acid and vinegar avoid these, and they should also ignore another typically Tunisian burning passion: *harissa*, a condiment based on locally grown chili peppers.

1. Mince the garlic. Heat 50 ml/3¹/₂ tbsp olive oil in a large pot. Tip the minced garlic into the hot oil. Cook 1 to 2 minutes over high heat, without letting it brown.

2. Dilute 4 tbsp tomato paste in 2 cups warm water. Pour into the pot with the garlic. Simmer for 5 minutes.

3. Add a stem of celery cut in half with its leaves chopped into small pieces. Stir.

with Capers

4. Blend 1 tbsp ground caraway and ground pepper into the soup. Stir with a wooden spoon to incorporate the spices.

5. In the palms of your hands, crush the leaves of dried mint over the pot. Finally, add 1 tsp hot chili sauce. Stir. Simmer for 5 minutes over high heat. Add 1 liter/1 quart cold water.

6. Pour the semolina into the pot, little by little, and stir constantly until it boils. Cook 20 minutes uncovered, over low heat. Away from the heat, remove the celery stem, add the preserved lemon quarters, and the capers. Serve hot.

Fish & Seafood

Clams in

Preparation time: 5 minutes
Cooking time: 15 minutes
Difficulty: ✶

Serves 4

For the vegetable bouillon:
1 leek
1 branch parsley
¼ onion

1 clove garlic
1 tbsp olive oil
1 chili pepper
1 tbsp flour
salt
pepper
500 g/generous 1 lb clams (almejas)
125 ml/½ cup dry white wine
parsley to garnish

Fished all along the Basque coasts, clams or *almejas* are the pride of the country, and enjoy a high status in Spanish gastronomy. In effect, the greatness of the shellfish is its flavor and the taste of the iodine contained within it.

Resembling the *palourdes* (a type of clam) with radiating thin grooves, *almejas* burst with flavor, and widely exceed the minimum size required for shellfish in the fishing world. Of a brownish-ivory color, the shell of this bivalve mollusk shelters an extremely flavorful soft roe. A lucky fishing trip may result in a catch including a few nice *palourdes* or cockles to make our green sauce.

Freshly caught *almejas* should be washed in running water immediately in order to retain their flavor. Open them quickly, fill with just a small amount of the sauce, and savor them hot, one after another. After adding a little vegetable bouillon to the sauce, then the flour and the shellfish, swirl the pan. As soon as the clams open, remove them from the heat and serve immediately. Like all shellfish, overcooked *almejas* become rubbery. Before serving, be careful to remove any clams that have remained obstinately closed: they have unquestionably died before reaching your kitchen. As for the green sauce, flavor it with parsley at the last moment before serving.

Times have changed since nobles banned cloves of garlic because of their odor. Nowadays, the most beautiful braided ropes of garlic come from La Mancha, which exports large quantities of them worldwide.

Rufino Manjarrès swears by eating his *almejas* all by themselves, in the mid-afternoon, just before the sublime moment of the siesta, when Spain languishes in the often oppressive afternoon heat.

1. Wash the leek. Remove the skin. Split it in two lengthwise. Cook 10 minutes in 250 ml/1 cup boiling water. Add the parsley and ¼ onion. Allow to simmer, then strain and retain the resulting vegetable bouillon.

2. Finely mince the garlic. Brown it rapidly in 1 tbsp very hot olive oil. Add the chili pepper, also minced. Cook for 2 minutes over low heat.

3. Sprinkle the flour directly into the pan with the olive oil, garlic and chili pepper. Add salt and pepper. Cook another 2 minutes on low heat, stirring constantly.

Green Sauce

4. Add a ladle of the vegetable bouillon. Stir. Allow to boil for 1 minute over high heat. Keep hot.

5. Wash the clams rapidly under water. Put them in the pan all at once. Allow to simmer over high heat, stirring.

6. Add the white wine to the pan and boil until the clam shells open. Remove them as soon as they open. Serve the clams in their sauce immediately, sprinkled with some fresh parsley.

Thai Lime

Preparation time: 45 minutes
Cooking time: 10 minutes
Difficulty: ★

Serves 4

2 kg/4½ lb sea bass
or 4 pieces, 500 g/generous 1 lb each
25 g/3 tbsp chopped fresh cilantro

30 g/¼ cup minced garlic
5 g/2 tsp fresh red pepper
2 limes
100 ml/7 tbsp fish sauce
30 g/¼ cup powdered sugar

For the garnish:
slices of lime

All along the canals that irrigate the heart of the towns in Thailand, Thai pirogues and rowboats catch the tourist's eye. Veritable floating marketplaces, these boat-boutiques offer a kaleidoscopic array of all kinds of products. But without question, the most surprising is the fish market. An important resource exported worldwide, fish abounds in the holds of these boats.

From the Andaman Sea and South China Sea to the Indian Ocean, the Thai people catch, sell and cook fish with elegance and beauty. Among the most prized fish, the barracuda and the *plaka pung* are worthy of note. The latter, a large fish with firm flesh, has an odd resemblance to the sea bass, which is more widespread in Western Europe. This lime sauce would also be appropriate for a mullet dish.

As for the sea bass, it must be carefully scaled, because its many little scales often go unnoticed. Next, the fish should be flavored with sauce and steamed lightly in its skin. The fresh but slightly sour flavor of the lime can be replaced with lemon juice, if needed. After cooking, our chef offers a choice of presentations: smaller sea bass remain whole, while larger fish are cut into separate pieces.

Blending the traditions of the East and West, Oth Sombath reserves a gourmet finish for the fish. After a steam bath and bereft of its skin, the fish is separated into two fillets. One slides over the other, allowing a white flesh spotted with red pepper to appear. Slices of lime adorn the sea bass as it lies on a bed of decorative greens. To give the dish an Asian flavor, take the time to prepare some steamed rice.

1. Place the fish on a chopping board. Use scissors to remove the ventral and tail fins. Gut the fish. Rinse the interior carefully under a stream of cold water. Dry lightly with paper towels.

2. Chop the cilantro finely, then tip into a small bowl. Add the garlic and pepper and mix thoroughly until completely combined.

3. Squeeze the limes. Measure the juice, adding 105 ml/7 tbsp to the cilantro mixture. Whisk thoroughly.

Sea Bass

4. Once the lime juice is well incorporated into the mixture, add the fish sauce and powdered sugar. Beat until the sauce is homogenous and fluid.

5. Put the fish on a dish that permits steaming. Use a small ladle to drizzle the sauce over the sea bass, adding a small quantity at a time.

6. Fill a long container with high sides ³/₄ full with water. Lay the dish containing the fish and sauce on top of this. Cover with plastic wrap. Steam the fish for 10 minutes on low heat. Serve garnished with slices of lime.

Andreoli-Style

Preparation time:	30 minutes
Cooking time:	45 minutes
Difficulty:	★

Serves 4

1 sea bass, ca. 1.5 kg/3¹/₄ lb
salt
pepper
1 shallot
60 g/¹/₄ cup butter

3 limes
2 pink grapefruit
2 oranges
100 ml/7 tbsp white wine
fresh dill

A noble fish with firm and delicate flesh is bathed in a sauce that is at once bittersweet and creamy, and garnished with pretty segments of pan-fried citrus fruit. Our chef was inspired to develop this recipe of citrus sea bass by southern Italy, a place where oranges, lemons and grapefruit are found in abundance. Sicilians have been cultivating citrus fruit on a large scale ever since Arab conquerors imported the first plants to the island.

The star of the recipe, the sea bass is prized by the Italians, who appreciate sea bream and tuna as well. This fish with great silver scales, also known as "the wolf", lives near the coast and travels in schools. Two species coexist, the common sea bass and the spotted bass.

We advise you to get striped bass if possible, wild fish that are traditionally caught with a trailing line or "bottom line". In terms of flavor, its flesh wins hands down in comparison to farmed fish. In Italy, the demand is so great that numerous fisheries have been established. This savory fish is prepared in the oven with potatoes and rosemary; in aluminum foil with parsley, garlic, lemon and fennel; or it can be grilled or turned into *carpaccio*. Sicilians cook it in saltwater.

The mild climes of Liguria, Sicily and Calabria produce the grapefruit used in this dish. The largest of the citrus fruits, grapefruit contains a lot of juice and vitamin C, but little sugar and no protein or fat at all. Here, our chef uses pink grapefruit with sweet flesh. Yellow grapefruit juice can also be used in the marinade to give it a little burst of tanginess.

Chef Andreoli recommends basting the bass regularly with the citrus and white wine sauce as it cooks to keep it moist and to permeate it with subtle flavors.

1. Gut the bass and rinse the interior well under running water. Carefully dry the body of the fish.

2. Place the bass in a large oval gratin dish. Salt and pepper the fish inside and out, on both sides.

3. Peel and chop the shallot. Cut 40 g/ 2¹/₂ tbsp of the butter into small cubes. Sprinkle the fish with the chopped shallot and small pieces of butter.

Citrus Sea Bass

4. Squeeze the juice of 1 lime, 1 grapefruit and 1 orange. Pour the citrus juice and white wine over the bass. Bake in the oven at 180°C/355°F for 30 minutes.

5. Peel the remaining limes, grapefruit and orange. Separate into segments with a small, sharp knife, running the blade along the length of each slice to remove the membranes.

6. Pan-fry the slices in the remaining butter over high heat for 2 to 3 minutes. In another pan, reduce the fish sauce to half its volume. Top the fish with sauce, surround it with fruit slices and garnish with fresh dill.

Bahia

Preparation time: 25 minutes
Cooking time: 1 hour 20 minutes
Difficulty: ★★

Serves 8

2 kg/4¹/₂ lb medium shrimp
juice of 1 lime
4 cloves garlic
salt
1 small onion, cut in rings
1 large carrot

250 ml/1 cup vinegar
1 small bunch cilantro
1.5 kg/3¹/₄ lb cassava (manioc)
3 tbsp red palm oil
500 ml/2 cups coconut milk
20 g/2 tbsp grated fresh ginger
Melegueta pepper
salt
Tabasco sauce (optional)

Built in the sixteenth century in northeast Brazil, Salvador da Bahia is a city with colonial charm and long white-sand beaches lined with coconut palms. The rich and varied cuisine of this town is famous throughout the world. Those who like to eat typical Bahian food choose shrimp bobo, *moqueca* fish stew or *acaraje*, small loaves of cornflower bread fried in palm oil, sliced and stuffed with crabmeat or shrimp.

The fishermen of the northeast bring back large quantities of shrimp, crab, prawn and other fish in their nets. The large shrimp are grilled. As for smaller shrimp, they are fried in oil seasoned with garlic, and are used to stuff fish and vegetables. Brazilians enjoy shrimp "à la milanaise" fried in breadcrumbs and accompanied with a tomato and onion sauce that can also be enriched with crème fraîche "à la Strogonoff". Cassava has

been enjoyed by the Brazilians since before colonization. Also known as manioc in English, in Brazil the plant is sometimes called *mandioca* and sometimes *aipim*. It is a tuber rich in starch, with white flesh and a brown skin, and belongs to the *Euphorbia* family. Brazilians make several important foods from cassava, eating it boiled, fried, milled (as tapioca flour) or puréed.

To season these dishes, our chef uses a lot of Melegueta pepper, a rare spice that is also called "Guinea pepper" or "Grains of Paradise". On seeing the little reddish-brown pyramid-shaped seeds, no one would guess that they grow on a sort of reed of the cardamom family. The dish may also be served with Tabasco sauce.

1. Wash the shrimp, then peel and devein them. In a dish, season the shrimp with lime juice, 2 cloves garlic and salt. Set aside in the refrigerator.

2. Immerse the heads and shells of the shrimp in a saucepan filled with 3 liters/3 quarts cold water. Add the onion rings, 2 cloves garlic, carrot, vinegar and cilantro (reserve a few leaves). Bring to the boil. Cover and simmer 30 minutes.

3. Drain the bouillon and remove the garnish. Add the cassava, peeled and diced. Bring to the boil, lower the heat and allow to cook 30 to 40 minutes until the cassava is tender.

Shrimp Bobo

4. Remove the diced cassava from the bouillon with a ladle. Tip into a blender. Add a ladleful of the shrimp bouillon. Mix to a homogenous and creamy purée.

5. Pour the purée into a saucepan. Add the palm oil and coconut milk. Stir over medium heat until the mixture becomes firm (crush the lumps with the end of a spatula).

6. Take the marinated shrimp from the refrigerator and add them to the soup, then the grated ginger, melegueta pepper and salt. Cook another 7 minutes. To finish, garnish with remaining cilantro leaves. Accompany with Tabasco sauce.

Cod Brandade

Preparation time: 1 hour
Cooking time: 40 minutes
Tenderizing fish: 20 minutes
Difficulty: ★★

Serves 4

For the brandade:
600 g/1¼ lb fresh cod fillets
30 g/1½ tbsp sea salt
200 g/7 oz potatoes
4 cloves garlic
1 bunch thyme
500 ml/2 cups crème fraîche
400 ml/1⅔ cups olive oil
pepper

For the egg vinaigrette:
juice of ½ lemon
salt, pepper

200 ml/generous ¾ cup olive oil
5 blades chive
50 g/1¾ oz black olives
1 hard-boiled egg

For the vegetables à la Provençale:
5 tomatoes
1 eggplant
2 shallots
16 basil leaves
50 ml/3½ tbsp olive oil
oil for frying

For the optional garnish:
salmon roe

Netted in the deep and cold waters of the Atlantic, the cod is reeled aboard the fishing boat, decapitated, gutted and filleted. Half the catch is salted in the hold, a process that raises it to the status of *morue*, salt cod, while the other half is frozen, and is known simply as "codfish". This fish, which can grow up to 1.5 meters (5 feet) in length, has a very delicate white flaky flesh. In our recipe, the chef prefers to make his own *morue*, by salting fresh cod.

For centuries, trading the salty cod made a fortune for the Breton and Norman fishermen, who caught them in Canada on the shores of Newfoundland. Nowadays, the majority of cod come from the coasts of Norway and Ireland.

Cooked in brandade flavored with black olives, salt cod long ago breached the ramparts of Nîmes. That is where Georges Rousset discovered it and brought it up to date with a flourish, alternating quenelles of brandade and rendered provençale

vegetables. The best fillets are found in the belly and the back of the fish where the flesh is denser and of better quality. The fishtail can be relegated to the next meal, when it may be fried and accompanied with miniature sautéed potatoes.

Salting the fillets will firm up the flesh. Do not hesitate to sprinkle generously with coarse sea salt, but do not soak for more than twenty minutes or the fish will become too soft. Next, rinse the fillets thoroughly, and do not add more salt while cooking.

The brandade should not be too smooth. Rather than crushing it, it can be worked with a fork while blending the olive oil to give it the texture of pâté.

The vegetables will be minced and cooked a few minutes in olive oil, accompanied by the fried basil leaves. At the last moment, pour the egg vinaigrette over the brandade.

1. Remove the skin of the cod and lift out the fillets. Scatter a dish with sea salt and place the fillets on top. Salt generously. Allow to stand for 20 minutes. Boil the potatoes 30 minutes in their skins, peel them and pass through a food mill.

2. Crush the chopped garlic and the thyme, then tie them into a piece of gauze. Pour the crème fraîche into a saucepan, add pepper and bring to the boil. Immerse the sachet of herbs in the mixture. Cook 3 minutes.

3. At the first boil, add the rinsed and diced fish fillets to the cream. Cook 4 to 5 minutes while stirring. Remove the sachet of herbs. The fish is cooked when it has absorbed the crème fraîche.

à la Provençale

4. Crush the fish in a mortar and transfer it to a saucepan. Gently incorporate the puréed potato. Blend everything to prepare the brandade. Pass the mixture through a food processor.

5. Add olive oil to the brandade: keep the consistency even and dense, with visible flakes of fish. Adjust the seasoning. In an oiled pan, render down the minced tomatoes, eggplant and shallots. Fry the basil.

6. For the vinaigrette, whisk the lemon juice, salt, pepper and olive oil. Blend in the chopped chives, crushed olives and minced egg. Arrange quenelles of the brandade and rendered vegetables on plates. Garnish with vinaigrette and salmon roe.

Sole Brochettes with

Preparation time: 40 minutes
Cooking time: 10 minutes
Difficulty: ★★

Serves 4

70 g/2¹/₂ oz black olive paste
zest and juice of 1 lemon
1 clove garlic, minced
300 g/11 oz fillets of sole
1 bunch chives
2 lemons, sliced
12 pitted green olives
cherry tomatoes

2 tbsp olive oil
salt
pepper
mixed greens to garnish (optional)

For the anchovy sauce:
1 clove garlic
50 g/1³/₄ oz flat-leaf parsley
30 g/1 oz basil
20 g/2¹/₂ tbsp capers
2 anchovy fillets
100 ml/7 tbsp olive oil
salt

Neglecting for once the valorization of the modest dishes of the Basilicata, his place of origin in the south of Italy, Donato Massaro looks to the sea for this recipe. In this case, the very aristocratic sole, which is featured in over 300 traditional recipes, is not encumbered with heavy sauces or an outdated presentation, but blends the aroma of black olives from the chef's native mountains with the tangy flavor of lemon zest.

Donato Massaro originally wanted to refine his recipe with citron, a citrus fruit with a thick skin and a unique taste. But it is so difficult to find citron at the market that our chef prepared this fish with lemon for greater convenience.

With all the sweetness of black olives, this sole lends itself well to a topping of extra virgin olive oil. Practically all regions of Italy produce their own olive oil. In the north of the country, the oil is more thin and fluid, with the taste of

almonds. Those of Lombardy, with a greenish color, are hearty and fruity. In the center of Italy the oils of Emilia-Romagna, Tuscany and Umbria are very flavorful and call to mind nuts and wild herbs. In the south, the majority of oils come from Abruzzo, Apulia, Sicily and Sardinia. A golden yellow color, they give off a pronounced aroma of olive and have a very fruity character.

Sometimes, the olive paste used to stuff our sole can be too heavy to work with. If that happens, we recommend heating a little olive oil in a pan over a very low heat, and mixing in the olive paste.

These brochettes make a very economical dish, especially if you replace the sole with ling, flounder or plaice, all which hold up well during cooking. By all means grill the brochettes in the garden as you enjoy a relaxing day in the sun.

1. Tip the olive paste, grated lemon zest and minced garlic into a pan. Mix well into a consistent paste and heat for a few minutes. Squeeze the lemon juice and set aside.

2. Stretch out the sole fillets on a chopping board. Garnish each fillet with the olive paste by spreading it carefully with the back of a spoon.

3. Roll the coated fillets starting with the nearest end. Secure each piece by winding a blade of chive twice round it and finishing with a knot.

Anchovy Sauce

4. Take a wooden skewer. Thread it alternately through the lemon slices, olives, sole and cherry tomatoes. Add salt and pepper. Then prepare the other brochettes.

5. Mix 1 tsp lemon juice with 2 tbsp olive oil (reserve the rest of the lemon juice for the sauce). Pour the sauce over the sole. Brown them 10 minutes under the grill or broiler.

6. For the sauce, mince the garlic, parsley, basil, capers and anchovies. Mix into the olive oil and the remaining lemon juice. Add salt and whisk rapidly. Eat the brochettes with the anchovy sauce on the side.

Carp

Preparation time: 35 minutes
Cooking time, fish: 40 minutes
Cooking time, potatoes: 30 minutes
Difficulty: ★

Serves 8

4 potatoes
1 carp, about 1 kg/2¼ lb
50 g/3½ tbsp butter
2 onions
2 carrots

1 head of celery (optional)
1 tbsp honey
salt
ground white and black pepper
100 ml/7 tbsp lager beer
2 bay leaves
white and black peppercorns
1 bunch curly-leaf parsley
1 bunch dill

In Russia, carp is most commonly prepared in lake and river regions such as those in central Russia, near Moscow, Kostroma, Saratova and Novgorod. The chain of Bear Lakes is especially well-known for the quality of fish that can be caught there. Many Russians legally fish in fresh water without taxation. They catch not only carp, but also trout, salmon, sturgeon and *riapouchka* or "fish of the tzar", long and slender with top-quality flesh.

Carp is readily available in Russia, and it remains a relatively economical fish. Those available on the market are fairly small in size (around 1.2 kg/2¾ lb), and larger pieces are rare. They are sold either fresh or smoked. Gourmets love to eat grilled carp at parties and picnics. They appreciate it equally well oven-cooked with a bitter cream and mushrooms, and will stuff

the fish with a mixture of mushrooms and tomatoes, or with bread and other fish. As for hunters, they will cook the fish on high heat in a sort of bouillabaisse, in cast iron pots surrounded by clay.

It is no surprise to find a Russian dish with a beer sauce. In fact, the country has a venerable tradition of beer production. This production was once a privilege reserved for the monasteries, but today businesses in the Vladimir and Novgorod regions are working to reintroduce several types of lager.

Russians tend to add buckwheat honey, with its rather dark color, to their dishes. But for this recipe, any type of honey will be suitable.

At the final garnishing, a few cooked green peas can be scattered on the potatoes to add a touch of additional color.

1. Boil the potatoes for 30 minutes. With fish scissors, cut the fins off the carp. Open the belly and empty it, remove the head and rinse the fish under running water. Dry off the fish.

2. Generously butter a large ovenproof dish. Put the fish in the dish.

3. Peel and mince the onions. Peel the carrots and chop into rounds. Chop the celery into sticks. Thin down the honey in a small bowl of water. Cover the fish with the vegetables and dissolved honey. Add salt and pepper.

in Beer

4. Pour the beer over the fish. Top with the bay leaves and the white and black peppercorns. Cover with a sheet of aluminum foil. Allow to cook for 40 minutes.

5. Using large spatulas, transfer the cooked carp onto a large serving dish. Peel the boiled potatoes, slice them in rings, and roll in melted butter, minced parsley and dill.

6. Place the herbed potatoes around the fish. Top it with the strained cooking sauce and eat while hot.

Stuffed Carp

Preparation: 45 minutes
Cooking time: 45 minutes
Chilling time, carp: 1 hour
Chilling time, jelly: 3 hours
Difficulty: ★★

Serves 4

1 carp, about 1.5 kg/3¼ lb
salt
pepper
100 g/3½ oz mushrooms

For the stuffing:
carp pieces
1 onion
1 clove garlic

½ sprig cilantro
1 tsp cumin
1 tsp paprika
salt

pepper
1 tsp harissa
1 tsp olive oil
1 egg
4 tbsp breadcrumbs

For the broth:
1 onion
3 cloves
2 carrots, peeled
½ sprig cilantro
1 celery stalk
1 large pinch dried saffron
salt
1 tbsp capers
juice of 1 lemon

When one imagines stuffed carp, one automatically thinks of the famous *gefilte fish*, the Yiddish name that designates this dish that originated in Eastern Europe, or more precisely, in Poland or Russia. By unalterable custom, on the principal Ashkenazi holidays this traditional dish honors the family table.

Ledicia Renassia, who demonstrates a veritable passion for this fish, underappreciated by the Jews of the Mediterranean, has boldly reconceived this basic recipe. Usually sweet, carp is brightened in this creation and unveils Mediterranean flavors.

Present in Israel, where it is raised in holding tanks, the carp is a fish from slow-flowing rivers. Capable of attaining a length of 75 cm/30 in, it is recognized by its heavyset body, covered in thick scales. Originating in Asia, it is appreciated by fish lovers for its firm and semi-fatty flesh. If it is live at the time of purchase, prefer those that are fattier. Be sure to remove the

venom sac, which can be difficult to extract from the bottom of the throat. It is also advised that you soak the fish, gutted and scaled, in several successive baths of vinegary water.

This recipe may also be prepared with perch or any other fish of the same family, according to taste.

Judiciously spiced, the stuffing masterfully complements the flavor of the fish. A major spice in oriental gastronomy, cumin unveils its hot, powerful and peppery flavor. This plant, originating in Turkistan, is an ideal complement for fish dishes. As for the saffron, its presence serves to enrich this dish, offering it character and a rich color. This spice, the most expensive in the world, comes from the purple crocus flower. It takes 200,000 flowers to obtain one kilogram or two pounds of saffron pistils!

Stuffed Carp in Saffron Glaze is a refined dish that really deserves to be discovered.

1. Cut off the head of the carp and gut the fish without opening the belly. Cut 6 steaks of 2 cm/¾ in thickness. Rinse, then salt them. Refrigerate for 1 hour. Set aside the remaining fish for the stuffing.

2. Prepare the stuffing by boning and mincing the rest of the carp with the onion, garlic and cilantro. Mix in a bowl. Sprinkle with cumin, paprika, salt and pepper. Add the harissa diluted in 1 tsp olive oil, the egg and the breadcrumbs.

3. Pepper the fish steaks. Using two spoons, fill the center with stuffing. Place a few slices of mushroom on top.

in Saffron Glaze

4. For the broth, fill the bottom of a roasting pan with water. Put in the onion studded with the cloves, the carrots, cilantro, celery, salt and saffron.

5. Arrange the fish steaks carefully in the broth. Cook on low heat for about 45 minutes. Five minutes before the fish is done, add the capers and pour the lemon juice on top. Allow to cool.

6. Place the steaks on plates. Remove the vegetables from the broth and cut the carrots into disks. Arrange them around the fish. Pour over the broth. Refrigerate 3 hours until a glaze is produced.

Swordfish

Preparation time: 40 minutes
Cooking time: ca.12 minutes
Marinating time: 30 minutes
Difficulty: ★

Serves 6

1.5 kg/3¹/₄ lb swordfish
2 lemons
2 onions
2 large tomatoes
3 long green bell peppers
10 bay leaves

For the marinade:
1 onion
100 ml/7 tbsp olive oil
5 bay leaves
1 tbsp tomato paste
2 cloves garlic
1 tbsp lemon juice
1 tsp salt
ground white pepper

The Black Sea, the Marmara Sea, the Aegean Sea and the Mediterranean Sea border the coasts of Turkey, making this country a paradise of fish. Winter is the best season for eating the local fish. Numerous species migrate from the Black Sea to the warmer waters of the Marmara Sea, and their flesh is well fattened, ideal for preparing grilled fish and brochettes.

Enjoying fish is strongly linked to Turkish conviviality. The inhabitants of Istanbul set off with friends or family for the taverns of the fishermen of the Bosphorus, Rumeli Kavağı at Kumkapı, or the fashionable restaurants between Tarabya and Bebek. Located on a seaside terrace, one treats oneself to *mezze* and grilled fish while talking around a glass of rakı. Along the docks near the Galata bridge, some fishermen offer grilled fish sandwiches right from their boats.

The Turkish much prefer the fish from the Black, Marmara and Northern Aegean Seas over those of the Southern Aegean and Mediterranean. Despite the pollution, the selection of species is still rather large: the swordfish (*kiliç*), Black Sea anchovy (*hamsı*), blue fish (*lüfer*) native to this region, the costly and enormous Black Sea turbot (*kalkan*), but also the dog mullet (*kefal*), bass (*levrek*) or even skipjack (*palamut*). All kinds of fish are cooked with red onions.

The swordfish chosen by our chef is the delight of Turkish brochette-lovers. This large fish is caught in the Aegean and Mediterranean Seas. It derives its name from the shape of its upper jawbone, which is extended by a long rostrum in the form of a sword. The Turks enjoy it grilled, steamed or cooked with onions in a tomato sauce. Its firm flesh allows it to be marinated in a mixture of lemon juice, olive oil, tomato paste and bay leaf before being cooked on a copper Turkish grill.

1. On a chopping board, cut off all the red portions of the swordfish flesh. Cut the piece of fish into large cubes of 3 to 4 cm (1¹/₄ –1¹/₂ in) each side.

2. Cut the lemons into semi-circles. Peel 3 onions, cut 2 of them into quarters and separate the layers. Cut the tomatoes into slices and the green peppers into rectangles of about 2 x 5 cm (³/₄ x 2 in). Set aside.

3. For the marinade, grate the remaining onion and squeeze it to gather the juice. Pour it into a bowl with olive oil, the bay leaves, the tomato paste, crushed garlic and lemon juice. Add salt and pepper. Whisk thoroughly.

Shish Kebabs

4. Place the cubes of fish in the marinade. Allow to marinate 30 minutes.

5. On a skewer, alternate a piece of swordfish then 1 bay leaf, 1 slice of lemon, 1 slice of tomato, pepper and onion and so on. Use about 4 swordfish pieces per skewer.

6. Grill the swordfish kebabs 3 minutes on each side on a barbecue, a portable Turkish grill, or under the kitchen grill or broiler.

Prawn

Preparation time: 20 minutes
Cooking time: 40 minutes
Difficulty: ★

Serves 4

750 g/1³/₄ lb tomatoes
2 chipotle smoked chili peppers
2 tbsp tomato paste
1 large onion
6 cloves garlic
10 sprigs parsley

50 g/3¹/₂ tbsp lard
32 large prawns
30 ml/2 tbsp tequila
1 liter/1 quart fish stock
250 g/9 oz canned cactus, in strips
5 or 6 leaves fresh lamb's-quarters
1 tsp dried oregano
salt
pepper
5 tbsp fine cornmeal

Originating in the region of Veracruz and Tampico, *chilpachole* is always served in the form of a thick sauce. It can be prepared with prawns, velvet swimming crabs, clams and a variety of shellfish.

In Mexico, the large fleshy pink prawns are caught in abundance on the Pacific coast as well as in the Gulf of Mexico. They are usually sautéed *à la diable* (deviled) in a spicy sauce. For this recipe, Tony Spinosa chose to pan-fry them in lard, which can be replaced with olive oil.

The chipotle chili pepper gives the sauce its rich and smoky flavor, which complements the cactus strips very well. When it is fresh, this spicy chili pepper, commonly found in Mexico, is called a jalapeno chili. About 12 cm/5 in long and of an average diameter, the pepper is green with narrow brown stripes.

Once dried and smoked, it becomes a chipotle chili with a brownish-red color and its flavor changes completely.

The lamb's-quarters brings an unusual note to the chilpachole. Called *epazote* in Mexico, this special variety of lamb's-quarters with finely serrated leaves is principally used in Mexican and Indian cuisine. In other countries, this plant is considered a weed. Sold fresh or dried, lamb's-quarters flavors fish dishes and black bean soups. In the *chilpachole*, our chef suggests that you replace it, if necessary, with dried oregano.

The cactus slices used for the garnish are from the tender young shoots of the India Fig, the tree represented on the Mexican flag. After harvesting, their thorns must be removed. Traditional cooks slice them into strips and boil them in salted water. These smoky-flavored leaves are also served from a can.

1. Cut the tomatoes into quarters. Pour them into a blender with ¹/₂ cup water. Add the smoked chili peppers and tomato paste then mix to obtain a sauce.

2. Peel and mince the onion and garlic. Mince the parsley. Melt the lard in a pan. Add the onions, garlic, prawns and half of the minced parsley. Pan-fry 5 minutes on high heat until the prawns turn orange.

3. Flambé the prawns in tequila. Pour the tomato sauce on top. Stir 2 to 3 minutes while heating.

Chilpachole

4. Add the fish stock. Simmer to reduce for 10 minutes until the sauce thickens a bit.

5. Strain the strips of cactus and rinse in warm water. Stir them into the prawns along with the remaining parsley, lamb's-quarters and dried oregano. Add salt and pepper. Cook 10 minutes on medium heat.

6. Dissolve the cornmeal in a bowl of water. Pour into the prawn mixture and allow to simmer 5 to 10 minutes.

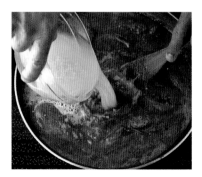

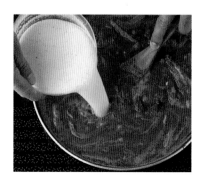

Cabbage Stuffed

Preparation time: 40 minutes
Cooking time: 1 hour 5 minutes
Difficulty: ★

Serves 4

1 green cabbage

For the stuffing:
700 g/1¹/₂ lb fillets of perch
1 onion
1 clove garlic
5 sprigs cilantro
1 tsp turmeric
1 tsp cumin
1 tsp paprika
salt, pepper

1 egg
1 tsp harissa
1 tsp olive oil
3 tbsp breadcrumbs

For the tomato sauce:
2 onions
1 clove garlic
3¹/₂ tbsp olive oil
1 kg/2¹/₄ lb tomatoes
1 tsp harissa
¹/₂ sprig cilantro
salt
pepper
6 dried mild red chili peppers
15 green olives in herbs
4 preserved lemons

For the garnish:
cilantro leaves

Inventive and passionate, Ledicia Renassia draws on various repertoires of the Jewish people of Israel for the recipes that she adapts with flair.

The preparation our chef proposes here is inspired by the famous stuffed cabbage, a dish highly prized amongst the Jewish families of Eastern Europe. This population generally eats stuffed cabbage on the weekly holy day of the Shabbat.

Wanting to pair this dish with Mediterranean flavors, Ledicia has replaced the original stuffing, which was made of beef, with spicy perch. In Israel, this freshwater fish, imported from Somalia, is sold canned. Highly sought-after for its lean, firm white flesh, perch has a delicate flavor. It can be substituted with cod.

Judiciously seasoned, the stuffing unveils flavors of the Orient. Cilantro, also called "Chinese parsley", is a flavorful plant used frequently in the Sephardic repertoire. As for the spices,

they add a ray of light. Also used to add color to dishes, the powdered form of turmeric root turns out to be a little more bitter than saffron. The preferred variety comes from Bengal, and releases its flavors when accompanied by other spices. Cumin is extracted from this plant, which tints milk-based products, candy, drinks and mustards.

Known throughout the world, harissa (hot chili sauce), a Tunisian specialty of Nabeul, is a purée of dried red chili peppers, ground and seasoned with salt, garlic, caraway seeds and olive oil. Use according to taste.

Unveiling its full mildness, green cabbage is an ideal accompaniment to spicy stuffing. This winter vegetable with a waffle-like texture should have thick leaves, without holes or cracks, and should be crisp and crunchy.

Cabbage Stuffed with Spicy Fish is a wonderful meal to enjoy at informal gatherings with friends.

1. To make the stuffing, mince together the perch fillets, onion, garlic and cilantro. Place them in a bowl. Add the turmeric, cumin and paprika. Add salt and pepper. Mix. Pour in the egg and the harissa diluted in olive oil. Sprinkle with breadcrumbs. Form into balls.

2. Wash the cabbage and remove the large leaves. Blanch the leaves for 4 or 5 minutes in boiling water. Chill them. Remove the central vein of the leaves and place a ball of stuffing in the center of each leaf. Close each leaf with wooden tooth picks.

3. For the tomato sauce, heat the onions and minced garlic in a frying pan with 3 tbsp olive oil. Add the tomatoes cut into slices. Cook and stew on low heat for about 20 minutes.

with Spicy Fish

4. Dilute the harissa with 1 tsp olive oil. Add it to the tomatoes and the chopped cilantro. Add salt and pepper.

5. Wash the dried chili peppers in cold water and deseed them. Place them gently in the tomato sauce. Add the green olives and quartered lemons.

6. Place the stuffed cabbage in the tomato sauce. Simmer on low heat, covered, for about 30 minutes. Place on a dish. Garnish with cilantro.

Fish Cigars

Preparation time:	30 minutes
Cooking time:	15 minutes
Difficulty:	★

Serves 4

200 g/7 oz shrimp
300 g/11 oz burbot
2 eggs
500 g/generous 1 lb phyllo dough
oil for frying

For the chermoula:
¹/₂ bunch parsley
1 lemon
100 g/7 tbsp butter
100 ml/7 tbsp oil
¹/₂ tsp paprika
1 tsp salt
¹/₂ tsp black pepper
1 pinch saffron

This recipe is quite similar to another stuffed phyllo pastry called *briouates*, except that the dough garnished with fish and shrimp stuffing is rolled in the form of cigars rather than folded into triangles. Fish cigars are served in the coastal regions. Casablanca is the top fishing port in Morocco, followed by Agadir and Tangier. There are more than 800 species of edible fish to be found in the ocean depths bordering Morocco, but only thirty of them are readily available. Moroccan gourmets particularly prize burbot, sardines, whiting, sea bream, ombrine, swordfish, skipjack and goatfish.

Only the inhabitants of the coastal regions near Asfi, Essaouira, Casablanca or Tangier regularly eat fish. With the modernization of transportation and food preservation, however, Moroccans who live in the mountain regions in the interior are beginning to discover the benefits of fish and different ways to prepare it.

The Moroccan coasts abound in shellfish, such as the little shrimp our chef has added to the stuffing of the cigars. Shrimp, crayfish, crabs, spider crabs, sea urchins and slipper lobsters are caught by great trawlers. In the Moroccan markets, the gray shrimp rubs elbows with pink shrimp, the black tiger shrimp caught in Madia (the port of Kenitra) and the royal shrimp. This large red shrimp is particular to Morocco and Senegal. Some countries now have fish farms that raise gray and tiger shrimp. All these little shellfish are prepared slowly in *tajines*, grilled on skewers or included in fillings for a wide variety of finger-food delicacies.

Moroccans enjoy filling their phyllo dough cigars with a variety of preparations, from ground chicken embellished with raisins to marzipan flavored with orange flower water. These fish cigars are often served while waiting for the arrival of the main course.

1. Remove the heads of the shrimps. Shell them. Dispose of the heads and shells. Chop the parsley and squeeze the lemon juice (set them aside).

2. Place the burbot on a chopping board. Cut into small pieces with a chef's knife.

3. For the chermoula, heat the butter and oil in a saucepan. Add the chopped parsley, lemon juice, paprika, black pepper, salt and saffron to the saucepan. Mix for a few moments over low heat. Set aside a little for dipping.

with Chermoula

4. Stir the burbot and shrimp into the sauce. Allow to cook briefly while stirring. Beat the eggs and add ¾ of them to the saucepan. Mix again. (The rest is used to seal the cigars).

5. Roll out a sheet of phyllo dough and cut it into equal halves. Place a little stuffing at the bottom of the sheet. Begin to roll, then fold in both sides of the leaf. Continue rolling to the end. Seal the end with a little beaten egg. Make the other cigars.

6. Heat the oil in a frying pan until it reaches 180°C/355°F. Dip the fish cigars into the oil and allow to brown for 10 minutes. Once they are cooked, transfer to paper towels to drain. Serve on a pretty serving dish.

Fish

Preparation time: 40 minutes
Cooking time: 1 hour
Marinating time: 10 minutes
Difficulty: ★

Serves 4

For the couscous:
500 g/2¹/₂ cups couscous
¹/₂ tbsp olive oil
1 pinch salt

For the sauce:
4 fresh tomatoes
¹/₂ tbsp tomato paste
4 onions, chopped
1 clove garlic

1 pinch cumin
1 pinch saffron
olive oil
salt, pepper

For the fish and garnish:
1 mullet, about 1.2 kg/2³/₄ lb
salt, pepper
1 clove garlic
1 pinch saffron
1 pinch cumin
olive oil
80 g/¹/₂ cup cooked chickpeas
80 g/10 tbsp golden raisins
4 red peppers, cut in strips
2 onions, sliced

Fish Couscous is a special variant of traditional couscous, the national dish of Tunisia, which is generally prepared with veal or chicken. This is a holiday dish that is enriched with grouper or mullet, accompanied by vegetables, chickpeas, raisins and slices of quince that give it a very fine flavor. We had to replace the quince with onions, here, because these fruit are difficult to find out of season.

In former times, Tunisian women prepared the couscous during the summer, as well as all kinds of foods that lasted all year long: *halalem* dough, olive oil, dried meat, olive conserve, spices and so on. In a traditional home, a special little room was reserved as a storeroom for all of these products, away from the humidity and the smoke of the kitchen.

To make couscous in the traditional way, pour a little salt, olive oil and water on the grain, then work it with your hands. The couscous must then be steamed. Tunisians have transformed the couscous to include fish because they are so fond of it. Favorites are grouper, sea bream, goatfish and whiting.

Of course couscous is served with the chickpeas that are found in a large number of dishes: with potato, zucchini or spinach ragout, *bnedr* meatballs, with mint or garlic, or *raēba* cakes. Do not hesitate to taste the astonishing *rzil bnet* covered in angel hair and wrapped in a sweet chickpea stuffing.

For extra flavor, our chef recommends cooking the fish heads with the flesh. The couscous will also take on wonderful flavor if a piece of cinnamon is added to it. Serve the couscous with side salads of fennel with vinegar, or with salty purple turnips spiced with lemon and hot chili sauce.

1. Mix the couscous, olive oil and salt. Pour some water into your hand and disperse it throughout the semolina. Continue until you have used ¹/₂ glass water.

2. Heat water in a couscous maker or other steamer. When it boils, pour the couscous into the upper basket and steam for 30 minutes.

3. Cut the fish into 4 slices. Peel the garlic and mince it. In a dish, coat the fish slices with the salt, pepper, garlic, saffron, cumin and olive oil. Allow to marinate for about 10 minutes.

Couscous

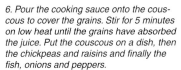

4. For the sauce, heat some oil and sauté the chopped onions. Mix the tomatoes with the paste and add to the onions. Heat 2 to 3 minutes, then add 2 liters/2 quarts water, the cumin, saffron, minced garlic, salt and pepper. Allow to cook for 10 minutes.

5. Pour the pieces of fish, the onion slices, red pepper strips, chickpeas and raisins into the sauce. Allow to cook another 10 minutes. Remove the cooked fish with a slotted spoon. Set aside the raisins and chickpeas.

6. Pour the cooking sauce onto the couscous to cover the grains. Stir for 5 minutes on low heat until the grains have absorbed the juice. Put the couscous on a dish, then the chickpeas and raisins and finally the fish, onions and peppers.

Jumbo Shrimp

Preparation time: 30 minutes
Cooking time: 15 minutes
Difficulty: ★★

Serves 4

20 g/2 tbsp fresh turmeric
1 bunch fresh cilantro
3 cloves garlic
20 g/1¹/₂ tbsp green curry paste
560 ml/2¹/₃ cups coconut milk
40 ml/2¹/₂ tbsp fish sauce

10 g/1 tbsp sugar
1 tsp white pepper
35 ml/2¹/₂ tbsp peanut oil
5 large scallions
4 celery stalks
1 large white onion
15 gray jumbo shrimp

Jumbo shrimp placed artistically on a bed of mild yet spicy sauce, colored with green Thai curry, may surprise those who are used to eating *kang kra rhi kung*. Ordinarily, Thai chefs present shrimp on a dish and drizzled with curry sauce.

The aromatic garnish composed of sliced scallions, celery stalk and white onions is a little extra by the chef, so rarified that Mr. Sombath's loyal patrons could never resist it. Although they look different, the scallions, celery stalks and white onions from Thailand are strangely reminiscent of their European homonyms. As for the ingredients that make up the sauce, apart from the sugar and oil, you will find them in specialized supermarkets that sell exotic products.

A large number of Thai dishes are enlivened with a red or green curry paste that is always comprised of chili peppers, fresh herbs and lemon grass. Red curry gets its color from fresh or dried red chili peppers, and is used to season rice and steamed chicken. Green curry, however, is made from green chili peppers and fresh cilantro. Red curry has a more powerful flavor, which marvelously enhances dishes with meat and shellfish. This paste is always cooked and well diluted in hot oil. Present in every curry sauce, coconut milk counteracts the power of the chili pepper.

A substitute for salt, mainly used by coastal populations, fish sauce, or *nam pla*, is an equivalent of the Vietnamese nuoc mam. Accompany the shrimp in the traditional way with small bowls of steamed rice. To make it authentic, eat the rice not with chopsticks, but in the style of the Thai people, who use a fork and spoon.

1. Slice the turmeric into fine disks. Cut off the stalk of the cilantro and weigh 5 g of leaves for the mixture. Peel the garlic. Mix all these ingredients together in a bowl until evenly distributed.

2. Place the green curry, coconut milk, fish sauce, sugar and pepper in separate ramekins. Pour the oil into a saucepan on high heat. When it is very hot, add the green curry paste. Mix till smooth with a wooden spatula.

3. When the scent of the curry is released, pour the turmeric mixture into the saucepan. Stir with the wooden spatula to mix all the ingredients. Bring to the boil.

in Green Curry

4. As soon as it boils, add the coconut milk, fish sauce and pepper. Mix lightly. When the sauce is smooth and even, add the sugar. Allow to simmer over very low heat until it is time to serve.

5. Cut the scallions, white onions and celery into fine disks. Place the shrimp on a plate. Remove their shells and devein.

6. Turn the shelled shrimp into the green curry sauce, then add the sliced vegetables. Allow to cook 10 minutes on low heat. As soon as the shrimp turn pink, remove them from the heat. Serve very hot.

Cameroon-Style

Preparation time: 20 minutes
Cooking time: 45 minutes
Difficulty: ★

Serves 4

1 kg/2¹/₄ lb jumbo shrimp
250 g/9 oz fresh tomatoes
1 small onion
200 ml/generous ³/₄ cup oil
1 pinch cayenne pepper
salt
1 sprig basil

In the traditional Cameroonian recipe for sautéed shrimp, the shrimp simmer in the company of tomatoes, onions and chili pepper. Marie Koffi-Nketsia put her personal touch on this dish by flavoring it with chopped basil.

In Cameroon, shrimp, crawfish, crabs and crayfish harvested by the local fishing industry are available for all kinds of side dishes. Among the shellfish, shrimp are the most prestigious and accompany the most famous dishes: they are used notably in *ngondo*, a dish based on pumpkin seeds cooked in parchment paper, and in *ndole*, which is a national dish prepared with leaves that resemble spinach. Cameroonians also eat grilled shrimp coated with a mixture of seven native spices.

The basil that augments this dish figures amongst the most frequently used herbs in Cameroonian cuisine. Thus our chef's idea is quite in keeping with the origin of this recipe. Her compatriots enthusiastically use basil in a sauce with *jansen* seeds for cooking fish, as well as with tomatoes for meat and fish dishes. Parsley and lemon balm are also customarily used to enhance their cooking.

To improve this traditional recipe even more, a Cameroonian would use peanut oil, which is manufactured in the north, where conditions are favorable for the cultivation of peanuts. But Cameroonians may also favor palm oil. Uncooked, this oil has a red color, but once it is heated over high heat, it whitens. It is then heated with tomatoes and onions to form the sauce for the sautéed shrimp. In some regions villagers produce highly flavorful local oil prepared with wild olives, but this is reserved for family use and is not available for purchase.

1. Take a shrimp in one hand and peel the tail section. Prepare the other shrimp in the same fashion.

2. Holding a shrimp in one hand, slice along its back with a small, sharp knife. Remove the entrails. Proceed in the same way with the remaining shrimp.

3. Cut the tomatoes into circles. Peel the onions and slice finely. Heat half the oil in a frying pan and stir-fry the onions for at least 15 to 20 minutes.

Sautéed Shrimp

4. When the onions are sufficiently brown, turn the tomato slices into the pan. Add salt and cayenne pepper. Cook 10 minutes on fairly high heat until the vegetables are well cooked.

5. Heat the remaining oil in a frying pan. Pour the shrimp into the pan and add salt. Fry them quickly over high heat for 4 to 5 minutes, turning several times.

6. Chop the basil. Combine it with the shrimp and fry 2 to 3 minutes, stirring with a spatula. Add the tomatoes, onions and a little cold water. Allow to cook for another 5 minutes, stirring often.

Andalusian

Preparation time: 20 minutes
Cooking time: 45 minutes
Difficulty: ★

Serves 4

For the fish:
1 sea bream, ca. 3 kg/6½ lb
1 kg/2¼ lb coarse sea salt

For the aïoli:
2 cloves garlic
1 tsp sea salt

1 egg yolk
juice of 1 lemon
150 ml/⅔ cup olive oil

For the accompaniments:
500 g/generous 1 lb potatoes
cherry tomatoes
lemon slices

Well known for their art of rhythm, Andalusians are also masters in the art of preparing fish. So it is fitting that José Luis Tarín Fernández, who originates from Seville, selected Andalusian Sea Bream or *pescado a la sal* for us from his repertoire.

The cooking method is simple, guaranteeing authentic flavors with a touch of sophistication. For best results, there is no need to gut or scale the fish. In this recipe, still complete with its scales, bones and fins, the sea bream is cooked on a bed of coarse sea salt. The fish you choose will depend on what is available: sea bream is a good choice, as is catfish, because any large-scaled fish will taste marvelous when cooked in coarse sea salt like this.

The first layer of salt should be about 1 cm (⅓ in) thick: this will protect the flesh of the fish while it is being cooked. The second layer covers the fish completely. Moistened, the salt helps to cook the sea bream. Sprinkle the fish with water from

your hands, then let it rest for a few minutes before placing it in the oven. This gives the salt time to absorb the water completely.

Well-cooked under its crust of salt, the sea bream is opened at the center of the table, before the attentive eyes of your guests. The first layer of salt is opened with the point of a knife, to reveal the fish. The solidified skin is easily detached from the flesh. Just pull it from the tail to the head in one delicate but firm movement.

Our chef recommends two possible ways to serve the sea bream: one piece per person, or presented whole once the skin has been removed.

In order to augment the taste of the fish, which has only been salted, aïoli gives it the right nod to southern flavor. Whipped like a garlic and lemon mayonnaise, our chef's aïoli can be garnished with a pinch of chopped curly-leaf parsley.

1. Take an ovenproof dish with high sides that is as long as the fish. Pour half the coarse sea salt into the dish. Spread it in a thick layer at the bottom of the dish.

2. Place the whole, non-gutted fish on the layer of sea salt. Pack the salt around it so that it can absorb the salt perfectly.

3. Pour the remaining sea salt over the fish. Spread by hand to cover the fish completely.

Sea Bream

4. Fill a small bowl with cold water. Sprinkle the top layer of salt with the water in small quantities. Put the fish in the oven at 190–200°C/375–390°F and cook for 45 minutes.

5. While the fish cooks, peel the potatoes. Quarter them and boil for 15 minutes. To prepare the aïoli, place the peeled cloves of garlic and sea salt in a bowl. Crush with a pestle to produce a smooth, even paste.

6. Add the egg yolk and lemon juice to the crushed garlic. Whip the aïoli by adding olive oil bit by bit until you obtain a thick, well-blended mixture. Serve with the potatoes and fish, garnished with slices of lemon and tomatoes.

Grilled Shizuoka

Preparation time: 40 minutes
Cooking time: 15 minutes
Marinating time: 20 minutes
Soaking time: 1 hour
Difficulty: ★

Serves 4

1 sea bream
1 bunch fresh white grapes
70 g/5 tbsp sugar
3 tbsp fine salt

For the sauce:
100 ml/ 7 tbsp mirin
100 ml/ 7 tbsp soy sauce
100 ml/ 7 tbsp sake

For the dashi bouillon:
2 strips konbu seaweed
30 g/1 oz flaked tuna

Grilled Shizuoka Sea Bream belongs to the top-of-the-line Japanese cuisine that accompanies the famed tea ceremony in Kyoto. Chefs place considerable importance on the various colors of the food, the distinct methods of cooking and the harmony between the serving pieces and the food. The dish in itself is savored as a delectable treat for the eye.

The Japanese have mastered a number of methods for grilling fish. The most simple, referred to as *shio yaki*, consists of coating the fish with salt and then cooking it on the grill. In the *saikyo yaki* method, the fish is covered in miso paste (fermented soy) before it is grilled. The method used by our chef is called *yu wan yaki*: the fish is marinated in a skipjack tuna bouillon (dashi bouillon) with sake, mirin and soy sauce before cooking.

This bouillon is obtained by heating two strips of konbu seaweed in a saucepan of water for 15 minutes. When the water begins to simmer, remove the konbu and add the flaked tuna and bring to the boil. The final step is to filter the bouillon and add seasonings.

Sea bream is the king of fish for the Japanese. Before preparing it, most native chefs bleed the sea bream so that the muscles remain supple and the flesh acquires a silky texture. The best fish come from the area surrounding Naruto in a strait between the islands of Shikoku and Awaji-Shima, where the waters of the Sea of Japan and the Pacific Ocean mingle. Indeed, the city of Naruto even has a pink sea bream on its official emblem.

The recipe presented by our chef, which includes grapes, is inspired by the region of Shizuoka on the Pacific coast, about 100 km (160 miles) south of Tokyo. It is, in fact, a viticultural area where table grapes and white wines are produced. Some rosé and red wines complete the range.

1. Remove the head of the sea bream. Open the fish along the belly and the back. Lift off the upper fillet by slicing along the central bone and pulling from the tail to the head. Then detach the other fillet. Set them aside with their skin intact.

2. For the sauce, mix the soy sauce, sake and mirin. Whisk to obtain a smooth, even sauce. Mix this with the dashi bouillon prepared earlier (see text above).

3. Hold the grapes between the thumb and index finger. Remove the skin with the point of a small knife. Remove the seeds by using a hair pin or a paperclip.

Sea Bream

4. Make a syrup with the sugar and 100 ml/ 7 tbsp water. Bring to the boil. When the sugar is dissolved, add the peeled grapes. Boil for 5 minutes, then remove from the heat and let the grapes marinate in the syrup for 1 hour.

5. Cut the sea bream fillets in the center, remove the bones and slice between the flesh and the skin. Open the pieces out flat. Add salt and allow to rest for 5 minutes. Rinse, then soak the fillets in the soy sauce for 15 minutes. Dry and garnish with 3 grapes. Roll each fillet around the grapes.

6. Place each filled roll of sea bream on a heated grill and cook 5 minutes on each side. Place gently on individual plates and eat while hot.

Cod with

Preparation time: 30 minutes
Cooking time: ca. 2 hours
Marinating time: 1 hour
Difficulty: ★★

Serves 4

4 pieces of cod, 180 g/6½ oz each
sea salt
16 young leeks
4 shallots
100 g/7 tbsp butter
100 ml/7 tbsp white wine

300 ml/1¼ cups crème fraîche
1 tbsp crushed coarse-grained mustard
2 tsp ground mustard
2 live blue lobsters, 350 g/¾ lb each
2 liters/2 quarts fish stock
peppercorns
1 bouquet garni
1 medium carrot, sliced
1 stalk celery, minced
100 ml/7 tbsp white balsamic vinegar
400 g/14 oz potatoes
fresh dill
120 g/4 oz lumpfish caviar

In the Danish tradition, cod and lobster are served separately at the New Year's meal. Our chef has united these two star ingredients and this combination is hugely successful at *Langelinie Pavillonen*, his restaurant in Copenhagen.

Cod is very popular in Denmark. Caught in the North Sea, it is cooked fresh. Except on the Faroe Islands, located near Iceland, cod is no longer salted. The Danes poach cod in salted water and serve it with potatoes or other robust tubers like Jerusalem artichokes.

Blue lobster is a delicious specialty of Danish fishing, caught in the Kattegat and Skagerrak Seas. The Danes, who are very proud of it, consider it the best lobster in the world! They boil it in broth and coat it with mayonnaise or a rouille sauce.

Potatoes are among the essential elements of Danish cuisine. They grow well in sandy soils and can be stored for a long time. More than fifty different varieties are cultivated and harvested from May to August. The earliest come from the island of Samsø, and are sometimes sold for exorbitant prices. The Danes principally use the King Edward and the *bintje* as well as *asparges kartofler*, or "asparagus potato", with its elongated shape. *Blølongo*, blue in color, are reserved first and foremost for the queen.

Whole cloves can be added to the broth, if desired. When the lobster is browned over the heat, it should remain somewhat undercooked inside. Place it in the oven still wearing its shell and do not remove the shell until the moment it is served. Garnish the dish with a bay leaf. On the plates, pour several drops of olive oil around the lobster and fish.

1. Place the cod in a dish with high sides. Use a brush to coat it with cold water. Sprinkle with sea salt and allow to marinate 1 hour. Cook the potatoes for 30 minutes in salted water. Blanch the leeks for 10 minutes, then slice lengthwise.

2. Peel the shallots. Set 2 aside and mince the remaining 2. Combine the minced shallots with a little butter in a saucepan and cook for 5 minutes until the shallots are transparent. Deglaze with white wine. Stir with a spatula.

3. Bring to the boil and then reduce for 10 minutes over high heat. Pour the crème fraîche into the sauce. Mix. Continue cooking the sauce for another 5 minutes on medium heat.

Lobster

4. Add the coarse-grained mustard and the ground mustard into the sauce. Stir rapidly with a whisk, then pass the sauce through a strainer. Kill the lobsters: thrust a knife between the head and the first section of the carapace. Then cut the crustaceans into chunks.

5. Bring the fish stock to the boil. Add the two reserved shallots, the peppercorn, cod, bouquet garni, carrots, celery and balsamic vinegar and poach for 20 minutes. Meanwhile, sauté the sliced potatoes with the dill for 20 minutes in a pan.

6. Pan-fry the pieces of lobster in butter for 5 minutes until they become red. Put them in the oven for 3 to 4 minutes. Place the potatoes, scallions, cod and one piece of shelled lobster on each plate. Add the mustard sauce and last of all the caviar.

Sea Bream

Preparation time: 50 minutes
Cooking time: 1 hour 10 minutes
Marinating time: 1 night
Difficulty: ★

Serves 4

4 gray sea bream, 400 g/11 oz each
600 g/1¼ lb new potatoes
100 ml/7 tbsp olive oil
700 g/1½ lb fresh tomatoes
2 red peppers
2 green peppers
pepper

4 preserved lemons
150 g/5½ oz marinated black olives

For the chermoula
20 sprigs cilantro, finely chopped
20 sprigs parsley, finely chopped
10 cloves garlic
salt
1 tbsp cayenne pepper
1 tbsp cumin
1 tbsp paprika
150 ml/⅔ cup peanut oil
6 lemons
pepper

M'charmel designates any dish that is marinated in *chermoula* sauce, a lemony mixture of spices, herbs and oil that is distinctively Moroccan. The town of Fez is far from the coast, and yet its most sophisticated cuisine includes many fish specialties. The people of Fez prepare sea bream and porgy in the oven with vegetables and a spicy sauce, as well as in pastries called *b'steeya*.

In Morocco, gray sea bream is caught in the waters of the Atlantic as well as those of the Mediterranean. The most popular fish in the country is the sardine, a specialty of the coastal town of Essaouira, closely followed by sea bream, anchovies, sole, whiting and ombrine. The fish is usually sprinkled with *chermoula*, cooked in the oven and served with peppers, potatoes and tomatoes. Roasted whole sea bream or sea bream cooked in special lidded clay pots called tajines may also be garnished with olives and preserved lemons. Finally, chefs sometimes stuff them with shrimp, squid and vermicelli.

In Moroccan cuisine, fresh lemon finds its way into salads and fish dishes, and preserved lemons are used to complement grilled fish. Many Moroccans are fortunate enough to have lemon, orange and olive trees growing in their gardens. Lemons, oranges, grapefruit and clementines are cultivated abundantly in every region of the country, and bitter orange trees line the streets.

Olives are harvested in the areas around Meknès and Marrakech. Industrious families tend to stock up with two or three boxes of olives when they are being picked, then marinate them for ten days or so in a lemon-based pickling juice. Preserved this way, the olives will keep for more than a year. The wide array of green, red, cracked, cured black and spicy or bitter purple olives makes a tempting display on the market stalls. For this recipe, we recommend boiling the olives for a few minutes if they are to be eaten warm.

1. Place the sea bream on a chopping board. Extend a fin with one hand and cut it off with fish scissors. Use the same method to cut off all the fins. Boil the potatoes 30 minutes in salted water, then set aside in the refrigerator in their skins.

2. Prepare the chermoula by combining the cilantro, parsley, crushed garlic, salt, cayenne pepper, cumin, paprika and peanut oil. Squeeze the lemons over the chermoula. (Set aside 3 cloves of garlic and 3 sprigs of cilantro and parsley).

3. Place the sea bream on a dish with high sides. Using a soup spoon, sprinkle the chermoula over the fish. Coat with olive oil. Allow to marinate overnight.

Fantasia M'Charmel

4. Remove the skins from the tomatoes by dipping them in boiling water. Deseed the tomatoes and peppers and cut into rounds. Line a gratin dish with pepper rings and the reserved garlic and herbs. Top with the sea bream and cover with tomatoes. Add pepper and the chermoula.

5. Bake the fish in an oven preheated to 180°C/355°F for 25 minutes. Cut the boiled potatoes in half. Place them in a saucepan. Use a spoon to drizzle with chermoula. Reheat for 2 to 3 minutes.

6. Cut the preserved lemons into strips and blanch the olives for 5 minutes. Pour the cooking juices from the fish, olives and lemons into a saucepan. Cook for 5 minutes over high heat. Present the fish atop the potatoes and peppers, decorated with olives and lemons.

Sautéed Fillet of

Preparation time: *1 hour*
Cooking time: *2 hours 40 minutes*
Difficulty: ★★

Serves 4

1 sea bream, ca. 1 kg/2$^{1}/_{4}$ lb
2 tbsp peanut oil

For the accompaniment:
500 g/generous 1 lb fresh shell beans
1 large carrot
1 onion
1 or 2 whole cloves
1 sprig thyme
1 bay leaf
2 or 3 sprigs parsley

scallion leaves
2 sprigs tarragon
sea salt
pepper

For the boiled sheep's foot:
$^{1}/_{2}$ sheep's foot
1 carrot
1 onion
1 whole clove
1 sprig thyme
1 bay leaf
2 or 3 stems parsley
sea salt

For the verjuice sauce:
3 or 4 shallots
150 ml/$^{2}/_{3}$ cup verjuice
200 ml/generous $^{3}/_{4}$ cup crème fraîche
50 g/3$^{1}/_{2}$ tbsp butter

Verjuice, a sour juice made from unripe fruit, was a highly regarded ingredient during the Middle Ages, and it is making a triumphant comeback. Back then, gourmets regularly regaled themselves with slowly simmered sour sauces based on the acidic juice of the green grape. Today, as well, the very special taste of verjuice works wonders in many sauces and creams. It can be found in gourmet and specialty stores, or if none is available, diluted cider vinegar, full-strength lemon juice, or even lime juice added to cream can serve as substitutes. Add two teaspoons of water to the lime juice then stop cooking: pure lime juice and crème fraîche do not blend well when heated.

The white beans should be cooked in two liters (two quarts) of water as you would cook any dry pulses. Tarbais, little dried

beans, will accompany the sheep's foot as well as fresh beans, and are the best choice because they do not split. The sprig of chopped tarragon brings a fine, delicate flavor to the verjuice cream. Without cooking, fresh tarragon flavors the beans, the diced sheep's foot and the cream, just as it complements the fish that accompanies them.

Dull-skinned and grayish, the gray sea bream cannot claim such fine, delicate flesh as the royal sea bream. Scaled, sliced behind the head, gutted, rinsed several times, then separated from its bones and fins, the sea bream should be cooked in its skin. Pan fried for five minutes, the fillets will become firm and rather crispy. As simply as that, the little gray sea bream goes astonishingly well with the luxuriant, creamy verjuice sauce with shell beans and diced sheep's foot.

1. Remove any bones from the sea bream with tweezers. Set aside. Tip the beans into 2 liters/2 quarts salted water. Add the carrot and the onion studded with cloves, then the thyme, bay leaf, parsley and scallion leaves. Allow to cook for 2 minutes on a low boil.

2. Poach the sheep's foot 2$^{1}/_{2}$ hours on low heat with the carrot, the onion studded with clove, thyme, bay leaf, parsley and salt. While it poaches, reduce the chopped shallots to $^{3}/_{4}$ in the verjuice. Add the cream, boil briefly, blend in the butter and set aside.

3. When tender, remove the sheep's foot from the cooking broth with a slotted spoon. Remove the bones. Dice the meat very finely.

Sea Bream in Verjuice

4. In a saucepan, combine the cooked beans, diced sheep's foot and verjuice cream. Heat gently for 2 minutes. Season. Add 2 sprigs of chopped tarragon. Keep warm.

5. Pan-fry the sea bream fillets, skin-side down, for 3 minutes in 2 tbsp peanut oil. When half cooked, flip the fillets and allow to cook 2 minutes more.

6. Place the sea bream fillets on plates. Accompany them with the beans and verjuice cream. Serve hot.

Fish Fillet in

Preparation time: 15 minutes
Cooking time: 15 minutes
Rehydrating time: 15 minutes
Difficulty: ★

Serves 4

5 dried black mushrooms
1 cod fillet
6 tbsp yellow Shaoxing wine
salt

$^1/_2$ egg white
2 tbsp potato flour
500 ml/2 cups oil for frying
3 tsp sugar
50 ml/3$^1/_2$ tbsp unsweetened condensed milk
5 blades chives

Fish in Chinese yellow wine is a specialty of the Zhejiang province on the eastern coast of China. The area surrounding Shanghai is a fertile region where rice, wheat, corn, barley, sweet potatoes and white cabbage grow. Pigs are raised there and fish, seafood and freshwater crabs are abundant.

The gastronomy of this region draws on flavors that are at once rich, soft and spicy. The town of Suzhou (formerly Wuhsien) is renowned for its candied sugar pork, Hangzhou for its fried rice, and Zhenhai for its flavored ham. Many of the dishes of eastern China are based on *hung-shao*, or "red cooking", a type of slow cooking in a tightly covered pan with a little liquid, often including local rice wine.

The rice wine that flavors our fish dish is produced near Shaoxing. Made from sticky rice, it has an alcohol content betwen 15 and 18 percent and an amber color. In the past it was served as a digestive between courses during long banquets. This alcohol is served at room temperature, or even hot in winter, in small glasses accompanied by plum preserves. It is sometimes flavored with plums, ginger or bamboo. In cooking, rice wine works as well with meat as with fish, and it adds a special flavor to sweetened soy sauces. It can, of course, be replaced with a semi-dry sherry.

The Chinese equally enjoy beer, *meiguilu jiu* (rose-flavored sorghum alcohol) and fruit liqueurs. "Give a man a fish and you feed him for a day. Teach him to fish, and you feed him for life" said the sage Confucius 2500 years ago. The Chinese have not only been fishing for millennia, but they have also been practicing pisciculture. Cod, turbots, bass, mullets and sea breams are the delight of Chinese gourmets. They also raise carp. The concept of fresh food is deeply ingrained in Chinese culinary culture: guests choose live, wriggling fish from holding tanks to be served for their lunch.

1. Soak the mushrooms in warm water for 15 minutes. With a chef's knife, slice the cod fillet into pieces of about 5 x 3 cm (2 x 1$^1/_4$ in).

2. Place the fish in a bowl. Pour 2 tbsp yellow wine over it and add salt. Pour in the $^1/_2$ egg white. Mix with your fingertips.

3. Sprinkle 1 tbsp flour over the cod with a spoon. Mix again with your hands until the fish is well covered. Strain the mushrooms and cut into small pieces.

Chinese Yellow Wine

4. Heat the oil in a pan. When hot, fry the fish pieces for 3 to 4 minutes without browning them.

5. In a saucepan, combine 150 ml/^{2}/$_3$ cup water, 4 tbsp yellow wine and salt. Heat, then use a spatula to put the fish in the sauce. Allow to simmer 2 minutes.

6. Add the mushrooms to the cod. Heat 2 to 3 minutes. Blend 1 tbsp flour in the condensed milk, sugar and 50 ml/3^1/$_2$ tbsp water. Pour on the cod, mix and allow to thicken for 5 minutes on high heat. Sprinkle with chives.

Zander Fillet

Preparation time: 20 minutes
Cooking time: 20 minutes
Difficulty: ★

Serves 4

For the garnish:
500 g/generous 1 lb leeks
1 pat butter
blades of chives

For the fish:
800 g/1³/₄ lb zander or walleye fillet with skin

salt, pepper
50 g/5 tbsp shallots, chopped
50 ml/3¹/₂ tbsp olive oil

For the sauce:
50 ml/3¹/₂ tbsp fish stock
50 ml/3¹/₂ tbsp dry white wine
1 shallot
50 ml/3¹/₂ tbsp liquid crème fraîche
salt
pepper
60 g/¹/₄ cup butter
2 medium tomatoes

The preparation for fish recipes often calls for precise and simple movements that we no longer have the time to perform: removing the scales and fins, gutting the fish and cutting the fillets off the bones. Jacky Morlon's presentation of Zander Fillet on a Bed of Leeks unites flavor, color and speed. Your fish merchant will fillet the zander (or walleye) for you and willingly give you the bones and head to use in fish stock. Be sure to ask for the skin to be left on the fillets.

A carnivorous freshwater fish in the perch family found in European waters, zander has a magnificent white flesh that tastes very much like its close relative, the North American walleye. It could also be replaced with pike, sole or salmon.

These different fish have always made a delicious marriage with leeks. You can use young leeks or scallions in the spring-time, or winter leeks, which have a more marked taste, both with delicious results.

The quickest way to prepare this dish is to make a fish stock from a bouillon cube, but a much better sauce is made from fish scraps. Bones and heads flavored with shallots and a bouquet garni are cooked in butter, then some water is added and everything heated. When it comes to a boil, add a generous amount of dry white wine and let the broth simmer for an hour. Strained, this fish stock will keep for fifteen days in an airtight jar in the refrigerator.

For those who must cook quickly, our chef suggests serving the zander or walleye fillet without its accompanying sauce. In any case, this fish should be drizzled in its cooking juices, which will give it a rich consistency and extra flavor.

1. Rinse and pare the leeks carefully. Separate the white and the green. Slice finely.

2. Heat a pat of butter in a saucepan. Add the sliced leeks. Heat 5 minutes while stirring. Remove from heat.

3. Slice each zander fillet diagonally into sections of about 8 to 10 cm (3–4 in). Preheat the oven to 180°C/355°F.

on a Bed of Leeks

4. Place the fish pieces in an earthenware dish. Add salt and pepper. Sprinkle with minced shallots and olive oil. Bake in the oven for 10 minutes.

5. For the sauce, reduce the fish stock and white wine by $^{3}/_{4}$ with 1 minced shallot in a saucepan. Pour the crème fraîche into the stock while whisking. Add salt and pepper. Add softened butter while stirring vigorously to obtain a thick sauce. Keep hot.

6. Finely dice the tomatoes and add to the sauce. Drain the cooking juices from the fish. Serve on a bed of leeks, garnished with sauce and blades of chives.

Brill Fillets

Preparation time: 1 hour
Cooking time, fish: 45 min
Cooking time, asparagus: 15 min
Difficulty: ★★

Serves 4

1 brill, ca. 1.5 kg/3¹/₄ lb
2 shallots
butter for the pan
salt, ground pepper
400 g/14 oz button mushrooms
1 bunch parsley
4 tomatoes
100 ml/7 tbsp white wine

1 bunch green asparagus
250 ml/1 cup liquid crème fraîche
100 g/7 tbsp butter
1 large onion
30 g/3 tbsp flour
200 ml/generous ³/₄ cup oil
2 or 3 sprigs chervil

For the fish stock:
brill bones
50 g/3¹/₂ tbsp butter
1 sprig parsley
1 large onion
150 ml/²/₃ cup white wine

The famous chef, Adolphe Dugléré, bequeathed a large number of his favorite recipes to the culinary heritage of France. Born in Bordeaux in 1805, he worked alternately for the Rothschild family, then at the *Trois frères provençaux*, a famous Parisian restaurant at the Palais Royal, and from 1867 until his death in 1884 at the *Café Anglais*, a gathering place for Europe's rich and famous at the time. Dugléré perfected Anna potatoes, chicken Albuféra, and *potage Germiny* (sorrel and cream soup), in addition to our pieces of brill simmered in the sauce named after him. This very flavorful and colorful sauce goes equally well with turbot, sole and bass, in addition to brill.

The brill is a large flatfish caught in the North Sea, the English Channel and the Atlantic Ocean from Boulogne-sur-Mer to Sables-d'Olonne. It is distinguished from its close relative, the turbot, by its oval shape and smooth dark gray skin, while the turbot is more diamond-shaped and has grayish-green skin and bony tubercles. Both of these fish have their eyes on the left side of their heads.

Brill can reach 30 to 50 cm (12–20 in) in length and weigh between 350 g and 2 kg (¾ lb–4½ lb). Their fine, firm, white flesh is particularly exquisite from May to June. Jean Bordier recommends choosing a single excellent fillet rather than two smaller ones, because smaller brill don't yield large enough pieces for this recipe. This fish can only tolerate a rapid and light cooking, and must be attentively monitored.

The brill stock presented in this recipe can also be enhanced by the addition of diced carrots, finely minced shallots, a bouquet garni, button mushrooms or peppercorns.

1. Fillet the brill and remove the skin. For the stock, crush the bones, rinse, dry and put in a saucepan with butter, parsley and minced onion. Allow to simmer. Add the white wine and reduce.

2. Cover with water, bring to the boil and cook for 15 minutes. Strain the stock and set aside. Meanwhile, peel and chop the shallots. Grease a baking dish with butter, sprinkle with salt, ground pepper and minced shallots.

3. Slice the mushrooms finely, mince the parsley leaves and dice the tomatoes. Add to the dish with the shallots. Sprinkle with the white wine.

à la Dugléré

4. Place the fish fillets on top. Add salt and pepper again. Cover with parchment paper and bake in the oven for 7 to 8 minutes at 180°C/355°F. Meanwhile, cook the asparagus and reserve the tips.

5. Set aside the brill fillets on a plate. Pour the garnish and cooking juices into a saucepan. Reduce by ⅔, add the crème fraîche, reduce again until the sauce is velvety. Heat with 100 g/7 tbsp butter. Season to taste.

6. Slice the onion into thin rings, dredge them in the flour and fry in the oil, heated to 170°C/340°F. Arrange the fillets on plates, drizzle with sauce, surround with the fried onion rings and asparagus tips. Garnish with minced chervil.

Fillets of Herring

Preparation time:	*45 minutes*
Cooking time, potatoes:	*30 minutes*
Total soaking time:	*20 hours*
Chilling time:	*12 hours*
Difficulty:	★★

Serves 4

4 herrings with roe
2 onions
4 lemons
2 bay leaves

10 g/4 tsp allspice
10 g/2 tbsp white peppercorns
300 ml/1¼ cups oil
250 ml/1 cup crème fraîche
1 tsp powdered sugar

For the garnish:
300 g/11 oz small potatoes
2 tsp cumin seeds
1 bunch dill or parsley (optional)

Herring is at its tastiest by far when it is spawning, and thus contains roe. The white interior pocket that contains the roe is a marvelous ingredient for omelets, whether poached or in a meunière sauce. The middle fillet of herring is bitter and should be removed before placing the egg casing in a sieve. Crush it lightly on the mesh of the sieve, turning once to extract all the richness: the lipid-rich white liquid will be blended with crème fraîche. In the absence of a sieve, use a strainer with a fine grid or a chinois. Crush the particles that gather at the bottom of the chinois thoroughly.

Herring must be soaked in two stages, each of which lasts ten hours. It is soaked whole the first time to wash away the brine in which it has been preserved. The second soaking, as de-boned fillets, will allow the fish to be completely rinsed. This preparation may seem unduly time-consumig, but those with discerning taste know how necessary it is.

Nevertheless, in consideration of those who prefer flavor with greater speed, our chef insists that non-macerated herring rinsed in running water will retain all its flavor. If herring with roe is difficult to find, you can use vacuum-packed fillets and marinate them in the same manner. Diced potatoes mixed with a blanched onion and a little cream will be an acceptable substitute for roe, but will not be as flavorful.

To complement the herring, choose a thick, non-acidic crème fraîche. Roe and lemon will be added in small quantities. Since not all palates are accustomed to the sweet-and-sour experience, taste often as you go, adding the ingredients until the perfect balance between sweetness and acidity is reached.

Accompany the herring fillets with boiled potatoes sprinkled with parsley or dill, a delicious supplement to the rich fish in cream sauce.

1. Soak the herrings for 10 hours in cold water. Open the fish and remove the roe (set it aside). Remove the head and central bone in a single movement. Take the two fillets from each herring and remove the small bones with tweezers. Soak for another 10 hours in cold water.

2. Slice the onions and 2 of the lemons and place the slices in a terrine. Cover them with 1 fillet of herring skin-side up and put a bay leaf on top. Repeat the process. Finish with onions, allspice and peppercorns. Fill the dish ³/₄ of the way with the oil, making sure to cover the herring. Set aside.

3. Set a sieve over a plate. With a plastic spreader, crush the egg casings and roe on the mesh. Squeeze the juice from the remaining lemons.

à la Crème

4. Pour the crème fraîche and lemon juice into a bowl. Beat. Add the roe to the cream while stirring vigorously. Add a pinch of powdered sugar, according to taste.

5. Cover the herrings in the terrine with this sauce. Refrigerate for 12 hours.

6. The day of the meal, boil the potatoes for 30 minutes in their skin. Peel them and toss in cumin and dill or parsley according to taste. Serve with the Fillets of Herring à la Crème.

Zander Fillets

Preparation time: 45 minutes
Cooking time: 1 hour 10 minutes
Difficulty: ★★

Serves 4

50 g/3^1/$_2$ tbsp butter
2 tbsp coarse sugar
60 ml/^{1}/$_4$ cup balsamic vinegar
500 ml/2 cups beet juice
5 fresh red beets

1 pinch ground cumin
salt
ground pepper
1 tsp cornstarch (optional)
1 sprig tarragon
oil for deep frying
 zander or walleye, ca. 600 g/1^1/$_4$ lb
butter, oil
250 ml/1 cup butter sauce

Marcel Vanic gives traditional foods a modern flair by pairing pan-fried zander with an astonishing preserved beet julienne. The fish fillets are served with crispy chips made from beet slices. Our chef accompanies them with a tarragon purée butter sauce, which creates a festive, colorful contrast and a delicate blend of flavors.

Many gourmets hold red beets in low esteem on account of their earthy aftertaste. In our recipe, the julienned strips of beet are steeped in a syrup of caramel, balsamic vinegar and beet juice that is reduced down to a glaze and gives them a highly unusual texture and flavor.

The beets should be sliced as finely as possible to ensure that they are good and crisp after frying: choose a very sharp chef's knife, a mandolin slicer or, better still, a meat slicer.

Zander is a popular eating fish in Europe. Very closely related and just as delicious is the walleye. First fry the zander or walleye fillets on the skin side to eliminate some of the fat from the fish. Then cook it rapidly on the other side. Our chef slashed the skin in several places to prevent the fillets from curling while cooking.

If the fish fillets are thick, letting them fry quite slowly over lower heat will produce crisp skin and moist flesh. If the fillets are thin, on the other hand, the temperature of the pan should be higher when the cooking begins, otherwise the skin will not crisp up.

Our chef accompanies the fish with a variation on the classic *beurre blanc*. He cooks shallots in butter, deglazes them with Noilly Prat (dry French vermouth) and a dry Riesling, and reduces them by half. He adds fish stock, reduces the liquid again, incorporates the cream, seasons and simmers the sauce briefly. Just before serving, he reheats the chilled *beurre blanc* and flavors it, for this recipe, with tarragon purée.

1. Prepare a caramel by melting the sugar and butter in a small saucepan on high heat. Once it is ready, thin it by gradually adding the balsamic vinegar, then beet juice. Bring to the boil. Reduce by half at a rolling boil.

2. Peel 300 g/11 oz of the beets. Cut them into narrow strips. Add them to the syrup prepared previously.

3. Season with cumin, salt and pepper. Reduce for about 20 minutes on high heat. If the syrup is too thin, thicken it with flour. While this reduces, mix the puréed tarragon with oil, salt and pepper (set aside).

with Beets and Tarragon

4. Peel the remaining beets. Slice into large but very thin rounds. Heat oil in a deep-fryer. When it is very hot, drop the beet slices into the oil and fry about 20 minutes.

5. Fillet the zander or walleye and discard the bones. Make slits in the skin of the fish at regular intervals. First, pan-fry skin side down in a mixture of oil and butter. When well done, turn and cook the other side for 3 to 4 minutes.

6. Warm the butter sauce. Add the tarragon purée and stir. Place a spoonful of the beet syrup at the center of each plate. Top with fried beet slices and then a fish fillet. Surround with tarragon sauce and garnish with sautéed tarragon.

Fillet of Brown

Preparation time: 40 minutes
Cooking time: 30 minutes
Difficulty: ★★

Serves 4

4 brown bullhead fillets, ca. 140 g/5 oz each
4 regular carrots
4 yellow carrots
4 green onions
4 small shallots
4 turnips
1 pinch sugar
12 small potatoes
1 pinch cumin seeds
100 g/7 tbsp butter

1 bunch chives
salt
ground pepper

For the horseradish beurre blanc:
5 or 6 shallots
250 ml/1 cup fish stock
250 ml/1 cup dry white wine
1 dash Noilly Prat (dry vermouth)
120 ml/¹/₂ cup liquid crème fraîche
120 g/8¹/₂ tbsp butter
1 tsp prepared horseradish
¹/₂ fresh horseradish root
salt
pepper

Impressive bullheads with long antennae fill the Austrian rivers and lakes. Every fisherman and every market sells them. They are usually eaten fresh as fillets pan-fried in butter or cooked in a paprika sauce.

Marcel Vanic presents golden diamonds of bullhead, nestled between braised vegetables and coated with a *beurre blanc* flavored with horseradish. The carrots of two different colors form an attractive duo. The yellow variety is a staple in Austrian cooking. Its taste is identical to that of orange carrots. When all the vegetables are cooked in the pan, remove them with a spoon and place them on a sheet of paper towel.

When browning the fish, be sure to sprinkle the fillets regularly with hot butter to decrease the cooking time and permeate the flesh with its flavor.

Our chef sets up his sauce by making a tasty fish stock. Generally, he cleans turbot carcasses which he then cooks in butter. He adds onions, leeks, tomatoes and mushrooms, browns them for a moment, and then sprinkles them with ice cubes. As he continues to cook, the ice cubes melt, slowly yielding a mousse containing all the impurities, while the melted water absorbs all the flavors. By skimming off the mousse, he is left with a very clear stock. Next, he cooks minced shallots in butter without browning them. These are deglazed in Noilly-Prat and dry Riesling and reduced by half. The fish stock is poured over this and continues to reduce. Finally, the crème fraîche is stirred into the sauce.

Just before serving, the cold *beurre blanc* sauce is reheated. In this particular recipe, our chef flavors the *beurre blanc* with prepared horseradish and grates a few shavings of fresh horseradish into it by scraping the peeled root with a small, well-sharpened knife.

1. Boil the potatoes for 20 minutes in water flavored with cumin. Peel the orange and yellow carrots, the turnips, small shallots and green onions (blanch the stems separately). Chop them all finely.

2. Melt some butter in a large saucepan. When it foams, pour the shallots, carrots, turnips and onions into the pan. Stir with a spatula to prevent sticking.

3. When the vegetables have begun to cook and are well coated with butter, add some water, salt and sugar to the pan. Bring to the boil, then simmer 2 to 3 minutes; they should remain crunchy.

Bullhead Weissensee

4. For the beurre blanc, heat the minced shallots in some butter. Deglaze with white wine and Noilly-Prat. Reduce, add the fish stock, reduce again and add the cream. Season. Finish reducing before whisking into butter.

5. Cut the bullhead fillets into diamond-shaped pieces. Add salt and pepper. Melt butter in a pan and brown the fillets, 3 to 4 minutes on each side. Pan-fry the boiled potatoes on the side.

6. Add the pickled horseradish and fresh grated horseradish to the butter sauce. Place the turnips, onions and shallots, a piece of bullhead, carrots and a second piece of bullhead on a plate. Garnish with onion tops, chives and beurre blanc.

Poached Turbot

Preparation time: 40 minutes
Cooking time: 40 minutes
Difficulty: ★★

Serves 4

1 small turbot, ca. 1.5 kg/3¼ lb
500 g/generous 1 lb potatoes
100 ml/7 tbsp milk
2 lemons
1 bunch curly-leaf parsley
sea salt

For the hollandaise sauce:
200 g/14 tbsp butter
3 egg yolks
juice of ½ lemon
1 pinch cayenne pepper
salt

Turbot fishing on the sandy beds of the French seashore is highly localized: in the North Sea near Boulogne, in the English Channel around Port-en-Bessin, in the Atlantic from Brest to Guilvinec, on the coast of the Vendée and in the gulf of Gascony. Mediterranean turbot is caught from Sète to Martigues.

The small turbot is a young turbot. This high-quality flatfish has a grayish-green skin punctuated by bony tubercles. Its flesh is fine and firm, and somewhat gelatinous. It can be differentiated from its cousin, the brill, because its body is diamond-shaped, while the brill is oval. It has no bones. The most common size is between 40 and 50 cm (16–20 in), and its weight varies from 500 g to 10 kg (1 lb to 22 lb).

The accompanying hollandaise sauce enhances the delicate flavor of the small turbot to perfection. Success with this high-class preparation requires care. Always use a saucepan of an appropriate size for the quantity of sauce: in an oversized pan, the eggs will coagulate before they can be whisked. If the sauce is too thick, thin it down with a little cold water. If it turns before or after the emulsion, that can be due to overheated clarified butter. In that case, add some cold water or an ice cube and whisk the sauce again. On the other hand, if the butter seems to have become too cold, try to recapture the hollandaise sauce by adding a dash of tepid water. When done, set it aside, covered, in a warm place but not in a bain-marie, because at more than 65°C/150°F the ingredients will separate out.

Designed for the turbot, this marvelous sauce will happily complement other noble fish, as well as asparagus, eggs and poached or steamed vegetables. You can easily transform it into a Maltese sauce, if you add the juice of two Maltese oranges from Tunisia and a pinch of their zests at the last minute.

1. Peel the potatoes. With a small knife, slice each potato while turning to give it an attractive, round shape. Cook in salted boiling water.

2. Separate the fish fillets from the skin with a large knife. Rinse the flesh, dry it and set aside on a plate until needed.

3. For the hollandaise sauce, melt the butter in a saucepan. Skim to remove the whey: this will produce clarified butter. Whisk the egg yolks in a bain-marie while adding 3 tbsp water to obtain a creamy butter paste.

in Hollandaise Sauce

4. Away from the heat, incorporate the clarified butter into the sauce bit by bit with a ladle. Season with a pinch of salt and cayenne pepper. Finish with the lemon juice.

5. Pour 1 liter/1 quart cold water into a saucepan large enough to hold the fillets. Add the milk, then a pinch of sea salt.

6. Place the turbot fillets in the saucepan and bring to the boil. Allow to simmer for 5 minutes. Strain the fish. Place each fillet on a plate with potatoes and coat with sauce. Garnish with parsley and slices of lemon.

Creole-Style

Preparation time: 30 minutes
Cooking time: 45 minutes
Difficulty: ★

Serves 4

1 kg/2¹/₄ lb large shrimp
2 onions
2 West Indian bay leaves
2 cloves garlic
1 green onion
2 tomatoes
30 ml/2 tbsp oil
1 small chili pepper
20 ml/4 tsp aged rum
salt
pepper

For the bouquet garni:
1 rib celery
1 sprig thyme
2 or 3 sprigs parsley
1 bay leaf

For the accompaniment:
2 large plantains
60 g/¹/₄ cup butter
60 g/7 tbsp flour
2 cups milk
1 pinch nutmeg
salt
pepper
grated Gruyère (optional)
400 g/2 cups rice (optional)
1 lemon (optional)

In Martinique, the local (large freshwater, raised) shrimp, *ouassous* and *cribiches*, prawns, langoustines and the majority of other shellfish can be fricasséed.

The *ouassous*, or *z'habitant*, is a shellfish in the shrimp family and resembles crayfish. Greenish-blue in color, it has antennae on its head and two large pincers replace the second pair of legs. People in Martinique catch the *ouassous* in rivers and ponds. When they are pan-fried, these shellfish take on an appetizing coral-red color. It is best to devein them (remove their entrails) before cooking to avoid all risk of bitterness. For this preparation, the *ouassous* can easily be replaced by shrimp or crayfish.

In this Creole-style fricassée, our chef has incorporated West Indian bay leaves, a local spice similar to large bay leaves with a rich flavor. They come from the *pimento racemosa*, a plant of

the *myrtacean* family. The West Indian bay leaf is used in the same way as the bay leaf in bouquets garnis, fish marinades and broths. Known throughout the world, the seeds of the flavorful West Indian bay tree instantly call to mind cinnamon, cloves, pepper and nutmeg and are called Jamaican pepper or allspice.

To prepare his purée au gratin, Eddy Gérald generally uses green dwarf bananas, also called *ti-nain*. When poached, this "vegetable" perfectly complements cod and meat dishes.

The *ouassous* should always be served in their shells. They can be placed on rolled banana leaves for a more sophisticated presentation. The color of the sauce can also be enhanced by adding tomato purée, and the banana gratin can be given a pretty golden color by sprinkling it with grated Gruyère before putting it in the oven.

1. Peel the onions, then chop them finely. Heat oil in a large pot. Brown the onions for about 5 minutes in the hot oil.

2. Rinse the shrimp carefully, then dry them. If possible, devein, then add to the pot on top of the onions.

3. Heat the shrimp in the onions for 2 to 3 minutes, turning them over when they have become a beautiful orange color on one side. Once they start to brown, remove from the pot and place them on a dish.

Fricasséed Shrimp

4. Peel and dice the tomatoes. Put the bouquet garni, diced tomatoes, chili pepper, minced garlic, green onion, West Indian bay leaves, salt and pepper, 150 ml/²⁄₃ cup water and, finally, the shrimp into the pot. Cook for 10 minutes.

5. At the end of the cooking, add a small glass of aged rum to the fricasséed shrimp. Stir. Keep warm until ready to serve. For the plantain gratin, poach the sliced plantains for 10 minutes.

6. In a separate pot, make a roux and thin it with warm milk. Thicken for 10 minutes into a béchamel. Add the plantains, salt, pepper and nutmeg. Pour into a small dish and brown in the oven for 5 minutes.

Maryland

Preparation time: 45 minutes
Cooking time: 45 minutes
Chilling time: 1 hour
Difficulty: ✶✶

Serves 4

3 hermit crabs, ca. 1 kg/2¼ lb each
½ onion
½ red chili pepper
1 bunch curly-leaf parsley
25 g/½ cup soft white breadcrumbs
60 ml/¼ cup crème fraîche
55 g/½ cup dry breadcrumbs
1 egg
120 g/8½ tbsp soft butter
1 pinch Old Bay Seasoning

½ tsp salt
1 pinch white peppercorn
1 or 2 large lemons

For the mayonnaise:
1 egg yolk
1 tsp mustard
250 ml/1 cup oil
1 tbsp vinegar

For the tartar sauce garnish:
1 shallot
1 large pickle
3 or 4 sprigs parsley
3 or 4 sprigs tarragon
2 tsp capers
50 g/1½ oz fromage blanc
½ lemon
1 pinch sea salt
1 pinch white pepper

Chesapeake Bay, at the center of the East Coast, is famous for the abundance and quality of its blue crabs. Considered the best American crab, this shellfish is caught from April to December using metal crab traps, along the Maryland and Virginia coasts. The male blue crabs are preferred because their tender flesh is more abundant than that of the females. For our recipe, however, hermit crabs are just as good.

To remove the meat, our chef simply poaches the crabs in boiling water. But in Maryland, they do something else: the shellfish are placed in enormous steamers and then covered and steamed for 15 minutes, until they become red.

These crab cakes, prepared in the traditional way, contain a large quantity of crab, a minimum of garnish, some soft white breadcrumbs and cream to prevent the cake from crumbling while it is cooking. If the crab meat appears a bit stringy, use more stale bread passed through a sifter. The soft white bread may be replaced by a variety of ingredients, such as mayonnaise, puréed sweet potatoes or grated red cheese from Holland.

The final touch of flavor is supplied by the Old Bay Seasoning, a mixture of spices for seafood made in Maryland: celery salt, mustard, red chili pepper, black pepper, bay leaf, ginger, mace, cardamom, paprika, cloves and allspice are all involved.

Crab cakes are always served with tartar sauce. The degree of herb flavoring will vary according to your taste. You may prefer to use large pickles "à la russe" (in mayonnaise) flavored with dill.

1. Peel and mince half an onion. Brown it in a saucepan in 20 g/4 tsp butter. Add half a diced red pepper and brown for 2 minutes. Set aside and keep at room temperature.

2. Prepare a mayonnaise with the listed ingredients. For the tartar sauce, mince the shallot, pickle, parsley, tarragon and capers. Add them to the mayonnaise as well as the fromage blanc and lemon juice. Season with salt and pepper. Set aside.

3. Beat an egg. Pour the onions and pepper into a bowl and add the egg, crème fraîche and Old Bay Seasoning. Season with salt and pepper.

Crab Cakes

4. Poach the hermit crabs for 15 minutes, then remove their shells. Add their meat to the preceding mixture. Sprinkle with soft white breadcrumbs and minced parsley. Knead the stuffing to mix all ingredients thoroughly. Cover and refrigerate for 1 hour.

5. Form small cakes with the crab mixture, by packing them well in the palms of your hands. Then put them in a bowl filled with dry breadcrumbs.

6. Melt 100 g/7 tbsp butter in a pan. When it is hot, brown the crab cakes in two batches of 6, for 4 to 6 minutes on each side. Pat them with paper towel. Serve accompanied by tartar sauce and slices of lemon.

Seafood

Preparation time: 1 hour 15 minutes
Cooking time: 1 hour 50 minutes
Difficulty: ★★

Serves 6

800 g/1³/₄ lb octopus
300 g/11 oz squid
300 g/11 oz shrimp
20 mussels
300 g/1¹/₂ cups orzo
400 g/14 oz tomatoes

1 sprig basil
1 onion
100 g/3¹/₂ oz eggplant
1 green chili pepper
150 ml/²/₃ cup retsina (Greek wine)
150 g/5¹/₂ oz Kasseri cheese
3 cloves garlic
10–12 tbsp olive oil
salt

For this seafood recipe, which he usually serves at *The Apollo* restaurant, Konstantinos Stamkopoulos nods at the *giouvetsi*, which is a kind of earthenware cooking brick. In his part of Macedonia, though, the *giouvetsi* is a stew based on a rabbit or veal stock that is baked in a high-sided casserole, and it has taken its name from the dish it was cooked in.

Octopuses abound in the Aegean and Ionian Seas. They have tentacles between 50 cm and 1 meter (20–40 in) long and very tough flesh. Fishermen say they must be beaten at least forty-four times against the rocks to tenderize them. They are usually served diced in salads and sauces, or grilled on the barbecue.

Smaller than octopuses, squid have shorter arms. In the Peloponnesian ports, they were once the thrill of tourist rubbernecks as the fishermen strung them up on lines to dry in the sun in preparation for Lent. Squid are served fried, grilled and sprinkled with lemon juice and olive oil, or cooked in a wine sauce with vegetables. Our chef has combined his vegetables with *kritharaki*, better known as orzo, a kind of oblong pasta very popular throughout the country. In the past, women would make this by hand. Nowadays, the most basic village grocer will sell them ready-made. The Greeks eat much less pasta than vegetables, but have a great choice of shapes at their disposal. A pasta dish called *pastitsio* is served at marriages. Soups are often enriched with vermicelli or crumbled pasta.

The retsina that flavors this dish is a traditional Greek wine infused with the strong taste of resin. Ancient Greeks coated the inside of their wine jars with pine tree resin to better preserve the wine. Greeks acquired a liking for it and still consume plenty of ice cold retsina wine each year. Resin crystals added to fermented grape juice give it its characteristic flavor.

1. Bring 2 liters/2 quarts water to the boil in a saucepan. When it begins to boil, add the octopus and cook for an hour. After 50 minutes, add the squid, shrimp and mussels. Continue cooking for 10 minutes.

2. Cut the squid and octopus into narrow strips. Shell the mussels and cooked shrimp.

3. Peel the eggplant. Cut it into long strips. Sauté for 5 minutes in hot oil. Set aside.

Giouvetsi Apollo

4. Peel the garlic and onion. Mince them along with the tomatoes, chili pepper and basil. Heat all these ingredients in the same pan for 15 minutes.

5. When the vegetables begin to melt, add the retsina and then the seafood. Heat for another 15 minutes. Cook the orzo for 10 minutes in salted boiling water.

6. Combine the vegetables, pasta and seafood in one pan. Reheat for a few minutes. Garnish with strips of eggplant and sprinkle with Kasseri. Finish by browning for 15 minutes in the oven.

Lobster

Preparation time: 30 minutes
Cooking time: 25 minutes
Difficulty: ★★

Serves 6

3 lobsters, ca. 600 g/1¹/₄ lb each
55 g/¹/₄ cup softened butter
2¹/₂ tbsp sherry
3 tbsp Cognac
350 ml/1¹/₂ cups crème fraîche
¹/₄ tsp grated nutmeg

¹/₄ tsp cayenne pepper
4 eggs
salt
soft white bread as accompaniment

Towards the year 1900, chef Alessandro Filippini, master of the famous New York restaurant *Delmonico's*, developed the recipe for Lobster Newburg in honor of Mr. Ben Wenburg, a regular of the establishment who particularly enjoyed seafood in cream sauce with beaten eggs. Since then, the recipe has been made in any number of variations, in the United States as well as in Europe.

Maine lobster is the most famous of American lobsters. In other states, prestigious restaurants have it sent to them still living, packed in ice or shut into a wooden box filled with straw. The inhabitants of New England are proud of their impressively-sized *homarus americanus*, which has a delicate and very flavorful meat. Progressing toward the warmer waters of Florida, the spiny lobster is found more often. This is a clawless lobster, closely related to crayfish. Americans recognize eight sizes of lobster for commercial purposes, ranging from the chicken lobster at 450 g/19 oz (the smallest size) to jumbo lobsters that weigh in at or above 1.125 kg (2½ lb). For this recipe, our chef has used large, or "select" lobsters, which are between 680 g and 1 kg (1½ to 2¼ lb).

In the United States, gourmets usually eat this prestigious shellfish boiled and dipped in melted butter. In restaurants, they are given a plastic bib to avoid staining their clothing, as well as a nutcracker and pick with which to extract the meat.

Newburg sauce has become a great classic of international cuisine. The most critical step is to ensure that the egg yolks do not overcook in the sauce. Mix them just for an instant, on very low heat, while whisking vigorously. It is essential not to reheat the sauce after they are added, or it will become lumpy. In the worst case, it can be rescued by mixing it in a blender. Some cooks make this sauce without adding any eggs.

1. Bring a large pot of lightly salted water to the boil. Place the live lobsters in the boiling water, cover and cook for about 10 to 15 minutes until they are bright red.

2. Remove the lobsters from the boiling water. Place them on a chopping board and slice them along the back, using a meat cleaver. Shell them and remove the meat from the body and the claws. Cut it into small cubes.

3. Melt the butter in a large pan. When it is good and hot, add the little pieces of lobster. Pan-fry for 2 minutes while stirring. Add 1 tbsp sherry and 3 tbsp Cognac.

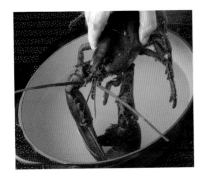

Newburg

4. With a slotted spoon, remove the lobster pieces from the cooking juices. Reserve them in a bowl.

5. Add the cream to the cooking juices whisking continuously on low heat to obtain a smooth and thick sauce. Add the remaining sherry, nutmeg and cayenne pepper.

6. Beat the eggs in a bowl. Pour them into the preceding mixture and whisk energetically for a few minutes to obtain a fine sauce. Finally, add the reserved lobster. Accompany with toasted slices of soft white bread.

Sfaxian

Preparation time:	20 minutes
Cooking time:	35 minutes
Difficulty:	★

Serves 4

1 sea bass, ca. 1.2 kg/2³/₄ lb
4 medium onions
4 tomatoes
1 yellow pepper, 1 red and 1 green
4 cloves garlic

70 ml/5 tbsp olive oil
2 tbsp tomato purée
1 preserved lemon
100 g/3¹/₂ oz black pitted olives
saffron
cumin
capers
salt
pepper

This fish and tomato stew is called *kabkabou* and comes to us from Sfax, the second largest port in Tunisia after Tunis. The best Tunisian fishes are caught in Sidi Déoud, Sfax and Bizerte. The absolute pick of the fish come from the Kerkennah islands, one hour from Sfax by boat. The fish there eat a special seaweed that gives their flesh a well-known taste.

Sea bass is greatly appreciated in Tunisia, but remains rather costly. It is a large fish with fine flesh that prospers in the Mediterranean and lives in the breakers near beaches and rocks. It hunts in groups and eats sardines, herring and pout. It is prepared in the oven whole, fried with chili peppers, fried tomatoes and potatoes, and served with eggs.

The preserved lemon adds a slight tang to this dish. Any good Tunisian cook prepares a large store of these lemons for winter.

She chooses medium lemons, washes them and makes four cuts half way through the flesh. She pours water and salt into a jar, puts an egg in with them and stirs: when the egg floats, the brine is ready. The preserved lemons are ready to be eaten after about a week. Whole small lemons, or large ones sliced into circles or quarters, can be used according to taste. They can be served in a tajine or on *kemia*, a Tunisian dish of raw vegetables.

Like the lemons, black olives are a traditional part of domestic cooking. After macerating for a week in salt, they are rinsed with oil. They are then poured into a jar filled with olive oil where they will be preserved for several months. When all the olives have been eaten, the oil in the jar can still be used to enrich salads.

1. Place the fish in a dish. Add salt and pepper. Sprinkle the saffron, cumin, minced garlic and capers on top of the fish. Drizzle with water. Rub the fish with the spices to make sure the flavors penetrate it and to obtain a sort of sauce.

2. Peel the onions and mince two of them. Heat oil in a saucepan and then cook the onions for 5 minutes, until they begin to brown. Meanwhile, mix 2 fresh tomatoes with the tomato purée.

3. Add the tomato mixture to the saucepan. Stir the sauce with a wooden spoon on low heat. Add 2 onions (quartered), the ground cumin, and salt and pepper. Cook for 15 to 20 minutes.

Kabkabou

4. Add the olives and capers to the dish containing the fish. Pour the hot tomato and onion sauce over the fish. Garnish with a slice each of green, yellow and red pepper. Cook another 10 minutes.

5. Remove the fish from the sauce with a spatula and transfer to an oval serving dish. Cut the remaining 2 tomatoes and the preserved lemon into slices.

6. With a soup spoon, arrange the olives, sliced tomato and preserved lemon, and the quartered onion evenly around the fish. Pour the sauce over the fish and serve hot.

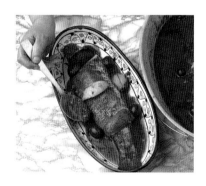

Spiny Lobster

Preparation time: 15 minutes
Cooking time: 15 minutes
Difficulty: ★

Serves 4

800 g/1¾ lb spiny lobster tails
20 g/1 tbsp salt
pepper
100 ml/7 tbsp oil

30 g/3 tbsp minced garlic
30 g/3 tbsp minced onions
30 g/3 tbsp diced green pepper
30 g/2 tbsp tomato purée
200 ml/generous ¾ cup white wine
ground cumin
200 ml/generous ¾ cup Carta Blanca rum

Varadero is home to some of the most beautiful tourist destinations on the island of Cuba. Varadero has beaches, luxury hotels, expensive villas built in the 1930s and casinos on a peninsula that extends 25 km (16 miles) into the ocean. Without a doubt, the best lobster dishes are served here.

Cuba has developed the most important network of spiny lobster—also known as rock lobster—fisheries in all of the Caribbean and South America. Spiny lobster differs from the lobster in its spiny brownish-red shell, lack of claws and very long antennae. Its fine, white and smooth-textured flesh has a slightly less pronounced taste than that of the lobster. Visitors to Cuba have the pleasure of tasting fresh spiny lobster, large quantities of which are exported in frozen form.

This shellfish is caught throughout the year in Cuba except between May and August, during the breeding period. The spiny lobster processing zones in Havana, Coloma and the Isle of Youth represent the country's most important industries.

Spiny lobster is sold fresh, freshly cooked or frozen in three different forms: whole, tails with their shell and meat removed from the shell.

The flavor of the spiny lobster can be enhanced by another prized local product: rum. *Ron* is the national drink of Cuba, which has a staggering number of distilleries. Rum was produced in Cuba as early as the sixteenth century, but its industrial boom dates from the mid-nineteenth century. The Carta Blanca used here is a light white rum that has been aged for three years in white oak barrels. Its light flavor makes it suitable for drinking on its own, or with fruit juices or carbonated beverages. There is also Carta de Oro, or gold rum, that has been aged for five years, and Añejo, which takes on a lovely brown color after aging for seven years.

Our chef recommends serving this dish with rice and cooked carrots. Garnish the dish with the spiny lobster tail ends lightly sautéed and a pinch of cumin.

1. Cut the tail tips off the spiny lobster. Using a chef's knife, slice the tails into rings at the joints. Remove the pieces of gray skin and the remaining bits of shell.

2. Place the lobster rings into a bowl, add salt and pepper. Heat the oil in a pan (you may need less than 100 ml/7 tbsp) and sauté the lobster pieces for 2 to 3 minutes.

3. Add the minced onion and garlic and diced green pepper to the pan. Brown the lobster with these vegetables for 5 minutes.

Varadero

4. When the lobster is nicely browned, add the tomato purée and white wine. Sprinkle with ground cumin to taste.

5. Blend the lobster, tomato purée and wine with a wooden spoon. Allow to simmer over medium heat for about 5 minutes, stirring regularly with the spoon.

6. When the sauce has reduced some, add the white rum. Cook for another 2 to 3 minutes, then serve the pieces of lobster well coated with sauce.

Primorska

Preparation time: 30 minutes
Cooking time: 15 minutes
Difficulty: ✷✷

Serves 2

4 large prawns
3 medium tomatoes
1 clove garlic
50 ml/3^1/$_2$ tbsp olive oil
50 g/5 tbsp minced shallots

50 g/3^1/$_2$ tbsp butter
50 ml/3^1/$_2$ tbsp white wine
salt
pepper
1 bay leaf
2 or 3 sprigs parsley

For the cheese gnocchi:
250 g/generous 1 cup cottage cheese
120 g/generous ^{3}/$_4$ cup wheat flour
2 eggs
70 g/5 tbsp butter
salt

Prawns with gnocchi are prepared in the coastal region of Slovenia, a short stretch located in the Gulf of Venice, adjacent to the Adriatic Sea. There are no fine sand beaches along the 26 km (16 miles) of Slovenian coast, but sunbathers nonetheless stretch out their towels on the rocks. Portorož is the main Slovenian sunbathing beach.

Prawns, also known as Dublin Bay prawns or langoustines, are caught in wire baskets by independent fishermen who find them mostly in Slovenian waters, but are just as likely to seek them out in the Italian waters to the south, near Croatia. Shrimp and crayfish are equally important products on the Slovenian market. In this country, prawns are enjoyed grilled, fried or simmered in tomato sauces or a white wine sauce called *buzzara*. Shellfish and squid can also be added to the *buzzara*.

Inspired by the cuisine of neighboring Italy, gnocchi have become very popular in Slovenia. Depending on the region, chefs flavor them with spinach, chestnuts, tomato purée and much more. Just before serving, they coat the steaming gnocchi with sauces of gorgonzola, mushrooms or even white truffles in June, and black truffles in autumn. Most often, gnocchi are made as a dish in their own right.

It is extremely important to pass the cottage cheese through a sieve so that it becomes fine and smooth, ensuring that the gnocchi will be firm with a consistent texture. Also be sure to soften the butter with a fork before blending it into the dough.

Our chef offers this tip to make the prawns' heads stand up at the center of the plate: take the soft part of some rye or wheat bread and roll it into little balls. Stick these to the bottom of the prawns' heads, moistening slightly. Then stand the heads of the prawns upright on the plates, pushing them firmly to make them stick.

1. Turn the raw prawns onto their backs. Use scissors to open the bellies.

2. Remove the flesh from the prawns. Place a toothpick down the middle of the flesh to prevent it curling as it cooks.

3. Peel and finely dice 2 tomatoes and the garlic. Heat the olive oil in a pan, then fry the shallots for 2 to 3 minutes. Add 30 g/ 2 tbsp of the butter in pieces, deglaze with white wine, and then add the tomatoes, garlic, salt, pepper and bay leaf. Cook for 5 minutes on medium heat.

Prawns

4. In another pan, melt the remaining butter and brown the prawns in it. For the gnocchi, press the cottage cheese through a sieve with the back of a soup spoon.

5. Transfer the strained cottage cheese into a bowl. Add the flour, eggs, softened butter and a little salt. Knead and then form a ball of gnocchi dough. Shape the dough into long rolls.

6. Slice each roll into pieces 3 to 4 cm (1¼–1½ in) long. Drop into boiling water for 6 to 7 minutes until the gnocchi rise to the surface. Serve the gnocchi and prawns on a bed of tomato sauce, with the prawn heads and half of the last tomato at the center. Sprinkle with minced parsley.

Prawns

Preparation time: 30 minutes
Cooking time: 40 minutes
Difficulty: ★

Serves 4

4 onions
4 carrots
4 ribs celery
3 lemons
2 bay leaves
1 sprig thyme
salt
peppercorns

20 medium prawns
12 radishes
12 cherry tomatoes
2 bulbs fennel
1 tbsp mustard
200 ml/generous ¾ cup olive oil
salt
ground pepper

Italians delight in their seafood. Shrimp and prawns frequently adorn their pasta and risotto dishes. They also love sea bass, sea bream and shellfish. In Italy, prawns are eaten fried, grilled in olive oil and garlic, or as an assortment of fritters known as *frito misto* with small fish and squid.

Prawns are much more closely related to the lobster than to the crayfish. It is best to buy them fresh, cook for a few minutes in a broth and then let them chill overnight in the refrigerator. This way, the flesh will be good and firm, which will make it easier to remove from the shells.

Fennel lends this dish a fresh taste that is much prized by our chef. He also enjoys creating recipes that include zucchini and eggplant. The fennel bulb, with a slight flavor of aniseed, cooks like a vegetable and is as adaptable as celery. In times past, Italians liked its sweetness so much that they frequently used it in desserts. In this country, it is available from autumn until spring. In northern Italy it is sliced, then baked in the oven, covered with butter and parmesan. In the south, however, it is more often finely minced and seasoned with olive oil and aïoli. Fennel can also be braised or made into fritters.

In the Italian language, the cherry tomato has the appealing name *pomodorino*. This delightful tomato, with its tiny size and acidic taste, grows in clusters and keeps well throughout the winter. Harvested in the regions of Apulia, Sicily and Calabria, it is eaten in salads or used by Italian *mammas* to make a quick pasta sauce. The *pomodorino di Cerignola* is the most sought-after variety.

1. Peel the onions. Peel the carrots and chop the celery. In a pot of boiling water, cook 1 carrot, 2 sliced lemons, 1 onion, 1 celery rib, the bay leaves, thyme, salt and peppercorns for 30 minutes. Set aside the remaining vegetables.

2. When the broth has taken on the flavors of these ingredients, add the prawns. Bring to the boil, and remove the prawns from the water after about 2 to 3 minutes. Set aside.

3. Cut the remaining carrots into strips. Wash the radishes and cherry tomatoes, then cut in half. Rinse the fennel and slice it into thin strips, along with the 3 remaining onions.

Sara

4. Squeeze the juice of the last lemon. In a bowl, mix it with the mustard. Pour the olive oil into the bowl little by little, whisking continuously. Add salt and pepper. Whisk until you have a fairly thick mustard sauce.

5. Place the prawns on a chopping board. Slice them down the back with a well-sharpened knife into two equal pieces.

6. Place prawn halves on each plate. Lay the vegetables between the prawns and drizzle with mustard sauce.

Steamed Sea Bass

Preparation time: 35 minutes
Cooking time: 15 minutes
Difficulty: ★

Serves 4

800 g/1¾ lb sea bass
1 bunch scallions
5 cm/2 in fresh ginger
3 tbsp peanut oil
salt
pepper
1 bunch cilantro

For the sauce:
1 tbsp peanut oil
salt
pepper
1 tbsp sugar
a few drops sesame oil
3 tbsp soy sauce

The cooks of the Guangzhou region, in the south of China, specialize in steamed bass with herbs. Usually, chefs brush the surface of the fish with oil mixed with ginger and scallions, then steam it in a bamboo basket placed over a pot of boiling water. Here we have cooked it using a more international method, on a fish platter placed in a bain-marie. According to Mr. Choi, steaming is the best cooking method to enhance the delicate flavor of the sea bass. He uses ginger to minimize any potentially fishy smell, and soy sauce brings out its natural flavor.

In China, the bass is very popular, but also expensive. It is called *lo yu, yu* meaning "fish" in Chinese. It is supplied either by sea fishing or aquatic farms, many of which are located in the delta of the Zhu Chu (or Pearl River), near Guangzhou. The fine flesh of this fish is sometimes fried, then stewed with pieces of fragrant mushrooms and chopped pork. Chinese chefs hesitate to add too many ingredients for fear of masking the subtle taste of the bass.

It is important to note that the Chinese are very exacting with regard to the freshness of fish. They buy it live from a tank or still wriggling on the fish merchant's stand. This is true not only of fish, but of all meat: butchers cut meat on demand, while at the market poultry move about in bamboo baskets as they wait for the next customer.

For this recipe, the bass may be replaced by any similarly-sized white fish of your choice (mullet, flounder, sea bream, etc.). The Chinese often use the wide range of yellow fish caught in the coastal rivers of the north.

In this dish, our chef has also used the salt-sugar mix that is part of almost all savory Chinese dishes.

1. Cut off the fins of the bass with fish scissors. Gut the fish, rinse and dry it. Place the prepared fish on a rectangular dish.

2. Slice the scallions lengthwise. Peel the ginger and slice it finely. Then cut these slices into long, thin strips.

3. Place half the scallions and ginger on the fish in alternation. Reserve the remaining half. Pour on 2 tbsp peanut oil. Add salt and pepper.

with Ginger and Scallions

4. Place the fish platter in a bain-marie and cook for 15 minutes.

5. For the sauce, mix 1 tbsp peanut oil, salt, pepper, sugar and sesame oil with 50 ml/3$^{1}/_{2}$ tbsp water in a bowl. Mix with a spoon. Add the soy sauce.

6. Remove the herbs that were cooked with the fish. Place the fish on a serving dish. Cover it with the reserved fresh ginger and scallions. Garnish with sprigs of cilantro, sprinkle it with the remaining 1 tbsp peanut oil and coat with the sauce.

Monkfish Casserole

Preparation time: 20 minutes
Cooking time: 25 minutes
Marinating time: 10 minutes
Difficulty: ★

Serves 4

1 monkfish tail
salt, pepper
150 ml/²/₃ cup rice wine
2 cloves garlic, minced
3 cm/1¹/₄ in fresh ginger, peeled and crushed

1 egg
1 tbsp potato flour
50 ml/3¹/₂ tbsp oil for the pan
50 g/3¹/₂ tbsp coconut sugar
100 ml/7 tbsp coconut juice
1 sprig fresh green peppercorns
30 ml/2 tbsp nuoc mam (fish sauce)
1 sprig Chinese lemongrass
2 or 3 blades scallion
3 or 4 sprigs cilantro

Hai Duong has created a savory monkfish casserole with coconut juice flavored with ginger and green peppercorns, the most successful specialty served at his restaurant. He has chosen monkfish, also called angler fish or sea devil, because it is most similar to the fish usually added to Vietnamese sauces. That fish is called *cá lôc* and is not available outside Vietnam. In fact, the Vietnamese have a wide variety of river and sea fish at their disposal, which they consume fresh, sun-dried, salted and smoked.

The main flavor of our recipe comes from soaking the fish with seasonings, enhanced by the slight acidity of the coconut juice. This dish can be kept and reheated, an important advantage in a country with a humid tropical climate, where not everyone has a refrigerator.

The coconut juice used in the sauce has a characteristically light acidic taste. Coconut juice is a whitish liquid that flows out when a green coconut is broken open. Unlike the coconut milk prepared from crushed coconuts, this juice is not thick, fatty or sugary. However, this recipe can indeed be made with coconut milk, which will produce a delicious creamy sauce with a totally different taste.

Our chef compensates for the lack of sweetness by adding a little coconut sugar to the sauce. This whitish, slightly gritty product is made by compressing coconut flesh. The juice is collected and then refined to extract the sugar. It differs from palm sugar, which is thick, has a reddish color and comes from the sap of certain palm trees.

Lastly, fresh ginger root brings a pleasantly spicy taste to this dish. The Vietnamese use it fresh, in strips that have been marinated in vinegar or even pickled. They frequently enrich fish or poultry broths and even desserts with its rich and powerful flavor.

1. Peel the monkfish tail. Cut it into large chunks and put into a basin. Add salt, pepper, 100 ml/7 tbsp rice wine, the minced garlic and 2 tbsp ground ginger. Marinate for 10 minutes. Then beat the egg and pour it over the fish.

2. Blend in the flour, then pan-fry the chunks of fish in hot oil for 5 minutes until they begin to brown.

3. Add the coconut sugar and coconut juice to the monkfish. Allow to dissolve over medium heat.

with Green Peppercorns

4. Next add the fresh green peppercorns to the pan.

5. Then add the nuoc mam and a thick slice of fresh ginger to the fish. Simmer until the mixture starts to caramelize.

6. Finally, pour 50 ml/3 ½ tbsp rice wine over the monkfish. Simmer for about 15 minutes. Slice the Chinese lemongrass and scallion finely, then add them to the fish. Garnish with cilantro leaves.

Alsatian

Preparation time: 45 minutes
Cooking time: 1 hour 40 minutes
Difficulty: ★★

Serves 4

For the fish:
500 g/generous 1 lb freshwater pike
500 g/generous 1 lb eel
500 g/generous 1 lb zander or walleye
400 g/14 oz carp
400 g/14 oz trout

For the broth:
2 or 3 sprigs parsley
1 sprig thyme
1 bay leaf

1 leek
1 small onion, sliced
2 shallots, sliced
300 ml/1¹/₂ cups Riesling

30 g/2 tbsp butter
1 clove garlic, crushed
salt, pepper

For the sauce:
50 g/3¹/₂ tbsp butter
90 g/10 tbsp flour
200 ml/generous ³/₄ cup liquid crème fraîche
salt, pepper
juice of ¹/₂ lemon

For the accompaniment:
200 g/7 oz pearl onions
200 g/7 oz button mushrooms
50 g/3¹/₂ tbsp butter
sliced soft white bread
fresh parsley, chives

Bordered by the Rhine River, Alsace has been enriched over time by the influences of its neighboring country, Germany. The original version of this recipe comes from the boatmen of the Rhine, who cooked the fish they caught during their travels up and down the river.

Alsatian Fish Stew brings together several savory freshwater fish in one dish. The basic recipe remains the same, whether you use freshwater or saltwater fish, as in recipes for Normandy fish stew. The heads, tails and bones of the fish are set aside to be used making the broth: in order to extract their full flavor, it is important to press the bones thoroughly when straining the broth in a chinois. There is no need to add salt to the broth, as this will be done at a later stage.

Sweet and aromatic, the leek greens and onions will not affect the flavor of the fish, but they are completely indispensable for broths and bouillons. The shallot, a close relative of the onion, has a subtler flavor, which is enhanced by mincing it finely. Shallots cook rapidly; they are added to melted butter as soon as the onions are lightly browned.

In terms of wines, Alsace has a well-deserved reputation. The vineyards of the greatest wines yield primarily white wines, which have a magnificent, powerful aroma. Our chefs have chosen the most prestigious of all: the Riesling, a wine named for the white grape variety with which it is made. Enhanced with Riesling, your sauce will have the slightly fruity flavor and the hint of minerals characteristic of this dish.

1. Descale, gut and wash the fish. Remove the central bones. Reserve the heads, tails and bones for the preparation of the broth. Remove the skin of the eel. Cut all the fish into slices about 4 cm/1¹/₂ in thick. Set aside.

2. For the broth, boil the fish cutoffs with a bouquet garni (parsley, thyme, bay leaf) in 2 liter/2 quarts water for 1 hour, then press through a chinois. Finely slice the leek greens. Fry in 30 g/2 tbsp melted butter with the onion for a few minutes, then add the shallots.

3. Pour on the Riesling. Fill the cooking pot to ³/₄ with the strained fish broth and crushed garlic. Reduce by ¹/₄ over high heat. Remove from the heat.

Fish Stew

4. Put the fish pieces into the broth. Bring to the boil, then reduce the heat and simmer for 20 minutes over low heat. Add salt and pepper.

5. Sauté the onions and mushrooms, separately, in butter for 5 minutes. Keep warm. For the sauce, melt 50 g/3^1/$_2$ tbsp butter, sprinkle on the flour, make a roux and stir in the fish broth. Bring to the boil. Add the crème fraîche, salt and pepper. Whisk.

6. Whisk the lemon juice into the sauce. Place the fish on a warm dish and coat with sauce. Serve with the mushrooms, pearl onions and croutons browned in butter. Sprinkle with fresh parsley and chives.

Majorcan-Style

Preparation time: 40 minutes
Cooking time: 50 minutes
Soaking time: 12 hours
Difficulty: ★★

Serves 6

1 kg/2¼ lb desalinated salt cod without skin
2 sprigs thyme
2 bay leaves
olive oil
50 g/6 tbsp golden raisins

1.2 kg/2¾ lb potatoes
3 tomatoes
2 cloves garlic
1 bunch parsley
salt
pepper
1 tbsp breadcrumbs

Discovered long ago by Basque whalers sailing in cold waters, cod was salted and stored in the holds of their fishing boats and quickly became part of Iberian cooking. Enthusiasm for this fish was so strong that its success transcended its natural boundaries. Because of how well it lends itself to being preserved, dried and salted, cod was soon found on menus in central Spain, a good distance from the rivers.

Firmly established in Iberian cuisine, salt cod quickly became a popular thing to serve during holidays, especially Easter. A favorite meal during lent, it is enjoyed in a number of savory preparations, transformed into spicy cumin stew, simmered in garlic and complemented with bread.

Majorcan cod comes from the Balearic Islands and is associated with the salty flavor of the fish and the sweeter flavor of sultanas, a large variety of raisin. Lightly enhanced, the addition of herbs greatly improves the dish. It's a specialty that is improved if it is cooked once, then sprinkled with a dash of olive oil and reheated. This allows the flavors of the salt cod, herbs, vegetables and raisins to become wonderfully blended. Go ahead and prepare this dish in large quantities, and then freeze some for later enjoyment.

To remove the excessive saltiness of dried salt cod, it must always be soaked in cold water for 12 hours, changing the water three or four times. Put the cod in a strainer below the surface of the water so that the salt falls to the bottom of the pot without re-permeating the fish. After straining, peel it and remove the bones by hand or with tweezers. For more impatient cooks, supermarkets sell cod already desalinated and without skin or bones, which can easily be substituted for the salt cod.

With such care given to preparing the fish, don't forget the wine: Chef Xavier Valero opts for a Somontano white.

1. Place the desalinated cod in a pot with 1 sprig of thyme, 1 bay leaf and a dash of olive oil. Cover with water and cook 10 minutes at a boil. Remove the bones and tease apart the flesh. Put the raisins in the water to cook and plump up.

2. Boil the potatoes and blanch the tomatoes. Allow to cool. Peel and crush the garlic. Mince the parsley, remove the thyme leaves, and crumble the second bay leaf. Peel the potatoes and cut into slices, then chop the tomatoes.

3. Preheat the oven to 180°C/355°F. Pour a layer of oil over the bottom of a high-sided casserole dish. Arrange the potato slices in a layer in the bottom of the dish.

Salt Cod

4. Top the potatoes with half the herbs, garlic and drained raisins. Sprinkle with a dash of oil. Cover with a layer of the cod. Add pepper and salt, and sprinkle again with oil.

5. Sprinkle with the rest of the herbs (reserving a little for garnish), garlic and raisins. Cover with a layer of tomato slices. Sprinkle oil over the top.

6. Sprinkle the tomatoes with the bread-crumbs, reserved herbs and a dash of oil. Bake in the oven for 15 to 20 minutes, then brown for several minutes under a grill or broiler. Serve very hot in the baking dish.

Char

Preparation time: 45 minutes
Cooking time: 35 minutes
Difficulty: ★★

Serves 4

120 g/¹/₂ cup butter
50 g/¹/₃ cup flour
200 g/7 oz green Chasselas grapes

2 char, 600–800 g/1¹/₄–1³/₄ lb each
120 g/³/₄ cup minced shallots
400 ml/1²/₃ cups white wine
100 ml/7 tbsp fish stock
400 ml/1²/₃ cups liquid crème fraîche
salt
pepper

Known as "the prince of the lakes," the char figures among the best fish of the Lake Geneva region. This close relative of the trout is characterized by its blue-green back scattered with touches of pink, its silvery-blue flanks and white stomach. Its pink flesh is a great delicacy and has a less pronounced taste than salmon. Around Lake Geneva, only professional anglers with permits are allowed to catch char, perch and salmon in large quantities.

The Swiss do not like bones in their fish, so char is usually served as fried fillets meunière, or seasoned, rolled in flour, fried in butter and served with lemon, parsley and hot melted butter. German-speaking Swiss people eat it with fried onions, while in Neuchâtel they more often add finely sliced bacon.

Our chef enhances this noble fish by pairing it with a sauce made with Dezaley, the famous white wine of Lavaux. The canton of Vaud, the second most important viticultural canton in Switzerland, is divided into three zones: Chablais, from

Martigny to Montreux; Lavaux, from Montreux to Lausanne on the shore of Lake Geneva; and Côte de l'Orbe, from Neuchâtel to the slopes of the Jura. The winery in the village of Dezaley was established in the thirteenth century by the monks of Cîteaux. Since then, the *Chasselas doré* grapes have grown on the small terraces called *parchets*. Dezaley wine offers hints of almond, toasted bread and notes of tea and honey.

This recipe can be prepared with a whole fish or fillets, with equally pleasing results. According to our chef, the fish has fewer and fewer bones as one progresses from the head to the tail. Most come away readily during the filleting process. The rest must be removed with tweezers.

Chef Marc Imbs suggests making the sauce more consistent by mixing it at the last minute using a hand-held blender that breaks the flour somewhat apart and makes the sauce light and very frothy. Serve the fish accompanied with buttered steamed potatoes sprinkled with parsley.

1. Cut 50 g/3¹/₂ tbsp butter into a dish and let it soften. Add the flour and mix with your fingertips to obtain an even beurre manié. Peel the grapes and set aside.

2. Slice through the fish just behind the gills. Lift the fillets by cutting along the central bone of the fish with a knife. Extract the bones from the fillets, one by one, with tweezers, pressing on the flesh with your thumb to make them come away more easily.

3. Heat 20 g/1¹/₂ tbsp butter in a pan and sweat the shallots for 5 minutes. Deglaze with the white wine. Let the liquid reduce by half (about 10 minutes) then add the fish stock. Allow to cook another 4 to 5 minutes.

Dezaley

4. Butter and salt a large rectangular dish. Place the char fillets on the dish. Spoon the well-heated white wine sauce through a sieve and pour over the fillets. Poach for 5 minutes over low heat.

5. Pour the poaching juices into a saucepan. Scoop some beurre manié from the bowl onto the tip of a whisk. Plunge the whisk into the saucepan and mix it with the liquid. Incorporate the rest of the beurre manié into the sauce the same way.

6. Stir the sauce 10 minutes over a low heat to yield a consistent texture. Add the crème fraîche and stir again over the heat to obtain a creamy sauce. Add salt and pepper. Fry the grapes in the remaining butter. Serve the fish topped with sauce and garnished with grapes.

Char with Potato

Preparation time: 30 minutes
Cooking time: 50 minutes
Difficulty: ★★

Serves 4

500 g/generous 1 lb char
100 g/7 tbsp butter, melted
salt
pepper
4 potatoes
oil to fry the fish

1 large onion
50 ml/3½ tbsp oil
100 g/3½ oz piece of smoked bacon
400 g/14 oz fresh sauerkraut
10 juniper berries
1 sprig thyme
2 bay leaves
125 ml/½ cup white wine
100 ml/7 tbsp fish stock
100 ml/7 tbsp liquid crème fraîche

The combination of sauerkraut and char has long been a highly appreciated dish in traditional German cooking. Our chef wished to give it a more personal touch by covering the fish fillets with fine potato scales. In this, he was inspired by the Mediterranean method of frying goatfish covered with fine slices of zucchini.

Char, a delicious fish with high-quality flesh, belongs to the same family as salmon and trout. It lives in deep water in cold lakes, below the level occupied by trout. In Germany, they can often be caught in the lakes of Bavaria and the Black Forest. The most traditional way to cook char is to grill or broil them with almonds, in the same way as trout. Our chef serves this recipe with an extra topping of Riesling sauce.

If char is unavailable, a trout or pike perch will work just as well with this recipe, but try to use one of the river fishes.

Sauerkraut, made of white cabbage that has been allowed to ferment, is a centuries-old German treat; the name *sauerkraut* literally means "sour herb". In the past, sauerkraut specialists visited homes throughout the countryside with a special utensil used for finely slicing the cabbage. Then, cooks let it ferment for several months between layers of salt in earthenware containers covered by a heavy stone to pack it down. Today, the process has been industrialized, and sauerkraut is almost always sold commercially prepared, rather than fresh.

To make sure the potato scales adhere well to the flesh of the fish, put the dish in the refrigerator to chill for a short time, just long enough for the butter to solidify. However, don't let it sit too long in the cold or it will blacken.

1. Open the char and remove the fillets. Remove the bones with tweezers. Cut the fillets in half across the center and remove the skin.

2. Using a brush, coat the fillets with some of the melted butter. Add salt and pepper. Peel the potatoes, then slice finely with a mandoline. Arrange them on the surface of the fillets to look like scales.

3. Heat the rest of the butter and some oil in a fish fryer. With a spatula, move the potato-garnished fillets into the fryer, flesh side down, and allow to cook. Turn gently with the potato side down and let them brown.

Scales and Sauerkraut

4. Peel and finely slice the onion. Brown in 50 ml/3¹/₂ tbsp oil with the chunk of bacon until everything is browned.

5. Add the uncooked sauerkraut to the onion along with a few juniper berries, the thyme and bay leaves. Sprinkle with the white wine and a dash of water. Cook for about 15 minutes, covered.

6. Reduce the fish stock in a small saucepan. Add the crème fraîche, bring to the boil and reduce over medium heat. Serve the fish with potato scales with the sauerkraut and bacon. Surround with wine sauce and garnish with juniper berries.

Squid

Preparation time: 45 minutes
Cooking time: 30 minutes
Difficulty: ★★

Serves 4

For the stuffed squid:
1/2 bunch flat-leaf parsley
1 bunch Swiss chard
1/2 bunch dill
2 cloves garlic, crushed
1 tbsp hot chili sauce
1 tsp coriander seeds

100 g/1 cup rice
1 tsp salt
1 tsp pepper
4 cleaned squid

For the sauce:
100 ml/7 tbsp olive oil
3 cloves garlic
100 g/3 1/2 oz tomato purée
1 tsp salt
1 tsp pepper
1 tsp dried coriander
1 tsp ground caraway seeds

"What good it does you, Mrs. Tunis, you who spend half your time feasting!" claims a popular Tunisian story. From the Rue de Marseille to the Rue de Lyon, at the market or on the patio, the city of Tunis celebrates late into the night. Its cuisine was developed amidst these celebrations and community gatherings. The market in Tunis abounds with octopus and squid, which our chef Rafik Tlati presents stuffed in the local style.

If possible, choose large, whole squid with a flexible body or "pocket", so that the stuffing does not come out while cooking. The stuffing, called *osbène*, has a subtle taste of young tender-leaved Swiss chard. When using Swiss chard, a plant closely related to spinach, Tunisians do not use the large leaves. Tunisian chards are, however, almost nonexistent in other parts of the world. They can be replaced with spinach leaves, according to taste. Either one will need to be very finely

minced in order to mix well in the stuffing that goes inside the squid. A veritable manna for Tunisian cooking, flat-leaf parsley is a basic ingredient in numerous dishes. To preserve the flavor, our chef recommends removing the leaves without washing them first.

When stuffed, the squid will bulge, so do not try to overstuff them, and be sure to remove any extra dressing at the edges of the pockets before sealing them with a toothpick. Leave a little empty space at this stage, because the squid will swell in the sauce and risk bursting open as the rice cooks. If the sauce seems too thin, uncover your cooking pot, then let it reduce until cooking is complete.

Whether whole or sliced, serve the squid pockets in generous portions and drizzled with the thickened sauce. Serve with delicious white rice.

1. Remove the leaves from the flat-leaf parsley; wash and chop the leaves. Separate the Swiss chard leaves. Rinse, drain and finely chop.

2. Place the Swiss chard and parsley in a large bowl. Add 1 tbsp chopped dill, the crushed garlic, hot chili sauce, coriander seeds and uncooked rice. Season with salt and pepper and mix.

3. Carefully wash the squid. Drain them and dry with a paper towel. Using a small spoon, fill each squid with the stuffing.

Pockets

4. Close each squid with a small toothpick. Pinch the edges of the opening together. Set aside.

5. To prepare the sauce, heat the olive oil in a pot and add the minced garlic cloves and tomato purée. Cook 3 minutes over high heat. Fill the pot about ¾ full with water and bring the mixture to the boil.

6. As soon as the sauce starts to boil, add the stuffed squid. Add salt, pepper, coriander and caraway seeds. Cook 30 minutes uncovered. Serve very hot with sauce.

Ô-Sun

Preparation time:	30 minutes
Cooking time:	30 minutes
Difficulty:	★★★

Serves 4

300 g/11 oz white fish
salt
white pepper
200 g/7 oz fresh spinach
sesame oil
4 eggs

3 tbsp cornstarch
1 carrot
7 fresh shiitake mushrooms
frying oil

For the sauce:
1 tsp mustard
50 ml/3¹/₂ tbsp soy sauce
1 tbsp sugar

Ô-Sun is a very aristocratic dish served with all the bones removed. A guest can sample the dish with pride, dipping the little fish portions into the sauce with chopsticks with no risk of finding a bone. This is a legacy from the royalty when it was inconceivable that a king or the nobles should pick their own bones out from a dish. The cooks of the court therefore performed this service for their illustrious masters. This recipe reflects another Korean specialization, the art of wrapping food. The cook envelopes central stuffing in a thin crepe-like pancake, or fragments of omelet, or the guest will do it for himself on his own plate, using whatever takes his fancy.

For this recipe, Mrs. Kim recommends a less expensive white-fleshed fish, such as whiting or pollock. These two fish belong to the *Gadidae* family, closely related to the cod.

The whiting is frequently eaten in Korea. In winter, people line-dry them for two months on the sea shore. Because the air is very dry, the whiting does not spoil, and its special texture, firm and supple, is highly valued for preparing soups.

Spinach is among the most commonly used vegetables in Korean cooking. Commonly used as a flavoring for vegetables, sesame oil brings the aroma of toasted hazelnuts. The sesame is an oil-producing plant that has been cultivated for more than 5,000 years, a plant harvested for its small, brown, oval-shaped seeds. One seed can contain up to 50% oil. Of a brownish-orange color, sesame oil is exceptionally resistant to rancidity. Only a small amount is necessary to add intense aroma and taste to a dish.

For a successful preparation of Ô-Sun, our chef strongly recommends letting the fish rolls refrigerate in the cloth before cutting them. Otherwise you risk crushing them while cutting. You can also let them sit in the freezer.

1. Slice the fish very finely. Salt and pepper it generously. Wash the spinach leaves and add salt and sesame oil. Set aside.

2. Beat the eggs, as in preparing an omelet, and cook them 10 minutes in a pan to make 4 very fine crêpes. Set aside. On a work surface, layer a bamboo sushi mat, then a cloth and finally a thin crêpe. Sprinkle it with cornstarch.

3. Place the finely sliced fish along the center of the crepe and scatter with cornstarch. Peel the carrot. Slice the carrot and the mushrooms into fine sticks and fry separately in a little oil, 5 minutes each.

4. On the fish slices, place a line of carrots, then a line of spinach, with a row of mushrooms in the middle. Add pepper.

5. Roll, keeping the cloth and sushi mat together. Carefully remove the sushi mat, then reroll the crêpe tightly. Tie the ends of the cloth and cook the roll inside it, steaming for 10 minutes. Repeat, making 3 additional rolls.

6. For the sauce, mix the mustard, soy sauce, 1 tbsp water and sugar. When the sushi rolls have been well-chilled, cut them into slices and serve topped with mustard-soy sauce.

Seafood

Preparation time: 15 minutes
Cooking time: 35 minutes
Difficulty: ★★★

Serves 4

300 g/11 oz monkfish
2 bunches flat-leaf parsley
1 onion
300 g/11 oz prawns
300 g/11 oz squid
500 ml/2 cups fish stock
1 rounded tsp saffron threads

salt
pepper
juice of 2 lemons
100 g/1¼ cups sliced button mushrooms
200 g/7 oz Chinese rice vermicelli
4 tbsp oil
paprika (optional)
3 eggs
5 or 6 b'steeya or phyllo leaves
2 tbsp butter

Decorated with a grid of minced flat-leaf parsley, paprika, pan-fried prawns, shaped lemons and black olives, this stuffed galette is exquisite. The garnish is a signature of our chef, Lahoucine Belmoufid.

This recipe for *b'steeya*, which takes its name from the more traditional dish composed of pigeons, almonds and cinnamon, is a new creation from Moroccan epicureans. About 10 years ago, chef Safi came up with this new version, and his success was so great that this recipe is now on the menus of all the best Moroccan chefs.

This *b'steeya* is unusually demanding in its preparation because of the seafood and fine fish that it requires. In exchange, however, this lower-calorie recipe is much healthier than the sugared *b'steeya*.

Our chef's recipe includes no sugar or almonds, but rather fresh fish and flat-leaf parsley to create a beautiful galette that

is served with the traditional *chermoula* sauce made of olive oil, salt, pepper, powdered chili pepper, cumin, lemon and cilantro that generally accompanies fish fried or cooked *en papillote* (in parchment paper).

To make this galette, you need to close it as shown in the last step below, tucking in the edges of the phyllo dough as if making a bed, tightly pressed together, and glazing each layer of pastry with melted butter.

Seafood B'steeya can be served as our chef presents it, or rolled in its pastry case like a Viennese strudel, or in any other way you prefer. Make sure that the stuffing is dry enough so that it doesn't saturate its envelope of delicate pastry.

Our chef recommends complementing this recipe with mesclun greens, in addition to *chermoula*: a salad made of leaf lettuce, romaine and Batavian lettuce cut in strips, and served with a light mustard vinaigrette dressing.

1. Remove the skin from the monkfish and rinse it in cold water. Drain. Chop the parsley and onion. Shell the prawns and blanch them 2 minutes in boiling water. Dice the monkfish, squid and prawns. Set everything aside.

2. In a saucepan, poach the squid in fish stock with saffron, salt, pepper and lemon juice. Add the sliced mushrooms to the saucepan with the vermicelli. Over low heat, reduce 2 to 3 minutes.

3. In a large pan, heat the oil and brown the onion for 2 minutes. Then add the cubes of monkfish and prawns and cook over medium heat 3 minutes while turning with a spatula.

B'Steeya

4. Scatter the monkfish and prawns with finely-minced parsley and ground paprika. The paprika is optional; it has a strong flavor, so it should be used according to taste.

5. In a bowl, beat the eggs as for an omelet. Pour the eggs over the monkfish and the prawn and allow to reduce until the liquid fully evaporates.

6. Lay out 3 sheets of phyllo in a buttered, circular baking pan. Place the seafood stuffing mixture in the middle of the phyllo, fold it over and seal the edges. Cover with another sheet of phyllo and melted butter. Bake for 20 minutes at 180°C/355°F.

Cod Pavé with

Preparation time: 25 minutes
Cooking time: 35 minutes
Difficulty: ★

Serves 4

For the fish:
1 cod, ca. 700 g/1 1/2 lb
salt
pepper
1 tbsp olive oil

For the endive compote:
2 onions
2 Belgian endives
1 small pat of butter

salt
150 g/1 1/4 cups blanched green beans
60 g/1/2 cup dried apricots
30 g/1/4 cup green walnut kernels

For the apple vinaigrette:
1 lime
2 Granny Smith apples
40 ml/2 1/2 tbsp balsamic vinegar
40 ml/2 1/2 tbsp walnut oil
60 ml/1/4 cup chicken stock
salt
ground pepper

For the garnish (optional):
sprigs of dill

When, for once, the fish does not take center stage in a recipe, it would be a pity not to make the most if it. When you know that cod only takes five effortless minutes to brown skin-side down, you might think that such simplicity must be hiding something. In fact, the sophistication lies in the wonderful compote of endive and dried fruit that is served with the cod.

In season from October to May, the endive is a winter vegetable in the chicory family that is forced in dark cellars to keep it white. Its green or white leaves are eaten cooked or in salads. Always choose young endives: their exquisite leaves, with a slightly bitter taste, are complemented by the onion's sweetness. 30 minutes' cooking over low heat is all it takes to give these two garden plants the compote touch. If bitterness does not suit your taste, leeks and Swiss chard work just as well. Mix their washed and finely-sliced leaves in the compote with the onions. The cooking time is the same as for the endives.

Chlorophyl and energy go hand in hand when Chef Michel Roth blends green beans, dried apricots and green walnuts. He recommends always using them in these exact proportions, without excess. Chopped finely, without allowing them to cook additionally, they give out their full flavor: the crunchiness of the walnuts, the sweetness of the apricots and the tenderness of the green beans blend well with the bitterness of the endive compote.

Michel Roth creatively accompanies the pan-fried cod with a unique vinaigrette flavored with apple juice and lime. The Granny Smith apple is known for its bold green color and for the acidity of its flesh. Cut into quarters, put through a blender and then filter the juice by pressing the pulp. Alternately, you can achieve the same effect more easily by using a centrifuge. The balsamic vinegar can be easily replaced with an apple cider vinegar for a subtle taste of apples.

1. Peel the onions; clean and pare the endives. Slice both finely. Place them in a pan with one pat of melted butter. Salt lightly. Cook for 25 minutes over low heat, stirring with a spatula.

2. Add the green beans, the dried apricots sliced into narrow strips and the crushed walnuts. Mix together and set aside on a hot plate, without letting them cook.

3. Fillet the cod without removing the skin. Cut each fillet into 4 pieces. Add salt and pepper, then set aside.

Endive Compote

4. In a frying pan, heat 1 tbsp olive oil. Brown each piece of cod for 5 minutes, skin side down. Turn them over and brown 3 minutes on the other side. The skin should be crusty and golden. Set aside.

5. Squeeze the lime, then extract the juice from the 2 apples cut into quarters. Mix the 2 juices with the balsamic vinegar, walnut oil and chicken stock. Add salt and pepper. Using a whisk, beat into a vinaigrette.

6. Place the hot cod pavé on plates and accompany with the vegetable compote. Decorate with several fine slices of dried apricots and a sprig of dill. Serve with the vinaigrette as garnish or on the side.

Djerban

Preparation time: 15 minutes
Cooking time: 45 minutes
Difficulty: ★★

Serves 4

1 sea bream or large grouper, ca. 2.5 kg/5¹/₂ lb
1 tsp sweet paprika
1 tsp coriander
1 tsp caraway
1 tsp turmeric
1 tsp cumin

2 white onions
100 ml/7 tbsp olive oil
1 tbsp tomato purée
2 bay leaves
2 cloves garlic
salt
2 lemons
pepper
1 tsp hot chili sauce
4 potatoes
3 tomatoes
2 green chili peppers

A blue fish tattooed on the hand, a good-luck charm sculpted or hung at the entrance of white houses: the traditional Phoenician custom of using fish to ward off the evil eye is still part of Tunisian culture.

Early in the morning, residents of the island of Djerba gather in large numbers at the fish market in search of large grouper that will be baked in the oven in a tomato sauce. Purchased ahead of time, the fish is scaled, gutted, cleaned and then thoroughly dried. It is important that the fish be quite dry so that it can fully absorb the spices and salt as it cooks. The fish is placed on a large plate for preparation. Four to six incisions are made diagonally across the skin; these openings are where the flesh will take on the flavor of a multitude of spices: *kammoun* (cumin), acrid and powerful; *karouya* (caraway), bitter and biting; the acidic and licorice-like *tabel* (coriander) and finally turmeric and paprika, suffusing the grouper with oriental flavors. One after the other, place a pinch of each spice into each incision. Then, turn the fish over to catch the excess spice on the plate. Finally, spread cumin generously over the entire surface of the grouper, but take care not to use too much or it will make the flesh overly bitter. Chill the fish so that the spices permeate the flesh thoroughly while you prepare the sauce.

A paste of crushed garlic and salt introduced into the belly of the fish completes the preparation. The tomato purée should always be diluted in water before adding it to the onions in the frying pan. Add hot chili sauce to taste. Pour the sauce over the entire fish to ensure that it does not dry out while baking. Chop the tomatoes and hot peppers in half and cook along with the potatoes so that they take on the flavor of the sauce and the spices in the fish.

1. Remove the scales, gut, wash and dry the fish. Remove the dorsal fin and place the fish on a chopping board. Using a knife, make 4 to 5 incisions across the flank of the fish, each about 1 cm (¹/₃ in) deep.

2. Into each incision, add a pinch of each spice: paprika, coriander, caraway and turmeric. Finish by rubbing cumin over the entire fish. Chill in the refrigerator. Peel the onions and chop them.

3. Coat a pan with olive oil. Tip in the chopped onions. Over high heat, cook the onions quickly without letting them brown. Add the tomato purée and bay leaves and mix well with the onions.

Baked Grouper

4. Over high heat, brown the onions and tomatoes. Add 1 tbsp olive oil and cover with water. Add 1 minced garlic clove. Simmer over low heat, uncovered. Crush 1 garlic clove, add salt, and stuff this mixture inside the fish.

5. Cut the lemons in thin slices and then semicircles. Side by side, place 2 slices into each incision in the fish (they will protrude slightly). Pour the onion and tomato sauce into a baking pan and place the fish in the center. Season with pepper, salt and hot chili sauce.

6. Peel and cut the potatoes in thick slices. Cut the tomatoes and hot green peppers in half. Place the tomatoes, hot peppers and potatoes in the sauce around the fish. Bake 20 to 30 minutes at 180°C/355°F. Serve hot.

Fish Cooked

Preparation time: 30 minutes
Cooking time: 45 minutes
Marinating time: 15 minutes
Difficulty: ★

Serves 4 or 5

4 or 5 potatoes
3 carrots (optional)
salt
1 kg/2¼ lb cod fillets
4 or 5 large gherkins or pickled cucumbers

½ celeriac
2 onions
1 bunch curly-leaf parsley
1 bunch tarragon
pepper
300 ml/1¼ cups brine from the pickles
1 bunch dill
60 g/¼ cup butter
60 g/4½ tbsp flour

Fish Cooked in Pickle Brine is one of the oldest and most authentic Russian recipes. Originally, before the era of trained chefs, people prepared this recipe by simmering it over the large wood-burning stove in the center of the main room of their home. The stove was thus used simultaneously for cooking and for heating the whole house.

Continental chefs prepare this dish with fish from lakes and rivers, while those from the maritime regions use fish from the sea. Ideally, the fish you select should have white flesh, rather firm like cod. However, whiting or goatfish may also be used. In Russia, people also enjoy this recipe prepared with lake sturgeon.

The Russians eat large quantities of pickles, which are stored in jars of brine. In a large container, pickles are alternated with layers that may include garlic, dill, tarragon, parsley, bay leaves, black currant leaves, whole black pepper and horseradish, according to the personal taste of the person making the pickles. Next, salty, cold water is added and the jars are left to marinate three days at room temperature. Finally, the pickles are tightly sealed in a jar and stored two months in a refrigerator before they are ready to be eaten.

Numerous recipes demonstrate the importance of these pickles. They are used in fish with sauce, in soups, in Russian salad with beets, mixed with smoked meats; or combined with potatoes, eggs, meat or fish, peas and onions and then topped with sour cream.

In the past, Russian women marinated their pickles in brine in oak barrels in the basement. This process took place during the autumn. Many of these salted vegetables were later presented on the table in cold entrées called *zakouskis*.

1. Boil the peeled potatoes and carrots for 20 minutes in salted water. Meanwhile, place the cod fillets in a large baking pan.

2. Place the large pickles on a chopping board. Slice finely.

3. Peel and chop the celeriac and onions. Sprinkle the fish with the celeriac, onions, pickle slices and a bunch of parsley sprigs and tarragon, tied together with kitchen string. Pepper generously.

in Pickle Brine

4. Pour the strained pickle brine over everything. Allow to marinate 15 minutes (if preferred, start to cook immediately without marinating). Then bake 10 to 15 minutes in a moderate oven.

5. Using a slotted spoon, place a piece of cod on each serving plate. Place the slices of boiled potato around the cod, sprinkle with minced dill, then add the carrots. Strain the cooking juices from the fish.

6. Melt the butter, then sprinkle in the flour to make a roux to absorb the cooking juices. Stir constantly over low heat for 10 minutes until the sauce is creamy. Top the fish with sauce and garnish with dill.

Chili-Spiced

Preparation time: 1 hour
Cooking time: 1 hour 25 minutes
Difficulty: ★★

Serves 6

200 g/generous ³/₄ cup tahini
2 lemons
salt
2 onions
olive oil
2 tbsp ground coriander
5 cloves garlic

1 green bell pepper
1 red bell pepper
¹/₂ green chili pepper
1 large tomato
1 tbsp tomato purée
pepper
¹/₂ tsp ground cumin
1¹/₂ bunches cilantro
50 g/6 tbsp pine nuts
1 sea bream, ca. 1 kg/2¹/₄ lb
2 bay leaves
50 g/scant ¹/₂ cup chopped green walnuts

Chili-spiced fish is among the most popular Lebanese dishes. In the hands of the chef, the sea bream is transformed into an exceptional specialty that is customarily served for festive and holiday meals. In fact, tradition requires that this fish, which is often among the largest items, be presented with both skin and bones removed, and surrounded with a red sauce and tahini; the cilantro sauce is served in a bowl on the side. For aesthetic reasons, the placement of the tahini and the cilantro have been reversed in the photo. The sea bream may be replaced with any fish that bakes well.

Well-known for its soothing qualities, a single spoonful of tahini is enough to mellow irritated throats. It consists entirely of sesame seeds that have simply been ground: rich in oil, they make a grayish-beige, fluid paste, naturally oily and quite

sweet. Tahini is sold ready-made in all Lebanese and Middle-Eastern specialty stores and is sometimes seen on the shelves of supermarkets.

Thinned with water and flavored with lemon juice, tahini is poured over Lebanese bread and served with fried fish. Whole sesame seeds are much less frequently used in Lebanon.

The small and elongated spicy chili peppers commonly found in the marketplace can be substituted with Tabasco or dried and powdered chili pepper, according to taste.

To be true to the traditions of Lebanon, this dish should certainly be preceded with a round of tabbouleh, a blend of bulghur, tomatoes, onions, fresh parsley and other flavors. Serve each dish with a glass of arrack, an alcohol with an anise flavor that complements both the fish and the tabbouleh.

1. In a small bowl, whisk together the tahini, the juice of 1 lemon, 1 tsp salt and 200 ml/ generous ³/₄ cup water. Slice the other lemon and set aside.

2. Peel and finely slice 1 onion. Brown in a saucepan in a small amount of oil until golden. Blend in the tahini mixture. Cook over low heat for 20 minutes, until thick. Season with a pinch of coriander. Chop the second onion and mince 2 garlic cloves.

3. Gently fry the chopped garlic and onion. Dice and add the bell peppers, chili pepper, tomato, tomato purée, salt, pepper and cumin. Pour in 400 ml/1²/₃ cups water. Cook 30 minutes over medium heat, adding ¹/₂ bunch cilantro mid-way through.

Fish from Byblos

4. Brown the pine nuts in olive oil and set aside. Place the sea bream in a baking pan, sprinkle olive oil over it, add 5 or 6 lemon slices, the bay leaves, salt and pepper. Bake 30 minutes at 200°C/390°F.

5. Chop the rest of the cilantro and mince the remaining 3 garlic cloves. Brown the garlic in 100 ml/7 tbsp oil, then add the cilantro and continue cooking over high heat for 5 minutes, stirring constantly.

6. Remove the skin and bones of the fish and place it on a serving platter. Pour the cilantro sauce on one side and vegetable sauce on the other. Pour the sesame sauce in a bowl and serve it on the side. Garnish with the toasted pine nuts and walnuts.

Tandoori

Preparation time: 30 minutes
Cooking time: 20 minutes
Resting time: 2 hours
Difficulty: ★★

Serves 4

1 whole turbot
1 lemon

For the marinade:
250 g/1 cup natural yogurt
1 tbsp tandoori powder
¹/₂ tsp cayenne pepper
1 cm/¹/₃ inch fresh ginger
2 cloves garlic
salt
pepper

Tandoori is a particular style of oven baking. That might not sound exciting, but the interesting part is that in India, this is done in a traditional oven that disperses an even heat that comes from glowing embers.

The tandoor oven resembles a long, narrow-necked, two-handled jar, or amphora, that is traditionally buried in the ground. Only the long neck, which serves as the opening, is above ground. Through this opening, meats, poultry or fish are placed on a spit in the middle of the stove. The coals must be red-hot before anything is put in the oven, so that the heat is evenly dispersed. The heat will gradually decrease as the embers die down.

A little Indian trick: to avoid the meat on the spit slipping and falling into the coals and destroying a successful dish, Indians thread a greased apple onto each end of the spit before placing the meat into the oven to hold the meat in case it should suddenly threaten to slide. This recipe for tandoori fish is only one variation among myriad possibilities, of which the most common is chicken tandoori.

Apart from the cooking style, tandoori requires a traditional preparation that can be varied according to region or the personal preferences of the chefs. In the south, for example, it would be made quite spicy with chili peppers and freshly ground or ground ginger.

The quality of this extremely popular Indian dish is a result of its traditional preparation. To achieve the best approximation of a tandoor oven, follow our chef's recommendations in the last step. To capitalize on the prized and ephemeral heat emanating from the coals, Indians rapidly knead their unleavened bread dough and press it against the interior wall of the oven to bake; they watch it closely so that it does not bake too quickly and blacken in the brazier's heat.

1. Prepare the marinade by mixing the yogurt and tandoori powder. Grate the ginger using a cheese grater, then blend in the minced garlic and lastly the cayenne pepper. Salt and pepper to taste.

2. Prepare the fish for cooking by removing all the skin. Be careful to avoid lifting away sections of the flesh while removing the skin; be sure to use a well-sharpened knife.

3. Make several incisions in the fish with your knife; cut in such a way that you form parallel, oblique slits. Then make cuts in the opposite direction, forming a grid. Turn the fish over and repeat.

Fish

4. Cut the lemon in half and rub it over the entire surface of the fish so that the juice flavors both sides; or, if preferred, squeeze the lemon juice by hand over the surface.

5. With a brush, coat the entire surface of the fish with the marinade, starting with one side of the fish. Do not coat the other side until it is on the grill. Let it stand 2 hours with one side coated.

6. In an oven heated to 180°C/355°F, place a metal rack over a baking dish. Half fill it with water to imitate the heat of a tandoori oven. Coat the other side of the fish with the marinade, place it on the grill and put in the oven. Bake 15 to 20 minutes.

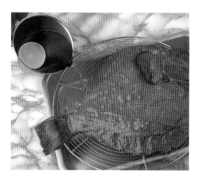

Acadian

Preparation time:	30 minutes	
Cooking time:	45 minutes	
Resting time, pastry:	30 minutes	
Difficulty:	★★	

Serves 5 or 6

For the filling:
4 potatoes
250 g/9 oz cooked lobster flesh
250 g/9 oz cooked shrimp
500 g/generous 1 lb raw cod fillets
500 g/generous 1 lb raw bay scallops

2 onions, chopped
salt
pepper
1 pinch savory
500 ml/2 cups fish stock

For the pastry:
200 g/generous 1 1/3 cups flour
1 tbsp baking powder
1 pinch salt
100 g/7 tbsp butter
1 egg
40 ml/2 1/2 tbsp milk

Pot pie has developed from hotpots of fish and seafood prepared in terrines. This recipe originates in Acadia, part of the Maritime Provinces region that includes New Brunswick, Prince Edward Island, Nova Scotia and the Magdalen Islands. The port of Halifax in Nova Scotia is renowned for its trade of Nordic shrimp, scallops, mussels and lobster.

Yet it is cod fishing that has dominated the fishing industry for centuries. In Quebec, cod is referred to as *morue* whether it is fresh or salted, though officially, the term *morue* means salt cod. In the past, freshly-caught fish was salted and then dried in the open air all along the coast of the Gaspé Peninsula. Then it was loaded into barrels and exported to Portugal, Spain or Italy. However, the size of the fish being caught decreased considerably as a result of commercial fishing, and the cod season became shorter and shorter. Today, fishermen value many kinds of fish and shellfish that they used to reject in favor of "his majesty", the cod.

A notable addition to this pot pie, the lobster, became fashionable in Quebec thanks to special promotion by Chef Paul Bocuse. The extremely cold waters in the St. Lawrence Gulf give the lobster flesh a delicious quality and taste. Excellent medium-sized shrimp also come from the Gaspé Peninsula, from the port of Matane.

In addition to lobster, the dish includes scallops, or *vaneaux*, which are sometimes mistakenly called Saint-Jacques scallops (sea scallops), although their meat is much smaller and of a lesser quality and their shells are quite different from the true Saint-Jacques. Quebec epicureans sometimes add eel, which is also caught in the Saint Lawrence estuary.

The top of this pot pie can be decorated with little leaves or any other shape cut out of the pastry scraps with a knife or cookie cutter.

1. Peel the potatoes. Slice them into thin circles. Blanch for 2 minutes. Drain and place 1/3 of the slices in a layer at the bottom of an ovenproof casserole dish.

2. Cover the potatoes with pieces of lobster, shelled shrimp, pieces of cod, scallops and chopped onions.

3. Add a second layer of potatoes, then top with a second layer of fish and seafood. Finish with a final layer of potatoes. Add salt, pepper and savory between each layer.

Pot Pie

4. Pour hot fish stock over the entire contents of the dish.

5. For the pastry, blend the flour, baking powder and salt. Dice the butter and then add to the flour, incorporating it with the aid of 2 knives. Finish by mixing with the tips of your fingers. Form a ball of dough and chill for 30 minutes in the refrigerator.

6. Roll out the dough and cut to fit the casserole dish. Place the pastry over the top layer of potatoes. Glaze with a mixture of beaten egg and milk. Bake for 30 minutes in the oven.

Potted

Preparation time: 40 minutes
Cooking time: 45 minutes
Difficulty: ★

Serves 4

2 onions
800 g/1¾ lb salmon fillets
800 g/1¾ lb potatoes
200 ml/generous ¾ cup milk
6 eggs

400 ml/1⅔ cups liquid crème fraîche
salt
white pepper
200 g/14 tbsp butter
200 g/7 oz fresh dill

Salmon is prepared throughout Sweden, where it is called *lax*. It is not a dish that Swedes prepare every day, however, but is reserved for major holidays like Christmas and Easter. Wild salmon is becoming increasingly rare. Baltic salmon has bright orange flesh, while those caught in the Skagerrak Sea have much redder flesh.

This fish is always part of the large Swedish buffet, called *smörgåsbord*, which is set up for all special occasions. The salmon dishes are marinated in salt, sugar and dill and are served with a Scanie mustard sauce. Nearby will probably be cold poached salmon and smoked salmon, both of which can be enjoyed on a slice of buttered pumpernickel bread. Dishes with shrimp and mussels are served alongside these different variations on salmon.

A Swedish meal is never complete without potatoes. Boiled, mashed, fried, gratin, in soup: they are served in every possible way. This tuber is grown in the southernmost part of Sweden, in Scanie, where the plains seem to go on forever. The range includes *Bintje*, *Sparis potatis* (asparagus potatoes) and red-skinned "almond" potatoes or *Asterix*.

Our chef enjoys seasoning with wild dill, or at least with organic herbs. Without question, dill is the herb most often found in Swedish cooking, and the umbels, flowers and seeds are all used.

This plant is equally delicious in the salmon marinade in this recipe as it is with crayfish, boiled potatoes and veal stew. The Swedes also make frequent use of other herbs, including parsley, thyme, chives, hyssop, rosemary and verbena.

The salmon "puddings" need to be flattened as they cook in a bain-marie. Our chef recommends filling small ramekins three-fourths full of water and placing one on top of each portion until they are cooked to compress them.

1. Peel the onions and potatoes. Slice them finely using a mandoline or a very sharp chef's knife. Set aside.

2. Remove the skin from the salmon. Using a tranchelard knife, finely slice the fish, slicing at a good angle and moving down the fillet as pictured below.

3. In a small mixing bowl, whisk the milk and eggs. Add the liquid crème fraîche, salt and pepper. Whisk again.

Salmon

4. Place small circular molds, pastry cutters or ramekins on your countertop. If using molds or pastry cutters, seal the bases with foil. In each circle, layer the potatoes, onions, 1 tbsp dill, and top with a piece of salmon.

5. Place the molds in a high-sided pan. Carefully make an opening in the center of the salmon and spoon in the cream. Fill the pan ¾ full of water and bake in the oven at 180°C/355°F for 30 to 35 minutes.

6. In a pan, melt the butter over high heat for 5 minutes until it foams and turns nut brown. Add the rest of the chopped dill and fry 2 to 3 minutes. Remove the puddings from their molds and top with dill butter.

Olhao Seafood

Preparation time:	40 minutes
Cooking time:	1 hour
Difficulty:	★★★

Serves 4

2 cloves garlic, chopped
1 onion, chopped
1 bunch parsley, leaves removed
olive oil
1 sprig thyme
1 bay leaf
200 g/2 cups long-grain rice
1 tbsp tomato purée
1 lobster, 500 g/generous 1 lb
salt

200 g/7 oz mussels
100 g/3¹/₂ oz cockles
200 g/7 oz medium clams
100 g/3¹/₂ oz cooked salad shrimp

For the court-bouillon:
1 carrot
1 onion
2 bay leaves
1 bunch parsley
10 peppercorns
250 ml/1 cup white wine
dash African chili sauce (pili-pili sauce)
salt

Portugal, a tongue of land running down the Atlantic with hundreds of kilometers of coastline, has an incredible range of choices for its cooking pots. Delicious seashore specialties are concocted with fish and shellfish taken directly from the fishing nets and baskets of seafarers and coastal fishermen. This seaside cuisine takes great pride in the numerous fish dishes oven-baked with vegetables and spices, or more simply grilled and topped with a butter sauce.

Originating in Algarve, this recipe of rice and seafood includes all the "treasures of the sea": white fish, shellfish, clams and large shrimp. And why not even add crayfish for a special meal? However, we advise against using sea scallops unless they have been pre-cooked. Each scallop has to be washed in a special way: if you purchase them with the grit already re-

moved, the scallops have been rinsed in running water for 15 minutes, subjected to a kind of pressure washing.

Of course, the lobster must be live when plunged into the court-bouillon. More hesitant chefs may want to deep-freeze the lobster before boiling, thus putting it to sleep. With regard to the rice, the ideal is to use rice imported directly from Portugal. However, if that is not possible, be sure not to use short-grain rice.

The *pili-pili* or *piri-piri* is actually an African condiment. *Pili* is a generic word for hot chili peppers, used to make a number of fiery sauces available in bottles. We recommend using it with caution, adding it sparingly and tasting after every drop. This type of pepper sauce is used particularly in the south of Portugal to season fish and meat.

1. Combine all the ingredients for the court-bouillon and set to simmer. Meanwhile, heat a small amount of olive oil in a casserole. Brown the chopped garlic and onion, parsley leaves, thyme and bay leaves.

2. Add the rice and tomato purée to the casserole, and fry gently until the rice become transparent. Set aside.

3. Plunge the lobster into the court-bouillon. Boil for 8 minutes. Set the lobster aside and strain the court-bouillon.

with Rice

4. Pour the strained court-bouillon into the casserole to just cover the rice. Add salt and bring to the boil, then lower the heat and continue cooking at a rolling boil, covered, for 20 minutes.

5. Pour a little more bouillon over the rice and add the mussels, cockles and clams. Over high heat, let them open and add seasoning to taste.

6. Shell the lobster: remove the flesh from the tail and claws. Cut the tail in round slices about 1.5 cm (½ in) thick. Add these slices to the casserole with the meat from the claws and the salad shrimps.

Indian Ocean

Preparation time: 15 minutes
Cooking time: 25 minutes
Difficulty: ★

Serves 4

12 large prawns
40 ml/2¹/₂ tbsp olive oil
4 cloves garlic
1 onion
60 g/²/₃ cup peeled, chopped fresh ginger
4 sprigs thyme

4 sprigs fresh parsley
500 g/generous 1 lb tomatoes
1 hot green pepper
1 tbsp tomato paste
salt
pepper
1 sprig cilantro

This traditional recipe has the advantage that it is quickly prepared. It is a family dish par excellence that the people of Mauritius prepare in a sort of wok called a *caraille*. The principle of the rougaille is simple: food is sautéed in a garlic-tomato sauce with onions, peppers and ginger. This method of preparation is a delicious way to cook a number of fish such as tuna, dolphin fish, parrot fish, or *sacré-chien* (a fish similar to red snapper).

The residents of Mauritius and the island of Réunion are also specialists of rougaille with sausage, beef, pork and young goat. To accompany the rougaille, they serve *achards*, all sorts of preserved vegetables or fruits marinated in a vinegar-based marinade.

In Mauritius, small shrimp are netted by fishermen in special boats called pirogues, or more commercially by trawlers. In India, Indonesia and Vietnam, on the other hand, the large shrimp varieties are important. Ordinarily, our chef prepares this rougaille with *camarons*, which are freshwater shrimp a little larger than prawns. As a result of pollution, however, wild *camarons* have disappeared from the island's rivers. Today, they are raised in holding tanks at the Château Riche-en-Eau. As in this recipe, they can easily be replaced by large prawns.

The best way to cook a rougaille is in a pan shaped like a Chinese wok, which allows the ingredients to be turned constantly and thus cook evenly. The mixture can be deglazed with a bisque, shrimp stock or even water.

For a final flavorful touch, our chef Vivek Ramdenee recommends adding a little finely chopped basil and a dash of pastis. Accompany with a timbale of rice with saffron and parsley.

1. Crack open the backs of the prawns using a small knife. Remove the entrails with the tip of a knife and discard.

2. Heat the oil in a saucepan. Brown the prawns for 2 to 3 minutes in the hot oil, turning frequently so they brown well on each side. They should turn pinkish-orange. Set aside.

3. To the same pan, add the peeled and chopped garlic, onion and ginger. Break up the thyme and add to the pan along with finely cut parsley. Brown for 5 minutes.

408 Vivek Ramdenee, Mauritius

Rougaille

4. Then add the tomatoes, peeled and cut into large segments, followed by the hot pepper and tomato paste. Brown 5 to 10 minutes over medium heat. Season with salt and pepper.

5. Add the prawns to the rougaille sauce. Cook an additional 5 minutes, gently tossing the pan frequently to mix all the flavors well.

6. When the prawns are fully cooked and the sauce well blended, sprinkle the rougaille with finely chopped cilantro. Serve the prawns hot in the rougaille.

Salmon Roulades with

Preparation time: 45 minutes
Cooking time: 35 minutes
Difficulty: ★★

Serves 4

200 g/7 oz salmon fillet
100 g/3¹/₂ oz zander or walleye
2 egg whites
50 ml/3¹/₂ tbsp heavy cream
¹/₂ lemon
dash Noilly Prat vermouth

salt
pepper
1 shallot
100 g/¹/₂ cup short-grain rice
50 g/²/₃ cup chopped chanterelles
1 pat butter
200 ml/generous ³/₄ cup chicken stock
250 ml/1 cup fish sauce
dill

Roulades are often part of a German meal. They are served as a delicacy made with a slice of beef that is seasoned and rolled, a roulade of cabbage, or even sole fillets garnished with a lobster stuffing. In this recipe our chef, Stefan Rottner, covers thin layers of salmon with zander or walleye flesh that is mixed with egg whites, cream, lemon juice and Noilly Prat.

The zander or walleye stuffing may be flavored and colored by adding basil, tarragon or saffron. For a more sophisticated effect, embellish it further with small shrimp, crab meat and even small pieces of lobster.

If zander or walleye is difficult to find, choose a fish with flesh that contains a large amount of albumin, like freshwater pike or cod. Coupled with the fish and cream gelatin, this ingredient contributes to the firmness of the stuffing.

When you begin to prepare the stuffing, all of the ingredients should be cold—they could even be put into the freezer for a short time. If they are too warm, the albumin will coagulate and will not bind correctly in the blender.

For the fish sauce, cook the finely-chopped shallots in white wine combined with the juices from cooking the fish. When this mixture has reduced by half, add the cream and bring it just to the boil. Add salt and pepper, and flavor with the lemon juice and Noilly Prat.

Our chef presents his salmon roulades on a rich bed of chanterelle risotto with Italian accents. In Germany, dishes are often accompanied by a generous serving of potatoes. However, the influence of the great number of Italian restaurants established in the country has made its mark, and German chefs are now also inspired by these foreign culinary traditions. In preparing the rice, you may use arborio or another short-grained variety.

1. Using a large tranchelard knife, carve fine, oblique slices from the salmon fillet.

2. Trim the zander or walleye fillet. Blend in a food processor. Add the raw egg whites, cream, lemon juice, Noilly Prat, salt and pepper. Blend to obtain a smooth white cream.

3. Place 2 slices of salmon on a square piece of aluminum foil. Salt and pepper. Spread some of the fish stuffing over them.

Chanterelle Risotto

4. Roll the fish around the stuffing and then in the aluminum foil. Close the ends tightly to fully enclose the roll. Poach for 8 minutes in simmering water.

5. In a saucepan, brown the chopped shallot in butter. Add the rice and then the chopped chanterelles. Stir for a few minutes over medium heat.

6. Heat the chicken stock until lukewarm and add to the rice. Cover and cook 20 minutes over medium heat. Unwrap the salmon roulades and slice into rounds. Reheat the fish sauce. Place the fish on a bed of chanterelle risotto and garnish with the sauce and sprigs of dill.

Roasted Sea Scallops

Preparation time: 40 minutes
Cooking time: 20 minutes
Difficulty: ★

Serves 4

20 sea scallops
1 kg/2¹/₄ lb porcini
70 g/5 tbsp butter
salt
pepper

500 ml/2 cups thick crème fraîche
or sour cream
1 tsp tomato paste
1 bunch chives
chervil leaves to garnish

Sea scallops are large shellfish that live on the sandy depths of coastal regions. If you buy them at an open-air market, their fan-shaped shells streaked with pink and brown should be tightly closed, a sign of their freshness. Opening sea scallops is not a complicated process. Insert the point of a knife just at the hinge that joins together the two shell halves, separating the muscle attaching the two shells with a jerk and removing the upper valve by pulling firmly. Then gently remove the muscle and the coral by sliding the blade of the knife underneath in order to remove them from the shell. Be sure to keep the muscle intact—it needs to be white and firm.

Remove the beards and internal organs from the scallop by cutting them away with kitchen scissors, and wash the shellfish very thoroughly with clear water. Drain the muscles and dry them before browning them rapidly in butter. Baking them quickly in a very hot oven completes the cooking process and turns them golden and crunchy.

Porcini, on the other hand, should not be washed. On contact with water, the mushrooms quickly soften and lose their strong woodsy flavor. Chop them coarsely immediately before cooking them in butter, a process that must be done quickly. Watch them carefully so they do not burn.

Tomato paste is added to give color and strengthen the flavor of the sauce. But if the paste seems rather thin, our chef recommends thickening it with a teaspoon of cornstarch dissolved in milk. In Normandy, people take extra special care in preparing their sauces, which are always creamy. They also blend the tomato paste with threads of saffron and cayenne pepper for more intensity and color. The resultant sauces vary and change according to the chef's taste.

1. Open the sea scallops by sliding the tip of a knife under the hinge that joins the two shells together and separate the muscle that attaches them. Use the knife as a lever to separate the shells. Remove the muscle and the coral, trim the beards, then dry with a paper towel.

2. Wipe the mushrooms thoroughly. Clean the stems and the caps speedily, using tweezers to remove the dirt. Chop finely.

3. Heat 20 g/1¹/₂ tbsp butter in a non-stick pan. Sauté the mushrooms rapidly in the hot butter for 4 minutes over high heat while turning constantly (the mushrooms should not change color). Set aside on a plate.

with Porcini

4. In another pan, melt 50 g/3½ tbsp butter. When it foams, place the scallops in the pan. Add salt and pepper. Quickly fry them 2 minutes on each side. Then bake for 4 minutes in an oven preheated to 180°C/355°F.

5. Heat the crème fraîche in a small saucepan. Add salt, pepper, the tomato paste and chopped chives. Stir for 3 minutes over low heat until the sauce is rich and even.

6. Pour a layer of sauce over each serving plate. Place 5 scallops on the sauce and garnish the center with the fried mushrooms. Decorate with leaves of chervil.

Fish and

Preparation time: 1 hour
Cooking time: 25 minutes
Difficulty: ★★★

Serves 4

4 prawns
16 salad shrimp
4 king prawns
1 live lobster, ca. 1 kg/2¼ lb
150 ml/²⁄₃ cup olive oil
200 g/7 oz monkfish
12 small squid or 3 large squid, cleaned
sea salt
1 green bell pepper
1 red bell pepper

3 green onions
1 tsp strong mustard
2 tbsp sherry vinegar
salt
pepper
8 small baby carrots
4 small turnips
1 rib celery
4 small zucchini

For the garnish:
3 or 4 sprigs parsley
1 small sprig thyme
1 rib celery
1 bay leaf
1 sprig dill

The intriguing name *salpicon* traditionally applies to a meat or mushroom preparation intended to be served as a garnish. For this recipe our chef, Alberto Herráiz, has replaced the meat with fish. There is a range of fish that will work well with this recipe, but avoid fish with a white, flaky flesh that tends to break apart easily while cooking. Instead, opt for a fish with firm flesh. The lobster may also be replaced with crayfish.

To kill the lobster, grip its body firmly, wait until its claws close, and then cut off the head with a large knife. The head can also be pulled off the body. To prevent the lobster from suffering, the best method is to push in the tip of a knife at the center of the cross marking on its back, cutting right through lengthways. The lobster is killed with this cut even if it continues to move for several minutes.

Chipirons are small squid sometimes found in the marketplace and very frequently found in the southwest of France. It is not necessary to gut them before preparing them: a simple rinsing is sufficient. A medium-sized squid or a cuttlefish can be used in place of the *chipirons*, if preferred.

As may be inferred from the photo of the finished dish, the baby carrots can be replaced or complemented by ordinary carrots. Concerning the shellfish oil, remember that it will be used with the raw meat of the head; this preparation will not be cooked at all.

During the summer, our chef invites you to visit his restaurant, *Fogón Saint Julien*, located in the 5th district of Paris, to try this Fish and Seafood Salpicon for yourself.

1. Remove the heads from the prawns, shrimp and king prawns. Remove the meat by scraping it out with a knife into a bowl. Cut the head off the lobster and remove its meat, too. Set aside the remains of the heads, along with the prawn claws and legs and the lobster legs.

2. Press the head meat through a strainer, pouring 100 ml/7 tbsp oil into the sieve in order to expedite the process. Set this shellfish oil aside. Cut the monkfish and squid into chunks. If using the small variety of squid, leave them whole.

3. Prepare a stock with the bodies, legs, claws, aromatic garnish and sea salt. Plunge the shrimp and squid into it for 2 minutes, the prawns and king prawns for 3 minutes, and the lobster for 5 minutes; let them cool. Cook the monkfish for 5 minutes.

Seafood Salpicon

4. Shell the shrimp, prawn, king prawn and the lobster tail and claws. Cut the lobster tail into circular chunks, then cut the shrimp, prawns and king prawns in half.

5. Peel the peppers, remove their seeds and finely chop half of them. Finely chop the onions. Mix the mustard with the vinegar, 50 ml/3$^{1}/_{2}$ tbsp oil, peppers and onions. Add salt and pepper. Set aside.

6. Peel the carrots, turnips and celery. Slice the zucchini and cut the carrots, celery and remaining peppers into sticks. Blanch all the vegetables. Prepare each serving plate with fish and vegetables. Top with the vinaigrette and surround with shellfish oil.

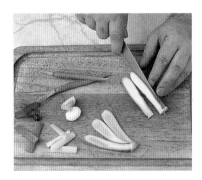

Bakony-Style

Preparation time: 30 minutes
Cooking time: 30 minutes
Difficulty: ★★

Serves 4

800 g/1³/₄ lb walleye or zander fillets
salt
130 g/scant 1 cup flour
2 tbsp oil
1 large onion
150 g/scant 2 cups quartered mushrooms
20 g/1¹/₂ tbsp butter

15 g/2 tbsp paprika
200 ml/generous ³/₄ cup crème fraîche

For the galuska (Hungarian noodles):
200 g/³/₄ cup + 2 tbsp flour
2 medium eggs
salt

For the garnish:
tomatoes
green Hungarian peppers
parsley

The mountains of Bakony rise from the north shore of Lake Balaton, in the eastern part of Hungary. In this recipe, our chef uses walleye from Lake Balaton and the Hungarian mushrooms often found in Bakony forests. This Bakony-Style Walleye is a dish regularly served almost everywhere in Hungary.

Balaton walleye (or pike perch) is a meat-eating fish from the *percide* family, a species that is exclusive to this large Hungarian lake. A one year old walleye that weighs about 1 kg (2¼ lb) is called *süllo*. Its name changes to *fogas* when it is 2 years old and weighs about 2 kg (4½ lb). Its very white flesh with a light hazelnut flavor is of a particularly high quality. A large number of professional fishermen concentrate on fishing walleye, the great local specialty. Hungarians enjoy this fish simply grilled whole over embers, or under an oven grill or broiler. It is eaten with a paprika cream sauce, tartar sauce, or a mayonnaise sauce. They also fry it, as we do in this recipe.

One hundred years ago, the famous Hungarian chef, Karoly Gundel, created the *fogas Gundel*, small chunks of walleye fried and then cooked on a bed of spinach with eggs and potatoes. The dish is then topped with a mix of white cheese and cream, and baked au gratin. Balaton fishermen also created a sort of bouillabaisse with paprika blended with carp, walleye and pike, which is called *halászlé*.

Although commercial button mushrooms can always be used, country people tend to gather their own mushrooms to dress up ordinary dishes. At the same time, therefore, they find not only porcini (*varganya*), ideal for enhancing a paprika stew, but also morels (*kucsmagomba*) and chanterelles (*rókagomba*).

Carp, poultry and even beef steak can all be prepared in the same way as the walleye in this recipe.

1. Salt the walleye fillets. In a dish filled with 100 g/²/₃ cup flour, coat each side uniformly with a layer of flour. Stir together all the ingredients for the Hungarian noodles with 150 ml/²/₃ cup water to make a smooth dough.

2. Brown the walleye fillets 5 minutes on each side in an oiled pan. On a chopping board, spread the noodle dough and cut it into small strips, then into pieces. Drop them into a pot of boiling water. When they rise to the surface, remove with a slotted spoon, drain and set aside.

3. Peel and finely chop the onions and quarter the mushrooms. In a saucepan over low heat, sweat the onions in butter for 5 minutes. When they start to become transparent, add the quartered mushrooms and paprika.

Walleye

4. Make this mixture more liquid by adding a little water. Add salt and cook for 5 minutes. While it is cooking, dice the tomatoes and peppers and mince the parsley. Set aside.

5. Mix 30 g/3 tbsp of the flour with the cream. Add this mixture to the mushrooms. Cook another 5 minutes over high heat, stirring constantly to prevent the sauce from sticking.

6. Top the walleye fillets with the sauce and finish by cooking another 5 minutes, covered. Place the fish onto serving plates with the mushroom sauce and Hungarian noodles. Decorate with peppers and tomatoes, and sprinkle the dish with parsley.

Walleye with Leeks

Preparation time: 45 minutes
Cooking time: 20 minutes
Difficulty: ★★

Serves 4

For the fish:
1 walleye or zander, ca. 1.5 kg/3¼ lb
2 tbsp olive oil

For the garnish:
4 leek whites
50 g/3½ tbsp butter
salt
pepper

For the sauce:
330 ml/generous 1⅓ cups brown
Chimay beer
200 ml/generous ¾ cup fish stock
100 g/7 tbsp butter

With nearly 120 breweries in operation, Belgium is the undisputed megacenter of beer. From the popular *Gueuze* to the somewhat more elaborate *Kriek*, which is flavored with cherries, the mountainous, foaming heads of these blonde, red or brown beers lend height to this otherwise flat country. The Chimay beer used in this recipe is a Trappist brown beer that has a light, bitter taste. Processed using the top-fermentation method, it is brewed at a temperature from about 15 to 20°C (60 to 70°F). Just six Belgian Trappist abbeys still brew their own beer according to traditional methods: Chimay, Orval, Westmalle, Rochefort, Westvleteren and Achel. These are the only breweries that have the right to use the appellation *Authentic Trappist Beer*.

The walleye (or pike perch), the great fish of lakes and running waters and relative of the perch, is marked by its grey-green tiger-striped skin and its rich, firm, white flesh. To protect this delicate flesh while cooking our chef, Michel Haquin, recommends leaving the skin on the fillets. Well-browned on the skin side, they will continue cooking in the oven while preserving their firm flesh. Zander, pike, perch and cod are several white-fleshed fish that can be substituted for walleye; they are cooked in the same manner.

To accompany such a simple, delicate fish, an apparently common but meltingly tender vegetable is essential. Cultivated by the Egyptians and Hebrews, leeks are Belgium's most popular national vegetable. With diuretic properties and low in calories, this garden plant is readily available all year long.

Delicious and tender new leeks, or winter leeks with a hazelnut taste, the choice is yours. Michel Haquin only uses the white parts of the leeks. Adding butter to the cooking water will make them richer. Their vitamins are preserved by cooking the leeks gently and quickly, just barely covered with water. This cooking liquid can then be added to the beer and fish stock in the last step of cooking.

1. Scale the fish. Then gut it and rinse well. Make an incision just behind the head and continue it along the back of the fish. Lift off the fillets and remove the central bone.

2. Chop the leeks, discarding the greens and keeping the whites. Cut the whites into 5 cm/2 in slices.

3. Place the leek whites into a saucepan with some dabs of butter. Cover with water and add salt and pepper. Cook over medium heat for 10 minutes.

and Chimay Beer

4. Place the walleye fillets on a chopping board, flesh-side down. On the skin side, cut each fillet into 4 equal sections.

5. In a non-stick pan, heat 2 tbsp olive oil. Place the fillet sections in the pan, skin side up. Brown 1 minute on each side before turning. Put them into the oven immediately and bake for 3 minutes at 200°C/390°F.

6. Pour the beer and fish stock into a saucepan. Reduce by half over high heat. Add the butter bit by bit while whisking briskly. Cover the plates with sauce and serve the walleye on top of their leek garnish.

Sashimi

Preparation time: 1 hour
Difficulty: ★★

Serves 4

1 crayfish
1 bass
60 g/2 oz salmon fillets
40 g/1⅓ oz red tuna
40 g/1⅓ oz medium-fatty tuna
40 g/1⅓ oz fatty tuna
30 g/1 oz wasabi

For the sauce:
2 sheets kombu seaweed
30 g/1 oz dried oceanic bonito shavings

1 tbsp rice vinegar
1 tbsp soy sauce
2 tbsp sake
2 tbsp mirin or rice wine

For the accompaniment:
carrot
daikon radish
cucumber
lime
lemon
shiso or mint leaves
scallions

Sashimi (sliced raw fish) is a typical Japanese dish that has been served in that country since the sixteenth century. Because it is eaten raw, the fish must be of the utmost freshness and exemplary quality: sole, sea bream, bass, salmon, lean and fatty tuna, turbot or even bonito are all excellent choices for this method of preparation. The Japanese customarily serve sashimi with wasabi, a green paste with a potent taste, prepared from a sort of wild horseradish that only grows in Japan. This plant is reputed to kill bacteria and thus helps reduce the risk of toxins from raw fish.

Many Japanese like to go out for a drink with colleagues or friends in small sashimi and sushi bars. The atmosphere in these bars is convivial, and after a few drinks, social hierarchies seem to recede. Customers ensconce themselves around an aquarium while a chef cuts and prepares the sashimi before

their eyes. It takes several years of apprenticeship for a chef to achieve perfect mastery of this type of preparation.

In Japan, bass is a summer fish that later migrates far offshore. Chefs serve it steamed, roasted, sliced for sashimi, or prepared in sushi (small rolls of fish and rice). It is usually salted and grilled on a kind of sieve set over hot coals. It is served with soy sauce seasoned with grated Japanese Daikon radish.

Our chef lays the lobster flesh on ice to firm it and mold the pieces into the shape they will take on the final serving platter. This is done so that the pieces do not fall apart during assembly. To cut the fish into fine, even strips, he presses the knife blade along the edge of the chopping board and uses a rocking motion to slice the block of fish. Similarly, he prepares the spiral-cut vegetables by soaking thin sheets of carrots or white radishes in a bowl of water filled with ice cubes.

1. Place the carrot, daikon radish and cucumber on a chopping board. Take a vegetable in your hand and pare it into a very fine spiral, using a very sharp slicing knife and turning the vegetable constantly in your hand. Then chop the thin "spirals" into very fine sticks.

2. Push the tip of your knife into the junction between the head and shell of the crayfish. Slice off the head. Slit the stomach and remove the membrane that covers the flesh. Remove the flesh from the shell.

3. Cut the crayfish flesh in two pieces and dice 60 g/2 oz of it very finely. Refresh at once in a bowl of cold water with ice cubes.

4. Cut the head off the bass. Slit the back and stomach of the fish. Remove the fillets by slicing along the backbone from the tail toward the head. Skin the fillets and set aside 60 g/2 oz of flesh. Repeat with the salmon.

5. For the tuna, cut the red portion, the medium-fatty portion and the fatty portion into strips. Make a bouillon with the kombu seaweed and bonito shavings. Strain through a sieve and add the vinegar, soy sauce, sake and mirin.

6. Cut oblique slices about 1 cm (¹/₃ in) thick from the strips of tuna and the bass fillet. Wrap a block of ice with a sheet of absorbent paper. Arrange strips of fish, slices of lemon, vegetable sticks, shiso leaves and scallions on top of it. Serve with the bouillon sauce and wasabi.

New Forest-Style

Preparation time: *35 minutes*
Cooking time: *15 minutes*
Difficulty: ★

Serves 4

130 g/4–5 oz chanterelle mushrooms
130 g/4–5 oz shiitake mushrooms
130 g/4–5 oz oyster mushrooms
fine white salt

12 sea scallops
300 g/1¹⁄₃ cups butter
500 g/generous 1 lb salmon fillets with skin
pepper
50 ml/3¹⁄₂ tbsp turkey stock
1 bunch chives
sea salt

Scottish rivers are well known for the quality of their wild salmon, which are fished from March through June. The small shrimp and shellfish that they eat during their migration to the sea give a characteristic orange color to their light, flavorful flesh. Wild salmon have noticeably different noses and tails from their farm-raised cousins. Their longer noses and larger tails help them swim against the strong ocean currents. In addition, a farm-raised salmon has plenty of fat, while wild salmon flesh is rather dry. British farms now produce so much salmon that wild Scottish salmon is mainly reserved for exclusive stores and restaurants as it is so expensive.

In the United Kingdom, sea scallops are caught in the North Sea and in the Atlantic Ocean during the winter months. The sea scallops that can be sampled at *Connaught*, our chef's favorite restaurant, come from a little port in Essex. They are sold fresh in reputable grocers and deep-frozen in supermarkets. British chefs prepare them boiled or even serve them in cottage pie, replacing the traditional ground beef with chopped sea scallops.

Great Britain is a well-forested country, and the woods of the New Forest in the south-west are regularly patrolled by avid mushroomers. Most notably, and to their greatest delight, they can gather full baskets of porcini (also called boletus) mushrooms during the autumn. For our recipe, the chanterelles may be substituted with morels, porcini or black chanterelle mushrooms and many more, according to taste and season. Why not enhance their flavor by frying a few shallots in the pan before adding the mushrooms?

1. Remove the stems from the mushrooms and then rinse and dry the caps. Blanch the mushrooms for 30 seconds in salted, boiling water and drain. Open the sea scallops, remove the flesh and set aside.

2. In the bottom of an ovenproof pan, melt 60 g/¹⁄₄ cup butter and add the salmon fillets, skin side down. Brown 30 seconds on the stovetop, then bake for 4 minutes in the oven, preheated to 200°C/390°F.

3. Place the salmon slices on a chopping board, skin side up. Remove the skin with the aid of a knife. Lay the skin flat and dry in the oven for 3 minutes at 200°C/390°F. Set aside.

Scottish Salmon

4. Melt 60 g/¹/₄ cup butter in a pan over high heat, shaking the pan to make the butter coat the bottom and bubble up.
Sauté the sea scallops with their egg sac for 3 minutes. Set aside.

5. In the same pan, add another 60 g/¹/₄ cup butter and melt. Add pepper to the mushrooms and sauté 5 minutes. Drain them and keep the cooking juice warm on the side. Heat the turkey stock.

6. Mix the juice from the mushrooms and the turkey stock. Beat 120 g/¹/₂ cup butter into the sauce with a hand whisk, making it lighter and frothier. Place the salmon, scallops and mushrooms on a serving dish. Decorate with chives, sea salt and dried salmon skins and coat with the sauce.

Planked

Preparation time:	30 minutes
Cooking time:	20 minutes
Marinating time:	15 to 20 minutes
Difficulty:	★

Serves 4

4 salmon fillets, 150 g/5¹/₂ oz each
50 g/3¹/₂ tbsp brown sugar
¹/₂ tsp dried thyme

1 tsp pepper
130 g/¹/₃ cup sea salt
1 lemon
60 g/¹/₄ cup butter, softened

In the American northwest, the Pacific Coast Indians developed an original way of cooking salmon, a fish they caught in abundance. They placed the fish on an alder plank positioned at an angle over red-hot embers. Modern Americans, who are great enthusiasts of family cookouts, are now more likely to prepare this recipe on a barbecue. Placing the plank among the coals, they close the grill and let the fish cook for 20 minutes. As it heats, the wooden plank gives the salmon a wonderful, unique flavor. With a barbecue it is possible to vary the type of wood used over the embers, and vine clippings bring an additional aroma to the salmon.

To make the preparation easier, the fish can be cooked on a wooden board in the oven, under the grill or broiler. Choose a plank of alder, cedar, oak or whatever is desired; experiment with different kinds. It is important that the wood has not been treated, and it must be resistant to heat. Make sure that the board is thoroughly moistened before putting it in the oven to prevent it from burning too quickly.

Five species of salmon are fished in the northwest and provide 99% of the wild salmon eaten in the United States, including the enormous Chinook or king salmon that weighs from 7 to 13 kg (15–30 lb), the sockeye with deep red flesh, the silver that is often processed and canned, the delicate pink-fleshed Alaskan pink variety, and finally the chum, with lean, pale flesh and little flavor. Salmon is harvested by hook or by net until about mid-June when it returns to the rivers to spawn.

The fish can be simply marinated in lemon juice flavored with dill, and does not need to be heavily coated with butter, thereby avoiding a large number of calories.

Salmon can be beautifully presented accompanied by wild rice embellished with oven-grilled, crushed hazelnuts. Decorate the dish with dried or fresh red currants.

1. Scale the salmon. Remove the fillets and chop each fillet into large slices. On the skin side of each slice, cut three diagonal incisions without cutting into the flesh underneath.

2. Mix the brown sugar with the minced thyme, pepper and salt. Pour half the mixture into a dish. Place the salmon on top, then sprinkle on the rest of the sugar mixture. Put into the refrigerator for 15 to 20 minutes.

3. To prepare the lemon butter, pour the juice from the lemon into a saucepan and heat. Add the butter and let it melt into the hot lemon juice. Remove from the heat and keep warm.

Northwest Salmon

4. When the fish has marinated, rinse well in cold water. Place the fish slices onto the wooden cooking board, skin side down.

5. Using a pastry brush, coat the top and sides of the salmon with the lemon butter.

6. Place the wooden board with the salmon on a grill pan or broiler pan under a very hot heat. Cook for 5 minutes under the grill or broiler. Coat the fish again with lemon butter and return to the heat for another 10 minutes.

Sautéed

Preparation time: 15 minutes
Cooking time: ca. 10 minutes
Soaking time, clams: 2 hours
Difficulty: ★

Serves 4

For the sautéed clams:
2 kg/4¹/₂ lb medium clams
2 cloves garlic
1 onion
1 bird chile

4 tomatoes
4 sprigs flat-leaf parsley
2 tbsp olive oil
100 ml/7 tbsp white wine

For the accompaniment:
1 small baguette
2 cloves garlic
dash olive oil
parsley sprigs

Italian fishermen draw the best seafood from the sea in the waters around Sicily and in the Gulf of Venice: *gambero* (lobster), *lumaca di mare* (sea snails), *ostrica* (oyster), *vongola* (medium-sized clams), *granciporro* (crab) and more mingle on their arrival in port.

Surrounded by a literal sea of blue, the Italian coast offers delicious, diverse and often very simple seafood recipes. The flavors of these dishes are deliberately unpretentious. According to the Italian chefs, every shellfish, like every fish, is a gift from the sea! An overly sophisticated presentation would be equivalent to a lack of respect.

Our recipe of Sautéed Clams is in keeping with this perspective. Respecting the natural clam flavors, the parsley stems flavor the cooking juices. The stems are removed as soon as the clam shells open, to avoid changing their original flavors. The cooked parsley stems are replaced with fresh leaves for a final flavor with a more discreet bouquet. The powerful bird

chile (or Thai chile) is left whole throughout the cooking process. Those who aren't partial to this degree of heat are welcome to replace the bird chili pepper with the tip of a large, seeded sweet pepper.

As with all shellfish, these medium-sized clams can have a lot of sand trapped in their shells. To remove it completely, let the clams soak for two hours in a large pot of clear water. Very fresh clams are recognized by their tightly closed, round shells. If they are living when purchased, they should be cooked very soon after you bring them home. They are excellent on bread and butter, whether cooked or raw.

Our chef recommends three different ways of presenting these delicious Sautéed Clams: in a soup made from their own cooking juices and white wine and served with grilled garlic bread; as antipasti consisting of several clams, followed by a lemon-grilled fish; or even preceded by a fresh pâté seasoned with garlic and basil.

1. Soak the clams 2 hours in a basin of cold, fresh water. Finely mince the garlic, onion and pepper. Cube the tomatoes. Reserve the parsley stems to use while cooking and the leaves for garnish. Heat the oil in a pan and begin to brown the garlic, onion and bird chile for 2 minutes.

2. Tip the clams onto the mixture in the oil, which should be hot, but not brown.

3. Add the tomato cubes and then the parsley stems. Shake the pan from side to side for 1 minute to make sure all the ingredients are evenly mixed.

Clams

4. Immediately pour in the white wine. Allow the cooking juices to absorb the wine at a low simmer.

5. As soon as the clams open, remove the parsley stems with a pair of tongs. Replace them with the parsley leaves reserved previously. Remove from the heat and set aside.

6. Slice the bread. Toast quickly. Rub each slice with a clove of peeled garlic and sprinkle with olive oil. Serve the garlic bread with the clams, still in their cooking juices. Decorate with minced parsley.

Port Said

Preparation time: 20 minutes
Cooking time: 45 minutes
Difficulty: ★★

Serves 4

2 onions
5 cloves garlic
50 g/3¹/₂ tbsp butter
2 tomatoes

5 sprigs flat-leaf parsley
5 sprigs cilantro
salt
pepper
2 tbsp olive oil
4 tilapia fillets, ca. 150 g/5–6 oz each

If a red sauce can cover a fish as blushes cover a bride, never has a fish so shamelessly reddened! Only the *bolti*, a form of tilapia, from the Red Sea itself, could carry it off. This fish, physically resembling the sea bream, swims in the depths of a mythical sea, never closed off from the worlds beneath. The Egyptians honored it by inventing the classic means of preparing fish called *sayyadieh*. Grouper and sea bream can be substituted for the *bolti*, a fish that apparently does not pass through the entrance of the Suez Canal.

The sauce is central to this *sayyadieh* recipe. Choose ripe, unblemished tomatoes that are juicy. The onions, cut into dice and cooked in butter with a little oil, should be brown but not burnt. Because garlic has a tendency to blacken rapidly, it is best to add it just as the onions are finishing browning.

Up to this point, the tomato sauce has not been surprising at all; a similar sauce is found in most Mediterranean cuisines. The aromatic herbs are what gives the sauce its special identity: flat-leaf parsley and cilantro flavor it with an oriental touch. Less elegant than traditional parsley, flat-leaf parsley is attracting more and more converts, and in the Orient people swear by this herb. Its distinct smell and flavor go well with almost every kind of sauce. Salted and peppered, the tomatoes, onions, cilantro and parsley simmer together to produce a very flavorful sauce.

If you purchase it already in fillets, the tilapia or sea bream is easy to prepare. Brown it rapidly on the skin side to preserve the fragile flesh before turning it over to cook the other side. When the fish is nicely colored and almost fully cooked, it finishes cooking in the oven. An alternative is to bake the fish covered with the tomato and herb sauce.

In Egypt, the *bolti* is served whole, completely covered with sauce. For a more aesthetically pleasing presentation, we prefer to place the fillets on a bed of sauce. The sauce may also be served on the side in a sauce boat.

1. Peel the onions and garlic and chop finely. Heat the butter in a saucepan. Add the onions and brown over medium heat while stirring. As soon as the onion finishes browning, add the chopped garlic. Let them brown together for 1 minute.

2. Blanch the tomatoes. Cut into quarters, then slices. Cut each slice into small cubes.

3. Tip the diced tomato into the saucepan with the onions and garlic. Mix well. Cook over medium heat to obtain a tomato purée. Thin the purée with a glass of water.

Sayyadieh

4. Chop the flat-leaf parsley and fresh cilantro together. Stir into the tomato mixture. Salt and pepper to taste and stir. Simmer gently, stirring constantly. Remove from the heat when the sauce is well blended.

5. Heat 2 tbsp olive oil in a non-stick pan. When it is hot, place the fish fillets, skin side down, in the pan. Brown for 1 minute. Turn the fish over and brown another minute on this side. Place the fillets in a baking dish.

6. Bake the fish in the oven for 20 to 25 minutes at 120°C/250°F. Pour a layer of sauce onto the bottom of a serving platter and place the fillets on top. Garnish the dish with finely chopped parsley.

Pan-Fried Catfish

Preparation time: 20 minutes
Cooking time: 35 minutes
Difficulty: ★

Serves 4

400 g/14 oz catfish fillets
16 unblemished sage leaves
8 strips smoked bacon
salt
pepper

50 ml/3¹/₂ tbsp olive oil
50 g/3¹/₂ tbsp butter
200 g/7 oz green beans
250 ml/1 cup fish sauce (see text)
100 ml/7 tbsp whipping cream
125 ml/¹/₂ cup chicken stock
several sprigs fresh savory

Like our chef, Franconian cooks enjoy preparing dishes with river fish. In this region, the catfish is now raised on fish farms, and in some places in Germany it can also be fished from tributaries of the Danube. Catfish are large, carnivorous fish, dark or even black in color, and have very distinctive barbels. The largest of the European catfish can attain lengths of up to 2.5 meters (over 8 feet) and can weigh up to 100 kg (220 lb)!

Generally, its high-quality flesh is served poached in a vinegar court-bouillon, served with potatoes topped with melted butter. Stefan Rottner's innovation is to wrap the pieces of catfish with sage leaves and bacon, which confer their characteristic flavors on the fish while cooking. These two ingredients also nicely complement the green beans.

To prepare the fish sauce called for in this recipe, first soak the fish bones to remove any impurities and viscous substances.

Then, in a saucepan, sauté some celery, leek whites, fennel and button mushroom caps, chopped and seasoned with lemon and bay leaf, without letting them brown. Add the fish bones and continue cooking, then deglaze with some white wine. Cover everything with water, bring to the boil, and allow this mixture to infuse for 20 minutes without letting it boil again. The albumin in the fish will rise to the surface, bringing with it the garnish and some foam. Strain the cooking liquid without pressing it. In a saucepan, reduce the strained fish stock by half and add shallot slices and white wine. Finally, incorporate a little liquid crème fraîche, stir, and season with lemon juice, salt, cayenne pepper and a dash of Noilly Prat.

If catfish is unavailable, it may be replaced by another firm-fleshed fish.

1. Cut the catfish fillets into very fine slices.

2. Place 2 catfish slices on top of each other. Top with 3 or 4 sage leaves. Wrap the whole with a slice of bacon. Add salt and pepper.

3. In a saucepan, heat 50 ml/3¹/₂ tbsp olive oil and 20 g/1¹/₂ tbsp of the butter. Add the fish roulades and gently brown on both sides.

with Bacon and Sage

4. Blanch the green beans in salted, boiling water. Using a slotted spoon, transfer them immediately into a bowl filled with cold water and ice cubes; this will preserve the beans' bright green color.

5. Heat up the fish sauce. Whip the cream and incorporate it into the fish sauce. Blend using a hand-held mixer.

6. In a saucepan, heat the remaining butter and the chicken stock, seasoned with salt, pepper and sprinkled with savory. Glaze the green beans with this mixture. Place them on each plate and top with the bacon-rolled fish. Surround with fish sauce.

Sushi

Preparation time: 1 hour
Cooking time: 15 minutes
Difficulty: ★★★

Serves 4 to 6

For the rice:
900 g/4¹/₂ cups sushi rice
25 g/1¹/₂ tbsp salt
90 g/6¹/₂ tbsp sugar
100 ml/7 tbsp sake
1 tbsp soy sauce
100 ml/7 tbsp rice vinegar

For the fish:
150 g/5–6 oz red tuna
150 g/5–6 oz fatty tuna

130 g/4–5 oz medium-fatty tuna
150 g/5–6 oz bass
250 g/9 oz salmon
wasabi
3 sheets nori seaweed
1 small jar salmon roe
4 or 5 sheets moist kombu seaweed

For the accompaniment (optional):
30 g dried tuna shavings
2 sheets dried kombu seaweed
12 cooked shrimp
pickled ginger (gari)
avocados

Sushi brings together rice and fish, the two basic elements of Japanese cuisine. Fine slivers of raw fish are placed on piles of rice with vinegar. The fish must be extremely fresh, as if it has just come out of the water.

Sushi of the kind currently prepared in Japan first appeared during the nineteenth century in small taverns in Tokyo. Before a Japanese chef can become a sushi master, he or she must go through several years of apprenticeship. Some chefs look to the paintings of the greatest artists for innovative ways to present their tiny morsels.

Some creative chefs have developed a range of sushi, each with its own name. The simplest, called *nigiri* sushi, is pile of moist rice rolled by hand and covered with fish. For *maki* sushi, a strip of fish wrapped in rice is rolled inside a piece of nori seaweed, with the aid of a bamboo sushi mat. With *oshi* sushi, the rice and the fish are packed together in a wooden box.

Finally, *chimaki* sushis blend rice with little pieces of raw fish that are wrapped in kuma bamboo and steamed.

With a constant eye to the tiniest details, Japanese chefs distinguish three parts of tuna flesh: the red part, the fatty part and the medium-fatty part, each of which is separated into distinct blocks. The lean red tuna (*kiwada maguro*) and the skipjack (*katsuho maguro*) are used in preparing sushi. On the other hand, white tuna (*mebachi maguro*) is used only for canned tuna. Tuna, mackerel, sardines, saurel, sea bream, bass, salmon and sepia are also easily adapted for sushi.

The rice used for sushi must be carefully prepared. First rinse it several times in a bowl of cold water until the water remains clear. Drain, let it stand for five minutes, and then tip it into a rice cooker. It should be cooked for 15 minutes and should have absorbed all of the steam.

1. Rinse the rice and then drain it. Tip into a saucepan equal amounts of rice and water. Cover the saucepan and cook for 10 to 15 minutes. At this point, the rice should have absorbed all the moisture.

2. Place a block of tuna on a chopping board. Divide it into separate chunks of red flesh, fatty flesh and medium-fatty flesh. Remove the fillets from the bass. Slice 130 g/4¹/₂ oz of the bass, the salmon and the 3 tuna varieties into narrow strips.

3. Prepare a sauce with the salt, sugar, sake, soy sauce and rice vinegar. Pour the cooked rice into a Japanese wooden tub, specially made for sushi preparation. Sprinkle it with the sauce and mix with a plastic spatula. Divide the rice into three portions.

4. Wet one hand. Take a small amount of rice and press it to form an oblong bar. Place this on a strip of tuna that has been seasoned with wasabi. Place it on a board, seam down. Make 32 more morsels in the same way, using about $1/3$ of the rice and 650 g/$1^1/_2$ lb assorted fish.

5. Place a half leaf of nori on a bamboo sushi mat. Spread $1/4$ of the second portion of rice on it and season with wasabi. Cover the rice with a small piece of salmon and roll. Make 3 more rolls, using the remaining tuna and bass. Wrap the salmon roe with a half sheet of nori. Cut each roll into 6 slices.

6. Place 100 g/$3^1/_2$ oz salmon in a wooden box. Cover with the remaining rice and press down, using the lid. Turn the contents over onto a board. Cover with moist kombu seaweed and cut into 10 parts. Serve with kombu and tuna sauces, shrimp, ginger and avocado.

Sea Bass Tajine

Preparation time:	20 minutes
Cooking time:	25 minutes
Difficulty:	★★

Serves 4

4 sea bass, 250–300 g/11 oz each
1 lemon
1 small bunch flat-leaf parsley
400 g/14 oz onions (about 3–4)

2 tbsp olive oil
1 tsp salt
1 tsp pepper
1 pinch saffron
6 cloves garlic
250 ml/1 cup fish stock, ready-made
300 g/11 oz dates (4 per person)
200 g/7 oz walnuts, for decoration

Fish prepared according to this recipe have been christened *t'faya* by the Moroccans because of the onions, sweet dates and nuts used in its preparation. *T'faya* is the name for the onion, fruit and nut mixture that forms the basis of this dish, and several chicken and lamb dishes as well. It is a traditional meal in the Oualidia region, a lively fishing port with very high-quality fish, shellfish and other seafood.

In that region, it is usually the conger eel that is prepared *t'faya*, but Chef Belmoufid and his team from the Casablanca *Sheraton* set their hearts on the sea bass caught in the Mediterranean. This version of the sweet and sour tajine may seem a little surprising at first, but you are sure to find it absolutely exquisite.

Sugar, in fact, is not actually one of the ingredients; the cooked dates alone sweeten and bind the sauce. Before baking the fish, cut two or three dates lengthwise and place them in the cooking juices.

Regarding the fish stock, this can be prepared at home or bought ready-made from the supermarket. A recommendation from our chef: do not let the fish cook too long, because the exquisite and tender flesh doesn't tolerate it well. Serve it as soon as it is removed from the oven. To prepare the dates, stuff them with walnuts before plunging them into boiling oil with the aid of a slotted spoon. Cook each date for about 2 minutes.

Be sure to remove the excess grease that will eventually rise to the top of the tajine. With the back of a spoon, spread a little of this oil over the fish to give them a special luster; this will enhance their appearance.

As an extra creative touch, our chef recommends garnishing the dish with lemon half-circles crowned with date halves.

1. Gut the fish and rinse under cold water. Rub with the juice of half a lemon. Cover with sprigs of parsley and set aside. Peel and finely chop the onions. Oil a tajine dish and place the onions in the bottom. Set over low heat.

2. Still over low heat, gently put in the fish and allow simmer slowly for 4 to 5 minutes. Stop cooking. Set the fish aside, away from the heat.

3. Prepare a marinade by mixing 1 tbsp olive oil, the juice of the other half lemon, salt, pepper, saffron, garlic, and finally the minced parsley.

with Dates and Walnuts

4. Coat the fish with ¾ of the marinade and pour the remainder around the fish to form the basis of the sauce.

5. Pour the fish stock into the tajine dish, taking care to pour it around the fish and not over the coated fish themselves, which would ruin the marination.

6. Bake 15 minutes in an oven preheated to 200°C/390°F. Meanwhile, fill the dates with the walnuts and deep-fry for 2 to 3 minutes. Serve the fish whole with the dates and walnuts.

Trout in

Preparation time: 45 minutes
Cooking time: 25 minutes
Difficulty: ★★

Serves 6

6 trout, ca. 200 g/7 oz each
1 leek
60 g/¼ cup butter
1 kg/2¼ lb fresh spinach, washed
6 red and green chili peppers

For the garnish:
2 large red bell peppers
200 ml/generous ¾ cup oil for frying
salt
pepper
1 small leek
3 tbsp flour

Tourists who discover San Carlos de Bariloche could think they were in the Swiss Alps. This city, founded by German, Swiss and Italian immigrants and located in the extreme northwest of Patagonia, similarly features mountain log cabins, chocolatiers and pottery shops. Nearby, its ski resort is a getaway for many students who come here to relax after exams.

Lake Nahuel Huapi surrounds the village and has its own claim to be the trout paradise. Along its shores, restaurants serve trout fried in butter, or with lemon and *fines herbes*. Incidentally, the lake is also home to the Nahuelito monster, a distant cousin of the Loch Ness monster.

The abundance of fish sustains a processing industry in the village, from which the fish emerge fumigated with *fines herbes*, preserved in oil or brine, or frozen. Lanin national park, which is located a little further to the north, attracts spear fishermen from around the world.

This fish from the *Salmonidae* family was the first to be bred in captivity. The markets sell only farm-raised rainbow trout, with its metallic blue back and flanks banded pink through purple. The only difficulty in this recipe will be to remove the bones carefully enough to avoid damaging the flesh.

The little chili pepper tucked into the green coat of the trout brings a surprising touch of life to the dish. This vegetable of Latin American origin is part of the *Solanaceae* family, along with such staples as potatoes, tomatoes and eggplant. Argentineans are blessed with many choices ranging from large, sweet peppers to the small, very spicy *puta pario*, whose name is taken from an Argentine insult.

Don't hesitate to reduce a little sherry vinegar in a saucepan; it will be excellent with the fried leeks.

1. Open the trout by slicing along the stomach. Carefully remove the spine and all the remaining bones. Cut the leek into long ribbons and blanch in boiling water for 2 to 3 minutes.

2. Heat 20 g/1½ tbsp butter in a large fish pan. Fry the trout in hot butter for 3 minutes on each side, just enough to dry the skin.

3. Place 2 or 3 spinach leaves onto a chopping board and then place a trout on top. Wrap the fish in the spinach leaves.

Spinach

4. Place a chili pepper on top of the trout. Wrap it up with a ribbon of blanched leek and tie securely. Repeat the process for each trout. Then place them in a baking pan, dot with the remaining butter, and bake for 7 minutes at 180°C/355°F.

5. For the garnish, cut the red bell peppers into long, narrow strips. Heat the oil in a pan. When it sizzles, sauté the peppers for 5 minutes. Add salt and pepper.

6. Julienne the small leek and coat with a layer of flour. Fry briefly in hot oil. Present the trout wrapped in its green coat and served with fried peppers and leeks.

Turbot with Potatoes

Preparation time:	30 minutes
Cooking time:	35 minutes
Difficulty:	★★★

Serves 4

For the fish:
50 g/3¹/₂ tbsp butter
4 turbot fillets, 150 g/5–6 oz each
2 sprigs rosemary
sea salt
pepper
100 ml/7 tbsp white wine

For the potato rosettes:
800 g/1³/₄ lb potatoes
20 g/1¹/₂ tbsp butter
sea salt
black pepper

For the ratatouille:
1 eggplant
2 red bell peppers
1 onion
2 zucchini
1 tbsp olive oil
1 sprig fresh mint

Because turbot is a flat fish with fine and fragile flesh, it is not easy to remove its fillets. The less-dexterous will, of course, accept the help of the fish monger. The rest will, with a single precise motion, obtain two large fillets from a good-sized turbot. For two adequate portions, cut each fillet in half.

Although the fish gives its name to the title, the fish itself is not, for once, the main feature in the recipe. Finely sliced and overlapping like rose petals, the potatoes can be browned as a unit in clarified butter. To prepare clarified butter, our chef eliminates the whitish whey foam that builds up on the surface of melted butter. This clarified butter will not blacken while cooking, leaving the potato rosette subtly bronzed.

Italians use their vegetables differently with meat or fish. Always diced evenly, the vegetables are seared almost al dente over high heat, thus preserving their original vitamins and fla-

vors. In this recipe, the eggplant and zucchini are diced finely into 2 cm (¾ in) cubes. Keeping the dice small allows them to cook quickly. The vegetables are easily removed from the pan with a slotted spoon. For a final touch of elegance and style, the ratatouille is presented shaped in small molds, so drain off all the cooking oil to make it easier to mold. For a healthier preparation, however, it can be cooked without any grease, in a non-stick pan. Ratatouille will keep for 24 hours or so in the refrigerator. Rapidly reheated, it will make a good meal, if needed.

Thin down the turbot cooking juices with white wine. Chicken stock may be used instead. Barely reduced, white wine and chicken stock just slightly reduced are served in a sauce boat, allowing people to use it according to their own taste.

1. To make the potato rosettes, peel the potatoes and slice with a mandoline. On a sheet of aluminum foil, arrange potato slices in an overlapping row and repeat to make 4 rows altogether.

2. Melt the butter in a small saucepan and remove the foam. Dip a brush in this clarified butter and coat the potato rosette generously with it. Repeat to make 3 more rosettes.

3. Use the remaining clarified butter to coat a non-stick pan, heating over high heat. Carefully take the aluminum foil and flip the rosette into the pan. Brown the potato rosette on each side, turning it with tongs. Add salt and pepper.

and Ratatouille

4. In a non-stick fish pan, heat the butter for the turbot over low heat. Place the fillets in the hot butter. Add rosemary, salt and pepper. Cook for 2 minutes on each side and baste with white wine. Cover the pan, remove from the heat and set aside.

5. Dice the eggplant, peppers, onion and zucchini very finely. Cook them in the olive oil with the fresh mint. Spoon the ratatouille into 4 small individual molds, packing it down well.

6. Gently remove the turbot fillets from the pan and place a fillet onto each individual plate. Use tongs to cover each fish with a potato rosette. Turn out one ratatouille mold beside each potato-covered fish. Coat with the turbot cooking juices and garnish with fresh mint.

Turbotine with

Preparation time: 45 minutes
Cooking time: 1 hour 15 minutes
Difficulty: ★★

Serves 4

4 turbotines (small turbots)
12 salsify roots
salt
pepper
150 g/²/₃ cup butter
600 g/1¹/₄ lb potatoes

1 celeriac, peeled and diced
2 shallots, peeled and minced
12 Jerusalem artichokes
500 ml/2 cups fish stock
1 bouquet garni
dried lavender flowers
1 lemon
200 ml/generous ³/₄ cup liquid crème fraîche
300 g/11 oz parsnip
500 g/generous 1 lb smoked bacon
¹/₂ bunch dill

A hint of countryside lavender is subtly added to this recipe from the land of the Vikings. In Danish cuisine, flat fish like the turbot, plaice and flounder are generally fried in a coating of breadcrumbs and served with a mayonnaise that is flavored with pickles.

The Danish accompany these fish with very robust tubers and sometimes with beets. The green vegetable season in Denmark is understandably short due to its rigorous climate. So the Danes have to fall back on vegetables that can be preserved for long periods of time, such as potatoes, beets, Jerusalem artichokes, oyster plants, parsnips and kohlrabi, all of which are easily found at the markets during the winter months. They are then cooked in water, for later use in soups, as side dishes for meat and fish entrées and for simmering in meat stews. They are also served grated and as crudités. All these vegetables are

a godsend for the Danish, great lovers of local-style open-faced sandwiches, called *smørrebrød*, that are eaten anytime from breakfast to dinner.

In Denmark, there are twice as many pigs as people, with over 10 million animals raised every year. Each Dane consumes an average of 70 kg (nearly 150 lb) of pork each year! So it is no surprise that Denmark is home to numerous butcher shops. Like English bacon, Danish bacon is made with smoked side meat that stays very rich while preserving its good taste. There are even pigs raised especially for this fatty delicacy. Danish farms also produce, in a descending order, cows, chickens, ducks, turkey and lamb.

For this recipe, toast may be substituted for the browned potato side dish.

1. Fillet the turbotine. Peel the salsify roots, cut them into chunks and poach for 20 minutes. Place the poached salsify in a baking dish. Add salt and pepper and pour 50 g/3¹/₂ tbsp clarified butter over the top. Bake in the oven for 10 to 12 minutes at 160°C/320°F.

2. Cut the potatoes into thin slices and brown in 20 g/1¹/₂ tbsp butter for 15 minutes. Brown the celeriac and shallots for 5 minutes in 20 g/1¹/₂ tbsp butter. Add the finely sliced Jerusalem artichokes and continue to brown for 5 minutes.

3. Baste with the fish stock and add the bouquet garni. Bring to the boil. Reduce this preparation until it is thick.

Lavender Sauce

4. As it thickens, add the dried lavender flowers. Stir briskly for 30 seconds over the heat to give the lavender time to add its flavor to the sauce.

5. In a small dish, whisk 60 g/¼ cup softened butter with the juice and zest of the lemon. Add this to the sauce, stirring briskly. Then incorporate the crème fraîche and reduce for 5 minutes over low heat. Peel the parsnips and finely chop them along with the bacon.

6. In a dry pan, brown the bacon and parsnips until golden. On each plate, place a serving of the salsify, turbotine, artichokes and potatoes. Sprinkle with the fried bacon and parsnips. Garnish with minced dill and the lavender sauce.

Roasted Turbot

Preparation time: 30 minutes
Cooking time: 45 minutes
Difficulty: ★

Serves 4

1 turbot, ca. 1.2 kg/2¾ lb
4 bay leaves
salt
pepper
2 tbsp olive oil
20 g/1½ tbsp butter

For the vegetables:
200 g/7 oz wild morels
40 g/2½ tbsp butter
2 shallots
200 ml/generous ¾ cup liquid crème fraîche
salt
pepper
200 g/7 oz fine green peas or petits pois
200 g/7 oz asparagus tips

For the garnish:
100 ml/7 tbsp veal juices
1 dash white wine vinegar

A ravenous fish from the cold waters of the Atlantic Ocean, the turbot is appreciated for its white, flaky flesh. Although classified as a bony fish, it is nonetheless easy to slice with simple but effective techniques before putting it to roast. Using a knife with a large blade, take the tail and cut the fish in two with a clean cut that follows the spine up to the head. The turbot has hard vertebrae that lend themselves easily to this technique.

It is customary to cook the turbot still enveloped in its fine and fragile, grey skin. It takes on a certain crispness, and holds the fish together during cooking. Sliced with its skin and bones, the turbot is salted and peppered on its white flesh and roasted on its grey skin. After cooking, let it slowly cool, then gently remove the blackened, crusty skin. Remove the bone before serving the turbot, browned and flavored with bay leaves.

There are innumerable varieties of mushrooms. Sheltered under the branches of pine trees, the morel is not an easy one to find. It is recognized by its conical, honeycombed cap that is either tan or brown. It is therefore essential to wash these mushrooms very carefully to make sure all the dirt is removed from its many pores.

Morel mushrooms must be cooked quickly. Cut in half, they are stirred in butter with shallots and crème fraîche to bring out their exquisite flavor. Gourmets agree in considering April the best season for turbot and morel mushrooms (the pick of the spring crop) alike. It is natural to combine these with the small, tender, green vegetables that appear fresh in the grocery stores and fresh produce markets in spring. Tied together in small bundles, the asparagus tips are boiled for 3 minutes. The petits pois are shelled and blanched for 5 minutes in salted water. But the real treat is the bay leaf, placed delicately between the two sides of the turbot and roasted inside.

1. Cut the turbot in two, following the central bone. Cut off the dorsal fin with kitchen scissors. Rinse with cold water and dry with a paper towel. With clean cuts, section the turbot into 4 slices, keeping the bone intact.

2. Using the tip of the knife, make an incision in the center of each turbot slice. Slide a bay leaf into the fish, between the flesh and the bone. Salt and pepper the white-skinned side.

3. In a pan, heat a mixture of olive oil and butter and brown the turbot slices for 25 minutes, starting with the grey-skinned side and turning over halfway through cooking. From time to time, spoon some of the cooking juices over each slice.

with Bay Leaves

4. For the vegetables, rinse the morels several times in warm water, then cut in half lengthwise. Brown for 2 to 3 minutes in 20 g/1¹/₂ tbsp melted butter with 1 tbsp finely chopped shallots. Pour in the crème fraîche; salt and pepper. Simmer for 10 minutes over low heat. Set aside.

5. Cook the peas and asparagus for 3 to 5 minutes in salted water. Drain and brown in the pan with the remaining butter. Place the cooked turbot slices on a chopping board. With a small knife, cut them in half horizontally, following the spine. Carefully remove the grey skin.

6. On each plate, place a serving of mushrooms in cream sauce crowned with 2 turbot fillets, accompanied with peas and asparagus tips. Decorate by surrounding the fish and mushrooms with a line of just warm veal juices with vinegar, and add the cooked bay leaves as garnish.

Red Snapper with

Preparation time:	20 minutes
Cooking time:	45 minutes
Difficulty:	★

Serves 4

2 cloves garlic
1 onion
3 sprigs parsley
3 green onions
2 whole cloves
1 hot pepper tip

1 bay leaf
1 red snapper, ca. 1.2 kg/2³/₄ lb
salt
pepper
500 g/generous 1 lb cassava root
500 g/generous 1 lb yellow bananas

For the coconut beurre blanc:
4 or 5 shallots
150 g/²/₃ cup unsalted butter
100 g/7 tbsp coconut milk

In this recipe, Joël Kichenin presents an opulent red snapper cooked *en blaff* and then topped with a coconut beurre blanc. *Blaff* is a true West Indian creation. The fish is poached in a bouillon perfumed with garlic and a local bouquet garni of parsley, spring or green onions and allspice or Jamaica pepper. Here, our chef has replaced this local spice with bay leaf. All West Indian fish and shellfish dishes lend themselves well to this *blaff* preparation.

The red snapper is a pinkish fish similar to a scorpion fish, and caught in the Caribbean and in Guyana. In Guadeloupe, people buy their fish directly from the fishermen as their boats arrive in port. Crew members are set up on the quayside or seashore to clean and gut the fish.

Few salty West Indian dishes are served with coconut milk, and this Asian custom is taking hold slowly in Guadeloupe. The coconut flesh is removed, dried and then powdered. It is then mixed with a little lukewarm water and pressed. Excellent quality ready-made coconut milk is available, in either liquid or dehydrated form.

Our chef serves his Red Snapper with Coconut Beurre Blanc accompanied by sweet cassava root, or *camanioc*. Guadeloupan chefs prepare delicious cassava root flat cakes filled with meat or with sweet coconut. For many years now, a Saint-Anne business has successfully promoted cassava in the form of flour, bread, chips, flat cakes and crêpes.

Our chef could not prepare a coconut beurre-blanc sauce with white wine because coconut milk reacts badly to acids, breaking down and curdling in an unappetizing way. Instead, he has replaced the wine with fish stock. Go ahead and replace the butter with a *beurre manié* (butter and flour paste) if you find it to be too liquid. At the end, sprinkle the sauce with a fine mince of red, yellow and green bell peppers.

1. Peel the garlic and onion, and chop finely. Pour 500 ml/2 cups cold water into a large saucepan. Add the onion, parsley, 2 green onions, cloves, hot pepper, bay leaf and garlic. Bring to the boil.

2. Cut the fish into large sections. Season with a chopped green onion, salt and pepper.

3. Place the red snapper pieces into this court-bouillon. Add salt and pepper and poach for 15 minutes. Peel the cassava root and bananas and cut into quarters. Cook for 20 minutes in salted boiling water.

Coconut Beurre Blanc

4. Prepare the coconut beurre-blanc. In a small saucepan, cook the shallots for 10 minutes in some of the bouillon in which the fish cooked, until there is no liquid remaining in the bottom of the saucepan.

5. Add the butter to the saucepan, bit by bit in small chunks, using a soup spoon. Stir over the heat by whisking briskly with a hand whisk. Heat the coconut milk in another saucepan.

6. Pour the warm coconut milk into the sauce with shallots. Mix, then strain finely or pass through a chinois. Place a section of red snapper on a serving plate with a helping of cassava root and bananas. Surround with coconut beurre blanc.

Belgian Fish

Preparation time: 1 hour
Cooking time, waterzooï: 35 minutes
Cooking time, potatoes: 30 minutes
Difficulty: ★★

Serves 4

2 carrots
3 leeks
1 rib celery
500 g/generous 1 lb potatoes

500 g/generous 1 lb cod fillets
200 g/7 oz fresh salmon
500 g/generous 1 lb whiting fillets
500 g/generous 1 lb mussels
500 g/generous 1 lb grey shrimp
250 ml/1 cup liquid crème fraîche
salt
pepper
1 bunch parsley

Originally, *waterzooï* (or *waterzoï*) was a delicious mixture of fish and shellfish from the North Sea cooked in a bouillon and flavored with seasonal vegetables. Fishermen from the Belgian coast would treat themselves to it thanks to a free basket from their boss on their return from fishing. The citizens of Gent, always creative and, of course, far from the sea, gave a new interpretation to *waterzooï*: chicken replaced fish and everything was smothered in cream. Cooks soon varied the recipe to include lobsters or crayfish.

For best results, be sure to talk to the fish merchant so that you get the fillets from choice fish: cod and whiting with their firm, white flesh and salmon with its refined, colorful flesh. The cooking process should be quick to keep the flesh whole and prevent it crumbling.

The fish may be poached in water seasoned with onions, carrots and bouquet garni. However, our chef seeks to add a sophisticated bouquet by poaching them in a mixture of the cooking juices from the mussels and shrimp. For that reason, he begins by cooking the shrimp and mussels. These can be prepared à la marinière by adding onions, shallots, white wine and a bouquet garni. As soon as the mussels open, remove them from the heat and set aside their juices.

The bouillon is the most important element of the *waterzooï*. With or without crème fraîche, it needs to be strongly flavored. You can also transform it into the creamy sauce that is much loved in Belgium. All that is necessary is to let it reduce over a high heat before adding the cream, and then carefully add the julienned vegetables.

Waterzooï is served according to a very precise ritual: shrimp and mussels should cover the bottom of a large serving platter. The poached cod, whiting and salmon should be barely flaky, and the bouillon, creamy and colored with julienned vegetables, should be thick enough to hide the fish and shellfish underneath it.

1. Peel the carrots and wash the leeks. Separate the celery, keeping the green parts. Julienne all the vegetables. Bring to the boil and cook for 5 minutes. Reserve the vegetables and cooking juices separately.

2. Cook the potatoes in their skins for 30 minutes in salted water. Keep hot. Cut the cod, salmon and whiting into large chunks, about 5 cm/2 in square. Cook the mussels and shrimp separately and set the cooking juices aside.

3. Remove the shells from the mussels and shrimp. Set them aside in separate bowls. Pour the cooking juices from the mussels, shrimp and vegetables into one large pan and bring to the boil. Immediately add the fish pieces and allow to cook for 4 to 5 minutes in the bouillon.

Waterzooï

4. Using a slotted spoon, remove the pieces of fish and transfer to a platter. Keep warm.

5. Boil the fish cooking juices again for 5 minutes on high heat. Allow to reduce by a quarter, then add the crème fraîche. Bring back to the boil for 4 to 5 minutes. Add salt and pepper.

6. Away from the heat, add the julienned vegetables to the sauce. Replace the pan on the stove and cook for 5 minutes. Serve the pieces of fish in a deep serving dish, accompanied by boiled potatoes. Top with sauce and sprinkle with chopped parsley.

Meat & Game

Roasted

Preparation time:	45 minutes
Cooking time:	45 minutes
Difficulty:	★

Serves 6

1 kg/2¼ lb rib steak
250 g/9 oz pork belly, sliced
2 bay leaves
oil
salt and pepper

For the Creole sauce for meat:
100 ml/7 tbsp vinegar
200 ml/generous ¾ cup olive oil
2 tomatoes, coarsely chopped
2 red bell peppers, diced

2 onions, minced
30 g/¼ cup fresh parsley, chopped
salt and pepper

For the salad:
20 g/1½ tbsp butter
1 pinch sugar
250 g/9 oz boiling onions
250 g/9 oz cherry tomatoes
olive oil
1 head Batavia lettuce
1 head lollo rossa lettuce

For the vinaigrette:
100 ml/7 tbsp raspberry vinegar
300 ml/1¼ cups olive oil
50 g/1¾ oz cheese, grated

Throughout Argentina, large herds of steer are able to graze freely on vast expanses of grass, corn, wheat and sunflower. Even if the gaucho has for the most part gone the way of his cousin, the cowboy, a legend to be shelved in a bookcase of memories, the Argentines have maintained a veritable "gaucho culture" and a penchant for beef derived from steer. Family and friends often gather every Sunday around an *asador*, a sort of giant barbecue.

This method of preparation requires lighting a fire at dawn, and cooking various cuts of meat to perfection makes it a great art. The Argentine method of cutting meat is different from that of Europeans. The Argentines prefer the long and fine section of the rib, which they call *tira de asado*.

The *bife de costilla*, the bones of which form a T and separate the fillet from the sirloin, is grilled in the same manner, as well as the *bife de lomo*, a very thick and tender fillet, and the *bife*

de chorizo, a cut of steak cooked in its own fat. A good Sunday meal of *asado* always includes many types of meat and organ meats such as tripe, calf's sweetbread, veal kidneys and liver. The beef is grilled on the *asador* according to regions, along with pieces of chicken, lamb or pork. Our chef has chosen pork belly in this case.

The Argentine pig, commonly referred to as *choncho*, strolls about the haciendas of Argentina, where space is never limited. The young suckling pig is stuffed, roasted whole, and served with its skin cooked to a crisp. They sometimes grill half of a full-grown pig instead.

To accompany this abundance of meat, the cooks serve *chimichuri*, an oil-based sauce with vinegar, parsley, dried hot peppers and paprika. This sauce may include up to 22 different flavors! It accompanies a Creole salad made of Batavia and lollo rossa lettuces, tomatoes and small onions.

1. Preheat the oven to 200°C/390°F. Place the rib steak on a solid surface to cut it. Cut through the bones with a meat saw, then use a butcher's knife to cut into slices 5 cm/2 in thick.

2. Arrange the pork belly and bay leaves in the bottom of a roasting pan. Add a rack to the pan and place the beef slices above the pork. Sprinkle with oil, pepper and salt on all sides. Bake in the oven for 30 minutes, turning midway through the cooking time.

3. For the Creole sauce, whisk together the vinegar and olive oil. Add the chopped tomatoes, peppers and onions. Sprinkle with the chopped parsley. Mix well, season with salt and pepper, and store in the refrigerator.

Cuts of Beef

4. To make the salad, melt 20 g/4 tsp butter in a pot. When it is sizzling, add a pinch of sugar and then the onions. Let them glaze for about 10 minutes, stirring constantly with a wooden spoon to prevent sticking.

5. With the point of a small knife, make cross slits in the cherry tomatoes. Dip them in boiling water, then in cold water. Peel and arrange on cookie sheet. Sprinkle with the olive oil and roast in the oven for 5 minutes.

6. Distribute the lettuces, in small pieces, among the salad bowl. Sprinkle with the raspberry vinegar and olive oil and top with the tomatoes, glazed onions and grated cheese. Serve the meat with the Creole sauce, with a bowl of salad.

Chicken

Preparation time: 25 minutes
Cooking time: 30 minutes
Difficulty: ★★

Serves 4

350 g/³/₄ lb chicken breast
1 large onion
oil for frying

For the biryani:
8–10 fresh curry leaves
¹/₂ tsp turmeric
¹/₂ tsp cumin
¹/₂ stick cinnamon
2 cardamom seeds

¹/₄ tsp ground coriander
¹/₄ tsp peppercorns, crushed
¹/₂ tsp fresh ginger

1 clove
¹/₂ green pepper
several cilantro leaves
30 g/2 tbsp butter
2 cloves garlic
225 g/8 oz plain yogurt
30 cashews
1 tsp flaked almonds
200 g/1 cup Basmati rice
salt
pepper

Optional:
10–20 g/1¹/₂ tbsp rice
food coloring
juice of 1 lemon

Like an invitation addressed to your taste buds, a cup of mango-flavored tea would be the perfect accompaniment for this Chicken *Biryani*. A rich and sophisticated holiday meal, it pleases both the eyes and the taste buds. The delicacy of the cashew nuts, the magic of fresh curry leaf, cardamom, cinnamon, ginger and other flavors blend into a stunning array of tastes and colors. Each plateful will include almonds, cashews, green lemons and hints of other ingredients.

The intoxicating aroma of the curry is sure to plunge guests into an infinitely exotic realm, especially since Chicken *Biryani* is traditionally served encircled by small bowls of different pickles or chutneys. The mixture in each bowl offers a unique taste: sweet, bitter, spicy, or pungent. The ideal is a good *masalchi*, or blend of spices.

It is by no means easy to make an excellent *biryani*, and our chef insists on using the unique flavor of the fresh curry leaf,

which has a taste quite different from that of dried curry powder. This highlights how important it is to be meticulous and pay rigorous attention to detail in order to master the cooking process.

For a truly authentic presentation, don't neglect the charming array of small bowls, full of mixtures both sweet and salty, and displayed elegantly on a platter called a *tali*. These will surely elicit compliments from your guests: a crowd-pleaser if ever there was one! Present your *tali* with the bowls of many flavors, and your *biryani* will be the crowning piece.

You can assuage the spiciness of the peppers, the acidity of the lemon and the robustness of the cloves and ginger by serving a mango *lassi*, a yogurt drink flavored with fresh fruit, such as pieces of mango.

If the cashews seem too soft at serving time, feel free to sprinkle a few fresh, crunchy ones around the *biryani*.

1. Cut the chicken breasts into small pieces, removing any excess fat. Peel and chop the onion.

2. In a frying pan, heat a little oil and fry the chopped onion and chicken over high heat for 3 minutes. Stir with a wooden spoon to prevent sticking.

3. Still over high heat, sprinkle the spices onto the chicken, one at a time, rubbing them between your fingers to distribute evenly to cover all the chicken. Add the green pepper (whole). Finally, add the finely chopped cilantro.

Biryani

4. Stir in the butter and chopped garlic. Pour the yogurt on top and blend well. Evenly mix in the cashews, then flaked almonds. Let cook over medium heat for 2 minutes.

5. Add the rice and stir for 1 minute. Pour water over the contents of the pan (use 1½ cups water for 1 cup rice). Cover the pan, wait until the water boils, then lower the heat and simmer over low heat for about 20 minutes.

6. For a beautiful presentation, top the biryani with 2 tbsp colored rice and sprinkle with lemon juice.

Scandinavian

Preparation time: 45 minutes
Cooking time, beef: 6 to 7 hours
Cooking time, garnish: 45 minutes
Difficulty: ★★

Serves 4

For the broth:
1 kg/2¼ lb beef brisket
1 head garlic, halved
1 onion, quartered
3 sprigs thyme
2 bay leaves
4 or 5 cloves
1 tsp ground cumin
sea salt
whole peppercorns

¼ celeriac
2 carrots

For the garnish:
2 turnips
4 potatoes
4 carrots
50 g/3½ tbsp butter
1 green cabbage
1 Savoy cabbage
1 cauliflower
brown stock
300 ml/1¼ cups heavy cream
1 small piece fresh horseradish
salt
crushed white pepper

It is a Danish custom to serve beef with horseradish sauce for the main Sunday meal. Pigs and chickens play a large part in Danish farming, but raising cattle remains a strong tradition, and beef has long been a fundamental part of the Danish diet. Hereford and Limousine cows are raised for meat on large industrial farms. In addition, beef is imported from Argentina, which is considered some of the best meat in the world.

Boiled "beef on a string" is a favorite item on the Danish menu. As a result of the added salt and a slow, seven-hour cooking process, the meat begins to come apart into thread-like strands. When the Danes aren't feasting on this tender, hot meat surrounded by an entourage of small vegetables, they transform beef into various other delicacies: stuffed cabbage leaves, pan-fried meat and onions, or black bread and butter topped with cooked red beets and slivers of boiled beef. In this manner, the *dyrloegens natmad*, "veterinarian's bread and butter", constitutes a Pantagruelian sandwich: buttered rye bread, liver pâté, beef, jelly and round slices of onions satisfy even the heartiest of appetites.

The Danes are fortunate that cabbage is a seasonal vegetable that preserves well. Cauliflower, kale and other cabbages are cultivated in abundance throughout the country. They make great soups, cooked in water and served smothered in melted butter. The cabbage is also boiled whole and then coated with a shrimp-flavored béchamel sauce. Also worth mentioning are white cabbage salad with cumin and apple slices, and stuffed cabbage with meat.

In his restaurant, our chef prefers to use wild horseradish, which has a richer taste than the cultivated variety. It is a plant belonging to the crucifer family, whose spicy root we eat when it is either yellow or gray. The blend of grated horseradish and cream is typical in Scandinavian cuisine.

1. Place the beef in a large pot. Add the garlic, onions, thyme, bay leaves, cloves, cumin, salt and peppercorns. Pour in cold water to completely cover the meat, then add the celeric and carrots, both peeled and cut in large pieces. Bring to the boil and cook slowly for 6 to 7 hours.

2. Peel the turnips, potatoes and carrots for the garnish. Use a small knife to cut the vegetables into hexagonal shapes. Cook in clear water for 30 minutes, drain, then add the butter.

3. Meanwhile, cut the Savoy cabbage in half, remove the core, and slice thinly. Remove the core from the green cabbage and cut the leaves into small triangles. Separate and chop the cauliflower florets. Blanch all of the cabbages for 5 minutes.

Beef and Potatoes

4. Warm some brown stock for 10 minutes. Strain the juices from the pot containing the meat and measure it. Add ⅓ of this quantity of brown stock to the meat juices.

5. Whip the cream. Grate the horseradish, then add it to the whipped cream. Season with salt and pepper, blending it in gently with a whisk.

6. Slice the beef brisket into thin, even pieces. Pour the sauce onto a serving plate. Place the meat in the center, surrounded by carrots, turnips, cabbages and potatoes. Garnish with the horseradish-cream mixture and fresh herbs.

Russian

Preparation time: 30 minutes
Cooking time: 2 hours 40 minutes
Difficulty: ★★

Serves 5 or 6

600–800 g/1¼–1¾ lb beef
4 thick pieces rye bread
½ celeriac
2 carrots
3 onions
150 g/5½ oz smoked bacon, sliced

60 g/7 tbsp flour
50 g/3½ tbsp butter
salt
freshly ground black peppercorns
2 or 3 bay leaves
400 ml/1⅔ cups beef broth
4–6 potatoes
100 ml/7 tbsp thick crème fraîche
parsley
dill

In Russia, it used to be that everyday meals usually consisted of minced meats in a crust, cabbage soups with beetroot, and thick, hearty stews. The first of such recipes in a more elaborate form appeared much later in Western Europe, however. Only wealthy people would have been able to serve large pieces of meat at their table. Russian gastronomy has preserved this tradition of serving thick pieces of beef and poultry, which unfold their full flavor in this succulent casserole that includes vegetables, bread and smoked bacon.

In the olden days, country folk would cook for hours, placing a large cast iron pot or a clay casserole dish in a huge oven in the center of their *isba*, or small wooden house. We have used more modern cooking methods, of course, using an enameled casserole dish and an electric oven. You may substitute pork for the rounds of rump steak or beef sirloin steaks. Due to the harsh climate in much of Russia, the growing season is too short for celeriac (celery root) to attain its maximum size, so it is often smaller than we are used to. Celeriac is used in this dish all the same.

In her beef casserole, Irina Sokolova uses a wonderful coriander flavored rye bread. Cooked in a bread pan, it develops a firm texture and dark brown color. It must be mentioned that Russians consume enormous quantities of bread, including many varieties such as wheat, rye and wholegrain. They flavor it with thyme, coriander, dill… and cook their dough in the form of rolls or molded into rectangles. Pieces of rye bread are often added to meat stews and stuffing—one could even say it has become a tradition.

1. Cut the beef into thin, even slices.

2. Cut the crust off the bread and cut the bread into small sticks. Peel the celery and 1 carrot and cut into julienne. Peel and dice the onions. Combine all the ingredients in a dish.

3. Cover the bottom of a casserole dish with the bacon strips, one overlapping the other. Dredge the slices of beef in the flour, then brown them in butter in a hot pan.

Beef Casserole

4. Place the browned slices of beef on top of bacon. Cover with alternating layers of vegetables and bread.

5. Season with salt and pepper. Add the bay leaves. Pour in the beef broth and cook in an oven preheated to 200°C/390°F for 2 to 2¹/₂ hours.

6. Cook the potatoes and remaining carrot in salted water for 20 minutes. 20 to 25 minutes before the stew is ready, stir in the crème fraîche. Serve the dish while hot, garnished with potatoes, carrots, parsley and dill.

Prekmurje Bograč

Preparation time:	*1 hour*
Cooking time, stew:	*45 minutes*
Cooking time, potatoes:	*30 minutes*
Cooking time, ravioli:	*10 minutes*
Resting time, dough:	*15 minutes*
Difficulty:	★★★

Serves 5

500 g/generous 1 lb onions
25 g/3¹/₂ tbsp chopped garlic
50 ml/3¹/₂ tbsp vegetable oil
350 g/³/₄ lb beef, chopped
25 g/3¹/₂ tbsp paprika
200 ml/generous ³/₄ cup red wine
1 sprig each: thyme, rosemary
1 pinch each: cumin, hot pepper

salt, pepper
800 g/1³/₄ lb potatoes
350 g/³/₄ lb pork, cubed
350 g/³/₄ lb venison, cubed

1 bay leaf
1 pepper

For the dough:
250 g/1³/₄ cups flour
1 egg
100 g/7 tbsp butter, whipped
15 g/1 tbsp sugar
5 g/1 tsp salt

For the filling:
200 g/7 oz smoked bacon
3 sprigs each: parsley, marjoram
2 eggs
60 g/2 oz sausage
1 pinch cinnamon
2 tbsp breadcrumbs

This meat stew served with ravioli is a local delicacy in the mountainous region of Idrija, to the west of Slovenia's capital, Ljubljana. Traditionally, the people there smoked many different types of meat, using the scraps to stuff the ravioli, called *žlikrofi*. The dough was made of potatoes that the cooks would roll into long strips and fill with dried meat. In our day and age, the dough is made of wheat flour and the potatoes are mixed in with the filling. In the central mountain region, the stuffing is always made with potatoes and smoked meat. It is prepared in differently in coastal areas, however, with seafood, scampi, truffles or mushrooms.

The inclusion of venison in this stew is evidence of the large wild game population in Slovenia. Mountain folk often cook meat from deer, stags and fawns. There are plenty of wild boar in the forests in the eastern part of the country, and fowl are often found on the northeastern plains. But the most prized meat of all comes from the bear. Bear meat is served as ham or processed into sausage, and the feet are used in the preparation of different sauces.

In the filled ravioli, our chef does not use ordinary sausage meat, but rather smoked bacon that is chopped and blended, resembling fatty potted meat. *Zaska* is fatty bacon that has been soaked in brine and then cold-smoked, and these odd-looking pieces of meat are either integrated into the stuffing or spread on bread with onions, salt and pepper. However, regular sausage would work just as well for these ravioli.

To make it more colorful, you can add two teaspoons of tomato concentrate to the sauce. And if you desire more thickness, you can also add a little flour.

1. Heat the oil in a heavy saucepan. Brown the onions and garlic for 5 minutes. Add the beef and paprika. Cook, stirring frequently, until browned. Add the water and wine, then the thyme, rosemary, cumin, hot pepper, salt and pepper. Cook for 15 minutes.

2. Boil the potatoes for 30 minutes in another pot. After the beef has cooked 15 minutes, add the pork and venison to it, then the bay leaf. Cook for another 15 minutes. Peel the potatoes and cut 500 g/1 lb into quarters (set aside the rest).

3. Dice the pepper and add to the pot along with the quartered potatoes. Cook for another 7 to 10 minutes, until the peppers have softened.

Stew with Žlikrofi

4. For the žlikrofi dough, tip the flour into a bowl and add the egg, butter, sugar and salt. Stir until all the ingredients are evenly mixed, and shape into a ball. Place in the refrigerator for 15 minutes.

5. For the filling, mash the rest of the potatoes. Chop the bacon, parsley and marjoram. Put the potatoes, bacon and herbs in a bowl, and add the eggs, sausage, salt, pepper, cinnamon and breadcrumbs. Stir well.

6. Roll out the dough. Place small balls of filling on the dough at 4–5 cm/2 in intervals and cut out squares around each ball. Fold the dough over and pinch together to form the žlikrofi. Boil water and poach the žlikrofi for 10 minutes. Serve the bograč in a fondue pot with a bowl of žlikrofi.

Bulgogi

Preparation time: 20 minutes
Cooking time: 10 minutes
Marinating time: 1 to 2 hours
Difficulty: ★

Serves 4

500 g/generous 1 lb beef fillet
1 pear
2 pinches sugar

2 cloves garlic
3 or 4 green onions
1 tbsp rice wine
1 tbsp sesame seeds, roasted
salt
pepper
1 tbsp sesame oil
3 tbsp water
3 tbsp soy sauce

The Koreans inherited an irresistible attraction to beef from the Mongols. Bulgogi is *the* quintessential national dish of South Korea. The meat is finely sliced and marinated in a very aromatic sauce. Traditionally, it is served on a hot plate over a brazier, and the hot meat is eaten between two pieces of lettuce. Our chef recommends using beef fillet, a particularly tender cut of meat taken from along the spine.

There are several varieties of soy sauces, which are separated into two groups: sweetened and non-sweetened. The most natural is made of fermented soy beans, salt, flour and water, without the addition of caramel or monosodium glutamate. In the past, Koreans would prepare their own non-sweetened, clear soy sauce.

You should have no trouble finding rice wine, a typically Asian product, at an Asian market, but you can easily substitute a dry white wine, since the color and flavor are very similar. In the original recipe, the meat is cooked on a tabletop grill, but we have decided to use a frying pan instead. In reality, few people own the correct Korean grill. You can cook the meat in an electric skillet or, even better, on a tabletop grill.

It is easy to alter this recipe to your liking. For example, you can cut the meat into large chunks, marinate the pieces, then grill them or cook them with vegetables on a skewer. The meat can also be marinated and then cut into thick slices to be cooked like a steak.

The Koreans like to accompany this dish with a basket containing an assortment of raw vegetables, such as cucumbers, lettuce, carrots and also chrysanthemum leaves. But you can also simply offer a bowl of rice.

1. Cut the beef into thin slices on a cutting board with a sharp butcher's knife. Put the pieces into a bowl.

2. Peel the pear and cut it into small, thin strips. Add the pear slices and 1 pinch of sugar to the meat. Mix.

3. Peel the garlic; chop it and the green onions. Mix with the rice wine, sesame seeds, salt and pepper. Add the sesame oil, water and 2 tbsp of the soy sauce.

4. Stir this marinade well with a spoon, then pour it into bowl with the meat.

5. Sprinkle the meat with the rest of the sugar. Add the last tbsp of soy sauce and mix together. Place the bowl in the refrigerator and let marinate for 1 or 2 hours.

6. Heat a large frying pan over high heat and brown the beef for 10 minutes. Serve immediately.

Veal Kebabs with

Preparation time:	25 minutes
Cooking time:	40 minutes
Marinating time:	20 minutes
Difficulty:	★

Serves 4

400 g/14 oz veal scallops
1 tsp potato flour
1 pinch sugar
several drops sesame oil
salt
pepper

For the Cantonese Rice:
380 g/2 cups rice
2 eggs

100 g/3½ oz small shrimp, cooked
4 chives
100 g/3½ oz ham, diced
50 g/⅓ cup peas, cooked
salt

For the sauce:
1 tsp potato flour
salt
pepper
2 tbsp tomato paste
2 tbsp water
1 tbsp Worcestershire sauce
1 dash vinegar
sesame oil
1 dash peanut oil
vegetable oil

The Chinese enjoy salads in the summertime, but for the winter season they love to treat themselves to kebabs. They grill them at home on small tabletop grills, or buy them from street vendors, hot and ready-to-eat. In fact, in China, kebabs are often eaten during the day as a snack. They are made with pork, beef, veal, chicken or shrimp. Here, we are adding rice to make it a main dish.

In China, oxen have long been considered working animals rather than a source of food. That is the simple reason why meals made with pork or chicken are more common. Chinese veal, though, is cooked with mushrooms, bamboo shoots and green vegetables.

The Yang Tse Kiang basin, located in the center of China, yields a harvest of rice each year. The most coveted rice cultivators, however, are those from the south (Canton), where the tropical climate yields rice up to two or even three times per year. The local chefs have since shared their famous Cantonese rice recipe with the rest of the world.

This dish can include small pieces of omelet, cooked beef, chicken, pork, fried jumbo shrimp, smoked sausage or broccoli. Some Chinese chefs even offer another, more refined recipe. The rice is mixed with carrots, smoked mushrooms, peas, shrimp and meat, then wrapped in lotus leaves and steamed. The rice thus takes on a subtle taste from the lotus.

1. Cut the veal into thin slices, then cut each slice in half again to make long, thin strips.

2. Place the meat in a bowl. Add the potato flour, sugar, sesame oil, salt and pepper. Mix the meat with the seasoning. Marinate for 20 minutes. Cook the rice in boiling salted water for 20 minutes.

3. Once marinated, thread pieces of veal onto wooden skewers.

Cantonese Rice

4. In a bowl, vigorously whisk together all of the sauce ingredients.

5. Scramble the eggs in a frying pan for about 5 minutes. Peel the shrimp and chop the chives. Add the rice, shrimp, scallions, ham and peas to the pan with the eggs, salt to taste, and cook for 5 minutes.

6. In a frying pan, brown the kebabs in vegetable oil over a high heat for 10 minutes. Serve with a bowl of Cantonese rice and a small dish of sauce.

Five-Spice

Preparation time: 25 minutes
Cooking time: 1 hour 5 minutes
Marinating time: 10 minutes
Difficulty: ★

Serves 4

2 tbsp five-spice powder
1/2 tsp curry powder
2 tsp sugar
salt

2 duck breasts
2 cm/1/2 in fresh ginger root
1 large onion
1 celery stalk
1 glass plus 200 ml/generous 3/4 cup water
1 1/2 tbsp soy sauce

Duck dishes are very popular in China, even though the more pronounced flavor of duck lends itself to fewer variations than its cousin, the chicken. Peking Duck, for example, is the most important part of a very precise, three-step ritual. The shiny, crispy duck is first presented whole, which always whets the guests' appetites. Then strips of baked skin are wrapped over wheat crêpes. The flesh is then served separately.

The inhabitants of Sichuan have learned to smoke duck over camphor wood or in a covered pot filled with tea leaves mixed with sugar and dry rice. The Chinese also like it cooked with bamboo shoots and black and flavorful mushrooms. But let's not forget the "Jeweled Duck", served with dates, walnuts, water chestnuts, lotus seeds, grapes, shallots and sticky rice.

In China, ginger root is usually used fresh, peeled and cut into small pieces to give a sweet scent to a dish, or in a marinade or as a dessert ingredient. Dried and ground ginger has a very different taste and is less highly esteemed. Ginger root is sometimes added to hide the scent of pork, which the Chinese find unpleasant.

The five-spice powder from which this recipe gets its name can be found in Asian markets or easily made at home. Though variations abound, it is most often comprised of equal parts of star anise, Sezchuan pepper, cinnamon, fennel seed and cloves. Its taste is so strong that we recommend adding just a little bit at a time.

1. In a bowl, mix together 1 tsp of the five-spice powder, the curry, 1 tsp of the sugar and a little salt.

2. Place the duck in a casserole dish with the skin down. With a small spoon, coat the whole breast with the mixed spices. Spread the spices evenly with your fingertips. Peel the ginger and onion.

3. Cut the ginger in thin slices and the onion into thin segments. Slice the celery in small sticks. Place the onions, celery and ginger over the duck breasts, alternating them. Pour over the glass of water and let marinate for 10 minutes. Bake at 170°C/350°F for 1 hour.

Duck

4. With a butcher's knife, cut the duck into thin, even slices.

5. Put the rest of the water in a pot. Add the soy sauce and the rest of the spices. Cook over low heat for 5 minutes or until the sauce has a nice brown color.

6. Place the duck on a serving dish, garnish and top with the five-spice sauce.

Rack of Lamb with

Preparation time: 1 hour
Cooking time: 1 hour 30 minutes
Difficulty: ★★

Serves 4

8 baby carrots
8 small turnips
8 small zucchini
100 g/3¹/₂ oz snow peas
2 racks of lamb, with 12 ribs apiece
1 carrot

1 onion
1 tomato
1 leek
150 ml/²/₃ cup olive oil
200 ml/generous ³/₄ cup red wine
1 sprig rosemary
salt
pepper
100 g/5 tbsp honey
50 ml/3¹/₂ tbsp red wine vinegar

Muslims in the city of Cordoba feasted on roasted lamb with herbs and honey as far back as the fifteenth century. And even after the Spanish regained this territory after 1492, this savory meal has remained a tradition there.

Our chef, faithful to his native region, uses an excellent breed of lamb from La Mancha, a place where the animal could roam freely on the plateaus of central Spain. Any high quality cut of lamb will go well with this recipe, which is cooked to taste. According to our chef, the loin is the best choice, but a leg could work just as well.

To make the presentation perfect, Alberto Herriáz deglazes the vegetables in a frying pan with a thick, red wine from La Mancha, and gets a superb reduction.

He also uses vinegar made from Cabernet Sauvignon, but which can be replaced by vinegar made from a sweet, red Bordeaux wine. The vinegar does not need to be acidic to go with this sauce. Finally, to match the finely spiced lamb, add a subtle touch of rosemary honey to the sauce.

If the sauce is too strong after being cooked in the oven, our chef recommends cooking it in a pan over high heat. You can also sprinkle it with a bit of flour before placing it in the oven.

The vegetables served with the lamb can vary according to the season. In winter, for example, simple steamed potatoes can be used instead of the small spring vegetables.

1. Peel the carrots and turnips. Peel the zucchini so it has stripes. Blanch the snow peas al dente, then refresh them in cold water. Blanch the zucchini, then the carrots and turnips together. Set aside all the vegetables.

2. Scrape and clean the long bones on the racks of lamb. Remove the main bone with a mincing knife and set aside. Remove the fat from the ribs.

3. Peel and chop the carrots, onion, tomato and leek. Chop up the small bones that were put aside. Warm the oil in an ovenproof frying pan with the vegetables and bones. Continue to cook for 15 minutes.

Rosemary and Honey

4. When the vegetables are all coated with oil, deglaze the pan with red wine. Add rosemary, salt and pepper. Place the frying pan in the oven and cook at 250°C/480°F for about 1 hour, or until the vegetables and bones are well blended and softened.

5. Generously salt and pepper the lamb on all sides. Brown in some oil in a frying pan. Place the frying pan in the oven and cook for 6 minutes on each side.

6. Stir the honey and vinegar into the vegetables and bones to make the sauce. Strain it; it should have the consistency of syrup. Cut up the lamb. Serve surrounded by the carrots, turnips, zucchini and snow peas, and coated in the sauce.

Rack of Lamb

Preparation time: 45 minutes
Cooking time: 20 minutes
Difficulty: ★★★

Serves 4

700 g/1¹/₂ lb rack of lamb
salt
pepper
olive oil
60 g/¹/₂ cup walnut halves

For the mint sauce:
250 ml/1 cup veal broth
¹/₂ bunch fresh mint
2 tomatoes, skinned
100 ml/7 tbsp heavy cream
2 tsp paprika
salt
pepper
50 g/3¹/₂ tbsp butter

Lamb and lamb cooked in milk head the list of southern Portuguese specialties. Lamb's tender and juicy flesh can be found at every holiday feast, from the Christmas roast to the Easter stew, an Alentejo specialty. In the north, it is served with rice. Placed over rice in a ceramic casserole dish, it is then seasoned with its own cooked fat.

In Portugal, the lamb is chosen with great care for this recipe, since it should have especially delicate flesh. It is not mandatory to add the trimmings to flavor the veal broth, and in this case, there is no need to strain the broth.

Aside from lamb dishes, walnuts are also used to stuff turkeys, as well as in some desserts. Like mint, they are a chef's delight in Alentejo. Meat and fish soups can be transformed by the addition of a few herbs and spices, which vary in strength and spiciness depending upon the sort. The Portuguese especially like to use a local mint called "river mint".

Those who love spicy flavors can sprinkle several pinches of paprika on the dish just before serving, which also adds a touch of color. Paprika is one of the most characteristic spices in Portuguese gastronomy. It comes from a sweet, bright red pepper that is dried and finely crushed. Its powerful flavor is present in many typical dishes, and it always has an appealing color. The delicious spice is easily mixed into *chouriço*, a forcemeat sausage.

1. Dress the lamb: with a knife, trim the meat and fat from ¹/₄ of each bone (or have this done by a butcher). Add these trimmings to the broth; they will flavor it nicely.

2. To prepare the sauce, bring the veal broth to the boil, lower the heat and reduce by half. Chop the mint leaves and tomatoes. Strain the broth, then add the mint, tomatoes, cream, paprika, salt and pepper.

3. Season the lamb and then brown it in hot olive oil.

Castelo Branco

4. Cut the butter into small cubes. With a whisk, mix into the mint sauce until uniform. Season to taste with more salt and pepper.

5. Brush the lamb generously with mint sauce.

6. Chop the walnuts coarsely and sprinkle them over the lamb. Place the lamb in a roasting pan greased with olive oil. Cook at 180°C/350°F for 10 to 20 minutes, depending on the desired degree of doneness.

Old English

Preparation time: 50 minutes
Cooking time: 2 hours 50 minutes
Difficulty: ★★

Serves 4

3 large onions
vegetable oil
100 g/1¼ cups sliced mushrooms
1 chicken, ca. 2.2 kg/5 lb
1 bouquet garni
100 ml/7 tbsp white wine

100 g flour, sifted
2 liters/2 quarts brown stock
8 slices smoked bacon
300 g/11 oz puff pastry
1 egg, beaten
1 tsp Worcestershire sauce
salt
pepper

Optional accompaniments:
Jersey royal potatoes with chopped parsley
4 quail eggs

Traditional English menus include several pies, which are often stews baked slowly in the oven in an oval dish covered with a crust. Steak and kidney pie has chopped beef kidneys cooked in beer. Apple pie contains delicious baked apples, and fish pie contains fish in sauce.

The English are not terribly sophisticated when it comes to preparing chicken and turkey. Local poultry, which comes from large poultry processing plants, receives no distinguishing labels or awards. Fried chicken is the most common method of preparation. This recipe is great because it is simple and easy to prepare. And all of the ingredients can be bought from an average grocer. Chicken fricassee, though, is served with white wine and a mushroom sauce. And let's not forget chicken served with gravy, a sauce made from chicken drippings and enriched with stock, flour, butter and sometimes milk, cream or Worcestershire sauce.

The slices of bacon wrapped around the chicken give it a smoked taste and a crisp texture. English-style bacon is made from smoked pork belly, which differs from the French-style, which uses pork loins instead. The English prefer their bacon for breakfast, fried with eggs. They also use it frequently in poultry dishes.

Our chef advises that you start by cooking the chicken with its skin side down first. This way, the drippings will soak into the meat, which will keep it from sticking to the frying pan.

The sauce for this Old English Chicken Pie, made of white wine and brown chicken stock, needs to be somewhat thick because the chicken is not completely cooked when it is placed in the pie. It will give off juices while being cooked under its lovely crust. Serve the chicken pie on a plate with some mustard and quail eggs.

1. Blanch the pork. Peel the onions and cut into thin slices. Chop 2 of the onions and sauté them in vegetable oil for 5 minutes. Set aside. Sauté the sliced mushrooms for 5 minutes over high heat, in another frying pan. Cut the chicken into 8 pieces. Remove the giblets and set aside.

2. In a pot with a little vegetable oil, cook the chicken for 2 minutes on each side over high heat, or until golden brown. The pieces should change color but not be completely cooked. Take the chicken out of the pot and set aside. Wipe off excess oil.

3. With the remaining cooking juices, brown the giblets over high heat for 5 minutes. Add the third onion and the bouquet garni. Let caramelize for 5 minutes, stirring. Deglaze with white wine. Let the wine evaporate for 5 minutes over high heat.

Chicken Pie

4. Sprinkle with flour. Mix briefly with a spatula and moisten with the stock. Cook over moderate heat for 1 hour. Meanwhile, wrap each chicken piece with a slice of bacon.

5. Strain the sauce and add the Worcestershire. Put the chicken pieces in a tall, oval cooking dish with the onions and mushrooms. Top with sauce and add salt and pepper.

6. Cover the dish with puff pastry, allowing it to hang over the sides. Glaze with egg. Cook for 20 minutes at 200°C/390°F, then for 1 hour at 150°C/300°F. After cooking, remove any extra crust that hangs from dish. Serve with potatoes and parsley, if desired.

Chiles

Preparation time: 40 minutes
Cooking time: 1 hour 20 minutes
Difficulty: ★★★

Serves 6 to 8

For the bouquet garni:
1 sprig thyme
2 or 3 sprigs parsley
1 rib celery
1 bay leaf

For the stuffing:
500 g/generous 1 lb veal
1 kg/2¹/₄ lb pork tenderloin
1 kg/2¹/₄ lb each: pears, Golden Delicious apples, peaches

2 plantains, very ripe
1 kg/2¹/₄ lb tomatoes, quartered
4 cloves
1 cinnamon stick

1 large onion, chopped
4 cloves garlic, chopped
250 g/2¹/₄ cups blanched, crushed almonds
250 g/scant 2 cups golden raisins
200 ml/generous ³/₄ cup veal broth

For the sauce:
500 ml/2 cups milk
300 ml/1¹/₄ cups crème fraîche
60 walnut halves
2 tsp sugar
200 ml/generous ³/₄ cup white wine
200 g/7 oz feta
1 pinch salt
8 poblano peppers, canned
1 pomegranate
parsley

Chiles en Nogada is traditionally a family holiday dish prepared to be shared by a group of about 15 people. The recipe was invented in Puebla, a colonial town about 100 km (60 miles) from the center of Mexico that is celebrated for its rich gastronomy. Pork tenderloin and boiled veal mixed with fruits and spices are cooked cordon-bleu style, stuffed inside large hot peppers and covered with a nut sauce.

The recipe is prepared with poblanos, round hot peppers with a dark green color and a spicy flavor. They are common in the city of Puebla and are usually used fresh in recipes throughout the country. You can make this dish with canned poblanos, or simply with red peppers. The filling can be varied in many ways, made with spiced beef, for example, or an assortment of cheeses. Everything could then be covered with a delicious tomato sauce.

Our chef strongly suggests preparing the stuffing the night before, so that the meat has enough time to fully take in all the flavors from the spices and fruits. After the meat is boiled, you can shred it or chop it with a knife.

When the meat and fruit mixture begins to reduce, add a pinch of sugar to reduce some of the acidity. If it happens to reduce too much, you can just add a little veal broth.

The *Chiles en Nogada* sauce is best when made with fresh walnuts. Remove the shells and put the nuts in boiling water. Then you can peel them easily with the tip of a small knife. This way, the sauce will not be too bitter.

Our chef has found a trick for easily removing seeds from pomegranates. He cuts the fruit in half, turns them upside down, and taps on the shell with the back of a knife until the seeds fall out.

1. Put the ingredients for the bouquet garni together and place in a large pot of water. Bring the water to the boil and add salt and pepper. Cut the veal and pork into large pieces and cook for 1 hour, then drain. Cool the meat, then shred it.

2. To prepare the stuffing, peel the pears, apples, peaches and plantains. Remove the seeds and cores, and cut the fruit into small cubes. Put aside in small bowls.

3. In a blender, purée the tomatoes with the cloves and cinnamon. In a large pot, brown the onion and garlic with the almonds. Add the tomatoes and bring to the boil, stirring continually. Stir in the fruit and raisins. Simmer for 5 minutes.

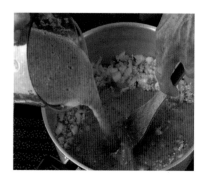

en Nogada

4. Add the minced meat to the pot with the fruit. Moisten with veal broth. Reduce for 10 to 15 minutes, then salt.

5. For the walnut sauce, put the milk, crème fraîche, feta, walnut halves, sugar, wine and salt in a blender. Blend until you have a uniform white mixture.

6. Slice open the peppers lengthwise. With a large spoon, fill them with the meat mixture. Top with walnut sauce and serve with pomegranate seeds and parsley.

Texas-Style

Preparation time: 30 minutes
Cooking time: 1 hour 35 minutes
Soaking time: 1 hour
Difficulty: ★★

Serves 8

6 dried red chili peppers
4 fresh Anaheim peppers
120 g/4 oz smoked bacon
2 cloves garlic
1.5 kg/3¹/₄ lb beef shoulder

750 ml/3¹/₄ cups water
1 tbsp salt
2 bay leaves
2 tsp powdered sugar
1 tbsp cumin seeds
1 tsp dried oregano
1 tbsp paprika
4 or 5 sprigs cilantro
100 g/scant 1 cup grated cheddar cheese
1 onion
2 small fresh serrano peppers

A beef stew with dried chili peppers and spices could be found as early as the start of the twentieth century in the city of San Antonio, Texas. The dish was without a doubt influenced by the Mexican immigrants who came to work on the local ranches. In their native tongue, the word *chili* means peppers and *carne* means meat.

Texans can be quite opinionated when it comes to how best to prepare their Chili con Carne. Traditionalists actually refuse to include kidney beans or tomatoes. They feel there should only be the flavor of stewed meat with a strong hot pepper and spice taste. Chili is sometimes made with pork, and sometimes with just beans and chili peppers for vegetarians. The recipe lends itself to a great deal of creativity. Under the patronage of the International Chili Appreciation Society, more than 400 tournaments are held each year, where thousands of participants prepare their Chili con Carne in front of the public. The most famous competition takes place each year in Terlingua, Texas.

The success of this dish is not that surprising when one considers the "monster appetite" that Americans have for beef. Texas is still famed for its vast cattle ranches. In the 1850s, cattle-ranchers began domesticating wild Longhorn bulls, descendants of those introduced by the Spanish back in the sixteenth century. Since their meat did not taste especially good, though, they were eventually replaced by Hereford and Angus cows. Today, the ratio of cattle to acreage is still such that cowboys have a lot of ground to cover in order to keep watch over them.

In our recipe, the chef has combined many types of hot peppers with the beef: the Anaheim, a long green pepper with mild spiciness, goes well with the powerful, dried red chili peppers and the equally hot fresh serrano peppers. They are sprinkled with spices and a handful of grated cheddar cheese, which melts invitingly atop individual serving bowls.

1. Soak the red peppers in a bowl of hot water for 1 hour. Keep the water when finished.

2. Slit open the peppers and remove the seeds. Remove the flesh by scraping across the skin lengthwise. Open the Anaheim peppers, deseed and chop the flesh.

3. Finely chop the bacon. Peel and chop the garlic. Dice the beef into 2 cm/³/₄ in square pieces. Warm a little bacon in a heatproof casserole. Brown the beef pieces over high heat for 5 minutes. Add the garlic, Anaheim pepper and some skin from the red pepper.

Chili Con Carne

4. Add the rest of the bacon.

5. Add the water plus the water used to soak the peppers, as well as the dried peppers, salt, bay leaves, sugar, cumin seeds, oregano and paprika. Cook for 1 to 1¹/₂ hours until thick.

6. Prepare the condiments: separate the cilantro leaves, grate the cheddar and peel and chop the onion and the serrano peppers. Place each ingredient in its own small bowl. Add them to the chili just before eating.

Choucroute

Preparation time: 1 hour
Cooking time: 4 hours 30 minutes
Difficulty: ★★

Serves 6

Choucroute Garni:
1.5 kg/3¼ lb raw sauerkraut
2 large onions
100 g/½ cup goose fat
3 or 4 cloves
400 g/14 oz smoked bacon
200 ml/generous ¾ cup dry white wine
1 clove garlic, crushed
5 juniper berries
750 g/1¾ lb salted pork belly
1 smoked, salted pork shoulder

1 semi-salted pork knuckle
pepper
10 potatoes

For the liver dumplings:
250 g/9 oz pork liver
150 g/5½ oz smoked bacon
5 sprigs parsley
2 sprigs chervil
2 onions, sliced
1 clove garlic, chopped
2 tbsp vegetable oil
3 eggs
100 g/3½ oz bread, crusts removed
50 g/5 tbsp fine semolina
1 pinch nutmeg
salt, pepper
1 liter/1 quart chicken stock

4 Strasbourg sausages
4 small blood sausages

Alsatian people have been eating sauerkraut since the Middle Ages. Over time, they began to garnish the fermented cabbage with an assortment of tempting meats, which nicely balance the somewhat acidic taste of the cabbage. This lively dish has become the greatest symbol of Alsatian gastronomy.

Fermented cabbage is the heart and soul of all types of sauerkraut. Alsatians produce nearly 25,000 tons of fermented cabbage per year. Huge white cabbages are cut into thin slices and left to soak in brine for three to seven weeks. While fermenting, the cabbage produces lactic acid, which accounts for its distinct flavor. To make the recipe a success, we advise that you use raw sauerkraut rather than pre-cooked varieties. After rinsing it three or four times to reduce the acidity, use your hands to squeeze all the water out.

For cooking, use a large pot that has enough room for many types of meat. The clove-studded onions are not absolutely necessary; thinly sliced onions browned in goose fat can work just as well. The juniper berries, wrapped in cheesecloth or muslin and sometimes accompanied by crushed garlic cloves, give off their strong scent throughout the course of cooking.

The Alsatians, always admirers of pork products, enjoy trying different types of meats and sometimes add to this mix Montbéliard smoked sausage, salted pork or saveloy, which resemble frankfurters. Preserved by salting, pork meats and cabbage always contain an abundance of salt. There is, therefore, no need to add any salt after cooking.

Depending upon one's taste, this hearty meal can be served with baked potatoes, mashed potatoes or even baked apples. The Alsatian artist Hansi, commenting on the famous Colmar sauerkraut, even suggests seasoning it with a glass of Kirsch half an hour before it is finished cooking.

1. Place the sauerkraut in a strainer. Plunge the bottom of the strainer into a pot of cold water 3 or 4 times. Drain the water.

2. Cut 1 onion into thin slices. In a large pot, sweat the onion in melted goose fat for 10 minutes. Stud the other onion with the cloves; add it and some of the bacon to the pot. Moisten with the white wine and enough water to fill the pot halfway. Spread out the sauerkraut in this mixture.

3. Add the garlic to the mixture, as well as the juniper berries, which should be enclosed in a cheesecloth. Mix well. Cook at 180°C/350°F for 1 hour.

Garni

4. Add the rest of the bacon as well as the pork belly, shoulder and knuckle. Pepper, cover and cook for 2¹/₂ hours over low heat. Peel the potatoes, place on top of the meat and cook for another 30 minutes over low heat.

5. For the dumplings, mix together the liver, bacon, parsley and chervil. Glaze the onions and garlic in the vegetable oil, then mix with the liver. Beat the eggs and add them, the bread, semolina, nutmeg, salt and pepper, and mix thoroughly.

6. Bring the broth to the boil. Take 1 tbsp of the dumpling mixture and pack down with another spoon. Repeat the process until all the dumpling mixture is used. Poach the dumplings in the broth for 10 minutes. In another pot, poach the sausages for 10 minutes. Serve with the sauerkraut.

Charlevoix-Style

Preparation time: 45 minutes
Cooking time: 4 hours
Soaking time: overnight
Difficulty: ★★★

Serves 6 to 8

For the marinade:
1 carrot
1 onion
2–3 sprigs thyme
1 bay leaf
500 ml/2 cups beer
500 ml/2 cups cider
12 whole peppercorns
$^1/_2$ tsp sea salt

For the pie:
1–2 partridges
450 g/1 lb hare saddle
450 g/1 lb pork
700 g/1$^1/_2$ lb pie pastry dough
125 g/4$^1/_2$ oz salt-cured fatback
1 kg/2$^1/_4$ lb potatoes
2 large onions
1 pinch savory
1 pinch thyme
1 bay leaf
pepper
salt
1 liter/1 quart beef broth

The Canadian regions of Charlevoix and Saguenay-Lac Saint Jean are great for fish and game. For as long as anyone can remember, they have been prized by hunters and fishermen from local Indian tribes, as well as by the French pioneers who joined them in the sixteenth century. The hunters particularly prize elk, roe deer and caribou. Small game is also common, such as hares, partridges and Canadian geese and ducks, especially since it is an important migratory route for birds. Over the centuries, the natives of Charlevoix, the "Charlevoisiens", have developed a cuisine that is quite different from the rest of Quebec. *Cipaille*, a layered meat pie, and soup made with *gourganes*, or "swamp beans", are good examples.

In the original recipe, *cipaille* included at least six layers of dough interspersed with pieces of wild game, meat and vegetables. To feed large families, the fresh game would be combined with home-raised pork and basic ingredients such as potatoes and bacon.

Since then, the pie has been "lightened" a little by only using pastry layers on the top and bottom. You can make it even simpler by not using the bottom or side layers at all. You should, however, keep the top layer for its nice crust.

To get the pastry to stick, moisten the sides of the pot with water and press the dough firmly against it. Cut off the extra dough with scissors and pinch the edges together to make a nice design. A small "chimney" in the center of the dough will allow steam to escape during cooking.

After removing the bones from the meat, you can use them to make a broth and add it to the *cipaille* with the marinade.

1. The evening before, peel and chop the onion and carrot. Place them in a bowl with the thyme and bay leaf. Add the beer, cider, pepper and salt.

2. With a butcher's knife, cut the partridges, hare saddle and pork into 4 or 5 pieces. Place them in the marinade. Marinate in the refrigerator overnight.

3. The next day, roll out the pastry dough into two sheets with a rolling pin. Place one sheet in a cast-iron pot, covering the bottom and sides. Tamp down well to prevent from slipping. Set aside the other sheet of pastry.

Cipaille Meat Pie

4. Cut one large slice of fatback. Place it inside the bottom layer of pastry like a lining and press down. Peel the potatoes and onions and cut them in thin slices.

5. Remove the bones from the marinated meat, then separate the meat into small pieces. Place half this meat on the bottom of the pot, over the fatback. Add some savory, thyme, bay leaf and pepper, then the potatoes, onions and salt.

6. Add another layer of meat, herbs, potatoes and onions. Strain the marinade and fill ³/₄ of the pot with it and the broth. Cover with the other pastry sheet, pressing down the edges. Cook at 230°C/450°F for 10 minutes, 180°C/350°F for 1 hour and 45 minutes, then at 120°C/250°F for 2 hours.

Lamb Colombo

Preparation time: 25 minutes
Cooking time, lamb: 40 minutes
Cooking time, rice: 20 minutes
Difficulty: ★

Serves 4

600 g/1¼ lb lamb shoulder
50 ml/3½ tbsp vegetable oil
salt
pepper
1 tsp mixed cumin, fenugreek
and mustard seeds
1 onion
2 cloves garlic
2 tbsp colombo powder

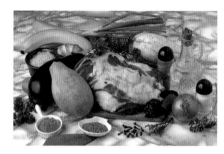

1 small hot pepper
1 Indian bay leaf
2 cloves
1 carrot
1 chayote
1 green papaya
1 eggplant
2 large yellow bananas

For the bouquet garni:
1 sprig thyme
2 or 3 sprigs parsley
several chives
1 bay leaf

400 g/2 cups white rice

In the mid-nineteenth century, many immigrants from India and Ceylon (now Sri Lanka) came to Martinique and Guadeloupe to work on the plantations. They brought with them a special mixture of spices they called colombo powder. Used in meat stews, its flavor was so good that the dish was named after it: now, a variety of *colombos* are made with lamb, chicken, pork, fish, shrimp or even scampi for a special occasion.

Colombo seasoning is sold either as a powder or a paste. Our chef advises using the powder form, because it more easily blends with the meat. In general, it is a combination of cumin, turmeric, coriander seeds, mustard, garlic, chili pepper, some fenugreek and saffron or ginger. Some Antillean cooks make their own colombo, adjusting the spices to achieve just the taste they want.

In this recipe, our chef has combined colombo powder with another spice mixture called *seeds à roussir*, which is a mixture of cumin, fenugreek and mustard that has become very rare on Martinique. Only a handful of old street vendors still offer it.

Our chef adds some country vegetables and fruits to this Lamb Colombo, which absorb the spicy juices but do not become overcooked. Among these fruits and vegetables, the green papaya is harvested from the female papaya tree before it has fully ripened; the male papaya tree does not produce any fruit. It can be eaten raw or cooked, in salads or as a garnish for meat. Make sure you carefully remove all of the skin and seeds, since they give the dish a bitter taste.

Finally, when buying the chayote, a vegetable from the cucumber family, make sure it has firm white skin, because green skin indicates that it is not yet fully ripe.

1. Cut the lamb into even cubes with a butcher's knife.

2. Heat the oil in a large pot. Place the lamb pieces in the pot, add salt and pepper and brown for about 5 minutes. Add the spice mix. Mix while it continues to brown.

3. Peel and chop the onion and garlic. Add both to the lamb and cook for 3 to 4 minutes or until golden brown.

à la Martinique

4. Sprinkle the meat with colombo powder. Make and add the bouquet garni, then add the whole hot pepper, Indian bay leaf and cloves. Fill the pot with water and cook for 20 minutes.

5. Peel the carrot, chayote, papaya, eggplant and bananas. Cut the bananas into even slices and the rest into cubes. Boil the rice for 20 minutes in a pan of salted water.

6. When the lamb has cooked for 20 minutes, add all of the vegetables and fruits. Cook for another 10 minutes. Remove the bouquet garni. Season to taste and serve with rice.

Country-Style

Preparation time: 40 minutes
Cooking time: 1 hour 50 minutes
Difficulty: ★ ★

Serves 4

1.5 kg/3¼ lb rooster or chicken
salt
freshly ground pepper
100 ml/7 tbsp olive oil
2 carrots
1 onion
3–4 sprigs parsley

1 sprig thyme
1 bay leaf
1 tbsp flour
50 ml/3½ tbsp brandy
6 whole black peppercorns
1.5 liters/1½ quarts red wine
3 cloves garlic
200 g/7 oz small potatoes
150 g/5½ oz white pearl onions
150 g/5½ oz fresh mushrooms
50 g/3½ tbsp butter
100 g/3½ oz slab bacon, in small pieces
2 sprigs chervil

A rather neglected figure, the French rooster is nowadays seen only as an image on sports teams' jerseys. It used to be a different story, though. This domestic bird, the male mate to the tender hens, used to play his role from dawn to dusk: his morning song would wake the slumbering countryside each morning, and the hens would lay their eggs for their owners. Worn down after a life well lived, the old rooster would eventually end up in a casserole, slowly tenderized in a wine sauce. Today, the proud rooster is more often replaced by a chicken, for a faster preparation of *Coq au Vin*.

Two ingredients face off in the pot: a young featherweight chicken and a robust red wine, rich in alcohol and tannins. With such a match going on, the other ingredients become spectators. Carrots cut into round slices add their vitamins. The bouquet garni, garlic and onions contribute their essential aromas, while the peppercorns and ground pepper give the sauce a spicy flavor.

The French countryside is full of spirits that are perfect for cooking the bird. Distilled fruits produce Kirsch, Mirabelle and pear brandy, cider becomes Calvados, and wine makes Cognac and Armagnac. Exactly which you choose to include depends on how you feel at the moment!

The pearl onions, mushrooms and bacon browned in butter should be kept warm. Small potatoes, with delicate skin and a savory flavor, are cooked whole. Overcome by the garnish, the young chicken can not escape from this final battle. It is too bad he hides himself at the bottom of the casserole dish!

1. Cut the chicken at the highest point on the leg joint to keep the legs and thighs as one piece. Separate the wings from body. Season with salt and pepper.

2. Heat the olive oil in a cast iron pot. Put the chicken pieces in the pot and brown rapidly, turning on all sides.

3. Cut the carrots into round slices, chop the onions and garlic and make a bouquet garni from the parsley, thyme and bay leaf. Add the vegetables and spices to the pot and stir for 5 minutes over medium-high heat. Sprinkle with the flour and mix well.

Coq au Vin

4. Add the brandy, peppercorns and red wine. Cover and cook for 50 minutes over medium heat, then remove the chicken from the sauce and keep it warm. Boil the potatoes in salted water for 30 minutes while the chicken is cooking. Set aside.

5. Cook the pearl onions in salted water for 10 minutes, then drain. In a frying pan, fry the onions, bacon and mushrooms in butter until golden brown. Keep warm.

6. Reduce the sauce by ¾ over medium-high heat. Add the mushrooms, onions and chicken. Cover the pieces of chicken with sauce, then add the potatoes sprinkled with chervil.

Chicken with Olives

Preparation time:	25 minutes
Cooking time:	1 hour
Difficulty:	★

Serves 4

3 onions
4 young chickens, 350 g/³/₄ lb apiece
1 pinch saffron
red food coloring
10 sprigs cilantro, chopped
salt

4 cloves garlic, chopped
150 ml/²/₃ cup peanut oil
1 cinnamon stick
1 tsp black pepper
200 g/2 sticks butter
1 pinch ginger
500 ml/2 cups cold water
4 preserved lemons
300 g/11 oz marinated red olives

This recipe for *m'qalli*, Chicken with Olives and Preserved Lemons, is one of the most traditional dishes in all of Moroccan cuisine. Usually, the chicken is cleaned in water and vinegar, then marinated in a flavorful *chermoula* sauce made with fresh coriander (cilantro), garlic and saffron. The chicken is braised in this sauce.

Served on a nicely decorated ceramic plate, often a tajine, which has a conical lid that looks like a pointed hat, the succulent chicken *m'qalli* blends the spicy flavors of its sauce with the slightly bitter taste of the olives and preserved lemons. Chicken and lamb are the two most widely used meats in Morocco. They are often cooked on skewers, or used to fill small fried triangles of pastry called *briouates*. In chicken *t'faya*, the meat is served on a bed of couscous and smothered in a sauce of caramelized raisins and onions.

Preserved lemons are one of the most typical Moroccan ingredients. Lemons are cut into quarters, marinated in brine and then sealed in jars. They need to stand at least two months before using them in tajines, especially with fish. Nowadays, some cooks drain and blanch the lemons to take away some of the bitterness before adding them to the chicken. Traditional cooks, though, still place them directly in with the chicken, adding a great deal of salt as well.

The red olives used by our chef are picked just before they turn black, which means that they are completely mature. Little incisions are made in them before they are crystallized and placed in the marinade with lemon juice. Moroccans eat these olives with salads, fish and tajines. The olives and lemons give the chicken an unmistakeable Oriental style.

1. Peel the onions and chop them. Clean the chickens. Remove and discard the feet and the tips of the wings.

2. In a bowl, mix together the saffron, red food coloring and some of the coriander, salt and garlic. Moisten with 100 ml/7 tbsp of the peanut oil. With your hands, take a little of the sauce from the bowl and spread it completely over the chickens.

3. In a large pot, combine the onions, cinnamon, ginger, pepper, butter and the rest of the peanut oil, coriander, garlic and salt. Add the chickens. Cook uncovered for 20 minutes, frequently turning the chicken in the sauce.

and Preserved Lemons

4. Pour 500 ml/2 cups cold water into the pot with chicken. Cover and simmer for 30 minutes over medium heat.

5. Blanch the olives for 5 minutes. Slice the preserved lemons into quarters. In another pot, cook the olives and lemon quarters with the cooking juices from the chicken over medium-high heat for 4 to 5 minutes.

6. Remove the chickens with a skimmer and arrange on a serving plate. Garnish with olives and lemon quarters.

Lamb Chops

Preparation time: 20 minutes
Cooking time: 30 minutes
Difficulty: ★★

Serves 4

For the stuffing:
200 g/7 oz bread, crusts removed
5 sprigs flat-leaf parsley, chopped
6 black olives, halved
1 clove garlic, minced
10 g/1½ tbsp grated pecorino cheese
2 egg yolks
1 sprig thyme
2 sprigs rosemary
salt, pepper

12 lamb chops
200 g/7 oz pork caul
olive oil

For the frittedda:
6 marinated artichokes
juice of 1 lemon
4 spring onions
3 tsp olive oil
500 g/generous 1 lb fresh beans
300 g/2 cups peas
2 tsp wine vinegar
1 tsp sugar
1 pinch nutmeg
12–15 fresh mint leaves, chopped
salt, pepper

Olive trees and herds of sheep dot the mountainous landscape of Basilicata, a province in southern Italy located between Pouilles and Calabre. The inhabitants of this region particularly enjoy oven-roasted lamb on a bed of potatoes filled with thyme and rosemary. They also prepare lamb with vegetables, which cooks for hours in an earthenware dish called a *pignata* in the fireplace. In another dish, lamb is again cooked for several hours, but surrounded with tomatoes, vegetables and many spices, until the meat is nice and tender.

Here our chef offers a lamb chop recipe from Potenza, the capital of Basilicata. The chops are delicately filled with herbs, bread and cheese and wrapped in caul fat to keep them moist. Caul, a thin, lacy layer of fat from the stomach of sheep or pigs, is what the people of Basilicata use to make stuffed scallops of lamb sweetbreads. Using caul reflects a time in

which no piece of meat, no matter how modest, was wasted. Today it is not readily available, but ask your butcher. Caul is not expensive and is easy to prepare. Before using it, soak it in a bowl of vinegar and ice water. Then rinse it under running water and spread it over a cloth to absorb the excess water. Handle it with care, as it tears easily.

To accompany the lamb chops, there is a *frittedda*, sautéed young green vegetables. It used to be a typical Sicilian recipe called *minestra di primavera*, because it celebrated the return of the spring season. It is prepared with similar sautéed vegetables throughout all of southern Italy.

You can make the same recipe with veal chops, but you would have to reduce the quantity of herbs, which would otherwise be too strong for the more delicate flavor of veal.

1. For the frittedda, remove the leaves from the artichokes. Soak the hearts in water and lemon juice. For the stuffing, crumble the bread. Combine the bread, half the chopped parsley and olives, the garlic, cheese, egg yolks and seasonings, and mix well.

2. Place the lamb chops on a chopping board. Spread a spoonful of stuffing on each lamb chop.

3. Place a sprig of parsley and half an olive on each lamb chop. Wrap each chop in a piece of caul fat.

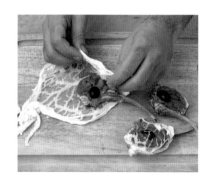

Potentina

4. For the frittedda, thinly slice the onions. In a frying pan, heat the olive oil and brown the onions for 5 minutes. Cut the artichoke hearts in thin slices and add them to the pan.

5. Shell the beans and then add them to the frying pan with the peas. Pour over a little water, cover, and cook for about 12 minutes.

6. Sear the lamb chops in a pan with olive oil. Put the vegetables in with the meat. Add the vinegar, some lemon juice, sugar, nutmeg, mint leaves, olive oil, salt and pepper. Cook for 12 minutes. Serve the lamb chops over a bed of green vegetables.

Venison Chops with

Preparation time: 30 minutes
Cooking time: 1 hour
Difficulty: ★

Serves 4

For the goat cheese custard:
100 ml/7 tbsp milk
100 g/3¹/₂ oz goat cheese
350 ml/1¹/₂ cups light cream
3 egg yolks
salt
pepper

20 g/1 tbsp honey
200 g/7 oz bilberries or small blueberries

For the venison chops:
oil
coarse salt
4 venison chops
2 shallots, chopped
100 ml/7 tbsp balsamic vinegar
200 ml/generous ³/₄ cup game stock
50 g/3¹/₂ tbsp butter
thyme

Nearly 80% of Sweden is covered with forests, mountains, lakes, bogs and other rugged terrain. This landscape accounts for the many elk (*älg*), stag (*hjort*), bucks (*rådjur*) and hares (*hare*) throughout the country.

Hunting, although strictly regulated, has grown in popularity among Swedes in recent years. Life slows down for hunters during the three week time period in October that is devoted to elk hunting. Hunters also bag woodcocks, pheasants and many types of wild ducks. In the south, people who own castles and large tracts of land have private hunting grounds that are fenced off from outsiders.

Combining venison chops with goat cheese custard may seem absurd in Sweden. According to our chef, though, the production of local cheeses is growing. Until the 1980s, the Swedes ate hard cheese made from cow's milk.

Small-scale producers of goat cheese have appeared in recent decades, notably on the island of Gotland. For this recipe, our chef prefers to use cheese from Borgvattnet, in the north of Sweden. As far as the variety of cheeses goes, there are even some farmers on the Kattegatt coast who produce a Roquefort-type of blue cheese from their sheep's milk.

The Swedes have been profiting from *allemansrätten* (every man's right) for a long time now. This right of free access to nature allows anyone to walk through woods and meadows and to pick mushrooms, berries or flowers without having to ask permission from the landowner. In autumn, many families hurry to the nearest woods to search for bilberries, blackberries and blueberries.

Bilberries, something like tiny, tart blueberries, are often stewed or made into jellies or sauces. Our chef also likes to use this berry when making parfaits, ice cream, Bavarian cream and crème brulée.

1. Warm the milk in a saucepan and crumble the goat cheese. Take the milk off the heat and add the goat cheese a little at a time. Whisk until the cheese is melted.

2. Mix the cream and egg yolks in a bowl. While whisking, add the milk and cheese. Stir rapidly to preventing the eggs from cooking, and add salt and pepper.

3. Pour the honey over half of the bilberries in a small saucepan. Stir with a spoon for 2 to 3 minutes over low heat.

Goat Cheese Custard

4. Place the warm bilberries in individual ramekins. Fill them with the goat cheese mixture. Cook in a waterbath in the oven at 120°C/250°F for 30 minutes.

5. Oil a grill pan and sprinkle with sea salt. Heat the pan and grill the venison chops for 1½ minutes on each side. In a pot, mix together the shallots, balsamic vinegar and game stock and bring to the boil.

6. Reduce the sauce by half, until syrupy. Thicken with the butter. Sauté the remaining bilberries with thyme over medium-high heat. Place the chops on plates with a ramekin of goat cheese custard. Top the meat and custard with bilberries.

Chicken

Preparation time: 30 minutes
Cooking time: 2 hours 25 minutes
Soaking time: overnight
Difficulty: ★★

Serves 6

250 g/1¼ cups chickpeas
250 g/scant 2 cups raisins
1 kg/2¼ lb onions
2 tomatoes
1 chicken, about 1.5 kg/3¼ lb
200 ml/generous ¾ cup vegetable oil

grated nutmeg
1 tsp ground ginger
1 pinch saffron
1 tsp salt
½ tsp white pepper
red food coloring
250 g/1 cup + 2 tbsp sugar
100 g/7 tbsp unsalted butter
½ tsp cinnamon
1¼ tsp gum arabic powder
1 kg/6 cups couscous
50 g/3½ tbsp salted butter

The chicken couscous dish known as *T'faya* is one of the most succulent dishes, an uncommon and satisfying blend of sweet and savory. The chicken, cooked in butter spiced with saffron, is served with couscous and a sauce made of onions and raisins strongly perfumed with cinnamon.

Traditionally a Friday dish, couscous has an infinite number of varieties. Couscous, usually made from hard wheat, can also be made from barley or corn. Lamb couscous with seven vegetables is one of the most common dishes (see preceding pages), but it is not unusual to find couscous prepared with chicken and olives, chicken and prunes, or any number of other combinations. There is also *sekkouk*, which is topped with whey; *medfoun*, which hides under a layer of lamb with onions and raisins; *baddaz* couscous with Essaouira and Safi fish; couscous from the Sahara with fresh figs; or *seffa*, which is sweet couscous sprinkled with powdered sugar and cinnamon.

Moroccan chickens, like those in Europe, are raised industrially. There are, however, also farm-raised chickens, called *beldi*. The city of Fez is renowned for its chicken *m'qalli* with olives and preserved lemon (see page 676). Fowl is also used in the filling for *b'steeya* meat pie, or on kebabs.

The raisins used here come from vineyards in Meknes and Agadir, which produce both golden raisins and sultana raisins. They are put into the couscous and *t'faya* alike. For the Muslim New Year and Aid el Miloud (the holiday that celebrates the birth of the Prophet Mohammed) Moroccans prepare large platters filled with raisins, walnuts, apricots, prunes, almonds and cashews.

You can make this recipe with either lamb or beef, in addition to poultry. Truly original, however, is when the people of Safi make it with conger eel.

1. The night before, soak the chickpeas and raisins in cold water. The day of the meal, poach the chickpeas for 30 minutes and then peel them if necessary. Peel and cut the onions into thin slices. Grate the tomatoes.

2. Place the chicken on a cutting board. Cut it in half lengthwise to separate it into 2 pieces, then cut it in 4.

3. In a large pot, mix together the chicken, 1 sliced onion, tomatoes, oil, nutmeg, ginger and saffron. Salt and pepper to taste. Pour in 1 liter/1 quart water, then cover and cook for 30 minutes.

T'faya

4. Tip the remaining onions into another pot and add ¹/₂ glass of water. Sprinkle with food coloring and cook for 5 minutes over low heat.

5. Add the sugar, unsalted butter, most of the raisins, cinnamon, nutmeg and gum arabic. Mix with a wooden spoon for 15 to 20 minutes over low heat, until the onions have a nice caramel color.

6. On a plate, work the couscous with your hands, adding the salted butter and 350 ml/ 1¹/₂ cups water. Steam three separate times for 20 minutes each. Place the couscous on a serving plate. Garnish with the rest of the raisins and top with the chicken and sauce. Sprinkle with chickpeas.

Daoud

Preparation time: 40 minutes
Cooking time: 1 hour 5 minutes
Difficulty: ★★

Serves 6

3 cloves garlic
500 g/generous 1 lb onions
1/2 bunch parsley
500 g/generous 1 lb lean ground beef
1/2 tsp salt
1/2 tsp pepper

1 tsp ground cinnamon
200 ml/generous 3/4 cup oil
500 g/2 1/2 cups long grain rice
2 ripe tomatoes, diced
70 g/ 1/4 cup tomato paste
1.2 liters/5 cups cold water
100 g/3–4 oz vermicelli
1/2 tsp dried mint, crumbled

While already renowned for their own cuisine, the Lebanese also have a wonderful knack for integrating recipes that originated in other cultures, such as Turkish, into their own. And that is the case with these succulent meatballs, the favorite dish of a Turkish general named Daoud Bacha, who governed Mount Lebanon during the rule of the Ottoman Empire. Nowadays, this dish is often prepared for receptions, alongside other meat and fish.

There is also an Egyptian variation called "Daoud Bacha meatballs". Despite the similarity in their names, however, the Egyptian dish differs in that the ground meat is flavored with coriander, aniseed and allspice. The meatballs are also larger in Egypt than in Lebanon.

Traditionally, the cooking juices are kept to be served in a soup bowl alongside the serving platter, but one can also simply pour some of the juice over the serving dish, or even thicken the juice with a little flour. To bring out the flavor of the vermicelli and rice, just add a pat of cold butter.

Different types of meat can be used to make the meatballs. Beef, lamb or a combination of the two work perfectly. Poultry should be avoided, however. It is also essential to use flat-leaf parsley for the garnish. It should be chopped finely by hand with a chef's knife, leaving the stems intact.

Daoud Bacha can be served with *arak*, an alcoholic drink made from aniseed. Our chef also suggests red wine, such as Kefraya or Château Musar.

1. Cut 1 garlic clove in thin slices, and finely chop 1 onion and the parsley. On a wooden cutting board, mix the meat with the onion, half of the garlic clove and the parsley. Add the salt, pepper and cinnamon.

2. Shape the meat into small meatballs (about 1 tsp each). Heat 100 ml/7 tbsp of the oil in a frying pan and cook the meatballs for 10 minutes until they are nicely browned.

3. Soak the rice in cold water. Cut the remaining onions into thin slices and dice them. Brown the onions and remaining garlic in 50 ml/3 1/2 tbsp oil. Add the tomatoes and tomato paste, then the meatballs.

Bacha

4. Pour in 600 ml/2 ½ cups cold water, stir, and cook for 15 minutes over low heat.

5. Heat the remaining 50 ml/3 ½ tbsp oil. Brown the vermicelli in the oil until golden brown. Strain the rice and add to the vermicelli. Add salt and 600 ml/2 ½ cups water. Bring to the boil, cover and simmer for 30 minutes.

6. Halfway through cooking the meatballs, sprinkle the mint over the sauce. Place the meatballs in a casserole dish and serve with vermicelli rice.

Mauritian

Preparation time: 25 minutes
Cooking time: 1 hour 55 minutes
Marinating time: 30 minutes
Difficulty: ★★

Serves 4

500 g/generous 1 lb lamb shoulder
salt
pepper
250 g/9 oz potatoes
2 onions
4 cloves garlic, chopped

3 g/1 tbsp crushed fresh ginger
½ tsp cumin powder
1 tbsp dried thyme
2 tbsp oil
1 cinnamon stick
2 cloves
2 cardamom pods
2 green chili peppers, crushed
4 tomatoes
1 pinch saffron
3–4 fresh mint leaves
1 sprig fresh chervil

The inhabitants of Mauritius are especially fond of casseroles, a tradition with origins in the French colonial period from 1721 to 1814. Hindus, who do not eat beef, make this dish with lamb, and Muslims (many of whom are of Hindu origin) make theirs with *halal* meat. Vegetarians replace the meat with soy when preparing this dish.

While sheep are raised on Mauritius, they are not enough to meet local demand, so the island must import sheep from the large populations raised in Australia and New Zealand. Mauritians especially like lamb when it is prepared as a stew with curry, grilled as chops, or *biryani*-style: in this recipe, which comes from northern India, the meat is cooked with rice and vegetables and seasoned with a blend of saffron, cinnamon and cardamom.

Strong-tasting chili peppers are harvested throughout the year on the island of Mauritius. They are pickled in brine, then pre-

served in oil with garlic and ginger, and make a wonderful addition to curries. Our chef, Vivek Ramdenee, often fries his green chili peppers, which are only moderately strong. He also stuffs them with seafood and serves them as an appetizer.

Cinnamon was introduced to the islands of Mauritius and Réunion in the 1770s by the intendant Pierre Poivre. Cinnamon is derived from a small tree in the laurel family, and can reach a height of 5 to 6 meters (16–23 feet) in hot and humid regions. The eight to ten lateral branches that extend from the base of the plant are cut after three years of growth, then peeled, dried and rolled into long sticks. The most famous cinnamon comes from Sri Lanka.

Our chef serves this lamb and rice casserole with a salad, chutney, tomatoes, mangos and Indian bread.

1. Cut the lamb shoulder into large cubes and remove the bones. Salt and pepper the meat. Peel the potatoes and cut in quarters. Place them in a bowl of cold water and set aside. Peel and quarter the onions.

2. Combine the garlic, ginger and half of the cumin and thyme. Coat the meat thoroughly with this mixture and marinate for 30 minutes.

3. Heat the oil in a pot. When it is hot, sear the lamb for 5 minutes until it starts to brown. Add the onions and cook for another 10 minutes.

Lamb Casserole

4. When they are golden brown, add the cinnamon stick, cloves, cardamom, chili peppers and the remaining cumin and thyme. In a food processor, blend the tomatoes with the saffron and add to the pot. Cook for 35 to 40 minutes.

5. Rinse the mint and chervil. Dry them and chop finely. Add to the meat. Cook for another 35 to 40 minutes.

6. Add the potatoes to the pot. Cook for another 15 minutes, until the vegetables are tender. Serve hot.

Sultan's

Preparation time: 35 minutes
Cooking time: 1 hour 20 minutes
Difficulty: ★★

Serves 6

2 medium onions
2 cloves garlic
3 tbsp butter
1 kg/2¼ lb leg of lamb
1 small green bell pepper
2 large tomatoes

1½ tsp salt
½ tsp peppercorns

1.5 kg/3¼ lb eggplant
oil to deep-fry

1 liter/1 quart milk
50 g/3½ tbsp butter
50 g/⅓ flour
1 pinch grated nutmeg
salt
pepper
20 g/3 tbsp hard cheese, grated

The Topkapi Palace in Istanbul, residence of the sultans, has been a splendid breeding ground for Turkish gastronomy. This particular recipe is called *hünkar beğendi* in Turkish, which means "Sultan's Delight" or "Sultan's Favorite". Around 1865, the empress Eugénie, wife of Napoléon III, visited the sultan Abdul Aziz and was so impressed with this dish that she sent her chef to obtain the precise recipe from the sultan's chef. But he came back empty-handed: "A great chef only requires his heart, his eyes and his nose", the Turkish chef is said to have responded to the request.

This mouth-watering dish made for the sultan is just one that demonstrates the sensual side of Turkish gastronomy, evident in the names: a "Maiden's Navel" is served with "Vizier's Fingers", "Luscious Lips" and the "Afflicted Imam" (even a religious person succumbs to delicious eggplant…).

Turkish people also use several terms of endearment that evoke different foods, such as "my little baklava" and "my little Turkish delight".

According to our chef, the meat with tomatoes and peppers gives the Sultan's Delight quite a different flavor than the eggplant purée served with salad. The béchamel sauce gives it a smooth texture.

There are three different ways to prepare the eggplant, but the inside should always be puréed. The first is to cut it in half, slit its skin with a knife, and roast it for 30 minutes in a hot oven. The second method consists of grilling the eggplant on a charcoal grill. The third method involves deep-frying the whole eggplant in hot oil.

When the meat stew is finished, you can sprinkle the entire dish with chopped parsley or crushed thyme.

1. Peel and chop the onions and garlic. In a large pot, brown the onions and garlic in butter for 2 to 3 minutes. Cut the lamb into cubes and add it to the onions. Brown for 15 minutes while stirring.

2. Dice the pepper and tomatoes and add to the meat. Mix together over low heat, then add salt and pepper. Fill halfway with water and cook for about 45 minutes.

3. For the eggplant purée, heat a pot of oil. Using a metal strainer, place the eggplant in the oil. Fry for about 5 minutes, until the skin is somewhat soft.

Delight

4. Bring the milk to the boil. In another pot, melt the butter and stir in the flour. Pour on the hot milk and stir for about 15 minutes over low heat into a smooth béchamel sauce. Season the sauce with nutmeg, salt and pepper.

5. Remove the eggplant from the oil. Grate the skin with the tip of a small knife. Slit the eggplant open to remove the seeds from the center. In a bowl, mash it with a fork to make a purée.

6. Add the eggplant to the béchamel sauce. Mix rapidly and sprinkle with the cheese, then mix a second time. Pour the sauce on a plate and top with the meat.

Thanksgiving

Preparation time: 2 hours
Cooking time: 4 hours 20 minutes
Difficulty: ★★★

Serves 12

1 turkey, 6–7 kg/13–15 lb
fresh sage
fresh marjoram
fresh thyme
fresh rosemary
115 g/$^1/_2$ cup unsalted butter, melted

For the cornbread stuffing:
300 g/generous 2 cups flour
350 g/2$^1/_2$ cups fine cornmeal
4 tsp active yeast

220 g/1 cup butter
1 tsp salt
100 g/7 tbsp sugar
2 eggs

500 ml/2 cups milk
225 g/8 oz sweet sausage
3 stalks celery
7 leeks
100 g/7 tbsp butter
salt, pepper
200 g/scant 2 cups pecans
4 sprigs parsley
500 ml/2 cups broth
200 g/2 cups fresh cranberries
55 g/$^1/_4$ cup white sugar

For the gravy:
1 large onion
40 g/5 tbsp flour
1 liter/1 quart turkey broth
125 ml/$^1/_2$ cup dry white wine

Every year, on the third Thursday in November, American families get together for a traditional meal that celebrates one of the biggest holidays of the year: Thanksgiving. This occasion is held in remembrance of the meal in 1621 when the newly arrived European settlers offered food in gratitude to the Native American Indians who helped them survive the first harsh winter there. Since Thanksgiving is neither religious nor related to any specific person or military victory, it is celebrated by nearly all ethnicities across the United States. On this special occasion, family members often travel hundreds of miles to be together. The huge feast, which is usually eaten in the afternoon, includes a stuffed and roasted turkey with thick gravy, cranberry sauce, sweet potatoes with marshmallow or mashed potatoes, pearl onions and green beans with bacon pieces. And for dessert, they invariably serve a pumpkin pie.

For Thanksgiving, it is common to cook an enormous turkey that could feed twenty people or more. In the evening, those who grow hungry again can use the leftover turkey to make delicious hot or cold sandwiches.

The turkey stuffing is usually made of pieces of bread, meat, vegetables and dried fruit. Our chef, wanting to stick to tradition, has used croutons made with home-baked cornbread. You can also serve the turkey with stuffing on the side.

1. Tie the turkey legs together. Put some fresh sage, marjoram, thyme and rosemary inside the turkey. Baste the bird with the melted butter. For the stuffing, prepare a cornbread: combine the flour, cornmeal, yeast, butter, salt and sugar in a bowl.

2. Beat the eggs in the milk and add to the preceding mixture. Mix the dough well and turn it into a pan lined with buttered parchment paper. Bake in the oven at 180°C/350°F for 50 minutes. Let it cool and cut it into cubes.

3. Peel the sausage. Chop the celery and leeks and brown them in butter. Mash the sausage and add to the pan. Salt and pepper. Brown for a moment. Roast the pecans in the oven and then chop them. Snip the parsley. Mix all the ingredients with the broth and the croutons. Cool.

Turkey

4. In a saucepan, cook the cranberries with the sugar until the berries pop open and begin to thicken. Add this to the previous mixture and blend well.

5. Using a spoon, fill the turkey with the stuffing. Salt and pepper the turkey. Roast in a hot oven for at least 3 hours, depending on the weight of the bird.

6. Chop the onion and brown it in the juice remaining from the cooked turkey. Add flour and make a roux. Dilute it with hot broth. Cook and stir. Add white wine, reduce and then season this gravy with salt and pepper. Serve the turkey with the gravy and stuffing.

Veal on Rösti,

Preparation time:	45 minutes
Cooking time:	55 minutes
Chilling time, potatoes:	overnight
Difficulty:	★★

Serves 4

For the Rösti:
1 kg/2¼ lb potatoes
200 g/1 cup lard
salt
pepper

400 g/14 oz veal fillet
250 g/9 oz veal kidney
150 g/scant 2 cups mushrooms, quartered
100 g/²/₃ cup flour
100 g/scant ¾ cup chopped shallots
100 ml/7 tbsp dry white wine
200 ml/generous ¾ cup veal stock
200 ml/generous ¾ cup crème fraîche
or light cream
oil

Cows—especially wearing cow bells and roaming the Alps—are one of the things typically associated with Switzerland. There are cattle everywhere, even just outside the major cities. In Valais, the cattle herds climb as high as 2,000 meters (6,500 feet) and cheese is produced high up in the mountains. Around October, the farmers bring their herds back down into the valleys for the winter.

The Swiss are expert at preparing excellent veal or beef dishes. In the country, veal is made into stuffed scallops, or cooked in cream, Swiss-German style. Depending on your taste, the veal dish presented here may or may not include veal kidneys.

The dish prepared by our chef simply had to be accompanied by *Rösti*, which is pronounced "reushty". These marvelous hash browns used to be standard breakfast fare for the French-speaking Swiss not long ago. The hash browns are placed in the middle of the table and eaten communally. Some people even dip a little in their coffee! Today, each town has its own *Rösti* specialty. They are served with bacon and local cheeses in Appenzell, with onions in Bale, and with bacon pieces in Bern and Schabziger in the canton of Glarus. On the other hand, people from Ticino use bacon cubes and rosemary, while in Zurich you'll find chopped onions and cumin. Once the potatoes have been grated, the grease works its way in, giving them a nice, golden color. To prevent the *Röstis* from becoming soggy or mashed, boil the potatoes the night before the meal. This way, they can completely dry in their skins before they are grated.

Rolling the kidneys in flour, which thickens the sauce, is optional. It all depends on how you like your sauce.

1. To make the Rösti, boil the potatoes in their skins for 30 minutes. Let them cool in the refrigerator overnight. Peel and grate them over a plate.

2. Heat the lard in a frying pan. Add the potatoes and salt and pepper them. Flatten the potatoes to make one large, uniform "pancake". Cook each side for 8 minutes.

3. Place the veal fillets on a chopping board. Cut them into long thin slices with a sharp knife. Set aside.

Zurich-Style

4. Place the veal kidneys on a chopping board. Remove any excess fat and cut the kidneys into thin slices. Dredge them in flour.

5. Sauté the veal in oil and remove from the pan. Repeat with the kidneys, shallots and mushrooms. Deglaze the pan with the white wine, veal stock and crème fraîche. Add the mushrooms to the sauce and let it thicken for 5 minutes.

6. Place the hot Rösti on a serving plate. Stir the meats together and add the shallots. Top this mixture with sauce and serve.

Eléni's

Preparation time: 45 minutes
Cooking time: 2 hours 20 minutes
Difficulty: ★★

Serves 3 or 4

1 shoulder of lamb
3 cloves garlic
200 ml/generous ¾ cup olive oil
dried oregano

salt
pepper
1 eggplant
1 kg/2¼ lb potatoes
4 carrots
1 zucchini
2 lemons
1 bunch parsley
4 cups cold water

On his restaurant's menu, our chef calls this recipe "Mama's Shoulder of Lamb", in homage to his mother, Eléni. This dish used to be made on Sundays in his hometown of Platanorema, Macedonia. The wonderful aroma of the lamb roasting in the oven made everyone within smelling distance want to eat it right away.

When Konstantinos Stamkopoulos was a child, many of the inhabitants of Platanorema still raised sheep in the surrounding mountains. Each family also had a goat that provided milk for the winter and a young kid for the Easter meal, and a pig that was slaughtered for Christmas. Sheep and goats adapt well to both the rocky mountains and the arid fields of Greece, which make up two-fifths of the country's landscape. Lamb is the Greeks' favorite type of meat: they especially enjoy its tender

meat cooked quite thoroughly. Lamb is also eaten for Easter, roasted whole on a spit. In the countryside, sheep's milk is made into feta and *touloumisio*, a creamy cheese that is similar to cottage cheese but stronger in flavor.

Macedonians use large, yellow-skinned potatoes grown in their region, even to make French fries. Nearby is the town of Polimilos (whose name means "many starches"), which is known throughout all of Greece for the superb quality of its potatoes. Other varieties of potatoes will taste equally good with Eléni's Shoulder of Lamb, though.

The roasting pan should be tightly covered with parchment paper and aluminum foil during cooking. Braising the meat allows it to cook well in its juices.

1. Rinse the lamb shoulder and pat it dry. Place it on a chopping board. Peel the garlic cloves and cut 2 of them into thin slices.

2. Make slits in the lamb and place the garlic pieces in the slits. Grate the remaining garlic clove over the lamb. Cover the meat with olive oil, oregano, salt and pepper.

3. Cook the meat at 180°C/350°F for 10 minutes. Turn it over and cook the other side for 10 minutes.

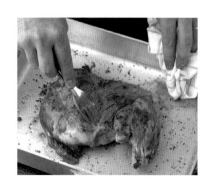

Shoulder of Lamb

4. Cut the eggplant in half lengthwise, then slice it and the potatoes. Chop the carrots and zucchini. Sprinkle the vegetables with salt, pepper and oregano.

5. Place the vegetables in the cooking dish around the lamb. Squeeze the lemons and add the juice to the meat. Chop the fresh parsley and sprinkle it over the meat and vegetables.

6. Pour water over the meat and vegetables. Place parchment paper over the meat and vegetables and then cover with aluminum foil. Bake at 180°C/350°F for 2 hours.

Roman-Style

Preparation time: 30 minutes
Cooking time: 20 minutes
Difficulty: ★★

Serves 4

500 g/generous 1 lb veal scallops, thinly sliced
50 g/¹/₃ cup flour
30 g/2 tbsp butter
salt
pepper

1 block buffalo mozzarella cheese
2 large slices Parma ham
100 ml/7 tbsp white wine
1 onion
2 zucchini
2 tbsp olive oil
3 sprigs tarragon
fine sea salt
sage leaves

Italian cooks have great ideas when it comes to cooking veal. Francesca Ciardi aims for simplicity in this recipe. Parma ham, which comes from the region of the same name, is known throughout Italy and beyond. The ham, which undergoes complex transformations, requires very particular conditions in order to achieve its unparalleled quality. It is said that the air in Parma caresses thousands of aging hams in their aerated storehouses, thus giving the meat its great aroma. Especially when thinly sliced, these hams are full of flavor.

Buffalo mozzarella, made in Campania, is often paired with Parma ham and is recognized as a cheese of exceptional quality. Its sweet flavor and soft texture are brought out nicely in this recipe as the cheese slowly melts on the stovetop, covered with aluminum foil. However, the recipe can also be made with mozzarella from cow's milk, which is more commonly sold outside of Italy.

In case these products are not available, an uncooked country ham (not too salty, though) and a mild cheese that melts well will work. White chicken meat could also replace the veal scallops.

In this recipe, the meat is flattened into delicious mouth-size bites. Francesca Ciardi cleverly uses a metal spatula, which helps prevent the meat from tearing.

While it is cooking, pour several spoonfuls of cooking juices over the scallops, ham and mozzarella so that they do not dry out. Since the Parma ham is already salty, our chef warns not to add too much salt to the scallops.

Brown the thin slices of zucchini for a moment to bring it *al dente*. Small zucchini are preferable as they take less time to cook. Browned in their skin, they remain crisp and retain their nutrients and perfect consistency.

1. Place the scallops on a cutting board. Beat each scallop as thin as possible, ideally to a thickness of 2 mm.

2. Cut the scallops into thin slices about 5 cm/2 in long. Leave them on the chopping board.

3. Tip the flour into a bowl. Using tongs, dredge each piece of meat in the flour. Brown the meat in butter in a frying pan. Salt one side of the meat, then turn over. Pepper the other side. Fry over low heat.

Veal Scallops

4. Cut the mozzarella into thin slices. Cut the Parma ham to the same size as the veal. Cover the peppered side of the veal with a piece of ham and a slice of mozzarella.

5. Pour on the white wine. Cook for 2 minutes over low heat. Cover the pan with aluminum foil, allowing the mozzarella to continue to melt.

6. Finely chop the onion. Cut the washed but unpeeled zucchini in slices. Heat the oil in a separate frying pan over medium-high heat. Add the zucchini, onion, tarragon and sea salt. Garnish with sage. Serve with the veal pieces.

Scallops and

Preparation time:	*45 minutes*
Cooking time:	*45 minutes*
Difficulty:	★★

Serves 4

200 g/7 oz pumpkin
crushed pepper
400 g/14 oz wild mushrooms
salt
400 g/1¾ cups butter
2 cloves garlic

2 shallots
4 large pickles in vinegar
1 fawn leg, bones removed
1 kg/2¼ lb potatoes
150 g/5½ oz Danish blue cheese, sliced
1 rack of fawn, cut in thin chops
1 parsnip, diced
300 ml/1¼ cups ale
200 ml/generous ¾ cup crème fraîche
500 ml/2 cups game stock
2 tbsp cranberry coulis

At the *Langelinie Pavillonen*, Charles-René Madsen's colorful fawn dish is one of his guests' favorites. The beautiful presentation includes tender fawn scallops that are filled with a mixture of shallots, garlic, mushrooms and pickles, served with a crown of potatoes and Danish blue cheese and slices of peppered pumpkin. Several drops of cranberry coulis add the perfect finishing touch.

Fawn meat is one of the most tender and flavorful types of game. When cooked, its subtle taste is not as gamey as deer meat or other types of game. Danish hunters regularly hunt deer, stag, wild duck and even pheasant and quail. There are also some farms that raise deer in Denmark.

Before cooking the rack of fawn, be sure to remove the ends of the bones and smooth down any rough edges. This will make

the final presentation all the more beautiful when it is served. When the meat has been browned in its skin, then cooked to perfection in the oven, transfer the meat to a chopping board and carefully carve the rack into individual cutlets.

Danes are avid fans of any variety of potato, and they also eat what some might consider "neglected" vegetables elsewhere. One example of these is the parsnip, from the *Umbelliferous* family, which is related to the carrot. This yellowish conical root, which has a slightly sweet taste, was already part of the ancient Greeks' diet. In this recipe, our chef uses it to flavor the meat while it is in the frying pan.

1. Peel the pumpkin, cut in thin slices, then add pepper to taste and set the pieces aside. Clean and chop the mushrooms. Melt 50 g/3½ tbsp of the butter and brown the mushrooms in it with some salt and pepper for 5 minutes.

2. Peel the garlic and shallots. Chop them and the pickles, as well. Add them to the mushrooms. Continue to sauté for 3 to 4 minutes over medium-high heat, stirring.

3. Cut scallops from the fawn leg. Place a little of the mushroom mixture in the center of each piece. Fold both sides of the scallop over the filling and then roll the meat. Secure with toothpicks.

Rack of Fawn

4. Peel and thinly slice the potatoes. Place a sheet of parchment paper and 4 small metal rings on a tray. Alternate layers of potatoes and cheese in the rings. Melt and clarify 200 g/14 tbsp butter and baste the potatoes and cheese with it. Bake at 220°C/425°F for 20 minutes.

5. Melt and clarify 50 g/3½ tbsp butter in a pot. Cook the pumpkin in it for 5 minutes. In a different pan, melt the same amount of butter and fry the fawn scallops and chops and the diced parsnip. Brown the chops in the frying pan, then roast them in a moderate oven for 5 minutes.

6. Deglaze the meat with the ale, crème fraîche and game stock. Bring this to the boil to thicken the sauce. Add the remaining butter. Arrange the scallops on top of the pumpkin slices, next to the chops and potatoes. Garnish with cranberry coulis and parsnip.

Aubrac Fillets with

Preparation time: *30 minutes*
Cooking time: *40 minutes*
Difficulty: ★★

Serves 4

4 strip steaks of beef, 200 g/7 oz each
20 g/1¹⁄₂ tbsp butter
50 ml/3¹⁄₂ tbsp oil
fine sea salt
freshly ground pepper

For the Swiss chard:
600 g/1¹⁄₄ lb Swiss chard
50 ml/3¹⁄₂ tbsp crème fraîche or light cream
30 ml/2 tbsp milk
30 g/1 oz Roquefort cheese
20 g/1¹⁄₂ tbsp butter

For the Porto reduction:
250 ml/1 cup Porto (port wine)
50 ml/3¹⁄₂ tbsp balsamic vinegar

Steer raised in Aubrac are not dumb. Ever conscious of their reputation, they are very aware of what they eat before they themselves are eaten. This breed of cattle, which produces a red meat of high quality and robust flavor, is native to the plains of the Massif Central, northeast of Aveyron, France. This ancient breed of cow has a coat that varies from the color of wheat to whitish gray. The outsides of its ears and the hairs on its tail are both black. More than a century before the French Revolution of 1789, monks from the Benedictine abbey of Aubrac were selectively breeding the best of these animals to improve the race.

When preparing this recipe, watch the reduction of the Porto and balsamic vinegar carefully to be sure it remains a syrupy juice. If this is your first attempt to tie meat, you may want to use a "butcher's-style" kitchen string. No one can expect miracles and there is no need to burden yourself with unnecessarily high expectations. Remove the string from the meat after it is cooked, before slicing it.

Measure out the ingredients for the Roquefort sauce precisely so that no one flavor overshadows the others. The sea salt and peppercorns are crushed and sprinkled over the meat just before serving so that they do not interfere, either.

The cooking time for the meat will vary depending on whether it is preferred rare or well done. We recommend keeping the freshly cooked meat at room temperature for thirty minutes; or better, wrap it separately in aluminum foil. It will thus have time to rest after the cooking and the juice will spread evenly throughout the meat, producing a delicious, tender meal.

1. Remove the stems from the Swiss chard. Wash them and chop into small sticks. Roughly chop the leaves. Cook the leaves in 2 liters/2 quarts salted water, and then the stems for 15 minutes. Strain both.

2. Reduce the Porto and vinegar to a syrup for 10 minutes over medium-high heat. In another pan, bring the crème fraîche, milk and chunks of Roquefort to the boil, stirring. Remove from the heat and keep hot.

3. Slice the meat into 2 pieces. In a very hot frying pan, sear the meat in butter and oil. Flip them over quickly. Once seared on both sides, keep over low heat.

Swiss Chard in Roquefort

4. Combine the Swiss chard stems and Roquefort cream in a saucepan. Reheat the Swiss chard leaves in some water and 20 g/1½ tbsp butter. Season and keep hot.

5. With a sharp knife, slice each piece of meat into long thin strips 3 cm/1 in wide.

6. Arrange 2 to 4 slices of meat on each plate, sprinkle with crushed sea salt and pepper, and add some Swiss chard and Roquefort sauce.

Venison with

Preparation time:	1 hour	
Cooking time:	1 hour	
Difficulty:	★★★	

Serves 4

100 ml/7 tbsp oil
salt
freshly ground pepper
800 g/1³/₄ lb venison fillets
100 g/3–4 oz (4 slices) bacon
1 dozen juniper berries
50 g/3¹/₂ tbsp butter
100 g/3–4 oz button mushrooms
100 g/3–4 oz black chanterelles

100 g/3–4 oz oyster mushrooms
100 g/3–4 oz pieds de mouton mushrooms
(also called hedgehog mushrooms)

For the walnut brioche:
55 g/6 tbsp flour
25 g/2 tbsp baker's yeast
250 ml/1 cup milk
125 g/4–5 oz small potatoes,
boiled and mashed
85 g/scant ²/₃ cup shelled hazelnuts
2 eggs
butter for the mold

For the mustard sauce:
500 ml/2 cups venison stock
2 slices bacon
4 tsp mustard seeds
4 tsp bilberry or blueberry jelly

Marcel Vanic has put together a tempting blend of tender venison fillets in mustard, wild pan-fried mushrooms, and brioche with hazelnuts.

In Austria, these small, light pieces of brioche are called *Buchteln*. They used to be eaten for dessert with sugar and vanilla sauce. With the addition of the baker's yeast, the dough will rise and can be divided into balls and placed in small cups. These are browned in the oven.

In contrast to the *Buchteln* prepared for dessert, our chef has added some mashed potatoes to the dough (in addition to the flour), which will give some heft to the mixture and make the brioche a little more substantive. You can roast the dry hazelnuts on a pan or under a broiler. If the dough is still too moist, just add more walnuts or flour.

Stag and deer are highly prized game in Austria. Our chef always buys his meat from hunters in order to obtain the highest quality. When selecting venison fillets, they should be very fresh but not gamey, which would become too starchy when cooked. Frozen game can be used because it is sure to have been frozen immediately after being butchered. Simply let it thaw in the refrigerator before preparing it.

Marcel Vanic prepares his mustard seed sauce in advance. He washes the dry seeds, then soaks them in lukewarm water for an hour and a half or so. He then cooks them in fresh water from an hour to 90 minutes.

He also uses a specific bilberry jelly. This fruit grows wild throughout much of Europe and is gathered from the forest with large rakes. Combined with crystallized sugar, the berries are stirred for one day and kept cold until they have the consistency of jam. They are closely related to blueberries, which can be used in their stead with wonderful results.

1. For the brioches, stir together the flour and crumbled yeast in a bowl. Pour in the lukewarm milk. Whisk thoroughly. Briefly heat the oven, then open the oven door and place the bowl on the door to start the process of fermentation, then place it on the stovetop and let rise.

2. During this time, roast the hazelnuts in the oven. Blend them in a food processor. Add the potatoes (boiled and mashed), hazelnuts and eggs to the yeast mixture. Whisk thoroughly. Cover with a cloth and let it double or triple in size near the heat.

3. Sprinkle some flour on one hand. With the other hand, take a spoonful of dough and form it into a ball. Place 3 or 4 balls into buttered cups or muffin tins. Cover and let rise again. Bake in the oven at 180°C/350°F until golden brown.

Hazelnut Brioche

4. Heat some oil in a pan. Add the salted and peppered venison fillets, chopped bacon and juniper berries. Start cooking on the stovetop, then continue in the oven. Add some butter while cooking.

5. Reheat the stock obtained from the venison. Cook the pieces of bacon in another pan. Add the stock, mustard seeds and bilberry jelly to the pan with the bacon.

6. Clean the mushrooms and sauté them in a pan with oil. Season them with salt, pepper and chopped parsley. Serve the venison fillets with a hazelnut brioche, berry jelly and mustard sauce.

Jacques Brel

Preparation time: 1 hour 20 minutes
Cooking time: 50 minutes
Difficulty: ★★

Serves 4

For the meat:
100 g/7 tbsp butter
600 g/1¼ lb suckling pig fillet

For the garnish:
1 large head Savoy cabbage
1 bunch red radishes
1 tsp baking soda

50 g/3½ tbsp butter
pepper
1 pinch nutmeg

For the sauce:
50 ml/3½ tbsp gin
500 ml/2 cups veal stock
250 ml/1 cup crème fraîche
6 juniper berries
salt
pepper
2 tbsp Ghent mustard

For the decoration:
5 sage leaves

Pierre Fonteyne preserves a touching memory of Jacques Brel in this recipe. He pays homage to the "great Jacques", author-composer, lyrical songwriter and singer, by describing his favorite "country food".

It was during a film shoot that the singer, who had a great appreciation for fine cuisine, set foot in Pierre Fonteyne's restaurant. As they shared drinks, good food and song, these piglet fillets were born in the composer's imagination. The cook takes care of the cooking with his loving partner, the recipe. The tenderness of suckling pig fillets is due to their delicate pink skin. Suckling pig has been a choice dish since the Middle Ages. If piglet fillets or suckling pig are unavailable, use pork tenderloin, which is actually the most tender cut of meat. Veal or lamb, which have a stronger taste, can also be used without ruining the flavor.

The red radishes and green kale go well together. Since radishes are Belgium's primary crop, it is not surprising that Pierre Fonteyne has chosen them to go with the fillets. These round radishes, completely red, are blanched and sautéed in butter. When you buy them, they should be firm and have a bright color, just like the kale.

When the fillets' skin becomes crisp and the meat becomes pink in the oven, they are almost done. Deglaze the cooking juices in gin or *peket*, which will flavor the sauce wonderfully. The latter is a product of malted barley, wheat and oats, that is flavored with juniper berries and has a strong 46-proof. According to legend, it was drunk already in Charlemagne's time and has been bought and sold in Flanders since the sixteenth century.

1. For the garnish, slice the cabbage in half. Remove the white stalk. Finely chop each half. Poach for 15 minutes in salted water. Strain and keep to the side.

2. Remove the stems from the radishes. Blanch them for 1 minute in salted water with the baking soda, then strain. Melt the butter in a pan and fry the radishes for 5 minutes. Set aside.

3. Melt 100 g/7 tbsp butter in a frying pan. Place the meat in the hot butter and fry for 2 minutes over medium-high heat, turning. Transfer the meat to the oven and roast at 180°C/350°F for 12 minutes until pink.

Suckling Pig Fillets

4. When the meat is golden brown, remove it from the pan and keep warm. Deglaze the bottom of the pan first with the gin, and then with the veal stock. Let it reduce by ¾ over medium-high heat, stirring.

5. Away from heat, pour the crème fraîche into the pan. Add the crushed juniper berries, salt and pepper. Return to the heat and boil for 4 to 5 minutes.

6. Away from heat, add the mustard to the sauce. Whisk to thicken. Reheat the cabbage in butter for 3 minutes. Add salt, pepper and grated nutmeg, and stir. Serve the meat and cabbage covered in the sauce along with the radishes, and garnish with fresh sage.

Stubica-Style

Preparation time: 30 minutes
Cooking time: 15 minutes
Marinating time, prunes: 3 to 4 hours
Difficulty: ★★

Serves 6

150 g/1 cup pitted prunes
100 ml/7 tbsp prune brandy
2 pork tenderloins
50 g/3^1/$_2$ tbsp butter

salt
pepper
1 tbsp sunflower oil
150 ml/^{2}/$_3$ cup white wine
1 tsp vegeta
200 ml/generous ^{3}/$_4$ cup crème fraîche
2 egg yolks
fresh parsley (optional)

These delicate tenderloins stuffed with prunes take their name from the city of Stubica, near Zagreb. Today Stubica is the main pork-raising city in Croatia.

Pork is an important food in Croatia, which has many meat production facilities. Croats especially like tenderloin as well as pork belly and shoulder. They often cut the meat into medallions and serve them with a creamy sauce made with mushrooms and white wine. Sliced into long narrow strips, pork cooks well in a sauce of fresh tomatoes and peppers. Lovers of dried meat, Croats also smoke fillet pieces and hang them in aerated attics to dry.

Plum trees grow primarily on the mainland of Croatia, producing plums and Ente prunes. About twenty years ago Croatia was the leading producer of prunes in Europe. Croats generally associate prunes with pork, veal and wild game. In desserts, they use the dried fruit to stuff *strudel* (rolled cakes) as well as potato *knädle*.

Our chef has flavored his prunes with an eau-de-vie locally known as *sljivovica*, but any spirit made from prunes would work for this recipe. An eau-de-vie made from grapes, similar to the Italian *grappa*, is also distilled in Croatia. Viljam Cvek also uses *Vegeta*, a strong condiment made from vegetable roots and spices. However, you can replace this with a blend of spices for the vegetable broth.

While cooking the tenderloin, be careful not to pierce the meat, which would allow the juices to escape. Serve Stubica-Style Pork Fillets with your choice of pasta.

1. Three or four hours before preparing the dish, soak the prunes in 5 tbsp spirits. Then, place the fillets on a chopping board. Use a sharpening steel to make a hole from one end of the fillet to the other, lengthwise.

2. Dice the butter. Squeeze the prunes between your fingers to remove the extra juice. Stuff each prune with a cube of butter, but reserve a few prunes for the sauce.

3. Fill the inside of the tenderloins with the stuffed prunes. Salt and pepper the tenderloins.

Pork Fillets

4. Heat oil in a large saucepan. Fry the tenderloins for several minutes until they are golden brown. Add the other prunes and moisten with 50 ml/3 1/2 tbsp water and the white wine. Sprinkle with vegeta. Cover, bring to the boil and allow to cook for 10 minutes.

5. Pour the crème fraîche over the tenderloins. Then pour on the egg yolks and 2 tsp of eau-de-vie. Stir over medium heat for 3 to 4 minutes to obtain a delicious sauce.

6. Dice the stuffed tenderloins and place them on a serving plate. Cover the plate with the prune sauce and sprinkle with chopped parsley according to taste.

Gemista

Preparation time: 30 minutes
Cooking time: 1 hour 5 minutes
Difficulty: ★

Serves 4

4 peppers
2 large onions
4 zucchini
1 bunch mint
1 bunch flat-leaf parsley
1 bunch dill

500 g/generous 1 lb ground meat
salt
pepper
6 tbsp rice
4 tomatoes
2 potatoes
olive oil

The Greeks eat stuffed zucchini, peppers and tomatoes daily, as they are a popular, economical family dish. They used to be stuffed with small vegetables and rice because meat was rare and expensive, but nowadays meat is often included in the fillings.

Zucchini is grown throughout Greece. The small varieties are cooked in lemon water and olive oil and used in salads. They are also used in ratatouille: added to eggplant, peppers, tomato sauce and basil to make a tasty stew. For this recipe you will use long, straight zucchini whose flesh is easily removed.

The peppers found in Greece are small and light green with fine skin. They are eaten stuffed, grilled, in salads, and in ratatouille. Long, fine peppers are grilled in olive oil, vinegar and garlic and eaten on the spot, or made into a sauce and added to feta. They are also stuffed with rice or meat, except during Lent, when observant Greek Orthodox are not allowed to eat meat.

The Greeks prepare many varieties of stuffing: zucchini flowers, vine leaves, or even cabbage leaves enclose delicious medleys of vegetables, beef, pork or rice. Pork gives the filling some extra taste and helps hold it together. It is served with a sauce called *avgolemono*, which is made with lemons and eggs and thickened with flour.

There will probably be stuffing left over after the vegetables are filled. This may be cooked in small portions and served along with the vegetables. These bits will absorb some of the juices from the vegetables, which will give them the same taste. The stuffing can then be served with feta cubes and a Greek salad.

1. Cut off the top section of the peppers. Remove the seeds and any extra pieces from the insides. Peel and chop the onions. Remove the insides of the zucchini. Finely chop the mint, parsley and dill.

2. Fry the onions in a frying pan with hot oil. Add the ground meat and fry for 2 to 3 minutes. Add the parsley, mint and dill. Season with salt and pepper. Cook for another 5 minutes.

3. Add the rice and 2 cups of water. Let it cook for 3 minutes.

4. Peel the tomatoes and dice them. Put them through a strainer. Add to the meat and cook for 5 minutes. Peel the potatoes and dice them.

5. Fill the peppers, tomatoes and zucchini with the meat stuffing. Place them in a pot and add the potatoes.

6. Pour in 2 or 3 cups of water and olive oil. Cook in a medium oven for 45 minutes.

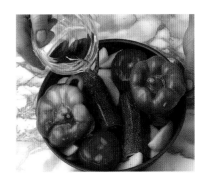

Irish

Preparation time:	45 minutes
Cooking time, stock:	1 hour 30 minutes
Cooking time, meat:	1 hour 15 minutes
Cooking time, sauce:	25 minutes
Cooking time, cabbage:	2 hours 25 minutes
Marinating time:	overnight
Difficulty:	★★★

Serves 4

1.6 kg/3^1/$_2$ lb neck of lamb

For the lamb stock:
neck of lamb offcuts
1 bouquet garni
1 large onion, halved
3 leeks, 1 clove garlic

1 bouquet garni
1 clove garlic
3 ribs celery, chopped
salt, pepper

For the vegetables for gravy:
1 kg/2^1/$_4$ lb potatoes
2–3 onions
6 leeks
butter for browning

For the cabbage:
1 red cabbage
2 onions, chopped
150 g/^{2}/$_3$ cup granulated sugar
1 bottle red wine
300 ml/1^1/$_4$ cups wine vinegar
50 g/^{1}/$_4$ cup lard
150 g/scant ^{1}/$_2$ cup red currant jelly
2 Braeburn apples, cooked

Irish Stew is Ireland's national dish. It used to be made with strong mutton, but is now more often made from one-year-old lamb that has already started feeding on rich pasture grasses.

Irish farms raise many sheep and pigs. For centuries sheep have been bred for their precious wool, while the English raised them for their butcher shops. Other regions of Great Britain are also known for their high quality of production. The Kentish lamb, raised in Kent in southern England, benefits from huge grazing pastures and generations of experience. It is also found in Wales and Scotland.

Other English recipes feature sautéed lamb with potatoes and onions, and some even like Lancashire hotpot, which is mutton cooked in beer and covered in oysters. Finally, let us not forget the famous leg of lamb with mint jelly.

The red cabbage served with this Irish Stew can be fried in lard or in oil, which is the traditional method. This cabbage is also very popular in Nordic countries' gastronomy. Other vegetables the English might serve with such a fine meal include broccoli and green cabbage or Savoy cabbage with butter. Other good sides for Irish Stew are new potatoes, pearl onion, and a sprinkling of fresh parsley or chervil.

The jelly is another English tradition. It is called jam when there are chunks of fruit still in it, and jelly when it is clear. English gardens and rural areas are full of all sorts of berries: red currants, raspberries, blackberries, elderberries, sloes and wild rose hips make exquisite jams, as well as enriching superb sauces for meat.

1. The night before, chop and dress the neck of lamb. In a large pot, stir the offcuts with the bouquet garni, halved onion, leeks and garlic. Fill with water and cook for 1 hour 30 minutes over low heat. Strain the stock and keep in the refrigerator.

2. Prepare the cabbage. Slice the red cabbage into long thin strips with a butcher's knife. Add to these the chopped onions, granulated sugar, red wine and vinegar. Leave to marinate overnight.

3. Place the dressed neck of lamb in a pot and fill with water. Bring to the boil and then strain. Return the lamb to the pot with a bouquet garni, 1 garlic clove, chopped celery, salt and pepper. Pour in the lamb stock made the night before. Cover and cook for 1 hour 15 minutes.

Stew

4. Caramelize the red currant jelly for 15 minutes. Drain the cabbage, reserving the marinade. Reduce the marinade over a medium heat for 20 minutes. Pour this into the caramelized jelly.

5. Sweat the cabbage in lard for 10 minutes. Add the jelly sauce and stir. Tip into a pot and cover with parchment paper. Put in the oven at 180°C/350°F for 1 hour 40 minutes. Remove from the oven and add the cooked apples to the cabbage.

6. For the gravy, boil and mash the potatoes. Mince the onions, leeks and celery and sweat in butter for 5 minutes. Add some stock from the cooked lamb. Blend to a cream in the pan and bring to the boil. Skim. Now blend in the mashed potatoes. Serve the lamb with gravy and cabbage garnish.

Braised Knuckle

Preparation time: 20 minutes
Cooking time: 2 hours
Difficulty: ★

Serves 4

4 knuckles of lamb
1 carrot
2 onions
¼ celeriac
thyme
rosemary

salt
pepper
2 tbsp tomato paste
500 ml/2 cups red wine
6 potatoes
4 shallots
oil

Knuckle (or fore shank) of lamb is a traditional German meal. It is less common, though, than pork and veal varieties, which are especially popular in southern Germany.

This unusual cut of lamb (which the French call the *souris*, or "mouse") is the muscular, gelatinous part that surrounds the leg bone. Cooks usually roast lamb knuckle in the oven until the meat separates from the bone, unlike a leg of lamb, which should be served rare.

In this recipe, Stefan Rottner prepares the knuckles by braising them and then serving them over a bed of small vegetables. When it is ready to be served, the meat should be tender enough that it can be eaten with a spoon, without even using a knife. According to our chef, "it is better to overcook it than to undercook". In his part of the country, people like to sprinkle it with thyme, rosemary and cumin.

You can make a strong sauce by choosing a robust wine that has a lot of personality. It is best to choose one that is rich in tannins and has a dry, fruity taste. In southern Germany, there are now thirty or forty wine producers known for the superb quality of their red wines.

These delicious potato cubes with shallots make a great side dish. It will have a hint of the flavor of the small vegetables that are added to season the meat and the sauce.

Braised Knuckle of Lamb with Shallots is not a one- or two-person dish: it is a dish made for get togethers. The longer the meat is fried, the better the sauce.

1. In a hot pan, fry the knuckles of lamb in a little oil for about 12 minutes.

2. Peel the carrot, onions, garlic and celeriac and cut all into cubes. Add the cubes to the meat along with some thyme and rosemary. Salt and pepper. Stir for 5 minutes over medium-high heat.

3. Add the tomato paste. Stir for a moment over medium-high heat.

# of Lamb with Shallots

4. Deglaze the preparation with the red wine. Fill with water. Cook in the oven at 200°C/390°F for 1 hour and 30 minutes.

5. Peel the potatoes and shallots. Cut both into cubes of similar size.

6. In hot oil, fry the shallots and salted and peppered potatoes. Serve the knuckles of lamb with their sauce, surrounded by the golden potatoes and shallots. Garnish with thyme and rosemary.

Knuckle of Veal

Preparation time:	20 minutes
Cooking time:	2 hours 40 minutes
Difficulty:	★

Serves 4

1 veal knuckle
1 carrot
1 onion
1 rib celery
1 leek
1 sprig thyme

2 bay leaves
200 g/7 oz slab smoked bacon
100 ml/7 tbsp balsamic vinegar
2 shallots
20 cloves garlic
100 g/3½ oz parsley
320 g/1½ cups butter
200 ml/generous ¾ cup chicken stock
salt
black pepper
200 g/7 oz chanterelle mushrooms, yellow

Less popular than the knuckle of pork, veal knuckle is a slow-cooked, savory dish, especially if covered (as suggested by our chef) with chopped parsley and garlic sauce.

In Sweden, beef production has increased in recent years, but is still only about one-third as much as the amount of pork produced. Veal accounts for slightly more than 5 percent of the beef consumed.

The region of Norrland produces the most meat and dairy products in all of Sweden. Several years ago, our chef bought his veal in another European country. He no longer needs to do this since he has discovered the immense array of livestock farms. Swedish veal is mainly raised in open fields. However, Swedish farmers are turning more and more to bio-intensive methods of raising livestock.

Recent statistics show that the Swedes are quite passionate about pork. They place pieces of bacon in almost everything,

along with vegetables and mushrooms, and make them into a brunoise to enrich the vinaigrette sauces that go with salads. People from southern Sweden enjoy eating a sort of soufflé with smoked and salted pork belly.

Large stretches of Sweden are covered in woodlands that are full of wild mushrooms, and Swedes therefore take advantage of the ancient law that allows them to pick mushrooms and berries freely.

And, of course, everyone has their secret "mushroom spot". Armed with their mycology manuals, families hurry to the nearest woods in the spring to gather different types of mushrooms, such as chanterelle, morel, St. George's, *coprins* and puffballs.

In the fall, mushroom-lovers go for the remaining porcini and chanterelles. There is such an abundance of mushrooms that there is never a shortage of them in our chef's restaurant.

1. In a large pot, place the knuckle of veal, the peeled carrot and onion, celery, leek, thyme and bay leaves. Fill with water. Bring to the boil, cover and cook for 2½ hours until the meat separates from the bone. During this time, slice the bacon into pieces.

2. Strain the knuckle of veal. Place it on a chopping board and chop the meat into large pieces with a chef's knife.

3. Brown the bacon in a pan with no additional fat for 5 minutes until golden-brown. Deglaze it in balsamic vinegar and set aside. Peel and chop the garlic and shallots.

in Parsley Butter

4. Bring the chicken stock to the boil with the shallots and garlic. Place the parsley and 300 g/1¹⁄₃ cups butter in a blender. Pour in the stock and blend. Season with salt and pepper.

5. Melt the remaining butter in a frying pan. Sauté the chanterelles for 5 minutes over medium-high heat.

6. Add the veal pieces to the parsley sauce, then the chanterelles (keep a handful for the garnish). Stir with a wooden spoon. Arrange all the food on serving plates with the mushrooms and bacon pieces, and serve hot.

Witloof-Style

Preparation time: 30 minutes
Cooking time, pheasant: 35 minutes
Cooking time, potatoes: 15 minutes
Difficulty: ★★

Serves 4

50 g/3¹/₂ tbsp butter
1 young hen pheasant, 1 kg/2¹/₄ lb
10 Belgian endives
1 clove garlic
2 shallots

salt
pepper
1 pinch nutmeg

For the garnish:
12 small potatoes
salt
pepper
50 g/3¹/₂ tbsp butter

Pierre Fonteyne presents an unusual combination of tastes, cooked simply to obtain an authentic cuisine. Known as *chicons* in the Walloon area of Belgium and *witloof* in Flanders, endives are a variety of chicory. They were perfected in the 1850s in the Botanical Gardens of Brussels, by an agronomist named Brezier. In 1872, the first Belgian endives were exported to France under the name "Brussels chicory".

Grown mainly in the region around Antwerp, this young endive with pale, narrow leaves is grown in the absence of sunlight in order to produce its characteristic creamy white color. Its slightly bitter taste is normal and requires some modifications: the endives must be stripped of any damaged leaves, soaked briefly in water, dried and have their stalks removed (they are the source of most of the bitterness). Chopped lengthwise, they will remain firm and whole throughout the cooking, surrounded by the hen pheasant.

Over the past century Belgians have become masters at cooking with poultry and wild game. They love to use pheasant, which is plentiful in Flemish territory. While the male pheasant lends itself to sophisticated recipes, the smaller, more tender female is perfect for simpler dishes.

For variation, Pierre Fonteyne suggests preparing this dish with woodcock or guinea fowl. However, it is difficult to replace such a bird, especially when served with delicious potatoes and butter: cooked briefly in water in their skins, these *rattes* (potatoes) keep their firm, yellow flesh.

Voilà! Three great Belgian recipes nestled together in one pot, and ready to be served.

1. Heat the butter in a cast-iron pot. Place the whole pheasant in the pot and brown on all sides. Cover. Cook for 35 minutes over low heat, basting occasionally with butter.

2. Remove hard pieces from the endives. Separate the leaves from the stalk and slice them lengthwise. Set aside in a salad bowl. Season with the garlic, snipped shallots, salt, pepper and nutmeg.

3. After the pheasant has cooked for 20 minutes, add the endives to the pot. Cover. Continue cooking for 10 minutes over medium-high heat, then 5 minutes over low heat until the endives brown.

Hen Pheasant

4. Cook the potatoes (in their skins) for 15 minutes in salted water. Cool slightly, then peel. Seasoning them with salt and pepper, then brown in a pan with butter. Leave them in the pan.

5. Place the pheasant on a chopping board. Cut off the thighs and wings at the joints. Chop the carcass in half.

6. Transfer the potatoes to the pot with the endives. Cover with the pieces of pheasant. Reheat if necessary. Serve the pheasant with endives in the pot.

Kamounia

Preparation time: 20 minutes
Cooking time: 35 minutes
Difficulty: ★

Serves 4

200 g/7 oz beef
100 g/3½ oz lamb
100 g/3½ oz beef or lamb kidney
200 g/7 oz lamb's liver
1 bay leaf
200 ml/generous ¾ cup olive oil
10 g/4 tsp ground caraway
10 g/4 tsp ground turmeric

10 g/4 tsp ground coriander
3 onions
salt
1 tbsp tomato paste
1 tomato
1 clove garlic
10 g/4 tsp ground cumin

For the garnish:
½ bunch flat-leaf parsley
1 onion
1 lemon
small, green hot peppers (optional)

Kamounia is the quintessential Tunisian stew. It is popular throughout the country, and is delicious with an assortment of meats and vegetables. Tunisians love stocking up on fresh meat: that is why *Kamounia* is traditionally prepared for large ceremonies during which a lamb is butchered to serve many guests. The meat and its giblets are supposed to give energy and vitality to young married couples, so that they can lead long and happy lives.

Another traditional *Kamounia* meal is celebrated with the family. It can be prepared the way our chef has, with slightly dried beef and kidneys. These must be washed well and have all extra membranes removed before being cut.

The liver is often purchased already sliced from a butcher's shop. It is then sliced further into long strips, diced and added

to the other meats at the end of the cooking—this will help it remain firm. However, if you can find one, it is preferable to use a whole lamb's liver, dice it into large pieces, and allow it to cook at the same time as the giblets.

Skimmed at the first boil, the water used to cook the meat is thus strained of its impurities. Seasoned with bay leaves and olive oil, it will become a spicy meat broth. Note well: the *Kamounia* sauce is best when it can be absorbed by bread, an indispensable quality for all Tunisian sauces. Cooked over low heat until the meat is thoroughly cooked, the sauce becomes red like a tomato, incorporates the caraway, and is spiced up by peeled garlic and turmeric. But the crowning moment is when the cumin infuses the delicious stew with its pungent aroma.

1. Slice the beef and lamb into large strips and then dice them into 2 cm/¾ in cubes. Remove the skin from the kidneys. Cut them in half lengthwise, then dice. Slice and then cube the liver.

2. Place the pieces of meat in 2 liters/ 2 quarts of water to cook. Add the bay leaf and the olive oil. Allow to boil.

3. When it first boils, skim the broth. Add the caraway, turmeric, coriander, chopped onions and some salt. Cook for 20 minutes, uncovered, over low heat.

4. When the meat is almost cooked, add the tomato paste, freshly chopped and peeled tomato and the crushed garlic. Cook for about 5 minutes over low heat until the meat is fully cooked. Adjust the seasoning.

5. Prepare the garnish: wash and remove stems from parsley. Peel the onion. Chop them together with a chef's knife. Set aside these condiments in a small bowl to garnish the kamounia.

6. Take the cooked meat off the heat. Add 2 good pinches of cumin. Serve in soup dishes while still hot. The parsley and chopped onions are served as a side dish or sprinkled over the kammounia. Garnish the meat with some lemon and fried hot peppers.

The Pasha's

Preparation time: 40 minutes
Cooking time: 30 minutes
Difficulty: ★★

Serves 5

For the kofta balls:
4 cloves garlic
4 onions
1 bunch flat-leaf parsley
1 bunch dill
1 bunch cilantro
1 kg/2^1/$_4$ lb lean lamb meat
salt

pepper
oil for frying

For the tomato sauce:
2 cloves garlic
1 onion
1 kg/2^1/$_4$ lb tomatoes
2 tsp caster sugar
2 tbsp tomato paste
1 tsp quatre épices (spice blend of ginger, nutmeg, white pepper and cloves)
salt
pepper
200 ml/generous ^{3}/$_4$ cup beef stock
dill

Bored with always having fancy meals, a certain Egyptian pasha began looking for a simple dish. His great effort and imagination produced some great results. He took lamb, parsley, cilantro and dill and formed them all into a ball. And thus was *kofta* born.

This famous Egyptian meal has since traveled far outside of its original borders. From Turkey to Morocco, it has been transformed according to each country's culinary tastes and preferences. The meat, which is always ground, can come from a lamb or a cow. Egyptians eat very little beef; lamb and mutton are eaten much more often. The fat is always removed from the meat before it is ground. The young lamb's flesh is the reason *kofta* is so tender.

Herbs are indispensable in making the *kofta* balls. Flat-leaf parsley is used complete with its stem so as to preserve all its vitamins. The cilantro, which is sometimes called "Chinese parsley" or "Italian parsley", enlivens all oriental cuisine with its distinctive aroma. It should be used sparingly, however since not everyone likes its strong aftertaste. The meat flavor can be enhanced instead with fine, green-plumed dill that has a slightly aniseed and lemon flavor.

Every expert chef has their own personal technique for making *kofta*. Mohamed Fawzi Kotb recommends wetting the hands before smoothing out the meat. Simply take a sufficient amount of the meat mixture in your hands and shape into a ball. It is then placed in very hot oil. When fried, the balls continue to cook slowly in the tomato sauce. A pinch of fine sugar or a sugar cube will reduce the sauce's acidity.

1. For the kofta balls, peel the garlic and onions. Wash and dry the flat-leaf parsley, dill and cilantro. Chop them separately on a chopping board along with the onions and garlic cloves.

2. Grind the lamb meat and place it in a large bowl. Season it with the prepared herbs, salt and pepper. Mash with your hands until uniformly blended.

3. Take small portions of the meat mixture in your hands and roll into small meatballs. Keep a small bowl of water nearby to moisten your hands. Place the meatballs on a large plate.

Kofta

4. For the sauce, peel and chop the garlic and onion. Purée the tomatoes in a blender. Sauté the onion in butter for 1 minute. Add the garlic, blended tomatoes, sugar, tomato paste, quatre épice, salt and pepper, then pour on the broth. Cook for 20 minutes over low heat.

5. Heat 500 ml/2 cups oil in a deep-fryer. When it is hot, add the meatballs one by one. Fry for 2 minutes. With a skimmer, remove the meatballs and place them on paper towels for 5 minutes.

6. Place the fried kofta meatballs in the tomato sauce. Heat for 5 minutes. Serve hot, garnished with dill.

Loc Lac

Preparation time: 15 minutes
Cooking time: 5 minutes
Marinating time: 20 minutes
Difficulty: ★

Serves 4

200 g/7 oz rump steak
1 tbsp potato flour
150 ml/²/₃ cup nuoc mam
pepper
oil for frying

50 ml/3¹/₂ tbsp rice wine
1 clove garlic
5–6 tbsp tomato paste
1 dash vinegar
1 dash oyster sauce
1 pinch sugar

For the accompaniment (optional):
1 head salad greens
2 or 3 large carrots
1 cucumber
white rice
lemon wedges

Loc Lac is a savory stew of diced beef flavored with tomatoes, nuoc mam, oyster sauce and rice wine. By analogy, the name reflects the game of dice, because the Vietnamese are great players and often gamble on a sheet marked with numbers from three to 18. When they shake three dice in bowls covered by a plate, it makes the noise "*loc lac*", and then they turn them over and see what numbers they've rolled. In cities, popular *Loc Lac* is served hot in the street by traveling vendors.

Our chef has enhanced the marinade with the powerful flavor of the popular nuoc mam. This amber colored sauce is made by letting small, salted fish macerate for a few months in the sun, in jars. A specialty of southern Vietnam, the very best nuoc mam comes from the island of Phu Quoc and from the city Phan Thiet.

The rice wine adds an unusual touch to the marinade. It is transparent, and can have an alcohol content of up to 30 proof.

The Vietnamese use it quite often in their cooking because there is no wine in the country. They also like to serve it as an after dinner drink.

Many Vietnamese dishes are inspired by the rich Chinese cuisine, because Vietnam was under Chinese influence for many centuries. So it is not surprising to find oyster sauce in this recipe. Of Cantonese origin, this condiment is made of fermented oysters, starch and soy sauce. It is dark brown and relatively thick.

Customarily, rice is added to the tomato sauce in *Loc Lac*, but we have served it separately for a more sophisticated presentation. This blend is not very common in Vietnamese cuisine, where it is traditional to enjoy the rice plain or with sugar. According to our chef, to do otherwise would be reminiscent of the European colonization.

1. Place the rump steak on a chopping board. With a chef's knife, slice it and then cut into cubes.

2. Put the cubes of meat in a bowl. Sprinkle with the potato flour and add a little water. Season with 100 ml/7 tbsp of the nuoc mam and pepper.

3. Pour over the oil and rice wine. Stir well, and allow to marinate for 20 minutes.

4. Heat oil in a pan with a little crushed garlic. Allow the cubes of meat to fry, turning often with a spatula, until the meat is browned but not completely cooked.

5. In a bowl, stir the tomato paste with a little cold water, vinegar, oyster sauce, 1 pinch sugar, 50 ml/3^1/$_2$ tbsp nuoc nam and the rest of the crushed garlic.

6. Heat the tomato sauce in the pan that you used to cook the meat. When it is caramelized, add the cubes of meat and allow to cook for a few minutes. Enjoy hot, accompanied by salad, vegetables or rice and lemon wedges.

Massaman

Preparation time: 1 hour
Cooking time: 40 minutes
Difficulty: ★★

Serves 4

For the fried meat:
10 lamb chops
30 ml/2 tbsp peanut oil

For the massaman sauce:
110 g/4 oz massaman curry paste
1 tsp ground coriander

1 cinnamon stick
1 tsp cardamom
1 tsp ground cumin
560 ml/2$^{1}/_{3}$ cups coconut milk
4 sweet potatoes
8 shallots
45 ml/3 tbsp fish sauce
50 ml/3$^{1}/_{2}$ tbsp tamarind juice
30 g/2 tbsp sugar
10 ml/2 tsp oil

Fired by a vast number of sauces, the favorite seasonings of gourmet Thais are red, green or yellow curry pastes. Essentially composed of small peppers, fresh seasonings and lemon grass, Thai curry pastes differ from Indian curries, which are flavored with dry spices. Cooks embellish red curry with small red peppers, shrimp paste, and the root and seeds of coriander, cumin and red shallots; green curry is tinted by green peppers, fresh cilantro (leaves, stems and roots) and lime.

Always diluted with oil, red curry enhances rice but easily takes over steamed dishes. More powerful, green curry must always be sweetened with coconut milk. There is also another curry, reddish-brown in color, reminiscent of Indian flavors. Made of dried pimentos, red shallots, ground cloves, galangal (also called Siamese ginger), lemon zest, coriander, cinnamon,

cardamom and nutmeg, *massaman* curry has character. In light of such powerful seasoning, the choice of meat is secondary in Thailand: beef, chicken or veal all work well with these spicy sauces. However, Oth Sombath prefers lamb for greater refinement.

In an easily crumbled brown pod, tamarind contains an acidic pulp. Dried or in paste, it can be soaked in hot water to extract its juice. You can replace it with lemon juice. Sweet and smooth, sweet potatoes sometimes replace rice. Those not familiar with exotic tastes may prefer classic potatoes. The *massaman* sauce will stay fresh for two days in an airtight jar. It will accompany grilled meat or cold chicken well. Fans of strong flavors enjoy the *massaman* sauce served very hot.

1. Set the lamb chops on a chopping board. French-cut them: hold the lamb chop flat on the chopping board. With the other hand, remove the excess fat at the tip of the bone. Push the meat down the bone for about 5 cm/2 in.

2. Pour the peanut oil into a pot and place over high heat. When the oil is hot, sear the lamb chops for 2 minutes on each side. Allow them to cool on a plate.

3. Place all the ingredients for the sauce in separate bowls. Place a large pot over high heat. Pour in 10 ml/2 tsp oil, then the massaman curry paste, coriander, cinnamon, cardamom and cumin. Fry for 5 min, stirring with a spatula.

Curried Lamb

4. When the blend has become red and even, add the coconut milk all at once. Stir well. Bring to the boil.

5. When it starts to boil, put the lamb chops in the sauce. Continue cooking for 5 minutes over high heat. Take out the meat and keep hot.

6. Peel and quarter the sweet potatoes. Chop the shallots. Add both to the sauce. Pour in the fish sauce and tamarind juice and add the sugar. Simmer for 25 minutes. Serve promptly with the lamb chops.

Cowboy

Preparation time: 30 minutes
Cooking time: 2 hours 10 minutes
Marinating time: 24 hours
Difficulty: ★

Serves 6

2 kg/4¹/₂ lb flank steak
2 cloves garlic
10 g/1 tbsp chopped parsley
salt
pepper

100 ml/7 tbsp olive oil
4 eggs
250 g/9 oz carrots
500 g/generous 1 lb fresh spinach
2 red bell peppers
1 pinch crushed pepper
1 pinch paprika
100 g/scant 1 cup shredded Gruyère
2 medium onions
2 bay leaves

The myth of the cowboy has indelibly marked the history of Argentina. The *gauchos*, or cowboys, traveled up and down the pampas to keep watch over their herds of free-range cattle. When they needed meat, the cowboys turned to the cows, aiming their *bolladora*, an Indian weapon made of three metal spheres linked by a braided leather straps.

In flight, the spheres move away from the center, and when the leather strap touches the cow it is immobilized immediately. The cowboy has only to approach the animal to kill it with his *faco*, a large knife carried in his belt. Afterwards, he first cuts the back of the cow to remove the shoulder, which represents the most precious piece of meat.

The *matambre*, based on shoulder steak rolled around fresh spinach, carrots and egg, often constitutes no more than a modest appetizer before grilled meat. In the past, the Indians cooked the roulade enveloped in fabric.

This way, the filling would not come out while cooking. Many Argentineans filled *matambre* with chard leaves, which are locally called *bunellos de aselga*. They are used more often than the spinach chosen by our chef to lend their color and taste to his recipe. But some people also put bacon, herbs or even peas in the filling.

The grated cheese brings a little moisture to the filling. Argentineans would use *creollo* cheese, which is made of cow's milk and firm enough to be grated. Elsewhere, Gruyère or Emmental are good choices for this recipe, as well. Argentinean dairies also sell *cremoso* cheese (a creamy paste), *mar del plata*, a semi-firm yet tender cheese, and *tafi*, which can be compared to cantal cheese. In the northwest and in the pampas, farmers who raise sheep often produce a few cheeses from the milk of ewes.

1. Spread the steak on a large chopping board. Using a small, sharp knife, clean the surface of the meat, removing all skin.

2. Place the steak in a shallow baking pan. Sprinkle with the finely chopped garlic, chopped parsley, salt and pepper. Sprinkle with olive oil. Place in the refrigerator and marinate 24 hours.

3. Boil the eggs for 10 minutes, then shell them. On the meat, evenly spread peeled carrot sticks, spinach leaves and halved eggs and then cover with strips of red pepper.

Matambre

4. Season the filling with crushed pepper and paprika. Cover with shredded Gruyère. Roll the steak around the filling, starting with the edge closest to you. Grip well, using both hands to keep all the filling inside.

5. Using a needle, pass a length of kitchen string through the meat to seal the edges of the steak. Sew along the length of the roulade and close the ends. Tie up like a roast.

6. Bring 4 liters/4 quarts water to the boil with carrots disks, onions and bay leaves. Lower the heat, place the roulade in the broth and simmer, covered, for 2 hours. Serve sliced.

Mechoui

Preparation time: 20 minutes
Cooking time: 1 hour 35 minutes
Difficulty: ★

Serves 4

1 tsp saffron threads
1 tsp ground cumin
red food coloring
1 tsp paprika
1 tsp salt
1/2 tsp pepper

oil for frying
2 kg/4 1/2 lb lamb shoulder
300 g/1 1/3 cups butter, in pieces
16 dried figs
16 walnuts
200 ml/generous 3/4 cup oil
5 or 6 sprigs fresh mint

The Berbers have prepared barbecued roast of lamb for centuries. The roast-master must carefully watch and tend the fire, over which a whole lamb will be roasted on his spit. The meat is often seasoned with melted and spiced butter, to allow the outside to become crisp while the inside remains tender.

Town-dwelling Moroccans never miss an opportunity to cook their lamb in the oven of the town baker. As for *mechoui m'bakher*, it is steamed and then finished in the oven. Guests bring the lamb to their mouths with three fingers of their right hand. Common courtesy is to offer the choice pieces to your neighbor.

In Morocco, there is no village where you cannot hear the bleat of sheep. Moroccans enjoy them in all forms, from head to foot. As well as kebabs, lamb is served in tajines with artichokes and peas, with turnips, with prunes and sesame seeds, by the Berbers with lots of vegetables or, in the Sefrou region,

with potatoes and olives. In *mrouzia*, the lamb meat is marinated in *ras-el-hanout*, ginger and saffron, cooked in butter with onions and cinnamon, then served with raisins, almonds, honey and cinnamon.

In Morocco, the season for fresh figs lasts from June until September. Market stalls offer them in pale brown, green and violet, all coming directly from the regions of Taounat and Ouazzane, known for the exceptional quality of their fruits. The Berbers have the custom of adding green figs to their couscous. A large part of the fig harvest is strung on ropes and dried in the sun for later use.

Although Mechoui Lamb is traditionally cooked out of doors over an open fire, with this recipe, the lamb cooked in your oven is sure to be an exquisite meal if you take care to baste the meat throughout the cooking.

1. Blend the saffron, cumin, red food coloring, paprika, salt, pepper and oil in a casserole dish filled with 1 liter/1 quart hot water. Stir this saffron sauce well.

2. Place the shoulder of lamb on a large baking sheet. Using a ladle, baste it with the saffron sauce. Arrange the pieces of butter on top of the lamb.

3. Seal the meat tightly in a few sheets of aluminum foil. Roast in the oven for 1 1/2 hours at 240°C/465°F.

Lamb with Figs

4. Place the figs on a chopping board. With a small knife, cut them in two without cutting completely through the flesh.

5. Carefully open the figs. Fill each one with a walnut.

6. Shortly before serving, heat a pan of oil to 180°C/355°F. Place the stuffed figs in the oil and fry for 5 minutes. Arrange the lamb on a serving plate, atop a bed of mint sprigs. Cover with fried figs.

Sorrento-Style

Preparation time: 20 minutes
Cooking time: 15 minutes
Difficulty: ★★

Serves 4

For the medallions:
4 large tomatoes
flour
8 veal scallops, 100 g/3¹/₂ oz each
2 tbsp olive oil
200 g/7 oz mozzarella
8 basil leaves for garnish

For the sauce:
50 g/3¹/₂ tbsp butter
1 bottle dry white wine
salt
pepper
1 pinch oregano

Astonishly varied, there is more to the preparation of Italian veal than simply the famous osso bucco. Other less familiar recipes that deserve to be enjoyed are Roman-style *saltimbocca*, Milan-style *involtini* deliciously rolled and filled, *piccatas* from Marsala hidden in their parcels, and the very special *farsumagru*, a signature recipe from Sicily.

In our chef's recipe, the veal is tenderized in the form of medallions. The scallops will become as thin as slices of Parma ham when flattened with a mallet. If you do not own a mallet, your butcher can do this for you. Fold up the veal and flatten it again a second time. This way, they will become crisp when fried. Here is an alternative trick to use in place of the mallet for this process: arrange the medallions in a freezer bag and vigorously roll over it with a rolling pin. Tomatoes and

mozzarella mark the medallions with the seal of the city of Sorrento, which is famous for its admirable setting, wonderfully juicy tomatoes and its prize-winning mozzarella.

Is it better to cook with butter or oil? Both are good, but our chef does not combine them. Oil is recommended to seal the medallions quickly. Butter is used when the meat continues cooking in the oven, decorated with tomatoes and cheese.

The mozzarella will not melt completely during cooking. Feel free to create a form other than the one proposed by Massimo Palermo to decorate the medallions. In the end, you will obtain a smoother sauce if you take care to pour it through a chinois sieve. Discerning palates will appreciate a sprinkle of oregano and basil, right before serving.

1. Slice the tomatoes 1 cm/¹/₃ in thick. Divide the scallops into 10-cm/4-in pieces, a little larger than the tomato slices.

2. Flour each scallop. Flatten with a mallet. Gently turn the four corners inward to give them the shape of a medallion. Flatten the reshaped pieces of veal with the mallet to give them the shape of the tomato slices. Set them aside.

3. Heat 2 tbsp olive oil in a pan. Carefully place the medallions in the oil. Sear them quickly, then turn them over. Set them aside on a plate.

Veal Medallions

4. Pour the oil out of the pan. Gently melt the butter over low heat. Put the veal medallions back in the pan with the butter. Add a pinch of oregano on each medallion. Pour over the white wine.

5. When the white wine is completely incorporated into the butter, cover each medallion with a slice of tomato. Season with salt and pepper.

6. Arrange the strips of mozzarella in crisscrosses. Bake in the oven for 2 minutes at 160°C/320°F. When the mozzarella is melted, sprinkle with basil and oregano, and top with the white wine sauce. Serve hot.

Medfouna Pigeon

Preparation time: 45 minutes
Cooking time: 35 minutes
Difficulty: ★★

Serves 4

4 pigeons
2 onions
olive oil
1/2 tsp salt

1 tsp pepper
1 tsp saffron threads
1 bunch fresh parsley
1 packet vermicelli
30 g/1 tbsp butter
100 g/²/₃ cup deep-fried almonds

Medfouna is the feminine form of the word *medfoun*, which means "buried" in Arabic. It is a fitting name for this dish, as it serves as a surprise for uninitiated guests, who find the pigeons as they taste their way through the nests of vermicelli on which they are arranged.

This very economical recipe is still prepared today in Morocco. The same base of pasta is often used to make traditional *seffa*, a dish of steamed vermicelli covered with confectioner's sugar and cinnamon and surrounded with a crown of candied raisins in sugar syrup.

Medfouna with Pigeons and Vermicelli is a variation of the traditional *seffa*, which is usually made with small-grain couscous. But the term is the same whether prepared with vermicelli or couscous. Since pasta is relatively rare in Moroccan gastronomy, our chef had designated *Medfouna* the "queen of the pastas", a sovereign who rules alone, without rival.

Other variations team well with this kind of vermicelli: lamb, chicken or beef can be prepared the same way as the pigeons. But pigeons are particularly prized in Morocco, and Moroccan farmers make every effort to satisfy the demand to produce small, tender, free-range pigeons that are not only delicious but organic, which is an added bonus.

Lahoucine Belmoufid suggests preparing vermicelli with a tomato sauce flavored with onions, parsley, cilantro, olive oil and saffron threads; this will have an Italian flair.

Here is a little trick to give your Pigeons with Vermicelli an extra level of flavor: if you can fit a steamer basket or colander over the pot in which the pigeons are cooked, steam the pasta in the steam of the food simmering below. This allows the pasta to be infused with all its aroma. Now you have a whole program of tricks and tempting ideas, to be discovered without delay.

1. Remove the pigeons' innards and rinse the birds with cold water. Cut each pigeon in two, discarding the wings, the ends of the leg bones and the sternum. Peel and chop the onions.

2. In a pot, sweat the onions in olive oil until soft, then add the pigeons. Pour in a little water, then the salt, pepper and saffron. Over medium heat, allow to cook for 10 minutes, maintaining a steady simmer.

3. Finely chop the parsley and sprinkle it over the pigeons and onions. If the liquid reduces, thin it with a bowl of hot water.

with Vermicelli

4. Spread out the vermicelli in a large, flat bowl. Sprinkle it with olive oil, and toss by hand for 2 minutes to distribute the oil.

5. Pour the vermicelli into the top of a couscous steam or other steamer and fill the lower part half way with water. Steam for 5 minutes. Repeat this process 3 more times: oil the vermicelli, then steam it.

6. Place the vermicelli in a deep dish, butter them and scoop a deep "nest" in which to nestle 4 of the pigeon halves. Sprinkle with the cooking juices, arrange the rest of the pigeon on top and cover with sauce. Garnish the dish with fried almonds.

Noisettes of Lamb

Preparation time: 50 minutes
Cooking time: 1 hour 25 minutes
Soaking time, morels: 30 minutes
Difficulty: ★★★

Serves 4

1 saddle of lamb
50 g/1³/₄ oz dried morels
16 baby carrots
16 baby turnips
50 g/3¹/₂ tbsp butter
16 snow peas
30 ml/2 tbsp oil
salt
freshly ground pepper

For the sauce:
lamb bones from the meat
50 ml/3¹/₂ tbsp oil
1 large onion
1 carrot
1 rib celery
salt
crushed white pepper
1 tomato
fresh tarragon
1 clove garlic
1 or 2 sprigs thyme
1 bay leaf
50 g/3¹/₂ tbsp butter

Most people associate the word lamb with young sheep under a year old. The French meat industry, however, recognizes several types of lamb. Among the most prestigious are salty meadow lamb, raised on the salt marshes of the Bay of Mont-Saint-Michel, with dark pink flesh and strongly iodized taste; and Pauillac lamb, from the Bordelaise region. Most of the meat from French lambs bears the national designation "Traditional Butcher's Lamb" when it is sold retail by butchers, and "French Shepherds' Lamb" for large and medium wholesale. In addition, there are a limited number of red quality labels that signify especially superb production. Others receive certification for "organic agriculture", and a number of producers have united in local brands to showcase the specific quality of their meat, tied to their region.

The attention-getting piece here is the "English saddle", or saddle of lamb, which will be carved into small medallions called noisettes. This cut of meat corresponds to the lumbar region of the animal, and follows the lower back bone. When the fillets are removed, they are sliced into noisettes of 50–60 g (1¾–2 oz) each. Allow two or three noisettes per guest. After cooking, the meat should be crisp on the outside and pink inside. Always allow it to rest for several moments before serving so that the juices can spread evenly through the meat, making it especially tender.

Our gravy, made from the cooking juices of the lamb, is enhanced with the unique flavor of morels. The first mushroom of the year (from March to June), this inhabitant of forests and mountains is easily recognizable by its conical, alveolate top. As its growth is somewhat capricious, they are rarely found fresh in markets. You can settle for dried morels, which you will have to rinse and then rehydrate before use.

1. Cut the meat off the saddle, removing the bones and gristle. Soak the morels for 30 minutes, rinse them in fresh water, then blanch them (reserve the cooking liquid). Finely chop the tarragon. Peel the baby carrots and baby turnips.

2. For the sauce, crush the lamb bones and gristle. Fry in the oil with the chopped onion, carrot and celery. Pour off excess oil and add 500 ml/2 cups water and the cooking liquid from the morels. Add salt, pepper, diced tomato and finely chopped tarragon. Cook for 30 minutes, then strain.

3. Sauté the morels in butter in another pan. Then briefly pan-fry the baby carrots, baby turnips and snow peas, one vegetable at a time, to be used in the garnish.

with Tarragon

4. In a pan, fry the salted and peppered fillets of lamb in a blend of oil and butter, 3 to 4 minutes on each side over medium heat. Allow them to rest between two plates for 12 minutes to obtain a pleasant rose tint.

5. Pour off the grease in the pan after cooking the meat. Add the sauce and reduce over low heat for 10 minutes. Strain the sauce and add finely chopped tarragon. Away from the heat, stir in 50 g/3½ tbsp butter, then the morels.

6. Reheat the vegetables and cut the lamb into medallions. Carefully arrange the meat, vegetables and sauce on each plate. Garnish with fresh tarragon leaves.

Duck Noisettes with

Preparation time: 25 minutes
Cooking time: 40 minutes
Difficulty: ★★

Serves 4

2 duck breasts, 600 g/1¼ lb each
coarse salt
4 slices bacon
2 Belle de Boskoop apples
40 g/1½ tbsp butter

For the wine sauce:
2 shallots
250 ml/1 cup red wine
250 ml/1 cup veal stock
1 tbsp sugar
1 tbsp vinegar

For the garnish:
1 sprig rosemary

Medallions of Duck with Apples is one of an established array of recipes from Normandy with a long tradition. The apple is loaded with symbolism, ever since Adam and Eve were forced to leave Paradise for biting into this fruit of knowledge. Always ready to enjoy a good meal, Gallics have transformed it into cider, too. Red, yellow, speckled or green, each kind of apple harbors a particular flavor. Our chef has chosen the Belle de Boskoop apple to accompany his medallions of duck. This large, slightly bumpy apple with thick, dark red skin marked with yellow-green, has juicy flesh with a sweet, tart flavor. Peeled, cored and quartered, they are briefly fried in butter.

The duck breasts are served with a succulent, wine-colored sauce flavored with shallots. After having been cooked dry, the apples are moistened with a full-bodied red wine, then reduced by three quarters before adding the veal stock. Combined with a little caramel, the reduction becomes a sweet blend of sweet and tart close to that of the apples. This specially flavored sauce brings a hint of autumn to the duck, and can be served with any grilled red meat of your choice.

Ready-made veal stock is easy to find in most supermarkets. Although useful for thickening a sauce, it cannot truly compare to a homemade veal stock made from veal bones and herbs. Made ahead of time, this can be kept in a tightly sealed jar in the refrigerator, or frozen in cubes.

The duck breasts are roasted in the oven in large pieces to guarantee an even cooking, then cut into medallions. Chefs usually serve them still slightly pink on the inside, but you can certainly continue cooking them a little longer if you prefer.

1. Remove the excess fat from the duck breasts and any small feathers that remain. Chop the breasts into two lengthwise.

2. For the sauce, peel and mince the shallots. Briefly heat them until dried in a saucepan with no added fat. Add the red wine. Reduce by ⅔ over high heat, then pour in the veal stock. Simmer for 15 minutes over low heat to obtain a wine sauce.

3. At the same time, caramelize 1 tbsp sugar with 1 tbsp vinegar in a small pan.

Apples and Bacon

4. Away from the heat, pour the wine sauce through a small sieve into the caramel. Beat thoroughly and set aside.

5. Place the halved duck breasts skin side up on a baking sheet. Sprinkle over some salt. Cook for 3 minutes under the broiler. Add the pieces of bacon to the pan alongside the duck and broil another 5 minutes. Quickly pan-fry the apple slices in butter.

6. Slice the breasts into 6 medallions. Serve napped with the wine sauce, accompanied by the cooked bacon and fried apples. Decorate with a sprig of rosemary.

Veal Sweetbread

Preparation time: 1 hour
Cooking time: 45 minutes
Difficulty: ★★

Serves 4

For the meat:
600 g/1¹/₄ lb veal sweetbread
100 g7 tbsp flour
150 g/²/₃ cup butter

For the salsify:
1 kg/2¹/₄ lb salsify
2 tbsp flour
juice of ¹/₂ lemon

For the breading:
2 eggs
50 g/3¹/₂ tbsp flour
50 g/¹/₂ cup dried bread crumbs
peanut oil

For the beurre blanc:
200 ml/generous ³/₄ cup white wine
200 ml/generous ³/₄ cup white vinegar
salt, pepper
1 bay leaf
2 shallots
250 g/1 cup + 2 tbsp butter
fresh thyme

For the garnish:
1 bunch fresh parsley

Not very attractive or easy to peel, salsify (also known as oyster plant) is gradually disappearing from markets. Frozen and canned foods are replacing fresh vegetables. Yet this root, whether in its black form or white, round or long, has long been appreciated for its luscious flesh.

Some advice to make peeling salsify easier: if you rinse and then soak them in cold water for an hour, the peel will come away without problems. Salsify is usually blanched in lemon juice or vinegar water before cooking. Slice or cut it as needed for your recipe, then cook it a second time in salted water.

Michel Haquin uses another method. He combines great taste with efficiency by serving salsify *au blanc* or *au blanc de cuisson*, meaning a small amount of flour is added to the cooking water through a strainer to avoid lumps. The lemon juice can be replaced by a spoonful of white vinegar.

Cooked in this way the salsify, lightly breaded, stays tender on the inside and crisp on the outside. To do this, the chef uses a blend of flour and breadcrumbs. Beaten egg holds the bread-crumbs in place and assures a perfect frying of the vegetable.

Michel Haquin leaves nothing to chance and feels that even the simplest things should be refined. He transforms the sauce into a *beurre blanc*. A classic accompaniment for meat and fish, this reduction of vinegar, white wine and shallots blended with fresh butter has a well-deserved reputation. For perfect results, the butter must be very fresh in order to result in a perfectly smooth sauce.

Such a sauce needs to be partnered with very tender and delicious veal sweetbread: barely blanched, test to see if they are cooked by inserting a fork into them; the meat should not catch on the fork.

1. Blanch the sweetbread 10 minutes in salted water. Drain and set aside. Wash and scrape the salsify. Cut into 10 cm/4 in sections, then slice each section in half lengthwise.

2. Place the flour in a small sieve. Hold the sieve over a small saucepan. Sprinkle the flour with some cold water, then with the lemon juice.

3. Heat the saucepan and add the salsify. Simmer for 20 minutes. For the sauce, in a separate pan, combine the white wine, vinegar, salt, pepper, bay leaf and finely sliced shallots. Reduce by half over high heat.

with Breaded Salsify

4. Add the butter to the sauce. Whisk vigorously until it is thick. Remove the beurre blanc from the heat and strain.

5. Slice the sweetbread into medallions 2 cm/³/₄ in thick. Coat them in the flour and fry them in hot butter, turning over to cook both sides.

6. To bread the salsify, beat 1 egg. Mix the breadcrumbs and flour in a small bowl. Roll each piece of salsify in egg, then the crumb mix. Sear for 2 minutes in hot peanut oil. Serve the medallions with pieces of breaded salsify and beurre blanc sauce.

Quail

Preparation time:	40 minutes
Cooking time:	1 hour 10 minutes
Difficulty:	★★★

Serves 4

8 quails
2 large onions
10 sprigs cilantro
15 sprigs parsley
1 pinch saffron threads
400 g/1¾ cups butter

100 ml/7 tbsp peanut oil
40 g1½ oz cinnamon stick
salt
ground black pepper
1 tsp ground ginger
400 g/2⅔ cups whole almonds
olive oil for frying
80 g/6 tbsp fine granulated sugar
3 tbsp ground cinnamon
8 eggs
8 sheets phyllo dough
30 g/¼ cup confectioner's sugar

Under a dusting of confectioner's sugar mixed with cinnamon and a crisp sheet of phyllo dough, this *Quail B'Steeya* reveals itself as a meal worthy of a thousand and one nights, in which roasted almonds team up with the subtle flavor of quails. The sheets of phyllo dough, called *warka* in Arabic, recall a recipe based on very thin pasta, prepared flat. White meat enveloped in phyllo dough is a lightly sweetened dish served on special occasions throughout Morocco, although it is less commonly made with quail than with farm-raised chicken or pigeon.

In Morocco, quail, which are migratory birds, are hunted in the month of June. They are also raised in the area around Marrakech. In Fez, quails are stuffed with almonds and onions and cooked in a *kadra* (the bottom of a couscous cooker separate from its perforated steamer) or prepared in a tajine with a medley of almonds and onions.

The recipe proposed by our chef makes wonderful use of herbs and spices. In Morocco, cilantro is featured in the preparation of red meat as well as fish and poultry. Among the other highly appreciated condiments are paprika, ginger, parsley, cinnamon, cayenne pepper, nutmeg, cumin and saffron. Too often for our chef's taste, however, the saffron is diluted with a synthetic red powder that imitates its brilliant color, and the cinnamon is replaced by a related bark called *cassia*.

In this phyllo dough pastry where nothing is wasted, you can add to the scrambled eggs all the fragments of quail flesh that cling to the bones. Our chef recommends allowing the eggs to rest on an inclined plate so that most of the liquid runs out. Fill any holes or tears in the sheets of phyllo dough with a mixture of flour and water. Finally, decorate the dish with mint leaves and crushed toasted almonds.

1. Cut the quails in half along their backs and gut them. Put them in a pot with the chopped onions, finely chopped cilantro and parsley, red food coloring, saffron, butter, peanut oil, cinnamon stick, salt, pepper and ginger. Cook for 10 minutes.

2. Add 1 liter/1 quart cold water to the pot. Stir to blend, then cover and simmer for 40 minutes. Meanwhile, blanch the almonds in boiling water, then rub between a clean towel and peel them.

3. Heat olive oil in a deep-fryer or deep pan. Place the almonds on a skimmer and lower into the hot oil. Allow them to brown briefly (2 to 3 minutes maximum). Repeat until all the almonds are fried. Grind them, then mix with the granulated sugar and ground cinnamon.

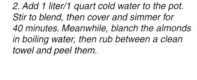

B'Steeya

4. Using a skimmer, take the quails out of the pot one by one. Reserve the stock from the pot (discard the cinnamon sticks).

5. Carefully detach the quail meat. Break the eggs into a bowl and beat them. Pour them into the quail stock, add salt and pepper, and whisk for 10 minutes over low heat to obtain scrambled eggs.

6. Lay 2 sheets of phyllo dough over a round baking dish. Fill with scrambled eggs, quail meat and almonds. Cover with 2 more sheets of phyllo dough and fillings. Close the phyllo dough and deep-fry for 5 minutes. Decorate with confectioner's sugar and cinnamon to taste.

Beef Roulades

Preparation time: 2 hours
Cooking time: 2 hours 30 minutes
Difficulty: ★★★

Serves 4

For the roulades:
500 g/generous 1 lb veal or beef
(brisket or rump roast)
4 tbsp mustard
100 g/3½ oz gherkins in brine
120 g/4–5 oz smoked bacon
10 g/4 tsp dried marjoram
salt, pepper

For the sauce:
50 g/generous ¼ cup chopped celery

50 g/3½ tbsp butter
50 g/generous ¼ cup chopped onions
10 g/2 tbsp dried wild mushrooms, minced
10 allspice berries

1 tsp salt
10 white peppercorns
1 bay leaf
400 ml/1⅔ cups turkey stock
1 tsp black pepper

For the beets:
50 g/generous ¼ cup chopped onions
50 g/3½ tbsp butter
50 g/3½ tbsp flour
500 g/generous 1 lb beets, cooked
juice of 1 lemon
1 tsp powdered sugar
1 tsp salt
1 tsp pepper
100 g/7 tbsp buckwheat

Arkadusz Zuchmanski has chosen two notorious products from his country: meat products and pickled gherkins. Sliced into matchsticks, the gherkins are lined up in the center of fine slices of meat, deliciously blending their flavors. Large quantities of sweet gherkins marinated in sea salt are consumed in Poland. They can be replaced with more vinegary crunchy gherkins, if you prefer. Choose a mild mustard to cover the scallops.

As for the veal or beef, choose a high-quality meat, tender and without fat. In place of a mallet to flatten the meat, use a chopping board: cover it with a cloth, place it on top of the piece of meat, then press hard: this technique is effective, but takes longer than using a mallet.

Those who prefer not to use this method must extend the cooking time of the roulades: it is important that they are well

seared before braising in the stock. Our chef recommends cooking everything in the same pot for maximum flavor, but the roulades can also be fried separately in a skillet. Just melt the butter for frying in a new pan and continue cooking the roulades as indicated in the recipe.

As for the sauce, it will be served fluid, light but smooth. A few simple actions will result in the most beautiful sauce: take the roulades out of the cooking pot and strain the sauce. Transfer the garnish left in the strainer to the bowl of a food processor. Mix gently while adding the strained bouillon a little at a time to obtain the texture of your choice.

The well-cooked beets and onions complement the roulades. Rapidly cooked, the hulled buckwheat will swell as it cooks in three times its volume of water. Serve it as you would rice and other grains.

1. Place a piece of meat on a chopping board. Using a chef's knife, slice the thickness in half. In this way, make 4 scallops 2 cm/¾ in thick. Flatten with a mallet or a chopping board as described above, making the meat as thin as possible.

2. Spread each scallop with mustard and smooth the surface.

3. Slice the gherkins and smoked bacon into narrow sticks. In the center of each scallop, alternate 3 sticks of gherkin and 3 sticks of bacon. Sprinkle with marjoram, salt and pepper.

with Hot Beets

4. Pull the two sides of the scallop over the filling. Roll the scallop from one end to the other, lengthwise. Secure each roulade with a toothpick.

5. In a saucepan, sear the roulades in butter for 3 minutes over high heat. Add the onions, celery, mushrooms, allspice, salt, peppercorns, bay leaf and turkey stock. Cook 30 to 40 minutes over low heat.

6. For the beets, sweat the onions in butter for 3 minutes and sprinkle with flour. Stir in the grated beets, lemon juice, sugar, salt and pepper. Add $1/2$ cup water halfway through cooking. Cook the buckwheat and serve with the roulades and sauce.

Andalusian Marinated

Preparation time: 45 minutes
Cooking time: 1 hour
Marinating time: 24 hours
Difficulty: ★★

Serves 4

4 partridges, 400 g/14 oz each
salt
ground pepper
2 onions
6 cloves garlic

300 ml/1¼ cups sherry vinegar
250 ml/1 cup fine sherry
2 bay leaves
2 cloves
a few peppercorns
2 juniper berries (optional)
500 ml/2 cups poultry stock
600 g/1¼ lb potatoes
500 g/generous 1 lb oyster mushrooms
olive oil

Contrary to popular belief, Spain (although better known for its coastal cuisine), has abundant high-quality game birds and animals that will be much appreciated by the culturally curious gourmand. The Andalusian menu features a distinctive sherry-partridge recipe. Traditionally, the potatoes and oyster mushrooms in this recipe are replaced by a few fresh grapes, for a fruity and sophisticated garnish.

During the hunting season, the displays in the butcher shops are decorated with the plumage and pelts of game birds and animals, whose brown and red tints agreeably dress the shop windows. Faced with this sight, temptation quickly gives way to question, then doubt and then retreat. For greater discernment, it helps to know that the ideal partridge will be quite firm to the touch—so do not hesitate to feel it for a better assessment. The bird shold be not too fatty, and equipped with a good plumage. If no male partridge is available, choose a delicious female. Be aware, however, that the cooking time will be longer.

Made from the acidic yellow wines of Andalusia, sherry vinegar ages in oak barrels for many years, and develops a powerful aroma. Concentrated, this scented elixir is used to deglaze meats and season vegetables. As for the sherry, dry or sweet, its reputation has nothing to do with it: the dry *fine* reveals a subtle flavor of almonds, while the mellow *dolorosa*, smooth and scented, offers a nutty flavor.

1. A day ahead of time, gut and singe the partridges. Arrange them in a bowl. Salt, pepper, and cover with the sliced onions and garlic. Add the vinegar, sherry, bay leaf, cloves, peppercorns and juniper. Pour on the poultry stock and allow to marinate.

2. The next day, peel the potatoes and slice them into fine disks. Clean the oyster mushrooms and cut them in half.

3. Place the partridges in a pot with their marinade. Bring to the boil. Lower the heat and continue cooking for 30 minutes.

and Roasted Partridge

4. Drain the partridges and reserve the stock. Chop the birds in half along their backs. Bone them, reserving the thigh and wing bones. Remove the brown impurities found inside of the bird.

5. Bring the stock to the boil, then add the potatoes and cook for 5 minutes. Using a skimmer, remove the potatoes and the aromatic garnish. Reduce the stock by $^{2}/_{3}$, to obtain a concentrated sauce.

6. Pour a little olive oil in a pan and fry the partridges, potatoes and oyster mushrooms. Arrange the partridges on plates. Garnish with potatoes and mushrooms. Surround with some of the aromatic garnish and the sauce.

Croatian-Style

Preparation time: 45 minutes
Cooking time, meat: 30 minutes
Cooking time, gnocchi: 35 minutes
Difficulty: ★★★

Serves 4

300 g/11 oz dry potatoes
800 g/1³/₄ lb turkey breast
40 g/¹/₂ cup button mushrooms, sliced
5 green asparagus
salt
pepper
3 eggs
60 g/2 oz black truffles

20 g/1 tbsp meadow honey
2 or 3 sprigs parsley
2 or 3 fresh basil leaves
1 liter/1 quart chicken stock
oil for the pan
100–130 g/²/₃–scant 1 cup white flour
1 whole egg and 1 yolk
20 g/2 tbsp blanched hazelnuts
30 ml/2 tbsp olive oil
salt

For the cream sauce:
200 ml/generous ³/₄ cup liquid crème fraîche
1 large handful pine nuts
1 egg yolk

Viljam Cvek invites you to savor this recipe, a dish worthy of the grandest restaurants: deliciously stuffed and colorful turkey in which the flavor of asparagus blends with slices of truffle.

The north of Istria, bordering Italy, is rather forested. This is the place in Croatia where you can find the delicate black and white truffles. These tuber mushrooms are dug up by dogs specially trained for this work, all through the year. Black truffles are more expensive than white. As in many countries, their gastronomical reputation and even aphrodisiacal properties have been established for a long time. The Croatians like to cook them with soft fresh cheese, or to preserve them in olive oil. Recently, chefs have been preparing small breads garnished with pieces of truffles.

Truffle blends well with the turkey, which has become the principal poultry consumed in Croatia. Sales of this bird are on the rise everywhere, since white meat has been deemed best for your health, lighter, etc. However, Croatians use many more fillets than whole turkeys. The fillets blend delightfully with asparagus, highly prized in Croatia, both in its cultivated and wild forms.

Honey is an equally indispensable element of Croatian cuisine. Whether the honey comes from from acacia blossoms, linden trees or meadow flowers, beehives are found in almost all regions. Croatians do not hesitate to flavor meat with honey or incorporate it into desserts and liqueurs, and they prefer to use it in place of sugar to sweeten their cakes. It is common to conserve figs or nuts in a pot of honey, for a snack. Fans of local *grappa* enjoy their brandy all the more after stirring a spoonful of honey into it.

1. Cook the potatoes 30 minutes in boiling water. During this time, divide the turkey fillets in half horizontally using a large, sharp knife. Flatten them as much as possible with a mallet.

2. Sear the sliced mushrooms and chopped asparagus 2 to 3 minutes in an oiled pan. Salt and pepper. Pour 3 beaten eggs over the mushrooms and stir as for scrambled eggs. Slice the truffle and add to the eggs, as well as the honey. Sprinkle with crushed parsley and basil.

3. Garnish each scallop with a large spoonful of egg filling. Form them into roulades by rolling each scallop around the filling.

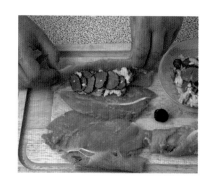

Turkey Breast

4. Place the rolls of meat on a square of aluminum foil. Close the foil over the meat and twist the ends like a parcel. Arrange them in a large pot and cover with poultry stock. Cover and cook 20 minutes.

5. For the gnocchi, run the cooked potatoes through a vegetable mill. Add the flour, eggs, ground hazelnuts, oil and salt. Knead, roll into long tubes, then cut into small sections. Poach the gnocchi until they rise to the surface of boiling water.

6. For the sauce, pour into a pot the cream, pine nuts and egg yolk. Salt, pepper and stir 1 to 2 minutes over low heat. Cut the turkey roulades into neat slices. Arrange on a plate with the gnocchi and cover with sauce. Decorate with the tips of asparagus.

Pigeon Breast

Preparation time:	1 hour 30 minutes
Cooking time:	2 hours 45 minutes
Difficulty:	★★★

Serves 4

For the roasted pigeon:
1 calf's foot
2 liters/2 quarts clear stock
4 pigeons, 300 g/11 oz each
or 2 pigeons, 600 g/1¼ lb each
1 onion
1 carrot
1 sprig thyme
3 or 4 sprigs parsley
1 bay leaf

Vegetables for the sauce:
2 turnips
2 carrots
500 g/3⅓ cups peas
salt

4 sheets phyllo dough
50 ml/3½ tbsp olive oil
50 g/3½ tbsp butter

For the sauce:
5 sprigs basil
2 cloves garlic
25 g/1 slice salted bacon
olive oil

This is one of those dishes that warms the soul and leaves us with indelible scents, like a stew that simmers for a long time. This recipe, which comes from the region of Languedoc, requires a few traditional steps. Thoroughly rinse the calf's foot to clean it of any possible dirt. Reserve the bones of the foot to enhance the flavor of the stock.

Anticipate a large quantity of stock, which can stay fresh for a few weeks when strained. It is important to take time to skim the surface throughout cooking. You can flavor it with carrots, onions, shallots, celery, leeks and a bouquet garni after it has simmered for one hour.

When you fillet the pigeon, you will reserve the carcasses for the preparation of the pigeon reduction. In a lightly oiled pot, melt a pat of butter. The mixture of oil and butter allows the moisture from the bird to evaporate and the bones of the carcass to fry without burning. Then add the vegetables, cut into small dice. It is the juices of the meat blended with the flavors of the chopped vegetables that forms the pigeon reduction.

The sauce will bring all the flavor of garlic and basil to the pigeon. It is not by chance that the ancient Greeks raised this plant to the rank of "royal herb". With its large, green leaves, basil combines perfectly with olive oil. Crush it gently, or grind it with a pestle.

Making the crisp calf's foot requires a bit of care. Cut bands of phyllo dough 10 cm/4 in wide. Fill each piece with a tablespoon of diced meat from the calf's foot, and fold at a right angle to form triangles. Fried in hot butter for just four minutes, they will glisten nicely under the pigeon breast. Accompany the pot-au-feu from Languedoc as our chef does, with a Mourvèdre red wine.

1. Boil the calf's foot 2 hours in the clear stock. Remove the wishbone from the pigeons. Cut in two along the back, leaving the two halves connected. Separate the bony part from the fillet. Remove the wings at the joint. Take out the giblets and reserve the thighs for another use.

2. Prepare the pigeon reduction by cooking the crushed wings and carcasses of the pigeons with the diced onion and carrots and the bouquet garni made of thyme, parsley and bay leaf. Deglaze the pan with some of the broth from cooking the calf's foot, and strain the resulting liquid.

3. Peel the turnips and carrots for the sauce. From these vegetables, scoop out small balls the size of peas. Blanch the balls of turnip, carrot and the peas, separately, for 3 to 5 minutes in salted water. Refresh them in ice water to retain their color. Drain.

Pot-au-Feu

4. After 2 hours of cooking, remove the calf's foot from the stock and drain. Detach the meat from the bone and cut into cubes. Arrange these on the phyllo dough, sliced into bands. Fold into triangular turnovers and fry them in a pan of butter.

5. In another pan, heat 50 ml/3½ tbsp oil and 50 g/3½ tbsp butter. Cook the pigeons 2 minutes on each side, starting with the skin side down. Moisten by covering with the pigeon reduction and cook another 4 minutes.

6. For the sauce, blend the basil, garlic and bacon in a food processor. Add the olive oil. Away from the heat, add this mixture to the pigeon reduction. Arrange the pigeons in the center of each plate, with the small vegetables covered in sauce.

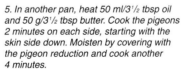

Polenta

Preparation time: 10 minutes
Cooking time, polenta: 45 minutes
Cooking time, quail: 20 minutes
Difficulty: ★★

Serves 4

500 ml/2 cups water
500 ml/2 cups milk
coarse salt
400 g/generous 2³/₄ cups cornmeal

8 quails
16 sage leaves
16 slices smoked bacon
200 ml/generous ³/₄ cup olive oil
fine salt
pepper
160 ml/²/₃ cup white wine
20 g/1¹/₂ tbsp butter

The basic idea behind polenta dates back to the time of the Romans, who nourished their legions with *pulmentum*, a porridge of boiled and seasoned wheat. Broad bean, spelt, millet, buckwheat or chickpeas were also eaten in this form. The first ground corn arrived in Venice around 1500, from the Americas. Venetian patrician Leonardo Emo Capodilista may have been the first to think of growing corn on his property, situated close to Trévise, in order to cheaply feed his numerous servants. Since then, corn polenta has become a staple food for the poor people of northern Italy.

In the past, the inhabitants of the country prepared polenta in a *paiolo*, a sort of large, copper cauldron. Using a long stick, they stirred the corn flour and water in the container hanging over the fire in the chimney, until it took on a thick consistency. They then poured it over a cloth and shaped it with a spatula before cutting with a thread.

Polenta is enjoyed hot, often in place of bread. You can serve it simply embellished with a pat of butter and grated Parmesan, with tomato sauce, or with a creamy cheese such as gorgonzola. It perfectly accompanies stews of rabbit, lamb, game and mushrooms. In Venice, polenta with Vicenza cod is also well known. In central Italy, it goes well with sweet sausages, whereas chefs in the Piedmonts are more likely to serve slices of it fried with an egg and strips of white truffles.

The recipe presented here is a *polenta e osei*, which means with small birds. It is a specialty of Lombardy. In Brescia, quails are cooked in a pan while in Bergamo, they are served as brochettes (on skewers). In the past, the small migratory bird was hunted at the end of August; today, only farm-raised quails are sold.

1. In a large pot, bring 500 ml/2 cups water to the boil with the milk and coarse salt. When the mixture boils, lower the heat and gradually pour in the cornmeal. Cook over low heat 40 to 45 minutes, stirring to avoid lumps.

2. During this time, clean the quails. Remove the giblets from the interior cavity of each bird. Neatly cut the end of the legs and neck. Remove any excess fat.

3. When they are well cleaned, truss the quails. Make a small slot in the skin on each side, next to the rump, and pass the legs through the slot.

and Quails

4. Place 2 or 3 sage leaves on each quail. Wrap with 2 slices of smoked bacon.

5. Heat the olive oil in a large pan. Salt and pepper the quails and fry them in the hot oil for 20 minutes until they are nicely browned.

6. Deglaze the quails with white wine. Scrape off the drippings to form a nice sauce. Present the birds on a bed of polenta with a little butter and topped with white wine sauce.

Stuffed Pork

Preparation time: 40 minutes
Cooking time: 1 hour 30 minutes
Marinating time: 3 hours
Difficulty: ★★

Serves 8

2 kg/4¹/₂ lb pork loin
juice of 1 lime
salt
black peppercorns
2¹/₂ onions
1 clove garlic, minced

2 green apples, about 200 g/7 oz each
250 g/9 oz mozzarella
90 g/¹/₂ cup pitted prunes
1 green bell pepper
1 red bell pepper
6 slices bread with no crust
500 ml/2 cups milk
4 egg yolks
50 g/scant ¹/₂ cup grated Parmesan
160 g/6 oz sliced smoked bacon
olive oil

For the accompaniment:
320 g/2¹/₄ cups cassava flour (tapioca flour)

The city of São Paulo, situated in the southeast of Brazil some 70 km (45 miles) from the sea, was founded in 1554 by the Jesuits. Today, it is an enormous and lively metropolis, and an important industrial and commercial crossroad. The stuffed, roasted pork proposed by our chef stems from the culinary tradition of this region.

In Portuguese, this recipe is called *lombinho de porco recheado*. It is a traditional dish for the Christmas feast, prepared a day in advance and served cold, surrounded by dried fruits such as nuts, figs, prunes or even pineapple. During this meal, which takes place during the hottest part of the year in Brazil, Brazilians also eat cold chicken and potato salads. The meal ends with succulent desserts such as chocolate tarts with coconut and tropical fruits. This tender, tasty roast might also be a treat for parties or birthdays.

Brazilians also appreciate other stuffed meat dishes. The beef shoulder top blade, sometimes called flat iron steak, a rather tough piece of beef, is dressed with salted and peppered onion, then simmered for a long time. As with chicken, it is stuffed with ground veal, onions, carrots and breadcrumbs.

Pork meat is so popular in Brazil that it always garnishes *feijõada*, the most celebrated regional dish, which combines several kinds of meat and side dishes. In the past, slaves prepared it with black beans and the scraps of meat left over from the owners' feasts: feet, ears, tails, ribs and fat. Today these meats are made delectable, sliced thinly, and complemented with sausage and beef brisket and sides of various greens and hot peppers.

You have a choice in the side dishes for the Stuffed Pork de São Paulo. You can serve the salted cassava flour in a small bowl next to the meat, or you can sauté some onions in palm oil, which the Brazilians call *farofa*. You can also simply serve white rice or a green salad.

1. Place the pork loin in a baking dish. With a spoon, moisten with the lime juice. Salt and pepper. Spread 1 chopped onion and the minced garlic over the surface. Cover with plastic wrap and set aside to marinate for 3 hours in the refrigerator.

2. Slice the potatoes and mozzarella, grate 1 onion and chop the prunes. Dice the bell peppers. Soak the bread in milk then squeeze out the excess with your hands. Combine the bread, onion, egg yolks, Parmesan, prunes and peppers.

3. Using a chef's knife, slice the meat open horizontally to make a large scallop. Slice it in half again. Salt and pepper.

de São Paulo

4. Spread out the meat on a chopping board. Arrange the slices of green apple and mozzarella on top, then use a spoon to spread the pepper filling over them.

5. Using both hands, carefully roll the meat over the filling. Tie it up like a roast with kitchen string.

6. Place the roll in an oiled roasting pan. Sprinkle with the remaining $1/2$ chopped onion then cover with slices of bacon. Cook in a 200°C/390°F oven for 1 hour 30 minutes. Slice and serve hot, accompanied by a small cup of salted manioc flour.

Savoy-Style Hotpot

Preparation time: 30 minutes
Cooking time: 5 to 6 hours
Difficulty: ★★

Serves 4

For the hotpot:
2 unsalted pork shins
4 pork sausages
2 carrots
4 turnips
8 potatoes
2 large onions
1 green Savoy cabbage
20 g/1¹/₂ tbsp butter
1 or 2 cloves
coarse salt

For the stock:
2 or 3 sprigs thyme
1 bay leaf
3 or 4 sprigs parsley
1 rib celery
750 ml/3¹/₄ cups dry white wine
1 liter/1 quart poultry stock

For the confit:
800 g/1³/₄ lb unsmoked slab bacon
1 kg/2¹/₄ lb duck fat
salt
pepper
4 duck thighs
flour
4 slices duck liver

In France, the hotpot represents a preparation of meat and vegetables cooked for a long time in an earthenware pot. Legend tells how the friendly giant, Gargantua, came to feast in Savoy one day. In bliss from the delectable meal, he fell asleep draped over one of the Alpine mountain tops, admiring the valley below. Clearly, he thought he was in heaven!

Potato, turnip and cabbage have long been part of the Savoy-Style Hotpot. Rich in potassium and magnesium, innumerable types of cabbage are grown all over the planet. Raw or cooked, it can be prepared in a number of ways. The Savoy cabbage lends its strong and generous flavor to this meal. Blanch it for two to three minutes in salted water to prevent the leaves from separating in the stock. Remove the hard stalk, then cut it into large pieces.

In keeping with tradition, Bernard Collon braises the quartered cabbage in a blend of white wine and poultry stock, assuring that the vegetables have a tender consistency from prolonged cooking. Like the cabbage, the turnip is a robust plant often used in soups and stews. Purple or white, the turnips absorb the fat from the meats.

Because it goes well with Savoy-style cuisine, pork is another ingredient in many one-dish stews. Bacon, belly, sausage, shin: all are conserved with salt. But the trademark of Savoy pork products remains the deliciously fresh, plump sausages called *diots*, often cooked in wine.

No part of the hotpot goes to waste. If there are vegetables leftover, you can serve them as a soup thinned with stock. If some of the stock remains, you can add vermicelli and serve it as a soup. And if there should happen to be some leftover stew, you can keep it cold until the next day. The duck *confit* lends an air of special Sunday dinner to this everyday hotpot, and the slices of duck liver make it a true celebratory meal.

1. Rinse the pork. Roll up the slab of pork and wrap a string around it. Make a first knot on top of the meat, then wrap the string around a few more times to maintain a tight roll. Tie a second time.

2. Melt the duck fat in a large pot over low heat. Add the salted and peppered duck thighs and rolled pork. Cover and cook 3 hours over low heat.

3. Peel the carrots, turnips, potatoes and onions. Chop the carrots and potatoes and slice 1 onion. Blanch the cabbage, cut in large pieces, for 3 minutes.

with Braised Cabbage

4. In a soup pot, fry the carrots and sliced onion in the butter for 3 minutes. Add the bouquet garni (the thyme, bay leaf, parsley, celery). Stir just until the vegetables darken, then add the blanched cabbage and cover with white wine and poultry stock.

5. Add the whole turnips, the second onion studded with cloves, the sausages, blanched pork shin and a pinch of coarse salt. Simmer 1 hour. Add the duck and bacon rolls. Continue cooking, covered, for 1 hour.

6. Coat the slices of duck liver in flour and fry them 2 minutes on each side. Drain them on absorbent paper. Arrange all the vegetables, meats and duck liver on plates and serve hot.

Southern-Style

Preparation time: 30 minutes
Cooking time: 35 minutes
Marinating time: 1 hour
Difficulty: ★★

Serves 4

1 whole chicken
250 ml/1 cup buttermilk or cottage cheese
1 tsp salt
500 ml/2 cups frying oil
150 g/generous 1 cup flour
1½ tsp dried sage
1 tsp dried thyme

1 tsp dried oregano
½ tsp ground cumin
1 tbsp salt
½ tsp black pepper

For the sauce:
2 onions
2 tbsp flour
250 ml/1 cup chicken stock
salt
pepper
250 ml/1 cup heavy cream

Fried chicken is a typical meal in the southern United States. Essentially, pieces of chicken are seasoned, floured and fried in a pan. The drippings are then incorporated into a creamy gravy. This recipe, very popular in Virginia, South Carolina, Georgia, Tennessee and Kentucky, can also be enjoyed at almost any restaurant. Over the course of his career, our chef has participated in many debates about the best way to prepare fried chicken. Recipes are often jealously guarded family secrets that are passed down from generation to generation. In the end, he arrived at the conclusion that the best recipe is a matter of personal taste.

In our version, Eric Beamesderfer seasons the chicken in an original way. He marinates the chicken in buttermilk inside a freezer bag; this is a very useful technique to cover the meat evenly without having to get your hands in the buttermilk.

Buttermilk is the whitish liquid that is left when cream is churned into butter. This can be replaced with cottage cheese made from cow's milk. Buttermilk or cottage cheese will help the flour and spices to stick to the surface of the chicken while it is fried.

Refrigerated inside the plastic bag in its marinade, the mix will have time to tenderize the flesh of the chicken and fill it with flavor. In addition, moistened meat will better withstand contact with the hot oil without drying out too much.

After that, cover the pieces of chicken in spiced flour inside a paper bag, because in a plastic bag, the marinade would tend to make all the spices adhere to the bag, rather than the chicken.

In the United States, fried chicken is traditionally served with mashed potatoes, rolls with butter, cornbread, or even succotash, a stew of corn with lima beans, onions and tomatoes.

1. Cut the chicken into 8 fairly even pieces.

2. Tip the buttermilk or cottage cheese into a plastic freezer bag. Add the pieces of chicken. Close the bag and manipulate it to thoroughly cover the chicken pieces with the marinade. Refrigerate for 1 hour.

3. Pour the flour into a bowl. Add the sage, thyme, oregano, cumin, salt and pepper. Blend well with a spoon. In a paper bag, cover the pieces of chicken with the spiced flour mixture.

Fried Chicken

4. Heat the oil in a cast-iron pot. When it bubbles, arrange the pieces of meat in it and fry them over high heat for 20 minutes, turning them over a few times. Set the chicken aside on a plate. Pour off some of the drippings.

5. Heat the pot with the remaining drippings. In it, fry the chopped onions. Stir in the flour, then thin with the chicken stock. Salt and pepper. Whisk over low heat until the gravy is smooth.

6. Finally, blend the cream into the sauce. Season to taste. Whisk one last time over low heat. Serve the pieces of fried chicken over a bed of sauce.

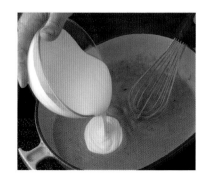

Satiny Chicken

Preparation time: 30 minutes
Cooking time: 15 minutes
Difficulty: ★

Serves 4

4 chicken thighs
oil for frying
2 pieces ginger, 5 cm/2 in each
1 small bunch chives
4 or 5 sprigs cilantro

4 tbsp sugar
1 tsp black pepper
1/2 tsp cayenne pepper
3 1/2 tbsp soy sauce
4 tbsp water
1/2 tbsp vinegar

Satiny Chicken with Chives and Ginger is among the most appreciated of Mr. So's specialties at *Grenelle de Pékin*, his restaurant in the prestigious ministries district of Paris.

Chicken and duck are the base of many familiar Chinese dishes. Chicken is cooked whole or in pieces, cubed, chopped, in fine strips or ground and incorporated into fillings for spring rolls or dumplings.

Regional chicken dishes readily blend with sesame, walnuts, water chestnuts, roasted peanuts, sweet peas, or peppers. When a whole braised or poached chicken is served in China, it is cooked such that you can easily remove the flesh with chopsticks. In fact, the Chinese prefer that their poultry be removed from the bones prior to serving. Nonetheless, in Chinese restaurants, the pieces of meat often are not de-boned, because the chefs believe the meat has more flavor when it is cooked with the bones. Therefore, a small plate is placed on the side to dispose of the scraps.

The soy sauce that flavors this dish is one of a varied ensemble of Chinese sauces with many different flavors. It is made from soybeans fermented in brine. The clear soy sauce, rather salty and delicious, works well with seafood. The darker and milder soy sauce is more commonly used with meats and mushrooms.

The Chinese also flavor their dishes with oyster sauce, made with oysters and soy sauce. As for hoisin sauce, it has a thicker texture and a slightly sweet note. It contains soy paste, sugar, garlic, sesame, chili peppers and sometimes prune compote.

Finally, let us not neglect to mention fish sauce with fermented anchovies, and pepper sauce, which should be used in moderation, since it has a strong flavor.

1. Chop the chicken thighs in half from the skin side. With a small, sharp knife, work all around the bone until it is completely detached it from the flesh.

2. Heat a pot full of oil. With a skimmer, immerse the chicken thighs into the very hot oil. Allow to cook at least 10 minutes until the skin is browned and crisp.

3. Peel and finely mince the ginger on a chopping board. Also mince the chives and cilantro with a chef's knife.

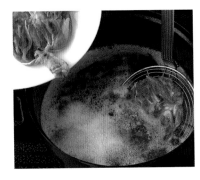

with Chives and Ginger

4. Remove the remaining small bones from the chicken thighs. Cut each thigh into even strips.

5. Pour into a pot the ginger, cilantro, chives, sugar, pepper and cayenne pepper. Add the soy sauce and 4 tbsp water. Stir over low heat until the sugar dissolves.

6. Add the vinegar to the sauce. Stir. Pour some of the sauce onto the bottom of a serving dish. Arrange the strips of chicken on top, decorate with minced ginger and chives and serve very hot.

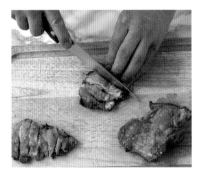

Chicken with

Preparation time: 20 minutes
Cooking time: 30 minutes
Difficulty: ★

Serves 4

4 large chicken thighs
2 tbsp peanut oil
salt
1 large onion
2 ripe tomatoes
250 g/scant 2 cups fresh shelled peanuts
2 tbsp peanut butter
1 pinch cayenne pepper

Chicken with Peanut Sauce is one of the most traditional foods of West Africa. In Cameroon this sauce is prepared with fresh peanuts, while in neighboring Senegal, cooks prefer to use a paste of roasted peanuts, like peanut butter.

Most of the chicken sold in stores comes from industrial farms. However, many Cameroonians praise the flesh and firm bones of free-range chickens, which spend their lives around the village. In addition to serving it with peanuts, they also enjoy chicken simmered in a sauce of tomatoes and onions or in red palm oil. They also marinate chicken in a mixture of seven local spices before grilling.

The peanuts that form the base of the sauce are grown in the north of Cameroon near Garoua and Maroua. These legumes, which bury themselves underground, were introduced in West Africa in the sixteenth century by Portuguese colonists who in turn brought them from Central America.

Unsalted peanuts, already shelled and blanched, are best. If you cannot find these, remove the shells and soak the peanuts in cold water for 24 hours, then roll them in a clean towel to remove their brown skins. As for the presentation, our chef advises you to always rinse the peanuts to remove all traces of dust and any remaining skin.

In the recipe presented here, Marie Koffi-Nketsia has blended the different flavors of fresh peanuts and roasted peanut paste. Ready-made paste, something like our peanut butter, is sold in metal bottles. In the markets, Cameroonians also offer this caramel- or chocolate-colored "cream", hand-made and sold in a gourd.

You can decorate your dish according to your taste with small pieces of tomatoes and crushed herbs. The same recipe works perfectly with cubes of beef, as well.

1. Place the chicken thighs on a chopping board. Chop each one in half.

2. Heat the oil in a saucepan. Add the pieces of chicken. Salt. Sear 5 minutes over high heat.

3. Peel the onion and cut into small cubes. Pour it over the seared chicken. Stir for 3 to 4 minutes over high heat while scraping the pan with a spoon to avoid sticking.

Peanut Sauce

4. When everything is well fried, cover with water. Cover and allow to cook 20 minutes. Cut the tomatoes into small cubes. Add them to the chicken while it is cooking.

5. Rinse the peanuts with cold water. In a blender or food processor, blend them into a thick, whitish paste. (Add a little cold water if necessary).

6. When the chicken is tender, add the white peanut paste, the peanut butter and a pinch of cayenne pepper. Thin with a little hot water, stirring a few minutes over low heat, taking care that it does not stick. Serve right away.

Goat Stew

Preparation time: 45 minutes
Cooking time: 50 minutes
Difficulty: ★★

Serves 6

1 kg/2¼ lb young goat
3 tbsp oil
salt
white pepper
1 onions
1 pinch chili pepper

1 pinch paprika
2 cloves
3 sprigs parsley
1 sprig thyme
3 green onions
2 kg/4½ lb yams
500 ml/2 cups milk
50 g/3½ tbsp butter
1 tsp ground nutmeg

The people of Guadeloupe and Martinique particularly favor the meat of young goats, which they call *cabri*. Goat stew is one of the most typical dishes. Each year in the month of August, the chefs in Guadeloupe organize a tremendous food festival under the name the *Fête des Cuisinières* (Festival of Women Cooks). It begins with a religious ceremony in which their most beautiful creations are presented on small pieces of furniture and brought to church to be blessed. Goat stews, *accras*, *rougailles*, Creole blood sausages and *tourments d'amour* compete for attention at the foot of the statue of Saint Lauren, patron saint of chefs.

In the countryside of Guadeloupe, some families still raise goats, pigs and some cattle. Goat meat is readily available in any butcher shop or grocery store. The families of Hindu tradition are used to sacrificing young goats for their ceremonies; they then prepare it in a special stew called *colombo*

(see pages 670 ff). The entire animal is consumed, including the organs, provided that it is cooked in the form of a stew, because the meat is too tough to be roasted.

A mousse of yams adds its discreet and subtle flavor to this meal. These tubercles of the *Dioscoreaceae* family are of Chinese and Japanese origin, and they grow in Guadeloupe, Martinique, Guyana and Réunion Island. Their taste is rather close to that of potatoes, but sweeter. Depending on the species, they can be round, long, or in the form of a hand and can sometimes weigh as much as 12 kg, or 26 lb!

Our chef suggests using the shoulder of a goat or even an entire small goat to make this dish. You can prepare the same recipe with chicken, pork or lamb.

Don't hesitate to thicken the sauce with a mixture of butter and flour if you find it too thin. To add a note of elegance to your dish, lightly sprinkle the roses of mousse with paprika.

1. Remove all the goat meat from the bones. With a chef's knife, cut the meat into cubes. Heat the oil in a pan and fry the meat for 15 minutes.

2. Add salt, pepper, chopped onion, red pepper, paprika, cloves and a West Indian bouquet garni composed of parsley, thyme and green onion tied with a piece of kitchen string.

3. Add 500 ml/2 cups cold water. Stir and bring to the boil over high heat. Simmer for 15 minutes, uncovered, to obtain a nice sauce.

with Yam Mousse

4. Cut the yams into large pieces. Peel them with a sharp kitchen knife. Cut them into smaller quarters, then steam for 15 minutes.

5. Heat the milk in a small pot with the butter and the nutmeg. Put the steamed yam in the bowl of a food processor and pour over the hot milk. Beat to obtain a purée that forms stiff peaks.

6. Using a piping bag, make rosettes of yam mousse on the corners of each serving plate. Grill for 5 minutes under a broiler. Arrange the very hot goat stew in the middle of the plates and serve.

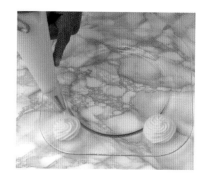

Pork Stew

Preparation time:	40 minutes
Cooking time, pork:	40 minutes
Cooking time, purée:	15 minutes
Cooking time, chayotes:	10 minutes
Difficulty:	★★

Serves 4

1 kg/2¹/₄ lb boneless pork tenderloin
40 ml/2¹/₂ tbsp oil
1 pimento
1 bunch curly-leaf parsley
1 green onion
1 onion
2 cloves
1 pinch quatre épices (blend of ginger, nutmeg, white pepper and cloves)

salt
pepper
4 tbsp granulated sugar
100 ml/7 tbsp wine vinegar

1 pineapple, ca. 2 kg/4¹/₂ lb
1 beef bouillon cube
1 red chili pepper

For the yam purée:
1 yam
1 egg yolk
3 cups milk
50 g/3¹/₂ tbsp butter
salt
pepper

For the chayotes:
2 chayotes (cristophines)
1 clove garlic
20 g/1¹/₂ tbsp butter
salt, pepper

This succulent Pork Stew with Pineapple spectacularly flavored with spices and caramel often accompanies Antillean celebrations, where the myriad subtle sweet and salty accents are greatly appreciated.

The Antilles established pork stew as an "institution" particularly prized during the Christmas season. Many people from the Martinique countryside make it with *cochon-planche*, a small black pig around 80 cm (30 in) high and 1 meter (3 feet) long, named for its raw-boned appearance. Raised in a pen close to the house where it is fed leftover fruits and vegetables, the animal is sacrificed just before Christmas.

Called *zannana* in Creole, pineapple is grown on more than 600 hectares (1,500 acres) in the north of Martinique, notably in Saint-Pierre, Gros-Morne and Morne-Rouge. At first green, the outer shell in the form of small scales becomes yellow-brown when the fruit is ripe. In Martinique, chefs also serve pork roast with pineapple, covered in a pineapple sauce that is blended with sugar, roasted in the oven and garnished with diced fruit. In this stew, our chef combines two peppers with different flavors. The first, the pimento, can be added as you begin cooking because it releases a nice pepper flavor without spiciness. The chili pepper, on the other hand, must be incorporated in the last ten minutes of cooking and removed before serving. In fact, if it should burst open during cooking, the stew will not be edible!

The *cristophine*, or chayote, that accompanies this dish is a pear-shaped vegetable with a white or green peel that grows on a climbing or creeping plant. After having eliminated the spines, you peel it like a potato and remove the central core (though the seed is edible). Cut the flesh into small pieces, blanch them for 10 minutes, then sweat them in a little melted butter with minced garlic. The yams au gratin are prepared in the manner of mashed potatoes au gratin.

1. Dice the pork tenderloin. Heat the oil in a heavy pot. When it is hot, tip in the pieces of meat and fry for about 5 minutes.

2. Add the crushed pimento, minced parsley, green onion and onion, the cloves, quatre épices, salt and pepper. Cook for 5 minutes longer.

3. Make a caramel with the granulated sugar and a little water. When it begins to brown, deglaze the with vinegar. Cook 2 minutes over low heat, stirring. Pour it into the pork stew.

with Pineapple

4. Peel the pineapple, making sure to remove all the small black points. Cut into quarters, then dice. Purée half the pineapple pieces and set aside the rest.

5. Pour the pineapple purée into the pork stew. Dissolve the bouillon cube in 150 ml/²/₃ cup water and add to the pot. Cover and cook another 20 minutes. When it is almost finished, cooking, add the chili pepper.

6. Add the remaining diced pineapple. Cook another 5 to 6 minutes, covered, then remove the spicy pepper. Serve the pork stew with a purée of yams and the diced chayotes sautéed in butter and garlic.

Alentejo-Style

Preparation time: 30 minutes
Cooking time: 2 hours 5 minutes
Difficulty: ★★

Serves 4

800 g/1³/₄ lb pork tenderloin
30 cockles (or small clams)
2 small onions

2 springs cilantro
30 g/2 tbsp tomato paste
250 ml/1 cup white wine
olive oil
salt
pepper

In the center of Portugal, where the region of Alentejo lies, cuisine harmoniously blends the bounty of the land with that of the sea. Notably, this is done through pork stew with cockles, small or medium-sized clams, *a alentejana*. The dish usually simmers in a special type of copper pan with an attached lid, a *cataplana*. This meal originates from the south of the country, where it used to be made with pork from Alentejo, known for its particular quality, but served in the inns of the Algarve. The shellfish were caught in the Algarve.

This preparation is just one of many that include pork, without a doubt the favorite Portugese meat. It is particularly sought after in regions where pastures are scarce. As in a number of other countries, butchering traditionally took place just before Christmas.

Some lean pieces, such as fillet are enjoyed fresh, covered in a garlic paste or flavored with seasonings and spices, marinated in wine and herbs and then grilled, or simmered in soups and stews. In the northern part of the country, pork seasoned with cumin is accompanied by boiled chestnuts. The rest of the meat is left to dry or be smoked: feet, ears, blood, liver, lean and fatty meat are all treated with the respect they deserve. The pig is sometimes surplanted by a suckling pig, with a finer and more delicious meat, roasted whole and diced before being garnished with vegetables.

Cockles are quite popular, as are medium-sized and small clams, whether braised, in soup or in stews. Firm and tasty, the small shellfish have to be thoroughly cleaned to remove every bit of sand and grit. In this recipe, you can replace the cockles with clams.

For the cilantro, you can also substitute parsley, which has a less pronounced taste. Another variation would be to add some potatoes three-quarters of the way through the cooking.

1. Wash the cockles under running water for 15 to 20 minutes, brushing them to remove all the grit. Set aside. Peel and slice the onions, then brown them gently in a pot with some olive oil.

2. Cut the pork tenderloin in small cubes.

3. Add the cubes of meat to the pot with the onions. Fry over high heat for around 10 minutes.

Pork Stew

4. Add the tomato paste to the pot and stir well to coat the meat.

5. Pour on the white wine and season with salt and pepper. Lower the heat and cover. Simmer covered for 1 hour 45 minutes.

6. Add the cockles to the pot, cover, and continue cooking over low heat for 10 minutes. During this time, pluck the leaves off the cilantro and chop them. Just before serving, sprinkle with the chopped cilantro.

Paella

Preparation time: 15 minutes
Cooking time: 30 minutes
Difficulty: ★

Serves 4

700 g/1½ lb rabbit
4 chicken thighs
150 ml/⅔ cup olive oil
150 g/5–6 oz flat beans
150 g/5–6 oz sugar snap peas
8 small artichokes

1 clove garlic
150 ml/⅔ cup tomato sauce
½ tsp paprika
1 pinch ground saffron
400 g/2 cups bomba rice
1 small sprig rosemary
50 g/scant ½ cup cooked white beans
60 g/2 oz small grey snails,
cooked and shelled

Spain boasts as many versions of *paella* as it does cities and villages. This satisfying meal derives its name from the large two-handled pan in which it is cooked, which allows a constant and even cooking. Originally prepared by agricultural workers in Valencia, it can be enriched with snails and vegetables, chicken, or even rabbit for special occasions. Traditionally cooked by the men for the Sunday meal, paella is a synonym for feasts. Each village and each family satiates itself with its own recipe, prepared with products offered by the surrounding environment: fish on the coasts, meat and pork products in the interior, and vegetables, spices and seasonings.

The only immutable ingredient in paella is the rice, specifically *bomba* rice, which is a round rice of exceptional quality grown in some parts of the country. In fact, *bomba calasparra* bears a label verifying its origin. What makes it so perfect for paella is its ability to absorb a great amount of liquid without bursting during cooking. It stays firm to the bite, without stickiness. At the same time, it absorbs all the flavors of the ingredients that surround it and acts as a vessel for them.

The secret of paella consists of giving the rice a unique taste, a savory combination of many flavors. The most common versions of paella are Valencia-style, rice cooked in stock flavored with rock fish, and rice with squid and ink. In our recipe, the chef adds large white lima beans called *garrafons*.

To savor a paella prepared according to the rules of the art, pay a visit to the Parisian restaurant *Fogón Saint Julien*, in the 5th district, where chef Alberto Herráiz, a true master of the dish and great defender of tradition, presides. To accompany it, he suggests serving a red *Valdepeñas* from La Mancha.

1. Using a large knife, cut the rabbit meat and chicken thighs into fairly small pieces.

2. Heat the oil in a paella pan (or very large skillet). Fry the pieces of meat in the hot oil until brown. During this time, remove the stems from sugar snap peas and cut them in half, then mince the garlic.

3. Add the white beans and sugar snap peas to the pan. Cut the base and tops of the artichokes, remove the small leaves, cut into quarters, and remove the choke. Add them to the pan. Fry over high heat until colored. Add the garlic.

Valencia-Style

4. Preheat the oven to 250°C/480°F. Pour the tomato sauce over the meat and vegetables and sprinkle on the paprika. Add 1.5 liters/1½ quarts water. Bring to the boil and reduce by one third.

5. Add the saffron, being careful to distribute it evenly.

6. Add the rice, again spreading it evenly. Blend into the other ingredients. Add the rosemary, white beans and snails. When the rice rises to the surface, put the pan in the oven and cook for 10 minutes.

Veal Roast

Preparation time:	*30 minutes*
Cooking time:	*1 hour 20 minutes*
Difficulty:	★★

Serves 4

For the roast:
¹/₂ bunch flat-leaf parsley
2 cloves garlic
1 kg/2¹/₄ lb veal round
100 ml/7 tbsp olive oil
sea salt
black pepper
10 g/2 tsp butter

For the olive sauce:
150 g/5–6 oz black olives
100 ml/7 tbsp poultry stock
3 drops lemon juice

For the accompaniment:
100 g/3¹/₂ oz dandelion greens
2 cloves garlic
1 pinch paprika
2 tbsp olive oil
1 pat butter
sea salt
black pepper

Francesca Ciardi chose to flavor this veal roast with two simple and classic seasonings, for a happy union of southern flavors: garlic and parsley, finely chopped and then slipped into pockets cut in the meat. Others that might also be used are left to your imagination, for example, basil, pesto or other diverse spices. Some people use less garlic to tone down the strong taste.

The veal round is the most tender part of a young cow. The loin and rump have similar qualities. As with all white meat, it is salted at the end of cooking. Also, for the roast to remain tender, take care to baste it regularly with its juices as it cooks. The roast can also be braised over low heat in a closed pot, surrounded by its olive sauce. Delicious in its own right, the olive sauce can be saved for a few days, if refrigerated in a well-sealed jar. It makes a quick sauce for cold meat, just like a condiment. Italians are especially fond of thin slices: pork products, cheese and meats are always sliced very thin to produce a subtler flavor, but also for overall refinement. Offer three slices of the roast on each plate, arranged in a row or in the form of a rose.

Originally slightly bitter, sprigs of dandelion greens are rapidly pan-fried in olive oil and butter, but potatoes or red pepper are simple and elegant alternatives. The accompaniment should be discreet when the veal roast is presented, nicely coated in olive sauce.

If any roast remains, cover it with plastic wrap and keep it for a couple days in the refrigerator. Cold roast between slices of fresh Italian bread make for a tasty sandwich.

1. Remove the stems from the parsley and rinse the leaves. Mince the parsley and the peeled garlic. Place the veal on a chopping board. Slide the blade of a knife along the length of the piece of meat and fill 4 or 5 incisions with the garlic-parsley blend.

2. In a pot, heat the oil over high heat. When the oil is very hot, sear the meat on all sides by turning it often. Salt and pepper the roast. Set aside away from the heat.

3. Line the bottom of a baking dish with a sheet of aluminum foil. Place the veal roast in it. Scatter small pats of butter over it and roast 1 hour at 200°C/390°F. After cooking, remove the roast from its cooking juice. Pour the juice into a small pan.

with Olive Sauce

4. Pit the olives and cut them in quarters. With a hand-held mixer, purée the olives. Set aside.

5. Combine the olive purée, poultry stock and lemon juice in the pot containing the juice from the roast. Reduce over high heat. This sauce should be quite thick. Cull the sprigs of dandelion greens.

6. Crush the garlic into coarse pieces, and add the paprika. Heat the olive oil and butter in a pan and stir fry the garlic and dandelion greens 2 minutes over high heat. Add salt and pepper. Serve al dente with the sliced roast of veal, covered in olive sauce.

Pork Roulade

Preparation time: 35 minutes
Cooking time: 1 hour 15 minutes
Marinating time: 15 minutes
Difficulty: ★★

Serves 4

1 fresh ham (pork leg)
40 g/¹/₄ cup chopped garlic
5 g/2 tsp oregano
5 g/2 tsp cumin
6 Seville oranges
200 g/7 oz slab bacon
40 g/2¹/₂ tbsp salt

Pork roulade is one of the recipes truly typical of Cuban restaurants. It offers a delicious contrast between the pronounced flavor of the smoked bacon and the mildness of the fresh pork, and with good reason is a perennial favorite of the patrons of *Bodeguita del Medio*, the most legendary restaurant in Havana. All kinds of stars, artists and prominent people have eaten at this establishment, which opened in 1942.

Pork is the most popular meat in Cuba along with chicken. On the island, pigs benefit from a natural diet of vegetables and small fruits from palm trees. The bacon that garnishes the roulade of pork is smoked pork belly taken either from the flank or the loin. The proportion of meat to fat differs, depending on the place and the cut of the meat.

Ham is here blended with the particular flavor of Seville oranges, which can be found easily in many gardens throughout Cuba. Every Cuban grandmother has "her" tree, whose oranges are superior to those growing on her neighbor's. This citrus fruit has a thick, rough skin and is quite bitter. Cubans prefer to season their food with bitter orange rather than with lemon, and use Seville oranges to make marmalade and jelly, as well. Its zest is what gives many orange liqueurs their intense orange flavor, and its leaves are the source of the essence used for perfumes and orange flower water.

If you have trouble finding bitter Seville oranges, our chef suggests that you replace them with a blend of sweet orange juice and vinegar.

When the pork roulade seems to be cooked, insert a skewer into the center, wait a few seconds, then remove it and touch the end to your lip. If it is hot and dry, the inside of the roast is cooked. Serve the slices of roulade over a bed of black beans and rice, garnished with fried onions, diced tomatoes and toasted croutons.

1. Using a large knife, divide the pork in half horizontally, not slicing all the way through. Open it up, then divide it in half two times. The meat should resemble a giant scallop.

2. Transfer the meat to a large baking dish. Sprinkle it with chopped garlic, oregano and cumin. Slice the oranges in half and squeeze them over the ham. Let the meat marinate 15 minutes.

3. Remove the skin from the slab bacon. Cut the bacon into thick slices, then into thin strips.

with Bacon

4. Arrange 2 or 3 strips of bacon, depending on the width, along one short end of the marinated meat. Roll it tightly around the bacon.

5. While holding the roulade firmly, wrap kitchen string around it as if you were tying a roast. End with a solid knot.

6. Transfer the roulade to a baking sheet and salt it. Rub it with chopped garlic. Cook in a 200°C/390°F oven for 1 hour 15 minutes. Remove the string. Slice and serve hot.

Roasted Duck

Preparation time:	*30 minutes*
Cooking time:	*1 hour 20 minutes*
First marinating:	*1 hour*
Second marinating:	*overnight*
Difficulty:	★★

Serves 4

1 duck, about 1.2 kg/2³/₄ lb
¹/₄ tsp ground cloves
2 bay leaves
2 sprigs thyme
1 cinnamon stick

4 cloves garlic
5 g/1 tbsp minced fresh ginger
salt
5 g/2 tsp crushed pepper
500 ml/2 cups red wine
1 pinch sugar
500 ml/2 cups oil
2 onions
3 dried red peppers
500 g/generous 1 lb tomatoes
1 or 2 sprigs parsley
160 g/generous ³/₄ cup rice (optional)

Monique, the mother of one of our chef's favorite colleagues, inspired him to make this dish. This traditional dish of roasted game with sauce made from its own juices is a veritable "cocktail" of Creole traditions from Mauritius. His compatriots also like to prepare this recipe with hare and stag, meats available in abundance in the country.

Duck is the favorite meat in Mauritius, where there are large industrial duck farms. There are even occasional Chinese ducks, used to prepare glazed duck. Partridges, wild turtle-doves and quails are also favorites.

Fresh ginger, named after the Indian city of Gingi, gives a pleasing bite to the sauce. Grown in Mauritius, it forms small bushes around 50 cm (20 in) high. It is an irregularly-formed tubercule with a white peel, pale yellow flesh and a strong scent of lemongrass, slightly spicy. Much of the ginger grown on the island is exported to Anglo-Saxon countries for the making of ginger ale, cookies and candies.

Whole cloves are the dried buds of a shrub called "clove tree". In the seventeenth century, this tree was grown on the Moluccas, also known as the Spice Islands, which were controlled by the Dutch. Pierre Poivre, an inhabitant of Mauritius from Reunion Island, at that time French colonies, organized an expedition in 1769 to steal clove trees from the island of Ceram. On the same occasion, he brought nutmeg to Mauritius. Today, cloves are imported from Madagascar and Zanzibar.

For the duck, the ideal would be to find a "cross-bred duck", a blend of duck from Nantes and wild duck with its characteristic flavor. But a simple small chicken will also do the trick. Finally, decorate the bird with small pieces of dried peppers.

1. Chop the duck into pieces and place them in a bowl. Add the ground cloves, bay leaves, thyme, cinnamon, garlic and peeled and chopped ginger. Salt and pepper generously. Marinate for 1 hour.

2. At the end of this time, moisten the duck with the red wine. Add a pinch of sugar and stir to combine thoroughly. Marinate at least overnight.

3. The next day, drain the duck, setting aside the marinade and seasonings. In a large pan, heat oil and fry the duck for 10 to 15 minutes. Peel and chop the onions, peppers and tomatoes.

à la Monique

4. Remove the duck pieces from the pan and put in the onions and peppers. Fry them for 5 minutes, then add the tomatoes and cook another 5 minutes. Add all the seasonings and cook another 5 minutes.

5. When everything is well cooked, pour the marinade into the pot. Bring to the boil and simmer 5 minutes over low heat.

6. Put the duck back into the sauce, cover the pan, and simmer 45 minutes. Arrange the duck on a plate and cover with the sauce seasoned with chopped parsley. Accompany with rice and parsley.

Baden-Baden Saddle

Preparation time: 1 hour
Cooking time: 40 minutes
Difficulty: ★★★

Serves 6

For the roasted venison saddle:
salt
pepper
1 venison saddle, 1.5 kg/3¼ lb
40 g/2½ tbsp butter
100 ml/7 tbsp oil

For the poached pears:
2 pears
250 ml/1 cup white wine
juice of 1 lemon

1 pinch sugar
1 vanilla bean
200 g/7 oz blueberries (jar)

For the spätzle:
500 g/3½ cups flour
6 eggs
salt

For the game sauce:
2 carrots
3 or 4 shallots
1 onion
2 sprigs thyme
2 bay leaves
1 pinch chopped parsley
4 or 5 juniper berries
400 g/14 oz chanterelles
200 ml/generous ¾ cup red wine
100 ml/7 tbsp cranberry juice
200 ml/generous ¾ cup brown duck stock

A saddle of roasted venison with the bones is a "royal dish" in Germany, just as foie gras and truffles are for the French gourmet. Otto Fehrenbacher suggests a recipe typical of the Black Forest region, one named for the hot springs town of Baden-Baden, in Baden-Württemberg. The venison is accompanied by poached pears garnished with cranberries and sautéed chanterelles, coated with a savory game sauce.

Our chef has made venison one of the great specialties in his restaurant. His recipes brought him so much renown that he uses almost one hundred animals every year, all from regional hunters. He roasts the saddle, serves the leg cut in noisettes and uses the neck and shoulder for stews.

Choose a variety of pear that holds up well during cooking, avoiding William pears, which tend to fall apart in the poaching syrup. As for the white wine, it should not be too dry so that it adds a hint of sweetness to the dish. A wine made from Chasselas grapes would work wonderfully.

Spätzle are one of the great culinary specialties from Swabia. These homemade noodles are an indispensable accompaniment to any number of meat dishes, and are often sprinkled with cheese just before serving. The *Spätzle* dough should be worked until it is firm and elastic. It is then placed on a chopping board and cut directly into a pot of boiling water in small bits. You will need to moisten the chopping board regularly as you cut, so that the dough can slide well. When the *Spätzle* rise to the water's surface, they are ready to be scooped out with a wire skimmer. They can be eaten plain, pan fried in a blend of butter and oil, or even better, in clarified butter, or layered with grated cheese and topped with blackened onions.

Take care to baste the venison saddle regularly in the oven, drawing from the cooking juices so that it does not dry out. The meat should be served pink.

1. Salt and pepper the venison. Brown it in a blend of butter and oil, then place it in a moderate oven for 12 minutes.

2. Peel the pears and halve them lengthwise. Remove the core. Poach them in a blend of water, white wine, lemon juice, sugar and vanilla. For the spätzle, pour the flour, eggs and salt into a bowl. Combine with your hands, then knead vigorously while stretching the dough.

3. Place a large piece of dough on a chopping board. Using a spatula, scrape off narrow bands of dough directly into a large pot of boiling water. When the spätzle rise to the surface, they are cooked. Immediately immerse them in cold water, then drain and set aside.

# of Venison with Spätzle

4. For the sauce, add the chopped carrots, shallots, onion, thyme, bay leaves, parsley, juniper berries and 2 or 3 chanterelles to the cooking juices and heat. Deglaze with red wine, then pour in the cranberry juice and game stock. Reduce slightly, then strain.

5. Arrange the cooked pears on a plate. Garnish with a teaspoon of drained berries.

6. Slice the saddle along the central bone and remove the meat. Slice the 2 fillets into strips. Pan-fry the rest of the chanterelles separately. On the serving plate, arrange the slices of meat, chanterelles, spätzle and surround with sauce.

Chicken Soufflé with

Preparation time: 30 minutes
Cooking time: 5 minutes
Difficulty: ★★

Serves 4

25 g/3 tbsp chopped garlic chives (ku chai)
1 sprig lemongrass
10 g/1 tbsp chopped fresh turmeric
3 g/1 tsp chopped fresh galangal
2 shallots
5 sprigs fresh cilantro

2 cloves garlic
250 g/9 oz white meat chicken
45 g/3 tbsp red curry paste
1 egg
40 g/3 tbsp caster sugar
90 ml/6 tbsp fish sauce
700 ml/3 cups coconut milk
2 fresh bergamot orange leaves

Grilled, steamed, flavored with curry, or chopped into kebabs, the meat of Thai chickens is used in many dishes, as diverse as they are sophisticated. Smaller than the chickens we are familiar with, this bird hides a dense and delicate flesh under its yellow skin. It is raised to be consumed in its entirety, and the Thais use everything, from head to toe. The carcasses are immersed into a stock flavored with lemongrass, and the fillets removed from along the back will compose a delicious soufflé.

Thai chickens are usually available in Asian grocery stores. The pre-cut presentation makes preparing them easier. Of course, the soufflé will also succeed with white meat chicken from another source.

On the other hand, our chef urges you not to make substitutions for any other ingredients in this recipe. Very common in

Thai food, coconut milk comes in two forms, one liquid and the other thicker and creamy. For the soufflé, you should choose the thicker kind. The coconut milk with a more liquid consistency lends itself to the preparation of desserts. Thai cuisine is renowned for its harmony of flavors. When chopped, each ingredient is weighed with precision. All of them can be kept for fifteen days in a hermetically sealed pot, making it easy to prepare a quick Asian dinner.

Like all soufflés, Thai *homok kaï* does not wait around. As soon as it puffs up from the action of the steam, turn it over onto a folded banana leaf to strengthen the bottom. Supported by a wooden pick, each corner is flattened out to form a bowl. Finally, turn out the soufflé onto the banana leaf. Tiny strips of red pepper will conceal the wooden picks.

1. Chop the garlic chives, lemongrass, turmeric, galangal, shallots, cilantro and garlic. Put them in the bowl of a food processor. Chop in successive "pulses" until everything is minced, but not puréed.

2. Add the chicken, cut into chunks. Blend until the meat is completely incorporated into the mixture.

3. Add the red curry paste to the blend and mix until it becomes a thick paste. Finally, add the egg, sugar and fish sauce to the food processor.

Coconut Milk and Spices

4. Pour the coconut milk into the paste all at once. Continue blending until you have a smooth yellow mixture.

5. Fill a deep, round bowl ¾ full with the chicken preparation. Sprinkle the surface with the chopped bergamot orange leaves.

6. Fill a large pot ¾ full of water. Bring to the boil. Place the bowl with the chicken mixture above the boiling water. Cook 5 minutes in this water bath, over medium heat. As soon as the soufflé puffs up, remove it from the heat and serve hot.

Duck and Corn

Preparation time: 20 minutes
Cooking time: 1 hour 40 minutes
Difficulty: ★

Serves 4

For the duck in sauce:
1 duck breast
50 ml/3¹/₂ tbsp sake
50 ml/3¹/₂ tbsp mirin (rice wine)
80 ml/¹/₃ cup soy sauce
juice of 1 orange (optional)
1 tsp rice vinegar
salt

30 g/1 oz dried, flaked bonito
2 strips konbu algae

For the corn flan:
100 g/²/₃ cup cooked corn kernels
500 ml/2 cups milk
4 egg yolks
salt

For the garnish:
1 large daikon (Japanese radish)
chives (optional)
1 red bell pepper
1 yellow bell pepper

The Japanese inherited little inclination to eat meat from their ancestors. In the year 675, a decree forbade practicing Buddhists from eating a wide range of animals. This ban was not lifted until Emperor Meiji did so in 1873. In addition, Japanese cuisine developed throughout the country based on dishes made with fish, rice, vegetables and noodles. However, the Japanese continued to cook some poultry raised at home.

Often, meat dishes prepared in Japan are derived from Chinese or European recipes, but soy sauce, miso and sake have given them an unmistakable Japanese touch. Today, the different sorts of meat remain expensive for the Japanese, and they are accordingly used in tiny quantities. They often enjoy duck breast sautéed in teriyaki sauce (sake, mirin, sugar and soy sauce), or marinated in these same ingredients and simmered with leeks.

The sake that flavors the *sunomono* sauce is one of a number of essential Japanese condiments. Next to tea, it is the Japanese's favorite drink, enjoyed hot or cold. In cooking, it lightens the iodized taste of fish and the flavor of some foods that are too salty. Sake is made from steamed rice, yeast and water. The traditional process of fermentation and brewing lasts one hundred days, resulting in a light, 15-proof wine. Its "cousin", mirin, is a sweet sake used solely in cooking.

To prepare his sauce, our chef begins with a classic bonito stock or *dashi*. The bonito, a small tuna, is skinned, sliced, cooked and then smoked. It is left to dry for six months until it resembles petrified wood. In the countryside, cooks regularly grate a few flakes off a block of bonito using a sort of plane. These days you can find bonito flakes in any Japanese or Asian supermarket.

1. Make a cooking utensil by sticking 5 or 6 wooden skewer halves through a chunk of radish. Poke the skin of the duck all over with the skewer tips.

2. Place the duck skin side down in a heated pan. Brown it on both sides in its own fat, 5 minutes on each side.

3. In a small pot, combine the sake, mirin and 50 ml/3¹/₂ tbsp of the soy sauce. Add the orange juice. Heat until the liquid is just about to boil.

Sunomono

4. Place the duck breast in the hot sauce. Bring to the boil and cook 15 minutes over low heat.

5. Purée the corn kernels. Stir in the milk and egg yolks and add salt. Pass through a fine sieve, then pour the mixture into ramekins and cook 1 hour in a water bath.

6. In a pot, combine the remaining soy sauce, the vinegar, water, salt, bonito and konbu. Cook 15 minutes. Strain the sauce and let it cool. Arrange in a dish a corn flan, strips of duck, minced chives, sliced bell peppers and grated radish.

Lamb Tajine with

Preparation time: 20 minutes
Cooking time: 55 minutes
Difficulty: ★★

Serves 4

1 leg of lamb, 1.5 kg/3¼ lb
salt
pepper
1 onion
oil
100 g/7 tbsp butter

1 tsp ginger
ground cinnamon
½ tsp saffron threads
ground nutmeg
1 kg/2¼ lb quinces
1 tbsp powdered sugar
20 g/3 tbsp black cumin seeds

Quinces, not widely used in cooking, still deserve high praise. Throughout Morocco, they fill the stands at fruit markets toward the end of summer. They are a favorite in Moroccan gastronomy, where fascinating blends of sweet and savory reign supreme. Of course, they can otherwise be prepared in jam, jelly, squeezed into refreshing juice, or dried in the sun like apples and pears to be saved and used later for cooking.

Black cumin seeds, those tiny, black, flavorful grains, are often used in cooking and baking in North Africa and the Middle East. In addition, they serve to decorate breads and garnish finished dishes.

Sprinkled over the quince, these seeds add a festive touch. They have a particularly Eastern taste when the small seeds crack under your teeth, combined with caramel from the quinces candied in the sauce.

The salted meat could be replaced by beef, cooked until very tender in a saffron stock and then fried in a pan. The quinces can be replaced by firm Anjou or William pears. In the preparation of this tajine, the lamb soaks up the very sweet taste of the fruits, giving it a strong, yet mild flavor.

While they cook, the quinces release a syrupy juice and they brown very quickly in the frying pan; they take on an amber brown color and the caramel gives them a golden covering. The saffron, with its triple contribution of color, flavor and aroma, plays an important role in the intermingling of multiple tastes, to create a sophisticated and enjoyable dish.

Beautifully presented, this dish is rich enough to hold its own in a festive menu preceded by fresh salads and followed by a refreshing dessert such as sherbet.

1. Cut the lamb into 4 or 5 pieces. Lightly salt and pepper each piece. Set aside.

2. Peel and chop the onion. In a large pot, heat the oil and add the butter. Fry the onion 5 minutes and then add the pieces of meat, one by one.

3. Salt, pepper and sprinkle with the ginger, cinnamon, saffron and nutmeg. Cook for 5 minutes. Pour in a bowl of water to thin the juiced released by the meat. Cover the pot and simmer 20 minutes over low heat.

590   Lahoucine Belmoufid, Morocco

Quince and Cumin Seeds

4. Peel the quinces, cut them in half, and remove the seeds. After the meat has simmered, add the quinces and cook 10 minutes over medium heat.

5. Remove the quinces from the stock. Caramelize them in a pan with the powdered sugar and a ladle-full of stock, with the rounded part of the fruit on the bottom. Reduce for 15 minutes. Turn them over half way through cooking.

6. Sprinkle black cumin seeds over the rounded side of each quince, trying not to drop the cumin seeds in the sauce or on the meat. Serve the tajine covered with juice and surrounded by a crown of quinces.

Budapest-Style

Preparation time: 20 minutes
Cooking time: 45 minutes
Difficulty: ★

Serves 4

2 large onions
3 tbsp oil
1 tsp paprika
1 tomato
1 bouillon cube
60 g/2 oz fatback

120 g/4 oz mushrooms
100 g/3¹/₂ oz raw goose liver
2 Hungarian green peppers
4 slices beef fillet, 100–120 g/3¹/₂–4 oz each
salt
pepper
100 g/²/₃ cup cooked peas
butter

For the accompaniment (optional):
400 g/2 cups rice
salt
parsley leaves

In the traditional recipe for Budapest-Style Tournedos, chefs cover the fillet with all of its mushroom sauce, small vegetables and goose liver. Our chef chose to create a more modern presentation. He dressed the plate with a thin bed of sauce and arranged the grilled tournedos on top of it. This dish was created in the 1930s by a Hungarian chef.

For everyday meals, Hungarians often eat pork or chicken, reserving beef for more special occasions. They like to pan-fry beef with a ratatouille made with peppers, tomatoes, onions, bacon and paprika. This dish is decorated with fried pieces of bacon cut into the shape of a cock's comb, and topped with an egg.

Pork fat is a mainstay in Hungarian cuisine. The fattiest part, taken from the back of the pig (hence the name fatback), is used primarily in dishes where other Europeans would use leaner bacon. After it is cut, the fat is salted and left to rest for a few hours. It is ideal if you can smoke it yourself. This sort of

bacon is typical of the Alföld Plain. In Hungarian novels, they write that cattle ranchers on the great plain nourished themselves with bread garnished with pork fat and onions. In the past, some of it was included in almost every meat dish. Today it is used less often, but it is an essential ingredient in *lebbencsleves*, for example, a traditional soup with pasta, peppers, potatoes and tomatoes.

The mushrooms called "button" are about the only ones grown in Hungary. Sometimes chefs prepare a meatless goulash made with mushrooms; they also make their way into salads and accompany meat. Our chef suggests another delicious idea for blending mushrooms and goose liver: fill two large mushroom caps with a goose liver mousse, reassemble the mushrooms, then dip them in a breading of egg, flour and semolina before frying. These could be served as an appetizer or as a main dish with rice.

1. Peel the onions, chop and fry them in oil. Add the paprika, diced tomato and the crumbled bouillon cube. Add 200 ml/generous ³/₄ cup water and cook 10 to 15 minutes. Cook the rice for 20 minutes in lightly salted boiling water.

2. In a second pan, cook the fatback until it is transparent. Add the mushrooms, cut in quarters, and fry 2 to 3 minutes.

3. Cut the goose liver and pepper into cubes. Add them to the mushrooms and cook 5 minutes over high heat.

Tournedos

4. Pour the onion and tomato mixture, with its sauce, into the pan of goose liver. Bring to the boil and simmer another 5 minutes.

5. Pan-fry the fillet of beef in hot butter, 5 minutes on each side. Season with salt and pepper.

6. Garnish the plates with mushroom and goose liver sauce and place a tournedos on each one. Garnish with the peas, and accompany if you like with rice and sprigs of fresh parsley.

Iberian Tripe,

Preparation time: 1 hour
Cooking time: 3 hours 5 minutes
Difficulty: ★★★

Serves 6

For the meat:
750 g/1³/₄ lb tripe
1 kg/2¹/₄ lb pork foot and muzzle
500 ml/2 cups white vinegar
1 onion
6 cloves
1 bouquet garni (thyme, bay leaf, parsley)
1 carrot

1 pepper bird
200 g/7 oz chorizo
200 g/7 oz blood sausage

For the refried sauce:
1 onion
1 clove garlic
6 tomatoes
50 ml/3¹/₂ tbsp olive oil
150 g/generous 1 cup flour
10 g/2¹/₂ tbsp sweet paprika
2 tsp salt
2 tsp pepper

With this recipe, José Luis Tarín Fernández pays homage to *cerdo ibérico*, the Spanish pig, without which so many local specialties appreciated by gourmets would not exist. Similar to a wild boar, this black animal runs freely and happily in the cork oak forests in Extremadura and the north of Andalusia.

Although it is washed and ready to use, the tripe should be blanched before cooking. Our chef suggests blanching all meats in water with white vinegar: two precautions are better than one. A long, gentle cooking produces soft and tender tripe. In Spain, the combination of tripe and pork foot and muzzle is often enjoyed simmered with potatoes.

When drained, let the meat cool on a chopping board. Meat cooked for a long time needs time to rest in order to keep its flavor. The well-cooked foot and muzzle of pork are easy to bone. Remove the skin before dicing it.

As for the tomatoes, they are an integral part of Andalusian cuisine. Buy them ripe and fragrant. Our chef adds them to the sauce with a pang of regret, as this is not quite authentic. The tomatoes of his Sévillian region taste so good that people prefer to consume them uncooked, as a fresh accompaniment to the tripe.

Garlic and onions are cooked in olive oil for a milder flavor. You can extend the cooking time from 10 to 20 minutes over very low heat. Because large dishes deserve a little time, add the stock to the sauce ladle by ladle.

Like all dishes that cook for a long time, tripe is tastier the next day. You can reheat it gently. Small potatoes sautéed in olive oil will make a perfect garnish.

1. Place the tripe, foot and muzzle in a large pot. Cover with cold water, filling the pot ³/₄ full. Add the vinegar. Bring to the boil and let cool.

2. Pour the mixture into a second large pot. Cover with cold water. Add 1 onion studded with the cloves, the bouquet garni, the peeled carrot and the pepper bird. Finish with the chorizo and blood sausage. Cover and cook 2¹/₂ hours over low heat.

3. Remove the meats from the pot with a skimmer. Let them cool on a chopping board. Reserve the water from cooking without the aromatic garnish. Slice the chorizo and blood sausage 2 cm/³/₄ in thick. Slice the tripe, foot and muzzle in dice of 2 cm/³/₄ in.

Chorizo and Blood Sausage

4. For the sauce, chop the onion and garlic and dice the tomatoes. Fry the onion and garlic in oil for 10 minutes over low heat. Add the tomatoes. Cook 1 minute while stirring. Mix in the flour, paprika, salt and pepper. Stir to obtain a smooth paste.

5. Quickly add the cooking water from the meat. Stir and bring to the boil. Add the tripe to the sauce. Allow to reduce for 10 minutes, uncovered, over high heat.

6. When the sauce is nicely reduced and thickened, add the diced meat along with the sliced chorizo and blood sausage. Cover and simmer 5 minutes. Serve hot.

Veal with Paprika

Preparation time: 30 minutes
Cooking time: 40 minutes
Difficulty: ★★

Serves 4

800 g/1¾ lb veal shoulder
1 large onion
oil
1 tsp ground paprika
1 tbsp tomato paste
1 tomato

2 Hungarian green peppers
salt
1 tsp flour
200 ml/generous ¾ cup heavy cream

For the galuska:
200 g/generous 1⅓ cups flour
2 medium eggs
salt

Veal with Paprika is a traditional dish widespread in Hungary. Chefs also prepare lamb, fish and chicken in the same manner. You can even use mushrooms instead of meat, making it a vegetarian meal.

Veal features in several very popular dishes in Hungary. It is enjoyed in goulash soup and in the stew called *pörkölt*. A less known variation of Turkish inspiration consists of cooking veal in a sauce with rice pilaf. It goes well with ratatouille, and chefs make delicious roasts with it. Budapest-Style Tournedos (see page 822), which is prepared with beef as well as with veal, is served in a mushroom sauce with tomatoes, pepper and goose or duck liver. In Budapest you might also get to taste the grilled, Estérazy-style rump steak, which is covered in a creamy sauce of onions, mustard and carrots.

The vegetables most commonly used in Hungarian cuisine include carrots, green and yellow beans, peppers, "white carrots" (better known as parsley root), tomatoes, cauliflower, green cabbage and Brussels sprouts. Often prepared with other vegetables in the form of ratatouille, tomatoes grown in Hungary are also exported to Germany and Austria.

Paprika is produced in two Hungarian regions that are very distinct: in the south near Szeged, and in Kalosca, a city in the east close to the Körös River. It is prepared from a very small, elongated, red pepper with a powerful flavor. In the months of September and October, the façades of many houses are adorned with strings of peppers left to dry in the sun for two to three weeks. Reduced into a powder, the best paprika comes from those who produce only small quantities.

When you serve Veal with Paprika and Galuska, pour a little cream over the meat and sprinkle it with paprika for an attractive touch of color.

1. Dice the boned shoulder of veal. Peel and chop the onion. Fry it 5 minutes in a saucepan with oil and a little paprika. Add the cubes of veal. Cook for 5 minutes.

2. Stir in the tomato paste and then add 400 ml/1⅔ cups water. Sprinkle with paprika. Bring to the boil and cook for about 10 minutes.

3. Add the diced tomato and the peppers sliced into rings. Salt. Stir, then cover the pan and cook for another 10 minutes.

and Galuska

4. Add the flour to the heavy cream and then salt. Pour this preparation into the pot with the veal. Stir with a spoon and bring to the boil. Cook another 5 to 10 minutes, stirring so it doesn't stick.

5. Prepare the galuska by mixing the flour, eggs and salt. Add 150 ml/²/₃ cup water. Stir with a spoon until you obtain a rather soft, pale yellow mass. Place the dough onto a chopping board.

6. Bring a pot of water to the boil. Using a plastic scraper, drop very small heaps of dough into the boiling water. When they rise to the surface, remove them with a skimmer and refresh in very cold water. Serve the veal stew accompanied by the galuska.

Desserts & Pastries

American

Preparation time: 1 hour
Cooking time: 1 hour
Chilling time, dough: 30 minutes
Difficulty: ★★

Serves 8

For the crust:
300 g/2¼ cups flour
1 tsp salt
180 g/13 tbsp butter, cut in small cubes
80 ml/⅓ cup cold water

For the filling:
45 g/⅓ cup flour
100 g/7 tbsp brown sugar
100 g/7 tbsp white sugar
1 tsp cinnamon
1 tsp allspice
2 tbsp lemon juice
1 egg
6 Granny Smith apples
3 tbsp butter

Apples have been cultivated abundantly in Europe and Asia for almost 2000 years, and cooks know how to turn them into literally countless delicacies. One might wonder where the expression "as American as apple pie" comes from. Many Americans have sweet memories of apple pies from their childhood, fresh out of the oven and placed on a windowsill to cool. A pie on the windowsill is an image still typically associated with farms, especially in the northeast United States.

Originally of English origin, apple pie is most often served as a dessert, but also makes a regal Yankee breakfast. It is filled with native apples, originally a cross of wild apples from New Orleans and a variety of European apples imported by the colonizers. For this recipe, you will want to choose apples that are quite tart, but ripe enough to produce their own sugar. You can even combine the apples with blueberries, blackberries, strawberries, rhubarb or raisins.

When making the dough, it is recommended that you use very cold butter, which will blend more easily with the flour. If the butter is too soft, the dough will be too smooth, almost sticky. For the same reason, the water should be ice cold, and you should not mix the dough too much. Once the pie is cooked, the texture of the crust will be quite flaky and will melt in your mouth. Some traditional apple pie masters replace the butter with lard. You can choose, depending on your own taste.

Don't hesitate to give expression to your artistic capabilities by making pretty designs on the top crust of the pie. Apple pie can be served with a scoop of vanilla ice cream, whipped cream or melted cheddar cheese.

1. To make the dough, place the flour and salt in a bowl. Add the butter and water. Rub the flour and butter between your fingertips, forming a dough. Make two balls of equal size and place them in the refrigerator for 30 minutes.

2. In a bowl, combine the flour, sugars, cinnamon, allspice, lemon juice and the egg. Mix well until caramel colored.

3. Peel the apples, cut them in half and remove the seeds. Cut into even slices. Add them to the bowl with the other ingredients and mix.

Apple Pie

4. Roll out the balls of dough with a rolling pin. Butter the pie pan, especially the sides, right up to the top. Press one of the rolled-out crusts into the pan.

5. Fill the pan to the top with the apples. Scatter some small pieces of butter over them.

6. Cover with the second crust. Fold over and press together the edges all the way around. Bake in the oven at 220°C/430°F for at least 1 hour.

Strudels with

Preparation time: 40 minutes
Cooking time: 30 minutes
Difficulty: ★★

Serves 4

For the strudels:
2 lemons
100 g/7 tbsp butter
2 eggs, separated
250 g/9 oz brioche
125 ml/¹/₂ cup milk
500 g/2 cups fromage blanc
50 g/3¹/₂ tbsp sugar
1 package strudel leaves

For the vanilla sauce:
500 ml/2 cups milk
2 vanilla beans
4 egg yolks
200 g/1³/₄ cups powdered sugar
20 g/3 tbsp powdered vanilla cream
or vanilla pudding mix

For the decoration:
25 g/3¹/₂ tbsp powdered sugar
red currants
raspberries
strawberries
mint leaves

Our chef here presents a spectacular and elegant way of presenting the traditional strudel in individual servings. These pouches are filled with a mixture of brioche, fromage blanc and lemon, and are further enhanced with a light sprinkling of powdered sugar crowned with red berries. Symbolic of Austrian gastronomy, the strudel is usually wrapped in a fine, supple pastry, made of flour, oil, salt and water. It is rolled around a sweet stuffing that might include apples, jam, plums, fromage blanc, poppy seeds, hazelnuts or walnuts. In this case, the dough is shaped like thin crêpes, which are then placed in circular pastry molds, filled with stuffing, then wrapped to form a pouch.

When you are ready to put the dough into the molds, fill the bottom of the mold with a small square of the strudel dough, then place the large square that will form the pouch over it.

This precaution ensures that the cake maintains its shape and prevents the filling from leaking. Our chef uses an unbeaten, thick Austrian fromage blanc with 10% fat content to make the filling. Another fresh cheese, well strained, would work just as well. If the cheese you are using is very moist, wrap it in a muslin cloth and let it drain for one to two days.

This filling can be given a special flavor by adding raisins that have been soaked in rum, crushed pistachios or pieces of apricot or plum. Before wrapping the dough over the stuffing, brush it with melted butter. Gently twist the top of the dough to form a pretty packet and top it again with a little butter. When baking, place a piece of aluminum foil over the pastry at the beginning so that the top does not turn golden too quickly. The vanilla sauce can be replaced with apricot sauce or a purée of red berries.

1. Squeeze the lemons and grate the peel. In a large bowl, beat the butter with the egg yolks, lemon juice and lemon zest.

2. Cut the brioche in small cubes. Sprinkle with the milk. Let the bread pieces soak for a while so that they absorb the milk. Stir in the fromage blanc. Mix with a spatula until this mixture has the consistency of a filling.

3. Pour the butter and lemon mixture into the fromage blanc mixture, and blend together. For the vanilla sauce, heat the milk with the vanilla. Beat the egg yolks with the powdered sugar and powdered cream. Blend.

Vanilla Sauce

4. Whip the egg whites until they are snow white. Add the sugar and continue whipping until you have a smooth, stiff meringue.

5. Delicately fold the meringue into the brioche mixture. Butter a pastry dish and put the pastry circles on it. Fill each circle first with a small square of dough, then a much larger one that extends far over the rim of the mold.

6. Spoon in the filling. Close the pastry to form a pouch. Bake for 20 minutes at 180°C/355°F. Carefully remove the circular molds. Place each pastry on a bed of vanilla sauce. Sprinkle with powdered sugar, and decorate with red berries and mint leaves.

Banana Flambé

Preparation time: 20 minutes
Cooking time: 30 minutes
Chilling time, ice cream: overnight
Difficulty: ★★

Serves 6

For the vanilla ice cream:
500 ml/2 cups milk
2 vanilla beans
8 egg yolks
250 g/2¹⁄₄ cups powdered sugar

For the bananas:
6 bananas
3 oranges
1 lemon
100 g/7 tbsp butter
200 g/³⁄₄ cup + 2 tbsp cane sugar
30 ml/2 tbsp aged rum

One of the most classic West Indian dishes, Banana Flambé with Aged Rum combines two of the leading products of Guadeloupe: cane sugar and bananas. Half of the arable land of the island is devoted to sugar cane production, and less than one-fourth is occupied by banana trees.

A famous proverb in Creole says *Si bon Die ti jette banane, fe'me pas tes yeux, ou've ta bouche,* which literally means "If the good Lord sends you bananas, don't close your eyes, open your mouth!" or, simplified, "If joy comes your way, take advantage of it!" The banana tree is actually a huge herb that grows to a height of 3 to 8 meters (10–26 feet); the fruit grows in "hands" that contain 10 to 25 bananas, also called "fingers." A whole bunch, which is called a stem, consists of several "hands" and can weigh up to 30 kg (66 lb) and contain 200 to 300 bananas. In Guadeloupe, bananas are cultivated mainly in Basse-Terre, not far from Capesterre. Almost all of the produce

is exported to metropolitan France. To make Banana Flambé, our chef recommends using regular *poyo* bananas, which are in fact the only ones exported. Sugar cane was first introduced in the West Indies in 1645 to replace the tobacco culture. Nowadays it occupies almost all the plains and the hillsides of the Grande-Terre, although the production of sugar is currently declining sharply.

The cane that does not leave for the sugar mills ends up at the agricultural rum distilleries. When the cane is crushed, it gives out a juice called *vesou*. This is fermented for 24 hours and then distilled. White rum is aged for three months in an oak barrel. After 6 to 18 months in a wooden barrel, it is called *rum paille*. The aged rum used by our chef needs to mature for at least three years. Guadeloupe produces around 66,500 hl (1.7 million gallons) of rum every year, of which 21,000 hl (550,000 gallons) are agricultural rum.

1. A day ahead, use the ice cream ingredients to make a custard sauce, then freeze. The day of serving, peel the bananas and cut them in two lengthwise. Squeeze out the orange and lemon juice and set them aside separately.

2. Melt the butter in a large frying pan and sprinkle the cane sugar over it. Simmer for 10 minutes until you have a pretty caramel-colored sauce.

3. Place half of the bananas in the sauce. Cook for 5 minutes over a hot flame.

with Aged Rum

4. When the syrup starts to caramelize and form small bubbles, carefully turn the bananas over so that they brown evenly.

5. When the bananas are well-cooked and caramelized, remove them from the frying pan. Deglaze the sauce by pouring orange and lemon juice over it. Reduce for 5 minutes over a hot flame.

6. Strain the sauce. Place the bananas on dessert plates, then top with sauce. Pour the rum over each serving and ignite it. Serve with a scoop of vanilla ice cream.

Chocolate

Preparation time: 30 minutes
Cooking time: 4 minutes
Difficulty: ★★

Serves 4

For the custard:
125 g/9 tbsp sugar
6 eggs
500 ml/2 cups milk
50 g/¹/₃ cup cornstarch

For the choux pastry:
250 ml/1 cup water
10 g/2 tsp salt
20 g/3 tbsp powdered sugar
75 g/¹/₃ cup butter
125 g/³/₄ cup + 2 tbsp flour
4 eggs
500 ml/2 cups peanut oil for frying
200 g/7 oz chocolate
100 ml/7 tbsp water
powdered sugar

What could be sweeter than waking up to the aroma of hot chocolate? The Spanish have a special predilection for this magic potion. Furthermore, when delicious *bunuelos* (donuts) or hot and golden-brown *churros* are served with chocolate, a Madrileno wakes up in a good mood.

The recipe for these Chocolate Cream Puffs is simple: just adhere to the quantity of the ingredients. One by one, blend the eggs into the warm choux pastry; dough that is too hot will prevent the eggs from mixing well.

When frying the dough, have a small bowl filled with cold water close by. Wetting the two spoons in between scooping up each portion of dough will keep it from sticking to the spoons and help it slide more easily into the hot oil.

As soon as the balls of dough puff up to the desired size, take them out of the oil just before they become brown. If they puff up with too much pride, they might collapse. When they have cooled down a little, fill them with the custard. Using just the dough, you can also make small balls, sprinkled with powdered sugar, or else profiteroles, in which the small puffs are filled with vanilla ice cream and topped with hot chocolate. The dough should be allowed to rest for two days in the refrigerator, covered with plastic wrap.

The filling of the profiteroles varies according to the chef's inspiration: vanilla, orange or cocoa custard, or chocolate ganache… all ideas are welcome.

As the Spanish are gourmands, Rufino Manjarrés has another fate in store for his pastries. Filled with custard or chocolate, he presents them on a bed of custard sauce and tops them with a chocolate sauce. A real treat to be enjoyed with friends or, even better, in secret!

1. Blend the ingredients for the custard, then store it in the refrigerator. In a saucepan, warm the water, salt, sugar and softened butter over medium heat for 2 minutes. Lower the heat as soon as the butter is melted.

2. Pour the flour gently into the mixture: beat thoroughly with a wooden spatula to form a homogenous dough. When it starts to pull away from the sides of the saucepan, take it off the heat.

3. Break the eggs one at a time into the dough, beating the dough after each egg has been added. Once all the eggs have been added, blend until smooth.

Cream Puffs

4. Heat the oil in a saucepan. Slide a spoonful of dough into the oil.

5. Fry the profiteroles for 1 minute. Take them out of the oil as soon as they turn golden and place them on paper towels to cool.

6. Fill a small piping bag with the custard. Use the nozzle of the bag to make a hole in each pastry and fill them with custard. Melt the chocolate with the water. Serve the cream puffs topped with the hot chocolate sauce or sprinkled with powdered sugar.

Banana Fritters

Preparation time: 30 minutes
Cooking time: 20 minutes
Difficulty: ★

Serves 4 (ca. 20 pieces)

For the banana fritters:
4 bananas
1 tbsp sugar
50 g/¹/₃ cup flour
1 pinch active yeast
1 pinch salt

oil for frying
100 g/7 tbsp sugar
¹/₂ tsp cinnamon powder

For the custard sauce:
1 vanilla bean
500 ml/2 cups milk
6 egg yolks
120 g/9 tbsp sugar

Mauritians, who are particularly fond of donuts, merrily call this dessert banana cake. The sweet fritters are just as delicious when made with pineapple or apples as with bananas. The Hindus of Mauritius treat themselves to potato cake filled with sweet potatoes and sweetened coconuts for the festival of Diwali, which celebrates the return of the god Rama from exile. There are even savory donuts, such as chili cake, which are served as appetizers.

On Mauritius, the banana trees are planted solely for local needs. Bananas, lychees, longans, mangoes and Chinese guavas are all found growing in gardens. Among the noteworthy species, the little banana sort called *zingili* is very sweet and slightly sour at the same time, and it has pink flesh.

Originally from Africa, large red bananas are used mostly for decoration because of its starchy fruit. In Mauritius, the bananas are made into fricassees, curries or chips, or are used to make pies or ice cream.

Vanilla is cultivated on Mauritius, Reunion, Madagascar and the Seychelles. The vanilla bean is the fruit of an orchid that climbs up the length of tree trunks. When they are harvested, the beans are yellow and don't have any smell. They are only sold after they have been dried for a long time. Visitors can explore the Vanilla Crocodile and Tortoise Park on Mauritius, which has information on the vanilla plant as well as a crocodile farm.

When frying the fritters, make sure that the oil is not too hot, or the dough will quickly brown on the outside while the inside remains uncooked.

To determine when the custard sauce, a classic crème anglaise, is ready, put a little on a spatula and pass the end of your index finger over the cream. It should neatly separate. The custard sauce can be replaced with strawberry purée, or you can mix the two together.

1. Peel the bananas. Mash them with a fork in a bowl. For the custard sauce, split the vanilla bean and warm it with the milk in a saucepan. Bring it to the boil and set aside.

2. To make the dough for the fritters, mix the sugar, flour, yeast and salt in a small bowl. Add all this to the banana purée.

3. Heat the oil in the fryer to 160°C/320°F. When it is ready, make small dumplings from the dough by rolling the banana mixture between two spoons.

with Custard Sauce

4. Drop the fritters into the hot oil. Fry until they become golden brown.

5. Place the fried fritters on paper towels to drain excess oil. Mix the sugar and cinnamon on a plate. Roll the hot fritters in this mixture to coat thoroughly.

6. To finish the sauce, whisk the egg yolks and sugar in a pan. Add the milk. Warm over low heat until it is thick enough to cover the spatula. Serve the fritters with warm custard sauce.

Caramelized

Preparation time: 20 minutes
Cooking time: 7 to 8 minutes
Difficulty: ★

Serves 4

1 egg
150 g/generous 1 cup flour
1 tsp active yeast
200 ml/generous ³/₄ cup water
4 Golden Delicious apples

120 g/9 tbsp sugar
1 handful white sesame seeds
oil for frying

Here our chef recommends a family recipe that is well known throughout China. These apple fritters, crispy and melting at the same time, are wrapped in a smooth caramel shell with a sprinkle of sesame seeds.

It is not a Chinese tradition to finish meals with a dessert. They prefer to eat sweets between their meals. At big ceremonial feasts, they serve sweets between the main dishes to refresh their palates; but everyday meals are more often rounded off with fruit.

China enjoys a huge variety of fruits, from the familiar to the exotic. Instead of classic apples in the fritters, in China it is also possible to make them with coconuts, bananas, the miniscule citrus fruit called kumquats, arbute berries (the fruit of the strawberry tree, which resemble giant strawberries), lychees flavored with violet or even mangoes, papayas or the unusual durian. The Chinese make some interesting things with

this green spiky fruit. When opened, it gives off such a strong smell that it is also quite aptly called the stinky fruit!

In Chinese kitchens, apples are generally cooked in the form of fritters, made into sauce to fill a tart, or even stuffed with dates and steamed. In savory dishes, they are exquisitely sautéed with crustaceans or blended with oranges in a sauce for spareribs.

To add a final touch to the fritters' caramel shell, Shing-Kwok So uses white sesame seeds. Chinese cuisine has been using sesame seeds for more than 2,000 years. They bread shrimp with these seeds, and roast them before adding them to a number of meat dishes.

You can enjoy different variations of these Chinese fritters by using pineapples, bananas or slices of yam in place of the apples.

1. Beat the egg in a small bowl as though for an omelet. Combine the flour and yeast in a separate dish. Add the egg and 100 ml/7 tbsp of the water. Whisk into an even batter.

2. Peel the apples. Cut off the top and the bottom of the apple, then cut each apple into four slices. Remove the core.

3. Dip the pieces of apple in the batter, letting them soak in a good amount of the mixture.

Apple Fritters

4. Heat the oil in a frying pan. Put in the apples when the oil is very hot: fry for about 2 minutes. Drain the fritters on paper towels.

5. In a saucepan, mix the sugar with the rest of the water. Cook over high heat, stirring constantly, until the sugar becomes thick and begins to froth. Add the sesame seeds and mix until you have a golden caramel.

6. Dip the fritters in the sesame caramel, coating well on all sides. Then, using chopsticks, dip each one in a bowl of ice water. Take them out of the water as soon as the coating has hardened: eat right away.

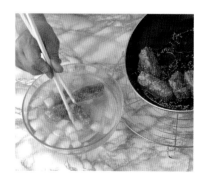

Almond Milk Pudding

Preparation time:	*30 minutes*
Cooking time:	*25 minutes*
Soaking time:	*20 minutes*
Chilling time:	*4 hours*
Difficulty:	★★

Serves 4

30 g/¹⁄₄ cup sultanas
150 ml/²⁄₃ cup muscatel wine
250 ml/1 cup milk
100 g/7 tbsp sugar

100 g/generous ³⁄₄ cup finely
ground almonds
2 sheets gelatin
cold water
250 ml/1 cup cream
2 ripe pears, Conference or similar
40 g/2¹⁄₂ tbsp butter

One of Spain's most famous products has to be almonds: produced in abundance, they are enjoyed just about everywhere. The consumption of almonds in Spain was probably influenced by the Arabs.

Covered in beautiful attire, they are lovely in sauces and hot dishes. They can also be used to make marzipan and the famous *turron*, a chewy nougat. Spaniards like to transform them into a thirst-quenching drink, most welcome in the summer to help withstand the heat of the sun. Made of skinned almonds, water and sugar, this drink goes well with its savory partner, a cold soup made of almonds, water, garlic and a dash of oil. The sweet almond is used in baked goods, in confectionaries and in the kitchen, while the bitter almond can only be used in processed form or small amounts, as it is potentially lethal. It is not available at all in the United States.

Once finely ground into powder, almonds should be conserved in a dry, airtight box. Almonds have a high calorie content—300 calories per 50 grams or ¹⁄₃ cup—but are also rich in minerals such as magnesium and potassium as well as protein.

In Catalonia, this dessert was once made with milk and a large quantity of almonds, and gelatin was only added to the recipe much later. Xavier Valero insists on the importance of choosing the right pears: they need to be very firm, and the most satisfactory and widely available type is Conference. Larger than currants, sultanas are golden raisins, less sweet and muskier than their "cousin". They are of Turkish origin.

The Almond Milk Pudding with Sultanas and Pears can also be made into an exquisite beverage, like the Xérès pale cream, which can end a wonderful meal on just the right note.

1. Place the sultanas in a bowl. Pour the muscatel over them and soak for about 20 minutes.

2. In a saucepan, bring the milk, sugar and ground almonds to the boil. While it cooks, soak the gelatin in cold water and whip the cream. Remove the milk from the heat and let cool slightly, until warm but not hot.

3. Dice the pears. In a frying pan, brown them slowly for 4 minutes in butter. Remove the pears from the pan and set aside. Also set aside the butter in which they were browned.

with Sultanas and Pears

4. Drain and press the gelatin, then blend it into the warm milk. Let cool.

5. Add the diced pears, most of the sultanas (save some for decoration), a quarter of the muscatel in which the sultanas soaked (save the rest for the sauce) and the whipped cream. Fill ramekins with the mixture and set in the refrigerator.

6. Make the sauce by reheating the butter with the remaining muscatel until it thickens. Turn the ramekins over onto plates. Top the pudding with sauce and decorate with sultanas.

Coconut Blancmange

Preparation time: 20 minutes
Cooking time: 30 minutes
Chilling time: overnight
Difficulty: ★

Serves 4

For the coconut pudding:
400 ml/1²/₃ cups coconut milk
50 g/3¹/₂ tbsp sugar
100 ml/7 tbsp sweetened condensed milk
6 sheets gelatin
cold water

1 pinch nutmeg
1 pinch cinnamon
2 drops orange blossom water

For the mango purée:
150 ml/²/₃ cup water
50 g/3¹/₂ tbsp sugar
700 g/1¹/₂ lb mangoes
20 ml/4 tsp aged rum
juice of 1 green lemon

For the garnish:
cherry preserves, preferably Bigarreaux
grated coconut

Blancmange is a popular and typical dessert in Martinique. Although this lovely, light pudding is traditionally made with coconut milk, our creative chef suggests using the juice from passion fruit, guava, strawberries or red currants.

Blancmange prepared with coconut milk has little flavor in itself, which explains why it is always accompanied by a flavored purée made from some of the juicy fruits cultivated in Martinique, like the mangoes chosen by our chef. He enhances the flavor of this pudding by incorporating orange blossom water, which you can replace with a teaspoon of almond extract, if you prefer.

People on Martinique most often use ready-made coconut milk to make this dessert, because making coconut milk from a whole coconut is a quite long and complex process. For the purée, you can use concentrated mango juice as well.

The puddings are baked in a water bath, and you should remove them from the oven as soon as the surface is able to withstand a finger pressing on it gently, while the inside is still quite wobbly. Since it contains gelatin, the blancmange will become firmer as it cools down in the refrigerator.

Generally, Eddy Gérald cooks his blancmange in small ramekins for individual servings. This also makes it easier to cook them precisely and to take them out of their molds. But this dessert can also be cooked in one large mold. To serve it, cut the blancmange in pretty slices. Our chef, however, doesn't recommend using a big round mold, as it is not easy to remove the pudding from it and the final presentation will suffer.

He usually places a small pudding in the middle of a dessert plate and surrounds it with a ladle of mango purée.

1. To make the pudding, pour the coconut milk in a saucepan. Add the sugar and then the sweetened condensed milk. Mix and bring to the boil.

2. Soften the gelatin in a cup of cold water. Then blend it into the boiling mixture. Whisk over medium heat until the gelatin is dissolved.

3. Remove from the heat and add the nutmeg, cinnamon and orange blossom water. Whip thoroughly, so that all the ingredients are well mixed.

with Mango Purée

4. With a small ladle, fill individual ramekins with the pudding. Cook for 15 minutes in a water bath. Then place the puddings in the refrigerator and let them set overnight.

5. For the purée, bring the water and sugar to the boil. Whip so that the sugar dissolves rapidly. Peel the mangoes, remove the seeds and cut the fruit into small cubes. Add to the syrup and cook for 10 minutes over high heat.

6. Stir the mango cubes in the syrup. Add the rum and lemon juice. Blend with a hand-held mixer, then let cool. Place the puddings on plates over a bed of mango purée. Decorate with preserved cherries and grated coconut.

The Tzar's Blini

Preparation time: 20 minutes
Cooking time: ca. 1 hour
Rising time: 1 hour
Difficulty: ★

Makes about 30 blini

500 ml/2 cups milk
10 g/2¹/₂ tsp baker's yeast
300 g/generous 2 cups flour
1 whole egg + 1 egg yolk
50 g/3¹/₂ tbsp butter, melted

120 ml/¹/₂ cup crème fraîche
1 tsp sugar
butter and honey, to taste
oil for the frying pan

Russian cooks always have to make a significant quantity of blini to satisfy the appetites of gourmands. These very small, rich pancakes are associated with religious traditions. Before the birth of the Eastern Orthodox religion, blini symbolized the sun, the rich harvest, a good marriage and healthy children. They were then tied to the festival that takes place before the beginning of Lent. Foreigners were often amazed by the large quantity of pancakes eaten on this occasion.

In those days, making dough was considered a sacred activity. They were made with a little bit of snow, when the crescent of the moon appeared in the sky, or even at the riverbank when the stars were at their brightest. Nowadays it is preferable to make the dough in an enamel or wooden container in order to facilitate the fermentation process, as the dough will be able to breath more easily. The pancakes are cooked in a cast-iron pan the size of a saucer.

These diminutive pancakes are so delicious that they are served frequently and in many variations. For dessert or with afternoon tea, they are topped with honey, jam or thick crème fraîche. On a cold buffet table they are served with salmon, sardines or caviar.

To make them even more attractive, split the pancakes in two and fill them with fromage blanc, fried meat or cabbage. This dish can be served as a hot appetizer or even as an entrée.

Our chef has used the most traditional method and ordinary wheat flour for the dough. However, pancakes made from buckwheat or rice flour fill Russian plates just as well.

Another variation of these crêpes is called "empty pancakes", a regal treat for pancake lovers. Made without yeast or butter, they have a pale yellow color once cooked.

1. Warm the milk over low heat. Measure 250 ml/1 cup of it and pour into a bowl. Add the yeast to the bowl little by little, crumbling it with your fingers if needed, and stirring vigorously so it dissolves well.

2. Add 150 g/generous 1 cup of the flour gradually and blend completely.

3. Cover the bowl with a cloth. Keep at room temperature until the dough has doubled or tripled its volume.

with Honey

4. When it has risen, add the eggs, butter and then the crème fraîche. Stir again.

5. Add the rest of the milk and flour, and then the sugar. Beat thoroughly. Again cover the dough with a cloth and let rise for 30 minutes.

6. Oil a small pan and when it is hot, pour in small portions of batter at a time and cook until brown on both sides. Put the pancakes on a plate, with butter on each one. Top with honey before serving.

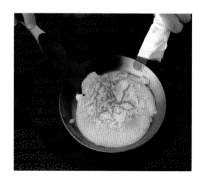

Bread and Butter

Preparation time: 30 minutes
Cooking time: 1 hour 20 minutes
Difficulty: ★

Serves 4

For the pudding:
1 vanilla bean
500 ml/2 cups half-skimmed milk
3 eggs
60 g/generous ¹/₂ cup powdered sugar
1 loaf plain sandwich bread

60 g/7 tbsp golden raisins
50 g/3¹/₂ tbsp butter
20 g/3 tbsp powdered sugar

For the garnish:
strawberries
raspberries
gooseberries
red currants
blackberries
mint leaves

Most of the English desserts that are somewhat elaborate are called puddings. The dishes can vary greatly, from dough made with suet to crumbles, breads, sponge cakes, layered pastries and even oat flour pastry. The most famous of all is still the Christmas pudding, a typical British specialty containing suet, spices, sugar, ginger, candied fruit, raisins, flour, eggs and white bread. Sponge pudding unites sponge cake with any manner of delicious toppings or fillings, while treacle pudding is flavored with golden syrup and ginger, and summer pudding includes bread and red fruits, ideal to eat in the summer in an English garden.

The British make many of their desserts with bread, which makes sense considering how much white bread they consume. This bread, which has a very supple consistency, slips into their meals from breakfast to supper. At teatime, small sandwiches filled with lemon curd, salmon or cucumber are often welcome.

Milk and other dairy products are also companions throughout the day for British citizens. At dawn, some of those who live in the countryside still find milk in recyclable glass bottles on their doorsteps, delivered by small electric vehicles from the neighboring dairy. The great British milk production is mostly provided by black and white Holstein and Friesian cows that generously produce the milk consumed all day long, at work or along with sandwiches at lunchtime.

After baking, this pudding, presented by Oliver Tucki, has the consistency of a rich milk flan.

1. For the pudding, split the vanilla bean and bring it and the milk to the boil. Beat the eggs and sugar in a bowl until the mixture lightens.

2. When the milk is boiling, add it slowly to the egg mixture, beating thoroughly with a whisk until blended. Strain this mixture and set aside.

3. Remove the crusts from the bread. With a serrated knife, cut the bread so you get a cylinder-shaped bread log. Slice it into small disks.

Pudding

4. Cover the bottom of an oval dish with raisins. Cover the raisins with overlapping slices of bread.

5. Pour the custard sauce over the bread. Slice the butter and top the pudding with it. Bake in the oven, in a water bath, for 1 hour and 20 minutes at 150°C/300°F.

6. Sprinkle the pudding with powdered sugar. Brown it under a broiler or with a special torch. Decorate the dessert with fruit and mint leaves.

Orange-Scented

Preparation time: 30 minutes
Cooking time: 5 minutes
Difficulty: ★★

Serves 4

800 g/2²/₃ cups whole almonds, shelled
400 g/generous 1³/₄ cups sugar
15 g/1¹/₂ tbsp gum arabic crystals
2 tbsp orange blossom water
8 leaves b'steeya or phyllo dough
80 g/¹/₃ cup butter

300 ml/1¹/₄ cups peanut oil
oil for frying
100 ml/7 tbsp honey
40 g/¹/₃ cup sesame seeds
mint leaves

Out of an assortment of Moroccan sweets, the *briouates*, wrapped in almond paste, are always the most appreciated. For a family party or just to enjoy among friends, they are presented in big baskets along with *ghribas* (flat cakes made of puff pastry) with almonds and semolina, *shebakia* honey braids, "gazelle horns" (see page 862) and more.

In Morocco, the best honey comes from the mountains, where it is harvested from beehives in the wild. There are also bees to be found elsewhere, of course. This is how our chef assesses the purity of honey: he spreads out some sand and then drops a little honey onto it. If it is really pure, the drop will roll over the sand without sticking. In the mornings, Mohammed Rifaï likes to fortify himself with a spoonful of honey.

The miniscule sesame seed with its delicate nutty flavor has made its way into all Moroccan sweets. They come from a plant which has been cultivated for over 2,000 years. During fructification the shell breaks, releasing the little seeds that are cherished in kitchens from Morocco to China. In Moroccan cuisine, sesame enriches lamb tajine with prunes and accents almond paste in a favorite dessert called *kaab al-ghzal*, literally "gazelle horns". Mixing sesame with almonds, eggs and flour makes great little appetizers.

Moroccan desserts are not complete without the sweetness of orange blossom water. Flowers from the bitter orange tree are distilled in steam in a machine similar to the one used to steam couscous. Its flavor is, in fact, stronger than that of the flower of the ordinary orange plant. On special occasions, Moroccans not only have the flavor of the orange blossom on their palates, but also spray the perfume onto fabrics in their homes.

1. Remove the almond skin by boiling the nuts in water, then peeling off the skin. Put the almonds in a food processor with the sugar and gum arabic. Pour in 1 tbsp orange blossom water.

2. Process into a pale yellow filling, then set aside in a small bowl. Place the pastry leaves on an oiled chopping board.

3. Melt the butter and mix it with the peanut oil. Cut a fine band from one side of a pastry leaf. Coat it with butter and oil. Put a little filling at one end of the band. Fold it into a triangle to form a briouate. Repeat to make more briouates.

Honey Briouates

4. Heat the oil in a frying pan. When it is boiling hot, add the briouates and fry for 2 to 3 minutes until they are golden brown.

5. Heat the honey in a small pan. Place the briouates in the hot honey. Add the rest of the orange blossom water and mix with a small spoon.

6. Place the honey-coated briouates on a serving plate. Sprinkle with the sesame seeds and decorate with sprigs of fresh mint leaves. To finish, top with some of the honey and orange blossom water mixture.

Chocolate Chip

Preparation time: 20 minutes
Cooking time: 35 minutes
Difficulty: ★

Makes 24

575 g/2¹/₂ cups chocolate chips
225 g/ butter, softened
5 eggs
100 g/7 tbsp brown sugar
200 g/1³/₄ cups sugar

100 g/²/₃ cup flour
1 tsp vanilla extract
salt
50 g/scant ¹/₂ cup chopped walnuts
butter for the pan

It seems that brownies originated with a cake recipe gone wrong. According to legend, a certain Miss Brownie Schrumpf, a library manager in a city on the east coast of the United States, one day served her guests a hopelessly flat cake. It was so rich and delicious, however, that her friends asked for the recipe and dubbed it "brownie". In the 1930s, Milton Hershey, the founder of the famous Hershey's chocolate factory in Pennsylvania, printed the recipe on packages of cocoa powder, chocolate chips and chocolate bars. Mothers find it a delicious and easy snack to make for their children. Even today, the success of this magic chocolate cake is still increasing. It is a favorite snack for children, and a great treat for young and old all over America.

This recipe can be made with semi-sweet chocolate, milk chocolate, cocoa powder or chocolate chips, depending on your own preference. Katia Davies-Kemmler here shares her own successful personal recipe, which is made with chocolate chips. Before sliding the brownies into the oven, she sprinkles chocolate chips over the top, too, making the brownies as rich outside as they are inside.

To speed up the process, you can refrigerate the chocolate-butter mixture in a bowl filled with ice. It is also possible to replace the butter with margarine.

Our chef has added chopped walnuts to the batter, but they can be replaced with pecans or left out altogether. Adding a little bit of coffee to the batter gives you an espresso brownie.

Freshly baked brownies are hard to cut, so try to wait until they have cooled down a little before digging in.

1. Melt 450 g/scant 2 cups of the chocolate chips in a bowl in a double boiler. When the chocolate is soft, add the butter and mix into a smooth cream. Cool.

2. Beat the eggs as for an omelet. Add the brown sugar, then the granulated sugar. Beat thoroughly.

3. Add the butter-chocolate mix to the egg mixture. Beat thoroughly to a uniform cream.

Brownies

4. Add the flour to the mixture, followed by the vanilla extract and salt, stirring well.

5. Add the chopped walnuts and stir one last time.

6. Pour the batter into a well-buttered baking pan. Sprinkle the rest of the chocolate chips on top. Bake for 25 to 30 minutes at 175°C/350°F. Cut into small squares before serving.

Dried Fruit Compote

Preparation time: 30 minutes
Cooking time: 35 minutes
Soaking time: 30 minutes
Chilling time: 1 hour
Difficulty: ★

Serves 4

For the compote:
400 g/14 oz various dried fruits, such as
prunes, apricots, pineapple, dates, raisins
warm water
1 vanilla bean
100 g/7 tbsp sugar

1 cinnamon stick
1 tbsp cornstarch
80 ml/¹/₃ cup water

For the vanilla aspic:
4 sheets gelatin
cold water
500 ml/2 cups crème fraîche
30 g/¹/₄ cup powdered sugar
1 vanilla bean

For the decoration:
cinnamon sticks
vanilla beans

Our chef recommends this delicious dessert, typical of old Danish estates, which he found in a local cookbook published towards the end of the nineteenth century. Traditionally, the fruit is often boiled until soft and served as dessert. In the summer, stewed berries (strawberries, raspberries or cherries) are served with cream, in a dish called *rødgrød med fløde*.

The Danish also like to stew dried prunes or apricots, often enjoyed simply topped with a dollop of cream. These fruits are also blended into the batter of several typical cakes, and are sometimes used as a filling in layered dough recipes.

Cinnamon, cloves, vanilla and cumin add flavor to Danish desserts and breads, but are otherwise used little in the local cuisine. Cardamom is added to bread made with milk and cumin is used in brown bread. Other white breads are topped with white poppy seeds.

The Danish are, after all, serious crème fraîche afficionados, and they don't hesitate to buy cartons of it at the supermarket. This cream is the freshest, because in Denmark it is not pasteurized. It can be incorporated into almost all typical desserts, either as an ingredient or as a garnish. The base of these desserts is often very sweet and therefore the cream is served without sugar to counterbalance the taste.

For this recipe, Charles-René Madsen pours the aspic cream in individual tart molds or petit fours molds. But you can also put all the cream in a large ring-shaped mold. If so, you will have to wait two or three hours for the aspic to set completely.

1. Place the dried fruit on a chopping board. Remove the pits from the dates. Cut all the fruit into large pieces. Soften the gelatin in a bowl with a little cold water.

2. Put all the fruit in a saucepan with warm water. Let soak for 30 minutes.

3. Split the vanilla bean open and add to the saucepan with the sugar and cinnamon. Bring to boil and cook for about 30 minutes.

with Vanilla Aspic

4. Dissolve the starch in 80 ml/¹/₃ cup water and then add to the cooked fruit mixture. Place it over the heat and cook for 5 minutes, stirring constantly, until the mixture is quite smooth.

5. Beat the cream with the powdered sugar and vanilla mark. Dissolve the softened gelatin in a small pan, then blend it into the cream. Pour into small molds and let it chill in the refrigerator for 1 hour to set.

6. With a slotted spoon, quickly dip the bottom of each mold in hot water and then remove the aspics from the molds. Put the compote on serving plates and top with vanilla aspic, cinnamon sticks and vanilla beans.

Gazelle

Preparation time: 45 minutes
Cooking time: 15 minutes
Resting time: 30 minutes
Difficulty: ★★

Serves 4

250 g/1³/₄ cups sifted flour
1 egg
2¹/₂ tbsp butter
2 tbsp orange blossom water
oil for the work surface

500 g/3¹/₃ cups whole almonds
250 g/1 cup + 2 tbsp sugar
1 lemon
1 pinch powdered gum arabic

In keeping with Morrocan tradition, Fatima Mouzoun serves Gazelle Horns, or *kaab al-ghzal*, on most festive occasions, including weddings, holy days and receptions. They are one of the classics among the Moroccan assortments of sweets, along with *briouates* and *m'hanchas* (see pages 856 and 922). They are often accompanied by generously sweetened mint tea.

In our recipe, the dough and filling are so fully flavored with the orange blossom water that they can be used separately in other recipes. You can make small ballet shoe shapes out of the dough, for example, and fill them with grape jam. In the city of Oujda, the dough is cut into little bands, then stuffed and made into the shape of a bracelet.

Of all the ingredients, the gum arabic is the only one not produced in Morocco. It comes from the resin of two species of acacia trees that grow in Egypt and Sudan. It is sold in small crystals or as a white powder, and is used to thicken fillings and sauces.

The dough for the gazelle horns should be separated into rolls before it is set aside to rest, because it is hard to separate it later without making it overly elastic. You will notice that the small rolls are much easier to roll out.

Some inexperienced cooks might be tempted to use a rolling pin. Our chef stretches the dough slowly with his fingertips, making it thinner than you can achieve with a rolling pin. As for the little sausage-shaped filling, rub your hands with oil and roll it between your palms.

Once out of the oven, the horns can be served by themselves or coated with powdered sugar mixed in orange blossom water. These cakes are also delicious rolled in crushed almonds or sesame seeds before baking.

1. Put the flour in a large, deep dish. Separate the egg yolk from the egg white. Melt ¹/₂ tbsp butter and add it, the egg white and 1 tbsp orange blossom water to a well in the middle of the flour.

2. Mix with your fingertips. Knead well until you have a soft, uniform dough. Separate it into 4 rolls. Let them rest for 30 minutes at room temperature on an oiled surface.

3. For the filling, place the almonds on a plate. Add the sugar and mix with your fingertips. Melt the rest of the butter in a small pan and grate the lemon peel.

Horns

4. Blend the sugared almonds in a food processor until they are a fine powder. Add the gum arabic, egg yolk, the rest of the orange blossom water, $1/2$ tbsp lemon zest and the butter. Mix again.

5. Transfer this filling to a plate. Knead with your hands until you have a pale yellow ball. Make small sausages about 5–6 cm/ 2–2$1/2$ in long and 1 cm/$1/3$ in around.

6. Flatten a piece of dough, place a filling sausage on it and close the dough over the filling. Cut the edges with a pastry wheel. Repeat with the rest of the dough. Bake for 15 minutes at 160°C/320°F, without opening the oven. Cool before serving.

Carrot Purée and

Preparation time: 20 minutes
Cooking time: 15 minutes
Freezing time, ice cream: overnight
Difficulty: ★

Serves 4

For the cinnamon ice cream:
2 egg yolks
60 g/4¹/₂ tbsp sugar
250 ml/1 cup milk
2 cinnamon sticks
30 ml/2 tbsp orange blossom water

For the carrot purée:
500 g/generous 1 lb carrots
1 lemon
1 orange
3 tbsp powdered sugar
water
2 tsp orange blossom water
4 fresh mint leaves

This refreshing dessert is an original creation by chef Lahoucine Belmoufid. It's a summer dessert, to be served in the evening, after a meal in which the spices have sufficiently tantalized our taste buds so that they are in need of coolness. What could be more delightful than the sweetness of vegetables and ice cream savored under palm trees, the fragrance of the beautiful nights in Marrakech or at the Oualidia beach in the air, listening to the waves of the Atlantic Ocean?

Carrots are the stars here. Presented like this in a dessert, their best qualities are highlighted: color, freshness, sweetness and crunch. Lemon further brings out their sweetness with its sharp acidity, which is always welcome after a meal.

Our chef, who never runs out of ideas, suggests grating the carrots, stewing them with sugar and cinnamon, decorating the dessert with chopped almonds and toasted sesame seeds, or even better, filling a sheet of b'steeya or phyllo dough with this compote and a scoop of vanilla ice cream. Roll the pastry, cook it quickly in hot oil, and garnish with some powdered sugar and cinnamon.

Cinnamon plays an important role in this recipe because it's the only spice. Cinnamon should be carefully measured because it is very strong and slightly spicy when too much of it is used. Its flavor should come through in desserts to the same extent as in main dishes.

How delicate, exotic and creative! This will amaze guests from all around the world. To further the pleasure of cooking and sharing, do not hesitate to accent your dish with mint leaves, seasonal flowers or anything else that comes to mind.

1. For the ice cream, beat the egg yolks and sugar until light. Bring the milk and cinnamon stick to the boil, and then infuse for 5 minutes off the heat. Remove the cinnamon. Beat the milk into the egg. Thicken the mixture by stirring for 10 minutes over low heat.

2. Add the orange blossom water to the milk mixture and beat one last time. Mix it in an ice cream maker and put it in the freezer.

3. Grate the carrots very finely with a four surface grater. This creates small carrot shavings.

Cinnamon Ice Cream

4. Squeeze the juice from the orange and lemon. Pour it over the carrots and sprinkle with 2 tbsp of the powdered sugar. Blend well.

5. In a pot, make a syrup from a little water and the rest of the sugar. Bring to the boil for 3 minutes.

6. Remove the syrup from the heat and add it to the carrots. Add the orange blossom water and stir to blend. Serve the carrot purée chilled, topped with a scoop of cinnamon ice cream and fresh mint leaves.

Ricotta Sundaes

Preparation time: 25 minutes
Chilling time: 1 hour minimum
Difficulty: ★

Serves 4 to 6

200 g/7 oz ricotta
50 g/6 tbsp mixed candied fruits
1 orange
80 g/6 tbsp sugar
2 tbsp water

4–5 tbsp Marsala wine
250 ml/1 cup heavy cream
1 tsp liquid vanilla
1 tsp orange blossom water
1 tbsp Strega herbal liqueur
350 g/³/₄ lb fresh raspberries
1 sprig mint leaves

A major product in Italian gastronomy, in this recipe ricotta is combined with cream and liqueur to create a creamy and lightly flavored mousse.

To give the mousse an extra touch, our chef uses Marsala. This dark red wine, as its name suggests, comes from the village of Marsala, in northwest Sicily. Its base is Passito, a white wine made from dried grapes. *L'eau de vie* (literally "water of life", otherwise known as brandy, which is usually fruit-based) and grape syrup are added, and then it is aged in barrels for two to five years. Marsala is divided into different categories, depending on the duration of the aging process and its alcohol and sugar content. Sometimes the wine is even flavored with almonds or eggs.

It is the cream, ideally a high-fat liquid cream, that gives this mousse its airy texture. It is important to make it really light and frothy, so be sure to use heavy cream, not a light or reduced fat version that will be hard to beat as desired. One hour before beating the cream, put all the tools and utensils you will use (the bowl and beater) in the freezer and the cream in the coldest place in the refrigerator to chill.

For a more decorative presentation, fill the bowls with the help of a pastry bag with a grooved tip so the mousse forms a pretty spiral. There is no reason why you cannot replace the raspberries with strawberries, wild strawberries or even a fruit purée. You can also sprinkle the sundaes with whatever you like: candied orange peels, fruit preserves, whole or chopped mint leaves, chopped nuts or almond pieces. Feel free to give your culinary imagination full rein. As a final touch you may want to serve little biscuits with the mousse. We recommend *tuiles* (delicate almond-flavored cookies), sugar wafers or any other small cakes or pastries of your choice.

1. Press the ricotta through a sieve.

2. Finely chop the fruit. Remove the orange zest and cut into thin long pieces. In a pan, combine it with 50 g/3¹/₂ tbsp of the sugar and the water. Cook over high heat until it becomes a thick syrup. Set aside.

3. Put the ricotta and fruit in a blender or food processor and blend. Add 2 tbsp of the Marsala and mix again.

with Raspberries

4. Beat the cream, then add the rest of the sugar and half the orange zest. Whisk until firm, then blend in the vanilla and most of the remaining orange zest (save some for decoration).

5. Fold the whipped cream into the ricotta. Add the orange blossom water and the herb liqueur. Mix well.

6. Fill dessert cups with the ricotta and chill them in the refrigerator for at least 1 hour. Just before serving, sprinkle with the rest of the Marsala. Garnish with raspberries, orange zest and mint leaves.

Crêpes

Preparation time:	30 minutes
Cooking time:	25 minutes
Resting time, batter:	1 hour
Difficulty:	★

Serves 4

For the batter:
2 eggs
200 ml/generous ³/₄ cup milk
3 tsp oil
salt
250 g/1³/₄ cups flour
sparkling water
oil for cooking

For the filling:
100 g/²/₃ cup shelled walnuts
70 g/5 tbsp sugar
70 g/9 tbsp raisins
100 ml/7 tbsp water
dash of rum

For the chocolate sauce:
500 ml/2 cups milk
1 vanilla bean
100 g/3¹/₂ oz chocolate
3 eggs
50 ml/3¹/₂ tbsp water
100 ml/7 tbsp crème fraîche
100 g/scant 1 cup powdered sugar
1 tbsp flour
dash of rum

In 1910, Jonas Gundel started an elegant restaurant in the Varosliget, the City Park in downtown Budapest. A few years later, his son Karoly created the new Hungarian cuisine. They founded a dynasty of great chefs, and influenced numerous talented cooks. Several dishes today carry their name, such as these crêpes and pickerel (a fish in the pike family). The Gundel restaurant still exists and enjoys international renown.

Hungarians love crêpes, at home or in restaurants. A true Hungarian creation, Crêpes Gundel are traditionally topped with a generous serving of chocolate sauce. To make the dish more appealing to the eye, we have presented the crêpes on a bed of chocolate sauce. You can also sprinkle powdered sugar or ground walnuts over them.

The local recipe for the crêpe batter is always the same, and includes a dash of carbonated water to make it lighter. Only the

filling is different. According to taste, Hungarian gourmands love to top the crêpes with fromage blanc, poppy seeds, walnuts or, more traditionally, chocolate or jam. There are also savory crêpes, like the Hortobagy crêpe. First a chicken *pörkölt* stew is made with a little more water than usual, then the meat is ground and filled into the crêpes. The cooking water plus flour and cream make a sauce.

The nuts and dried fruits used in Hungarian cuisine are not especially varied; walnuts, dried apples and prunes are the most commonly used in desserts. For fromage blanc crêpes, prunes are mixed with a large quantity of ground nuts. Hungarians also love to treat themselves to *begli*, roulades filled with poppy seeds and ground walnuts, which is the traditional dessert served on Christmas Eve.

1. Break the eggs into a bowl. Add the milk, 1 tsp of the oil and the salt. Start stirring, then add the flour. Whisk until the batter is uniform and pale yellow.

2. Add sparkling water gradually, until the batter is thick but still quite liquid. Beat again and let it rest in the refrigerator for 1 hour.

3. Pour the batter in an oiled and heated saucepan a portion at a time and cook the crêpes for 3 minutes on each side.

Gundel

4. Grind the nuts. Turn them into a pot with the sugar, raisins and water. Cook over high heat for about 5 minutes, to make a walnut batter. Add the rum. Put this filling into each crêpe. Fold or roll the crêpes.

5. Bring the milk to boil with the vanilla. After the milk is warm, remove the vanilla bean. Melt the chocolate over low heat in a small pan. Remove from the heat and add the eggs and milk. Mix well.

6. Blend in the crème fraîche, sugar and flour. Beat over low heat until the chocolate cream becomes thick. Add the rum. Place 2 crêpes on each plate on a bed of chocolate sauce and decorate with additional sauce.

Berber

Preparation time: 25 minutes
Cooking time: ca. 2 minutes/crêpe
Resting time: 1 hour
Difficulty: ★

Serves 4

For the batter:
60 g/7 tbsp flour
2 tsp active dry yeast
½ tsp salt
270 g/generous 1½ cups semolina
10 g/1 tbsp baker's yeast
500 ml/2 cups milk

For the sauce:
250 g/1⅔ cups whole almonds
oil for frying
10 ml/2 tsp argan oil
20 g/3 tbsp cinnamon
300 g/scant 1 cup honey
mint leaves

Moroccans enjoy these Berber Crêpes, called *beghrir*, for breakfast or in the evening at tea time. What a pleasure to take a bite of crêpes, dripping with honey as you devour them.

There are also other types of pancakes cherished by the Moroccans: *harcha*, made from fine semolina and topped with butter and honey, *rghaēf*, filled with minced meat and *mlaoui*, similar to *rghaēf* but without the filling. *Beghrir* are covered in *amelou*, a delicious sauce made from almonds, argan oil and honey. This quite fluid sauce brings to mind the color and flavor of peanut butter.

When working with the flour and semolina, take care not to mix it too much. According to our chef, the semolina "breaks up" the otherwise smooth batter, resulting in crêpes filled with attractive little holes, like a beehive. Semolina can also be used to make pancakes such as *harcha* and *ghriba* with almonds, as well as mint semolina soup.

A necessary ingredient for the *amelou* sauce, argan oil is made from the fruit of the argan tree, which only grows in the region of Essaouira, in southwestern Morocco, where the Berber people live. After they are picked, the argans are dried and the green skin is removed. The fruit is then pressed between millstones to win the oil. The color of argan oil is similar to that of sesame oil, and the flavor reminds one of hazelnuts. Walnut or hazelnut oil are good substitutes if argan oil is not available.

The Moroccans traditionally cook *beghrir* on a heated ceramic pan above a gas flame or over the ashes of an old-fashioned coal heater. This pan diffuses the heat to a greater degree than an ordinary frying pan, but the pancakes can also be cooked in a non-stick pan over very low heat.

1. In a bowl, mix the flour with the active dry yeast, salt and semolina. Sprinkle the baker's yeast over the flour by breaking it between your fingers. Mix with your fingertips.

2. Add the milk. Mix well with a hand whisk, then let it rest for 1 hour. Blanche the almonds in boiling water, then remove their skins and set the nuts aside.

3. Heat a small pan with no oil. Pour a small ladle of batter into the pan, spread it evenly, and cook for around 2 minutes. Use all the batter to make crêpes.

Crêpes

4. Use a slotted spoon to fry 200 g/1⅓ cups of the almonds by dipping them into simmering oil. Drain them. Blend them with the cinnamon in a food processor and set aside.

5. Again in the food processor, mix the rest of the almonds with the argan oil and honey to make amelou sauce.

6. Place a crêpe on a plate. Sprinkle with the cinnamon almonds and some amelou sauce. Cover with another crêpe. Continue layering until everything has been used. Garnish with a sprig of mint leaves.

Blueberry

Preparation time: 20 minutes
Cooking time: 35 minutes
Difficulty: ★

Serves 6 to 8

40 g/2¹/₂ tbsp butter for the dish
500 g/generous 1 lb blueberries
40 g/3 tbsp sugar
150 g/generous 1 cup flour
110 g/¹/₂ cup brown sugar
and 1 pinch for decoration
150 g/²/₃ cup cold butter, in small pieces

Richard Bizier has made a delectable dessert in which small, juicy and full-flavored blueberries are buried under a crunchy, crumbly, golden brown crust.

This fruit is so abundant in the area around Saguenay-lac Saint-Jean that people who live there are nicknamed "the blueberries". Every Saguenian or Jeananian has a personal blueberry tale to tell, and every family jealously guards their best recipe for the "blue pearl".

Very similar to huckleberries, blueberries are fleshier and sweeter. From the end of July until the end of August, seemingly infinite quantities of wild blueberries grow in clearings, especially in places where the ground has been burned. They grow on small shrubs amidst moss and lichens. Some families make expeditions into the forest during blueberry season and collect them in big enough quantities to sell them wholesale.

In Canada, they are available frozen throughout the year, and there are also cultivated varieties. Canadians eat blueberries simply sprinkled with sugar and topped with a little bit of whipped cream, tossed with pieces of pound cake to make a trifle, in tarts, jam or in liqueur, or with ice cream.

This dessert, quite similar to English crumbles, can certainly be made with any other kind of wild berries: huckleberries, bilberries, blackberries, raspberries or strawberries. The people of Quebec sometimes replace the blueberries with other local berries, such as cranberries or cloudberries, also known there as *chikoutai*.

It is possible to replace the flour in the topping with oats. As for the sugar, you can use either brown sugar extracted from sugar cane or demerara sugar.

1. Generously brush a ceramic or glass baking dish with melted butter.

2. Rinse and cull the berries. Turn them a few at a time into the dish.

3. Sprinkle the sugar evenly over the berries.

Crumble

4. To make the crumble topping, pour the flour into a bowl. Add the brown sugar and then blend in the butter.

5. Crumble the dough by rubbing it with your fingertips, until it forms small pieces.

6. Cover the berries with the topping. Bake for 30 minutes at 180°C/355°F. Sprinkle with the rest of the brown sugar and bake for 4 or 5 minutes more.

Almond-Filled

Preparation time: 1 hour
Cooking time: 1 hour 10 minutes
Difficulty: ★

Serves 4

For the apple chips:
3 Granny Smith apples
100 g/scant 1 cup powdered sugar

For the filling:
60 g/¼ cup butter, softened
60 g/generous ½ cup powdered sugar

60 g/½ cup finely ground almonds
15 g/1½ tbsp flour
1 egg
1 drop almond extract

For the apricot purée:
80 g/6 tbsp sugar
500 ml/2 cups water
50 g/2½ tbsp apricot pulp or jam

12 figs
100 g/3½ oz thyme sorbet

With their soft skin of black, violet or green and tender white or pink flesh, used in a thousand ways, figs have seduced civilizations since antiquity. Dried figs are more readily available, but fresh figs can be found on produce stands during certain months of the year.

The sunlit, warm lands of the Mediterranean basin are where figs soak in all the vitamins they contain when ripe. Choose good quality figs; the fruit should be heavy and slightly soft, with purple skin, flavorful and plump so they hold up well in the oven.

The apples should be smooth and without any blemishes. You can replace the Granny Smith apples with Jona Gold. Their flesh cooks easily when cut into chips. Powdered sugar facilitates evaporation of the moisture. Do not bake the apple chips for more than an hour; the chips should not brown.

If you are fortunate enough to live in a sunny region, make the purée from fresh apricots: poach the ripe apricots, cut them into two, remove the stones and add sugar according to taste. But the results are just as good with jam or even dried and rehydrated apricots.

The almond extract must be used carefully in the almond cream. Test the flavor of the cream; too much of the powerful extract will spoil the recipe.

In order to fully enjoy all the flavors of the countryside in this dessert, be sure to include the chef's crowning touch: thyme sorbet. Thyme is an herb that, according to legend, originated from one teardrop from the beautiful Helen of Troy. The magic of thyme is that it combines the flavors of cloves, camphor and mint with a soft orange taste. And what could be more appropriate than to have some light, natural, amber wine to include yet another enchanting aspect of the Provence countryside?

1. Peel the apples and remove the cores. Cut the apples in round slices. Spread out 8 slices on parchment paper laid on a flat tray. Sprinkle with powdered sugar, then dry in the oven at 80°C/175°F.

2. To make the almond cream, combine the butter, powdered sugar, ground almonds, flour and egg. Add the almond extract. Mix thoroughly with a whisk.

3. In a pot, boil the sugar and water for 3 minutes. Cool the syrup, then gradually stir it into the apricot jam to get a light but thick purée.

Roasted Figs

4. Gently wipe the figs. Carefully cut the tops off. Scrape out the inside of the fruit with a melon baller, leaving a little bit of the pulp at the bottom. The removed pulp can be used in another recipe.

5. Fill the inside of each fig with almond cream. Smooth the cream with a spatula. Place the figs and fig tops on a tray. Bake for 5 to 6 minutes at 250°C/480°F, until the almond cream starts to darken.

6. Cover the figs with their tops. Put 3 figs on each plate. Add a scoop of thyme sorbet between 2 apple chips. Garnish with apricot purée.

Dulce de

Preparation time: 15 minutes
Cooking time: 1 hour 55 minutes
Difficulty: ★

Serves 6

For the flan:
2 liters/2 quarts milk
1 kg/4¹/₂ cups sugar
1 vanilla bean
17 egg yolks plus 1 whole egg
1 tsp powdered sugar (optional)

For the caramel:
200 g/³/₄ cup + 2 tbsp sugar
100 ml/7 tbsp water
powdered sugar (optional)

Just about every Argentinean household has a jar of *dulce de leche* in the refrigerator. It is so widespread, Argentineans can even buy it at newspaper stands. This delicious caramel flavored, milk-based spread is used in many different ways: to fill tarts, top pancakes or crêpes, to make chocolate desserts richer, or simply spread on bread like jam. There is one very famous delicacy called *alfajor*, which has layers of both chocolate batter and *dulce de leche*.

Dulce de leche is generally served alongside a milk flan, but our chef prefers to integrate it directly into the custard.

According to legend, it was a French immigrant, Jacques de Liniers, who made *dulce de leche* so famous in Argentina. Jacques, who adored this dessert made by his companion, played a big role in the history of Argentina. In 1806 and 1807, he twice saved Buenos Aires from English invasion by encouraging the inhabitants to revolt. They bombarded the British

with tiles and burning hot oil and were successful in chasing them away. The king of Spain, Charles IV, became the count of Buenos Aires. To build up agriculture in their country, the Argentineans imported Aberdeen Angus oxen for meat, and cows from Holland for milk. They could then produce various dairy products, including cheeses, yogurt, fromage blanc and dried and condensed milk.

Milk flan is always made with vanilla or caramel or with a raspberry sauce.

There is not a tremendous array of Argentinean desserts. Specialties include black caramel cake with spices, *milloras* with layers of *dulce de leche* and even Cordoba chocolate macaroons with milk cream.

Nevertheless, everyday meals often end with fresh fruit or a fruit salad. You may enjoy whipped cream or a scoop of vanilla ice cream with your flan.

1. For the flan, first make dulce de leche by pouring the milk and sugar into a pot. Split the vanilla bean and add it. Bring the milk to the boil, and simmer uncovered, over medium heat, for 1 hour until you get a syrupy, light brown cream.

2. Put the yolks and the whole egg in a large bowl. Whisk as for an omelet.

3. Cool the dulce de leche and remove the vanilla bean. Then pour into the beaten eggs. Beat thoroughly to a smooth cream.

Leche Flan

4. In another saucepan, cook the sugar and water over high heat for 10 minutes, until it becomes caramel.

5. When the caramel starts to darken, remove it from the heat and immediately pour it into small flan molds. Tap the molds on all sides so the caramel spreads out evenly.

6. With a small ladle, pour the cream into the molds. Place them in a water bath and bake for 45 minutes at 90°C/195°F. Then refrigerate. Serve chilled, with powdered sugar if desired.

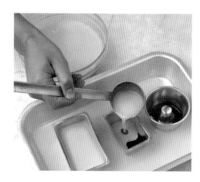

Baleares

Preparation time: 45 minutes
Cooking time: 30 minutes
Difficulty: ★

Serves 6

For the dough:
200 g/generous 1⅓ cups flour
20 g/1½ tbsp sugar
100 ml/7 tbsp milk
1 pinch ground cinnamon
a few drops anis liqueur

10 g/2½ tsp baker's yeast
70 g/5 tbsp butter

For the filling:
6 fresh mint leaves
4 eggs
250 g/1 cup + 2 tbsp sugar
500 g/2 cups chilled fromage blanc
50 ml/3½ tbsp anis liqueur
lemon zest (optional)

In celebration of Easter, Spanish chefs have traditionally made this *flao*, a generously-sized tart filled with ewe's milk cheese or unripened cheese made by heating whey. However, this tart is also greatly welcomed in the summer: the fromage blanc makes it refreshingly cool, and the mint flavor envigorates.

The Spanish have a penchant for aniseed and greatly enjoy liqueur made from it. Del Mono is the most well-known and is widely used as a digestif. There are other liqueurs that enhance Spanish meals throughout the year, especially fruit liqueurs, such as apple, apricot or prune. If you cannot find distilled anis, don't hesitate to replace it with a pastis or sambuco.

Mint, which bears the lovely name *hierbabuena* in Spanish, gives this dessert most of its flavor. It is often used in its wild form in Spain, in large leaves. Our chef has even decorated the

tart with several perfect mint leaves, taking the time to brush the leaves with egg white to protect them from the heat of the oven. The finished dessert is sprinkled with powdered sugar.

Strained cheese, fromage blanc and farmer's cheese, all fresh (unripened) cheeses, are all equally good choices for this type of recipe. The important thing is that the cheese be carefully strained, or else it will give off a significant amount of liquid when baked. Adding some thinly grated lemon zest to the filling complements the flavor nicely.

The dough used by our chef can be replaced by a ready-made one from the supermarket. However, it will not have the same crispiness, or the subtle aniseed taste that is the special charm of the recipe.

1. Tip the flour onto a counter and form a well in the middle of it. Add the sugar, milk, cinnamon, anis liqueur and yeast. Knead the dough with your fingertips. Work in 50 g/3½ tbsp butter, then set aside the ball of dough.

2. Rinse the mint leaves and squeeze out excess water. Cut into fine strips.

3. In a bowl, beat the eggs and sugar until the mixture lightens.

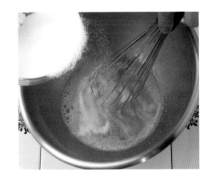

Flan

4. Blend in the fromage blanc, mint and anis liqueur. Mix with a whisk to form a smooth and even cream.

5. Preheat the oven to 160°C/320°F. Roll out the dough with a rolling pin to a thickness of 3 mm/¹⁄₈ in. Butter a tart mold with a diameter of 26 cm/10 in and line it with the dough. Decorate the edges as desired.

6. Fill the tart with the fromage blanc mixture and bake for 25 to 30 minutes.

Black Forest Ice Cream

Preparation time: 1 hour
Cooking time: 50 minutes
Difficulty: ★★

Serves 6

For the cherry ice cream:
500 ml/2 cups crème fraîche
1 vanilla bean
200 g/scant 1 cup sugar
8 egg yolks
500 ml/2 cups milk
30 ml/2 tbsp Kirsch
50 g/1³/₄ oz chocolate, melted

For the cherries:
500 ml/2 cups red wine

1 cinnamon stick
100 g/7 tbsp sugar
50 g/¹/₃ cup cornstarch
water

200 g/generous 1 cup pitted cherries
Kirsch

For the chocolate sponge cake:
240 g/1 cup + 2 tbsp sugar
5 eggs
190 g/6¹/₂ oz couverture chocolate
150 g/²/₃ cup butter
80 g/9 tbsp flour

For the garnish:
500 ml/2 cups whipped cream
chocolate shavings
cherries macerated in Kirsch
mint leaves

The delicious Black Forest Cake has crossed the German borders, to the great pleasure of millions of fans. It has inspired Otto Fehrenbacher to create his own dessert, combining chocolate sponge cake, ice cream enhanced with Kirsch, cherries and whipped cream.

There is an abundance of cherries in the region where our chef resides, at the northern end of the Black Forest. The cherries that grow there are not necessarily pretty, but they are very black, quite small, delicious and very sweet. They are used to make the famous *kirschwasser*, or cherry-flavored brandy, that adds flavor to the ice cream and the sponge cake. The areas around Baden-Baden and Bühl are known for production of cherry and quetsch (a sort of small plum) brandy. Also made there is *Sauerkirsch*, a more acidic variety of kirsch, which is a mixture of ordinary Kirsch and Morello cherry brandy.

To make the ice cream with its small chocolate spangles, when the ice cream starts to freeze in the ice cream maker, slowly pour in the melted chocolate while the blade continues to turn.

To make the sponge cake, beat the eggs and sugar vigorously in a bowl. Then whisk the mixture for ten minutes over a water bath. In a separate pan, melt the chocolate and butter, then add it to the eggs and sugar mixture. Gently fold in the flour. Again whisk for ten minutes over the water bath. Pour the batter into small individual molds or ramekins lined with parchment paper and bake as described below.

Grate a block of chocolate to make chocolate shavings for the garnish. Gently place the shavings around the whipped cream, working quickly so they don't melt.

1. Heat the crème fraîche and vanilla bean. Beat the sugar and egg yolks, then add the milk and crème fraîche. Beat well over low heat to thicken. Chill in ice water. Remove vanilla bean. Add the brandy and pour into an ice cream maker. Add the melted chocolate once the ice cream starts to freeze.

2. Heat the red wine with the cinnamon and sugar. Mix the starch and water in a small bowl. When the wine starts to boil, add the starch and beat thoroughly. Let thicken over low heat. Add the cherries, coating them with the sauce. Once the wine starts to boil again, remove from the heat and cool.

3. Prepare the sponge cakes as described in the text above. Bake for 30 minutes at 180°C/355°F, then allow to cool before removing them from the molds and cutting each cake into 3 or 4 slices.

with Cherry Brandy

4. Soak half of the sponge cake slices with some Kirsch.

5. Place a scoop of ice cream on these slices. Top with some cherries. Place a second slice of cake on top and press gently.

6. Cover the cake with whipped cream. Decorate with chocolate shavings and cherries marinated in Kirsch and dipped in chocolate. Surround the cake with more cherries and small mint leaves.

Old Danish

Preparation time: 40 minutes
Cooking time: 1 hour 40 minutes
Difficulty: ★

Serves 4

8 slices rye bread
6 tbsp sugar
90 g/6 tbsp butter, softened
1 lemon
4 apples

1 tbsp brown sugar
500 ml/2 cups clabber or buttermilk
1 vanilla bean
1 egg yolk
3 sheets gelatin
400 ml/1²/₃ cups heavy cream

According to our chef, this Danish dessert, made of layers of bread and apples, has been passed on since the Middle Ages! Traditionally, the cook makes a thick mush of boiled apples. Some of the compote is tipped onto a plate, covered with breadcrumbs that have been fried with sugar and butter, then topped with additional layers of apple compote. Our chef decorates the dessert with clabber, a form of thickened milk very similar to crème fraîche, and fruit.

For a more modern presentation of the dessert, our chef offers alternating layers of apple compote, a jelled cream and circular pieces of rye bread.

Apples and pears are amongst the favorite fruits in Denmark. The Danish are very fond of apple compote topped with crème fraîche or milk, and delicacies in which apples alternate with bread. These fruits are also used to make pies or tarts in which the thick dough is rich with dried fruit.

A savory mixture of rye bread, sugar and butter form the base of this dessert. In Denmark, an amazing number of different types of rye bread are widely available. The Danish enjoy this bread during all meals, often in the form of toasted bread garnished with butter, sliced meats, vegetables or fish.

To add a hint of tartness to the dessert, our chef suggests a sauce made with soured milk. This is also the basis of a typically Danish dessert called *koldskål*, which is sour milk or buttermilk flavored with vanilla, sugar and lemon. It has relatively few calories and is quite filling. Because it is so refreshing, it is eaten especially often in the summer, sometimes with small biscuits called *kammerjunkere*.

When you are assembling this dessert, a good way to level off the surface of the cream is with the back of a spoon that has been dipped in water.

1. Cut the bread into cubes. In a food processor, combine the bread, 2 tbsp of the sugar and 60 g/¹/₄ cup of the butter. Mix well.

2. Place parchment paper on a flat surface and place metal rings on it. Fill them with the bread mixture. Smooth the surface with a spatula. Bake for 15 minutes at 180°C/355°F.

3. Squeeze the lemon juice. Peel the apples and cut 3 of them into equal quarters, reserving 1 apple for later. In a pan, melt the remaining butter, then brown the apples with 1 tbsp lemon juice and the brown sugar.

Cake

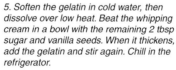

4. Mix the clabber or buttermilk, 2 tbsp sugar and half the vanilla mark in a pan with a hand whisk. Add the yolk and beat. Warm over low heat for 15 minutes to form a creamy sauce. Let chill in the refrigerator.

5. Soften the gelatin in cold water, then dissolve over low heat. Beat the whipping cream in a bowl with the remaining 2 tbsp sugar and vanilla seeds. When it thickens, add the gelatin and stir again. Chill in the refrigerator.

6. Cut the last apple thinly with a mandolin. Dry the slices for 1 hour in a 110°C/225°F oven. Place a layer of jelled cream on the bread in the rings, then remove the rings. Top with apples. Layer 2 small cakes on top of each other and decorate with apple chips and sauce.

Mexican

Preparation time: 20 minutes
Cooking time: 45 minutes
Difficulty: ★

Serves 6

500 g/generous 1 lb corn kernels
100 ml/7 tbsp milk
250 g/1 cup + 2 tbsp butter
5 eggs
150 g/²/₃ cup sugar
1 pinch salt

200 g/generous 1¹/₃ cups flour
1¹/₂ tbsp baking powder
several drops vanilla extract
butter and flour for greasing the pan

This easy and delicious cake is eaten throughout Mexico, where it is often made with kernels of fresh corn that are scraped straight from the cob. However, you can also use canned kernels of corn instead.

Grown for centuries, corn is as fundamental to the Mexicans as rice is for the Chinese or wheat for Egyptians. According to their mythology, the Aztecs believed that corn was a son of the sun god, who dropped small browned kernels like rain to give daily nourishment to the people. The Aztecs would dry and then roast the kernels before crushing them with a grindstone and preparing a flour called *pinole*, an ingredient in many dishes that is also eaten as a simple delicacy in itself.

Today, more than 800 varieties of corn are grown every year around the country: golden, white, red, brown, blue, black and multicolored. Mexicans eat roasted corn as street food, or use the kernels to prepare tortillas, a versatile flat bread that they top with meat or guacamole, or *tamales*, a kind of filling wrapped in corn leaves and cooked in paper or banana leaves.

The vanilla that flavors this Mexican Corn Cake also has Mexican origins. Long before colonization, the Totonacas Indians, who lived in the region that is now Veracruz, devoted themselves to raising and harvesting the fruit of this climbing plant. Today, Veracruz is the indisputable vanilla capital of Mexico. Only several drops of its concentrated extract are necessary to enrich your cake.

The cooking time can vary from 45 minutes to 1 hour, depending on your oven. When the cake looks golden, stick a toothpick into the center. The toothpick will come out clean if the cake is done.

For a real treat, serve the cake with a scoop of rum raisin or vanilla ice cream or with custard. It is also delicious cooled and topped with whipped cream.

1. Pour the kernels of corn into a blender and add the milk. Blend to a pale-yellow mixture.

2. Cut the butter into small pieces and melt in a small saucepan. In a large mixing bowl, beat the eggs and sugar with a whisk. Add the melted butter and then the salt.

3. Incorporate the corn mixture into the batter and blend.

Corn Cake

4. Mix the flour with the baking powder and add this to the batter, along with the vanilla. Whisk briskly just until the batter has been evenly mixed.

5. Grease and flour a round cake pan and pour the batter into the pan. Bake for 45 minutes at 180°C/355°F until it is golden and firm.

6. Remove the corn cake from the pan and flip it over onto a cooling rack. Cool before serving and eating.

Villareal

Preparation time: 40 minutes
Cooking time: 15 minutes
Chilling time: 1 hour 30 minutes
(may be prepared the night before)
Difficulty: ★

Serves 6

200 g/7 oz soft honey almond nougat,
such as Jijona
100 g/3¹/₂ oz hard nougat,
such as Alicante

4 sheets gelatin
cold water
330 ml/scant 1¹/₂ cups heavy cream
3 egg whites
60 g/4¹/₂ tbsp sugar
300 g/11 oz fresh fruit

As a change from the ordinary assortment of nougats that are often on the dessert menu in Spanish restaurants, Alberto Herráiz created this refined recipe that mixes hard nougat with soft nougat, and adds the sweetness of whipped cream and the airiness of egg whites.

A delicacy from times past, people in Catalonia say that nougat was invented by a confectioner named Pablo Turrons. It is said that he was the first to make nougat with almonds, a food that sustained Barcelona during a siege in the war of the Spanish Succession, when the only products available were almonds and honey. Others think it more likely that nougat, called *turrón*, is related to the Turkish and Middle Eastern *halva*, and is part of the region's Arab heritage. Eaten most often at Christmastime, nougat is still prepared by local craftsmen in the capital of Catalonia, Jijona, a town close to Valencia.

There are two basic kinds: the tender Jijona variety, or *turrón blando* (soft nougat), and the harder Alicante nougat, or *turrón*

duro (hard nougat), both made with blanched and crushed almonds, honey and egg whites.

Cut into large slices, this delicacy is covered with a thin wafer before being wrapped and packaged. Today, there are a wide range of nougats based on hazelnuts, pine nuts, coconut, almond paste, candied fruits and/or chocolate.

Turrones merchants were already widespread at the end of the nineteenth century, and there have always been specialty stores called *turronerias*, specializing in the preparation and sale of this typically Iberian delicacy. *Turrón* also emigrated with the Spanish, to North Africa and other colonies.

Correctly preparing this recipe depends on how you mix the nougat cream with the whipped cream and the beaten egg whites. It is important not to stir them, but rather fold the mixtures together gently, so that the cream and eggs don't lose their airiness. This will ensure that the dessert maintains its lightness.

1. Cut the soft nougat into 1 cm/¹/₃ in cubes. Cut the hard nougat the same way, as much as possible, because hard nougat tends to break apart. Keep both the cubes and the broken pieces.

2. Soak the gelatin in a little water. Place 6 round molds 5 cm/2 in high on a plate or a board. Put a layer of hard nougat cubes and pieces in the bottom of each mold.

3. Bring 100 ml/7 tbsp of the cream to the boil. Lower the heat and add the soft nougat. Stir just until you get a rich texture. Remove from the heat, add the gelatin, and allow to cool down.

Nougat Cake

4. Whip the rest of the cream. Beat the eggs until they are stiff, then add the sugar.

5. Incorporate the whipped cream into the cooled nougat by gently folding it in. Then delicately incorporate the egg whites.

6. Fill the circular molds with this nougat mixture. Refrigerate for about 1¹/₂ hours. Remove from the molds, place on serving plates, sprinkle with pieces of hard nougat, and garnish with pieces of fresh fruit.

Chocolate

Preparation time: 1 hour
Cooking time: 20 minutes
Difficulty: ★★

Serves 6

225 g/8 oz dark chocolate,
preferably 72% cocoa
70 g/5 tbsp butter
4 eggs
85 g/6 tbsp sugar
1 pinch salt (optional)

15 g/1½ tbsp flour
40 g/7 tbsp cocoa powder
plus some for decoration
100 ml/7 tbsp heavy cream,
preferably 35% fat
mint leaves

This Chocolate Mousse Cake was created at the *Golf Club du Domaine Impérial*, where our chef practices his craft. His cake is an indisputable success and graces the dessert buffet every day. What makes it stand out from other chocolate cakes is that it is covered with a firm layer of chocolate mousse. The dessert is prepared with a base of chocolate that is separated into parts; one portion is mixed with flour to make the cake batter, and the other is combined with whipped cream to make mousse.

It wouldn't be fitting not to present a chocolate dessert from the country where so many contemporary chocolate specialties were first concocted. Chocolate was brought to Switzerland by a resident of Zurich, Henri Escher, who discovered it in 1697 in Brussels. In Belgium, Philippe Suchard established the first industrial chocolate factory in the nineteenth century.

In 1830 in Switzerland, Charles-Amédée Kohler made chocolate with hazelnuts for the first time. Then, pharmacist Henri Nestlé teamed up with a candy maker to create the first milk chocolate. And in 1879, Rodolphe Lindt discovered the process of conching, a special production method that gives chocolate its moist and melt-in-your-mouth texture. Today, the Swiss consume up to 24 pounds of chocolate per person per year, a world record. They use chocolate in cakes, mousses, ganaches and soufflés. Only the Swiss could invent chocolate fondue, into which pieces of fruit, cookies and cake are dipped.

You can get excellent cake batter by paying careful attention to the quantity of eggs. For this recipe, use 4 eggs if they are very large, or 5 if they are smaller. Make sure that the cake is fully cooked in the center by pricking it with a toothpick. It will come out clean if the cake is baked completely. In any case, if it has been cooked too long, brush the cake with Kirsch, rum, port or orange juice to moisten it.

1. Break the chocolate into a double boiler. Cut the butter into small cubes and add to the chocolate. Place the double boiler over a pan of boiling water and mix the butter and chocolate until melted and well blended.

2. Separate the egg whites from the yolks. Beat the yolks and sugar in a mixing bowl with a whisk or an electric mixer until the mixture is pale.

3. Add a pinch of salt to the egg whites. Beat them with an electric mixer until they are stiff. Gently fold into the egg yolk and sugar mixture, then add the melted chocolate. Pour 60% of this batter into another mixing bowl and save 40%; chill the smaller portion in the refrigerator.

Mousse Cake

4. Sift the flour and pour it into the mixing bowl with 60% of the batter. Then sift the cocoa into the bowl. Blend very gently so that all of the ingredients are combined without breaking down the egg whites.

5. Pour the batter into a large pastry circle placed on top of a pastry board. Bake in the oven for 15 minutes at 170°C/340°F. Vigorously whip the cream and blend it with the smaller portion of batter. Return to the refrigerator.

6. Run a knife around the edge of the cake pan to help ease the cake away from the side, then remove the ring. Let the cake cool on a cooling rack. Cover the cake with the chocolate mousse. Sprinkle with cocoa and garnish with a sprig of mint.

Honey

Preparation time: 30 minutes
Cooking time: 10 minutes
Difficulty: ★★

Serves 4

5 cm (2 in) piece fresh ginger root
130 g/scant 1 cup flour
140 ml/9 tbsp water
1 pinch salt

500 ml/2 cups vegetable oil for frying
140 g/scant $^1/_2$ cup liquid honey
1 tbsp pine nuts
60 g/4$^1/_2$ tbsp sugar (optional)

Desserts like those we are accustomed to in the West are not included on Korean menus. To round off a meal, they are often content with fruits such as pears, prunes, persimmons or apples, or possibly walnuts, along with roasted barley tea or an invigorating ginseng infusion. Small cakes are sometimes served with a glass of tea. European-style bakeries are starting to establish themselves in Seoul; however, they remain something exotic for the majority of Koreans.

In this recipe, Madame Kim presents small pastry twists that have quite a curious origin. Their Korean name, *me dja kwa*, signals the appearance of the traditional matchmaker in Korean society. In the past, matchmakers were employed to marry young Koreans. If two families reached a marriage agreement, the family of the bride would send a packet of various cakes, including these twisted pastries, to the groom's family.

The twisted cakes baked by our chef are flavored with ginger. Ginger is the root of a hardy, perennial herbaceous plant in the Zingiberaceae family and has a zesty and spicy flavor. A root that has dull, brownish skin and is limp will be stringy and dry, so leave it in the store. Ginger adds an exquisite touch to exotic dishes, cakes and curries.

Chef Kim enriches her twists by coating them with honey. In the past, Koreans bought the entire honeycomb complete with the wax. They then had to melt and filter it to gain the sweet golden liquid. Today, of course, honey is sold in jars in every supermarket. However, our chef's mother believes that the traditional honey is more natural and has more flavor than "commercial" honey.

Before frying your pastries, make sure that the dough is not too limp because the twists have a tendency to stick together while cooking. Fry them slowly; otherwise, the cakes will be too brown and poorly cooked.

1. Peel the ginger and chop it into large pieces. In a food processor, blend just until it is puréed. Remove the purée and strain through a dish towel to extract all the juice.

2. Put the flour on a flat surface and make a well in the center. Slowly add 40 ml/ 2$^1/_2$ tbsp of the water, the ginger juice and salt. Knead into an even dough and then shape the dough into a ball.

3. Roll out the dough. Cut into strips about 4 cm/1$^1/_2$ in long and 2 cm/$^3/_4$ in wide. With the point of a knife, cut 3 parallel slits along the length of each strip. Open at the middle and bring one end of the strip through this middle hole to form twists.

Twists

4. In a fryer, heat the oil to 150°C/300°F. Brown the pastry twists slowly, turning them often. They should cook until golden, about 10 minutes. Crush the pine nuts.

5. Drain excess oil from the cooked twists with a paper towel. Place them in a shallow dish with the honey. Turn the twists so they are well coated by the honey. If you like, make a syrup by boiling the rest of the water with the sugar and dipping half of the twists in it.

6. When the twists are completely coated with honey, sprinkle with pine nuts. Serve and eat them right away.

Red Fruit

Preparation time: 15 minutes
Cooking time: 2 minutes
Difficulty: ★

Serves 4

200 g/7 oz strawberries
100 g/3¹/₂ oz raspberries
100 g/3¹/₂ oz blueberries

2 liters/2 quarts water
6 egg yolks
250 g/1 cup + 2 tbsp sugar
120 ml/¹/₂ cup Marsala
120 ml/¹/₂ cup dry white wine

Baking a zabaglione au gratin lets you serve a light delicacy embellished with a touch of elegance, a sophisticated treat that will happily surprise your guests. Francesca Ciardi is Roman, and her taste, simplicity and imagination all contribute to her creative culinary genius. A dessert of Italian origin, zabaglione is made of eggs, sugar, white wine and a flavored liqueur. Served with a golden crust on top, this zabaglione is a specialty of the house at the *Café Greco* in Rome.

The term zabaglione (or sabayon in French) has been used to describe all sorts of mousses with sauce, generally sprinkled with wine and served after fish and crustacean dishes to top off elegant meals. In this recipe, Francesca Ciardi presents a zabaglione in the true Italian tradition. Strawberries, blueberries and raspberries, or a mixture of them, come together in this gratin. Red currants are another option.

The cooking process is quite quick: the simmering bain-marie and a preheated oven should be hot and ready to go. When you remove the zabaglione from the oven, it should be presented and served in its baking dish.

Making a successful zabaglione depends on thickening the mixture without cooking it: the gente heat of a bain-marie does just that. If you think the water is too hot, you can remove the zabaglione for a minute and continue to beat it away from the heat. Once whipped, the zabaglione is a light and creamy mass. Put it in the oven to bake lightly right away.

Among all the Italian dessert wines, Marsala is without a doubt the best known. Made with white wine flavored with *Passito* raisins and brandy, *Marsala vergine* (white) is mixed with grape syrup and caramel. Its brown color and unmatchable sweetness play a part in many favorite Italian desserts.

1. Rinse and carefully dry the berries. Gently distribute them on the bottom of 4 round baking pans. Set aside. Preheat the oven to 250°C/480°F.

2. Bring the water to the boil in a saucepan. Put the egg yolks and sugar into a large mixing bowl.

3. Add the Marsala.

Zabaglione

4. Add the white wine. Quickly whisk the mixture until you get a pale yellow mousse.

5. Immediately place the mixing bowl containing the mousse over the saucepan of boiling water. Continue to whisk the mixture without stopping until it becomes a thick mousse-like cream; make sure the mixture does not start to cook.

6. Pour the zabaglione into the small baking dishes containing the fruit. Place the dishes in the oven right away. Bake up to 2 minutes. Serve the dessert once it has cooled slightly.

Gulab

Preparation time: 30 minutes
Cooking time: 30 minutes
Chilling time: 4 hours
Difficulty: ★

Serves 4

For the syrup:
500 ml/2 cups water
800 g/3²/₃ cups sugar
1 tbsp rosewater

For the dough:
180 g/scant 1¹/₂ cups dry milk
50 g/¹/₃ cup flour
1 tsp baking powder
1 tsp ground cardamom
1 tbsp peanut oil
150 ml/²/₃ cup fresh milk, room temperature
oil for frying

This typical Indian dessert comes from Rajasthan, but is known throughout the country.

The rose is the queen of flowers all around the world, thanks to its beauty and scent. In India, it blooms throughout the country, and is also appreciated for its taste. Indians add rose, or at least its petals, when making jellies, syrups and desserts. In addition, for a lovely aesthetic touch, white, pink or red rose petals are strewn on the table or encircle serving plates like a crown for the best-tasting dishes. These noble and majestic flowers are highly prized by women, who often wear them in their hair and on their sari. And if it is not roses, it's jasmine: these small white flowers with their heady scent flavor teas and desserts.

Gulab Jamun is an ideal recipe for a dessert, but it can also be enjoyed as a fresh taste during the summer months if served with Earl Grey, the afternoon tea. Earl Grey is a tea known around the world, and although it is often present on the afternoon tea tray in England and served with milk, it is actually Indian. It first came from India, where it is still grown in 1001 varieties.

Indians often stress that the period of British colonization has not left its mark on Indian cuisine: to the contrary, the English returned to England with traditionally Indian foods like pickles or chutneys, small jars of sugared or salted preserves that are not at all English except for their name.

Even if the British have not tried to take the credit for these creations, newcomers to Indian cuisine unknowingly attribute much to the English, which is a disservice to India. It is an error to be avoided so that you do not offend either the English or the great chefs of India.

Our chef says that when it comes to *Gulab Jamun*, it is best if the small dough balls are saturated with syrup so that the dessert becomes even richer.

1. Boil the water and sugar for 15 minutes, gently whisking to melt the sugar. Remove the saucepan from the heat and add the rosewater.

2. In a large mixing bowl, mix the dry milk, flour, baking powder, cardamom and oil well.

3. Add the milk to the mixing bowl. Begin to mix the liquid with the dry ingredients, then knead the mixture into an even and slightly sticky dough. Set aside for 15 minutes.

Jamun

4. After 15 minutes, take the dough and, using your hands, roll it into balls about 3 cm/1¹/₂ in around; place the balls on a clean cloth.

5. In a fryer or a large pot filled with oil, fry the small balls of dough until well browned. Remove them using a slotted spoon and place on 2 sheets of paper towel to drain.

6. Place the saucepan with syrup over medium heat. When it starts to boil, add the fried balls of dough and coat with the syrup. Put the balls in small serving bowls half-filled with syrup and chill in the refrigerator for 4 hours.

Wildberry

Preparation time: *30 minutes*
Cooking time: *20 minutes*
Difficulty: ★

Serves 6 or 7

For the kissel:
60 g/2 oz strawberries
60 g/2 oz blueberries
60 g/2 oz raspberries
60 g/2 oz cranberries

1.5 liters/1¹⁄₂ quarts water, plus a little more
120 g/9 tbsp sugar
3 tbsp potato flour

For the decoration:
berries
mint leaves

A dessert that is particularly enjoyed throughout Russia, kissel is a red fruit coulis cooked and thickened with flour. Formerly, kissel referred to an everyday, unsweetened liquid beverage made from peas. In the age of Peter the Great, at the end of the seventeenth century, cooks began to use fruit purées and syrups to prepare fresh and dried fruit kissel.

Any fruit can be made into kissel, whether berries or apples or pears. Russians harvest raspberries from the forest, blueberries and strawberries from the woods, and forage the marshes in search of cranberries in the fall. You can add red currants, strawberries, black currants and raspberries, all commonly grown in gardens, in any combination that suits your taste.

Cranberry kissel wins all the votes from the Russian palace. These small, wild fruits are closely related to blueberries. They are used particularly in sauces for meats, coulis, pickled cabbage, in jellies and in all sorts of cakes.

The thickness of the kissel varies according to what you add to it. If you add a very small amount of flour, it will remain relatively liquid and you can even drink it as a refreshing beverage. In Russia, it's used as a sauce for small, round slices of cheese sautéed in butter.

With more flour, the texture ranges from a rich coulis just up to a thick cream that you can serve as a cold dessert. It is generally accompanied by cakes, cookies, small pies or as part of a larger pie stuffed with jelly.

For an even richer dessert, add a large spoonful of heavy cream to each bowl of Wildberry Kissel.

1. Rinse and dry off all of the fruit. Blend them in a food processor to a purée. Crush the purée through a sieve into a small dish and set the juice aside.

2. Pour the pulp from the fruit into a saucepan. Add 1.5 l/1¹⁄₂ quarts water and stir quickly.

3. Add the sugar to the saucepan. Bring to the boil and cook 4 to 5 minutes. Using a slotted spoon, remove the foam that forms on the surface.

Kissel

4. Filter the mixture though a sieve above a saucepan. Set the pulp aside and bring the filtered juice to the boil.

5. Dilute the flour in a small dish of water. Add to the hot juice, whisking briskly in order to break apart the flour. Let thicken over low heat while stirring constantly.

6. Pour the pressed juice and the fruit pulp into the thickened sauce. Mix, pour into a dish and cool. Serve chilled, decorated with berries and small mint leaves.

Konafa

Preparation time: 45 minutes
Cooking time: 50 minutes
Difficulty: ★

Serves 5

For the konafa:
1 kg/2¹/₄ lb fine konafa pastry
1 kg/2¹/₄ lb unsalted butter
100 g/1 cup walnuts
100 g/²/₃ cup almonds
100 g/²/₃ cup hazelnuts

100 g/³/₄ cup raisins
100 g/generous 1 cup flaked coconut

For the syrup:
1.5 kg/3¹/₄ lb powdered sugar
750 ml/3¹/₄ cups water
1 slice lemon

Used in a number of Middle Eastern countries, *Konafa* is presented in many different forms: rolled like cigars in Lebanon, in crispy triangles in Turkey and in flat cakes in Egypt. Very fine, like angel hair, this particular variety of pastry dough is made simply of flour, salt and water.

Konafa is sold in a compact package, and should be untangled with the tips of your fingers so that it can better absorb the melted butter. Cover the bottom of a round baking pan with half of the buttered *konafa* and bake in the oven. After 10 minutes, garnish with almonds, hazelnuts and walnuts. The second half of the *konafa* should be cooked alone in a mold.

Middle Easterners are masters at the art of grazing, or nibbling on food throughout the day. Renowned as a great source of energy, dried fruits are a popular snack. Our chef suggests boiling raisins or other dried fruit in water for a minute before using them in recipes.

Great fans of pastries, Egyptians give *Konafa* an extra touch by topping it with syrup. If possible, you may want to prepare this syrup before making the rest of the dessert. Made simply from sugar and water, it should simmer for half an hour to an hour over low heat. Adding a slice of lemon to the syrup will help maintain a constant boil and will make the sugar and water come together in a thick but fluid mixture.

Once the *Konafa* is baked, with a quick and accurate motion, flip it over so that it fully covers the dried fruit stuffing. At this time you can saturate the entire cake with syrup. You have two options: pouring the cold syrup over the hot dessert, or heating the syrup and pouring it over the chilled dessert.

During the festival of Ramadan, it is not unusual to see individual servings of *Konafa* in the front windows of pastry shops, accompanied with a glass of sweetened milk. Fans of this dessert cannot resist the golden and sugary pastry.

1. Turn the entire package of konafa onto a plate. Untangle it with your fingers and place in a mixing bowl.

2. Slowly melt the butter in a saucepan and then pour into the mixing bowl with the konafa. Mix together with the tips of your fingers until the butter has been fully absorbed.

3. Put half of the buttered konafa in the bottom of a circular baking pan and set the other half aside. Bake the konafa for 10 minutes in a moderate oven. Then flip it over onto a plate and return it to the same baking pan with the opposite side facing up.

4. Crush the walnuts, almonds and hazelnuts, then mix them together in a bowl. In another bowl, mix the raisins and coconut. Sprinkle the baked konafa with a layer of nuts, then with a layer of coconut and raisins. Set aside.

5. Bake the other half of the konafa. After it is fully baked, invert it onto a plate, then place it on top of the konafa garnished with fruits and nuts.

6. Prior to this, make the syrup by boiling the sugar, water and lemon together (see text). Soak the konafa with half of this syrup and put the other half in a serving bowl. Serve the cake in slices accompanied by the bowl of syrup.

Kirsch-Glazed

Preparation time: 30 minutes
Cooking time: 5 minutes
Chilling time: 12 hours
Difficulty: ★★

Serves 4

250 ml/1 cup water
375 g/3¹/₂ cups powdered sugar
6 egg yolks

75 ml/¹/₃ cup heavy cream
110 ml/7 tbsp kirsch
15 Morello cherries in alcohol
raspberry coulis

Franck Mischler and Mickaël Wolf chose to create an opulent dessert inspired by *Gugelhupf* from Alsace (also spelled *Kugelhopf*). This is a light cake in the same family as brioche that is often enhanced with raisins or other dried fruits and cooked in a high crown-shaped mold with decorative grooves. However, their version resembles the traditional dessert mainly in its distinctive shape. Frothy, refreshing and perfectly flavored, the *Gugelhupf* created by our chefs requires precision, flexibility and knowledge of the techniques used in the recipe. Make sure to choose very fresh and good-sized eggs.

Chilling the heavy cream ahead of time makes it easier to whip. Franck Mischler suggests an infallible trick: put several ice cubes in a bowl, and then place the bottom of the mixing bowl containing the cream above the ice and beat vigorously with a large whisk.

Gently incorporate the whipped cream into the dessert batter, adding it bit by bit using the tip of the whisk. The cream should be perfectly whipped so that it does not break apart in the beaten eggs.

Then add the kirsch to this light batter. Produced in Alsace, this cherry brandy is a key element in many well-loved desserts. Its powerful fragrance and refined taste mix well with Morello cherries. You can replace it with another clear alcohol, such as pear brandy or plum liqueur; the alcohol should complement the fruit you choose for the *Gugelhupf*. The recipe adapts to any season: cherries, peaches, plums, berries or any other fruit could be used.

Whether it is portioned out into individual molds or made in a large family-sized dish, our chefs' *Gugelhupf* needs to be frozen. After freezing, turn it over onto a serving plate and remove it from the mold with several taps on the bottom of the pan; then the *Gugelhupf* will be ready to eat. Crowned with Morello cherries and topped with a raspberry coulis, this is truly a royal dessert.

1. Bring the water to the boil and add the sugar. Mix with a whisk until it becomes a syrup. Remove from the heat. With an electric mixer, beat the yolks until firm and frothy.

2. Briefly return the pan with the syrup to the heat, then add it all at once to the egg yolks. Beat just until it cools down. Set aside.

3. Pour the heavy cream into a high-sided mixing bowl and beat with a large whisk until the cream is thick and light.

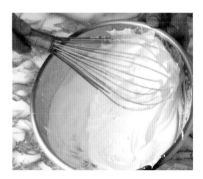

Gugelhupf

4. As soon as the cream is firm, carefully fold it into the yolks.

5. Slowly pour the kirsch into the mixture. With each addition of kirsch, make sure to blend carefully with your whisk.

6. Cut the cherries in half and garnish the bottom of small gugelhupf molds with them. Pour the mixture over the cherries. Freeze overnight. After they are frozen, remove the gugelhupf from the molds. Purée fresh raspberries and top the dessert with the coulis and more cherries.

Baklava

Preparation time:	45 minutes
Cooking time:	35 minutes
Resting time, dough:	10 minutes
Difficulty:	★★★

Serves 6

For the baklava:
1 kg/7 cups flour
2 tsp butter
$^1/_2$ tsp salt
300 ml/1$^1/_4$ cups water
100 g/$^2/_3$ cup cornstarch

200 g/generous 1$^1/_3$ cups cashews
300 g/1$^1/_3$ cups concentrated margarine
or butter

For the syrup:
100 g/7 tbsp sugar
100 ml/7 tbsp water
1 splash lemon juice
1 drop orange blossom water

100 g/scant 1 cup pistachios

Hussein Fakih presents the preeminent Lebanese dessert, as renowned as it is demanding. Everyone will recognize baklava from seeing it in the windows of bakeries or in Middle Eastern markets. If you encounter any difficulty preparing the pastry itself, you can always buy ready-made pastry in a Lebanese or Middle Eastern grocery store. In the traditional recipe, a dozen pastry disks are piled on top of each other, then crushed with a large rolling pin, transforming the piled leaves into a single leaf of large diameter. For greater convenience, and to prepare the recipe as traditionally as possible, it is preferable to use fewer pastry disks.

Baklava can take a variety of shapes. For the cigar shape, place a pencil in the center of a 10 x 15 cm (4 x 6 in) rectangle of pastry. Fold one half of the rectangle onto the other over the pencil. Spread nut stuffing on the pastry the length of the pencil. Roll the pastry around the stuffing (into a cigar) and gently pull out the pencil. You can also make baklava as a little turnover, cut out with an oval cookie cutter.

Although cashews are traditional, almonds and pistachios can be substituted in the fillings. The traditional sugar syrup has a serious rival in honey, which is greatly appreciated in Lebanon even though more costly. It is preferable to use a flower honey. Hussein Fakih also uses a concentrated margarine in this dessert, rather than butter. You can find it in Lebanese grocery stores.

Generally, baklava is enjoyed after meals, or on festive occasions, accompanied by mint tea. Our chef serves the baklava with delicious Turkish coffee or espresso. Baklava will hold for five or six days at room temperature.

1. Put the flour into a large bowl. Add the butter and salt. Mix, adding the water a little at a time.

2. On a surface sprinkled with cornstarch, shape the pastry into a large sausage and cut into 12 disks that are 2 cm/$^3/_4$ in thick. Let it rest for 10 minutes. Roll out each disk 1 cm/$^1/_3$ in thick. Pile them on top of each other and roll out, crushing them and rolling them into a thin puff pastry.

3. Placing the rolling pin directly on the pastry, cut strips the width of the rolling pin. Repeat until the pastry is cut into long strips. Turn the rolling pin in the opposite direction and cut again, making even squares.

4. For the filling, finely chop the cashews. Place a spoonful of cashews on each pastry square. Pinch the four corners of the pastry together, taking care they do not stick to each other. Make little open-topped pouches, with the stuffing still visible.

5. Place the baklava on a baking sheet. Melt the butter and spoon it over the baklava squares. Bake 30 minutes at 200°C/390°F. Prepare a syrup by boiling the sugar and water, then adding the lemon juice and orange blossom water.

6. Chop the pistachios. Take the baklava from the oven and sprinkle with syrup and chopped pistachios. Allow the baklava to cool before serving.

Cuban

Preparation time: 30 minutes
Cooking time: 1 hour
Difficulty: ★

Serves 4

1 kg/2¹/₄ lb grapefruit
1 kg/2¹/₄ lb ripe guava
2 oranges
3 liters/3 quarts water
1.5 kg/7 cups sugar
fresh mint leaves

This grapefruit and guava recipe is one of Cuba's favorite desserts. It is an everyday family treat and quite economical, as many people have grapefruit or guava trees growing near their homes. They only have to run out to the garden to replenish their supply.

Cubans serve grapefruit in entrées and in salads with vegetables. They also enjoy them in delicious desserts such as the recipe we are presenting here.

Just as clementines are often confused with mandarin oranges, there has been some confusion about grapefruit and pomelos. Pomelos are an ancient ancestor of grapefruit, brought from the Far East to the West Indies around 1700. The pomelo that grow in Cuba are smaller than grapefruit—unlike pomelo in the Far East, which are much larger—and no one knows whether they were a natural mutation of the grapefruit, or the product of crossing grapefruit with something else.

In this recipe, grapefruit shells are tenderized and sweetened by syrup before receiving the preserved guavas. This little yellow fruit with succulent sweet flesh belongs, curiously, to the same botanical family as cloves, cinnamon and nutmeg: the Myrtaceae family. Myrtaceae are trees and shrubs found in the tropics, subtropics and temperate Australia.

There are more than a hundred species of guava. They can be divided into two categories: the first, which resemble the pear, has pink pulp and is quite sweet. The second looks more like the apple, and has a clear rosy salmon color and a pronounced flavor. Guava is eaten fresh but is also made into jams, fruit pastes, juice, sorbets and preserves.

1. Peel off the grapefruit's outer skin with a very sharp knife, leaving the white inner skin intact. Cut the grapefruit in half.

2. Peel the guavas. Cut them in half across the thickest part. With a melon baller or grapefruit spoon, remove the seeds from the center.

3. Cook the grapefruit in 1.5 l/1¹/₂ quarts water and half of the sugar for 15 minutes. Remove the grapefruit from the syrup. Carefully turn each piece inside out, removing the pulp. In a separate pot, cook the guavas in the same manner with the same amount of water and sugar.

Delights

4. Refresh the grapefruit shells by dipping them in cold water. Gently press each shell between your hands, pressing out as much liquid as possible to remove any bitterness that may remain. Discard the cold water and set aside the grapefruit shells.

5. Scoop out the cooked guavas, draining the sugar-water syrup back into the pan. Set the guavas aside. Pour half the guava syrup into another saucepan, add the grapefruit shells and bring to the boil. Heat to 120°C/250°F, then reduce the heat and simmer for 20 minutes.

6. Cut the oranges in thin slices. Put them in the second pan of guava syrup and cook for 15 minutes. Serve the grapefruit shells filled with cooked guava, surrounded by slices of orange and garnished with a sprig of mint.

Cherry

Preparation time: 40 minutes
Cooking time: 45 minutes
Resting time, dough: 1 hour
Difficulty: ★★

Serves 4

For the sweet pastry:
125 g/³/₄ cup + 2 tbsp flour
50 g/3¹/₂ tbsp sugar
1 pinch salt
75 g/¹/₃ cup butter
1 egg

For the millat:
60 g/7 tbsp flour
100 g/scant 1 cup powdered sugar
5 g/1 tbsp ground almonds
2 eggs
2 tsp yeast
100 ml/7 tbsp milk
100 ml/7 tbsp cream
1 pinch salt
400 g/14 oz cherries

For the raspberry sauce:
100 g/3¹/₂ oz raspberries
50 g/3¹/₂ tbsp sugar

Red, beautiful, appealing to the eye: their very appearance makes sweet, juicy cherries a pleasure to behold. Rich in liquid, vitamins and fiber, cherries lead us on the road to alimentary balance. Since the Middle Ages, two species have been cultivated in Europe: sweet cherries and sour cherries. Today, among the 2,000 varieties in existence, only about a dozen are currently on the market. Alas, the cherry season is very brief; the beautiful red Burlat announces the arrival of spring, while the white Griotte, translucent and tangy, hails the end of the summer. For the Cherry Millat, Jacky Morlon prefers to use the beautiful Pigeon Heart cherry—fat, carmine red and full of sugar—that one finds at French market stalls at the beginning of June.

Cherries are more delicate than one might think: they must be handled and pitted with great care. It is important to note that cherries should never be eaten cold, but they should be stored in the vegetable drawer.

This creamy dessert, similar to a clafouti, gets its name from the preparation: a mixture of flour, sugar, almond powder, eggs, milk and cream. In bygone days, the *millat* was nothing more than a thick porridge of millet or corn flour, cooked on the stove in the shape of a *galette* (a flat thin cake). Our chef has created a lighter and more modern version. The cream should thicken for 20 minutes before being poured over the cherries, which have been arranged atop the sweet pastry. When cherries are not in season, any fruit can be used for a *millat*: pears, mulberries, apples, bilberries, blueberries, strawberries or plums, according to availability.

This delicious dessert reminiscent of childhood is served lukewarm, accompanied by raspberries blended with sugar. The coulis, or fruit sauce, can be thinned out or made more liquid by adding up to two tablespoons of water, a little at a time. A few drops of lemon juice for those who love that acid tang, and your raspberry sauce is ready.

1. For the pastry, combine the flour, sugar and salt and make a well in the center. Melt the butter and add it and the egg to the well. Mix to a dough with your fingertips. Shape it into a ball and cover with waxed paper or plastic wrap. Chill for an hour.

2. For the millat, combine the flour, sugar, ground almonds, eggs, yeast, milk, cream and salt in a large mixing bowl. Whisk together. Let stand for 20 minutes.

3. Lightly sprinkle the work surface with flour. Roll the pastry into a circle about 5 mm/¹/₅ in thick and 16 cm/6¹/₄ inches in diameter.

Millat

4. Line a small, deep baking dish with the dough. Trim off the excess.

5. Wash the cherries and remove the stems and pits. Put them into the pastry shell.

6. Pour the millat mixture over the cherries. It should fill the baking dish about ¾ full. Bake for 45 minutes at 180°C/350°F. Meanwhile, blend the raspberries and sugar into a sauce. When the millat is ready, serve it warm, sprinkled with powdered sugar and accompanied by the sauce.

Orange Pieces

Preparation time: 1 hour
Cooking time: 50 minutes
Chilling time: 45 minutes
Difficulty: ★★

Serves 4

For the fried milk:
500 ml/2 cups milk
1 vanilla bean
4 egg yolks
120 g/9 tbsp sugar, divided
40 g/5 tbsp cornstarch
zest of 1 lemon
oil for baking pan
3 whole eggs

100 g/²/₃ cup flour
¹/₂ tsp cinnamon
50 ml/3¹/₂ tbsp oil for frying

For the pieces of heaven:
260 g/scant 1¹/₄ cups sugar + 2 tbsp
125 ml/¹/₂ cup orange juice
8 egg yolks
1 tsp lemon juice

For the red sauce:
125 ml/¹/₂ cup water
150 g/²/₃ cup sugar
zest of 1 lemon, julienned
zest of 1 orange, julienned
¹/₄ stick cinnamon
¹/₈ tsp black pepper
4 tsp wine vinegar
50 g/ca. 2 oz each: red currants, strawberries, raspberries

Harmony of flavor is the operative term for this suite of desserts brought to us by chef Alberto Herráiz. A well-known sweet especially enjoyed on holidays, the "piece of heaven", better known as *tocino de cielo*, requires a large number of egg yolks. It is said that the winemakers of the past who created fine sherry needed many egg whites to clarify the beverage as it was being prepared. They handed over the unused egg yolks to their wives, who then used them to create this dessert.

Orange juice replaces water, the liquid originally used in this recipe. Taking advantage of the acidity of the orange juice, as well as that of the red fruits in the sauce, the chef achieves a balance of flavors. Rather than juice from a bottle or carton, it is best to use freshly squeezed and strained orange juice.

As for the fried milk, it is said that the recipe for these creamy bread-like rectangles comes directly from monastery kitchens, where it used to be prepared on a regular basis. Don't forget to roll the pieces of fried milk in cinnamon sugar, which perks it up quite pleasantly.

It is imperative to use organic, untreated lemons and oranges for the zest. Use a sharp paring knife or zester. Slice off and use only the outer layer of peel; if any of the white pith is used, the flavor may be changed.

This dessert must be served chilled. Unmold one of the orange juice creams onto a large plate, then put two portions of fried milk beside it. The red fruit sauce, which the chef likes to call "soup", is not poured on top of everything, but surrounds the pieces of fried milk like a broad ribbon, with the zests garnishing it. No one will want to miss this dessert!

1. Split and scrape out the vanilla bean and put it in the milk. Scald, then set aside. Mix the egg yolks with 80 g/6 tbsp sugar and the cornstarch. Slowly whisk the milk into the egg yolk mixture. Place in a bain-marie or double boiler. Add the lemon zest.

2. Oil the bottom and sides of a baking pan. Pour in the egg-milk mixture and smooth to an even thickness of 3 cm/1¹/₄ in. Let cool at room temperature for 45 minutes. Beat the 3 whole eggs well and set aside. Put the flour in one bowl, and mix the rest of the sugar with the cinnamon in a second.

3. Heat the cooking oil. Cut the cooled egg-milk mixture into 8 rectangular portions. Dip each into the beaten egg, then flour, and brown in the hot oil. Drain the pieces and roll in the cinnamon sugar. Set aside.

# of Heaven

4. For the "pieces of heaven", boil 260 g/ scant 1¼ cups sugar and the orange juice together. In a deep bowl, whip the egg yolks, and pour the orange juice syrup into them.

5. Cook 2 tbsp sugar in a heavy saucepan over medium heat until it melts and turns golden. Add the lemon juice. Pour this caramel into 4 small steep-sided custard cups. Divide the egg mixture among them. Steam for 7 minutes, placing a cloth under the cover to absorb condensed steam.

6. For the red sauce, bring the water to the boil, then add the sugar, lemon and orange zests, cinnamon, pepper and vinegar. Add the fruit in pieces and let cool. Place the unmolded creams and the fried milk on individual dessert plates. Surround with the red fruit sauce.

Chocolate Mousse

Preparation time: 45 minutes
Difficulty: ★★

Serves 4

For the chocolate mousse:
150 g/5^1/$_2$ oz dark chocolate, melted
2 eggs
250 ml/1 cup heavy cream, chilled
40 g/6 tbsp sugar

For the nougatine:
150 g/^{2}/$_3$ cup sugar
80 g/^{2}/$_3$ cup almonds, crushed
50 ml/3^1/$_2$ tbsp Mandarine Napoléon liqueur

For the garnish:
mint leaves
julienned candied orange zest

Invented in France in the seventeenth century, Cognac made the fortune of the distilleries of Charentes. But it was in Belgium that the great Napoléon Cognac, aged for thirty years, was wed to the flavor of tangerines. In one of the country's greatest distilleries, Mandarine Napoléon was born in the shadow of the distilling devices, by the steeping of tangerine zest in French Cognac. With his fine-tuned Belgian palate, Pierre Fonteyne did not hesitate to unite this alcohol with another local culinary passion: chocolate. He offers us sumptuous, creamy chocolate mousse served on a bed of liqueur enhanced by nougatine.

But all chocolate is not equal: its quality depends upon the numerous primary ingredients that make up the final product. Good balance between the quantity of cocoa butter and the proportion of pure cocoa, and the quality of the conchage, the method used to separate the cacao bean from its outer hull,

make chocolate meltingly sweet on the tongue. Some people enjoy mousse that is rich in sugar and light in chocolate, while others swear by mousse that is rich in cocoa, with a very robust flavor. When you choose baking chocolate, be certain to verify the amount of cocoa in it: this can vary greatly from one brand to another.

Chocolate cream becomes mousse with the addition of eggs. In a flash, stiff-beaten egg whites are folded in with a light hand. The chocolate of the mousse is muted by beaten egg whites and whipped cream. Its bitterness becomes sweetness, and its robust flavor, lightness.

A nougat fondant hides under this mouth-watering mousse. To make it, prepare a caramel by cooking some sugar in a heavy saucepan over medium heat until it starts melting and turning golden, then pour some crushed almonds and hazelnuts into the middle of it.

1. Chop the chocolate and place it in a small saucepan. Place this into a larger saucepan partially filled with warm, not boiling, water. Let the chocolate melt over low heat.

2. Separate the egg whites from the egg yolks. Add the yolks to the melted chocolate and stir briskly. Set aside and allow to cool.

3. Whip the cream with a mixer or whisk until stiff peaks form. Fold it gently into the chocolate/egg yolk mixture.

with Mandarine Napoléon

4. Beat the egg whites until firm, but not stiff or dry. Add the sugar and continue beating until you have a firm meringue. Fold gently into the chocolate mixture. Set aside.

5. Prepare the nougatine as directed in the main text: make caramel and then add nuts. Spread it on a slab of cold marble or a greased baking sheet. When cooled, break into small pieces. Cover the bottom of dessert goblets with pieces of nougatine.

6. Pour the liqueur over the nougatine in the dishes, filling them about ¼ of the way. Using a pastry bag, fill the goblets the rest of the way with mousse. Decorate each serving with mint leaves and orange zest.

Recife Passion

Preparation time: 20 minutes
Cooking time: 5 minutes
Freezing time: 1 hour or more
Setting time, mousse: 2 hours or more
Difficulty: ★

Serves 6

For the mousse:
250 ml/1 cup passion fruit juice
120 g/9 tbsp sugar

12 g/1¹/₂ envelopes granulated gelatin
250 ml/1 cup boiling water
3 egg whites
350 ml/1¹/₂ cups whipping cream

For the syrup:
120 ml/¹/₂ cup passion fruit juice
90 g/6¹/₂ tbsp sugar
¹/₄ tsp cornstarch
120 ml/¹/₂ cup water
1 tsp dried passion fruit grains

Recife is the capital of the state of Pernambuco, in northeastern Brazil. This city, which was founded in the sixteenth century, boasts more than a hundred historical monuments and the magnificent beaches of Boa Viagem and Pina, bordered with coral reefs. If the local gastronomy is particularly renowned for its fish dishes, it is also rich in numerous dessert sweets like *cartola* (fried bananas with cheese), compotes, sorbets and mousses based on tropical fruits. This passion fruit mousse is reminiscent of a very popular Brazilian family dessert. Using the basic recipe, epicures can revel in mousses made with pineapple, lime, mango, tangerine, orange, guava or *azeroles*, an Amazonian fruit.

Passion fruit, called *maracudja* by Brazilians, is cultivated in the tropical northeast of Brazil. When they were first evangelizing the country, Jesuit priests employed the unusual flower of the passion fruit to explain to the Indians the symbols of the Passion of Christ.

Available in Brazil from December through February (the warmest season of the year), *maracudjas* have chestnut-grey skin and yellow-green flesh that is like a firm jelly. At the time of purchase, the skin of the *maracudja* ought to have a little give to it and be a bit wrinkled, a sign that the fruit is fully ripe. Passion fruit is rarely eaten out of hand because it is very juicy and full of seeds. In Brazil, cooks prize the juice for use in mousses, sorbets, cakes garnished with *maracudja* cream or ice cream, or they use it chilled and iced or in cocktails.

Passion fruit juice is readily available in all Brazilian food markets. If you can't find it in your local store, you can make it yourself by pressing several passion fruit, then filtering the juice. Sweeten to taste.

1. Pour the passion fruit juice into an ice cube tray. Place in the freezer and leave for at least an hour.

2. In a blender, combine the sugar, gelatin and boiling water. Blend immediately until the mixture has the consistency of syrup.

3. Add the egg whites and cream to the blender. Mix until it becomes a well-blended, homogenous white cream.

Fruit Mousse

4. Finally, with a spoon, add the cubes of frozen passion fruit juice to the blender. Blend one last time. Pour the resulting mousse into decorative individual dishes. Place them in the refrigerator for at least 2 hours or until the mousse is well jelled.

5. For the sauce, mix the second portion of passion fruit juice, sugar, cornstarch and water. Bring to the boil, stirring continuously. Remove from the heat and allow the liquid to cool.

6. Stir the passion fruit grains into the syrup. Decorate the dishes of mousse with the syrup and serve.

Ice Cream with

Preparation time: 30 minutes
Cooking time: 50 minutes
Difficulty: ☆

Serves 4

For the vanilla ice cream:
6 egg yolks
125 g/9 tbsp sugar
500 ml/2 cups milk
1 vanilla bean

For the sauce:
1 fresh pineapple
250 g/1 cup + 2 tbsp sugar
water (start with ¹/₄ cup)
50 g/generous ¹/₂ cup peppercorns,
mixed white and black
1 vanilla bean
2 cinnamon sticks
30 ml/2 tbsp coffee liqueur

When she puts her signature on dishes prepared for the patrons of her restaurant, Marie Koffi-Nketsia's goal is to promote products that originate in Africa by using them in new ways, or by creating completely new recipes. Here, she offers us her *Nana au Poivre*, or Ice Cream with Pepper-Pineapple Sauce, a delicately spiced, caramelized pineapple sauce with which she blankets rich ice cream.

European desserts are not part of the Cameroonian culinary culture. Meals are completed with a mango or a piece of pineapple, but these fruits are often eaten in celebration at harvest time as well. Beignets are another sweet that must be served straight from the oven, like this dessert.

Cameroon was the first African country to promote its very sweet and flavorful pineapples. Large pineapple plantations are found in the southwestern region called Penja. Pineapples are cultivated here so that they are available all year long. The outer skin of pineapples grown for export have a chestnut-yellow color when they are ripe.

In Cameroon, industrial cane sugar plantations are clustered around Bandjock, not far from Yaoundé, the capital city. Produced primarily for export, cane sugar is rather expensive in the local markets. It is commercially produced in the form of brown sugar or as a white powder similar to beet sugar. In this recipe, you can substitute the white sugar with brown sugar, which will enhance the flavor of the caramel.

When you prepare your dessert, you can certainly make the ice cream yourself, or purchase it from the grocery. Some guests may hesitate when they discover whole peppercorns in the sauce, so take care to remove them before the sauce is completely cooked. This way you will retain the flavor and avoid the bother of the peppercorns.

1. Prepare a custard whisk together the egg yolks and sugar, while heating the milk and vanilla seeds over medium heat just to boiling. Cool the milk slightly, then stir into the egg yolks. Cook over low heat until thick. Freeze for 24 hours. On the day of serving, cut the top and outer skin off the pineapple.

2. Cut the bottom section in thick rings. Cut out all the little black points remaining in the flesh of the pineapple. With a small cookie cutter or sharp knife, remove the heart section from the middle of each slice.

3. Cut the pineapple slices into small cubes. Set aside.

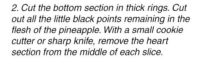

Pepper-Pineapple Sauce

4. Pour the sugar into a small skillet or heavy saucepan with a little water. Cook for 10 minutes on high heat to obtain a caramel, adding more water if necessary. When it is just done, add the pineapple cubes and coat well.

5. Add the peppercorns, cinnamon sticks and vanilla bean to the pineapple caramel. Cook for 30 minutes, then remove the peppercorns, cinnamon sticks and vanilla bean.

6. To serve the dessert, place 2 small scoops of ice cream on each dessert plate. Top with the pineapple caramel. Heat the coffee liqueur in a small saucepan and pour over each serving. Light the alcohol and serve immediately.

Preparation time:	20 minutes
Cooking time:	30 minutes
Soaking time, raisins:	10 minutes
Difficulty:	★

Serves 4

250 g/9 oz puff pastry

For the filling:
150 g/5–6 oz nuts (walnuts, hazelnuts, almonds)
50 g/¹/₄ cup raisins (golden or dark), *or* other dried fruits

100 g/generous 1 cup grated coconut
1 liter/1 quart milk
200 g/1³/₄ cups powdered sugar
150 ml/²/₃ cup whipping cream, lightly whipped

For the decoration.
2 tsp mixed nuts and raisins
boiling water
2 tsp grated coconut

The Lighthouse of Alexandria may well have disappeared in a storm, but one cannot say the same for the cuisine of Egypt. Truly inimitable, it stands out from the rest of the Orient with strength and sweetness. *Om Ali,* literally "Ali's Mother", is a brilliant reflection of Egyptian cuisine. Composed of puff pastry, nuts and dried fruits, this rich and crunchy dessert is the creative echo of a mother's love! The legend says that Ali's mother looked on her son's marriage with a jaundiced eye. Finally, the promise was warded off by the sweetness, energy and warmth of this maternal dessert.

For the pastry, there is no need for complicated ingredients. To simplify things, our chef uses ready-made puff pastry, which is rolled out quickly before being browned in the oven. This pastry has a tendency to puff up during cooking. Chef Mohamed Fawzi Kotb wisely avoids this by resting a grill on top of the pastry. The pastry cooks under the grill, without

puffing up. This way the cooked pastry can be broken into pieces without crumbling.

As for the nuts and dried fruit, five to ten minutes in boiling water softens them. Concentrated sunshine, full of natural sugar, dried fruits and nuts hold pride of place in Egyptian cuisine, as in all cuisines in the Mediterranean basin.

In preparing the *Om Ali,* your choice of dried fruits will depend upon the time of year. Whether you use a single type of fruit or nut, or a variety, they must be mixed quickly to maintain their texture, with the exception of the raisins. Whether from Smyrna, Corinth or Malaga, golden, black or brown, large or small, translucent or dried up, all raisins can be used to good effect in *Om Ali.*

The sweet white flesh of the coconut is greatly appreciated by Egyptians. Used ground or grated, it is found in numerous desserts and drinks.

1. Bake the puff pastry for 10 minutes according to package directions. Then break it with your hands into medium-sized pieces.

2. Put half the pieces of baked pastry into the baking dish that the dessert will be served in. Reserve the rest for the last stage of preparation.

3. Soak the nuts and raisins in boiling water for 10 minutes. Put the nuts in a blender or food processor and roughly chop them. Pour into a bowl and mix in the raisins and grated coconut. Tip this mixture over the broken pastry pieces and cover with the rest of the pastry.

Ali

4. Heat the milk and sugar. Pour ³/₄ of the milk over the mixture in the baking dish. Bake in the oven at 150°C/300°F for 15 minutes. Add the remainder of the milk and return to the oven for another 15 minutes.

5. Soak the raisins to be used as decoration in boiling water for 5 minutes. Drain and set aside.

6. Remove the dessert from the oven. Cover it with the cream, smoothing out the surface with a spatula. Return to hot oven for 3 minutes to lightly brown the surface. Serve the Om Ali in the baking dish, decorated with raisins and coconut.

Pistachio Opéra

Preparation time:	1 hour
Cooking time:	ca. 30 minutes
Chilling time:	10 hours
Difficulty:	★★★

Serves 4

For the cake:
5 whole eggs + 4 egg whites
100 g/generous ³/₄ cup ground almonds
100 g/scant 1 cup powdered sugar
35 g/2¹/₂ tbsp sugar
35 g/2¹/₂ tbsp butter + to grease baking sheet
65 g/7 tbsp flour

For the coffee butter cream:
1 egg
190 g/6¹/₂ tbsp sugar, divided in half

400 ml/1²/₃ cups milk
400 g/1³/₄ cups unsalted butter
4 or 5 drops very strong coffee

For the chocolate ganache:
400 ml/1²/₃ cups whipping cream
350 g/³/₄ lb dark chocolate, in small pieces
50 g/3¹/₂ tbsp butter

For the coffee syrup:
600 ml/2¹/₂ cups water
50 g/3¹/₂ tbsp sugar
3 or 4 drops coffee extract

For the icing:
300 g/11 oz dark chocolate
2 tbsp + 2 tsp peanut oil

For the decoration:
100 g/generous ³/₄ cup shelled pistachios
pistachio cream
crème anglaise (custard sauce)

The traditional *Opéra* cake was created in homage to the sumptuous Garnier opera house, built in the center of Paris in 1875. All of Paris was astonished because the opera was built adjacent to a highly unlikely neighbor, the Bastille. Here chef Michel Roth combines the concept of both buildings. He cleverly moves from the classic to the modern, carried by the harmony of creams: buttered, caffeinated, chocolate and pistachio. Each plays the diva without a false note!

As with all pastry, the ingredients must be measured precisely. Composed of flour, sugar, butter, egg yolks and almond-flavored egg whites, the pastry dough is spread in a fine mousse-like sheet on a buttered baking sheet and baked for five minutes in a hot oven. Once cooked, it can be stored for two to five days in the freezer. After the dessert rosettes are cut out, the excess dough makes a delicious little snack when warmed for a few minutes and topped with a dab of custard sauce.

For the *Opéra*, both the butter cream and custard sauce start off in the same way. But watch out! The two take different turns. Once thickened over high heat and mixed with butter, the first is removed from the heat and beaten with an electric mixer. The second is a classic crème anglaise, which must be stirred constantly as it thickens slowly over low heat.

Whether full-bodied *Robusta* coffee or *Arabica* with its sweet subtle flavor, the quantity of coffee used to flavor the cream differs according to each cook's taste. The coffee extract that is usually found in stores is highly concentrated; just a few drops suffice to flavor the cream without making it too bitter. To make the coffee syrup, bring the water and sugar to the boil. When it has reached 100°C/220°F on a candy thermometer, remove it from the heat and stir in the coffee extract.

1. Preheat the oven to 250°C/480°F. For the cake, blend the whole eggs, almond powder and powdered sugar. In another bowl, beat the egg whites and sugar until stiff. Delicately fold the whites into the first mixture to obtain a mousse-like dough.

2. Melt the butter and set aside. Add the flour carefully to the first mixture. Incorporate the melted butter little by little. Butter a cookie sheet and cover with wax or parchment paper. Spread the dough on the paper with a spatula. Bake for 5 minutes and set aside.

3. For the butter cream, beat the egg and half the sugar. Bring the milk and remaining sugar to the boil. Pour the first mixture into the second. Cook over high heat so it thickens. Remove from heat and beat for 5 minutes, then add the butter and beat at a high speed for 10 minutes. Add the coffee.

Bastille Cake

4. To make the ganache, bring cream to the boil. Pour gradually over the chocolate. Stir from the center of the bowl outward until shiny and uniform. Incorporate the butter in small pieces. Let it melt, and set aside. Prepare the coffee syrup as described in the text.

5. Peel the paper off the cake. With a bowl or other round object, cut 3 disks of equal size. Soak one in the coffee syrup. Cover another disk with butter cream, then top it with the first one. Add a layer of ganache and smooth it out. Put the third disk on top and smooth buttercream on it. Chill.

6. Melt the chocolate for the icing in a bain-marie or double boiler. Remove from heat and add the peanut oil. Warm the mixture. Place the cake on a serving plate and ice it with the chocolate. Refrigerate until just before serving. Decorate with pistachios, custard sauce and pistachio cream.

Vanilla

Preparation time: 15 minutes
Cooking time: 10 minutes
Chilling time: 8 hours
Difficulty: ★

Serves 4

For the panna cotta:
1 vanilla bean
50 g/3½ tbsp sugar
200 ml/generous ¾ cup cream
1½ sheets gelatin

For the sauce:
300 g/11 oz raspberries

For the garnish:
mint leaves

As in most southern countries, Italian gastronomy does not offer a great variety of desserts, since meals are often rounded off with fresh, ripe fruit. So it takes a special occasion for there to be a cooked dessert after a meal. It's not until deep into a celebratory evening that guests at the table turn to the pleasure of a *dolce*, or sweet treat.

However, there are a number of really tasty creations in the register of Italian desserts, including tiramisu, panettone, *crostata*, *frutta di martorana* (fruit and almond paste) and *monte blanco* (chestnut purée and cream). *Panna cotta* is one of the Italian desserts best consumed at the end of a hot day. This dessert is surprising in its simplicity and authentic taste.

Sugar and cream are heated together over a low flame, but should never boil. The vanilla bean can be replaced with a few drops of vanilla extract, but it would be a shame to forego the little specks of vanilla bean and the natural flavor that prettily mark the unmolded flan.

We suggest using thin leaves or sheets of edible unflavored gelatin. Francesca Ciardi recommends that you break them gently before adding them to the cream. That way, the gelatin can blend well with the very hot mixture. You can also let them soften in a bowl of warm water, then wring them out and add them to the crème.

Chilled in individual brioche molds, or in a single large mold, the panna cotta will have a firm consistency and a pleasing appearance. If there is any panna cotta left over, you can put it in the freezer and serve it like ice cream. Try serving both with a red berry sauce.

1. With the point of a knife, cut the vanilla bean lengthwise and split it in two. Scrape the interior to reveal the mark.

2. Pour the sugar into a saucepan and scrape the vanilla seeds into it. Add the cream.

3. Put the saucepan over low heat. Let it heat without boiling. Stir with a wire whisk. Holding the gelatin leaf above the saucepan, break it into little pieces and add to the pan. Stir gently. When the mixture is blended, remove it from the heat and allow to cool.

Panna Cotta

4. Using a small ladle, fill each mold with vanilla cream. Refrigerate immediately for 8 hours.

5. Carefully rinse and wipe dry the raspberries. Put them in a mixer and mix at low speed until liquid. Strain the resulting coulis into a small bowl. Refrigerate.

6. Bring a large pan of water to the boil. Remove the molds from the refrigerator. Dip the bottom of each in the hot water for 1 minute, then turn out onto the dessert plate. Decorate the panna cotta with the raspberry sauce and some mint leaves.

Paris-Brest

Preparation time: 40 minutes
Cooking time: 40 minutes
Chilling time: 20 minutes
Difficulty: ★★

Serves 4

For the choux pastry:
80 ml/$\frac{1}{3}$ cup milk
100 ml/7 tbsp water
100 g/7 tbsp butter
4 tsp sugar
3 g/$\frac{1}{2}$ tsp salt
110 g/$\frac{3}{4}$ cup flour
4 whole eggs
1 egg yolk
50 g/7 tbsp slivered almonds

For the hazelnut pastry cream:
250 ml/1 cup milk
60 g/4$\frac{1}{2}$ tbsp sugar, divided equally
2 egg yolks
60 g/7 tbsp flour
70 g/2$\frac{1}{2}$ oz praline paste (nuts glazed in caramel, dried, then made into a paste)
125 g/8$\frac{1}{2}$ tbsp unsalted butter

For the orange juice:
juice of 2 oranges
1 vanilla bean

For the decoration:
powdered sugar
orange zest
cinnamon

Created in 1891, this dessert owes its renown to a baker whose name is lost in the mists of history. At that time, a widely hailed bicycle race between Paris and the town of Brest created a rivalry between the two cities. Caught up in the fervor, the baker created a little round cream puff reminiscent of the wheels of a bicycle. Our chef brings them to us updated in the form of creamy bite-size morsels.

The choux pastry is not an easy one to make. It is made in a different way from other dough, and it must be prepared at the same time as the whole recipe; it cannot be made ahead of time. Before adding the eggs, chill the pastry enough that the eggs can be incorporated without being cooked in the process. You must stir them in carefully, one at a time, using a spatula or wooden spoon.

Do not open the oven door until the little tear-shaped puffs are completely expanded and nicely browned.

France would not be the country of dining pleasures that it is without its multiple creams. Pastry cream is the essence of many seductive pastry concoctions, such as eclairs, *mille-feuilles* and fruit tarts. Its success is based on one secret: "it must cook without cooking", says our chef. It is important to understand that pastry cream must never acquire color during cooking. Beat it energetically in the mixing bowl so that it thickens while being blended, without sticking to the bottom of the bowl. Then the warm cream is combined with the praline paste and butter.

Puff pastries look as if they were wearing little hats. Filled with hazelnut cream and dusted with powdered sugar, Michel Roth's little "tears" have the flavor of the Paris-Brest, but not their shape.

Epicures will happily dip the pastries into vanilla-flecked orange juice. You can also sprinkle them with cinnamon.

1. Preheat the oven to 180°C/355°F. In a saucepan, bring the milk, water, butter, sugar and salt to the boil. Add the flour, beating energetically. Over low heat, work dough with a spatula or wooden spoon until it pulls away from the sides of the pan. Chill. When cool, beat in the eggs, one at a time.

2. Butter a baking sheet and cover with parchment paper. Halfway fill a pastry bag fitted with a number 7 nozzle. Form tear-shaped pastries 3 cm/1¼ in long by 1 cm/⅓ in wide, spacing them carefully on the sheet.

3. Beat an egg yolk and spread it on the pastries with a soft pastry brush. Sprinkle with slivered almonds. Bake for 30 minutes. Let cool for 5 minutes after taking the baking sheet out of the oven.

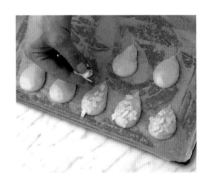

Morsels

4. Cut off the top of each pastry. Set aside. For the cream, bring the milk and 30 g/2 tbsp sugar to the boil. Separately, whisk together the egg yolks, remaining sugar and flour. Mix the milk into the yolk mixture and bring to the boil, beating with a whisk, until the cream thickens. Remove from the heat quickly.

5. Tip the pastry cream into a bowl and add the praline paste. Vigorously work in the butter to obtain a smooth, uniform cream. Refrigerate for 20 minutes. Reduce the orange juice by $3/4$ over high heat. Scrape the seeds from the vanilla bean and add. Let boil for 10 minutes. Refrigerate.

6. Fill the cream puffs with the hazelnut cream using a number 7 ridged nozzle (or another one). Cover them with their lids. Sprinkle with powdered sugar. Arrange 5 pastries on each plate and decorate with the orange-vanilla sauce, and cinnamon and orange zest, if desired.

Custard

Preparation time: 30 minutes
Cooking time: 50 minutes
Difficulty: ★★

Serves 6

300 g/11 oz puff pastry
500 ml/2 cups milk
2 tbsp cornstarch
200 g/³⁄₄ cup + 2 tbsp sugar
¹⁄₂ vanilla bean
6 egg yolks

In Portugal, pastry shops and cafés offer passers-by any number of tempting sweet delights to be savored at any time of day: at breakfast with coffee, on the way to the office, or mid-afternoon, while tranquilly seated on a terrace. But feast days and celebrations remain the preferred time for enjoying these foods. The *pasteis de nata*, a small tart filled with custard, is always on display in the windows of Lisbon's *pastelarias*, or pastry shops. Custard-based desserts are legion, as they are in Aveiro, where the tender pastries are filled and tenderly imprinted with the shape of a fish or star.

What marks Portuguese desserts specifically is the use of eggs, and especially the yolks, which are the unique ingredient in certain desserts. Cooked, or even raw, they are generally enveloped in a thick sugar syrup. Since the nuns in the convents in north and central Portugal used to use egg whites to stiffen their headpieces, they had to find a way to use the yolks: sugar and a few additional tasty ingredients, and voilà! A solution was found. So you find *"filets d'œufs"* soaked in syrup, yolks mixed with sugar and almonds and then fashioned into rolls, or stuffed between wafer-like pastry leaves, made into omelets or integrated in cakes cooked gently in a bain-marie, or broiled, fried or baked.

This list of Portuguese desserts is never-ending: rice with milk, almond paste, almond cake, squash jam, honey cake, Kings' Cake, crowns with candied fruits, Easter nests, cakes shaped like nests covered with a pastry cross, sweets sprinkled with a spicy veil of ground cinnamon, and more.

Alain Beirao points out that traditionally, pastry molds with a diameter of just 7 cm (2¾ in) are used for this dessert, making the smallest possible tarts.

1. Roll out the puff pastry. With a cup, glass, or another object with a 12 cm/5 in diameter, cut out 6 pastry disks. Fit each one into an ungreased tart mold with a diameter of 10 cm/4 in.

2. With the tines of a fork, gently poke holes in the bottom and around the sides of the pastry. Preheat the oven to 180°C/350°F.

3. Pour the milk into a saucepan. Before heating, whisk in the cornstarch and sugar. Break open the vanilla bean. Scrape the mark into the milk and toss in the bean itself. Bring the milk to the boil. Lower the heat and cook, stirring, until thick, about 20 minutes.

Tarts

4. Remove the saucepan from the heat and let the contents cool. When the milk mixture has cooled to barely warm, whisk the egg yolks into it.

5. Return to the heat and bring to a simmer. Whisk continuously until the mixture has the thick texture of a pastry cream.

6. Pour the custard into the tart molds. Take care to fill them only ¾ full as the mixture will expand while baking. Bake for 20 minutes or until golden brown.

Coconut

Preparation time: 45 minutes
Cooking time: 1 hour 10 minutes
Difficulty: ★★

Serves 4

For the dough:
200 g/1¹/₃ cups sweet rice flour (mochiko)
100 g/7 tbsp sugar
250 ml/1 cup water

For the egg filling:
150 g/²/₃ cup sugar
100 g/²/₃ cup flour
100 g/generous ³/₄ cup custard powder
100 g/generous ³/₄ cup dry milk
2 eggs
50 ml/3¹/₂ tbsp sweetened condensed milk
200 g/14 tbsp butter
60–70 ml/4–5 tbsp water

100 g/generous 1 cup grated coconut

On the fifteenth day of the New Year, temples, parks and Chinese homes are decorated with a multitude of multicolored paper lanterns. The Feast of Lanterns closes the New Year festivities, and celebrates the beginning of the agricultural year. On this occasion, families enjoy little balls of sticky short grain rice, *yuanxiao,* and boiled taro root. The "pearls" proposed by our chef, with their delicious coconut covering, have migrated beyond China's borders and are found as desserts in Chinese restaurants around the world. The rather gelatinous dough covering the "pearls" never varies. On the other hand, the filling may be based on lotus paste, peanut paste, black or white sesame paste or soybean paste. The balls are often poached in a sugar syrup.

Chinese cooks use wheat flour, soy flour and rice flour. Among the varieties of rice cultivated in China, short-grain rice, called *nuo mi,* is given pride of place. Its high starch content helps hold all the various "pearls", fillings and porridges together. Sweet rice flour, made from this sticky rice, is used to make savory steamed dumplings filled with chicken, pork or beef, or for making little sugared cakes that are fried or steamed. The Chinese also use sticky, short-grain rice to make *huan jiu* and *shaoxing jin,* two alcohols used for marinades and sauces. In fact, short-grain rice is a symbol of prosperity and of family cohesion.

As the final step, the "pearls" are rolled in coconut. Coconuts are produced in the extreme south of China, which enjoys a tropical climate, but are not widely distributed. The Chinese enjoy thin strips of coconut meat cooked and soaked in a sugar syrup as a delicacy given at New Year's. They don't hesitate to add a little coconut cream to their curried noodles.

1. To prepare the dough for the coating, mix the rice flour and sugar, then thin with water, using a wire whisk, until you have a uniform and somewhat liquid batter.

2. Put some water in the bottom of a steamer and bring to the boil. Then put the mixing bowl with the dough in the upper part of the steamer, cover, and let cook for 30 minutes. Set the dough aside.

3. For the egg filling, mix the sugar, flour, custard powder and dry milk. Stir in the eggs, sweetened condensed milk, butter and then the water.

Pearls

4. Again bring the water in the bottom of the steamer to the boil. Put the bowl with the egg filling in the upper basket. Let cook for 30 to 40 minutes, until the filling is compact.

5. Cut the dough into large pieces. Roll them in a little coconut so they won't stick to your fingers. Cut into small pieces with a plastic knife or food scraper.

6. To make the pearls, take a small piece of dough and push a little ball of filling into the center with your thumb. Close the dough over the filling and shape gently into a ball. Roll generously in coconut and serve.

Chinese

Preparation time:	30 minutes
Cooking time:	2-3 minutes per batch
Difficulty:	★

Serves 4

200 g/generous 1¹/₃ cups flour
1 egg
120 g/9 tbsp sugar
10 g/2¹/₂ tsp yeast

50 ml/3¹/₂ tbsp water
100 ml/7 tbsp peanut oil
300 g/2 cups sesame seeds
oil for frying

Little pastries with sesame seeds are New Year's delicacies in China. The Chinese New Year celebration, a four-day national holiday dedicated to rejoicing, is a major occasion for receiving friends and family. Relatives and neighbors come to share steamed dumplings, rice cakes, spring rolls, New Year cakes and sesame puffs. These round sweets symbolize the unity of the family circle. During the rest of the year, Chinese people eat sesame puffs for an afternoon snack with beet paste and jasmine tea. Sesame puffs are frequently associated with *dim sum*, dumplings served at tea houses or restaurants.

In Chinese gastronomy, frying, called *zha*, figures among the twenty-some cooking methods, each of which has a specific name. The most frequent method is sautéing (*chao*), which consists of cooking small pieces of food in a very hot wok.

Cooks also use steam (*zheng*), simmering (*men*), cooking with plain water (*zhu*), poaching in starchy water (*hui*), smoking (*xun*) and roasting (*kao*).

Chinese homemakers frequently use sesame seeds to decorate delicacies and biscuits. At the market, they can buy white, golden and black sesame seeds. The flavor is the same; the choice is made according to the desired appearance. Notice that the coating of these little Chinese delicacies varies very little: sesame seeds, grated coconut, crushed peanuts or flour mixed with ground hazelnuts.

The Chinese people have used sesame seeds in their cooking for at least 2,000 years. China and India are the two principal producers of this oily plant, a source of gastronomic delight around the world.

1. Pour the flour onto the work surface and make a well in the center. Break the egg into the well, then add the sugar and yeast. Work the water into this, a little at a time, mixing everything together with the tips of your fingers. Knead as for a pie crust.

2. Flatten the dough a bit and form a flat space in the center. Little by little, pour in the peanut oil. With a plastic scraper, knead the dough a few times, folding it into the center, until all the oil is incorporated.

3. Cut the dough into several large pieces. Roll them into several long sausages.

Sesame Puffs

4. Cut the sausages into small chunks of equal size with a plastic scraper.

5. Fill a bowl with the sesame seeds. Roll each chunk of pastry in the seeds, and roll into a ball in the palm of your hand.

6. Heat the cooking oil in a deep-fryer. When it comes to a rolling boil, plunge the sesame balls into it. Allow to cook for several minutes, or until they are golden brown. Serve warm.

Fromage Blanc

Preparation time: 1 hour 15 minutes
Cooking time: 30 minutes
Resting time: 30 minutes
Difficulty: ★★

Serves 4

For the apple pierogi pastry:
250 g/1³/₄ cups flour
2 eggs
¹/₂ tsp salt

For the filling:
350 g/³/₄ lb Golden Delicious apples
30 g/2 tbsp butter
30 g/2 tbsp brown sugar
10 g/4 tsp cinnamon

For the fromage blanc pierogi pastry:
500 g/3¹/₂ cups flour
1 egg
1 egg yolk

30 g/2 tsp butter
100 ml/7 tbsp water
¹/₂ tsp salt

For the filling:
60 g/7 tbsp raisins
water and/or vodka
50 g/6 tbsp candied orange peel
400 g/scant 1²/₃ cups fromage blanc, drained
70 g/5 tbsp sugar
2 egg yolks

2 liters/2 quarts water

For the decoration:
cinnamon

Two doughs, two stuffings, one single cooking session, ravioli-shaped and dusted with cinnamon: several good reasons for you to try your hand at Polish pastry!

The Poles probably learned the art of pastry from the Italians, and ever since then *pierogi* have been eaten salted or sugared, stuffed with delicious meat fillings or enjoyed while still warm and moist as apple turnovers.

In our chef's recipe, the apples are browned in butter until golden and covered in a caramel sauce. A thick pastry is called for to contain such ingredients. In order to keep the dough compact, the pastry is made practically without liquid, and it is worked with the fingertips to obtain lighter results. The *pierogi* will crumble in your mouth after they have been cooked. Pinching the edges of the pastry together lets you seal the edges without using egg white.

The sweet Golden Delicious apple is a marvel when it comes to browning in butter. Its tender flesh caramelizes effortlessly in the saucepan. Aim to make smaller *pierogi*: you can wrap entire quarter-apples. The chef offers you his trick: round off the outer side of the apple quarter with a knife. When you fold the pastry over it, it will fit in perfectly.

Some sweet fresh cheeses won't maintain enough of a shape to stuff a *pierogi*. If you have a choice, try to use an old-fashioned fromage blanc that comes in a wrapper. Depending on who will be eating the fruits of your labors, you can soak the raisins in a dish of vodka rather than water.

Similar to ravioli, *pierogi* are cooked in water. Here's an infallible timing trick: scoop the *pierogi* out of the water as soon as they rise to the surface. Then dust them with a cloud of cinnamon and enjoy.

1. For each pastry dough, mound the flour on a work surface. Make a well in the center. Break the eggs into it and add the salt. For the apple dough, work ingredients together with fingertips. For the cheese pierogi, mix in the water and butter and work with both hands. Chill the balls of dough 30 minutes.

2. For the apple filling, peel the apples and cut into sixths. Melt the butter in a skillet and add the brown sugar. Turn the burner to a high heat and add the apple slices. Brown for about 3 minutes, stirring to coat all sides. Dust with cinnamon, then put on a plate and set aside.

3. For the cheese filling, soak the raisins in warm water and/or vodka and set aside. Cut the orange peel into very thin slices. Pour the cheese, sugar, raisins, half the orange peel and the egg yolks into a bowl. Mix well. Chill for 30 minutes.

and Apple Pierogi

4. Remove the 2 balls of dough from the refrigerator. Roll them out to a thickness of 1 cm/⅓ in. With a cookie cutter or glass of 10 cm/4 in diameter, cut circles out of the dough. Remove the excess pastry and line up the circles for stuffing.

5. Using the dough for the apple filling, place one apple slice in the center of each circle with a fork. For the second batch, place 2 tsp of cheese mixture into the center of each pastry circle. Close each pierogi over its filling.

6. Finish by crimping the edges between thumb and forefinger. Bring a large pot of water to the boil. Drop the pierogis into the boiling water and let cook for 10 minutes. Only cook enough pierogi at a time to form one layer, to prevent sticking. Drain. Sprinkle with cinnamon and serve warm.

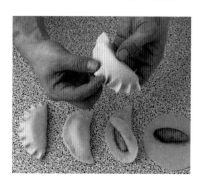

Piquenchâgne

Preparation time: 30 minutes
Cooking time: 45 minutes
Chilling time, pastry: 1 hour
Difficulty: ★★

Serves 4

For the pastry:
250 g/1³/₄ cups flour
60 g/¹/₄ cup butter
20 g/1¹/₂ tbsp sugar
10 g/4 tsp yeast
40 ml/2¹/₂ tbsp milk
1 egg
1 pinch salt

For the filling:
400 g/14 oz pears
10 g/2 tsp unsalted butter
80 g/6 tbsp sugar
1 egg yolk, beaten
80 ml/¹/₃ cup whipping cream

The fact that *piquenchâgne* means "make the pear tree" in the dialect spoken in the Allier region of France is no coincidence. Unquestionably, this Bourbonnais specialty can only be made with pears. The base is a short pastry with a high fat content. What's different is the use of yeast in the pastry. Dissolved in the milk before being mixed into the other ingredients, the yeast makes the pastry resemble brioche as it cooks.

The Montluçon pear is green and has a high sugar content. Its firm flesh makes it a perfect cooking pear. Other varieties, such as the Conference or William pear, can also be used in the *piquenchâgne*. Remember that the pear is a very delicate fruit. Choose fruit that has no blemishes, and peel it gently, with the help of a fine blade, without cutting into the flesh.

The *piquenchâgne* consists of two pastry disks and a filling made of pears. The smaller pastry disk covers the bottom of a tart tin, while the larger disk covers the fruit. It is important to plan for sufficient dough to make the two disks and the small strips which surround the decorative pear tops.

Akin to deep-dish pies and to tarts, the *piquenchâgne* is part of the rustic line of French cuisine. French provinces take delight in many varieties of tart; all of them have an important place at the table as classic entrées or desserts, depending upon whether the filling is salty or sweet.

The *piquenchâgne* includes a blend of heavy cream and pears for a perfect harmony of flavors. It can certainly be made without the cream, but it would be a shame to deprive your taste buds of such a combination. Browned and allowed to cool slightly, the *piquenchâgne* is cut open to reveal the firm cooked pears with their unique perfume.

1. Mix the ingredients for the dough, forming a ball. Let it rest for 1 hour in the refrigerator. Cut off the top of each pear 1 cm/¹/₃ in below the stem. Retain the stem and set aside for later decorative use. Peel the pear and cut into thick slices.

2. Divide the dough into two segments, one a little larger than the other. Roll them out into circles about 4 mm/¹/₆ in thick. The smaller circle should have a diameter of 16 cm/6 in, the larger 18 cm/7 in. Preheat the oven to 200°C/390°F.

3. Place the smaller pastry round in the bottom of the tart tin, then cover the dough with the pear slices. Sprinkle with pieces of butter and sugar. Brush the outer edges of the pastry with a small amount of water

with Montluçon Pears

4. Cover with the second disk of pastry, and bind them by pressing very gently on the outer edge; the water helps them stick. Arrange the pear tops on the crust. Cut strips from the extra dough. Brush one side of them with water, then use to secure the pear tops to the crust.

5. Bake 45 minutes in the preheated oven. When finished, let the piquenchâgne cool for 5 minutes. Carefully cut out and remove the top crust, leaving about 5 cm/2 in around the outer edge untouched.

6. Fill the interior generously with cream, and replace the top crust. Serve warm.

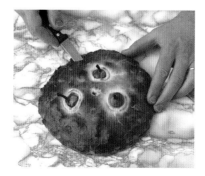

Chapala

Preparation time: 15 minutes
Cooking time: 35 minutes
Chilling time, pears: 2 hours
Difficulty: ★

Serves 6

6 William or Conference pears
1 lime
500 ml/2 cups water
500 g/2¹/₂ cups brown sugar
3 cinnamon sticks
1 clove
100 ml/7 tbsp tequila

Our chef brings you an exquisite new recipe that will delight all gourmands. The recipe can be modified according to whatever fruit is in season: pears, peaches, plums, pineapples and even mangoes lend themselves to this style. Its ease of preparation makes this use of ripe fruit an excellent alternative to making jam.

To serve this, Mexicans usually scrape ice into little dishes, then cover it with fruit that has been cooked in a sugar syrup. Numerous wandering street vendors sell a wide array of flavors of this refreshing treat, which they call *raspados*.

To prepare this recipe, you should choose large William pears, which have juicy and flavorful flesh, or Conference pears, which are long with creamy white flesh and a slightly acidic flavor. These two types hold up well during cooking.

To sweeten his dessert, our chef uses a Mexican loaf sugar because he believes its flavor is more distinctive than that of brown or muscovado sugar. The loaf sugar is a compact product of unrefined cane sugar, commercially available as a small caramel-colored pyramid. You will also get good results with brown sugar.

The flavor of spices can be heightened with the use of a vanilla bean. Our chef brings a definitively Mexican touch by adding tequila, a clear alcohol made from the extract of the bluish agave cactus.

You will know whether or not your pears are perfectly cooked by using a thin skewer. If it goes into the pear as into butter, they are done. Cooking time varies considerably according to the variety of pear and how ripe they are.

1. Carefully peel the whole pears, taking care to leave the stems in place.

2. With a small kitchen knife, slice off the bottom end of each pear so they will stand upright when served. Peel off the outer skin of the lime and place the zest in a bowl.

3. In a saucepan, mix the water, sugar, cinnamon sticks, clove and about ¹/₄ of the lime zest. Bring to the boil and cook over high heat for 5 minutes or until it has reduced to a syrup consistency.

Pears

4. Plunge the pears into the syrup. Bring the liquid back to the boil and let cook about 30 minutes. Pour the pears and syrup into a casserole, handling the pears with a large spoon or ladle, and chill in the refrigerator for about 2 hours.

5. Remove the pears from the syrup. Place on paper towels to drain.

6. Place the pears in dessert dishes. With a small ladle, coat the pears with syrup. Decorate each pear with a few strips of lime zest. Sprinkle with tequila and serve well chilled.

Prekmurska

Preparation time:	1 hour
Cooking time:	1 hour
Difficulty:	✶

Serves 8

For the poppy seed filling:
200 g/1¹/₂ cups poppy seeds
50 g/3¹/₂ tbsp sugar; 1 pinch cinnamon
100 ml/7 tbsp cream

For the cottage cheese filling:
400 g/scant 1²/₃ cups small curd cottage cheese
2 egg yolks
70 g/5 tbsp vanilla sugar
grated peel of 1 lemon peel
100 ml/7 tbsp whipping cream

For the walnut filling:
250 g/2 cups chopped walnuts
50 g/3¹/₂ tbsp sugar
70 g/5 tbsp vanilla sugar

100 ml/7 tbsp cream
¹/₂ tsp rum

For the apple filling:
500 g/generous 1 lb apples
70 g/5 tbsp sugar
1 pinch each vanilla sugar and cinnamon
80 g/10 tbsp raisins

For the pastry:
10 sheets gibanica or phyllo pastry
200 g/14 tbsp clarified butter

For the topping:
butter
cream

Prekmurska gibanica is a specialty from Prekmurje, the easternmost region of Slovenia. Literally translated, *prekmurska gibanica* means "trans-Mura moving cake". It showcases all the specialties of the region, and was originally served primarily at weddings or at the harvest festival. Today, it has become a dessert of national renown.

In Slovenia, poppy is grown on the plains near the Hungarian and Croatian borders, although to a lesser extent on the Hungarian side. In olden days, farmers collected the wild poppies that grew naturally in the midst of wheat fields. As its seeds are smaller than those of the cultivated poppy, it was necessary to collect many more flowers to make *prekmurska gibanica* than is the case today. Poppy seeds are used in many dessert fillings, as well as for sprinkling on loaves of bread before baking. As poppy seeds are not sold ground, you'll have to grind them yourself in an electric coffee grinder or with a

mortar and pestle. If not done well, it can form an oily paste that is difficult to work with.

The pastry used for authentic *gibanica*, which resembles the phyllo dough used in Greek pastries, is based on flour and water and has a very delicate texture. *Gibanica* is also used in Slovenian desserts to make apple strudels and rolled fruit cakes, or with meat and vegetable fillings.

As a base for the fillings, our chef uses cottage cheese, which has a pebbly texture rather close to that of the white Slovenian cheese called *skuta*. Strained cottage cheese will make a finer and more uniform filling than other soft white cheeses. You can thicken a filling that you find too runny by adding some fine breadcrumbs.

To make the upper pastry layer, invert the baking tin on the phyllo dough and cut around the edge of the pan. Butter this before covering it with the topping. Serve the cake warm.

1. Prepare the poppy seed filling by grinding the seeds into a very fine powder. In a mixing bowl, blend the powder with the sugar and cinnamon. Add the cream and blend well.

2. For the cottage cheese filling, pour the cottage cheese into a bowl. Add the egg yolks, vanilla sugar, lemon zest, sugar and cream. Blend well and set aside.

3. In a third bowl, stir together the walnuts and sugars. Add the cream and rum. Set aside.

Gibanica

4. Peel and slice the apples for the last filling. Toss with the sugars, cinnamon and raisins. In a tart tin or springform pan, place 2 sheets of buttered pastry, a layer of cheese filling, 2 more sheets of buttered pastry, then the apple filling, 2 more sheets of buttered pastry and finally the nut filling.

5. Press the top of the cake gently with the palms of your hands to compress it. Place the last 2 sheets of pastry on top.

6. Cover the top with butter and cream. Bake for an hour at 175°C/350°F. The top should be nicely browned.

Wine-Poached Plums with

Preparation time: 40 minutes
Cooking time, ice cream: 20 minutes
Cooking time, plums: 20 minutes
Chilling time, ice cream: overnight
Difficulty: ★★

Serves 4

For the lemon thyme ice cream:
250 ml/1 cup cream
125 ml/¹/₂ cup milk
1 bunch lemon thyme
3 eggs
60 g/4¹/₂ tbsp sugar

For the wine-poached plums:
250 ml/1 cup red wine
2 whole cloves
50 g/3¹/₂ tbsp sugar
1 cinnamon stick
20 quetsch or other plums
mint leaves
lemon thyme

A dessert of plums poached in wine and accompanied by lemon thyme ice cream is one of the specialties of the house at the *Gasthaus Rottner* near Nuremberg. The recipe was created by Irma Rottner, the mother of our chef, Stefan, who has presided over the kitchen for many years.

Irma Rottner greatly furthered the culinary reputation of the *Gasthaus Rottner*, formerly a country inn in Grossreuth near Schweinau, which has been open since 1812. This talented cook created numerous desserts and mouth-watering cakes, some of which are still on the menu, tempting a new generation of Nuremberg's food lovers.

The orchards of Franconia produce plums, apples, pears, peaches and quinces. The quetsch is part of the plum family. It is a small, juicy, violet fruit, oblong in form, with a sweet fragrance. It lends itself well to cakes, pies, marmalades and liqueurs. The quetsch becomes sweeter through cooking, un-

like some other plums, which have the tendency to become more acidic when cooked. In our recipe, spiced and sweetened red wine is heated to a high temperature until it becomes syrupy. The plums are cooked in the syrup and served at room temperature. Served here as a dessert, they also make a marvelous side dish for grilled duck breasts or venison medallions.

A unique, which is not to say eccentric, recipe, lemon thyme ice cream can be served in little cups on the side of the dessert plate, with the poached plums nestled next to it, garnished with mint leaves. You can also adjust the ice cream recipe to create a parfait, which does not require the use of an ice cream maker. To make a parfait, beat the milk with the sugar until frothy, crumble the lemon thyme into it, then whisk the mixture in a double-boiler or bain-marie until thick. Remove from the heat and continue to whisk briskly until the mixture has cooled down. Whip the cream, fold it in and freeze.

1. Mix the cream and milk in a saucepan. Immerse the sprigs of lemon thyme into the mixture and let simmer for about 10 minutes.

2. Beat the eggs in another saucepan. Add the sugar and whip until the mixture is frothy.

3. Strain the milk mixture into the eggs. Beat well to fully blend the ingredients. Cook the mixture over low heat and stir until thick. Process in an ice cream maker according to directions, and freeze overnight.

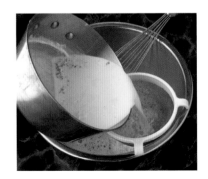

Lemon Thyme Ice Cream

4. Pour the wine into a saucepan, then add the cloves, sugar and cinnamon stick. Bring to the boil. Add the plums and bring to the boil again.

5. With a slotted spoon, remove the plums and put them in a separate bowl.

6. Reduce the poaching wine to a syrup over medium heat. Stir the plums into this syrup, then place 5 or 6 on each dessert plate. Place a generous scoop of ice cream among or near the plums and garnish with mint leaves and small sprigs of lemon thyme.

Revani

Preparation time: 30 minutes
Cooking time: 55 minutes
Difficulty: ★

Serves 10

For the syrup:
600 ml/2^1/$_2$ cups water
300 g/generous 1^1/$_3$ cups sugar
juice of 1 orange
1 cinnamon stick

For the cake:
150 g/^{2}/$_3$ cup sugar
60 g/^{1}/$_4$ cup butter, softened
and cut in small pieces
110 g/7 tbsp yogurt, drained in a strainer
lined with cheese cloth or coffee filters
3 eggs, separated
1 tsp yeast
grated zest of 1 orange
180 g/generous 1 cup fine semolina
or farina

Revani bears the sweet name of a sixteenth-century Turkish poet. This semolina-based cake with orange syrup is prepared throughout Greece. It is the specialty of Vergina, which is situated between Thessalonica and Kozani. There, it is usually eaten at tea time, in the late afternoon.

For this recipe, our chef uses yogurt that he makes himself, then drains to remove excess liquid. Genuine Greek yogurt has a thick and compact texture, and the best yogurt is made from sheep's milk. Delicious mixed with cucumbers and garlic as tzatziki sauce, yogurt is also used in cookies, and is an epicurean treat in itself simply drizzled with good honey.

Finely-ground semolina made from hard wheat is what gives this cake its unique texture. Greeks use it primarily for making desserts, including *melomacarona* cookies with honey syrup, which are served at Christmas, and *halva* with pine nuts,

almonds and cinnamon. Certain flavors are used again and again in Greek desserts: vanilla, cinnamon, honey, orange blossom water and rosewater. Our chefs have chosen cinnamon to flavor their Revani. Greek cooks frequently use geranium petals to flavor jam.

Chrysanti Stamkopoulos recommends that you pour the orange syrup over the cake while it is still hot, as it will absorb the syrup better that way. For variations, you can use lemon or blood orange juice and zest instead of orange, you can add almonds, or you can substitute farina for some of the semolina. You can also bake it in a shell of phyllo dough.

Serve this simple, delightful Revani with unsweetened whole milk yogurt, whipped cream or a scoop of vanilla ice cream. The cake can be stored for up to a week in the refrigerator and keeps very well when frozen.

1. In a large saucepan, combine the water and sugar. Add the orange juice and the cinnamon stick. Bring to the boil, reduce the heat and simmer for 13 to 15 minutes to obtain a syrup.

2. For the cake, pour the sugar into a mixing bowl and add the butter. Mix well with a stiff wire whisk.

3. Add the yogurt and egg whites. Whip briskly until the mixture is a creamy white batter.

4. Add the yeast and blend well. Stir in the orange zest, semolina and egg yolks. Mix thoroughly.

5. Pour the mixture into a buttered cake pan or straight-sided tart mold. Bake at 180°C/350°F for 40 minutes or until golden brown and a toothpick inserted in the center comes out clean.

6. Remove the cake pan from the oven and pour the orange syrup over it. Wait until the cake has absorbed the syrup. Serve when the cake has cooled.

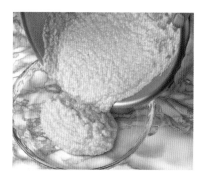

Dubrovnik

Preparation time:	20 minutes
Cooking time:	40 minutes
Resting time:	overnight
Difficulty:	★

Serves 6

500 ml/2 cups milk
200 g/³/₄ cup + 2 tbsp sugar
1 tbsp vanilla sugar
zest of 1 lemon, finely grated
4 whole eggs

2 egg yolks
40 g/2¹/₂ tbsp butter
rosewater

For the decoration:
blanched almonds
raisins
rose petals

A specialty of the city of Dubrovnik, this caramel flan called *rozata* gets its name from the rosewater that is sprinkled on it before it is enjoyed. It's a light dessert that is easily digested, and it is prepared all year long.

For centuries, Dubrovnik has been a wealthy, lively port, inhabited by clever business people who were often forced to purchase their freedom from numerous invaders. Over the years, they learned how to protect and preserve their ancient buildings and culinary customs. Like Venice, Dubrovnik was open to Eastern influences, and that's how it developed an interest in desserts made with rosewater.

This clear, delicately perfumed liquid comes from the distillation of small, highly fragrant roses. You only need to use a small drop, because its flavor can be overwhelming. If you are not accustomed to the flavor of rosewater, you might prefer to sprinkle your flan with a drop of good-quality orange blossom water, instead.

You will know that your flans are sufficiently cooked when the surface takes on a golden hue, and when the cream feels a bit firm when lightly pressed with the tip of your finger. You can also insert a very fine skewer into one of the dishes. A night in the refrigerator will complete the transformation of your dessert into perfect little caramel flans.

As well as the *rozata*, Dubrovnik offers gourmets *fritule*, fritters made with raisins and lemon zest, and *fiochi*, which are long, flat "tongues" of sugared lasagna noodles rolled up like a rose and fried. At Christmas, *pinca* are served, little cakes of raised dough made with raisins blessed at midnight mass.

1. Bring the milk to the boil in a saucepan. When it is hot, add 150 g/²/₃ cup of the sugar, the vanilla sugar and lemon zest. Whisk briskly. Turn off the heat.

2. Break the eggs into a mixing bowl. Add the yolks. Beat until frothy. Pour into the milk slowly, stirring continuously. Continue to whisk for a few moments over low heat.

3. In a small saucepan, cook the remaining sugar with a little water for 10 minutes over high heat to form a caramel. Remove from heat. Butter the ramekins and coat the bottom of each with the caramel.

Rozata

4. Pour the creamy mixture into the ramekins.

5. Set the ramekins in a deep baking pan. Pour enough warm water in the pan to cover the bottom and the sides of the ramekins. Bake for 30 minutes at 220°C/425°F. Let the desserts cool, and refrigerate until the next day.

6. Unmold the caramel flans onto dessert plates. Just before serving, sprinkle them with just a drop of rosewater. Decorate the rozata with raisins, almonds and rose petals.

Sabayon with

Preparation time: 20 minutes
Cooking time: 15 minutes
Difficulty: ★★

Serves 4

For the filling:
750 g/1³/₄ lb pitted cherries in syrup
2 tsp cornstarch
¹/₂ glass cold water (ca. 80 ml/¹/₃ cup)
2 tsp clover honey
200 g/7 oz gingerbread, cut in small cubes

For the sabayon:
8 egg yolks
300 g/generous 1¹/₃ cups sugar
500 ml/2 cups dark Belgian beer
mint leaves

Pierre Fonteyn brings us a creative and colorful dessert that blends Italian art and Flemish culture.

Sabayon is one of the most delicious culinary creations of the Italians, who call it zabaglione. This light, airy custard is made with wine (often Marsala), sugar and egg yolks, and it has become a much-appreciated dish. It is a marvelous accompaniment to all sorts of desserts, poached fruits, pastries or ice creams.

The egg yolks and sugar must be cooked very gently in the alcohol so that they don't end up as a crumb-like curd. That is why we recommend cooking the sabayon in a bain-marie or double boiler, over low heat, stirring constantly until the thickened mixture forms a "ribbon" when a spoonful is raised from the pan. As soon as it is ready, pour the sabayon into dessert dishes, on top of the cherries.

But beware! Not one drop of Marsala should touch this Belgian-accented dessert. Our chef has prepared his sabayon with the local cherry-flavored Kriek beer, instead. Two Belgian breweries currently market this beer, which owes its name to the city of Kriek, known for its delicious little cherries. Kriek beer is only made in the Senne Valley, near Brussels, and it is brewed by "spontaneous fermentation" (no yeast is added). Cherry juice is added to it later in the process for a unique fruity flavor. In the past, brewers let Griotte cherries steep with the beer in the kegs for six months.

In case you cannot find Kriek, Pierre Fonteyne offers you this little magic trick: take half the juice from a jar of cherries, and pour it into a Gueuze, another beer. The effect is astonishing!

Honey and gingerbread meet and combine flavors in the sweetness of this dessert. Creamy white clover honey is available all summer in Belgium, but as it has no particular flavor, it can be replaced with pine honey, which is darker. However, beware of using a highly flavored honey, since it could have an unwanted effect on the subtleties of the sabayon.

1. Strain the cherries. Set the cherries aside and bring the cherry juice to the boil over high heat.

2. Dilute the cornstarch in the water, then add to the cherry juice and stir. Let thicken for 2 minutes over low heat.

3. Add the honey and gingerbread, mixing with a wooden spoon. Remove from the heat and let cool.

Belgian Beer and Cherries

4. Cover the bottom of the dessert dishes with the cherries, reserving a few. Place the gingerbread cubes on top, and spoon the juice over the gingerbread.

5. Put the reserved cherries on top of the gingerbread.

6. In the top of a double boiler, beat the egg yolks and sugar together, then add the beer. Cook until thick, whisking constantly. Pour over the cherries and gingerbread and garnish with mint leaves.

Zabaglione Ice Cream

Preparation time: 15 minutes
Cooking time: 20 minutes
Chilling time: 10 hours
Difficulty: ★★

Serves 4

For the zabaglione:
10 egg yolks
150 g/²/₃ cup sugar
200 ml/generous ³/₄ cup Marsala
150 ml/²/₃ cup whipping cream, very cold

For the chocolate sauce:
200 g/7 oz dark chocolate
100 ml/7 tbsp milk
small strawberries
4 sprigs fresh mint

Zabaglione with Marsala originated in the Piedmont region, where it once pleased the palates of the princes of Savoy. Our chef has transformed this classic recipe into a divine ice cream, swimming in a rich chocolate sauce. Italians are literally "crazy" about ice cream. The smallest merchant offers 30 to 40 fresh, appetizing varieties of rather soft ice cream, which is whipped with a spatula before being served. You can also treat yourself to enormous portions of fruit-flavored ice, simple ice cream, tiramisu, zabaglione or panna cotta.

Marsala wine lends this zabaglione its amazing, subtle flavor of alcohol. Marsala is the best-known wine in Sicily, produced in the Trapani region. There are several classes of Marsala, according to the percentage of alcohol, how long it has been aged and how much sugar it contains. It may be made from white grapes or red (*oro* and *rubino*, respectively) and labeled *fino* (aged 1 year), *superiore* (2 years), *vergine* (5 years) or *vergine stravecchio* (aged at least 10 years). Marsala is used in

Italian desserts and also in sauces for meat. Around 1800, the Woodhouse brothers imported Marsala to Great Britain to supply Admiral Nelson's troops, and they popularized this beverage there.

This recipe demands your full attention, especially if you have never made zabaglione before. You must heat the cream very gently in a double boiler or bain-marie, stirring constantly so that the egg yolks don't cook to the point of separation from the cream, which would form curds. Once the zabaglione is rather thick, you should pour it into a lasagna pan or similar dish to give it greater exposure to the air for quicker cooling. When the zabaglione has completely cooled, fold in the whipped cream. If you fold it in too soon, the cream will rise to the surface rather than blending in fully.

You can substitute Asti Spumante or Moscato d'Asti for the Marsala, if you wish.

1. Beat the egg yolks in a large mixing bowl or saucepan with a whisk. Mix in the sugar and Marsala.

2. Put the mixing bowl or saucepan over simmering water in a bain-marie or double boiler. Lower the heat. Beat the cream briskly for about 15 minutes, or until the zabaglione is pale yellow and frothy. Draw the whisk through it; it should leave a path.

3. Pour the zabaglione into a large bowl and let it cool. Whip the cream and fold it gently into the zabaglione.

with Chocolate Sauce

4. Put individual molds on a baking sheet and fill them with zabaglione. Freeze for at least 10 hours.

5. Before serving, break up the chocolate and put it in a saucepan with the milk. Using a bain-marie or double boiler, stir the sauce with a spoon for 5 minutes until it is smooth and uniform.

6. Spoon chocolate sauce over each dessert plate. Unmold a zabaglione onto each plate by applying a cloth moistened with hot water to the bottom of the mold. Garnish each serving with a strawberry and a sprig of mint.

The Old Man from

Preparation time: 30 minutes
Cooking time: 5 minutes
Steeping time: 3 days or more
Difficulty: ★

Serves 4

For the syrup:
500 g/2¼ cups sugar
1 liter/1 quart water
150 ml/⅔ cup brandy

For the fruit salad:
2 apricots
2 peaches
2 nectarines
2 plums
100 g/3–4 oz red currants
100 g/3–4 oz mulberries
100 g/3–4 oz blueberries

These two were made to go together: she, rich in vitamins, painted with the color of summer fruits and flavored with brandy; and he, a country boy, bringing with him a taste for the land where he was born.

Michel Haquin has married the two in a perfect balance of color and sweetness. For lively color, you can choose all sorts of berries: red currants, mulberries, blueberries, black currants or raspberries. Profit from the late summer harvest by stocking up on them! Remember that damson and mirabelle plums also offer a lot of color.

For sweetness, there is also a wide choice of fruits. There is no end to the varieties of apricots. Tender, high in sugar, sweetly scented and not especially juicy, the apricot is a delicate fruit. Choose them at their peak. You must wash and wipe them dry immediately as their velvety skin doesn't like water. As for peaches, they have always been enjoyed as a table fruit, or in delicate desserts. Fragile but flavorful white peaches or hardy, less juicy yellow ones: the two varieties take equally to brandy. Whether distilled commercially or at home the old-fashioned way, brandy retains its distinctive flavor. Which brandy to use depends upon your taste, but plum brandy is a perfect match for summer fruit. The quantity of sugar syrup may surprise you, but it is necessary in order to prevent the fruit from fermenting. Sealed, steeped from the end of summer to the beginning of winter, this fruit salad holds all the flavor of the Ardennes earth. Deep in his Ardennes village, the old man pours the brandy and sugar syrup over the fruit with abandon, perhaps recalling his old conquests...

1. In a saucepan, mix together the sugar and water. Boil for 5 minutes over high heat. Remove from the heat, pour into a mixing bowl and chill.

2. Wash the fruit and berries, wiping them dry carefully. Quarter the fruit and discard the pits. Pick over the berries, discarding any that are not perfect.

3. When the syrup is chilled, stir in the brandy.

Ardennes' Fruit Salad

4. Gently pour all the fruit into the syrup.

5. Mix the fruit and berries in the syrup without crushing them. The syrup must fully cover the fruits. Let steep for a minimum of 72 hours.

6. Serve the fruit salad in individual cups with a generous portion of syrup.

Nut

Preparation time: 30 minutes
Cooking time: 10 minutes
Difficulty: ★★

Serves 4

300 g/2 cups whole almonds
100 g/generous ¾ cup pistachios, shelled
100 g/⅔ cup whole hazelnuts
50 g/scant ½ cup walnut halves

100 g/scant 1 cup powdered sugar
2 tsp orange blossom water
4 sheets phyllo dough
or spring roll wrappers
1 egg white, beaten
butter

The fried pastry pakets known as *brik* arrived in the Mahgreb a long time ago, coming from the countries of the Levant. But it took all the know-how of the Tunisians to make it one of the most appreciated foods in the country. Nut Samsas are just one of many delights served on copper platters at tea-time, bringing families and friends together: others include *makroud* date cakes, filled "cigars" and beignets.

Whether crescents, triangles or cigars, the shape and name of these little pastry cakes varies according to the baker's imagination, and the sweet or savory mixture with which they are filled. Making the dough actually used in Tunisia, though it consists of the simple ingredients of flour, salt, oil and water, is a complex enterprise. It is kneaded thoroughly, then stretched thin and heated on a specially designed pan to transform the dough into incredibly fine sheets called *warka* or *malsouka*.

Energy-giving nuts make up the filling in this recipe. Roasted whole and finely ground, or bought ground for quicker preparation, the nuts make a subtly flavored stuffing when blended with orange blossom water. A product of the bitter orange, a fresh supply of orange blossom water is distilled each spring in most Tunisian homes. Used primarily for mouth-watering cakes, this flower essence also perfumes the neck and hands of engaged women, or calms the force of boiling hot coffee.

Today, orange blossom water, protected by its traditional blue bottle, is still known for its soothing properties. Its bitter orange scent and flavor have an amazing effect: in the samsa stuffing, a single drop is sufficient to flavor the whole cake.

These samsa are coated in butter and baked in the oven, which browns the little triangles without making them excessively oily. Serve your samsa warm with very sweet mint tea in little gilded glasses, or with a very hot Arabic coffee.

1. Toast the nuts, then chop them finely in a blender or food processor. Pour them in a mixing bowl and add the powdered sugar, then the orange blossom water. Mix well to form a dense paste. Set aside.

2. Cut the rounded edges off the pastry sheets, about 1 cm/⅓ in. Cut the remaining large square into long strips that are 7 cm/2¾ in wide.

3. Place the strips of pastry in front of you. Put a spoonful of the nut paste at one end of the pastry strip, with enough pastry at that end to cover the paste.

Samsas

4. Fold the end of the pastry over the filling, turning it so it forms a triangle at that end. Fold the triangle over several times, maintaining the triangular shape. Leave the last 2 cm/³/₄ in of the pastry extended.

5. With a pastry brush, paint egg white on the pastry end. Fold it over, "gluing" it to the filled triangle. Repeat steps 3 through 5 until you have used all the pastry.

6. Butter aluminum foil and cover a baking tray with it. Then put the samsas on top, taking care that they don't touch each other. Top each with a small knob of butter. Bake at 180°C/350°F for 10 minutes or until golden. Serve when cooled.

Sévriolaine

Preparation time: 20 minutes
Cooking time: 2 minutes
Jelling time: 4 to 8 hours
Difficulty: ★★★

Serves 4

For the pastry cream:
2 egg yolks
50 g/3¹/₂ tbsp sugar
30 g/3 tbsp flour
250 ml/1 cup milk

¹/₂ vanilla bean
200 ml/generous ³/₄ cup whipping cream
25 g/2 tbsp sugar
100 g/scant 1 cup chopped walnuts
2 egg whites
parchment paper

In creating the Sévriolaine Custard, Bernard Collon wanted to pay homage to his home village, Sévrier, a little town in Savoie, south of Annecy. The end result is a worthy tribute. His dessert was quite a success when presented in Japan, and the flavor of sake mixed with that of the Sévriolaine was quite unexpected!

Nuts harvested in the Dauphiné region give this dessert its unique texture. It is important not to chop the nuts overly finely, because they are what gives the Sévriolaine its surprising crunch.

The whipped cream requires high-quality whole cream, and it must be very cold. You should also place the mixing bowl in the freezer well before use. This way you will be able to whip the cream very quickly before folding it in with the pastry cream. If you don't have pastry circles, pour the Sévriolaine

into custard cups. Don't forget to butter the bottoms and sides of the cups and then to line them with parchment paper to facilitate unmolding. A springform pan is also very useful for this dessert.

Place the Sévriolaine Custard in the freezer for a minimum of 4 hours and no more than 8, and serve it straight from the freezer. If you decide to serve it at the end of a meal that requires a lot of time and energy to prepare, it would be wise to make the dessert a day ahead of time.

For the ultimate in refinement, a light caramel made with demerara sugar or some chocolate shavings will highlight your efforts. The chef also suggests a coulis of fresh strawberries or a chocolate sauce to make the dessert a bit more sophisticated. A scoop of vanilla ice cream on the side will bring out the vanilla in this dessert.

1. Beat the egg yolks and sugar well with a whisk. Add the flour and mix well.

2. Boil the milk with the vanilla bean. Remove from the heat and let steep. When cooled, mix the vanilla milk into the egg and sugar mixture, stirring energetically. Cook for 2 minutes over high heat, stirring vigorously while the mixture thickens. Remove from the heat and let cool.

3. In a mixing bowl, beat the cream vigorously with a large whisk. Still beating, add the sugar. When the whipped cream is thick, smooth and somewhat stiff, it is ready.

Custard

4. Chop the walnuts coarsely. Carefully add them to the pastry cream, then fold in the whipped cream.

5. Gently stir the ingredients to blend without breaking down the air in the whipped cream. Beat the egg whites until firm and fold into the pastry cream mixture.

6. Cover a baking sheet with parchment paper. Set 6 cm/2¹/₂ in pastry circles on the paper and pour some cream into each one. Smooth out with a spatula. Place the tray in the freezer for 4 to 8 hours. Just before serving, caramelize the tops with a crème brulée iron, or under a broiler.

Sfogliatelle with

Preparation time: 40 minutes
Cooking time: 20 minutes
Resting time, pastry: 30 minutes
Difficulty: ★★

Serves 4

For the pastry:
200 g/generous 1¹/₃ cups flour
80 g/6 tbsp sugar
100 g/7 tbsp butter, softened, in pieces
2 egg yolks
50 ml/3¹/₂ tbsp milk

For the filling:
500 ml/2 cups water
1 pinch salt
150 g/1 cup + 2 tbsp fine semolina
150 g/10 tbsp ricotta
1 egg
150 g/1¹/₃ cups powdered sugar
1 tbsp vanilla sugar
80 g/10 tbsp candied fruits, diced

For the decoration:
1 egg yolk, beaten
powdered sugar

Three things bind Neapolitans to their home town: the sea, Vesuvius and *sfogliatelle*. While the Tyrrhenian Sea and Mount Vesuvius are attached eternally to the Neapolitans' visual memory, sfogliatelle leave an indelible imprint on their taste buds. Despite this, a majority of Italians, known for their love of fine cooking, are little given to the pleasures of good pastries. Copious and ever generous, Italian meals often end with fresh fruit, kissed by the sun and full of vitamins.

Sfogliatelle are usually prepared as rolled pastry, stuffed with small pieces of candied fruit that contrast with the smooth sweetness of the ricotta cheese. Ricotta, made from sheep's, cow's or goat's milk, insinuates itself into all aspects of Italian gastronomy, whether sweet or savory. Nothing is richer than a lemony ricotta filling with candied fruits.

Massimo Palermo's round *sfogliatelle* cakes have been made with shortbread pastry, which is known locally as *pasta frolla*. However, there is no reason why you couldn't use phyllo dough or pie dough. All of these sit side-by-side on supermarket shelves, ready to be unrolled to receive a delicious little Neapolitan stuffing.

Well-browned and still warm from the oven, mouth-wateringly delicious *sfogliatelle* will disappear in two bites. You can serve them with a cup of the dark Corsican coffee to which Italians are passionately devoted.

1. Mound the flour and make a well in it. Pour in the sugar, blend with your fingers. Make another well and add the butter. Again mix with your fingers. Mix the egg yolks and milk, then work that liquid into the pastry, blending without overworking the pastry. Cover and refrigerate 30 minutes.

2. Bring the water and salt to the boil. Pour the semolina like rain into the boiling water, stirring constantly. Cook for 5 minutes over high heat. Remove from the heat, turn into a mixing bowl and refrigerate to chill.

3. Press the ricotta through a sieve. Take out the mixing bowl with the chilled semolina, then add the ricotta, egg and sugars. Sprinkle with the candied fruit. Mix well with a wooden spoon or spatula. Set aside.

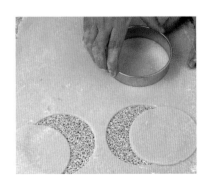

Ricotta Filling

4. Dust your work surface with flour. Roll out the dough to a thickness of 3 mm/¹⁄₈ in. With an 8 cm/3 in round cookie cutter or glass, cut 20 circles from the pastry.

5. Put a tablespoon of ricotta filling in the center of 10 circles. Cover each one with another circle. Press the edges with your thumbs to close the sfogliatelle or brush the outer edge of each bottom piece with beaten egg white as a glue.

6. Using a slightly smaller cookie cutter or glass, trim any uneven excess pastry from each cake. Glaze with egg yolk. Place the sfogliatelle on a baking sheet and bake for 15 minutes at 160°C/325°F.

Sherry

Preparation time: 45 minutes
Cooking time: 35 minutes
Difficulty: ★

Serves 4

For the sponge cake:
4 eggs
125 g/9 tbsp sugar
125 g/³/₄ cup + 2 tbsp flour, sifted
butter and flour for the baking pan
350 g/generous 1 cup English cherry jam

For the pastry cream:
500 ml/2 cups milk
3 eggs plus 1 yolk

60 g/4¹/₂ tbsp sugar
12 g/1¹/₂ tbsp custard powder
or dry whole milk

For the syrup:
75 g/¹/₃ cup sugar
75 ml/¹/₃ cup sherry
30 ml/2 tbsp dark rum

For the whipped cream:
400 ml/1²/₃ cups whipping cream
40 g/6 tbsp powdered sugar
¹/₃ tsp vanilla extract

For the decoration:
slivered almonds
pistachios
red berries, such as cherries or currants
mint leaves
apricot jam

In traditional English gastronomy, the trifle is a rich and delectable dessert created in stages. Wally Ladd, who was head pastry chef at the *Connaught Hotel* for 43 years, invented the sherry trifle around 1913. This dessert is as constant on the Connaught's menu as rice pudding, crumbles, and bread and butter pudding.

The sponge cake in this recipe is frequently used for making jelly rolls, a dessert made of cake slathered with jelly or jam and then rolled into a log shape. It is a very simple sponge cake that does not have to be whisked above a double boiler, as some more elaborate sponges must.

The United Kingdom, and particularly Scotland and the county of Kent, has an outstanding reputation for the making of jams. English jams such as raspberry, red currant or cranberry and marmalades are served on little cakes called scones, or between layers of soft sponge cake.

A clever merchant in the eighteenth century introduced Spanish Jeres wine to Admiral Nelson's troops; the English then developed a passion for this subtle alcohol and introduced it to the rest of the world. They rebaptized it "sherry" and appreciate it particularly as a flavoring for cakes. In other English desserts, favored alcohols are white or dark rum, juniper liqueur (Pimms), brandy, Cognac, port, Irish whiskey or Scotch.

Oliver Tucki suggests that you carefully butter and flour the baking pan for the sponge cake; this not only helps the cake to rise, but also prevents the cake from breaking when it is turned out of the pan.

If you don't have time to prepare the sponge cake yourself, you may be able to find it ready-made at a bakery or in the supermarket. You can even make this dessert with a simple yogurt cake.

1. For the sponge cake, beat the eggs and sugar in an electric mixer until frothy. Gently blend in the flour. Butter and flour the cake pan, pour in the batter and bake for 20 to 25 minutes at 180°C/350°F. Let cool for 5 minutes in the pan, then turn out onto a wire rack and let cool completely.

2. For the pastry cream, boil the milk and then set the pan on low heat. Beat the eggs and yolk with the sugar. Add the custard powder. Mix, adding in the hot milk. Whisk briskly, and cook for 10 minutes until the cream is thick. Cover and put in the refrigerator to chill.

3. Cut the cooled sponge cake in half horizontally. Spread the cherry jam on the bottom layer. Replace the top layer, then set aside. Prepare the syrup by boiling the sugar, sherry and rum together. Cook until somewhat reduced in volume.

Trifle

4. Cut the layered sponge "sandwich" into cubes of about 4 cm/1¹/₂ in on each side. Place them in a large serving bowl with high sides, pressing down gently but firmly. Pour the syrup over the cake and let stand while the syrup is absorbed.

5. With a spatula, spread the pastry cream evenly over the cake. Whip the cream with the powdered sugar and vanilla extract.

6. With a pastry bag, make a woven pattern of whipped cream on top of the pastry cream, or simply spoon it on and smooth with a spatula. Decorate with almonds, pistachios, berries and fresh mint leaves.

Sod

Preparation time: 30 minutes
Cooking time: 10 minutes
Difficulty: ★★

Serves 4

For the filling:
1 fresh coconut
500 g/2¼ cups sugar
water

For the wrapper:
250 g/1⅔ cups sweet rice flour (mochiko)
200 ml/generous ¾ cup water

For the coconut cream:
560 ml/2¼ cups coconut milk
50 g/⅓ cup sweet rice flour (mochiko)
12 g/2 tsp salt

500 g/generous 1 lb banana leaves

Here is a warm dessert, greatly appreciated on royal tables, that blends all of Thailand's sweetest flavors.

Coconuts are useful in several ways. Covered with a shell that changes from green to brown as it ages, the interior white nutmeat's freshness is completely protected. The shell protects the pulp and juice, which differ from one another in flavor as well as in appearance. The thick and somewhat creamy "milk", extracted from the pulp, is used in sauces and desserts. The colorless and thirst-quenching juice contains little sugar and is used like other fresh fruit juices. Everyone has their preferred method of opening a coconut; some people buy their coconuts already opened. If the juice has been drained off, do not buy the coconut if the white pulp has dried out.

As soon as you have poured the caramel on the grated coconut, refrigerate the mixture; the "meat" absorbs the caramel as it becomes cold. As sweet rice flour thickens rapidly, pour the

water into it in very small quantities. The mixture is ready when it has a thick, gluey consistency, but is still fluid.

Make the dumpling wrappers larger than the caramel-coconut balls, as the balls must be completely wrapped. Gently roll each wrapped dumpling in the palms of your hands to assure complete coverage and a seamless whole. The wrapped *Sod Sai* parcels need to steam for 5 to 10 minutes depending on the kind of container used: a *couscousier*, an Asian bamboo steam basket or aluminum vegetable cooker. When the banana leaf has turned yellow, the *Sod Sai* are cooked.

If you are leery of steaming with banana leaves, know that this dessert can easily be made in whatever kind of mold you have on hand. The presentation will be different: place three balls of caramel-coconut in a mold and blanket with coconut cream. Cover the mold with plastic wrap and steam the whole thing in a vegetable steamer.

1. Break the coconut open. Use a small-bladed grater to scrape out all the coconut meat, down to the hard shell. Set the grated coconut in a saucepan. In a heavy sauce-pan or skillet, melt the sugar slowly. When it becomes reddish, add a little water slowly, and boil for a few minutes.

2. While the caramel is being made, place the saucepan containing the coconut over high heat and stir for 3 minutes. As soon as the caramel is ready, pour it over the warm coconut. Stir, remove from the heat and let cool for 5 minutes.

3. For the wrappers, pour the rice flour into a mixing bowl. Add the water a little at a time, stirring. Mix until you have a thick and sticky dough. Flatten it, separate into pieces and set aside.

Sai

4. With the tips of your fingers, take small quantities of the caramel-coconut and form balls the size of a walnut. Set on a plate.

5. For the cream, warm the coconut milk in a saucepan over low heat, then add the rice flour and salt all at once, whisking briskly. Bring to the boil. Remove from the heat and set aside.

6. Cover each coconut ball with one of the wrappers. Place the dumplings on pieces of banana leaf. Cover each with a spoonful of coconut cream. Fold the banana leaf over the dumplings and close with a toothpick. Steam for 10 minutes and serve warm.

Elderberry Blossom

Preparation time:	*35 minutes*
Cooking time:	*20 minutes*
Resting time, pastry:	*30 minutes*
Chilling time, sorbet:	*overnight*
Difficulty:	★★

Serves 4

For the elderberry blossom sorbet:
2 lemons
300 ml/1¼ cups water
240 g/1 cup + 2 tbsp sugar
1 large bunch elderberry blossoms

For the shortcrust pastry:
500 g/3½ cups flour
5 egg yolks plus 1 whole egg
135 g/9 tbsp butter
135 g/1¼ cups powdered sugar

For the chocolate ganache:
450 g/1 lb dark chocolate
500 ml/2 cups cream
50 g/2½ tbsp honey
175 g/¾ cup butter, cubed
a few elderberry leaves or blossoms

Some Swedes really enjoy sorbets, while others remain faithful to the more classic cream-based ice creams. Today you can find sorbets and ice creams flavored with a variety of fruits, berries and herbs, including cloudberries, blueberries, raspberries, sea buckthorn or elderberry blossoms.

The white elderberry tree belongs to the honeysuckle family (*Caprifoliaciae*). It is found growing wild in all the uncultivated corners of Sweden. The elder is a majestic tree that blossoms in large clusters of tiny white flowers in June. The flowers have a very strong, fresh scent. In autumn, the tree bears little violet-brown berries.

Swedish cooks use the elder flower, called *fläderblom,* to make sorbets and syrups that are mixed with water to make cold, refreshing summer drinks. Our chef likes to flavor his crème brulée with this wonderful syrup.

Elderberries make excellent jam, especially when mixed with blackberries. Swedes also use the berries in schnapps.

Swedes have such a penchant for sweets that they seldom miss an opportunity to partake of cream pastries, cheese cakes or desserts made with red berries or apples. In the chocolate line, brownies are very popular both at home and in restaurants. In this recipe, the refreshing flavor of elderberry blossom sorbet is a perfect counterbalance to the strong flavor and heavy texture of a dark chocolate ganache.

In addition to this excellent elder-chocolate combination, we have a few variations to suggest: you can make a double Bavarian cream in which one part of the cream is flavored with elderberry flowers and the other with chocolate. Or, more simply, serve a brownie on a bed of custard sauce that has been flavored with elder blossoms.

1. To make the sorbet, grate the rind of 1 lemon and squeeze the juice of both into a saucepan. Stir in the water and sugar, then add the elderberry blossoms.

2. Bring the mixture to the boil. Let steep for 5 minutes over low heat. Strain the liquid into a mixing bowl, then pour into an ice tray and freeze overnight.

3. To make the pastry, combine the flour, eggs, butter and sugar. Beat with a whisk to form a homogeneous pastry. Knead briefly, then cover and let rest for half an hour.

Sorbet with Chocolate Tart

4. Butter the tart mold(s). Roll out the pastry with a rolling pin. Line the mold(s) with the pastry and then line the interior with aluminum foil and fill with dried beans or ceramic baking beads and bake for 15 minutes at 180°C/350°F.

5. Make the ganache: chop the chocolate. Mix the cream and honey in a heavy saucepan and cook over medium heat until quite warm. Add the chocolate bits and butter. Whisk or stir briskly until you have a smooth, well-blended ganache.

6. Ladle the ganache into the tart shell(s). Cool slightly. Serve the individual tartlets or slices with a scoop of sorbet. Decorate with a few leaves from the elderberry tree.

Mango Sorbet with

Preparation time: 20 minutes
Cooking time: 10 minutes
Chilling sorbet: overnight
Difficulty: ★

Serves 4

For the sorbet:
50 g/3¹/₂ tbsp sugar
250 ml/1 cup water
2 mangoes
2 Key limes
10 ml/2 tsp coconut liqueur

Fruit:
oranges
bananas
kiwis
strawberries
star fruit
passion fruit

The inhabitants of Mauritius and the tourists who come to relax on its beautiful beaches enjoy a wide variety of sorbets. Numerous local fruits offer a range of flavors: mango, coconut, tamarind, pineapple, guava, melon, papaya and passion fruit are just some of them.

In Mauritius, mangoes are picked from October to April, during the summer. They are so abundant that cooks find many uses for them: sorbets, jams, custard creams and purées. At the end of the summer, the last ripe mangoes lie uncollected at the foot of the mango trees. The island exports whole mangoes, mango juice and mango jam.

There are many varieties of mango and their names are evocative: the Dauphiné is yellow-green in color; the Maison-Rouge (Red House) is vermilion; the Baissac is almost violet;

the long saber mango, now quite rare, boasts a magnificent mixture of oranges, yellows and greens; and there are further varieties called Adèle, Lacorde, Aristide and José.

Oranges, limes and Key limes are also cultivated on Mauritius. The Key lime is a very small lime with a particularly refined flavor. Its delicious juice enhances ices, punch and fish marinades. Key limes can be preserved in pickles or used in *achards* (Indian seasonings, similar to chutneys). This last goes particularly well with grilled fish. You can substitute regular limes for the Key limes.

Coconut liqueur is made from coconut and rum. It is the basis of numerous cocktails like pineapple and orange punches, and of course, piña colada. Mauritians also add it to fruit sauces, and use it to make desserts *flambé*.

1. Put the sugar and water in a saucepan and boil for 10 minutes over high heat to make a syrup.

2. Cut the mangoes in half lengthwise. With a sharp knife, cut out the seed and remove the peel. Cut the flesh in cubes.

3. Mix the cubed mango in the blender until the fruit is puréed. Squeeze the juice from the limes and add to the purée.

Coconut Liqueur

4. Add the coconut liqueur to the purée and blend again.

5. Finally, add the syrup to the purée. Mix it in thoroughly.

6. Pour the mango purée into a sorbet maker and freeze according to the manufacturer's directions. Trim and cut the fruit. Serve scoops of mango sorbet with pieces of fresh fruit.

Almond Soufflé

Preparation time: 30 minutes
Cooking time: 20 minutes
Chilling time: 3 hours
Marinating time: 2 hours
Difficulty: ★★

Serves 4

For the soufflé:
50 g/3¹/₂ tbsp butter
50 g/¹/₃ cup flour
250 ml/1 cup milk
juice from 1 lemon
10 ml/2 tsp amaretto

50 g/1³/₄ oz almond paste
4 egg yolks
5 egg whites
a pinch salt
butter and sugar for the mold

For the cloudberry sauce:
400 g/14 oz cloudberries
60 g/4¹/₂ tbsp sugar

For the rosemary garnish:
4 sprigs rosemary
50 ml/3¹/₂ tbsp oil
sugar

For Swedish diners, a soufflé made with almond paste, caramel or vanilla is a rather unusual, but very welcome treat. Almond paste, called *mandelmassa*, is used frequently in Swedish desserts, as are distinctive spices such as cinnamon, cardamom, star anise and cloves. Almond paste or marzipan are mixed into cake dough, ice creams and ices. Our chef particularly recommends almond ice cream served with plums and port, as well as a Swedish specialty called *choklad biskvi*, a small round of baked almond paste topped with chocolate cream and served in a chocolate shell. These are served with coffee.

The Swedish climate doesn't lend itself to cultivating a wide range of fruits, but there are apples, pears, currants, blackcurrants and cherries in the southernmost parts of the country. On weekends, many Swedes take great pleasure in wandering through woods and fields gathering blueberries, wild cranberries, wild plums, wild strawberries and cloudberries, which embellish their desserts.

Cloudberries, also called "Lapp berries", grow in the northern reaches of Sweden. They are collected from the end of August through the beginning of October. Their acidic taste is rather different from that of the common raspberry, to which it is related. Swedes often eat these berries in the simplest possible way, just sprinkled with a bit of sugar. Cloudberries are also used in desserts, sauces and jams, and cloudberry jam with vanilla ice cream is a special favorite.

The principle problem associated with soufflés is whether they will puff up. Soufflés succeed best when baked in small dishes, because the center of the soufflé cooks most easily when small containers are used.

Furthermore, the soufflé will not rise well unless the sides of the mold are coated with butter and sugar. Finally, one *must not* open the oven door until a soufflé is completely cooked and well risen.

1. For the soufflé mixture, melt the butter in a saucepan. Add the flour and mix with a whisk, then stir in the milk, lemon juice and amaretto. Whisk into a homogenous paste.

2. Remove the saucepan from the heat, add in the almond paste, and beat briskly. Stir in the egg yolks and whisk energetically.

3. In another bowl, whisk the egg whites with a pinch of salt until firm. Butter and dust the baking dishes with sugar.

with Cloudberry Sauce

4. Carefully fold the egg whites into the other mixture with a wooden or plastic spatula.

5. With a spoon, fill the baking dishes with the soufflé. Refrigerate for 3 hours. Fry the sprigs of rosemary for the garnish in oil, then roll them in powdered sugar. Set aside.

6. Mix the cloudberries and sugar, crushing the berries with the whisk. Let stand for 2 hours. Bake the soufflés in a bain-marie at 200°C/390°F for 10 to 12 minutes. Serve immediately with a sprig of rosemary and a spoonful of cloudberry sauce.

Orchard

Preparation time: 1 hour
Difficulty: ★

Serves 4

For the soup:
2 pomegranates
2 oranges
2 grapefruits
4 tsp sugar

For the fruit salad:
2 large oranges
2 grapefruits
1 pint strawberries
3 kiwis
1 mango
1 bunch dark red grapes
1 melon
2 tsp orange blossom extract
fresh mint leaves

Plants that stretch as far as the eye can see and an ingenious irrigation system allow Israel to grow an abundance of fruit. Such is the image of the Holy Land, which has become a veritable orchard, *pardess* in Hebrew. Visit this land in the spring and wander the endless rows of fruit trees, breathing in the many scents. Ledicia Renassia uses this dessert to take you on a tour through this magnificent bounty.

Loaded with vitamins, this fruit soup is wonderfully refreshing. Well-known around the world, Jaffa grapefruits and oranges unveil their incomparable taste. These juicy, sun-ripened citrus fruits are esteemed for their tender flesh, so high in natural sugar. Choose the heaviest ones, with smooth skins.

The splendid carmine red of the pomegranates brightens the visual effect of this mixture. These fruits have a gentle and nicely perfumed flavor. In this recipe, they are used both for their juice and as decoration.

Our chef recommends that you quarter the pomegranates carefully to release the seeds. According to Jewish mysticism, these seeds should number 613, corresponding to the 613 commandments of the Hebrew religion! The fine white skin is very bitter and must be completely removed.

This festival of colors and flavors, highlighted by a dash of orange blossom extract, also shows off the kiwi, grapes and strawberries. Israelis grow strawberries in sandy soil in greenhouses and have succeeded in creating a variety as large as an apricot!

When you serve the fruit, don't hesitate to adjust the amount of sugar you use according to the sweetness of the fruits.

The ultimate in refinement, Orchard Fruit Soup should be served in beautiful crystal dishes so that it will shine on the table with the light of a thousand fires.

1. Cut the pomegranates in quarters and extract the seeds, taking care to remove all the white skin. Put ²/₃ of the seeds in one bowl for juice, and set aside the rest for later use. Run the seeds through a blender, straining the juice into a large bowl.

2. Squeeze the juice from the oranges and grapefruits. Add to the pomegranate juice. Stir in the sugar and set aside.

3. Carefully peel the remaining oranges and grapefruits. Remove the fruit from the skin and put in a bowl. Set aside.

Fruit Soup

4. Rinse, hull and quarter the strawberries. Peel the kiwis and cut into disks about 5 mm/$^1/_5$ in thick. Set aside.

5. Peel the mango and cut the flesh into cubes. Wash the grapes and cut each one in half. Peel the melon and make small balls with a melon baller.

6. Blend together all the fruit in a salad bowl. Sprinkle with orange blossom extract and the fruit juice. Serve in small bowls, decorate with whole or slivered mint leaves and the reserved pomegranate seeds.

Apple Strudel

Preparation time:	1 hour
Cooking time:	1 hour 10 minutes
Resting time, dough:	1 to 2 hours
Difficulty:	★★

Serves 4

For the dough:
300 g/generous 2 cups flour
80 g/¹/₃ cup butter
1 egg
1 pinch sugar
salt
a little water

For the vanilla sauce:
6 egg yolks
200 g/³/₄ cup + 2 tbsp sugar
500 ml/2 cups milk

500 ml/2 cups crème fraîche
2 vanilla beans, opened

For the filling:
3 apples
200 g/14 tbsp butter
200 g/³/₄ cup + 2 tbsp sugar
50 g/6 tbsp raisins
25 g/3 tbsp chopped hazelnuts
25 g/3 tbsp crushed almonds

30 g/2 tbsp butter, to spread on the dough

For the decoration:
powdered sugar
red apples
fresh mint, cinnamon

Apfelstrudel, a delicious flaky pastry stuffed with apples, is one of the most traditional of the German, Austrian and central European desserts. Generally, German meals end with a cup of coffee rather than a dessert, and gourmands treat themselves to a piece of *strudel* in the afternoon for a snack.

After making the dough, do not forget to let it rest for an hour or two in the refrigerator, covered with plastic wrap. This allows moisture to spread uniformly throughout the dough and makes it more supple.

The thinner the crust, the lighter and crispier the final product. First place the ball of dough on a piece of cloth; otherwise, it will stick to the counter and you will not be able to roll it out. After rolling it out, stretch the dough over the palms of your hands and stretch it delicately, turning and stretching it until it is extremely thin.

The compote is sure to have an excellent texture if you use Golden Delicious or Belles de Boskop apples. They should be quite soft and should break up easily when cooked. According to taste, you could flavor the compote with a touch of cinnamon or vanilla. Hazelnuts and almonds have complementary flavors and add crunch. However, do not add too many and make sure they are not bitter. Instead of apples, you can vary the recipe by using pears. Juicy fruits, though, are not suitable.

When the strudel is filled, it is possible that the dough may be too thin to contain all of the relatively heavy filling. If so, you can cover it with another layer of very thin dough.

Baking the strudel is a very delicate matter. While it is being baked, regularly remove any sugary juice that drips out. The strudel, when ready, should be quite firm and slightly golden.

1. Mix all ingredients for the dough. Knead thoroughly and form into a ball. Wrap in plastic wrap and chill 1 to 2 hours in the fridge. For the sauce, make a classic custard sauce: whisk the egg yolks and sugar. Heat the milk, crème fraîche and vanilla pods over medium heat just to the boil.

2. Let the milk cool slightly, then slowly stir into the egg yolks. Cook over low heat, stirring, until it thickens. Prepare the filling: peel the apples, remove the seeds and cut the apples into very thin pieces.

3. Melt the butter in a saucepan. When it starts to foam, add the apples and sprinkle with sugar. Turn up the heat, then add the raisins, hazelnuts and almonds. Let it cook into compote over medium heat.

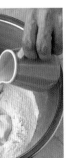

with Vanilla Sauce

4. Knead the chilled dough. Place it on a cloth and roll it out as thin as possible with a rolling pin. Then use your fingers to lift and stretch the dough. Mend in any holes that might appear and brush with melted butter.

5. Spoon the apple filling over the dough. Spread out uniformly with a spatula. Using a cloth, roll the dough quickly around the filling. Place it on a baking sheet and bake at 200°C/390°F for 30 to 45 minutes, depending on the oven.

6. Place the baked strudel on a cutting board. Sprinkle with powdered sugar. Cut the strudel into generous pieces, decorate with apples, mint and cinnamon, and serve with the vanilla custard sauce.

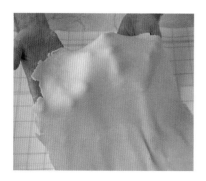

Royal

Preparation time: 45 minutes
Cooking time: 15 minutes
Chilling time: 2 hours 30 minutes
Difficulty: ★★★

Serves 4

200 g/7 oz water chestnuts
5 pandanus leaves to make baskets (optional)

For the green cream:
3 pandanus leaves
700 ml/3 cups water

300 g/generous 1⅓ cups sugar
30 g/3 tbsp rice flour
25 g/3 tbsp tapioca flour
(also called cassava flour)
8 g/1 tsp gelatin or 2 g/¼ tsp agar-agar

For the white cream:
670 ml/scant 3 cups coconut milk
25 g/3 tbsp tapioca flour
25 g/2½ tbsp rice flour
50 g/3½ tbsp sugar
5 g/1 tsp salt
2 g/¼ tsp gelatin (or 1 pinch agar-agar)

In one of his poems, King Rama II tells a story about how a Thai queen is driven out of the palace by her rival. The rightful queen returns to the palace and slips into the kitchen disguised as a kitchen helper. So that her son, the prince, will recognize her, she skillfully sculpts fruits and vegetables that are presented on the royal dinner table. Her son does indeed recognize her. Perhaps this story explains the fascinating abilities of Thai ladies, who tend to sculpt, carve, braid and decorate everything that enters the kitchen and graces their tables. Madam Sombath works in keeping with this ancestral tradition; while the *tako* is being prepared, she braids small baskets that serve as containers for the regal dessert.

To make your own elegant vessels, cut the pandanus leaves in half lengthwise. Each half leaf is notched in five places, evenly spaced, and then braided together to form small baskets. The use of the pandanus leaf in cooking is common all over Asia.

The Malaysians cook rice in it, Indonesians use it to present a complete meal of rice, meat and vegetables, and the Thai reserve the pandanus leaf for ceremonial desserts. In place of this elaborate presentation, however, you can also use several small individual molds.

An aquatic plant, the water chestnut is no larger than a walnut. Its dark shell shelters a soft, white meat. They are most often available in cans here. Surrounded by coconut cream, they give *tako* the most subtle of flavors.

Thai gelatin is jelled with agar-agar, rather than gelatin. It is a flavorless seaweed, sold in powdered form or in blocks, that has greater jelling power than our gelatin, so use it sparingly. Blended into cream, it becomes firm when chilled, preserving the creamy quality of the dessert. With or without the small braided baskets, *tako* is always served cold. Eaten with a small spoon, it gives your palate something royal to savor.

1. Drain and dice the water chestnuts. Reserve them for later. Make braided pandanus baskets, if desired.

2. For the green cream, use scissors with notched blades to cut the pandanus leaves lengthwise in strips. Trim each strip to a fine strip of 2 cm/¾ in, then dice them.

3. Blend the water and pandanus in an electric blender, then filter. Tip the juice into a saucepan. Warm over low heat, add the sugar and whisk.

Tako

4. Add both of the flours and gelatin to the pandanus juice. Stir continuously until the mixture boils, then lower the heat for a few minutes. Let it cool. When it has set, spoon it into small pandanus baskets or molds. Chill in the refrigerator for 1 hour.

5. Warm the coconut milk over low heat, then add the flours, sugar, salt and gelatin. Whip with a whisk and take off the heat.

6. When the green cream is quite solid in the baskets or molds, sprinkle the water chestnuts over it. Cover with 1 tablespoon of the white cream. Refrigerate for 1 hour and 30 minutes. Serve cold.

Skirmisher's

Preparation time: 10 to 15 minutes
Cooking time: 20 minutes
Difficulty: ★

Serves 4

For the corn pudding:
80 g/9 tbsp cornstarch
500 ml/2 cups milk
4 tbsp powdered sugar
3 tbsp rosewater

150 g/1¼ cups unshelled pistachios

For the meringue:
3 tbsp powdered sugar
3 egg yolks

The name of this dessert is believed to come from an old aristocratic lady who confused the various military ranks. The cake consists of a white layer of corn pudding, a green layer made of pistachios, and finally a layer of meringue. These three colors are similar to the stripes worn by colonels in the Tunisian army. Thus, it was named *kholozek el lioma* or "The Colonel's Cake". As she was probably not aware of the colors used by the army, the noble woman renamed it "The Skirmisher's Cake", which is *tarayoune* in Arabic. The musical sound of this word might explain why this name has been used ever since.

The pistachio cream is the central part of this cake. Originally found in Asia, the first pistachio trees, which grow to heights of 5 to 10 meters (15–30 feet), were planted on the shores of the Mediterranean more than 200 years ago. The most famous ones come from Iran and Turkey. Pistachio nuts are picked with bare hands, then soaked in water to get rid of their pulpy outer shell and dried in the sun. The only part eaten is the green part in the middle of the nut, which is covered with a thin brownish layer and a beige shell that opens when the fruit is ripe.

Rosewater, which is made by distilling petals from a tiny, strong-smelling rose, gives the dessert a smooth, distinctive taste. There are three different qualities of rosewater found in Tunisia. The first and best quality is used for the most prestigious desserts. The third grade is only used to add flavor to strawberries or fruit salads. You can find rosewater in some pharmacies, but make sure it does not contain preservatives or toxic materials.

You can make Skirmisher's Cake as a large cake or in small individual molds. Let it cool down for a while before you remove it from the mold/s, and serve it with tea or coffee.

1. Combine the cornstarch and milk. Strain it to remove any lumps. Add the sugar and cook over low heat for 10 minutes while stirring constantly, until you get a thick cream. Then add the rosewater.

2. Place a small rectangular mold on a non-stick pastry plate. Pour the corn pudding into the mold and let it cool in the refrigerator.

3. When the pudding is quite cold, take it out of the refrigerator. Chop the pistachios into small pieces and sprinkle them on top.

Cake

4. With a whisk, beat the powdered sugar and the egg yolks in a bowl until they are light in color.

5. Pour this mixture over the pistachios. Bake for 10 minutes at 150°C/300°F.

6. When the top of the dessert forms a light crust, take it out of the oven and let it cool. Remove from the mold and serve.

Ewe's Milk

Preparation time: 30 minutes
Cooking time: 35 minutes
Resting time, dough: 1 hour
Difficulty: ★

Serves 8

For the dough:
250 g/1¾ cups flour
125 g/8½ tbsp butter,
softened and cut in pieces
1 pinch salt
50 ml/3½ tbsp water
110 g/½ cup sugar

grated zest of 1 orange
grated zest of 1 lemon
1 egg

For the filling:
500 g/generous 1 lb white sheep's milk
cheese, chilled
125 g/9 tbsp sugar
2 eggs
4 egg yolks
½ tsp to 2 tsp bitter orange extract, to taste

When Georges Rousset prepares his Ewe's Milk Tart, he takes us back with him to the little town of Lodève, near Cévennes, to the time when his grandmother made this same tart. His grandmother made "recooked" cheese from the whey that drained off during the cheesemaking process and was collected, boiled and strained through cheesecloth. The foam that this yields is wonderful for making flan, an afternoon snack that pleases children.

Even if the homemade sheep's cheese of yesterday is replaced by today's commercial products, this tart still retains the old recipe's balance of ingredients. The flour, the liquid in the cheese and the butter give the pastry its elasticity; the egg yolks lend richness while the whites give it texture. The pinch of salt contributes to the color; and the citrus zests infuse it with their aroma.

This tart pastry is seductive. You can prepare it a day ahead of time: let it rest overnight in the refrigerator covered with plastic wrap, and roll it out as soon as you take it out of the refrigerator. Pre-baking the tart shell makes it less likely that the filling will make the bottom of the tart soggy.

If you find the sheep's cheese too dense, feel free to thin it out with some cream.

Don't be surprised if the tart looks like a flan when you take it out of the oven. All the ingredients conspire to make it so, in the purest tradition of the area it comes from. You can even top it with caramel.

Easy to prepare, this rustic tart is delicious accompanied by a spoonful of honey or maple syrup. And what could be more authentic than to serve it warm or at room temperature, with a glass of orange wine with its beautiful amber hue.

1. Pour the flour onto a work surface and make a well in the center of it. Put the butter, salt, water, sugar, zests and egg in the well. Work the mixture together rapidly with your fingers and form a ball of dough. Refrigerate for an hour.

2. In a blender, mix all the ingredients for the filling: the cheese, sugar, eggs and bitter orange extract.

3. Flour the work surface. Roll out the pastry dough to a thickness of 2–3 mm. The pastry should be larger than the tart form.

Tart

4. Fit the pastry into the pan by rolling it onto the rolling pin and then onto the pan. Let the excess pastry hang over the pan; this pastry has a tendency to shrink once rolled out. Cut the excess only after the pastry has been pressed into the dish, leaving a small margin.

5. Cover the pastry with parchment paper and fill with dried beans or pie weights. Be sure to cover the entire bottom of the pastry shell. Cook for 6 minutes at 175°C/350°C.

6. When baked, remove the parchment paper and beans. Immediately pour the filling into the warm tart shell. Bake for 40 minutes at 140°C/285°F.

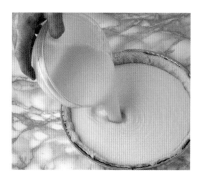

Caramel Juniper

Preparation time: 1 hour 30 minutes
Cooking time: 2 hours 50 minutes
Freezing time: overnight
Difficulty: ★★★

Serves 4

For the coffee ice cream:
250 ml/1 cup milk
250 ml/1 cup coffee
3 egg yolks
150 g/²/₃ cup sugar
150 ml/²/₃ cup heavy cream

For the sweet pastry:
250 g/1³/₄ cups flour
125 g/8¹/₂ tbsp butter

20 g/1¹/₂ tbsp sugar
1 egg
pinch salt

For the juniper caramel:
sugar
water
7 eggs, separated
170 ml/³/₄ cup milk
17 ml/³/₄ cup cream
100 ml/7 tbsp coffee
1 pinch ground juniper

For the topping:
1 banana
1 tsp brown sugar or cassonade

Caramel is nothing other than sugar that gets darker and darker the longer it is cooked. Heated beyond 150°C/300°F it loses its sweet flavor, and if the caramel is overcooked it becomes so bitter as to be inedible. That is why the chef needs to keep a close eye on the color as it cooks. When the sugar looks brown and translucent, it can be called caramel. For this particular tart, this is the moment to pour in the milk. The caramel is then immediately incorporated into the egg yolks, creating a flan-like mixture that is flavored with juniper berries. Used whole or crushed in stuffing for turkey or fish, the little black juniper berry is more often used in ground form for desserts. The juniper lends its peppery and resinous aroma to the caramel.

The custard is poured into a mold and then put in the oven. It takes two and a half hours for the custard to rise, swell and achieve its golden color. Completely chilled, the flan can be unmolded on the cooked pastry and decorated with slices of banana.

The ice cream served with it is a simple crème anglaise flavored with coffee, chilled, then enhanced with whipped cream. To make this, boil the milk and coffee in one pan and separately beat the egg yolks and sugar. Very slowly pour the hot milk into the egg and sugar mixture, then cook over low heat, stirring continuously, until thick. When this has cooled, fold in the whipped cream. Freeze this custard overnight to get a rich ice cream. You could also serve cinnamon ice cream: simply to cook the milk for the crème anglaise with a stick of cinnamon. Sprinkle this ice cream with ground cinnamon for a pretty visual effect.

1. Make the coffee ice cream as described above and freeze. Mix the ingredients for the sweet pastry. Roll out the dough and fit it onto the bottom of a tart mold; this is a flat disk, with no sides. Bake for 10 minutes. Cool, then chill. Prepare a caramel with sugar and water as described above.

2. When the caramel has cooled slightly, add the milk, cream and coffee to it. Warm over low heat for 5 minutes, stirring to totally dissolve the caramel.

3. Pour the caramel and milk mixture over the egg yolks. Whisk together well to blend all the ingredients. Add the ground juniper.

Tart with Bananas

4. Pour the mixture into a mold the same size as the pastry. Bake for 2 ½ hours in a moderate oven, then allow to cool. Cover with the baked pastry and chill. Unmold the pastry and flan onto a serving dish.

5. Peel and slice the bananas into disks. Arrange them, slightly overlapping, into a rosette on top of the tart; there should be 2 concentric circles with 1 piece flat in the center.

6. Sprinkle the bananas with brown sugar. Caramelize them with a crème brulée iron by passing the very hot iron about 2 cm/ ¾ in above the sugared banana slices with a circular movement. Serve the tart with scoops of coffee ice cream.

Maple Syrup

Preparation time: 20 minutes
Cooking time: 40 minutes
Resting time, pastry: 30 minutes
Difficulty: ☆

Serves 6

For the pie crust:
250 g/1¾ cups flour
20 g/1½ tbsp sugar
1 pinch salt
1 egg

125 g/8½ tbsp butter,
chilled and cut into cubes
4 tsp very cold water
butter for tart mold

For the filling:
40–45 g/scant ½ cup walnuts
3 eggs
2 tsp flour
2 pinches salt
250 ml/1 cup maple syrup
4 tbsp butter

Maple Syrup Pie is a delicacy typical of Quebec, a major center of maple syrup production. The art of transforming the sap of the maple tree into a savory, caramel-colored sugar syrup is a legacy of the Native Americans that the colonists of New France appreciated and quickly adoped.

Canadians are masters at using the natural maple forests. Most of these are situated in the part of Quebec known as the Beauce, on the south bank of the Saint Lawrence River and all along the Chaudière River. In the spring, as soon as the snow begins to melt, maple syrup producers drill holes in the trunks of the trees, place taps in them and collect the sap in buckets. The sap travels from the buckets through tubes and pumps to reservoirs. Then the liquid is cooked in "sugar huts". When the sap is boiled, first the syrup is made, and then by successive reductions it reaches the "pull" stage (with a consistency like taffy), and finally dried into maple sugar. Until the 1890s, maple production was concentrated on maple sugar, rather than the syrup.

Today, Quebec furnishes three-quarters of the world's maple syrup. A good syrup must contain at least 60% solid matter and its water content cannot exceed 35%. The addition of colorants or any other substance is strictly forbidden by Canadian law.

You can give your pie a rich brown color by sprinkling a little brown sugar on it. If you can find it, feel free to use maple sugar, which has a distinct flavor, a light caramel color and a lightly moist texture. In this recipe, the bottom of the maple pie is lined with walnuts, but they are not obligatory.

We suggest topping the pie with a maple leaf cut out of the pastry. Brush it with beaten egg before baking the tart.

1. Put the flour, sugar and salt into a mixing bowl. Break the egg into the center. Then add the butter. Knead the dough with the water, form a ball and chill for 30 minutes in the refrigerator.

2. Roll out the dough very thinly. Butter a tart mold or pie pan and fit the dough into it.

3. Line the dough evenly with the walnut pieces.

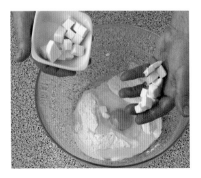

Pie with Walnuts

4. Beat the eggs and whisk them with the flour and salt until smooth. Add the maple syrup a little at a time, whisking constantly.

5. Melt the butter in a small saucepan. Add it to the filling, again stirring thoroughly.

6. Pour the maple syrup cream onto the nut-covered dough. Bake at 200°C/400°F for 15 minutes, then reduce the heat to 180°C/350°F for 25 minutes.

Pecan

Preparation time: 40 minutes
Cooking time: 50 minutes
Difficulty: ★

Serves 8

For the pie crust:
180 g/1¹/₄ cups flour
180 g/13 tbsp butter
¹/₃ tsp salt
60 ml/¹/₄ cup ice water

For the filling:
1 pinch flour
100 g/scant 1 cup chopped pecans
2 eggs
150 g/²/₃ cup brown sugar
100 g/7 tbsp butter, melted
250 ml/1 cup golden or dark corn syrup
¹/₂ tsp vanilla extract
¹/₄ tsp salt
100 g/scant 1 cup pecans, whole
200 ml/generous ³/₄ cup whipped cream
(optional)

This pie is prepared all across the southern part of the United States. It is filled with locally cultivated pecans and topped with a custard made of butter, eggs, sugar and corn syrup. For this recipe, you can substitute sorghum or molasses for the corn syrup for a stronger flavor. Other variations of this very sweet pie are the substitution of maple syrup or honey for the brown sugar. Inhabitants of Kentucky happily flavor it with Bourbon, while other people add raisins or chocolate.

The pecan is indigenous to North America. The wild pecan tree, part of the family of hickory trees, first grew along the rivers in what is now the state of Texas (it is also the state tree of Texas). In the language of the Algonquin Indians, "pecan" means "nut with the hard shell". This oblong caramel-colored nut is enclosed in a smooth, light brown shell. The majority of commercially produced pecans are grown in the state of Georgia, where the stable temperature, which is usually fairly

constant night and day, is important to the development of the nut. Pecans play a very significant role in the cuisine of the South: they are transformed into pies, biscuits, pralines and chocolate candy. Mixed with spices, they work well in salads and as stuffing for fowl. You can crush the nuts and add parsley and lemon juice as an accompaniment to fried catfish or trout.

Our chef suggests baking the pie in a large, shallow mold or pie pan, and that the filling be rather thin. If it is too thick, it takes too long to cook, and the nuts on the surface can get burned before the custard filling is completely cooked. The filling should be sufficiently spread out so that while a bite melts sweetly in your mouth, it is solid and almost crusty.

Connoisseurs of pecan pie serve it with a bowl of vanilla ice cream, and may even supplement the ice cream with a dash of chocolate syrup.

1. Mix the pie crust ingredients. Form a ball, and then roll out the dough. Fill a mold or pie pan with the dough, pushing it against the edge at regular intervals or crimping it between your forefinger and thumb to create a nice pattern.

2. Lightly flour the bottom of the pastry crust. Spread the crushed pecans evenly across the bottom of the crust with the flat of your hand.

3. Break the eggs into a mixing bowl. Beat them with a fork as for an omelet. Add the brown sugar and whip the mixture.

Pie

4. Add the butter, corn syrup, vanilla and salt. Beat energetically.

5. Gently spread the liquid mixture over the nuts.

6. Arrange the whole pecans decoratively on the surface of the custard. Bake for 10 minutes at 220°C/425°F, then lower the heat to 160°C/325°F and bake for another 40 minutes. Serve with whipped cream, if desired.

Hazelnut

Preparation time: 40 minutes
Cooking time: 40 minutes
Difficulty: ★★

Serves 4

1 kg/2¼ lb apples
100 g/7 tbsp butter
150 g/⅔ cup sugar
30 g/¼ cup chopped hazelnuts
1 package puff pastry

Numerous culinary specialties are the result of simple mistakes. In 1898, Stéphanie Tatin and her sister Caroline ran an inn across the street from the train station in Lamotte-Beuvron, in Loir-et-Cher, France. Stéphanie was renowned for her melt-in-your-mouth, caramelized apple tart. One day when the restaurant was full, the usual apple tart was not ready in time. Whether by miracle or in confusion, Stéphanie Tatin put her tart in the oven upside down: apples, sugar and butter on the bottom of the pan, and the pastry covering them on top. Her guests approved of the results. One of them, a certain Louis Vaudable, hurried back to Paris in order to put this tart on the menu of his restaurant, the famous *Maxim's*.

The success of the *demoiselles* Tatins' tart cannot be denied. On the centenary of this dessert, celebrated in 1998, the people of Lamotte-Beuvron prepared the largest Tarte Tatin ever created: with a diameter of 2.5 meters (8.2 feet), it used 250 kg (550 lb) apples, 30 kg (66 lb) sugar and 7 kg (15½ lb) butter!

The perfection of this dessert rests with the judicious choice of apples. They must have a high sugar content and be both firm and soft. Our chef Jean Bordier admits his preference for Reinettes. The grey Reinette of Canada is a large, tart fruit with slightly rough skin, grey-bronze color, soft flesh and a distinct flavor. The Reinette is available in markets from late fall through winter, and the Queen of Reinettes, reddish with yellow stripes, is ripe for a few months before it. It is crisp, juicy, and both sweet and slightly tart. Their cousin, the Reinette Clochard, is a specialty of the Gâtine area of Poitevin, available in France from the end of November through the end of May. Its skin is a patchy yellow, and its flesh is sweet, firm and flavorful.

Squeeze as many apple slices as possible into the pan, because the heat makes them shrink. If necessary, add a few more apple slices during cooking to maintain a uniform crown.

1. Peel the apples. Core and quarter them. Set aside a few quarters to insert into the "crown" of apples during baking.

2. Melt the butter in a non-stick cake pan over low heat. Add the sugar and cook until you have a golden butter caramel.

3. Arrange the apples in a crown in the butter caramel. Crowd them in, overlapping one slice against the next to make an attractive presentation when unmolded. Cook lightly over low heat.

Tarte Tatin

4. Scatter the hazelnuts over the apple slices, and then bake for 25 minutes at 180°C/350°F. Remove from oven.

5. Roll out a sheet of ready-made puff pastry. Cut out a piece slightly larger than the cake pan. Fit it over the apples using a fork or the back of a spoon. Gently push the pastry down around the edge, between the apples and the pan. Return to the oven for about 10 minutes.

6. Remove the tart from the oven and wait until it has completely cooled. Just before unmolding it, heat the pan slightly over low heat, to loosen up the caramel on the bottom of the pan.

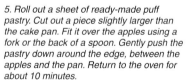

Cassava Cake

Preparation time:	30 minutes
Cooking time:	50 minutes
Soaking time:	30 minutes
Difficulty:	★★

Serves 6

For the cake:
500 g/generous 1 lb cassava
1 glass cold water
4 eggs
250 g/1 cup + 2 tbsp sugar
4 tsp yeast

For the coconut sauce:
freshly grated flesh of 1 coconut
500 ml/2 cups milk
4 egg yolks
150 g/²/₃ cup sugar

Yaka-yaka used to be an unpretentious dessert made of grated and sugared cassava, cooked in a bain-marie in little tins. Cameroonian mothers frequently prepared it for their children. Looking for a cake reminiscent of her native Cameroon, our chef recalled the childhood treat, and created this Cassava Cake. To make it more mellow and savory, she topped it with a coconut sauce.

Few desserts are prepared daily in Cameroon, with the exception of treats like crêpes or beignets that are eaten as snacks at any time of day. The people who eat European-style cakes purchased from bakeries are mainly those who live in cities and who have had some exposure to European ways.

Cassava flour (better known commercially as tapioca flour) is the principal ingredient of this delicious cake. Our chef makes it herself from the long, brown cassava roots. Its white flesh is chopped, ground in a blender with water, strained and then crumbled. At the market, she can easily determine which cassava is the right one for this cake by scratching the outer skin lightly with a fingernail. If she sees a deep pink skin, she knows she has chosen a cassava with a high sugar content. There is another variety of cassava that has a much lower sugar content, and its inner skin is white.

After straining the cassava paste, you can use the juice that remains as a thickening agent in other recipes. Simply let it stand until the starch falls to the bottom of the bowl.

Your cake will be even more of a treat for the eyes if you sprinkle it with cocoa, or top the coconut sauce with a rich chocolate sauce.

1. With a heavy knife or other tool, cut the cassava root into thick slices. Carefully cut off the thick brown skin.

2. Cut the slices in two lengthwise. Cut out and discard the hard core.

3. Chop the cassava into small 1½ cm/ ½ in cubes. Put them in a sieve and rinse thoroughly with cold running water. Put the pieces in a blender with the water and blend until the mixture is thick. Line a strainer with 4 layers of cheesecloth or a clean cotton dish towel.

with Coconut Sauce

4. Put some of the paste in the cloth and press out the liquid into a bowl. What remains in the cloth should be a sort of thick flour. Repeat until the liquid is strained from all the paste. Save the liquid. With the tips of your fingers, crumble the flour until it resembles rich pastry dough.

5. In the blender, mix the cassava flour with the eggs, sugar and yeast. Pour the mixture into a buttered brioche mold and bake at 180°C/350°F for 25 minutes. Finish by cooking the brioche mold in a bain-marie for 15 minutes, then let chill.

6. Boil the milk, then remove from heat and steep the grated coconut in it for 30 minutes. Strain the milk and return to the boil. In another pan, whip the egg yolks and sugar, then pour in the hot milk. Stir over low heat until thick, about 10 minutes. Let cool. Ladle the sauce over slices of cake.

Zriga Cigars

Preparation time: 20 minutes
Cooking time: 20 minutes
Difficulty: ★★

Serves 4

For the zriga cigars:
200 g/1²/₃ cups ground almonds
200 g/2¹/₂ cups ground hazelnuts
250 g/1 cup + 2 tbsp sugar
3 tbsp + 1 tsp rosewater
1 egg white

4 sheets phyllo dough
or spring roll wrappers
oil for frying

For the cream sauce:
2 tbsp + 2 tsp cornstarch
150 g/1¹/₃ cups powdered sugar
1 liter/1 quart milk
2 tsp rosewater
pistachios, chopped

Manoubia Hassairi proposes a true fantasy dessert: cigars made of ultra-thin pastry stuffed with almonds and hazelnuts, coated with a rosewater-flavored cream and sprinkled with pistachios. There are other fabulous Tunisian creams for adventurous gourmands to try, as well: a tri-color cream with almonds, pistachios and hazelnuts; *hachoura* with rose water; *baluza* with hazelnuts; or *assida,* made with flour and pine nuts.

Pistachios, almonds, pine nuts and hazelnuts flavor and decorate all of Tunisia's little cakes, such as *baklava du bey* ("the chief's baklava"), not to mention hazelnut dumplings. These little cakes never contain crème fraîche or vanilla as they do in the Western world, but rather a great deal of dried fruit, nuts, sugar and honey.

In Tunisia, the pistachio finds its way into every culinary creation. Aside from desserts, our chef can cite several couscous recipes that highlight them. In the white couscous of Beja,

mutton is prepared with pine nuts, almonds and pistachios, all roasted and dripping with butter. Mazouf couscous, sweet and served as a dessert, is rich with raisins, pine nuts and pistachios. It is also prepared the way the *zriga* are, with a white cream sauce.

Our chef suggests that the cooking oil be only moderately hot. If the pastry-covered cigars are cooked too much, they will dry out or take on a dark color. Once cooked and drained, the *zriga* are easier to cut when they have cooled a bit, rather than straight out of the hot oil. You need a little patience to enjoy this treat!

Once fried, the *zriga* can be refrigerated for up to a week without the cream sauce. Then you can use these little stuffed pastries as the need arises, or as your hunger dictates. You can also decorate the dessert with chopped pine nuts and whole almonds.

1. Mix the almonds, hazelnuts and sugar with your fingers, form a mound and make a well in the center. Add the rosewater little by little, stirring lightly with your fingertips.

2. Knead the nut mixture well into a uniform paste. Roll it into long, thin cylinders with the tips of your fingers.

3. Beat the egg white and then brush it over the edges of each sheet of pastry or spring roll wrapper. Put the roll of nut filling on the lower edge of the pastry. Fold in the left and right edges and roll it into a cigar.

with Cream Sauce

4. Seal the edges of the cigars with egg white. Fry them for 5 minutes in a pan of hot oil. Let them cool, then cut into small 2 cm/³/₄ in logs. Place a few in each of the dessert bowls.

5. For the cream, whisk the cornstarch and sugar in the cold milk. Warm over low heat, stirring constantly, until it begins to thicken. Stir in the rosewater, then finish cooking. The cream should have a thick consistency. This takes about 15 minutes.

6. Ladle the rosewater cream into the dessert bowls containing the pieces of fried cigar. Chill. Just before serving, sprinkle with chopped pistachios.

The Chefs

Gustavo Andreoli
Italy

Eric Beamesderfer
United States

Alain Beirao
Portugal

Lahoucine Belmoufid
Morocco

Richard Bizier
Canada (Quebec)

Jean Bordier
France

Mohamed Boussabah
Tunisia

Ling Choï
China

Francesca Ciardi
Italy

Bernard Collon
France

Viljam Cvek
Croatia

Diogo Damian
Brazil

Katia Davies-Kemmler
United States

Haï Duong
Vietnam

Nicole Fagegaltier
France

Hussein Fakih
Lebanon

Mohamed Fawzi Kotb
Egypt

Otto Fehrenbacher
Germany

Pierre Fonteyne
Belgium

Philippe Fouchard
France

Eddy Gérald
France (Martinique)

Michel Haquin
Belgium

Manoubia Hassairi
Tunisia

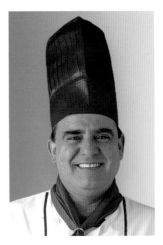

Enrique Hernandez Hernandez
Cuba

Alberto Herráiz
Spain

Marc Imbs
Switzerland

Yilmaz Kalayci
Turkey

Joël Kichenin
France (Guadeloupe)

Mi-Kyeung Kim
South Korea

Marie Koffi-Nketsia
Cameroon

Stefan Linde
Sweden

Charles-René Madsen
Denmark

Rufino Manjarrés
Spain

Donato Massaro
Italy

Kiyotaka Matsunaga
Japan

Franck Mischler & Mickaël Wolf
France

Jacky Morlon
France

Fatima Mouzoun
Morocco

Josef Oseli
Slovenia

Massimo Palermo
Italy

Vivek Ramdenee
Mauritius

Ledicia Renassia
Israel

Mohammed Rifaï
Morocco

Michel Roth
France

Stefan Rottner
Germany

Georges Rousset
France

Djegaradjou Sinniamourd
India

Shing-Kwok So
China

Irina Sokolova
Russia

Oth Sombath
Thailand

Mátyás Somogyvári
Hungary

Tony Spinosa
Mexico

Konstantinos & Chrysanti
Stamkopoulos
Greece

José Luis Tarín Fernández
Spain

Rafik Tlatli
Tunisia

Oliver Tucki
Great Britain

Xavier Valero
Spain

Marcel Vanic
Austria

Vanina Villareal
Argentina

Arkadiusz Zuchmanski
Poland

Glossary

ADJUST: To taste and correct the seasoning of a dish toward the end of cooking by adding neutralizing elements (such as sugar, cream or a vegetable purée) or by increasing the seasoning (salt, pepper or other spices).

ASPIC: Stock or juice mixed with gelatin. Often used as a decorative glaze for pâté or chilled meat, or as the basis for terrines.

BAIN-MARIE: See water bath.

BARD: To surround a piece of meat or fowl with thin strips of lard or bacon to prevent the meat from drying out during cooking.

BEAT: To stir vigorously with a whisk, especially egg-based preparations, or to vigorously combine ingredients until homogenous.

BEURRE MANIÉ: French term that literally means "kneaded butter". This is a mixture of softened butter and flour, which is incorporated into a liquid sauce to thicken it.

BIND: To bond ingredients to each other by adding a thickening or smoothing agent, such as egg yolks, flour, starch or cream.

BLANCH: To immerse food briefly in boiling water, then immediately rinse it in cold water to stop the cooking process. This is done to facilitate peeling (of tomatoes, for example) or reduce the bitterness of an ingredient (calves feet, Brussels sprouts).

BLEND: To gently incorporate a new element into a mixture.

BOUQUET GARNI: A small bundle of herbs, tied together with a thin string or inside a cloth, usually used to flavor a stock or a stew. The classic combination of herbs includes a sprig of thyme, a bay leaf, parsley and sometimes a leek or 4-inch piece of celery, but the exact blend may vary from recipe to recipe.

BRAISE: A method of cooking meat, fish or fowl slowly, in a tightly covered casserole with little or no added fat or liquid. This method can be done on the stovetop or in the oven. Foods with a high water content are best cooked this way; their own liquid condenses on the inside of the cooking vessel and keeps the food moist.

BREAD: To coat a food in a layer of breadcrumbs, often seasoned, before cooking. This preparation is usually dipped into a mixture of beaten eggs immediately before being cooked (often sautéed or fried).

BROIL: A method of cooking food by direct exposure to a source of heat above or below the food, often a part of an oven. Broiling is a good way to melt a cheese topping or add color to food in the last few minutes of cooking (UK: grill).

BROWN: To cook ingredients in oil or butter in a frying pan to give the surface a golden or brown color.

BRUNOISE: A mixture of vegetables (such as carrots, onions, beets, radish) cut into small dice of 1 to 2 cm (⅓–¾ in), then slowly fried in butter. The brunoise is then used to flavor soups, sauces, fillings, etc.

BUTTER: To apply soft or melted butter to a mold or baking dish to prevent food from sticking during cooking.

CARAMEL: Caramel is simply sugar that has been heated slowly until it melts and turns golden or brown. It can be thinned with water, milk or cream. It tends to burn quickly, and care must be taken when adding liquid to a hot caramel.

CARAMELIZE: To melt sugar to make caramel (see above); also to cook foods with a form of sugar until they turn brown and slightly sweet, such as onions in Moroccan cooking.

CHINOIS: A deep, cone-shaped strainer with very fine holes, most commonly made of metal. Food is pressed through the holes to extract every bit of flavor while holding back the solids.

CHOP: To cut food into pieces that are small, but not as small as diced or minced foods.

CLARIFIED BUTTER: Butter is melted and allowed to separate; the liquid portion (the clarified butter) is poured off, leaving the solids and milk residues in the pan. Clarified butter can be heated to higher temperatures than regular butter without burning.

CLARIFY: To remove impurities from a stock or jelly using a mixture of egg whites and herb garnish, which attract and bond with the impurities. When the egg white is removed, the broth or jelly is translucent and free of residue.

COMPOTE: Fruit or vegetables cooked slowly over a low heat in juice or syrup until the food is quite soft, but the pieces are still intact.

CONDENSATION: Water vapor released during cooking.

CONFIT: Meat that is cooked and preserved in its own fat, especially duck or goose.

COULIS: A purée, generally of one ingredient, or a simple sauce made of an ingredient for a dish that includes that ingredient. For example, a raspberry coulis (puréed raspberries) might be served with a dish that has raspberries as its main ingredient, or as a sauce for raspberry ice.

COURT-BOUILLON: In French, literally "short stock"; a clear broth to which onions, celery, carrots, bouquet garni, lemon or garlic may be added, used in the cooking of fish or meat.

COUVERTURE: Also called coating chocolate, this kind of chocolate has a high cocoa butter content, giving it just the right properties to melt and form a thin, glossy glaze over cakes and other desserts.

CREAM: To beat one or more ingredients vigorously until they are fully integrated, for example butter and sugar, or until the ingredient is very smooth and light.

CRÈME ANGLAISE: The French term for a basic custard sauce (see Custard).

CRÈME FRAÎCHE: A dairy product common in European cooking, this thickened cream has a texture something like sour cream but with less tang and is ideal for thickening sauces because it does not curdle when boiled. While a close approximation is sometimes found in specialty markets in the United States, you can make your own by combining 1 cup heavy cream and 1 tbsp buttermilk or plain yogurt with active cultures and leaving it at room temperature overnight. Then stir and refrigerate.

CUSTARD, CUSTARD SAUCE: A creamy sauce made by beating egg yolks and sugar, then whisking in milk that has been heated with vanilla. This mixture is set over gentle heat and stirred continuously until the custard is thickened (do not allow to boil).

CUTTINGS: Small pieces trimmed or cut off dough, meat or fish during the preparation of a dish. The meat and fish trimmings are often used to make sauces or stocks.

DEGLAZE: To add small amounts of water, wine, alcohol, vinegar or other liquid to a pan in which other food has been cooked so that the cooked-on remains in the pan are incorporated into the liquid (for use in a sauce or as seasoning).

DICE: To cut food into small cubes of approximately even size. Diced food is smaller than chopped food, but not as small as minced food.

DOUBLE BOILER: A method of cooking food in a pan suspended over (not in) a second pan that contains hot water. The gentle heat of the steaming water is perfect for melting chocolate and making delicate sauces without letting them curdle.

DRESS: To remove the inedible parts of meat or fish before cooking to achieve a more attractive presentation.

DUXELLES: A preparation of mushrooms chopped and braised with shallots and thinly sliced onions, used as a base for stuffings.

EMULSION: The incorporation of a fatty ingredient into another preparation by whipping vigorously. Mayonnaise (oil into eggs) or a hollandaise sauce (butter into eggs) are examples of emulsions.

ESCALLOPE: See Scallop.

FILTER: To pass a liquid through a strainer, sometimes lined with cheesecloth, to eliminate particles left in suspension.

FLAMBÉ: A French term that literally means "to flame". To set fire to food that has been coated with an alcohol glaze, or simply with alcohol, for example meat, cooked fruit or crêpes.

FLAVOR: To enhance a preparation by adding herbs, spices, alcohol or other flavoring substances.

FLOUR: To sprinkle a mold, baking pan or cooking dish with a light coating of flour to prevent food from sticking. Usually sprinkled on after the pan or dish has been buttered or greased.

FROMAGE BLANC: A very fresh, unripened cheese with the texture of sour cream but a mild, neutral flavor. Quark or Greek yoghurt (full fat) are close; or you can purée a blend of plain yoghurt and cottage cheese until it is perfectly smooth.

GARNISH: To add small enhancements to a dish just before it is served; also the food used to decorate in this way. This can be anything from fresh herbs or slices of toast or vegetables to a glaze or coating of sauce to chocolate shavings.

GELATIN(E): A clear, flavorless jelling agent derived from animal protein. It is available in envelopes of granules or in sheets (also called leaves). Four leaves of gelatin can jell approximately the same amount of liquid as one ¼-ounce envelope of granulated gelatin. Both forms are soaked in liquid before they are added to the other ingredients and heated to dissolve.

GLAZE: (verb and noun) To pour or brush something on the surface of food to give it a gleaming appearance. For sweet foods this can be done with an icing, jelly, sugar syrup, couverture or beaten eggs. For savory foods it might be a sauce, reduction or an aspic.

GREASE: To coat a mold or pan or utensil with butter or oil to prevent food from sticking to it.

GRILL: A method of cooking food placed on a metal wire rack over a fire or coals, also called barbecuing.

GUM ARABIC: A mild jelling agent derived from certain species of acacia tree. Although it is more commonly used in commercial production of gum and candies in the West, it is used for cooking in some other cultures. It is available in powdered or crystal form.

INFUSE: To blend an aromatic ingredient into liquid (usually very hot) to impart the flavor into the liquid. Tea is one familiar example, or the use of a bouquet garni to flavor stocks or sauces.

JULIENNE: (verb and noun) Foods cut into very small, thin and regular stick-shaped pieces (vegetables especially, but also meat and truffles).

Knead: To work several ingredients together, traditionally with the hands, to blend them thoroughly and create a homogenous paste or dough.

Macerate: To soak fruit, most often dried fruits, in a liquid to "plump" them as they absorb some of it. The liquid is usually alcohol, sugar syrup or an alcohol-based mixture.

Marinade, marinate: Foods are marinated, that is, allowed to steep in an aromatic liquid called a marinade, in order to take on the flavors of the marinade before cooking. This also tenderizes tougher cuts of meat and adds liquid to those that tend to be dry.

Mayonnaise: An emulsion of egg yolks and oil, seasoned with vinegar, lemon juice and other flavors. To make it, whisk the egg yolks and seasonings, then gradually drizzle in the oil while whisking constantly until the mixture is thick and creamy. Mayonnaise is the base for a number of sauces, including tartar sauce (for fish), aioli (with garlic) and rouille (a spicy sauce served with fish).

Mince: To cut meat, vegetables or fruit in very small and evenly-sized pieces, smaller than chopped or diced food.

Mirepoix: A mixture of finely diced carrots, onions and celery used to accompany roasts or as a side dish, usually sweated in butter. See also Brunoise.

Moisten: To add a liquid to a preparation during its cooking.

Nap: To complete an entrée or dessert by covering it lightly with a sauce, a jelly or an icing.

Offal: See Variety meats.

Papillote, en papillote: A method of cooking food inside an envelope of parchment paper, which traps the steam and helps keep food moist.

Poach: To cook a food by immersing it into simmering liquid.

Preserve: To prepare ingredients in such a way that they keep for a relatively long time. Fruits are commonly preserved in sugar syrup. Vegetables may be preserved in brine or mixtures of oil and other seasonings; meat, especially duck, is preserved in its own fat or in alcohol.

Purée: (verb and noun) To blend or process food (in a blender or food processor or with a hand-held mixer or even a fork) until it becomes a smooth, homogenous mass with no discernable lumps or pieces.

Quenelle: A small, light dumpling, classically made of a stuffing of fish and egg, that is poached in stock.

Reduce, Reduction: To reduce the volume of a sauce, cream or juice in order to intensify its flavor. The liquid is kept at the boil, uncovered, until evaporation has reduced the volume to the desired amount. The thickened liquid is called a reduction.

Refresh: To chill heated food rapidly by immersing it (usually the entire pan) in ice-cold water, thus preventing it from continuing to cook.

Rise: To increase the volume of a preparation, especially doughs that contain yeast.

Roast: (verb and noun) A method of cooking food in the dry heat of an oven. The food is typically a large cut of meat, which is also called a roast; since food can dry out while roasting, it is best suited to juicy foods.

Roulade: A thin piece of meat rolled around some kind of stuffing, most often vegetables or other meats, and held in place with toothpicks or string before cooking.

Roux: A mixture of butter and flour cooked slowly in a skillet or saucepan until the desired color (white, golden or brown) is obtained. Liquid is then added to the roux. A roux is the first step in the preparation of many sauces, and is also used to thicken soups and sauces.

Sabayon: The French word for Zabaglione (see Zabaglione).

Sauté: To cook food in a small amount of fat over high heat.

Scallop: A very thin piece of meat. Also called escallope.

Seal or Sear: To quickly cook food (mainly meat or fowl) in very hot fat, creating an exterior crust that seals in its juices, before a second and longer cooking period.

Set: To chill a mixture in order to thicken it or to make it jell.

Simmer: To bring a liquid to a point just below the boil. Also called a "slow boil".

Skim: To remove the fat or impurities that rise to the surface of a stock, sauce or a food cooked in liquid.

Soak: To immerse foods in clean water and let them stand for a length of time, either to rehydrate (dried mushrooms, beans) or remove salt (such as salt cod) or to remove blood or bitterness from variety meats (giblets, brains, liver, tripe).

Strain: To pour liquid or press solid ingredients through a sieve or strainer to remove solid matter. The amount of solid matter withheld will vary with the fineness of the openings in the strainer. If the mixture being strained is fairly dense, such as a tomato sauce or a purée, you may need to press the mixture through the openings with the back of a spoon or other implement.

Stud: To insert small plugs of lard, seasonings or truffles into a piece of meat or fish, or cloves into an onion or orange.

SUGAR SYRUP: A combination of sugar and water (in varying proportions) heated gently until the sugar dissolves completely, and then boiled briefly. Syrup reaches various stages of density at different temperatures, depending on how long it is cooked.

SWEAT: To cook meat or vegetables over a gentle heat in a covered pan (uncovered for mushrooms), thus retaining the food's natural water content.

THICKEN: To give a smooth sauce a more dense and very homogenous consistency. This can be done by allowing more liquid to evaporate (see Reduction) or by adding a binding agent (see Bind), such as egg yolk, cream, starch or a purée.

TRUSS: To draw the legs and wings of a fowl tightly to the body and hold them in place there by means of string, skewers or a trussing needle and thread to prevent them from spreading and burning during cooking.

VANILLA SUGAR: Sugar that has been infused with the aroma of vanilla is widely available in Europe and a frequent ingredient in European recipes. You can easily make vanilla sugar by putting one or two whole vanilla beans into a closed container of granulated sugar; after several days the sugar will take on the flavor of vanilla. The beans can be removed from the sugar and reused many times.

VARIETY MEATS: Called offal in the UK, this term refers to all kinds of internal organs and other parts of animals, including the liver, kidneys, lungs, tripe (tongue), tail, sweetbread (thymus gland) and more.

WATER BATH: A method of cooking in which a dish of food is set inside a larger pan or dish that is half-filled with water to cook (can be in the oven or on the stovetop). The heat of the warm water surrounds the food, allowing a gentle cooking.

WHIP: To vigorously whisk or beat ingredients together (cream, eggs, butter) to incorporate air into them and thus make them lighter and frothier, often with a whisk.

ZABAGLIONE: A light and airy concoction consisting of egg yolks, sugar and wine (traditionally Marsala) whisked over a double boiler into a delicious froth.

ZEST: The finely grated, scraped or cut peel of citrus fruits, used to flavor various dishes.

British Cookery Terms

US	UK
arugula	rocket (rocket salad)
bacon slices	streaky bacon, streaky rashers
baking soda	bicarbonate of soda
beet	beetroot
Belgian endive	chicory
blood sausage	black pudding
bok choy	Chinese leaves
bouillon cube	stock cube
broil, broiler	grill, oven grill
chicory	endive
chili pepper; chile	chilli pepper
cilantro	fresh coriander leaves
coconut, shredded or grated	desiccated coconut
cookie	biscuit (sweet)
corn	maize, sweetcorn
corned beef	salt beef
cornstarch	cornflour
eggplant	aubergine
extract	essence
flounder	plaice
flour, all-purpose	plain flour
flour, bread	strong flour
flour, cake	superfine flour
flour, whole wheat	wholemeal flour
French fries	chips
gelatin	gelatine
golden raisins	sultanas
grill	barbecue
ground beef or pork	minced meat or mince
ham (cured)	gammon
heavy (whipping) cream	double cream
jelly	jam

US	UK
kiwi	kiwi fruit
ladyfingers	sponge fingers
molasses	treacle
offal	variety meats
papaya	papaw
parsley root	Hamburg parsley
peanut, peanut oil	groundnut, groundnut oil
phyllo dough	filo dough
pit	stone (of fruits)
porcini	ceps, boletus or penny bun mushrooms
powdered sugar	icing sugar
rise	prove
rutabaga	Swede
salad shrimp	shrimp
scallop	escalope (thin slice of meat)
seed	pip
semi-sweet chocolate	plain chocolate
shrimp	prawn
slivered almonds	flaked almonds
snow peas, sugar peas	mangetout
streusel	crumble
sugar, very fine granulated	caster sugar
Swiss chard	chard
tart	flan
tofu	beancurd
tomato paste	tomato puree
vanilla bean	vanilla pod
vanilla seeds or mark	vanilla pulp
whole milk	full-cream milk
whole wheat	wholemeal
zucchini	courgette

Index of Recipes